World History

by
Wayne E. King and Marcel Lewinski

PEARSON
AGS Globe

Shoreview, Minnesota

About the Authors

Wayne E. King is currently the Academic Dean at the Baltimore School for the Arts. He earned his Bachelor of Science and Master of Science degrees from The Johns Hopkins University. He has taught history and social studies at all educational levels. With extensive experience as a curriculum writer, he has served as a consultant to schools, museums, and federal agencies. He has lectured at numerous national and international conferences on the teaching of history and cultural studies.

Marcel Lewinski is an Assistant Adjunct Professor of History Education at Illinois State University. Previously, he was an award-winning high school social studies teacher. He taught a wide range of subjects including geography, world history, economics, political science, sociology, and contemporary problems. Lewinski is professionally active in many organizations and has given presentations at many state, regional, and national conferences. He has conducted numerous workshops for social studies teachers and has traveled all over the world. As author of several textbooks in the social studies, Mr. Lewinski acts as a consultant to school systems and has often contributed to educational publications.

Reading Consultant

Timothy Shanahan, Ph.D., Professor of Urban Education, Director of the Center for Literacy, University of Illinois at Chicago; Author, AMP Reading System

Reviewers

The publisher wishes to thank the following educators for their helpful comments during the review process for *World History*. Their assistance has been invaluable.

Lois Barnes (Content Reviewer), Assistant Superintendent of Curriculum and Instruction, Woodford County Board of Education, Versailles, KY; **Phyllis Berman,** Supervisor/Coordinator, Scott School Assistant Center, Toledo Public Schools, Toledo, OH; **Elizabeth Burley,** Itinerant Resource Teacher, Ager Road Center, Hyattsville, MD; **Anita Dearing,** Resource Teacher, Oak Ridge High School, Oak Ridge, TN; **Tom Ferrara**, Teacher/Education Coordinator, South Bend Juvenile Correctional Facility, South Bend, IN; **Debora Hartzell,** Lead Teacher for Special Education, Lakeside High School, Atlanta, GA; **Patricia Henry,** Instructional Specialist, Special Education Programs, Montgomery County Public Schools, Rockville, MD; **Anne Hoffman,** Teacher, Santana High School, Santana, CA; **Lenore Heino Hoyt,** Social Studies Teacher, Centennial High School, Circle Pines, MN; **Larry Manchester,** Lead Resource Teacher, St. Andrews School, St. Paul, MN; **Russell F. Maruna,** Supervisor of Social Studies, Cleveland Municipal School District, Cleveland, OH; **Debby Persky,** Teacher, City of Angels, Los Angeles, CA; **Alice Richardson,** Special Education Teacher, Central High School, Detroit, MI; **Carolyn Scott,** Special Education Coordinator, Terrebonne Parish Schools, Houma, LA; **Craig Viscardi**, Special Education Teacher, Pasadena High School, Pasadena, TX; **J. B. Whitten,** Exceptional Student Education Teacher, Lennard High School, Ruskin, FL

Acknowledgments appear on pages 858–860, which constitutes an extension of this copyright page.

ISBN-13: 978-0-7854-6405-1

ISBN-10: 0-7854-6405-0

5 6 7 8 9 10   13 12 11 10 09

1-800-992-0244
www.agsglobe.com

Contents

Biography

History in Your Life

Communication in History

Technology Connection

Then and Now

Writing About History

Writing About History

Document-Based Reading

Spotlight Stories

Map Skills

Map Studies

Map Studies

How to Use This Book: A Study Guide

Welcome to the study of world history. You may be asking yourself, "Why do I need to know about people, places, and events that happened a long time before I was even born?" When we study the past, we can have a better understanding of why some things happened the way they did. We can learn from the mistakes and the successes of the past. It is important that we know about our world and about the people who live in it. Everyone can help make the world a better place to live.

This book is a story about the world. As you read the units, chapters and lessons of this book, you will learn about some of the important people and events that shaped world history.

Before you start to read this book, it is important that you understand how to use it. It is also important that you know how to be successful in this course. Information in this first section can help you achieve these things.

How to Study

These tips can help you study more effectively:

- Plan a regular time to study.

- Choose a desk or table in a quiet place where you will not be distracted. Find a spot that has good lighting.

- Gather all the books, pencils, paper, and other equipment you will need to complete your assignments.

- Decide on a goal. For example: "I will finish reading and taking notes on Chapter 1, Lesson 1, by 8:00."

- Take a five- to ten-minute break every hour to keep alert.

- If you start to feel sleepy, take a break and get some fresh air.

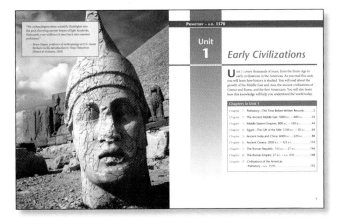

Before Beginning Each Unit

◆ Read the unit title and study the photograph. Do you recognize anything in the photo?

◆ Read the quotation.

◆ Read the opening paragraphs.

◆ Read the titles of the chapters in the unit.

◆ Read the Chapter Summaries and Unit Summary to help you identify key ideas.

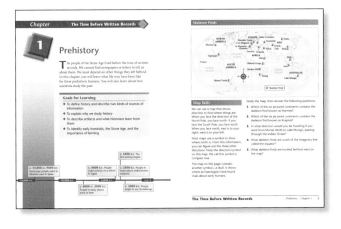

Before Beginning Each Chapter

◆ Read the chapter title and dates.

◆ Read the opening paragraphs.

◆ Study the Goals for Learning. The Chapter Review and tests will ask questions related to these goals.

◆ Study the timeline. These help you see when key events occurred. The timeline covers the years in the chapter title.

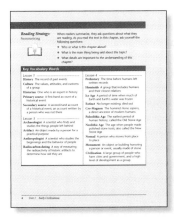

◆ Read the paragraph and bullets on the Reading Strategy page. The strategy will help you become a better reader. Reading Strategy Notes in each lesson will help you apply the strategy as you read

◆ Read the words and definitions in the Key Vocabulary Words box. The words in this list are important vocabulary words in the chapter.

◆ Read the Chapter Summary to identify key issues.

◆ Look at the Chapter Review. The questions cover the most important information in the chapter.

Note These Features

You can find complete listings of these features in this textbook's table of contents.

Biography
Highlights people who have played
a part in the history of the world

History in Your Life
Relates history to the modern world

Writing About History
Provides history topics to write
about in each chapter

Then and Now
Compares and contrasts something existing
now to how it existed in the past

Technology Connection
Highlights inventions at the time
that made life better or easier

Document-Based Reading
Presents primary- and secondary-source
documents related to each chapter

Spotlight Story
Tells about an important part of history
related to the content of the chapter

Skill Builder
Focuses on social studies skills

Before Beginning Each Lesson

Read the lesson title and restate it in the form of a question. example, write: *What is the meaning of history?*

Look over the entire lesson, noting the following:

◆ bold words

◆ text organization

◆ photos and illustrations

◆ maps

◆ graphs and charts

◆ Lesson Review questions

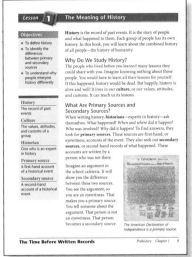

As You Read the Lesson

◆ Read the major headings.

◆ Read the subheads and paragraphs that follow.

◆ Study the maps, graphs, and charts.

◆ Before moving on to the next lesson, see if you understand the concepts you read. If you do not, reread the lesson. If you are still unsure, ask for help.

◆ Practice what you have learned by completing the Lesson Reviews.

Using the Bold Words

History

The record of past events

Knowing the meaning of all the boxed words in the left column will help you understand what you read.

These **vocabulary words** appear in **bold type** the first time they appear in the text and are often defined in the paragraph.

> **History** is the record of past events

All of the words in the left column are also defined in the **Glossary.**

> **History** (his´ tər ē) The record of past events (p. 5)

Word Study Tips

◆ Start a vocabulary file with index cards to use for review.

◆ Write one term on the front of each card. Write the chapter number, lesson number, and definition on the back.

◆ You can use these cards as flash cards by yourself or with a study partner to test your knowledge.

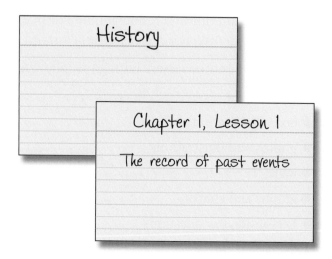

History

Chapter 1, Lesson 1

The record of past events

Taking Notes in Class

◆ Outline each lesson using the subheads as the main points.

◆ Always write the main ideas and supporting details.

◆ Keep your notes brief.

◆ Write down important information only.

◆ Use your own words.

◆ Do not be concerned about writing in complete sentences. Use phrases.

◆ Do not try to write everything the teacher says.

◆ Use the same method all the time. Then when you study for a test, you will know where to go to find the information you need to review.

◆ Review your notes to fill in possible gaps as soon as you can after class.

Using a Three-Column Chart

One good way to take notes is to use a three-column chart. Make your own three-column chart by dividing a sheet of notebook paper into three parts. In Column 1, write the topic you are reading about or studying. In Column 2, write what you learned about this topic as you read or listened to your teacher. In Column 3, write questions, observations, or opinions about the topic, or write a detail that will help you remember the topic. Here are some examples of different ways to take notes using the three-column chart.

The topic I am studying	What I learned from reading the text or class discussion	Questions, observations, or ideas I have about the topic
Information resources	• two sources of information • asks what, when, where, who, why	• This book contains both primary and secondary information • I wonder what primary sources are in this book

Vocabulary Word	Definition	Sentence with Vocabulary Word
Primary source	A first-hand account of a historical event	A primary source account of an event is told by someone who was there.

Topic	Facts	Page Number
the study of history	the past lives on in our culture (values, attitudes, customs)	p. 5
	different sources: primary: newspapers, diaries, letters secondary: books about events in the past	p. 6
	history as family tree of human race	p. 7

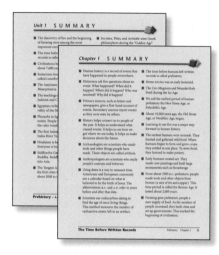

Using the Summaries

◆ Read each Chapter Summary to be sure you understand the chapter's main ideas.

◆ Review your notes and test yourself on vocabulary words and key ideas.

◆ Practice writing about some of the main events from the chapter.

◆ At the end of each unit, read the Unit Summary to be sure you understand the unit's main ideas.

Using the Reviews

◆ Answer the questions in the Lesson Reviews.

◆ In the Chapter Reviews, answer each fill-in-the-blank, multiple choice, short-answer question.

◆ Review the Test-Taking Tips.

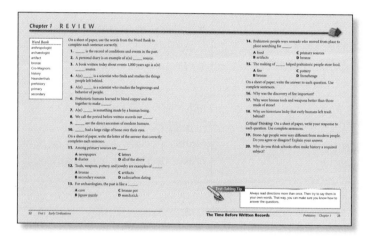

Preparing for Tests

◆ Complete the Lesson Reviews and Chapter Reviews. Make up similar questions to practice what you have learned. You may want to do this with a classmate and share your questions.

◆ Review your answers to Lesson Reviews and Chapter Reviews.

◆ Reread the Chapter Summaries.

◆ Test yourself on vocabulary words and key ideas.

Reading Checklist

Good readers do not just read with their eyes. They read with their brains turned on. In other words, they are active readers. Good readers use strategies as they read to keep them on their toes. The following strategies will help you to check your understanding of what you read. A strategy appears at the beginning of each chapter of this book.

■ **Summarizing** To summarize a text, stop often as you read. Notice these things: the topic, the main thing being said about the topic, important details that support the main idea. Try to sum up the author's message using your own words.

■ **Questioning** Ask yourself questions about the text and read to answer them. Here are some useful questions to ask: Why did the author include this information? Is this like anything I have experienced? Am I learning what I hoped I would learn?

■ **Predicting** As you read, think about what might come next. Add in what you already know about the topic. Predict what the text will say. Then, as you read, notice whether your prediction is right. If not, change your prediction.

■ **Text Structure** Pay attention to how a text is organized. Find parts that stand out. They are probably the most important ideas or facts. Think about why the author organized ideas this way. Is the author showing a sequence of events? Is the author explaining a solution or the effect of something?

■ **Visualizing** Picture what is happening in a text or what is being described. Make a movie out of it in your mind. If you can picture it clearly, then you know you understand it. Visualizing what you read will also help you remember it later.

■ **Inferencing** The meaning of a text may not be stated. Instead, the author may give clues and hints. It is up to you to put them together with what you already know about the topic. Then you make an inference—you conclude what the author means.

■ **Metacognition** Think about your thinking patterns as you read. Before reading a text, preview it. Think about what you can do to get the most out of it. Think about what you already know about the topic. Write down any questions you have. After you read, ask yourself: Did that make sense? If not, read it again.

Using Globes and Maps

A globe is a model of Earth. Looking at the globe, you can see that Earth is round. You can see Earth's features and surfaces. A globe is the best way to show Earth. However, how do you show the round features of a globe on a flat page? You use a map.

You also can see that geographers divide Earth into halves or **hemispheres**. The **equator** divides Earth into the Northern Hemisphere and the Southern Hemisphere. The equator is an imaginary line that circles the middle of Earth.

The **prime meridian** and the **international date line** divide Earth into the Eastern Hemisphere and the Western Hemisphere. The prime meridian is an imaginary line that circles Earth from the North Pole to the South Pole. The international date line is on the side of Earth you cannot see here. It is directly opposite the prime meridian.

Geographers measure distances from the equator and the prime meridian. These distances are imaginary lines called **latitude** and **longitude**.

The Hemispheres

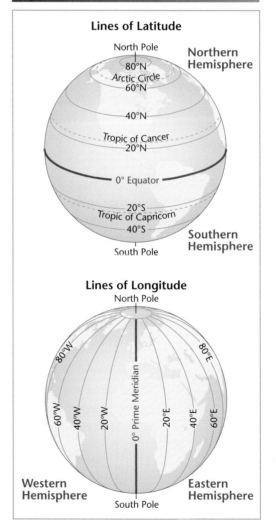

Lines of Latitude

Lines of Longitude

Cartographers, or **mapmakers**, have created different map projections. Some of these map projections show the true size of a place, but distort, or change, the shape. Others show the true shape, but distort the size. All maps show some kind of distortion. Therefore, geographers must choose the best maps for their purposes.

A **Mercator projection** stretches the lines of latitude apart. It does not show the true size of landmasses. A Mercator projection does show true shape, however.

Landmasses in a **Robinson projection** are not as distorted as in a Mercator projection. However, there is some distortion in the size of the landmasses.

Mercator Projection

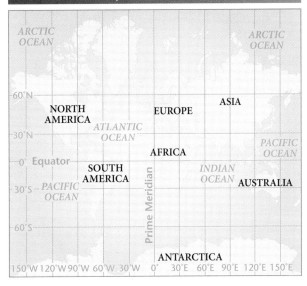

Robinson Projection

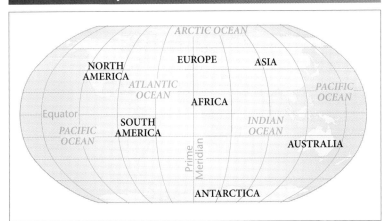

Critical Thinking

Why would a mapmaker choose to use a Robinson projection instead of a Mercator projection?

Reading a Map

To understand geography, you need to know how to read maps. To read a map, you need to understand its parts. The main parts of a map are a title, a key, a compass rose, and a scale. Many of the maps you see are **general purpose maps**. These are political maps and physical maps. A **political map** shows features that people determine, such as country boundaries, cities, and capitals.

The **title** of a map tells the area the map covers. →

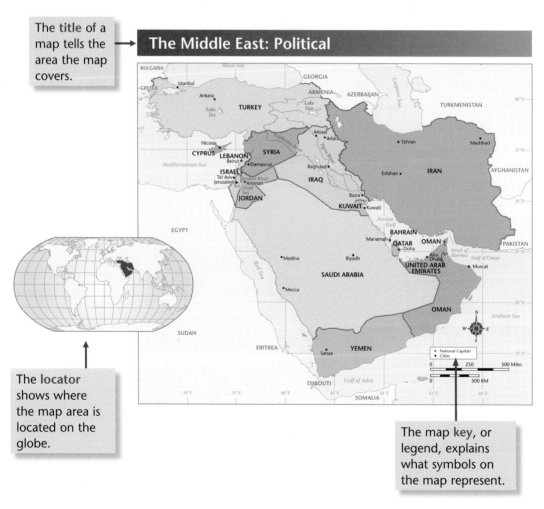

The **locator** shows where the map area is located on the globe.

The map **key**, or legend, explains what symbols on the map represent.

A **physical map** shows how high a landmass is. It also shows natural features such as rivers and oceans. Some of the maps you see show specific kinds of information. These maps are called **special purpose maps**. There are many types of special purpose maps. For example, a climate map is a special purpose map. It shows the typical weather in a place.

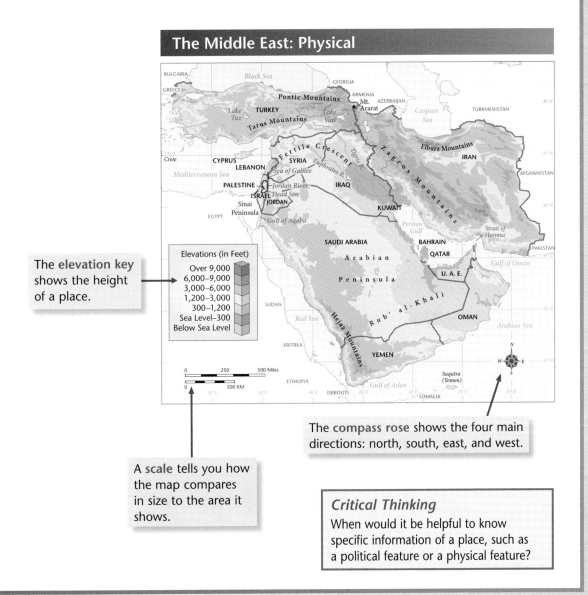

The Middle East: Physical

The **elevation key** shows the height of a place.

The **compass rose** shows the four main directions: north, south, east, and west.

A **scale** tells you how the map compares in size to the area it shows.

Critical Thinking

When would it be helpful to know specific information of a place, such as a political feature or a physical feature?

Reading Graphs and Charts

Graphs and charts organize and present information in a visual way. There are different types of graphs and charts.

A **circle graph** is sometimes called a pie graph. It is a good way to show the sizes of parts as compared to a single whole. This single whole is represented as a circle. Each piece of the circle represents a part of the whole.

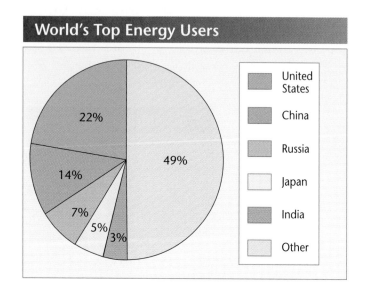

World's Top Energy Users

- United States — 49%
- China — 22%
- Russia — 14%
- Japan — 7%
- India — 5%
- Other — 3%

A **bar graph** is a good way to show information visually. Each bar represents a set of facts. You can compare sets of facts by looking at the different sizes of the bars.

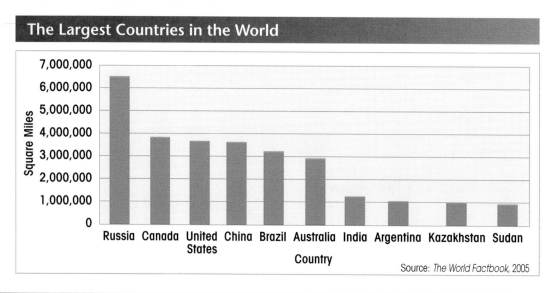

The Largest Countries in the World

Square Miles / Country

Source: *The World Factbook*, 2005

World Facts

Fact	Place	Location	Size
Highest Mountain	Mount Everest	Nepal and China	29,035 feet high
Longest River	Nile	North and East Africa	4,160 miles long
Largest Island	Greenland	North Atlantic	840,000 square miles
Largest Body of Water	Pacific Ocean	From west of North and South America to east of Asia and Australia	63,800,000 square miles

A **chart** can also be called a table. Charts are organized into rows and columns. Charts can help you to compare information.

A **line graph** shows the relationship between two sets of information. A point is placed at the intersection of every fact. When all the points are on the graph, a line is drawn to connect them. You can get a quick idea as to the trend, or direction, of information by looking at the ups and downs of the line.

World Population Growth: Historical

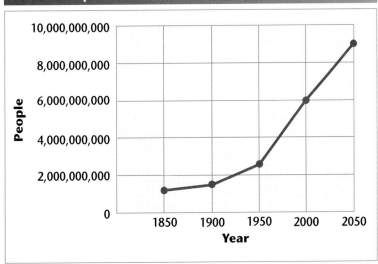

Critical Thinking

If you were to organize information about your classmates into categories such as age and gender, would you use a chart or a graph? Explain.

"We archaeologists shine scientific flashlights into the past, throwing narrow beams of light hundreds, thousands, even millions of years back into remotest prehistory."

~ *Brian Fagan, professor of anthropology at U.C. Santa Barbara in his introduction to Time Detectives (Simon & Schuster, 1995)*

Unit

1

Early Civilizations

Unit 1 covers thousands of years, from the Stone Age to early civilizations in the Americas. As you read this unit, you will learn how history is studied. You will read about the growth of the Middle East and Asia, the ancient civilizations of Greece and Rome, and the first Americans. You will also learn how this knowledge will help you understand the world today.

Prehistory

The people of the Stone Age lived before the time of written records. We cannot find newspapers or letters to tell us about them. We must depend on other things they left behind. In this chapter, you will learn what life may have been like for these prehistoric humans. You will also learn about how scientists study the past.

Goals for Learning

◆ To define history and describe two kinds of sources of information

◆ To explain why we study history

◆ To describe artifacts and what historians learn from them

◆ To identify early hominids, the Stone Age, and the importance of farming

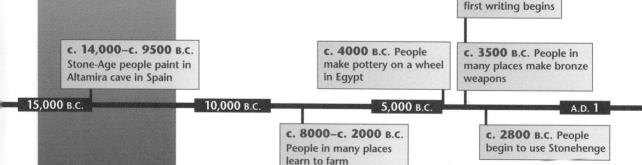

c. 14,000–c. 9500 B.C. Stone-Age people paint in Altamira cave in Spain

c. 4000 B.C. People make pottery on a wheel in Egypt

c. 3500 B.C. The first writing begins

c. 3500 B.C. People in many places make bronze weapons

15,000 B.C.   10,000 B.C.   5,000 B.C.   A.D. 1

c. 8000–c. 2000 B.C. People in many places learn to farm

c. 2800 B.C. People begin to use Stonehenge

Skeleton Finds

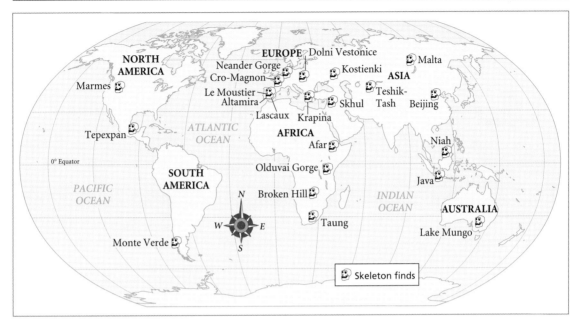

Map Skills

We can use a map that shows direction to find where things are. When you face the direction of the North Pole, you face north. If you face the South Pole, you face south. When you face north, east is to your right; west is to your left.

Most maps use a symbol to show where north is. From this information, you can figure out the three other directions. Note the direction symbol on this map. We call this symbol a compass rose.

The map on this page contains another symbol—a skull. It shows where archaeologists have found clues about early humans.

Study the map, then answer the following questions:

1. Which of the six pictured continents contains the skeleton find known as Marmes?

2. Which of the six pictured continents contains the skeleton find known as Krapina?

3. In what direction would you be traveling if you went from Monte Verde to Lake Mungo, passing through the Indian Ocean?

4. What skeleton finds are south of the imaginary line called the equator?

5. What skeleton finds are located farthest west on the map?

Reading Strategy:
Summarizing

When readers summarize, they ask questions about what they are reading. As you read the text in this chapter, ask yourself the following questions:

◆ Who or what is this chapter about?

◆ What is the main thing being said about this topic?

◆ What details are important to the understanding of this chapter?

Key Vocabulary Words

Lesson 1
History The record of past events

Culture The values, attitudes, and customs of a group

Historian One who is an expert in history

Primary source A first-hand account of a historical event

Secondary source A second-hand account of a historical event; an account written by a person who was not there

Lesson 3
Archaeologist A scientist who finds and studies the things people left behind

Artifact An object made by a person for a practical purpose

Anthropologist A scientist who studies the beginnings and the behavior of people

Radiocarbon dating A way of measuring the radioactivity of historic artifacts to determine how old they are

Lesson 4
Prehistory The time before humans left written records

Hominids A group that includes humans and their closest relatives

Ice Age A period of time when much of Earth and Earth's water was frozen

Extinct No longer existing; died out

Cro-Magnon The hominid *Homo sapiens,* a direct ancestor of modern humans

Paleolithic Age The earliest period of human history; called the Old Stone Age

Neolithic Age The age when people made polished stone tools; also called the New Stone Age

Nomad A person who moves from place to place

Monument An object or building honoring a person or event, usually made of stone

Civilization A large group of people who have cities and government, and a high level of development as a group

History

The record of past events

Culture

The values, attitudes, and customs of a group

Historian

One who is an expert in history

Primary source

A first-hand account of a historical event

Secondary source

A second-hand account of a historical event

History is the record of past events. It is the story of people and what happened to them. Each group of people has its own history. In this book, you will learn about the combined history of all people—the history of humanity.

Why Do We Study History?

The people who lived before you learned many lessons they could share with you. Imagine knowing nothing about those people. You would have to learn all their lessons for yourself. If this happened, history would be dead. But happily, history is alive and well! It lives in our **culture,** or our values, attitudes, and customs. It can teach us its lessons.

What Are Primary Sources and Secondary Sources?

When writing history, **historians**—experts in history—ask themselves: *What* happened? *When* and *where* did it happen? *Who* was involved? *Why* did it happen? To find answers, they look for **primary sources.** These sources are first-hand, or eyewitness, accounts of the event. They also seek out **secondary sources,** or second-hand records of what happened. These accounts are written by a person who was not there.

Imagine an argument in the school cafeteria. It will show you the difference between these two sources. You see the argument, so you are an eyewitness. That makes you a primary source. You tell someone about the argument. That person is not an eyewitness. That person becomes a secondary source.

The American Declaration of Independence is a primary source.

Reading Strategy:
Summarizing

How does this lesson help you understand what you will be studying in this book?

How Do Historians Use Sources?

A historian writing about the American Revolution would read what people living at the time wrote. These primary sources would include newspapers; diaries, or daily personal records; and letters.

The same historian would also read what recent historians have written about the war. Their books are secondary sources because these historians were not eyewitnesses.

You have used secondary sources ever since you started school. This textbook is a secondary source. But you are a primary source for what you actually see and hear each day.

How Do We Interpret History?

Individual people, like yourself, record history. Because people differ, what they record differs. You interpret, or explain, the cafeteria argument one way. Another eyewitness interprets it another way. Your two interpretations, or explanations of the meaning, differ. Secondary sources differ in their interpretations too.

This lesson of your history book is a secondary source. After reading it, each of your classmates will interpret it differently. Check out your various views.

Lesson 1 Review On a sheet of paper, use the words from the Word bank to complete each sentence correctly.

1. History is the record of _____ events.

2. Historians ask _____ questions that begin with *W*.

3. _____ sources are second-hand accounts of what happened.

4. _____ sources might include what an eyewitness wrote in newspapers, diaries, and letters.

5. History lives in our _____ and our customs.

Word Bank

culture

five

past

primary

secondary

What do you think

Why do history books sometimes say different things about the same subject?

History helps us remember our past. It also helps us understand how we got to the present. This knowledge helps us figure out what to do tomorrow.

What Can We Learn About People?

History tells us the story of all the people in every country of the world. We discover their new ideas. We realize that they did great things.

History helps us understand their problems. Remember that cafeteria argument? To really understand what caused it, we need to question each person involved. Then we discover all the things that caused the argument. The same is true with history.

How Does History Connect Us to the Past?

History connects us to all the people who have ever lived. Much happened before our lives began. Much will happen after our lives end. But the past gives us roots.

Objectives

◆ To describe how the study of history connects you to the past

◆ To explain how you are part of the global community

Reading Strategy:
Summarizing

This lesson summarizes the reasons for studying history. What does it tell you about the importance of learning about history?

Roots anchor, or hold, a tree in the ground. A family tree helps you understand who you are. The family tree, or history, of the world helps you understand the human race. You are a part of the global community. The global community involves the whole world. It stretches back through time to the beginning of humanity.

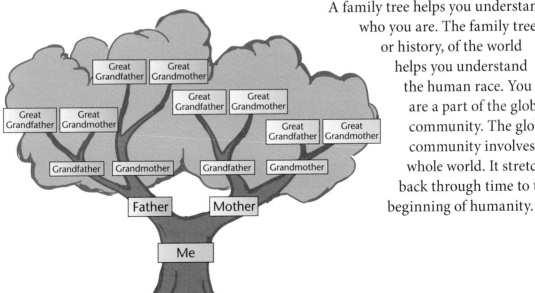

Reading Strategy:
Summarizing

What is the main idea of this lesson?

Lesson 2 Review On a sheet of paper, use the words from the Word Bank to complete each sentence correctly.

1. We study _____ to help us understand how we got where we are today.

2. History helps us understand how we got to the _____.

3. The past gives us _____. These anchor, or hold, us to those people who have gone before us.

4. History gives us a sense of being connected with the _____ of the past.

5. By knowing the past, we may be able to decide what to do in the _____.

What do you think ?

How does history help us understand what is happening today?

Then and Now

A Human's Best Friend

You may have something in common with early humans—a dog. Dogs have lived with humans for more than 9,000 years. At first, an orphan wolf cub may have found food near a human campsite. Because wolves are used to living in a pack, the cub stayed nearby. Gradually the wolf became tamer. It guarded the camp against other animals and began to help the humans hunt.

Dogs soon became very different from their wolf ancestors. People bred different breeds for certain qualities. Dogs with a keen sense of smell made good hunting dogs. Some dogs were bred for strength, to pull heavy sleds. Today some dogs are trained for police work. Others act as guides for the blind. About 400 different breeds of dogs exist. They live everywhere in the world with their best friends—humans.

Objectives

◆ To describe how historians use artifacts to learn about the past

◆ To understand why there are different calendars

◆ To explain how radiocarbon dating is used

Archaeologist

A scientist who finds and studies the things people left behind

Artifact

An object made by a person for a practical purpose

Anthropologist

A scientist who studies the beginnings and the behavior of people

Historians write about history. To do this, they study written sources that earlier people left behind. But early people did not write books, newspapers, or letters. What tells us about them?

Who Explores the Past?

Archaeologists are scientists who find and study things people left behind. These things are **artifacts,** or objects made for a practical purpose. They include tools, weapons, pottery, and jewelry.

Anthropologists are scientists who study the beginnings and the behavior of people. For example, they may study the garbage Americans throw out! The garbage tells them about the eating habits of Americans. It also tells them what Americans do for fun, what they read, and much more.

Why Are Dates Important?

Most students think that history is nothing but dates: 2186 B.C. and A.D. 1096. But dates help us measure time. Dates tell us when things happened. For example, a great earthquake shook India in 1897. By dating it, we know that this event happened over 100 years ago.

Archaeologists study things that are left behind from the past—even human remains.

The Time Before Written Records

Why Do We Have Different Calendars?

Calendars help us keep track of time. Throughout the world, people use different calendars. Each is based on a different event.

The calendar used in many parts of the world is based on the birth of Jesus, who Christians believe is the "Christ." This kind of calendar lists some historical events as B.C., or "Before Christ." It lists other events as A.D. The letters A.D. stand for the Latin words *anno Domini*. This means "in the year of our Lord." So, A.D. 1776 is "in the year of our Lord 1776." The Jewish calendar begins with the year in which the Jews believe God created the world. Many Muslims use a calendar based on the date of Muhammad's flight from Mecca to Medina.

What Is Radiocarbon Dating?

All living things contain carbon. A small number of carbon atoms in living things are radioactive. Some of these atoms stay in animals and plants for thousands of years after they die. Scientists use **radiocarbon dating** to determine the age of an artifact. That is, they measure the radioactivity of historic artifacts to determine how old they are.

Radiocarbon dating

A way of measuring the radioactivity of historic artifacts to determine how old they are

Reading Strategy:
Summarizing

What tools do archaeologists and anthropologists use to determine the date of an object?

History in Your Life

What Can You Learn from Bones?

A trained scientist would say you can learn a lot from bones. Scientists carefully study the bones and teeth of early humans. Bones are clues to diet, health, and lifestyles. The prehistoric man known as "the Iceman" was a Bronze-Age hiker. His 4,000-year-old frozen body was found in the Alps in 1991. The Iceman's worn-down teeth showed that he ate tough, raw foods. Scientists also analyze the chemicals in bones. Some experiments showed when early Americans stopped eating wild plants and began to eat corn. That meant they had become farmers.

Bones and teeth give other clues. They can show whether a person had a good diet or certain diseases. A fractured skull may mean that someone died violently. The long thigh bone is a good clue to a person's height. Measuring that bone can tell how tall or short people were in the past.

Biography

Louis Leakey: 1903–1972
Mary Leakey: 1913–1996

Louis and Mary Leakey made exciting discoveries about early humans. Louis Leakey believed that humankind had developed in Africa. The two British scientists worked in East Africa for about 40 years. They collected stone tools and pieces of bone, skulls, and teeth. These were clues to what early people were like. One major site was Olduvai Gorge, Tanzania. Mary Leakey found a large piece of skull there. Tests showed it was 1.75 million years old. That was much older than other human-type fossils. Later she found footprints more than 3 million years old. These showed that hominids (almost-humans) were walking upright that long ago.

How Else Do Archaeologists Date Artifacts?

Sometimes, archaeologists must guess the age of an object. They do this by studying where they found the object. For example, they might find one object near another one made of plastic. Plastic is a fairly new invention. So both objects are probably fairly new. In the same way, an archaeologist might find an object near ancient bones. Because the bones are old, the object probably is too.

Archaeologists must figure out how ancient people lived. To do this, they become detectives who use artifacts as clues. For example, an artifact is made of a certain material. We find this material in only a few areas of the world. The archaeologists can find out where the object may have been made. They may also be able to figure out where the people who used it came from.

How Is the Past Like a Jigsaw Puzzle?

For some periods of history, historians have few artifacts. That makes learning about people from the past hard. It is like a 1,000-piece jigsaw puzzle with no picture and only a few pieces. Historians can only guess what the finished puzzle of the past might look like.

But their guess can change. Sometimes, archaeologists discover new artifacts. They gather more missing pieces. Then their guess about the finished puzzle may change.

Lesson 3 Review On a sheet of paper, write the answer to each question. Use complete sentences.

1. What does an archaeologist do?

2. What does an anthropologist do?

3. What is an artifact?

4. Why are dates necessary to historians?

5. What does B.C. tell you about a date?

What do you think ?

How are artifacts like pieces in a jigsaw puzzle?

Objectives

◆ To identify early hominids, Neanderthals, and Cro-Magnons

◆ To describe the Old and New Stone Ages

◆ To understand the importance of farming

◆ To explain the Bronze Age

Prehistory

The time before humans left written records

Hominids

A group that includes humans and their closest relatives

Ice Age

A period of time when much of Earth and Earth's water was frozen

Extinct

No longer existing; died out

We know little about the earliest people who lived on Earth. Why? Because they left no written records. We have written records for only about the last 5,500 years. Scientists learned about prehistoric times by finding ancient bones and stone tools buried in the earth. The long, long time before humans left written records is our **prehistory.**

Who Was "Java Man"?

In 1891, on the island of Java in Asia, scientists discovered humanlike bones. It was determined that the bones were not those of a modern human. The bones of "Java Man" were thought to be around 2 million years old. "Java Man" was given the scientific name *Homo erectus,* meaning "upright man." Over the years, *Homo erectus* bones were found throughout Africa, Asia, and Europe. It is believed that *Homo erectus* was the first **hominid** to use fire. Hominids are a group that includes humans and their closest relatives. The bones of several hominids different from *Homo erectus* have also been discovered. These hominids were older in appearance and had smaller brains. They lived a million or more years before *Homo erectus.*

Who Were the Neanderthals?

In 1856, in Germany's Neander valley, the bones of a close relative to modern humans were discovered. Because of where the bones were found, it was given the name *Neanderthal.* Many more bones of the Neanderthals were found in Europe. Neanderthals appeared about 250,000 years ago. During this time, the climate changed from being mild to very cold. This cold period when much of Earth was frozen is called the **Ice Age.** Neanderthals were about 5 feet tall, stocky, and very strong. They had a large ridge of bone over their eyes. Their body shape helped them survive the harsh weather. They made different kinds of tools out of animal bones and stones. They skinned animals for clothing. They buried their dead. They may have been able to speak. Sometime between 20,000 and 30,000 years ago, the Neanderthals became **extinct,** or died out.

Who Were the Cro-Magnons?

Cro-Magnons, like all modern humans, are *Homo sapiens,* meaning "wise man." In 1868, five skeletons were found in a Cro-Magnon cave in France. The bones showed that the general body shape of these people was like that of modern humans. The Cro-Magnons appeared in Europe about 40,000 years ago. Unlike the Neanderthals, the Cro-Magnons are our direct ancestor. They had a spoken language. They were skillful hunters and toolmakers. On a piece of bone or stone, they kept count of the phases of the moon. This was a simple calendar. They were creative artists. They wore jewelry made of ivory and shells. On the walls of caves they painted colorful pictures of animals and simple figures of themselves.

What Are the Old and New Stone Ages?

We call the earliest period of human history the Old Stone Age, or **Paleolithic Age.** It is called the Old Stone Age because people made weapons and tools from stone. They shaped the earliest stone tools from obsidian, a volcanic glass. They also made hand axes and spears. People during the Paleolithic Age lived in small groups and moved frequently from place to place in search of food.

Communication in History

Humans Learn to Say "Hello"

What did early humans sound like? What language did they speak? No one can be sure. Anthropologists think that humans developed language over millions of years. Very early humans probably used a "call system." They made sounds with a certain meaning, like those that some animals use. Calls showed feelings. "Look out! There's a lion!" "I'm scared." "This plant tastes good."

Then life changed for early humans. For one thing, they began to walk upright on two feet. This freed their hands to make tools. People also began to live in larger groups. They worked together to find wild plants. Groups of hunters tracked animals. Now people needed a better way to share ideas. Hunters had to plan for the next day's hunt. A skillful potter needed to teach younger workers the craft. Humans also changed physically. Their brains and larynx, or voice box, developed. By about 100,000 years ago, some early humans were ready for complex human speech.

How Did Early Humans Use Fire?

The discovery of fire is one of the most important events in human history. Stone-Age humans knew that lightning caused fire. At some point, they learned that fire creates heat. With fire, they could warm themselves.

Much later, these early people learned how to move a fire inside a cave. They learned how to keep the embers, or glowing remains of the fire, burning. With these embers, they could start a new fire. Finally, they learned to cook with fire.

What Was the Neolithic Age?

About 10,000 years ago, the New Stone Age, or **Neolithic Age,** began. During this time, people made polished stone tools. They learned how to plant seeds and grow their own food. This allowed them to settle in one place. They also began to tame animals and raise them for food. The earliest humans were **nomads.** They moved from place to place to hunt and gather food. When people began to produce their own food, they were able to create settled communities. As time passed, these communities became villages and then cities. This important historical change is known as the agriculture, or farming, revolution. People lived in these farming communities for thousands of years. This would not change until the 1700s and 1800s, when the Industrial Revolution once again completely changed the way people lived.

How Did Early Humans Use Pottery?

Growing food created a new problem for these Stone-Age humans. They harvested crops once or twice a year. But how could they store the grains for later use?

Prehistoric humans solved their problem by making pottery. They made pottery jars out of clay from riverbeds. These pottery jars protected food from insects, mice, and dampness. Today, the broken parts of this pottery are like puzzle pieces. They help scholars calculate the dates a certain people lived.

Monument

An object or building honoring a person or event, usually made of stone

What Art Did Early Humans Create?

Prehistoric humans left no written records. However, they did leave us some important artwork. In 1859, a young girl and her father explored a cave in northern Spain. They discovered beautiful pictures on the cave walls. The drawings pictured animals—deer, wild boar, horses, and bison, or buffalo.

Today, most scholars believe that Stone-Age artists painted these pictures. They probably used twigs or bits of moss for brushes. To make the paint, they mixed meat grease with colored clay and vegetable colorings.

Reading Strategy:
Summarizing

What do you already know about Stonehenge? Was it helpful in understanding these paragraphs?

What Is Stonehenge?

Stonehenge is a famous prehistoric **monument.** It stands near the city of Salisbury in England. It consists of a series of great stone circles. Over 30 huge stones make up the circles. Each stone weighs over 35 tons.

Scientists have discovered that the stones at Stonehenge came from as far away as 135 miles. About 250 workers would have had to move each stone that long distance. How could early humans do this before the invention of the wheel?

The piled-up bank of earth around Stonehenge had a ridge nearly six feet high. A ditch six feet deep lay outside it. Prehistoric people worked with simple tools. How many people worked to build this bank and this ditch? And for how long did they work? We do not know.

Stonehenge is a puzzling prehistoric monument near Salisbury, England. Today, experts can only guess what this ancient mass of huge stones was used for long ago.

Stonehenge was in use for more than 1,700 years. Most scholars think prehistoric people honored their gods there. Or Stonehenge might have helped people guess when an eclipse, such as the moon hiding the sun, would happen.

How Did the Stone Age Become the Bronze Age?

Because stone tools broke easily, prehistoric humans looked for other materials for their tools. First, they used the metal copper. Later they discovered how to make bronze. Bronze is a harder metal made of an alloy, or blend, of copper and tin. It also holds a sharper cutting edge.

From about 3500 B.C., prehistoric people made their tools from bronze. They used it for the next 2,000 years. We call this time period the "Bronze Age."

How Did Bronze Change Life?

Bronze does not break easily. With it, ancient people invented many new tools. These made their lives easier. Bronze-Age people also invented a sled to carry things on land. They hollowed out logs and made canoes to carry things on water.

Where Does Prehistory Lead?

Prehistory is an exciting period of humanity's story. At first, humans were nomads. They moved from place to place to hunt and gather food. Then they learned to grow crops. They settled close to their fields and formed small groups.

Now prehistoric humans had a sure supply of food. Because of this, their population grew more quickly. This began a chain of fast changes. These changes brought about the first **civilizations,** in which people built cities and set up governments. People who belong to a civilization have a high level of development.

Lesson 4 Review On a sheet of paper, write the letter of the answer that correctly completes each sentence.

1. The scientific name of "Java Man" is _____.

   A Neanderthal   **C** *Homo sapiens*

   B *Homo erectus*   **D** Neolithic Man

2. The discovery of _____ helped ancient people cook food and stay warm.

   A fire   **B** pottery   **C** painting   **D** monuments

3. Drawings in _____ tell us something about the life of prehistoric people.

   A riverbeds   **B** bronze   **C** caves   **D** tools

4. Because they learned to _____, early people stopped being nomads.

   A make drawings   **C** farm
   B make bronze   **D** make pottery

5. Bronze is a mixture of copper and _____.

   A obsidian   **B** clay   **C** stone   **D** tin

What do you think ?

What do cave drawings and Stonehenge tell you about prehistoric people?

"In the Beginning . . ."

The Bible (this name comes from the Greek word meaning "book") is a special book of Jews and Christians. It is a collection of smaller books written over many years. Most existed as spoken stories before they were written down. They were written down over a period of more than 1,000 years.

The Jewish Bible is mostly about the history of the Hebrew, or Jewish, people in the Middle East. Most of it is set in Palestine or Israel. Christians usually call the Jewish Bible the Old Testament.

What Christians call the New Testament is about the teaching of Jesus and his followers, who started the Christian church. It was mostly written between A.D. 50 and A.D. 100.

The Bible was not written in English. It was written in the Hebrew, Aramaic, and Greek languages. It has been translated into many other languages. The following reading is from the first book, Genesis. That name means "beginning." In a poetic way Genesis describes the creation of the world. Read the excerpt below. Then answer the questions that follow.

In the beginning when God created the heavens and the earth, the earth was a formless void. . . . And God said, "Let there be light"; and there was light. God called the light Day and the darkness he called Night. . . .

And God said, "Let the waters under the heavens be gathered together into one place, and let the dry land appear." And it was so. God called the dry land Earth and the waters . . . he called Seas. . . . And God said, "Let the earth put forth vegetation . . . and fruit trees." . . . And it was so. . . .

"Let there be light . . . to separate the day from the night; and let them be for signs and for seasons and for days and years. . . ." And it was so. . . .

So God created . . . every living creature that moves, of every kind, with which the waters swarm, and every winged bird. . . .

Then God said, "Let us make humankind in our image, according to our likeness; and let them have dominion over . . . every creeping thing that creeps upon the earth." . . . God saw everything that he had made, and indeed, it was very good. . . .

And on the seventh day God finished the work that he had done, and he rested on the seventh day from all the work that he had done.

Document-Based Questions

1. What two religions consider the Bible a very special book?

2. What names did God give the waters and the dry land?

3. What do you think were the "lights" that separated day from night?

4. What do you think is meant by "dominion" (power) over "every creeping thing"?

5. According to Genesis, what happened on the seventh day?

Source: Quotes are from New Revised Standard Version.

The Search for the Truth

The ancient Greeks had two ways of thinking about the truth. They called them by different terms: *logos* and *mythos.* Logos meant the kind of truth that can be found through argument and demonstrations. You can see the word *logos* in the ending of words like *archaeology* and *anthropology.* These refer to careful study. Scientists in these fields study evidence and make experiments. They try to find the truth about human origins.

Poseidon, Greek god of the sea, was a key part of Greek mythology—stories that spoke the truth for ancient Greeks.

Mythos meant a different kind of truth. These were stories that everyone accepted as true. They were not questioned. Today, we use the word *myth* for made-up stories. That is the opposite of what the Greeks meant.

Like the Greeks, other people in history have asked basic questions about themselves and their world. When did the world begin? Where did human beings come from?

Scientists look for answers to these questions. They accept evidence showing that the earth is about 4.5 billion years old. They also agree with the evidence that life on earth began about 1.5 billion years later, with simple organisms. More complex forms of life developed gradually over time.

Many cultures explain how the world began in non-scientific ways. One creation story comes from the Navaho of the American Southwest.

It says there were once smaller worlds inside the earth. The story tells how people escaped to the earth's surface by climbing up a reed.

The Chinese have another story. It begins with a great void, or emptiness. Yin and yang were opposing forces in the void. Yin is the force of stillness. Yang is the force of action. Yin and yang combined and created the world.

In the Bible, the book of Genesis describes how God created the world and all life in six days. Because of this account, some Christians reject scientific explanations for human origins. Other Christians accept both scientific evidence and the biblical story.

Other peoples in other places have other explanations. Humans still seek the truth about themselves. In different ways, they will go on looking for answers to important questions.

Wrap-Up

1. What methods did the ancient Greeks use to find the truth of "logos?"

2. How was "mythos" different from "logos?"

3. What methods do scientists use to determine the truth?

4. What were the two forces in Chinese myth?

5. What book of the Bible describes the creation?

Chapter 1   S U M M A R Y

- Human history is a record of events that have happened to people everywhere.

- Historians ask five questions about an event: *What* happened? *When* did it happen? *Where* did it happen? *Who* was involved? *Why* did it happen?

- Primary sources, such as letters and newspapers, give a first-hand account of events. Secondary sources report events as they were seen by others.

- History helps connect us to people of the past. It helps us understand what caused events. It helps us see how we got where we are today. It helps us make decisions about the future.

- Archaeologists are scientists who study tools and other things people have made. These objects are called artifacts.

- Anthropologists are scientists who study people's customs and behavior.

- Using dates is a way to measure time. Americans and Europeans commonly use a calendar based on what is believed to be the birth of Jesus. The abbreviations B.C. and A.D. refer to years before and after that date.

- Scientists use radiocarbon dating to find the age of once-living things. This method measures the number of radioactive atoms left in an artifact.

- The time before humans left written records is called prehistory.

- *Homo erectus* was an early hominid.

- The Cro-Magnons and Neanderthals lived during the Ice Age.

- We call the earliest period of human prehistory the Old Stone Age, or Paleolithic Age.

- About 10,000 years ago, the New Stone Age, or Neolithic Age, began.

- Learning to use fire was a major step forward in human history.

- The earliest humans were nomads. They hunted and gathered wild food. When humans began to farm and grow crops, they settled in one place. To store food, they learned to make pottery.

- Early humans created art. They made cave paintings and built large monuments such as Stonehenge.

- From about 3500 B.C. prehistoric people made tools and other objects from bronze (a mix of tin and copper). This time period is called the Bronze Age. It lasted about 2,000 years.

- Farming gave prehistoric people a sure supply of food. As the number of people increased, they built cities and set up governments. This marked the beginning of civilization.

Chapter 1 R E V I E W

Word Bank

anthropologist

archaeologist

artifact

bronze

Cro-Magnons

history

Neanderthals

prehistory

primary

secondary

On a sheet of paper, use the words from the Word Bank to complete each sentence correctly.

1. _____ is the record of conditions and events in the past.

2. A personal diary is an example of a(n) _____ source.

3. A book written today about events 1,000 years ago is a(n) _____ source.

4. A(n) _____ is a scientist who finds and studies the things people left behind.

5. A(n) _____ is a scientist who studies the beginnings and behavior of people.

6. Prehistoric humans learned to blend copper and tin together to make _____.

7. A(n) _____ is something made by a human being.

8. We call the period before written records our _____.

9. _____ are the direct ancestors of modern humans.

10. _____ had a large ridge of bone over their eyes.

On a sheet of paper, write the letter of the answer that correctly completes each sentence.

11. Among primary sources are _____.

    A newspapers   **C** letters
    B diaries   **D** all of the above

12. Tools, weapons, pottery, and jewelry are examples of _____.

    A bronze   **C** artifacts
    B secondary sources   **D** radiocarbon dating

13. For archaeologists, the past is like a _____.

    A cave   **C** bronze pot
    B jigsaw puzzle   **D** matchstick

14. Prehistoric people were nomads who moved from place to place searching for _____.

    A food   **C** primary sources

    B artifacts   **D** bronze

15. The making of _____ helped prehistoric people store food.

    A fire   **C** pottery

    B bronze   **D** Stonehenge

On a sheet of paper, write the answer to each question. Use complete sentences.

16. Why was the discovery of fire important?

17. Why were bronze tools and weapons better than those made of stone?

18. Why are historians lucky that early humans left trash behind?

Critical Thinking On a sheet of paper, write your response to each question. Use complete sentences.

19. Stone-Age people were very different from modern people. Do you agree or disagree? Explain your answer.

20. Why do you think schools often make history a required subject?

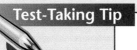

Test-Taking Tip

Always read directions more than once. Then try to say them in your own words. That way, you can make sure you know how to answer the questions.

The Time Before Written Records   *Prehistory*   *Chapter 1*   **23**

2

The Ancient Middle East

A s early as 7,000 years ago, civilization began to develop in the Middle East. Many people settled along the Tigris and the Euphrates Rivers there. We call this area Mesopotamia, a word that means "land between the rivers." Mesopotamia and the land to its east form the "Fertile Crescent." In this chapter, you will learn about the people who lived along the Fertile Crescent. You will also discover the gifts they gave to us.

Goals for Learning

◆ To describe life in Sumer and identify the Sumerians' contributions to the world

◆ To describe Akkadian and Babylonian civilizations in Mesopotamia and analyze the rule of Hammurabi

◆ To evaluate the role of the Phoenicians and the Hebrews in world civilization

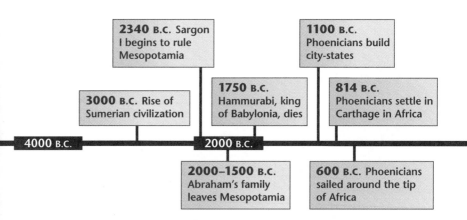

2340 B.C. Sargon I begins to rule Mesopotamia

1100 B.C. Phoenicians build city-states

3000 B.C. Rise of Sumerian civilization

1750 B.C. Hammurabi, king of Babylonia, dies

814 B.C. Phoenicians settle in Carthage in Africa

| 6000 B.C. | 4000 B.C. | 2000 B.C. |

5000 B.C. Sumerians begin to farm in Mesopotamia

2000–1500 B.C. Abraham's family leaves Mesopotamia

600 B.C. Phoenicians sailed around the tip of Africa

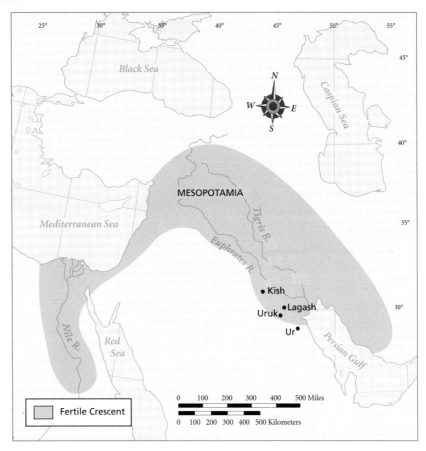

Map Skills

We have given Mesopotamia, the "land between the rivers," many names. Since the first great civilizations developed there, we called it "the cradle of civilization." We also called it the "Fertile Crescent." Why? Because Mesopotamia and the land to its west is shaped like a crescent, or quarter, moon. Also, it is fertile, or able to provide plentiful crops.

Because of the oil in this area, the Fertile Crescent is important to the whole world today.

Study the map, then answer the following questions:

1. What are the names of the five seas shown on the map?

2. What four cities appear on the map?

3. What two great rivers flow in Mesopotamia?

4. About how many miles long is the Fertile Crescent?

5. In what direction is Mesopotamia from the Mediterranean Sea?

Reading Strategy:
Questioning

Asking questions as you read will help you understand and remember more of the information. Questioning the text will also help you to be a more active reader. As you read, ask yourself:

◆ What is my reason for reading this text?

◆ What decisions can I make about the facts and details in this text?

◆ What connections can I make between this text and my own life?

Key Vocabulary Words

Lesson 1

City-state A city surrounded by smaller villages

Military Having to do with the army

Temple A place in which to honor gods

Worship To honor and praise a god

Priest A religious leader

Cuneiform The writing invented by Sumerians

Lesson 2

Translate To change the words of one language into those of another

Reign To rule; the period of time a king or queen rules

Lesson 3

Fertile Crescent The area in the Middle East shaped like a quarter moon (crescent) where one of the earliest civilizations developed

Bible The Hebrew and Christian book that is thought to be holy

Famine A time when crops do not grow and there is no food

Commandment A rule, or a way to act

Judaism The religion of the Hebrews that Jews practice today

Covenant An agreement

Objectives

◆ To describe life in Sumer

◆ To identify four things the Sumerians added to world civilization

City-state

A city surrounded by smaller villages

Military

Having to do with the army

Reading Strategy: Questioning

What do you think you will learn about by reading this lesson?

About 7,000 years ago, several groups of people settled between the Tigris and the Euphrates Rivers. The place where they settled is called Mesopotamia. Mesopotamia means "the land between the rivers."

Every spring the rivers flooded their banks and made the land fertile. The rivers helped people raise crops and care for their goats, cows, and sheep. Few trees grew there, and there was little stone for building. Yet in this place, an unusual people—the Sumerians—began to build a great civilization. Their civilization is called Sumer.

Who Were the Sumerians?

At first, the Sumerians lived in the hills northeast of Mesopotamia. Gradually they moved into the river valleys. The Sumerians shared a common language and religion. They were one of many different tribes that lived in this area.

The Sumerians built several large **city-states,** or cities surrounded by smaller villages. More than 20,000 people lived in the largest cities. They built strong, protective walls around the cities. They also built canals and dikes—banks of earth that keep out water. Then they drained the nearby water-soaked land and irrigated the farmlands.

Each city had its own government. In the beginning, the people chose their leader. But then the city-states began to fight with each other. Leaders of the **military,** or army, became their rulers.

What Was Life Like in Sumer?

Sumerians lived far better than prehistoric humans had. Even the poorest citizens owned their own farm or house. Women had many legal, or lawful, rights. They could own property and run a business. Sumerian slaves could set up a business, borrow money, and buy their freedom. Children had to obey. If they disobeyed, their parents could sell them into slavery! In school, teachers could beat children who made mistakes. The children's parents chose whom they would marry.

What Was a Sumerian Home Like?

The Sumerians learned to make bricks by putting clay in molds. Then they baked the bricks in the hot sun. They used these clay bricks to build one-story houses. Each had several rooms surrounding an open patio.

People with more money built larger, two-story houses. They coated the walls with a mixture of water, sand, and perhaps other materials. Then they painted the inside and the outside of their house white.

What Were Ziggurats?

The main building in each Sumerian city was its **temple.** There, the people **worshiped,** or honored, their gods. Each temple was in a ziggurat, or pyramid, shape with four sides. A temple ziggurat was up to six or seven stories high.

Inside the temple, the Sumerians built rooms for their **priests,** or religious leaders. The priests made sure that the workers built the ziggurat correctly. Building was expensive, so the priests asked for and received a part of each farmer's crop.

The ziggurat was the main part of every Sumerian city. It was a temple with rooms inside for priests and worship. Some ziggurats are still standing today.

What Were the Sumerian Gods Like?

Like most people at that time, the Sumerians believed in gods who had human feelings. They believed that when the gods became angry, they punished the Sumerians. They made rivers flood and crops fail.

To keep their many gods happy, the Sumerians built ziggurats in which to worship them. They kept statues of the gods in these temples. They also sacrificed animals daily to their gods.

What Is the Most Important Sumerian Invention?

The Sumerians invented writing. We call their writing **cuneiform.** Writing probably began when the priests started to keep records. Later, the Sumerians made cuneiform more simple by creating a different symbol for each sound or word. They created about 600 characters, or symbols.

The Sumerians had no paper. They wrote on soft clay tablets with a sharp, pointed tool called a stylus. Then they baked the tablets to make them hard.

History in Your Life

The Story of Gilgamesh

The story of Gilgamesh is the world's oldest known written literature. It is a long poem, or epic, that tells Sumerian myths. It is on clay tablets written about 4,000 years ago. The story itself is even older. Gilgamesh was a real person. He probably ruled Uruk, a city in Mesopotamia, before 2500 B.C. The myth makes him a hero king. He is part god and part human. The poem centers on his hunt for a way to live forever. There are battles with spirits and divine animals. Enkidu is another character. He lived in the forest with animals.

Gilgamesh beat him in a fight. Then Enkidu became his friend and companion.

Some stories in the Gilgamesh epic are similar to those in the Bible. One story tells about a great flood in Mesopotamia. A man tells Gilgamesh how he built a boat and lived through the flood. This is similar to the story of Noah and the Great Flood from the Bible.

Archaeologists have found many of these tablets. Most of them are legal and business records. About 5,000 of them, however, contain our oldest known writings—hymns, stories, and poems. Some tablets list the names of cities, trees, insects, and many other things. This means the Sumerians were the first people to write down history.

What Other Gifts Did the Sumerians Give Us?

The Sumerians may have been the first people to use a plow and a sailboat. They were the first to put wheels on carts. They also invented the potter's wheel. On this wheel, they could make more useful pottery shapes.

Sumerians created arches and ramps. These curved openings and smooth stairways helped them build taller and stronger buildings. To do this, they needed to know arithmetic. They based their arithmetic on the number 60. Even today, we use this number to measure time. For example, we have a 60-second minute and a 60-minute hour.

Reading Strategy:
Questioning

Ask yourself: "Did I understand what I just read about the Sumerians?" If not, read the material again.

Word Bank

bricks

cuneiform

Sumerians

temple

20,000

Lesson 1 Review On a sheet of paper, use the words from the Word Bank to complete each sentence correctly.

1. The _____ were one of many different tribes that lived in the Middle East.

2. The largest Sumerian cities had more than _____ people.

3. A ziggurat is the name for a Sumerian _____.

4. The Sumerians built with _____.

5. The Sumerians invented writing called _____.

What do you think ?

What do you think was the most important invention of the Sumerians? Why do you think this?

Translate

To change the words of one language into those of another

Years after the Sumerians built their city-states in Mesopotamia, Sargon I united them. He ruled a kingdom north of the Sumerians called Akkad. Because his Akkadian army used bronze weapons, they were stronger than other armies.

In time, Sargon's kingdom spread from the shores of the Mediterranean Sea eastward. It covered all of the Tigris and Euphrates River Valleys to the Persian Gulf. For the first time in history, one person ruled all this land. He ruled for about 35 years, from around 2340 B.C. to 2305 B.C.

What Did Sargon I Borrow from the Sumerians?

Sargon I borrowed many ideas from the Sumerians. The most important was their way of writing. The Akkadians had their own language, but they used the Sumerian cuneiform to make written records.

Scribes **translated** many Sumerian writings. That is, they changed the Sumerian words into their own Akkadian ones. In this way, the Akkadians discovered many of Sumer's ideas about religion and government.

Sargon I was a strong leader. He repaired dikes and made the irrigation systems longer. His army protected important trade routes. Sargon I died in 2305 B.C.

Think about the
purpose of this
text. Ask yourself:
"Am I finding out
the information I
expected to when I
began reading?"

Who Were the Babylonians?

Around 1800 B.C., a new city-state called Babylon arose. People feared its powerful army. Hammurabi, the king of Babylon, fought both the Akkadians and the Sumerians and won. His kingdom stretched from the Persian Gulf northward through Mesopotamia.

This memorial made of marble shows the Babylonian king (left) and the Lord Mayor of Babylon (right). Above them are cuneiform symbols of different gods.

Hammurabi built a giant ziggurat to honor the god Marduk. He also built a wall around Babylon to protect it. The wall was 11 miles long and nearly 80 feet wide. He improved roads and helped develop trade. Merchants, or traders, from as far away as India and China came to Babylon to do business.

Reign

To rule; the period of time a king or queen rules

Then and Now

"An Eye for an Eye"

Hammurabi's Code shows what life in Babylonia was like. Property was important. Ordinary people were valued less than nobles. Harming a common person brought a small fine. Harming a noble meant harsh punishment. This code was important because the laws were written out. Written laws were fairer because people knew what the law was. A ruler could not change laws without telling people. Laws were the same from case to case. People could defend themselves.

Today nearly every modern country has a written code of laws. Ideas about the laws have changed over time, though. In general, penalties for small crimes are not harsh like those in Hammurabi's Code.

Why Do We Remember Hammurabi?

People today remember Hammurabi because he created the first system of laws. We call these laws "Hammurabi's Code." He looked at the laws of all the lands he ruled. Then he collected what he thought were the best ones. Hammurabi put these into a code, or group of laws. He expected everyone in his kingdom to obey them. He also expected his government to carry out these laws.

Hammurabi ruled, or **reigned,** for almost 40 years. He was proud of all he had done during that time. Near the end of his reign, he ordered a scribe to carve his record on a large block of stone. In this way everyone knew his laws. The scribe carved nearly 300 laws on the stone. Archaeologists found it buried in the sands of Iran in 1902.

We call Hammurabi's reign the Golden Age of Babylon. After his death in 1750 B.C., the Babylonians lost their power. Then Mesopotamia was again divided into small city-states.

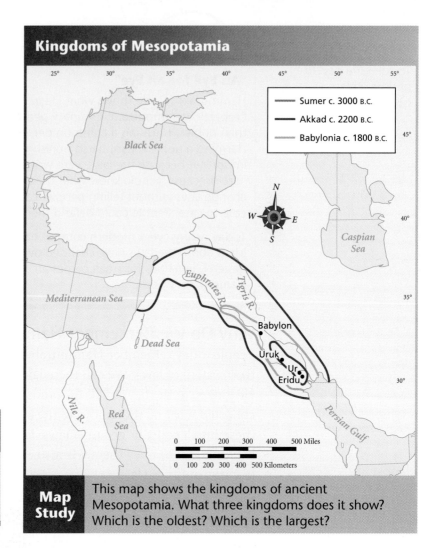

Kingdoms of Mesopotamia

Sumer c. 3000 B.C.
Akkad c. 2200 B.C.
Babylonia c. 1800 B.C.

Black Sea

Caspian Sea

Mediterranean Sea

Euphrates R.

Tigris R.

Babylon

Dead Sea

Uruk

Ur

Eridu

Nile R.

Red Sea

Persian Gulf

0   100   200   300   400   500 Miles

0   100 200 300 400 500 Kilometers

Map Study This map shows the kingdoms of ancient Mesopotamia. What three kingdoms does it show? Which is the oldest? Which is the largest?

What do you think ?

What made Sargon I and Hammurabi great leaders?

Word Bank

Akkadians
Babylon
code
Hammurabi
Sargon I

Lesson 2 Review On a sheet of paper, use the words from the Word Bank to complete each sentence correctly.

1. The first ruler to unite the city-states of Mesopotamia was _____.

2. He was the leader of the _____.

3. Around 1800 B.C. a new city-state called _____ came to power.

4. One of its great leaders was _____.

5. He collected laws from many groups of people and put them into a _____.

Fertile Crescent

The area in the Middle East shaped like a quarter moon (crescent) where one of the earliest civilizations developed

Geography Note

The rich soil in the Fertile Crescent provided those who lived there with foods such as wild wheat, barley, and nuts. Gazelle were among the wild animals available for food.

The **Fertile Crescent** is a part of the Middle East where one of the earliest civilizations developed. It is shaped like a quarter moon, or crescent, and it provides plentiful crops. Historians call its western tip Canaan and its eastern end Mesopotamia.

Why Did the Phoenicians Become Sailors?

Around 1100 B.C., a people we call the Phoenicians built a number of city-states in Canaan. Phoenicia was a narrow civilization squeezed between the mountains and the Mediterranean Sea. It had little land for farming.

The Phoenicians did, however, live in an area with many tall cedar trees. The Phoenicians used these to build ships. Soon they became sea traders. The merchants and traders became rich and built the great cities of Tyre and Sidon.

These traders sold cloth, glass, wood, and beautiful metal objects to people in other lands. Phoenician sailors carried this cargo in their ships. Then they sailed back home with ivory, metals, weapons, slaves, and wine.

Where Did the Phoenician Sailors Travel?

Phoenician sailors traveled to places no one else had been. They sailed to England in search of tin and copper. They traveled to Africa to trade for ivory. During their travels, they founded colonies in places such as France and Spain.

About 814 B.C., some Phoenicians settled in Carthage in northern Africa. Around 600 B.C., Phoenician sailors may have sailed around the tip of Africa. Some historians believe they even sailed across the ocean to America!

Phoenicians sailed in ships with a single sail. Many sailors pushed and pulled the oars that moved the ship forward. Phoenician sailors could sail far and wide because they mapped sea routes. They also used the North Star to navigate, or steer, their boats. They were the first sailors to do this.

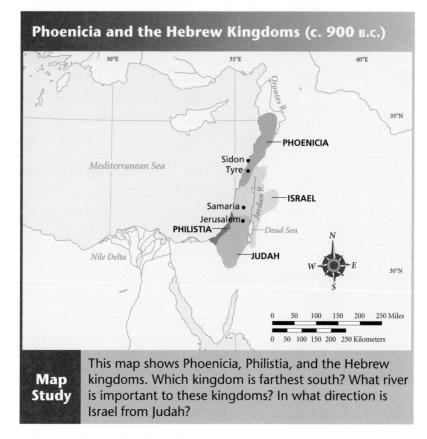

Phoenicia and the Hebrew Kingdoms (c. 900 B.C.)

Map Study

This map shows Phoenicia, Philistia, and the Hebrew kingdoms. Which kingdom is farthest south? What river is important to these kingdoms? In what direction is Israel from Judah?

What Gifts Did the Phoenicians Give Us?

We remember the Phoenicians for two important reasons: First, they developed a simple alphabet of 22 letters. These few letters took the place of the nearly 600 letters of the cuneiform alphabet. The Greeks and Romans used this alphabet to build their own. The English and Spanish languages also use it. Second, the Phoenicians spread the culture and the products of the Middle East to many places. They did this through their trade and their colonies. Because of this, important ideas spread around the world.

What Is the Holy Book of the Hebrews?

The Hebrews are another Middle Eastern people. For many centuries, Hebrew scribes wrote books to tell their story. These books have been collected into one large book that we call the **Bible.** Jews and Christians believe the Bible is holy. We find the story of the Hebrew people in the first part of Christian Bibles.

Where Did the Hebrews Come From?

Abraham was the first leader of the Hebrew people. The Hebrew part of the Bible says that God called Abraham's family out of Mesopotamia. With his family and relatives, he was to go to a new country. Historians think that this happened sometime between 2000 and 1500 B.C.

For many years, they wandered the deserts as nomads. During a **famine**—a time when crops do not grow and there is no food—they traveled to Egypt. Years passed, and the Hebrews grew large in number. The Egyptian rulers made them slaves.

Who Led the Hebrew People Out of Slavery?

A Hebrew leader named Moses led his people out of Egypt sometime between 1300 and 1200 B.C. According to the Bible, the people wandered in the desert to the east of Egypt. There Moses climbed Mount Sinai to pray.

There, the Hebrew god—Yahweh—gave Moses the Ten Commandments. These rules told the Hebrews what to do to live peacefully with God, themselves, and other people. The **commandments** became the roots of the religion of the Hebrews. Today, we call this religion **Judaism.** We now call the Hebrew people Jews.

Biography

Solomon: Ruled c. Mid–900s B.C.

Solomon was the son of King David and the greatest king of ancient Israel. According to the Bible, he ruled for 40 years. Solomon became a famous ruler.

To keep the throne, Solomon had his enemies killed. Then he made Israel a rich empire. His ships traded with other countries for gold and silver. The king had new cities built in the lands he ruled. His most famous building was the magnificent temple in Jerusalem. Thousands of workers cut cedar wood for it. They brought huge blocks of stones. The temple was richly carved and covered with gold.

What Covenant Did the Hebrews Make?

The Hebrew people believed that their god had made a **covenant,** or agreement, with them. They promised to honor Yahweh's commandments and worship him alone. In return, God promised to protect the Jews. The land of Canaan would belong to them forever.

After many years of wandering, the Hebrews came to Canaan. There they fought the people who lived in Philistia, along the coast of the Mediterranean Sea. In time, the Hebrews settled two kingdoms in Canaan—Judah and Israel. Later, invading armies destroyed both kingdoms. Today, we call this land Palestine. A large part of Palestine is the Jewish state of Israel.

What Gifts Did the Hebrews Give Us?

The Hebrews were the first people to believe in one all-powerful god. They set a high standard of behavior toward others. The Ten Commandments still influence many people.

Lesson 3 Review On a sheet of paper, write the letter of the answer that correctly completes each sentence.

1. The Phoenicians lived in _____.

    A Egypt   **B** Sumer   **C** Babylon   **D** Canaan

2. The Phoenicians became famous as _____.

    A sailors   **B** soldiers   **C** painters   **D** lawyers

3. The Phoenicians were the first people to use the _____ to help them navigate.

    A North Star   **B** compass   **C** astrolabe   **D** Orion

4. The holy book of the Hebrew people is called the _____.

    A Vegas   **B** Bible   **C** Ziggurat   **D** Cedar

5. The Hebrews differed from other ancient people because they believed in one _____.

    A commandment   **C** god

    B Marduk   **D** Sanskrit

Hammurabi's Code

Hammurabi was very concerned about justice. Having a written code of laws was fairer to his people. The laws applied to everyone. They dealt with all parts of daily life. Some laws set rules for business and trade. Others listed punishments for crimes. Still others protected women's rights. Hammurabi's Code was an important step forward in government. Many systems of laws that came later were based on Hammurabi's Code.

1. If a man destroys the eye of another man, they shall destroy his eye.

2. If he breaks a man's bone, they shall break his bone.

3. If he destroys the eye of a common man or breaks a bone of a common man, he shall pay one mina of silver.

4. If a man knocks out a tooth of a man of his own rank, they shall knock out his tooth.

5. If he knocks out a tooth of a common man, he shall pay one-third mina of silver.

6. If a house falls in and kills the owner's son, the son of the builder shall be put to death.

7. If a man strikes his father, they shall cut off his hand.

8. If a man is robbed and the robber is not caught, the governor of the city shall give the victim the value of the stolen goods.

9. If a man has stolen goods from a temple or house, he shall be put to death.

10. If a man has broken into a house, he shall be killed in front of the place where he broke through and buried there.

11. If a man wishes to divorce his wife who did not bear him children, he shall return to her the dowry [the property a woman brings to the husband at marriage] that she brought from her father's house and then he may divorce her.

Document-Based Questions

1. Compare the third law with the first and second. How were laws different for ordinary people and people of high rank?

2. Think about the saying "an eye for an eye, a tooth for a tooth." How do these laws fit with Hammurabi's Code?

3. What did Babylonians seem to value more—human life or property? Explain.

4. How was a careless builder punished? Do you think this punishment fits the crime?

5. How was a childless woman protected in a divorce?

Technology Moves Ahead

Technology is the use of knowledge to solve practical problems. Before 1500 B.C., technology was moving ahead in the ancient Middle East. People learned to control floods. They built impressive buildings. Clever, curious people have always made inventions and discoveries.

One giant step was learning to work with iron. Much earlier, people had mixed copper and tin to make bronze. Iron, however, was stronger than bronze. It made better knives and tools. Iron swords had a sharper edge. But it was harder to work with, too. It took a very hot fire to melt, or smelt, iron out of the rock. Then a worker called a smith hammered it into shape while it was red-hot.

We know little about the Hittites. Their craftsmen, however, were the first in the Middle East to work with iron. Hittites probably came from central Europe to what is now Turkey. Iron swords and horse-drawn war chariots helped them conquer their neighbors. The Hittite empire fell about 1200 B.C. After that, the secret of iron spread to others. Iron could then be used for new purposes. In Israel, farmers had iron-tipped plows. They used iron sickles to harvest grain. Carpenters had sharper iron tools.

Trade also encouraged the development of new technology for better transportation. For example, tin was scarce. People had to travel long distances to find it. Trading ships of the time had both a sail and oars. Most of the time, human crews rowed the ship. Large crews, however, were not practical for long trips. Then the Phoenicians turned a problem into an advantage.

They did not have much good farmland, but they did have tall cedar trees. Phoenicians used them to make sturdy wooden ships. Instead of rowers, their ships had one large, square sail. The Phoenicians had developed the technology to sail long distances.

In the 1300s B.C., traders sailed all over the eastern Mediterranean Sea. Usually they stayed within sight of land, the stars their only navigation tools. Traders from different cultures exchanged goods. Caravans brought goods to the coast from far inland. Hardwoods and gold came from Africa. Amber came from the Baltic Sea. Traders might bring a new ship into a region. Then others would copy it, further spreading the technology.

Wrap-Up

1. Why was iron more useful than bronze?

2. Describe how iron tools were made.

3. What people in the Middle East were the first to work with iron?

4. How did Phoenicians change the way ships were made? Why?

5. Describe how trade and technology worked together.

Chapter 2 SUMMARY

- Civilization developed in Mesopotamia about 7,000 years ago. People settled the land between two rivers—the Tigris and the Euphrates. Floods made the land good for farming. People built canals and dikes to control the water.

- The Sumerians were a tribe in Mesopotamia. They built walled city-states. Most people in Sumer could own property. Women and slaves had legal rights. Sumerians built houses out of baked clay bricks.

- Sumerians feared their gods. A ziggurat, or temple, was the most important building in a city. Their buildings had ramps and arches.

- Sumerian inventions included a writing system called cuneiform. They used a stylus to make symbols on clay tablets. They were the first to use the wheel on carts. Their counting system was based on the number 60.

- Sargon I was the ruler of Akkad in about 2340 B.C. He made the Sumerian city-states part of his lands. The Akkadians learned cuneiform.

- Hammurabi ruled the city-state of Babylon from about 1800 B.C. to his death in 1750 B.C. He organized his laws into a system, or code. They applied everywhere in the kingdom. This time is called the Golden Age of Babylon.

- The term "Fertile Crescent" refers to an area in the Middle East. It is a crescent-shaped area of land from Mesopotamia to the Mediterranean Sea.

- The Phoenicians built city-states in Canaan. They became shipbuilders and sea traders. Their main cities were Sidon and Tyre. Phoenicians also built the city of Carthage in North Africa. They made maps of the seas. They used the North Star for navigation.

- The Phoenicians developed a 22-letter alphabet. It is the ancestor of the alphabet we use today. They took ideas from the Middle East to many places.

- The first books of the Bible tell the history of the Hebrews. Their first great leader was Abraham. He led them out of Mesopotamia, probably between 2000 and 1500 B.C.

- The Hebrews were desert nomads for many years. Then they became slaves in Egypt. A leader named Moses led them out of Egypt.

- The Hebrews settled in Canaan. They believed God had promised them this land. They divided it into the kingdoms of Judah and Israel.

Chapter 2   R E V I E W

Word Bank

Hammurabi

Hebrews

Marduk

Mesopotamia

Phoenicians

Sargon I

Sumerians

wheels

Yahweh

ziggurats

On a sheet of paper, use the words from the Word Bank to complete each sentence correctly.

1. The Sumerians built _____, which were pyramid-shaped buildings.

2. We call the region between the Tigris and the Euphrates rivers _____.

3. _____, the king of Akkad, united the city-states of the Middle East.

4. _____ developed the first code of law.

5. The _____ were the first great sailors and traders.

6. The _____ were the first people to believe in one all-powerful god.

7. The _____ invented writing.

8. The name of the chief Babylonian god was _____.

9. The name of the Hebrew god was _____.

10. The Sumerians were the first people to put _____ on carts.

On a sheet of paper, write the letter of the answer that correctly completes each sentence.

11. The Sumerians built _____.

   A city-states   **C** the Bible
   B boats   **D** a code

12. The Akkadians _____ Sumerian writings into their own language.

   A translated   **C** stylus
   B cuneiform   **D** painted

13. The Babylonian king Hammurabi collected laws into a _____.

   A Bible   **C** ziggurat
   B Vedas   **D** code

14. The Phoenicians built boats of _____.

    A jade   **C** clay

    B marble   **D** cedar

15. The Hebrews became slaves in _____.

    A Egypt   **C** Phoenicia

    B Canaan   **D** Palestine

On a sheet of paper, write the answer to each question. Use complete sentences.

16. What gifts did the Sumerians give us?

17. Why do we remember Hammurabi?

18. In what way did the Hebrew people differ from other ancient people?

Critical Thinking On a sheet of paper, write your response to each question. Use complete sentences.

19. Which country or group of people in the ancient Middle East gave us the greatest gifts? Explain your answer.

20. Why is the invention of writing an important step in world civilization?

Test-Taking Tip

When a teacher announces a test, listen carefully. Write down the lessons that will be included. Write down any specific topics the teacher says to review.

3

Middle Eastern Empires

The Middle East was home to many city-states and kingdoms. For hundreds of years, they made war against each other. Finally, one group—the Assyrians—controlled most of the area. In fact, they controlled so much land that they became an empire. This chapter introduces you to the Assyrian Empire and to the Chaldean and Persian Empires that followed it. One by one, these empires controlled much of the Middle East.

Goals for Learning

◆ To describe the life, army, and government of the Assyrians

◆ To describe the life, army, and government of the Chaldeans

◆ To explain the ways the Persians unified their great empire and describe Zoroastrianism

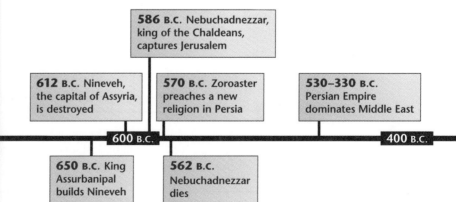

586 B.C. Nebuchadnezzar, king of the Chaldeans, captures Jerusalem

800 B.C. Assyrian Empire expands in Mesopotamia

612 B.C. Nineveh, the capital of Assyria, is destroyed

570 B.C. Zoroaster preaches a new religion in Persia

530–330 B.C. Persian Empire dominates Middle East

800 B.C.   **600 B.C.**   **400 B.C.**

650 B.C. King Assurbanipal builds Nineveh

562 B.C. Nebuchadnezzar dies

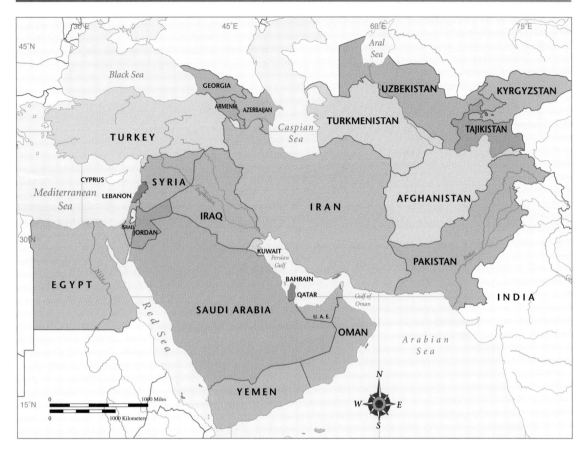

Map Skills

Many seas touch the shores of the Middle East. Many rivers flow through it. Deserts stretch for miles, and mountains stand tall. This geography has helped to shape the cultural and political history of the region.

Study the map, then answer the following questions:

1. What Egyptian river empties into the Mediterranean Sea?

2. What are the names of three countries that border the Mediterranean Sea?

3. What body of water separates Iran from Saudi Arabia?

4. Which country is farther south—Yemen or Egypt?

5. Which country is farther east—Iraq or Iran?

Reading Strategy:
Predicting

Previewing a text helps readers think about what they already know about a subject. It also prepares readers to look for new information—to predict what will come next. Keep this in mind as you make predictions:

◆ Make your best guess about what might happen next.

◆ Add details about what you think will happen.

◆ Check your predictions. You may have to change your predictions as you learn more information.

Key Vocabulary Words

Lesson 1

Empire A large area of land ruled by one person

Dominate To control

Artisan A person who works with his or her hands to create something

Chariot A two-wheeled, horse-drawn carriage

Cavalry Soldiers on horseback

Archer A soldier who fights with a bow and arrows

Tribute A payment given by a weaker ruler or nation to a stronger ruler or nation

Capital The city from which a ruler, or emperor, rules

Govern To rule

Province An area, such as a state, that is part of a larger country

Rebel To disobey or fight against

Alliance An agreement to help one another

Lesson 2

Terraced Going upward like steps

Astronomer A person who keeps track of the sun, the planets, and the stars

Lesson 3

Inspector A person who looks at how things are being done

Unify To bring together as one

Objectives

◆ To identify why the Assyrian army was so feared

◆ To describe the way the Assyrians treated conquered peoples

Reading Strategy:
Predicting

Read the heading of the next section. What do you think you'll find out about the Assyrians?

Empire

A large area of land ruled by one person

Dominate

To control

Artisan

A person who works with his or her hands to create something

Chariot

A two-wheeled, horse-drawn carriage

Cavalry

Soldiers on horseback

Archer

A soldier who fights with a bow and arrows

Between 900 B.C. and 700 B.C., the Assyrian **Empire** began to develop in Mesopotamia. An empire is a large area of land ruled by one person. It developed on the eastern side of the Fertile Crescent in the Tigris River Valley. The Assyrians were a fierce tribe of warriors. Their enemies hated and feared them. For several hundred years, they **dominated,** or controlled, the cities and trading routes of Mesopotamia.

Why Did People Fear the Assyrians?

Assyrian soldiers had iron weapons. The Assyrians had learned to smelt iron from the people known as the Hittites. The smelting process required three steps. First, the **artisan,** or person who works with his or her hands, heated the iron until it was red hot. Second, the artisan hammered the iron to remove unwanted materials. Third, the artisan quickly cooled the iron. Then the iron was shaped into weapons. These were harder and stronger than the copper and bronze weapons other armies used.

The Assyrian army divided itself into groups. Some became charioteers who drove **chariots**—two-wheeled, horse-drawn carriages. The army also had a **cavalry.** These soldiers on horseback were the first of their kind. The most feared soldiers were the **archers,** who fought with bows and arrows.

How Did the Assyrian Army Attack?

With its iron weapons, the Assyrian army became a fighting machine. On the field of battle, the soldiers marched forward shoulder to shoulder. Then they let fly a shower of iron-tipped arrows. These killed and wounded the enemy.

Next, the cavalry and the charioteers attacked. They wore iron helmets and breast plates; they carried iron spears and swords. Their weapons and their skill forced the enemy to run back into the city and hide behind its walls.

Walls did not stop the Assyrians. They battered down the gates with a thick iron-tipped tree trunk! Sometimes they tunneled under the walls or climbed over them on ladders.

Tribute

A payment given to a stronger ruler or nation

Capital

The city from which a ruler, or emperor, rules

What Did the Assyrians Do When They Won?

After beating their enemies, the Assyrians burned some alive or cut their heads off. They made others into slaves. Then they forced them to move to lands far from home. Next, the Assyrians stole everything they wanted. Finally, they burned the captured city to the ground.

Where Was the Assyrian Capital?

Everyone in Mesopotamia feared the Assyrians. Who could win against them? Some paid **tribute** rather than fight. That is, they gave a payment to the kings of Assyria. This tribute, the loot won in war, and taxes made the Assyrian kings rich. One of these kings used this money to build a mighty **capital.** From this city, he ruled his empire.

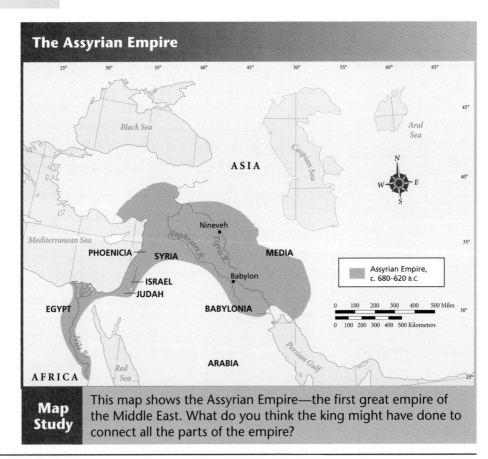

Map Study

This map shows the Assyrian Empire—the first great empire of the Middle East. What do you think the king might have done to connect all the parts of the empire?

Nineveh, on the Tigris River, was the largest city of its day. In 650 B.C., King Assurbanipal made it the showplace of the ancient world. Assurbanipal was one of the most powerful kings on earth. He boasted "I am Assurbanipal, the Great King, the Mighty King . . . King of Kings." He had a scribe carve these words on stone.

How Did King Assurbanipal Help Historians?

At his palace in Nineveh, Assurbanipal set up a library. There he collected and saved the ancient writings from the old Mesopotamian kingdoms of Sumer and Akkad. Hundreds of years later, in A.D. 1852, an archaeologist uncovered what was left of this library. He found 22,000 clay tablets!

These tablets contained dictionaries, which gave the same words in different languages. Some listed names of kings and important events in the ancient world. Still others contained songs and stories about the past. These tablets helped historians learn about life in the ancient Middle East.

Assurbanipal (shooting the bow) was the last great Assyrian king. Assyrians were mighty fighters and were the first to use cavalry.

Govern
To rule
Province
An area, such as a state, that is part of a larger country
Rebel
To disobey or fight against
Alliance
An agreement to help one another

How Did the King Govern the Empire?

The Assyrian Empire included all of Mesopotamia, the Fertile Crescent, and Egypt. To help **govern,** or rule, all this land, the Assyrian king divided it into **provinces.** (Provinces are areas similar to states.) Then he chose a governor for each province. This governor collected taxes and made sure that everyone obeyed the king's laws.

The king needed to control his empire and keep it connected. The Assyrians built a road system. They made all the roads level so that chariots traveled easily on them. Because of these roads, merchants and soldiers moved quickly from Nineveh to the provinces.

Why Did the Assyrian Empire Fall?

The Assyrian Empire became too large to govern. The people who had lost wars against the Assyrians began to **rebel,** or disobey, them. Fighting began. Soon the Chaldeans from Babylon and the Medes from Persia made an **alliance.** They agreed to help one another fight the Assyrians.

In 612 B.C., the Babylonians, Medes, and other armies captured the city of Nineveh and destroyed it. People throughout the empire celebrated!

Lesson 1 Review On a sheet of paper, write the answer to each question. Use complete sentences.

1. How did the Assyrians make their weapons?

2. What was the cavalry?

3. Why was Nineveh important to the Assyrians?

4. How did the Assyrians connect their empire?

5. What happened that destroyed the Assyrian Empire?

What do you think?

Why is the library of Assurbanipal important to historians?

Objectives

◆ To describe the beauty of the city of Babylon

◆ To explain the fall of the Chaldean Empire

Like the Assyrians, the Chaldeans defeated many different peoples. After destroying Nineveh, they became the leading Middle Eastern empire. We often call their society Neo-Babylonia or the new Babylonia. Their ancestors were the people Hammurabi ruled hundreds of years before.

Who Did King Nebuchadnezzar Defeat?

One of the greatest Chaldean kings was Nebuchadnezzar. Under his rule, the Chaldean empire grew as far west as Syria and Canaan.

Nebuchadnezzar defeated the army of Egypt when it tried to take over Syria and Phoenicia. He ruled the Hebrew, or Jewish, people too. After years of warfare, his armies defeated the Jews in 586 B.C. The soldiers destroyed Jerusalem and its temple. They marched 15,000 Jews to Babylon as slaves.

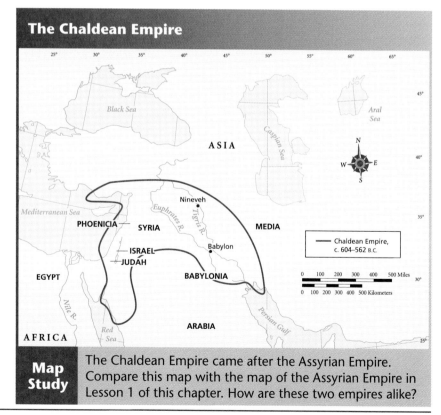

The Chaldean Empire

Chaldean Empire, c. 604–562 B.C.

Map Study The Chaldean Empire came after the Assyrian Empire. Compare this map with the map of the Assyrian Empire in Lesson 1 of this chapter. How are these two empires alike?

Reading Strategy:
Predicting

What kinds of things do you predict will be mentioned in the next paragraphs?

Terraced

Going upward like steps

What Made Babylon Beautiful?

Nebuchadnezzar made the city of Babylon the most beautiful city in the ancient Middle East. In A.D. 1899, a German archaeologist found ancient Babylon. He discovered that a long wall—300 feet high and 80

Bulls and dragons decorate the Ishtar gate in Babylon, the city Nebuchadnezzar made beautiful.

feet wide—surrounded the city! The wall was so wide that a chariot with four horses could turn around on top of it! From its 250 towers, soldiers watched for the enemy. People and chariots entered the city through several bronze gates.

A broad street ran down the center of Babylon. At one end stood a beautiful gate of bricks coated with a blue glaze, or shiny polish. This gate is called the Ishtar gate. Animal sculptures, or carvings from stone, decorated the gate. Red-brick sidewalks ran down both sides of this long street. Carved into each brick was the message "I am Nebuchadnezzar, king of Babylon, who made this."

Reading Strategy:
Predicting

Think about your prediction. Were you accurate?

What Were the Hanging Gardens?

Nebuchadnezzar's palace had walls covered with brightly colored tiles. The most famous part of the palace was the Hanging Gardens. Some say that Nebuchadnezzar built the gardens for a queen who had lived in a mountainous country.

The king built **terraced,** or stepped, gardens, which rose upward like a mountain. In them, he planted the flowers and bushes of the queen's homeland. He had well water pumped up to the terraces to water the plants.

Astronomer

A person who keeps track of the sun, the planets, and the stars

How Did Priests Use the Ziggurat of Babylon?

The highest building in Babylon was a 300-foot-high ziggurat. From the top of this great temple, the Chaldean priests studied the night sky. These early **astronomers** mapped the heavens and tracked the sun, the planets, and the stars.

Some groups of stars brought pictures to the astronomers' minds. They called these star pictures constellations. In fact, they saw 12 constellations evenly spaced across the sky. These became the zodiac. The astronomers believed that the stars told the future. They thought that stars had power over a person's life.

For many years the Chaldean priests viewed the night sky. They broke time into seven-day weeks. They also figured out the length of the year.

Why Did the Chaldean Empire Fall?

While Nebuchadnezzar ruled, the city of Babylon was a great trading and learning center. But after he died in 562 B.C., war broke out. The Chaldeans and the people they had defeated did not like the kings who followed Nebuchadnezzar.

Writing About History

Imagine you are a reporter for the *Mesopotamian Times*. In your notebook, write an article. Tell about an event in this chapter, such as the building of the Hanging Gardens.

Then and Now

Reading Signs in the Stars

People today read their horoscopes for clues to the future. This idea goes back to ancient Babylonia. There, priests were also astronomers. They studied the movements of the sun, moon, and stars. During a year, the sun seemed to circle through 12 constellations. The priests named these star patterns mostly after animals, such as the goat (Capricornus).

Using the sun and stars, priests predicted natural events. They also set the times for holidays. About the 6th century B.C., Chaldean priests began to make horoscopes. They told the future for rulers and nobles. A horoscope was based on the time of birth and the sun's position. Later the Greeks conquered Babylon. They gave the 12 star signs the names we use today. They named this circle of constellations the "zodiac."

Few written accounts of the fall of Babylon exist. One source, the Book of Daniel, offers one description. The Book of Daniel in the Hebrew Bible describes how, in 538 B.C., King Belshazzar held a great feast. Suddenly, a strange hand appeared and wrote mysterious words on the wall. No one except Daniel, a young Hebrew, could interpret the writing. Daniel told the king what the words meant: His days were coming to an end, and the Persian army would defeat his empire.

That night the Persians killed Belshazzar. Cyrus the Great, king of Persia, captured Babylon. The Chaldean Empire then became part of the great Persian Empire.

Lesson 2 Review On a sheet of paper, use the words from the Word Bank to complete each sentence correctly.

Word Bank
astronomers
Babylon
Chaldean Empire
Hanging Gardens
Nebuchadnezzar

1. The Middle Eastern empire that Nebuchadnezzar ruled was the _____.

2. The capital of his empire was _____.

3. One of the wonders of this capital was its _____.

4. _____ died in 562 B.C.

5. The Chaldean priests became _____, for they mapped the night skies.

What do you think ?

Why did Nebuchadnezzar carve his name on the red bricks of Babylon's sidewalks?

- To explain how the Persians' system of roads helped them
- To identify the two forces that Zoroaster said existed in the world

Inspector

A person who looks at how things are being done

Unify

To bring together as one

In 538 B.C., Cyrus the Great, king of Persia, defeated the Chaldeans. In a few years, he conquered all his neighbors. Under later kings, the Persian Empire stretched more than 3,000 miles—from the Nile River of Egypt to the Indus River of India.

Because the Persian Empire was large, Darius I, another king, divided it into 20 provinces. A governor ruled each province. To keep an eye on his governors, he hired government **inspectors.** These people looked at how things were being done. They became "the eyes and ears of the king." Traveling around the empire, they reported back to the king.

How Did the Persians Keep Their Empire Together?

To hold their empire together, the Persians built a great system of roads. One road stretched for more than 1,600 miles! It took merchants three months to go from one end to the other. Messages from the king went faster than this.

Horseback riders carried these messages across the empire. They could stop at 100 different places to change horses. The Persians could relay, or pass along, messages in one week, not three months! Another way to **unify,** or bring together, the empire was to use the same weights and measures throughout the land. Because of this, doing business was easier.

How Did Coins Help Traders?

From a people called the Lydians, the Persians got the idea of using metal coins. Then two people no longer had to barter, or trade things. The problem with bartering is that both people must want to trade something of equal worth. Money took care of this problem.

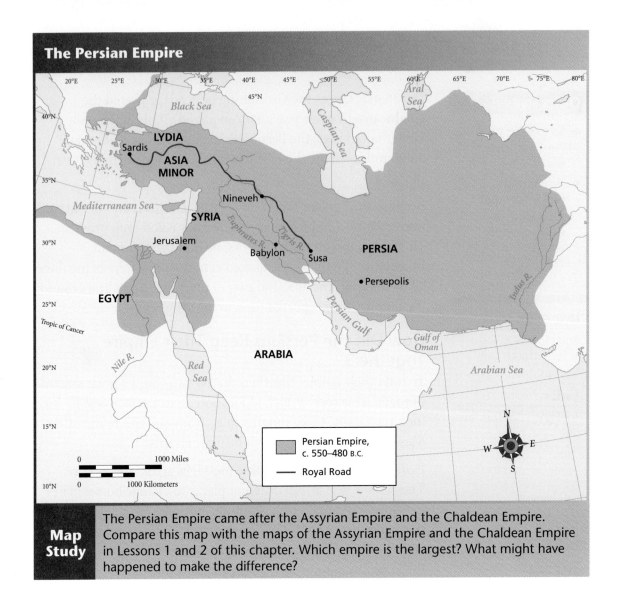

The Persian Empire

Persian Empire, c. 550–480 B.C.
—— Royal Road

Map Study

The Persian Empire came after the Assyrian Empire and the Chaldean Empire. Compare this map with the maps of the Assyrian Empire and the Chaldean Empire in Lessons 1 and 2 of this chapter. Which empire is the largest? What might have happened to make the difference?

Reading Strategy:
Predicting

Think about what you just read. What do you predict you will learn about how Persians treated others?

How Did the Persians Treat Others?

The Persians treated other people fairly. They did not destroy a city when they conquered it. They also did not loot from the people they defeated. They let conquered people keep their own language and religion. They even allowed some groups to follow their own laws. The Persians did ask everyone to pay taxes. But the taxes were small.

How Did the Persians Live?

The art of Persia tells us how people lived. It shows rich men on horseback. Slaves carried others on litters, or stretchers. The men often had long beards and wore makeup on their faces and eyelids.

Women were not allowed much freedom. They lived apart from the men. Girls were taught to be good wives and mothers. Boys were taught to ride horses, use the bow and arrow, and speak the truth.

The Persians protected merchants, but they refused to become traders. Why? They thought that buying or selling made people selfish. It made them lie and cheat other people. Instead, Persians became soldiers, farmers, or shepherds.

Who Was Zoroaster?

The Persians worshipped many gods. Then, in about 570 B.C., a religious leader called Zoroaster began to preach. He talked about the gods and told people how to live. He told people that there were two forces in the world. One force was goodness and light; the other, evil and dark. Zoroastrianism had a strong effect on other religions, especially Judaism and Christianity. Both religions share the idea of life after death and a final reward or punishment.

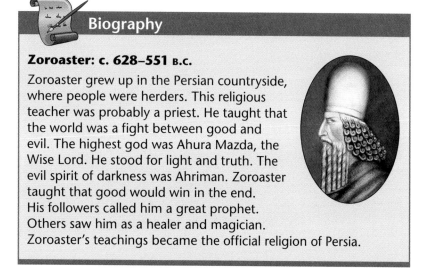

Biography

Zoroaster: c. 628–551 B.C.

Zoroaster grew up in the Persian countryside, where people were herders. This religious teacher was probably a priest. He taught that the world was a fight between good and evil. The highest god was Ahura Mazda, the Wise Lord. He stood for light and truth. The evil spirit of darkness was Ahriman. Zoroaster taught that good would win in the end. His followers called him a great prophet. Others saw him as a healer and magician. Zoroaster's teachings became the official religion of Persia.

Lesson 3 Review On a sheet of paper, write the letter of the answer that correctly completes each sentence.

1. One great king of the Persian Empire was _____.

   A Hammurabi   **C** Daniel

   B Nebuchadnezzar   **D** Cyrus the Great

2. The Persian Empire stretched from Egypt to _____.

   A China   **C** India

   B England   **D** Phoenicia

3. The Persian Empire had _____ provinces.

   A 20   **B** 100   **C** 1,600   **D** 3,000

4. The Persians built a system of _____.

   A dikes   **B** litters   **C** canals   **D** roads

5. To trade things without using money is to _____.

   A barter   **B** govern   **C** litter   **D** tribute

What do you think ?

How would a system of weights and measures help to unify a country?

A Few Words from the "Great King"

Darius I and an attendant are pictured in this carving.

Two Persian kings (Cyrus and Darius) are known as "the Great." Starting in about 550 B.C., Cyrus the Great built the Persian Empire. It became the largest empire ever known in the region. Cyrus died in battle about 529 B.C. His son became king, but others fought for the throne. Darius, a general, became king in 522 B.C. He was an outstanding leader. The empire grew. Darius found ways to run the huge empire efficiently. Darius wanted to make sure he was remembered as "the Great." He planned a great tomb for himself. Then he wrote what he wanted carved on it. The excerpt below is part of what he wrote.

A great god is Ahura Mazda, who created this earth, who created yonder sky, who created man, who created happiness for man, who made Darius king, one king of many, one lord of many.

I am Darius the great King, king of kings, king of countries containing all kinds of men, king in this great earth far and wide. . . .

Saith Darius the King: By the Favor of Ahura Mazda these are the countries which I seized outside Persia, I ruled over them; they bore tribute to me; what was said to them by me, that they did; my law—that held them firm:

Media, Elam, Parthia, Aria, Bactria, Sogdiana, Chorasmia, Drangiana, Arachosia, Sattagydia, Gandara, Amyrgian, Sind, Scythians with pointed caps, Babylonia, Assyria, Arabia, Egypt, Armenia, Cappadocia, Sardis, Ionia, Scythians who are across the sea, Skudra, petasos-wearing Ionians, Libyans, Ethiopians, men of Maka, Carians.

Saith Darius the King: Much which was ill-done, that I made good. Provinces were in commotion; one man was smiting another. The following I brought about by the favor of Ahura Mazda, that the one does not smite the other at all, each one has his place. My law—of that they feel fear, so that the stronger does not smite nor destroy the weak.

Saith Darius the King: By the favor of Ahura Mazda, much handiwork which previously had been put out of its place, that I put in its place . . . .

Saith Darius the King: May Ahura Mazda, together with the gods protect me and my royal house, and what has been inscribed by me.

Document-Based Questions

1. Who is Ahura Mazda?

2. According to Darius, who gave him the right to rule as king?

3. What titles does Darius give himself?

4. What did Darius require people in conquered countries to do?

5. List two things of which Darius is proud.

The Babylonian Captivity

The Bible tells us a lot about Middle Eastern history. Several books are about the history of the Jews. They tell about the Jewish kingdoms. The Bible also talks about neighboring rulers. In the 6th century B.C., the Chaldeans of Babylonia conquered the Jewish kingdom. But the Jews rebelled against their rule. The Bible tells how the king of Babylon put down the rebels. Nebuchadnezzar's soldiers attacked Jerusalem. His soldiers captured the Jewish king and his family. They were taken to Babylon as prisoners. So were thousands of skilled craftsworkers. Strong men were taken for the army. These Jews were kept in Babylon for many years. This period is known as the Babylonian Captivity.

Jewish houses of worship are called synagogues. This ancient synagogue is at Capernaum.

Meanwhile, the Jews rebelled again a few years later in 586 B.C. Again the Babylonians attacked Jerusalem. They burned the Great Temple. They destroyed the city. They took away most of the city's people. Only poor people and farmers were left in the country. The Babylonians also took gold and silver from the temple.

The Jews suffered greatly in Babylon. Psalm 137 tells how sad they were. "By the rivers of Babylon, . . . we wept, when we remembered our Zion. . . ." (*Zion* is another name for Jerusalem.) The Babylonian Captivity was an important time in Jewish history. It tested the strength of the Jews' faith. They were in a strange place with different customs. There was pressure to change their religion and culture. Through many years away from home, they never lost their faith. Their leaders set up houses of worship, or synagogues.

People observed the Sabbath and religious holidays. Their communities stayed strong.

At the same time, the Jewish people learned new skills in Babylon. They learned to be traders. They learned about banking. They slowly gave up farming in favor of business.

In 538 B.C., Persian armies led by Cyrus the Great conquered Babylon. The next year, Cyrus sent the Jews home to Jerusalem. In the Bible, Cyrus is praised for his actions. He gave the Jews money to rebuild the temple.

Wrap-Up

1. Why did Nebuchadnezzar attack Jerusalem?

2. What was the Babylonian Captivity?

3. What did the Jews do to keep their religion in Babylon?

4. What did the Jews learn from the Babylonians?

5. What events ended the Babylonian Captivity?

- The Assyrians were a warrior tribe in Mesopotamia. They built an empire between 900 and 700 B.C. People feared the Assyrian armies. They had iron weapons. Other armies only had bronze weapons. The Assyrian army also had archers, war chariots, and cavalry. The Assyrians were cruel to defeated peoples.

- Nineveh was the capital of Assyria. Assurbanipal was king in 650 B.C. He built a huge library. It included writings from earlier kingdoms in Mesopotamia.

- Assyrian kings divided their empire into provinces. They built roads to link its parts. Then the empire got too large to rule. Conquered peoples banded together against Assyria. They captured Nineveh in 612 B.C.

- The Chaldeans were next. Their capital was Babylon. Nebuchadnezzar made it beautiful. One feature was its Hanging Gardens.

- Nebuchadnezzar expanded the Chaldean Empire. He defeated Egypt and the Jews. He brought the Jews to Babylon as slaves.

- Chaldean priests were astronomers. They studied the stars. They named the constellations of the zodiac. They set up a seven-day week.

- Nebuchadnezzar died in 562 B.C. Then wars broke out. In 538 B.C., the Persians captured Babylon.

- Cyrus the Great was king of Persia. He conquered the peoples around him. At its largest, the Persian Empire stretched from Egypt to India. King Darius divided it into 20 provinces. His inspectors kept track of governors. Good roads connected all parts of the empire. Relays of messengers on horseback carried news quickly.

- Persian rulers treated other people well. They could keep their own language and religion.

- The Persians were not merchants. They did, however, encourage trade. Metal coins were used throughout the empire. Everyone used the same weights and measures for trade.

- Men and women lived separately in Persian society. Men had more freedom.

- Zoroaster brought a new religion to Persia. He saw life as a fight between good and evil. His teachings influenced Judaism and Christianity.

Chapter 3 REVIEW

Word Bank

alliance

astronomers

barter

cavalry

chariots

iron

litters

provinces

terraced

zodiac

On a sheet of paper, use the words from the Word Bank to complete each sentence correctly.

1. Everyone feared the Assyrian army because it had weapons made of _____.

2. The Assyrian army was the first to use a(n) _____ with its soldiers riding war horses.

3. Some Assyrian soldiers drove horse-drawn _____.

4. Both the Assyrians and the Persian kings divided their kingdoms into _____, or smaller areas.

5. The Chaldeans and the Medes formed a(n) _____ and agreed to help one another defeat the Assyrians.

6. Nebuchadnezzar, the king of the Chaldeans, built a(n) _____, or stepped, garden for his queen.

7. The Chaldean priests became the first _____, for they mapped the night sky.

8. These priests saw 12 constellations, or star pictures in the night sky, which would later become the _____.

9. People in the Persian Empire had coins, so they no longer needed to _____, or trade things without money.

10. From Persian art, we learn that slaves sometimes carried Persian men on _____, or stretchers.

On a sheet of paper, write the letter of the answer that correctly completes each sentence.

11. The first great empire of the Middle East was the _____.

   A Assyrian   **B** Chaldean   **C** Persian   **D** Hebrew

12. The largest city of the Assyrian Empire was _____.

   A Babylon   **B** Jerusalem   **C** Nineveh   **D** Canaan

13. One powerful king of Assyria was _____.

    A Hammurabi   **C** Nebuchadnezzar

    B Assurbanipal   **D** Cyrus the Great

14. One powerful king of the Chaldeans was _____.

    A Nebuchadnezzar   **C** Cyrus

    B Daniel   **D** Darius

15. One powerful king of the Persians was _____.

    A Daniel   **B** Cyrus   **C** Moses   **D** Zoroaster

On a sheet of paper, write the answer to each question. Use complete sentences.

16. What helped the Assyrians become a war machine?

17. What was the difference between the way the Assyrians treated defeated people and the way the Persians did?

Critical Thinking On a sheet of paper, write your response to each question. Use complete sentences.

18. Why do you think so many people in the Assyrian Empire were happy when the Chaldeans captured and destroyed Nineveh?

19. Think about the Persian religion of Zoroastrianism. What influence might it have had on the way Persians treated the people they conquered?

20. Which of the Middle Eastern peoples described in this chapter have influenced the course of world history the most? Explain your opinion.

Test-Taking Tip

Schedule short study periods that are easy to manage. Take breaks between study periods.

4

Egypt—The Gift of the Nile

Y ou have read about some of the people of the ancient Middle East. These people lived in an area known as the Fertile Crescent. Their city-states did not last long. However, the Egyptian civilization, which grew along the Nile River, lasted for more than 3,000 years! In this chapter, you will learn about the three kingdoms of the Egyptians: the Old Kingdom, the Middle Kingdom, and the New Kingdom.

Goals for Learning

◆ To explain why Egypt is "the gift of the Nile"

◆ To describe how Egypt was united in the Old Kingdom and explain how and why the pyramids were built

◆ To identify differences between the Old and the Middle Kingdoms

◆ To compare the New Kingdom with earlier periods of Egyptian history

◆ To list key contributions Egypt has made to world civilization

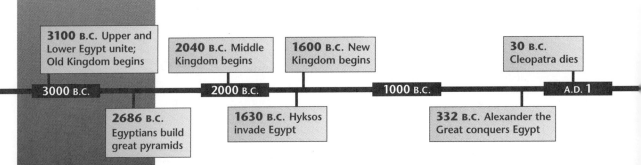

3100 B.C. Upper and Lower Egypt unite; Old Kingdom begins

2040 B.C. Middle Kingdom begins

1600 B.C. New Kingdom begins

30 B.C. Cleopatra dies

3000 B.C.　　　　　2000 B.C.　　　　　1000 B.C.　　　　　A.D. 1

2686 B.C. Egyptians build great pyramids

1630 B.C. Hyksos invade Egypt

332 B.C. Alexander the Great conquers Egypt

Ancient Egypt (c. 3000-2000 B.C.)

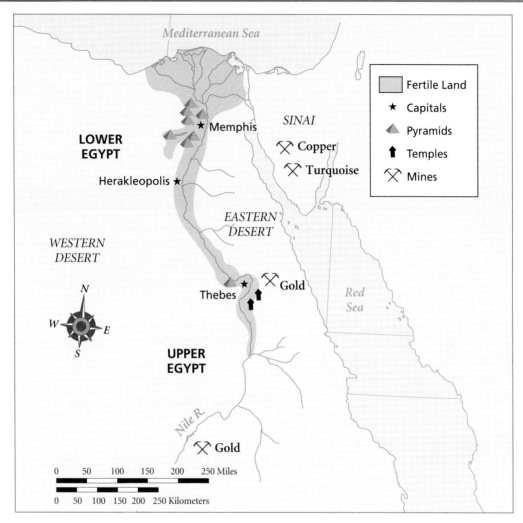

Map Skills

The Nile River dominates the geography of Egypt. Since ancient times, the river has provided water for irrigation. It also serves as a highway that unified Upper and Lower Egypt. The ancient Egyptians built their main cities and temples in the Nile Valley.

Study the map carefully, then answer the following questions:

1. Upper Egypt is in what direction from Lower Egypt?

2. What two deserts protected Egypt from invaders?

3. What are the names of the three Egyptian capitals shown on the map?

4. About how far is Thebes from Memphis?

5. What sea lies to the north of Lower Egypt?

Reading Strategy:
Text Structure

Understanding how text is organized helps readers decide which information is most important. Before you begin reading this chapter, look at how it is organized.

- ◆ Look at the title, headings, boldfaced words, and photographs.

- ◆ Ask yourself: Is the text a problem and solution, description, or sequence? Is it compare and contrast or cause and effect?

- ◆ Summarize the text by thinking about its structure.

Key Vocabulary Words

Lesson 1

Delta An area of fertile land at the mouth of a river

Silt A rich layer of soil left behind after a flood

Lesson 2

Unite To bring together as one

Caravan A group of traders traveling together, often through deserts

Pharaoh An Egyptian ruler

Abundant More than enough

Civil war Fighting between people within their own country

Economy The system of making and trading things

Lesson 3

Mummify To wrap a dead body in strips of cloth to keep the body from decaying

Armor A strong metal covering that protects the body in battle

Lesson 4

Annex To take over; to add a piece of land to one's country

Obelisk A tall, pointed stone pillar

Hieroglyphics A kind of picture writing in Egypt

Lesson 5

Papyrus A reed from the Nile River used to make paper

Scroll A roll of papyrus

Cubit A measurement that is the length of an arm from the end of the middle finger to the elbow

Objectives

◆ To identify some facts about the Nile River

◆ To describe the way Egyptians used floodwaters from the Nile

Delta

An area of fertile land at the mouth of a river

Silt

A rich layer of soil left behind after a flood

Reading Strategy:
Text Structure

Preview this lesson. Notice the headings, features, and boldfaced words.

The Egyptian civilization, like earlier civilizations, developed in a river valley. Historians call Egypt "the gift of the Nile." The Nile River is the longest in the world. It begins in the mountains of central Africa. Then it flows northward to the Mediterranean Sea.

How Long Is the Nile River?

For most of its 4,000 miles, the Nile cuts through desert. It seldom branches out, but this changes just before it reaches the Mediterranean. There, it forms a triangular-shaped area of fertile land. We call such an area at the mouth of a river a **delta.**

How Did the Egyptians Use Floods?

Every spring, snow melts in the mountains of eastern Africa. Rain falls. Then the Nile floods. Most people think that floods are disasters. However, the ancient Egyptians used these floodwaters to irrigate their fields. When the floodwater went down, it left behind a rich layer of **silt.** Because of this, the Egyptians harvested two, and sometimes three, crops a year.

Along the banks of the Nile, Egyptian farmers grew wheat, barley, and many other crops. They had more than enough food for themselves. They traded their extra food for the things they did not have.

How Did the Nile Unify Egypt?

The Nile became an excellent "highway" for trade. Going north on it was easy because the Nile flows north. To go south, the Egyptians put large sails on their boats. These sails caught the winds that blew from north to south. Egyptian traders, government workers, and the rulers easily traveled up and down the river.

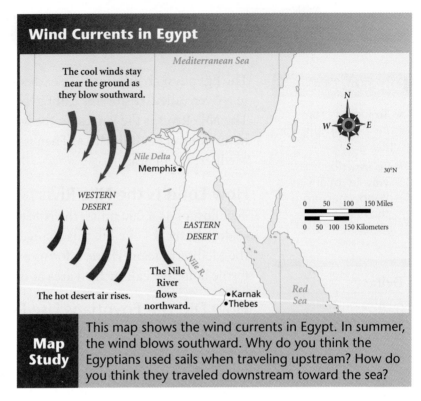

Wind Currents in Egypt

The cool winds stay near the ground as they blow southward.

Mediterranean Sea

Nile Delta
Memphis

WESTERN DESERT

EASTERN DESERT

The hot desert air rises.

The Nile River flows northward.

•Karnak
•Thebes

Red Sea

Nile R.

30°N

0 50 100 150 Miles

0 50 100 150 Kilometers

Map Study

This map shows the wind currents in Egypt. In summer, the wind blows southward. Why do you think the Egyptians used sails when traveling upstream? How do you think they traveled downstream toward the sea?

What do you think ❓

Why do you think historians call Egypt "the gift of the Nile"?

Lesson 1 Review On a sheet of paper, write the letter of the answer that correctly completes each sentence.

1. Like other ancient people, the Egyptians settled in _____ valleys.

   A desert   **B** dry   **C** river   **D** warm

2. The Nile River is about _____ miles long.

   A 2,000   **B** 4,000   **C** 6,000   **D** 6,500

3. Each year the Nile River floods, and this _____ the farmers.

   A surprises   **B** helps   **C** harms   **D** saddened

4. For traveling _____ on the Nile, the Egyptians put sails on their boats.

   A North   **B** South   **C** East   **D** West

5. The Nile River empties into the _____ Sea.

   A Black   **B** Mediterranean   **C** Red   **D** Dead

Objectives

- ♦ To identify two important gods that ancient Egyptians worshiped
- ♦ To describe why the Old Kingdom ended

Unite

To bring together as one

Caravan

A group of traders traveling together, often through deserts

At first, the ancient Egyptians lived in small villages. The people of the north, or Lower Egypt, lived near the Nile delta. Swampy marshland cut them off from one another.

The Egyptians living in the south, or Upper Egypt, began big irrigation projects. To finish these projects, they needed to work together. Upper Egypt was already unified around 3400 B.C.

Who United Egypt?

We do not know who **united,** or brought together, Upper and Lower Egypt. One story says that a god-king named Menes conquered Lower Egypt around 3100 B.C. He built his capital where Upper Egypt and Lower Egypt meet and called it Memphis. It is near Egypt's present capital—Cairo.

Menes wanted to show that Egypt was now united. He put the red crown of Lower Egypt and the white crown of Upper Egypt together into one crown. Pictures often show the later rulers of Egypt wearing this double crown.

We do not know if Menes was a real person. But Menes and the kings who followed him made up the first dynasty of Egypt. During the following 2,500 years, Egypt had 30 different dynasties!

What Was Life Like in the Old Kingdom?

Historians call the time from about 3100 B.C. to 2186 B.C. the Old Kingdom. During this time, Egyptian cities became centers of business. Groups of traders, called **caravans,** traveled together to Sumer to trade things. They also traveled to parts of Africa and the Mediterranean to trade.

Some Egyptians were traders, but most were farmers. They lived in mud-brick houses in small villages. They built their homes on the highest land. This protected them from the yearly floods. Because of the heat, people often slept on the roof.

One of the most well-known monuments of the Old Kingdom is the stone Sphinx at Giza, Egypt. It was built about 2500 B.C.

How Powerful Were Egyptian Pharaohs?

The Egyptian rulers were called **pharaohs.** They were both kings and priests. In Mesopotamia, the kings spoke for the gods. In Egypt, the people thought the kings were gods.

The pharaoh of the Old Kingdom controlled the lives of his people. He owned all the land and water. The Egyptians believed that he even made the waters of the Nile rise and fall. Because life depended on the Nile, who would turn against this god-king? No one.

Why Did the Egyptians Build Pyramids?

The Egyptians believed that pharaohs continued to rule even after they died. They built great tombs, or places to bury the dead rulers. They were in the shape of a pyramid. To make these tombs last forever, the Egyptians built with stone. About 75 pyramids still stand in the Egyptian desert. The three most famous are in an area called Giza, outside modern Cairo.

Building the pyramids was hard work. The builders had no iron tools to cut the stone. They had no wheels or work animals to carry the huge stone blocks, which weighed about 5,000 pounds each. It took thousands of skilled workers many years to build a pyramid.

How to Build a Pyramid

◆ Work 20,000 men for 20 years; feed them.

◆ Have 10,000 workers make about 26 million mud bricks for the inside of the pyramid.

◆ Have the other 10,000 workers cut huge stone blocks.

◆ Transport these blocks—about 12,600 of them—up the river to the building site.

◆ Dig a canal to connect the site to the river.

◆ Find a rock base, clear it of sand, and make it level.

◆ Make the sides of the stone blocks smooth; polish them.

◆ Build ramps upon which to haul the stone blocks higher and higher.

◆ Remove the building ramps as you work back downward.

◆ Build a funeral temple, the surrounding walls, a valley temple, and smaller pyramids for family members.

What Was the Afterlife?

The ancient Egyptians had two important gods. They called the sun god Ra and the river god Hapi. These gods were important because the Egyptians knew that the sun and the flooding of the Nile River provided their **abundant** food crops. This meant that they had more than enough to eat. This allowed most Egyptians to live well.

The Egyptians also believed that there was life after death. If people had led good lives before they died, they lived happily in an afterlife forever. They thought that if they had lived bad lives, a monster would eat them. The Egyptians wanted their dead pharaohs to be comfortable in the afterlife. They filled their tombs with treasure: food, clothing, jewelry, furniture, and beautiful art.

The Egyptians painted pictures of the king's friends and servants on the walls. They thought that the pharaoh would want these people with him in the afterlife. They believed everything pictured on the walls would magically come alive.

The towering pyramids at Giza are amazing examples of Egyptian architecture.

How Did the Egyptians Protect Pharaohs?

The Egyptians buried the dead pharaoh in rooms deep within a pyramid. Then they sealed the rooms with huge stone blocks. However, robbers broke into the tombs and stole the treasures there. Even though the treasures are gone, archaeologists can still learn from a pyramid. Its wall paintings tell us much of what we know about ancient Egypt.

Why Did the Old Kingdom Fall?

Around the year 2186 B.C., the Old Kingdom ended. The pharaohs had lost power and government officials had become more powerful. The city leaders began to fight each other. Then **civil war** broke out as the people within Egypt began to fight each other.

Some historians believe that natural disasters may have caused the troubles in Egypt. Perhaps little rain fell for many years. Perhaps the people then began to doubt that the pharaoh controlled the rain. Egypt's **economy,** or system of making and trading things, collapsed.

Word Bank

afterlife

farmers

Hapi

Menes

pyramids

Lesson 2 Review On a sheet of paper, use the words from the Word Bank to complete each sentence correctly.

1. According to an old story, _____ united Upper and Lower Egypt.

2. Most Egyptians in the Old Kingdom were _____.

3. The Egyptians believed in a(n) _____ that was like the life they lived on earth.

4. Ra and _____ were two important gods.

5. The Egyptians built wonderful tombs, or _____, for their pharaohs.

What do you think ?

How does the building of pyramids show that the pharaohs had money and power?

Communication in History

The Rosetta Stone

Scribes in ancient Egypt wrote with picture symbols. This writing system is called hieroglyphics. The term comes from the Greek words for "sacred carving." As time passed, though, people could no longer read them. Centuries later, the key to hieroglyphics was found. It was a stone tablet we now call the Rosetta Stone.

In 1799 Napoleon's army was in Egypt. French engineers were working near the Nile River. They dug up a tablet carved with three kinds of writing. One was Greek. One was a newer form of Egyptian writing. The third was hieroglyphics.

Jean François Champollion, a French scholar, knew many languages. He found that the inscriptions in Greek and the new Egyptian writing were the same. Then he compared the hieroglyphics with the Greek. After a long time, Champollion could read many of the symbols. The Rosetta Stone opened the door to learning about ancient Egypt.

Objectives

♦ To identify ways that the Egyptians changed their surroundings

♦ To describe the nomads from Asia who invaded Egypt

Reading Strategy:
Text Structure

Read the next heading. How do you know the section will contrast two different things?

Mummify

To wrap a dead body in strips of cloth to keep the body from decaying

Around 2040 B.C., a new dynasty of powerful pharaohs reunited Egypt. This was the beginning of the Middle Kingdom. Its capital was Thebes.

Once again, traders sold artifacts and other products in faraway places. To help trade and transportation, the Egyptians dug a long canal. It joined the Nile River with business centers near the Red Sea.

They also emptied out many swampy marshes to create vast areas of farmable land. The water they drew from these swamps flowed to a large natural basin. In this bowl-like place, they kept the water from the swamp. During dry months, farmers used it for irrigation. Once again, the Egyptians had more than enough food for everyone.

How Did the Two Kingdoms Differ?

The Old Kingdom and the Middle Kingdom differed in three ways. First, the Old Kingdom Egyptians thought their pharaohs were gods. People of the Middle Kingdom still thought this, but their pharaohs no longer had complete power. They had to share their power with other officials.

Second, the people of the Old Kingdom thought that only the pharaoh would live forever. However, the Middle Kingdom Egyptians thought that *all* people would live forever. They **mummified** everyone after death. They wrapped the dead body in strips of cloth to keep it from decaying.

Third, the Egyptians buried the Old Kingdom pharaohs in pyramids. However, they buried later pharaohs in tombs cut into cliffs near Thebes.

Who Invaded Egypt?

About 1630 B.C., nomads from Asia known as the Hyksos invaded Egypt. The Egyptians knew medicine and arithmetic, but the Hyksos knew war. They had horse-drawn chariots,

Armor

A strong metal covering that protects the body in battle

bronze and iron weapons, and **armor.** This strong covering of metal protected their bodies. Because of all this, the Hyksos easily defeated the Egyptians. For the first time in Egypt's history, foreigners, or people from another country, ruled.

How Long Did the Hyksos Rule?

The Hyksos were mean rulers. They buried some Egyptian cities and destroyed temples. The Egyptians were not happy with their new rulers. However, they learned a lot from the Hyksos, such as how to make bronze, new weapons, chariots, and armor, and how to weave. Meanwhile, the Egyptians began to use the weapons, chariots, and armor of the Hyksos. In 1570 B.C., the Egyptians drove out the foreign invaders.

What do you think

Why do you think the Egyptians took so long to drive out the Hyksos?

Lesson 3 Review On a sheet of paper, write the answer to each question. Use complete sentences.

1. What did Middle Kingdom pharaohs do with swamps and canals?

2. How did Middle Kingdom pharaohs help traders?

3. What are three differences between the Old Kingdom and the Middle Kingdom?

4. Why were the Hyksos able to conquer Egypt?

5. What did the Egyptians learn from the Hyksos?

History in Your Life

Farming Along the Nile

Egypt's success depended on thousands of peasants. But raising good crops depended on the Nile flooding every year. These floodwaters covered the land along its banks, making a strip of rich farmland. The rich soil came from farther up the river. The Nile also provided water for irrigation. The rest of Egypt was desert.

Men and women worked in the fields during the day. They grew grains such as wheat and barley. The flour from these grains was mixed with honey to make sweet bread. Farmers grew grapevines and picked dates too. Other peasants tended herds of sheep, goats, or cattle. They also hunted deer and water birds.

Besides food crops, Egyptian farmers grew cotton and flax, a plant that was used for its fibers. They spun the fibers to make cotton and linen cloth. Most farmwork was done by hand. Tomb paintings show farmers using metal tools to cut grain. Oxen were used for heavy work, such as turning water wheels.

Objectives

◆ To explain accomplishments of the New Kingdom

◆ To describe why Egyptians lost control of Egypt

Annex

To take over; to add a piece of land to one's country

In about 1600 B.C., the New Kingdom began. During that time, strong pharaohs ruled Egypt. Like the pharaohs of the Old Kingdom, they controlled the people of Egypt.

Who Was the First Woman Pharaoh?

With its strong army, Egypt began to expand. It **annexed,** or took over, lands next to the upper Nile and along the eastern Mediterranean. Hatshepsut—the first woman pharaoh—spread the influence of Egypt down into the heart of Africa. From there, traders got products such as beautiful wood, animal skins, and feathers.

What Pharaoh Was a Great Conqueror?

When Hatshepsut died, Thutmose III became pharaoh. He spread Egypt's influence all the way to the Euphrates River. Almost every year for 20 years, his soldiers won victories in Asia. As they did so, he built army bases in all the lands he controlled. He also organized, or set up, a navy to conquer the cities along the eastern Mediterranean.

Biography

Hatshepsut: Reigned c. 1490–1469 B.C.

Most people think of Egypt's pharaohs as men. Most were. The most famous woman pharaoh was Hatshepsut. She was a pharaoh's daughter. As was the custom, she married her half-brother, Thutmose II. He died suddenly about 1490 B.C. For a while, Hatshepsut ruled in the name of her young stepson. Then she had herself crowned pharaoh, calling herself a daughter of the god Amon. Statues show her with a false beard, a sign of power. Hatshepsut ruled for about 20 years. During that time, Egypt had a long period of peace. She had many great temples and monuments built.

Under Thutmose, Egypt's empire stretched far and wide. For this reason, historians sometimes call the period of the New Kingdom the "empire age." The many people the Egyptians conquered paid tribute, or taxes, to the pharaohs. The rulers and the nobles became rich.

What Did the New Kingdom Pharaohs Build?

The rulers and nobles of the New Kingdom used their money to build temples, palaces, and statues. Hatshepsut built a beautiful temple near Thebes, the capital of the New Kingdom. Artists painted and carved the story of Egypt's victories on the temple's walls.

Obelisks are tall pillars carved from a single stone. This one is from the ancient Egyptian village of Karnak.

Thutmose III used slaves to build great palaces and to rebuild temples. Tall, pointed stone pillars called **obelisks** were also built. Artists carved **hieroglyphics,** or picture writing, on the sides of these pillars.

The Egyptians honored their pharaohs by building giant statues, which stood many stories high. With its beautiful palaces and temples, Thebes became the most wonderful city in the ancient world.

Where Did Egyptian Children Go to School?

The Egyptians built great temples to honor their gods. These were both religious centers and schools. In them, the children of Egyptian nobles and those from conquered lands learned what Egyptians believed. The pharaohs hoped that these schools would make the children faithful to Egypt when they got older. The schools trained boys as young as five years old to be scribes. These scribes kept important records and wrote down religious laws.

Writing About History

A time machine has taken you to ancient Egypt. You can go anywhere and see anything. What impresses you most? In your notebook, write a letter to a friend. Tell about your visit to Egypt.

How Did Ikhnaton Change the Egyptian Religion?

The people of Thebes worshiped many gods. Sometimes they combined gods. That is, they put them together into one. For instance, they combined Amon, the god of the wind, with Ra, the sun god. The two became one. In fact, Amon-Ra became the most powerful god of all. He had power over both the sun and the air.

Around 1372 B.C., Amonhotep IV became pharaoh. He believed that the sun god, now called Aton, was the only god. To honor Aton, he changed his name to *Ikhnaton,* which means, "It is well with Aton." The new pharaoh closed the temples of the other gods. He took power away from the priests.

Ikhnaton built new temples that were completely open to the light and air. Often, Egyptian art shows this pharaoh and his wife, Nefertiti, giving gifts to Aton. The rays of the sun god beam down on them.

Reading Strategy:
Text Structure

As you read the next section, make a list of causes and effects as Egypt lost its power.

How Did Egypt Lose Its Power?

Many Egyptians did not like the new religion with its one god. The priests became angry and jealous because they had lost power. Soon they began to fight with the pharaoh. When that happened, he could not pay as much attention to the empire. The conquered people in many parts of the empire began to rebel against Egypt.

A later pharaoh, Ramses III, rebuilt the empire, but the weakened Egypt never became as powerful as it had once been. He built many obelisks, giant statues, and beautiful temples. He was the last great ruler of Egypt.

Who Conquered Egypt in 332 B.C.?

Egypt could no longer defend itself. Over the years, many people invaded the land—Ethiopians from farther south in Africa; Babylonians; Assyrians; and, Persians.

The Persians ruled Egypt until Alexander the Great defeated them in 332 B.C. Many years later, in 30 B.C., Queen Cleopatra killed herself to avoid surrendering Egypt to the Romans. The wonder of ancient Egypt ended with her death.

Lesson 4 Review On a sheet of paper, write the letter of the answer that correctly completes each sentence.

1. The first woman pharaoh was _____.

    A Cleopatra   **C** Ramses III

    B Hatshepsut   **D** Ikhnaton

2. The capital of the New Kingdom was _____.

    A Memphis   **B** Cairo   **C** Thebes   **D** Persia

3. Thutmose III organized a _____ to help him conquer other lands.

    A caravan   **B** obelisk   **C** navy   **D** religion

4. The name of the one god worshiped by Ikhnaton was _____.

    A Aton   **B** Ra   **C** Amon   **D** Amon-Ra

5. The glory of ancient Egypt ended in _____ B.C.

    A 1600   **B** 1372   **C** 332   **D** 30

What do you think ?

Why do you think Ikhnaton's new religion was unpopular?

Reading Strategy:
Text Structure

Notice the title of this lesson. What do you expect to learn in the lesson?

Objectives

◆ To describe the way Egyptians advanced medicine, building, and artwork
◆ To identify the counting system that the Egyptians invented

Papyrus

A reed from the Nile River used to make paper

Scroll

A roll of papyrus

Cubit

A measurement that is the length of an arm from the end of the middle finger to the elbow

Egyptian civilization has given many gifts to the modern world. As early as 3000 B.C., the Egyptians learned how to use **papyrus,** a reed from the Nile River, to make paper. (The English word *paper* comes from the word *papyrus.*) Their paper was so well made that even today we can still read the writing on it!

This invention was important because writing on paper is much easier than writing on stone. Of course, in order to write on paper, they also had to invent ink.

What Did the Egyptians Know About Medicine?

The Egyptians made papyrus **scrolls,** or rolls. Archaeologists have discovered some of these in Egyptian tombs. One of the most famous papyrus scrolls shows the Egyptians' interest in medicine. The scroll describes how to set broken bones, how to check for a heartbeat, and how to deal with fevers and accidents. People who lived at later times learned much of their medicine from these ancient Egyptians.

What Were Egyptian Temples Like?

The Egyptians were skilled builders. Some of their statues, temples, and pyramids stood several stories high! People from all over the world still come to see their size and beauty. However, most of the great temples that the Egyptians built are in ruins today.

How Much Arithmetic Did the Egyptians Know?

The Egyptians invented a system of counting based on ten. This helped them add and subtract. They used this system to collect taxes. They also invented a system for measurement and weights. They measured things in **cubits**—the length of an arm from the end of the middle finger to the elbow. They used geometry to survey, or measure, land.

What Artwork Did Egyptian Artists Produce?

Egyptian artists carved huge statues from stone. Many had heads about twelve feet high, with ears three feet long! They made small figures of people and animals from wood, bronze, or copper.

These same artists decorated temples with many drawings. We can still see much of their beautifully colored artwork today. Archaeologists have also found beautiful jewelry, pottery, and furniture in the pharaohs' tombs.

Egyptian pectoral jewelry, such as this "Sacred Animals of Thot" pectoral, was worn on the wearer's chest.

There were strict rules for Egyptian artists to follow. One rule was that important people had to be the largest figures in a piece of art. For example, a pharaoh would appear larger than a lesser god. Another rule said that figures in paintings and sculpture should be facing forward. However, the arms and legs of a figure should be turned to the side so they would be easier to see. The style of art in Egypt stayed this way for thousands of years.

Egyptian figures such as this one of the goddess, Isus, and her child, Horus, show that Egyptians were talented artisans.

Lesson 5 Review On a sheet of paper, use the words from the Word Bank to complete each sentence correctly.

1. The Egyptians made paper from a reed called _____.

2. The Egyptians built tall _____, temples, and pyramids.

3. An ancient _____ describes the Egyptians' interest in medicine.

4. The Egyptians decorated their temples with _____.

5. The Egyptians used _____ to survey their land.

What do you think ?

What is good and what is bad about measuring something in cubits?

Then and Now

The First Solar Calendar

Ancient Egyptians carefully watched the regular rise and fall of the Nile River. It stood for the cycle of birth and death. It also gave people a way to measure time. Egyptians discovered that the time between floods averaged about 365 days. So, nearly 5,000 years ago, they developed a calendar. It had 12 months, each 30 days long. An extra five days were added at the end of the year as holidays. This calendar was almost perfectly in tune with the solar year. That's the time it takes the earth to circle the sun—365 1/4 days. Today's calendar is a solar calendar, too. It has 12 months and 365 days, except in leap year.

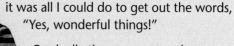
Opening King Tut's Tomb

Tutankhamen was eight when he became pharaoh of Egypt. He ruled for about 11 years. Then he died suddenly about 1352 B.C. For thousands of years, his tomb was lost. Grave robbers broke in, but they never reached the main room. As a result, this tomb kept almost all its original contents. It is the only pharaoh's tomb ever found in this condition.

"King Tut" was not a powerful ruler, but he is famous today. The reason is the discovery of his tomb in 1922 by British archaeologist Howard Carter. This is Carter's retelling of the event.

The gold mask of Tutankhamen.

The day following (November 26th) was the day of days, the most wonderful that I have ever lived through. . . . In the middle of the afternoon, 30 feet down from the outer door, we came upon a second sealed doorway. . . .

With trembling hands I made a tiny breach in the upper left-hand corner. Darkness and blank space . . . showed that whatever lay beyond was empty. . . . Widening the hole a little, I inserted the candle and peered in. . . . As my eyes grew accustomed to the light, details of the room within emerged slowly from the mist, strange animals, statues, and gold— everywhere the glint of gold.

For the moment . . . I was struck dumb with amazement. When Lord Carnarvon, unable to stand the suspense any longer, inquired anxiously, "Can you see anything?"

it was all I could do to get out the words, "Yes, wonderful things!"

Gradually the scene grew clearer, and we could pick out individual objects. First, right opposite to us . . . were three great gilt couches, their sides carved in the form of monstrous animals. . . . Next . . . two statues caught and held our attention: two life-sized figures of a king in black, facing each other like sentinels. . . .

These were the dominant objects that caught the eye at first. Between them, around them, piled on top of them, there were countless others— exquisitely painted and inlaid caskets; alabaster vases, some beautifully carved . . . a golden inlaid throne; . . . on the left a confused pile of overturned chariots, glistening with gold and inlay; and peeping from behind them another portrait of a king.

Document-Based Questions

1. Why was the discovery of this tomb important to historians?

2. Is this reading a primary source or a secondary source? Why?

3. What did Carter see all around after he got used to the darkness?

4. How did Carter answer Lord Carnarvon?

5. List three things found in the tomb.

Source: The Tomb of Tut-Ankh-Amen, *by Howard Carter.*

Burying the Dead

The people of ancient Egypt saw their pharaohs as god-kings. They believed that each pharaoh was the human form of a god. Egyptians also believed in an afterlife. It was much like life on earth. After death, a pharaoh would continue to rule in the next life.

The Egyptians believed that a dead person's body must not decay. Otherwise a person could not enjoy the afterlife. To protect the body, Egyptians used a process called embalming.

Embalming took time. First, the embalmers removed all the internal organs. The heart and other important organs were put in small jars. These are called canopic jars. Then the body was put in a pine box. It was covered with a salty liquid called natron. The natron removed most of the water in the body, making it shrink. That took about 70 days. Then the body was wrapped with bandages of wax-covered cloth. The wrapped body was now a mummy. It was placed in a decorated coffin and put in a tomb.

The tombs of the pharaohs were meant to last forever. They were decorated like a palace. The tombs were filled with things the dead might need in the next life. That would include food, furniture, jewels, and cosmetics. A ruler needed servants, too. Early in Egypt's history, servants were buried with the ruler. They were probably smothered or given poison. The pharaoh Djer ruled Egypt around 2900 B.C. When he died, about 580 members of the court may have been buried with him. Later, Egyptians buried small pottery figures in tombs to act as servants, instead of killing actual servants.

Mummies were prepared with great care. This one is an Egyptian priestess from about 100 B.C., with the original wood coffin.

Ancient embalmers were very skillful. Thousands of years later, many mummies are well preserved. You can see some in museums. Today scientists are also interested in mummies. They examine their bones, hair, and other parts. Research on mummies can discover much about the lives and health of ancient Egyptians.

Wrap-Up

1. What did the ancient Egyptians think of their pharaoh?

2. What did the Egyptians believe happened after death?

3. Why did the Egyptians not want the body to decay?

4. Why were things like food and furniture placed in a tomb?

5. What can scientists learn from mummies?

- Egyptian civilization developed in the valley of the Nile River. The river runs north from central Africa. The Nile's yearly floods made the soil rich. Farmers could grow many crops in a year. The river was also a good route for trade.

- Upper Egypt, in the south, was unified by about 3400 B.C. Stories say that Menes, a god-king, conquered Lower Egypt about 3100 B.C. He unified Upper and Lower Egypt. The symbol for this new Egypt was the double crown. Its capital was Memphis. His rule began Egypt's first dynasty.

- The Old Kingdom in Egypt began about 3100 B.C. The rulers were called pharaohs. They were all-powerful. People believed they were gods. Trade became important.

- Egyptians believed in an afterlife that was much like life on earth. Pharaohs built pyramids for tombs. People filled them with things the ruler would need in the afterlife.

- The pharaohs lost power. Then civil war broke out. The economy collapsed. As a result, the Old Kingdom ended about 2100 B.C.

- Egypt was reunited about 2040 B.C. The Middle Kingdom began. Its capital was at Thebes. The pharaohs had less power than in the Old Kingdom.

- Beliefs about the afterlife changed in the Middle Kingdom. Pharaohs were buried in tombs cut into cliffs. Ordinary people could share the afterlife.

- Egyptians had many gods. Ra was the sun-god. Hapi was the river god.

- The Hyksos from Asia ended the Middle Kingdom about 1630 B.C. They had iron weapons and metal armor. They ruled until 1570 B.C.

- The New Kingdom began about 1600 B.C. Egypt took over more land. Hatshepsut, the first woman pharaoh, encouraged trade. Thutmose III made the empire much larger.

- The pharaoh Amonhotep IV tried to change Egypt's religion. He believed in only one god. The fight over religion that followed made Egypt weak. Other peoples invaded it. Persia ruled Egypt until 332 B.C.

- The ancient Egyptians made paper from the papyrus reed.

- Egyptian doctors were skillful. They knew how to set broken bones and deal with fevers.

- Egyptian artists carved huge statues. They created jewelry, pottery, and artwork. They invented a counting system based on 10. They used geometry.

Chapter 4   R E V I E W

Word Bank

Hatshepsut

hieroglyphics

Ikhnaton

Menes

mummy

papyrus

pharaoh

Ra

Ramses III

Thutmose III

On a sheet of paper, use the words from the Word Bank to complete each sentence correctly.

1. The reed from which the Egyptians made paper is _____.

2. The Egyptians made a _____ by wrapping a dead body in cloth strips to keep it from decaying.

3. The Egyptians used _____, which is a kind of picture writing.

4. The Egyptians called their king or ruler a _____.

5. _____ was the god-king who unified Upper and Lower Egypt and began the Old Kingdom.

6. _____ was the Egyptian sun-god.

7. _____ was the first woman pharaoh.

8. _____ was the pharaoh who enlarged the Egyptian empire to its greatest size.

9. _____ was the last great ruler of Egypt.

10. The Egyptian pharaoh _____ believed in only one god.

On a sheet of paper, write the letter of the answer that correctly completes each sentence.

11. Upper Egypt was the _____ part of Egypt.

   A northern   **C** southern
   B eastern   **D** western

12. Lower Egypt was the _____ part of Egypt.

   A northern   **C** southern
   B eastern   **D** western

13. The Egyptians thought their rulers were _____.

   A children   **C** wind
   B gods   **D** sun

14. Building a pyramid took about _____ years.

A 3	**C** 13
B 7	**D** 20

15. The _____ invaded Egypt in 1630 B.C.

A Persians	**C** Assyrians
B Babylonians	**D** Hyksos

On a sheet of paper, write the answer to each question. Use complete sentences.

16. Why was the Nile River so important to the Egyptians?

17. How did the three kingdoms of Egypt differ?

18. Why were the Hyksos and later invaders able to defeat the Egyptians?

Critical Thinking On a sheet of paper, write your response to each question. Use complete sentences.

19. The Egyptians buried treasures with pharaohs when they died. We learn about the Egyptian society from this treasure. Think of things that would tell other people about our society. What five things from our society would you choose to put in your tomb? Explain your choices.

20. What gift from the ancient Egyptians do you think is best? Why do you think so?

Test-Taking Tip

Organize a study group to study a subject. Each person can share his or her notes on a different part of the subject.

5

Ancient India and China

Thousands of years ago, civilization developed in India and China. In India, villages grew into cities in the Indus River Valley. In China, small towns grew large in the Yangtze River and the Huang He Valleys. In this chapter, you will learn that ancient people in India planned their two large cities and that the Chinese people became great builders and artisans. You will also learn about Hinduism and Buddhism, two religions that developed.

Goals for Learning

◆ To explain the importance of geography in the history of civilization

◆ To describe India's first civilization

◆ To describe Hinduism and castes

◆ To compare Hinduism and Buddhism and describe the four noble truths of Buddhism.

◆ To explain two wonders of ancient China

◆ To describe the Shang, Qin, and Han dynasties

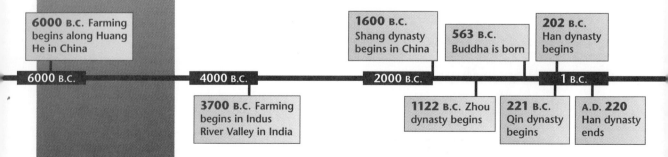

6000 B.C. Farming begins along Huang He in China

1600 B.C. Shang dynasty begins in China

563 B.C. Buddha is born

202 B.C. Han dynasty begins

6000 B.C.

4000 B.C.

2000 B.C.

1 B.C.

3700 B.C. Farming begins in Indus River Valley in India

1122 B.C. Zhou dynasty begins

221 B.C. Qin dynasty begins

A.D. 220 Han dynasty ends

Map Skills

Civilization began thousands of years ago along the river valleys of Asia. Geography, or the land and the weather, was important in the history of India and China. Both countries are large. Mountains cut them off from other countries. The people get water from the rivers and use them for travel.

Study the map, then answer the following questions:

1. Name the large desert in Mongolia.

2. Name two rivers in China.

3. Name one river in India.

4. What country is directly south of Mongolia?

5. Mountains separate China from the West. How do you think this has affected China's history?

Reading Strategy:
Visualizing

Visualizing is another strategy that helps readers understand what they are reading. It is like creating a movie in your mind. Use the following ways to visualize a text:

◆ Look at the photographs, illustrations, and descriptive words.

◆ Think about experiences in your own life that may add to the images.

◆ Notice the order in which things are happening and what you think might happen next.

Key Vocabulary Words

Lesson 1

Geography The science that deals with land, weather, bodies of water, and plant and animal life

Peninsula A piece of land surrounded on three sides by water

Subcontinent A large landmass that is somewhat smaller than a continent

Monsoon A seasonal wind

Lesson 2

Irrigate To bring water to crops

Pictogram A figure that tells a story

Lesson 3

Hinduism The main religion of India, which stresses the belief in the Vedas

Reincarnation The rebirth of the soul into a new body

Cycle The events that keep happening, one after another

Caste A class of people in India

Lesson 4

Buddha A name meaning the "Enlightened One"; the name given to Siddhartha Gautama, the founder of Buddhism

Enlightened Knowing the truth

Desire To wish for something

Nirvana A condition of complete emptiness in which a person's soul finds perfect peace

Soul A person's spirit

Lesson 5

Isolate To keep apart or away from others

Plateau A flat area that rises above the land close by

Canal A waterway made by humans

Invade To attack or march into another country

Lesson 6

Dynasty A family that rules a country over a long period of time

Noble A person of high birth

Artisan A person who makes beautiful objects for everyday use

Symbol Something that stands for something else

Scribe A person from ancient times who could read and write

Society A group of people whose members live together for the good of all

Objectives

◆ To describe why ancient towns formed along river valleys

◆ To describe the climate of India

Geography

The science that deals with land, weather, bodies of water, and plant and animal life

Peninsula

A piece of land surrounded on three sides by water

Subcontinent

A large landmass that is somewhat smaller than a continent

The civilization of India is one of the oldest in the world. **Geography**—land, weather, bodies of water, plant and animal life—shapes all civilizations. India has a very interesting geography. It is a **peninsula** surrounded on three sides by water. India is often called a **subcontinent** because it is so large. From north to south, India extends about 2,000 miles. It has the world's highest mountains, called the Himalayas. The Ganges and Indus are two great rivers. Great seasonal winds called monsoons are very important to life in India.

What Has Geography Done for India?

Most of the time, geography has protected India. However, many armies have marched into India over the past 4,000 years. These armies reached India through passes, or openings, in the mountains. The best known passage into India is the Khyber Pass.

The people who came through these passes changed India's history. Each group brought new ideas. The newcomers sometimes married the people who had come before. Indian culture became a blend of many different groups.

What Rivers Are Important to India?

The Indian subcontinent has many rivers. The three most important are the Ganges, the Brahmaputra, and the Indus Rivers. The Ganges River is so important to the Indians that they call it "Mother Ganges."

Writing About History

Geography influenced ancient India and China. What is the land like where you live? In your notebook, write an essay. Tell how rivers, mountains, or other features have affected the way people live in your area.

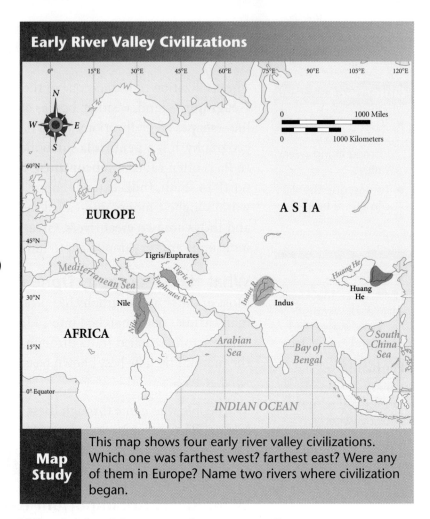

Early River Valley Civilizations

Map Study

This map shows four early river valley civilizations. Which one was farthest west? farthest east? Were any of them in Europe? Name two rivers where civilization began.

Monsoon

A seasonal wind

Reading Strategy: **Visualizing**

What words in this paragraph help you visualize the geography of India?

Why Is the Monsoon Important?

Life in India depends on seasonal winds called **monsoons.** In the summer, wind blows over the warm waters of the Indian Ocean. When this air reaches land, rain falls. Sometimes rain pours down for weeks. In fact, 90 percent of India's yearly rain comes from the summer monsoon. Sometimes the monsoon is late or little rain falls. Then crops fail, and many people go hungry.

India is hot most of the year. The temperature usually stays above freezing. Its two seasons depend on the rain. Summer is the rainy season; winter is the dry season.

Word Bank

geography

Indus

Khyber Pass

monsoon

subcontinent

Lesson 1 Review On a sheet of paper, use the words from the Word Bank to complete each sentence correctly.

1. We sometimes call India a _____.

2. Two important rivers in India are the Ganges and the _____.

3. A _____ is a seasonal wind that brings rain to India.

4. Armies marched into India through the _____.

5. _____ is the study of how land, bodies of water, weather, plants, and animals change people's lives.

What do you think ?

In what ways has its geography helped or hurt the people of India?

The Indus River is an important river in India.

Objectives

◆ To describe the farming, art, homes, and writing of the civilization

◆ To explain possible reasons why this civilization suddenly ended

India's first civilization developed in the Indus River Valley. This river begins in the Himalayas. When the snow melts, the river floods. Later, the water retreats and leaves silt, or a rich layer of soil, behind. Because this silt makes the soil fertile, people settled along the Indus River.

Two cities, Harappa and Mohenjo-Daro, looked like modern, planned cities. Their streets were wide and straight. The people built with clay bricks, which were all exactly the same.

How Did These Ancient People Live?

The people of the Indus River Valley raised grains and vegetables in their rich soil. They learned how to **irrigate,** or bring water to, their fields during the dry season.

Irrigate

To bring water to crops

The farmers grew enough food to feed everyone. Because of this, the city people could make pottery, cloth, jewelry, and metal tools. How do we know? Because archaeologists have dug up beautifully painted pottery, stone carvings, and gold and silver jewelry. We also know that Indians made the first cotton cloth.

Archaeologists have also found things from faraway in the ruins of ancient India. This early civilization traded goods with other civilizations.

What Were the Homes Like?

Reading Strategy:
Visualizing

How could this paragraph be written differently to create a stronger picture of these homes in your mind?

In the cities, people's homes were sometimes two stories high. Most had a patio, or rooms open to the sky. Stairs led up to the roof. The people built alabaster windows. This marblelike stone allowed light to shine through. Some homes had indoor bathrooms and toilets. Dirty water drained away through clay pipes.

Reading Strategy:
Visualizing

Draw a picture to help you visualize what this paragraph is about. How does this image help you picture a city in ancient India?

Pictogram

A figure that tells a story

Why Were the Cities Walled?

A great wall surrounded each city and protected it. Towers were built into the walls. From these towers, people could see any enemy. In the center of the city was another walled area. Behind the wall stood a fort, a place to store food, and a large bath. The people may have used this area as a place to honor their gods.

Did These People Have a Written Language?

Archaeologists have discovered many clay tablets in the Indus River Valley. On them are **pictograms**—figures that tell a story. They have also found hundreds of small carved markers. Did business people use these to stamp the things they sold? We do not know because at this time no one can read the Harappan language.

What Caused This Ancient Civilization to End?

About 1500 B.C. this civilization suddenly ended. Perhaps the coastline changed so trading became harder. Maybe the monsoon failed. Maybe disease, an earthquake, or a flood struck. Perhaps farmers could no longer grow enough food. Or maybe armies from central Asia invaded.

It is not known what these pictograms mean. No one can read the writing of the Indus Valley civilization.

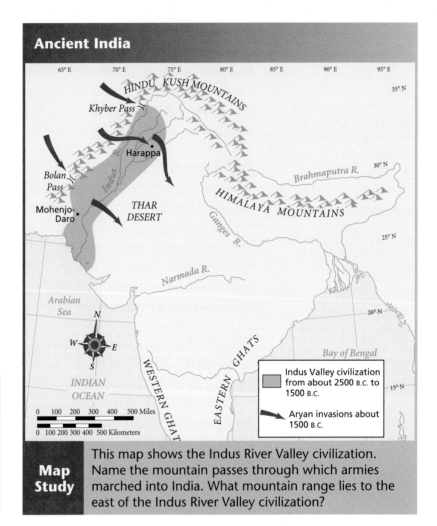

Ancient India

This map shows the Indus River Valley civilization. Name the mountain passes through which armies marched into India. What mountain range lies to the east of the Indus River Valley civilization?

Map Study

Indus Valley civilization from about 2500 B.C. to 1500 B.C.

Aryan invasions about 1500 B.C.

Word Bank

alabaster
Harappa
Indus
pictograms
silt

Lesson 2 Review On a sheet of paper, use the words from the Word Bank to complete each sentence correctly.

1. The first civilization in India grew up along the _____ River Valley.

2. This happened because of the rich _____ that the spring floods left behind in the valley.

3. The two great cities of this civilization were _____ and Mohenjo-Daro.

4. People in these cities built _____ windows to let in light.

5. In this valley, archaeologists have discovered clay pads with _____, or pictures, on them.

Objectives

- To identify the major features of Hinduism
- To understand the importance of Sanskrit to India
- To explain the purpose of castes

Hinduism

The main religion of India that stresses the belief in the Vedas

Reincarnation

The rebirth of the soul into a new body

Cycle

The events that keep happening, one after another

Reading Strategy:
Visualizing

What words in this paragraph help you understand what you are reading?

For the next 500 years, people fought wars in the Indus River Valley. Many soldiers wandered into India. They fought with each other and with the people who came before them. Over hundreds of years, these people married one another. Eventually, they developed a new set of beliefs and practices called **Hinduism.** Hinduism is the main religion of modern India.

What Do Hindus Believe?

The Hindus, or the people who practice Hinduism, believe that everything is God, or Brahman. The Vedas, their holy writings, explain "Brahman is one, and yet expresses itself as many." The word *Vedas* means "books of knowledge." Hindus believe that Brahman, Vishnu, and Shiva are different faces of God. Brahma creates, or makes, life. Vishnu preserves life, and Shiva destroys it. Hindus believe that these three faces express the main powers of God.

The Hindu god Vishnu preserves life.

What Is Rebirth?

Hindus believe that all living things—weeds, water, insects, animals, and people—have souls. Hindus believe in **reincarnation,** or the rebirth of the soul into a new body. The **cycle** of birth, death, and rebirth keeps happening until a soul becomes perfect. Then the cycle ends, and a soul becomes one with Brahman. Hindus do not kill animals. They believe that cows are especially holy.

Caste

A class of people in India

What Is a Caste?

Hinduism teaches that people are born into **castes,** or classes of people. Hindus have four main castes:

1. the Brahmin caste made up of religious leaders

2. the ruler and warrior caste

3. the shopkeeper, landowner, and skilled-worker caste

4. the farmer, unskilled worker, servant, and slave caste

The Brahmin caste is the highest; the fourth caste listed is the lowest. Over thousands of years, the Hindus have divided their four main castes into smaller and smaller groups. They divide according to work, money, skin color, and religious beliefs.

There are many religious temples in India. This is the Vimal Vasahi Temple at Mount Abu, India. It is from the Jainist religion, which uses parts of Hinduism.

Why Were Castes Important?

The members of each caste remained in the caste for life and followed its rules. For example, a person could marry only within the same caste. Another rule was that all the people in a caste did the same kind of work. When people broke these rules, they were thrown out from the caste. People called them "outcaste," because they are outside any caste.

What Is Sanskrit?

Sanskrit was the language of ancient India. It is one of the oldest languages in the Indo-European family. Latin, English, German, Spanish, Greek, and Persian are also in this language family. The languages have many words in common. For example, *mata* is the Sanskrit word for "mother."

Lesson 3 Review On a sheet of paper, write the answer to each question. Use complete sentences.

1. What are the Vedas?

2. What does the saying "Brahman is One, and yet expresses itself as many" mean?

3. Why do some Hindus not kill animals?

4. What is an Indian caste?

5. What does Sanskrit have to do with the English language?

What do you think ?

What can the Hindu religion teach us?

Objectives

◆ To explain how Siddhartha Gautama founded Buddhism

◆ To explain how and where Buddhism spread

Buddha

A name meaning the "Enlightened One"; the name given to Siddhartha Gautama, the founder of Buddhism

Enlightened

The state of knowing the truth

Hinduism developed over a long period of time. Later in India, a man named Siddhartha Gautama began to question Hindu beliefs. He explained his beliefs to others. These beliefs are the basis of Buddhism.

How Did Gautama Become the Buddha?

Gautama was born around 563 B.C. His family was very rich. As a young man he began to feel sorry for the poor people in India. According to an old story, Gautama left his palace one day with his servant. They saw a crippled man, a sick man, a dead man, and a holy man. His servant said, "Such is the way of life, to that we must all come." This led Gautama to realize that birth, old age, sickness, and death come to everyone. The next day Gautama left his wife and newborn son. For several years, he walked the countryside and studied the Hindu holy books.

One day, while sitting under a giant tree, Gautama discovered four noble truths about life. From then on, he was known as the **Buddha,** or the "**Enlightened** One." To be enlightened is to know the truth.

What Are the Four Noble Truths Buddha Discovered?

For the rest of his life, Buddha taught and preached. He walked from village to village, dressed in a yellow robe. He trusted others to give him the food and shelter he needed.

Many statues and sculptures honor Buddha. This one is from the second or third century B.C.

Reading Strategy:
Visualizing

What clues on this page help you visualize the four "Noble Truths"?

Desire

To wish for something

Nirvana

A condition of complete emptiness in which a person's soul finds perfect peace

Soul

A person's spirit

Reading Strategy:
Visualizing

Create a graphic organizer to show how Buddhism and Hinduism are alike and different.

Buddha preached four "Noble Truths" about the meaning of life:

1. Our life is full of suffering.

2. Our own selfish wishes cause this suffering.

3. We stop suffering when we stop being jealous, greedy, and selfish.

4. We can stop wishing for, or desiring, more.

To stop wanting more and more, Buddha said that people must follow the "Eightfold Path." To stop wanting so much a person must believe, think, speak, wish, enjoy, act, try, and live in the right way. When all **desires** finally end, a person enters the spiritual place called **nirvana.** In nirvana, a person's **soul,** or spirit, finds perfect peace.

How Are Buddhism and Hinduism Alike and Different?

Gautama was born a Hindu, so many Buddhist beliefs are the same as those of Hinduism. Both religions believe that life is sad and evil. Both believe in reincarnation. Many followers of both religions refuse to kill an animal or eat meat.

A big difference between the two religions is that Buddhists do not believe in the caste system. Buddha treated all people the same. He believed that when people follow the Eightfold Path, they reach nirvana in their own lifetime.

Where Did Buddhism Spread?

Buddha founded several groups of monks. These holy men lived in monasteries that became important centers of learning. Buddhism spread from India into Burma, Thailand, Southeast Asia, China, Korea, and Japan.

Who Was Ashoka?

The first Indian empire, the Maurya, was created in 321 B.C. Ashoka was its third emperor. At first, Ashoka fought wars to expand his empire. In one military victory, more than 100,000 people died. Seeing this, he realized the evil of war. He became *shoka,* or powerful. He accepted the teachings of Buddhism. Because of his change of heart, he was called "without sorrow," or *ashoka.* Ashoka is remembered as an emperor who tried to rule with justice and wisdom.

Lesson 4 Review On a sheet of paper, write the letter of the answer that correctly completes each sentence.

1. Siddhartha Gautama was born _____.

    A rich   **B** poor   **C** small   **D** large

2. Another name for the Buddha is _____ One.

    A Channa   **B** Allah   **C** Enlightened   **D** Nirvana

3. Gautama preached _____ "Noble Truths."

    A two   **B** four   **C** six   **D** eight

4. Buddhists give up _____ when they reach nirvana.

    A desire   **B** religion   **C** food   **D** labor

5. Some Buddhist beliefs are similar to _____ beliefs.

    A Christian   **B** Muslim   **C** Orthodox   **D** Hindu

What do you think

Why do you think that some Hindus became Buddhists?

Then and Now

Buddhism, Yesterday and Today

Buddhism spread quickly throughout Asia. Buddhism started in India, but it has nearly disappeared there today. Worldwide, there are about 353 million Buddhists.

Buddhism has split into three main groups: Tibetan, Pure Land, and Zen.

The major difference among them has to do with how a person can reach enlightenment.

Buddhism spread to America in the 1900s. Why? Partly because many people from Asia moved to the United States. Also, Buddhism appealed to some Americans who were looking for a new kind of religious experience and expression.

Objectives

◆ To describe the geography of China

◆ To explain how the Yangtze River and Huang He have influenced life in China

Isolate

To keep apart or away from others

Plateau

A flat area that rises above the land close by

People have lived in China for thousands of years. Its geography made China a safe and productive place to live. In fact, farming began there more than 1,000 years ago. These farm villages eventually grew into cities. The first Chinese cities began near the Huang He about 2000 B.C. The ancient Chinese were also great builders.

What Is China's Geography?

China is huge. In ancient times, its geography **isolated** or kept it away from other peoples. The enormous Gobi Desert lies to the north. The Tibetan mountain **plateau**—a flat area that rises above the land close by—stretches toward the west. The mighty Himalayas rise in the southwest. The sea guards the east and south.

What Keeps the Yangtze from Flooding?

The Yangtze is the longest and most important river in China. Because it is deep and runs swiftly, it hardly ever floods. In fact, it is the world's deepest river. Large ships travel inland on it as far as 600 miles. The Yangtze flows through southern China. It has been one of China's main trade routes since ancient times.

Why Does the Huang He Flood?

The Huang He flows across northern China. Because the river is shallow, it often floods. Throughout the years, it has destroyed both cities and farms. Since 600 B.C., it has flooded more than 1,500 times. Hunger, disease, and death follow. For this reason, it is sometimes called "China's Sorrow."

The Huang He in China is about 3,000 miles long. The first Chinese civilization began near the Yellow River in about 2000 B.C.

Canal

Canal

A waterway made by humans

Invade

To attack or march into another country

Reading Strategy:
Visualizing

What words in this paragraph help you visualize the building of a canal?

Why Did the Chinese Build a Grand Canal?

A great wonder of the ancient world was the Grand **Canal**. Most of China's rivers flow from west to east. The Chinese rulers built a 1,100-mile canal, or waterway, that flowed north and south. It joined the Huang He and the Yangtze River.

The Chinese used the canal to transport grain and other supplies from the fertile south to the north.

Who Built the Canal?

The Chinese rulers began the canal more than 2,400 years ago. More than 5 million people worked on it. In some areas, the rulers forced all men between the ages of 15 and 50 to work on the canal. An army of 50,000 guards beat and sometimes beheaded those who refused to work.

One person in every five families had to supply and prepare food for the workers and guards. During the building of the canal, 2 million workers died, became ill, or ran away.

Why Did the Chinese Build a Great Wall?

In ancient times, nomads **invaded,** or attacked, China on its northern and western frontier. Rulers built walls to keep them out. Two rulers joined all the walls together and created the Great Wall of China. It is another wonder of the ancient world.

How Big Is the Great Wall?

Builders started work on the wall over 2,000 years ago. It stretches nearly 1,500 miles from the Yellow Sea westward. It is really a collection of short walls. In some places, it stands about 35 feet high. Its base was 15 to 30 feet thick. The workers built towers along the wall. From these, guards looked far to the north and to the west. They watched for signs of invaders.

An ancient Chinese historian says 300,000 workers built the Great Wall of China. Others believe that 1 million people worked on it and that 400,000 of them died while building the wall.

Lesson 5 Review On a sheet of paper, write the letter of the answer that correctly completes each sentence.

1. For nearly 1,000 years China was nearly cut off from the rest of the world because of _____.

    A the Gobi Desert   **C** the Himalayan Mountains
    B the Tibetan plateau   **D** all of the above

2. The _____ River is the deepest river in China and in the world.

    A Yangtze   **B** Huang   **C** Ganges   **D** Indus

3. The _____ joins together the Yangtze River and the Huang He.

    A Great Wall of China   **C** Gobi Desert
    B Grand Canal   **D** Tibetan mountain plateau

4. The Great Wall protected the Chinese from invaders from the north and the _____.

    A east   **B** west   **C** south   **D** all of the above

5. "China's Sorrow" is another name for the _____.

    A Great Wall of China   **C** Huang He
    B Grand Canal   **D** Yangtze River

What do you think

Why do people think that the Great Wall of China is a wonder?

History in Your Life

The Huang He, Sweet and Sour

Many popular Chinese dishes mix sweet and sour flavors. China's Huang He has "sweet and sour" traits too. This river flows out of the western mountains across the flat North China Plain. For farmers, the river can be "sweet." It waters the fields. It also brings loess, a rich yellow soil, from the mountains. The yellow mud gave the river its Western name. It also makes the soil the most fertile in China.

Sometimes, though, the river turns "sour." It overflows its banks and floods the plains. Then it becomes deadly. More than 1,500 floods have been recorded in the past 3,000 years. One terrible flood in 1887 killed almost a million people. The Chinese people have built dikes and dams to control the river. Even today, the floodwaters of the Huang He can be a "sour" threat.

Dynasty

A family that rules a country over a long period of time

Noble

A person of high birth

Symbol

Something that stands for something else

Reading Strategy:
Visualizing

Create a symbol that has two parts, like a Chinese character. How does this help you visualize a Chinese character?

In ancient times in the valley of the Huang He, many rulers fought one another. Around 1600 B.C., one powerful ruling family took over the whole plain. This family ruled for many years. A family that rules a country for a long period of time is called a **dynasty.** We call China's first dynasty the Shang.

What Was a Shang City Like?

Like the people of ancient India, the ancient Chinese built cities. The people of the Indus River Valley in India built brick homes. However, the people of the Yellow River Valley in China built wooden ones.

Archaeologists have discovered over 130 Shang villages and cities. Among the most important was Anyang, which was carved out of a forest. A palace and a temple stood in its center.

Near these important buildings, the **nobles**—people of high birth—lived. Their homes were large rectangles. Anyang had a business area with shops and government buildings.

What Is a Chinese Character?

During the Shang dynasty, the Chinese developed writing. At first, they wrote pictograms. Later they included **symbols.** These figures stood for something else. It was a difficult language with over 3,000 characters, or symbols.

Each Chinese character includes two parts. One gives the meaning of the character. The other tells how to pronounce it. The language of modern China still uses the same characters the Shang dynasty used.

The Shang made beautiful things out of bronze, such as this kettle.

Who Were the Scribes?

The written language of the Shang dynasty was difficult. Only a few people could read and write. We call these people **scribes.** Shang scribes wrote on long, narrow bamboo strips. Scribes wrote the characters up and down the strip rather than across.

What Is Ancestor Worship?

The Shang people believed that the gods controlled all things. They believed that the spirits of nature gave their rulers power. Among these spirits were the spirits of dead ancestors. When bad things happened, families thought that dead ancestors were not pleased with them. Ancestor worship was an important part of the Shang religion.

Why Did the Shang Decline?

The Shang dynasty lasted over 500 years. Then in 1122 B.C., the Zhou people captured the city of Anyang. The Shang **society** was sharply divided into rich and poor people. A society is a group of people whose members live together for the good of all.

The rich nobles lived in large houses in the cities. They owned bronze weapons. They were proud of their beautiful silk clothes and jade jewelry. But the poor lived in small huts or in caves. They owned no land. They could only work the land the nobles owned. When invaders came, the poor may have welcomed them. Perhaps because of this, the Shang dynasty fell apart.

Technology Connection

Early Earthquake Detection

A man named Zhang Heng thought he could predict that an earthquake was about to occur. In about A.D. 132, he created what is believed to be the world's first earthquake detector.

Zhang Heng's instrument was shaped like a large vase. Its copper-domed top featured eight dragons' heads around its edge. Each of these heads held a bronze ball.

A pendulum under the dome would swing if the earth shook. As the pendulum swung, it caused a ball to drop from a dragon's mouth into the mouth of a bronze toad beneath it.

The loud sound of the falling ball warned of an impending earthquake. The position of the dragon showed the direction of the earthquake's epicenter. The epicenter is the point where an earthquake begins.

What Were the Accomplishments of the Qin Dynasty?

The Qin dynasty ruled China for only a short time, from 221 to 206 B.C. It was the first to unite China with a strong central government. *Qin* is pronounced as Ch'in. This may be why the land is called China. Before the Qin dynasty took control, there was no central ruler of China. The Qin leader, Shi Huangdi, named himself First Emperor. For 2,000 years after Shi Huangdi, Chinese rulers took the title of Emperor. The First Emperor is known for many accomplishments. Writing became more uniform. This allowed people in different areas to better communicate. The same system of laws was created throughout the land. New roads and canals were built. Nearly 2000 miles of the Great Wall of China was built to protect the country from northern enemies.

However, the Qin Dynasty did not last long. When the First Emperor died, he was buried in a tomb beneath a huge mound of earth. Buried near the tomb in a large pit were more than 6,000 life-size clay statues of warriors and horses. When the First Emperor died, his son became the Second Emperor. At this time, the peasants were unhappy with high taxes and harsh treatment by the Qin rulers. The peasants rebelled. In 206 B.C., Liu Bang, a peasant, who became the Prince of Han, defeated the Emperor's army. Under the Han Dynasty, China entered its first Golden Age.

Why Is the Han Dynasty Known as the First Golden Age of China?

The Han Dynasty changed China in important ways. Beginning in 206 B.C., the Han military expanded China's empire by conquering Vietnam, Korea, and much of what is now western China. The Han created a trade route called the Silk Road. It increased trade with central Asia, western Asia, Africa, and, later, Europe. The Silk Road brought China a new religion called Buddhism. Buddhism began in India. It taught how to escape the hardships of life. Many Chinese became Buddhist.

Besides military conquest and economic progress, the Han Dynasty had many other achievements. The Han learned how to make paper out of wood pulp. Chinese writers wrote history books and dictionaries printed on paper. They learned how to mass produce iron and steel farming tools. They invented sundials, water clocks, wheelbarrows, and compasses.

Before the Han Dynasty, government workers were selected by the influence of family and friends. Under the Han Dynasty, government workers were selected for their knowledge and skills. They had to be honest and respectable. It was thought that this would make the government more stable. Each worker had to pass an examination based on the teachings of Confucius, a very important Chinese philosopher.

He taught that a ruler should govern by good example. Confucius thought that if a ruler used force to govern, the ruler had failed. The teachings of Confucius were so important that they became the state religion of China.

The Han dynasty ended in A.D. 220, but the influence of the Han can still be seen in the culture and people of China. Today, more than 90 percent of the Chinese people identify themselves as the "People of the Han."

Biography

Confucius: c. 551–479 B.C.

Confucius was China's greatest teacher. (In Chinese, he was called "Master Kung.") Confucius did not teach religion, but he advised local rulers. His students later wrote down his sayings.

China was in great disorder when Confucius was alive. He hoped his ideas would bring back order. Confucius thought each person had a place in society. People owed respect to a superior, such as a ruler or a father. They should obey him or her. In turn, that person should set a good example. Confucius also taught his students to be loyal and honest. Culture and polite behavior were important too.

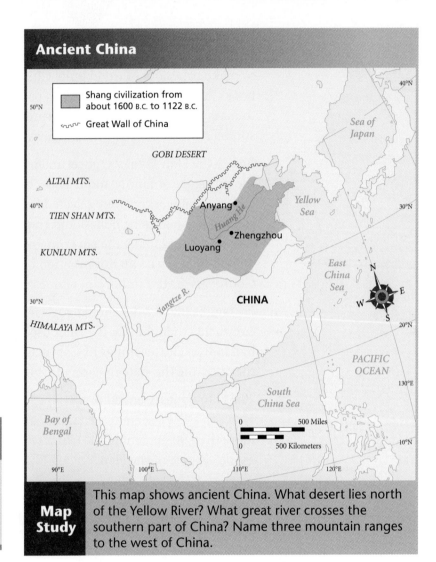

Ancient China

Shang civilization from about 1600 B.C. to 1122 B.C.

Great Wall of China

GOBI DESERT

ALTAI MTS.

TIEN SHAN MTS.

KUNLUN MTS.

HIMALAYA MTS.

Anyang

Zhengzhou

Luoyang

Huang He

Yangtze R.

CHINA

Sea of Japan

Yellow Sea

East China Sea

PACIFIC OCEAN

South China Sea

Bay of Bengal

0   500 Miles

0   500 Kilometers

Map Study This map shows ancient China. What desert lies north of the Yellow River? What great river crosses the southern part of China? Name three mountain ranges to the west of China.

What do you think ?

Why would the division of society into the rich and the poor cause problems?

Word Bank

characters
dynasty
Han
Qin
Shang

Lesson 6 Review On a sheet of paper, use the words from the Word Bank to complete each sentence correctly.

1. A _____ is a family that rules a country over a long period of time.

2. The _____ was the first dynasty in China.

3. In their writing, the Chinese use _____.

4. The _____ dynasty was the first to unite China with a strong central government.

5. The _____ invented paper out of wood pulp.

The Bhagavad Gita

Hinduism is the major religion of India. Over 80 percent of India's more than one billion people follow it. Hinduism is one of the oldest of the great world religions. It is different from the others in several ways. Hinduism is not based on the teachings of one person. It grew slowly over hundreds of years. It also does not have one holy book, such as the Bible or the Qur'an. Instead, there are many religious hymns and poems.

In Hinduism, there are many hymns and poems in the Vedas. This drawing shows Vishnu, one of the three main faces of Brahman.

whatever God [the eternal spirit] gives him, and he has risen beyond the two contraries here below; he is without jealousy, and in success or in failure he is one: his works bind him not.

He has attained liberation: he is free from all bonds, his mind has found peace in wisdom, and his work is a holy sacrifice. The work of such a man is pure.

This excerpt is from the Bhagavad Gita. The name means "Song of the Lord." This poem was probably written about A.D. 100. It is part of an older epic, or long poem. In it, the god Krishna teaches lessons about life and death.

What is work? What is beyond work? Even some seers [wise men] see this [incorrectly]. I will teach thee the truth of pure work, and this truth shall make thee free.

He whose undertakings are free from anxious desire and fanciful thought, whose work is made pure in the fire of wisdom: he is called wise by those who see. In whatever work he does such a man in truth has peace: he expects nothing, he relies on nothing, and ever has fullness of joy.

He has no vain hopes, he is the master of his soul, he surrenders all he has, only his body works: he is free from sin. He is glad with

Greater is thine own work, even if this be humble, than the work of another, even if this be great. When a man does the work God gives him, no sin can touch this man.

And a man should not abandon his work, even if he cannot achieve it in full perfection; because in all work there may be imperfection, even as in all fire there is smoke.

Document-Based Questions

1. What does the speaker want to teach?

2. Who is a wise man?

3. Why should a person do his or her own work?

4. Should a person give up a job if he or she is not good at it? Why or why not?

5. How does the advice in this reading relate to the caste system?

Family Ties—The Ties That Bind

The family has always been the backbone of Chinese society. In ancient China, people thought that the dead were still part of the family. Living family members honored those who had died. People offered them food and drink. They took care of family graves. These ancestors were seen as powerful spirits. Families hoped their ancestors could help them gain the gods' approval. That would bring good luck.

During the Shang dynasty, ancestors had a special role. People asked their help before making decisions. Even rulers asked their advice. People would go to a priest and ask him a question. To answer, priests used animal bones or tortoise shells. These were called oracle bones. The priest scratched a question on a bone. Next, he touched it with a red-hot bronze rod. The heat made cracks in the bone. These lines were the ancestors' answer. The priest studied the shape of the cracks. Then he explained what they meant.

Traditional Chinese families were very close. The family made sure every member was taken care of. It provided work, especially in farming areas. In turn, people were loyal to their families. A person's actions affected his or her whole family. If one member did wrong, it would shame them all.

The Chinese had great respect for old age. Children were expected to care for aging parents and grandparents. Older members of the family also had the most power. The teachings of Confucius made such relationships very important. A father had authority over his children and wife. Men were seen as better than women.

In the past, families arranged marriages for their children. Often the groom and bride met for the first time at their wedding!

Chinese society has changed a lot in recent times. In general, families are smaller. The government makes some decisions that families used to make. But even in modern times, Chinese family ties remain strong.

Wrap-Up

1. What is the backbone of Chinese society?

2. How did the ancient Chinese people show respect for their ancestors?

3. How were oracle bones used?

4. In general, what did the Chinese think of older family members?

5. How did Confucius affect beliefs about the family?

- India is a large peninsula in south Asia. The world's highest mountains are in the north.

- India gets water from the Ganges and Indus rivers. Seasonal storms called monsoons also bring rain.

- The first Indian civilization began in the Indus River Valley. The largest cities were Harappa and Mohenjo-Daro.

- Harappa and Mohenjo-Daro were walled cities. The careful planning of these cities shows their people knew mathematics.

- People in the Indus River Valley irrigated crops. They made pottery and cotton cloth. They traded with other peoples and wrote pictograms on clay tablets. The civilization ended suddenly about 1500 B.C.

- A set of religious beliefs and practices called Hinduism developed. The Vedas contains some of its holy writings.

- The Hindus believe that everything is god, or Brahman. Hindus believe in a cycle of birth, death, and rebirth (reincarnation).

- Hindus developed a spoken and written language called Sanskrit. It belongs to the same language family as many European languages.

- Hinduism is based on castes, or classes. Everyone is born into a caste. A person's job and way of life depend on this.

- The Indian Siddhartha Gautama became the Buddha. He taught the four "Noble Truths." He said that people should follow the "Eightfold Path" to reach nirvana.

- Buddhism shares some beliefs with Hinduism, but not the caste system. Buddhism spread from India into other parts of Asia.

- China is a huge region. A desert, mountains, and oceans kept it isolated. Chinese rulers built the Great Wall to keep out invaders.

- The Yangtze, in southern China, is its longest river. The Huang He (the Yellow River), in northern China, often floods. The first cities were built along this river about 2000 B.C.

- The Shang was China's first dynasty. It began about 1600 B.C. Its center was in the Huang He Valley.

- Shang society was sharply divided between rich and poor.

- The Shang developed a written language. Only scribes could read and write it. It is still used today.

- Ancestor worship was an important part of the Shang religion.

- The Qin dynasty was the first to unite China with a strong central government.

- The Han dynasty is known as the first golden age of China.

Chapter 5 REVIEW

Word Bank

Grand Canal

Han

Harappa

Hinduism

monsoons

planned

Sanskrit

Shang

Vedas

Yangtze

On a sheet of paper, use the words from the Word Bank to complete each sentence correctly.

1. The ancient language of India is _____.

2. _____ was one of the two big cities of the Indus River Valley civilization.

3. Farming in India depends on the _____, or seasonal winds.

4. Mohenjo-Daro in the Indus River Valley is a _____ city.

5. One religion practiced in India is _____.

6. The earliest written record in India comes from the _____ or "books of knowledge."

7. The two most important rivers in China are the Huang He and the _____.

8. The two great wonders of ancient China are its Great Wall and its _____.

9. Under the _____ dynasty, government workers were selected for their knowledge and skills.

10. The first dynasty, or ruling family, in China was the _____.

On a sheet of paper, write the letter of the answer that correctly completes each sentence.

11. The _____ are in the northern part of India.

    A Huang He and Yangtze Rivers
    B Himalayan Mountains
    C Sahara and Gobi desert
    D all of the above

12. Civilizations developed along rivers because _____.

    A people can travel on them to other places
    B people can send objects and food on them to other places
    C they connect the villages and cities of the country
    D all of the above

13. When rivers flood and the water retreats, they leave behind rich dirt called _____.

   A bronze   **B** silt   **C** jade   **D** monsoon

14. The first villages in India and China grew up around _____.

   A deserts   **C** oceans
   B river valleys   **D** mountains

15. The Hindus believe that they are born or reborn into one of _____ castes.

   A two   **B** three   **C** four   **D** five

On a sheet of paper, write the answer to each question. Use complete sentences.

16. Why did ancient civilizations all start in river valleys?

17. Why is geography important to history? (Hint: Use the geography of China and India to explain your answer.)

18. What are three facts about Hinduism?

Critical Thinking On a sheet of paper, write your response to each question. Use complete sentences.

19. What does the saying "the monsoon means life or death to the Indian people" mean?

20. What was the same about life in ancient India and life in ancient China? What was different? (Hint: You might think about where the cities grew up, city life, and religion.)

Test-Taking Tip

Study test material with a partner. Take turns quizzing each other on the material.

6

Ancient Greece

The civilizations of India, China, and the Middle East developed in river valleys. However, the Greek civilization developed on a rocky peninsula. This geography greatly influenced the Greek people. In this chapter, you will learn about the city-states that developed because of this geography. You will also discover the many gifts the Greeks have contributed to our life.

Goals for Learning

◆ To describe early Greek civilizations

◆ To explain why the Greek city-states developed

◆ To describe democracy in Athens

◆ To describe life in Sparta

◆ To explain why democracy came to an end in Greece

◆ To list the contributions the ancient Greeks made to world civilization

◆ To explain the importance of Alexander the Great

490 B.C. Athenians defeat the Persians at Marathon

336 B.C. Alexander the Great begins to rule

2000 B.C. People move from the north into Greece

480 B.C. Greeks defeat the Persian army and navy

323 B.C. Alexander the Great dies

| 2000 B.C. | 1500 B.C. | 1000 B.C. | 500 B.C. | A.D. 1 |

1200 B.C. Beginning of the Trojan War

750 B.C. Homer writes the *Iliad* and the *Odyssey*

404 B.C. Sparta destroys Athens

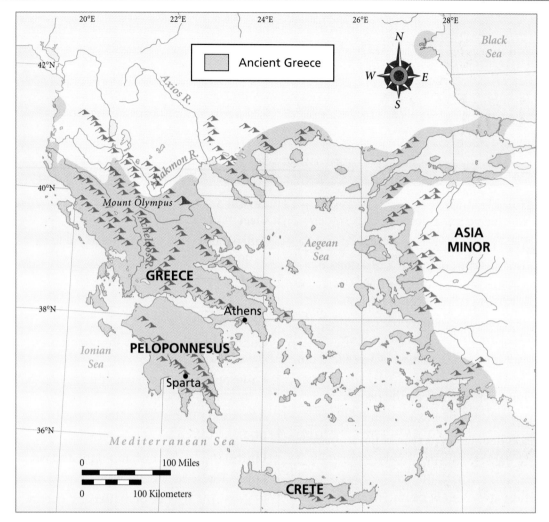

Map Skills

The geography of Greece has had an effect on its growth and its history. Its mountains made traveling by land hard. The Greeks took to the seas, which surrounded them on three sides, and became sailors. The geography of Greece helps us understand how each city-state developed its own culture.

Study the map, then answer the following questions:

1. What Greek city-state is located closest to the Aegean Sea?

2. Many islands surround Greece. What is the name of the largest island that lies near Greece?

3. What three seas surround Greece?

4. What tall mountain stands in the north of Greece?

5. What city-state is located in Peloponnesus?

Reading Strategy:
Inferencing

Sometimes the meaning of a text is not directly stated. You have to make an inference to figure out what the text means.

◆ What You Know + What You Read = Inference

◆ To make inferences, you have to think "beyond the text." Predicting what will happen next and explaining cause and effect are helpful strategies for making inferences.

Key Vocabulary Words

Lesson 1
Heroic Being brave and bold

Lesson 2
Polis The Greek name for a city-state

Acropolis A hill on which the people in a Greek city built their main temple

Aristocrat A member of the powerful ruling class

Tyrant A leader who rules by force and not by law

Democracy The rule by the people

Lesson 3
Direct democracy A type of government in which each citizen votes on everything

Assembly A meeting

Lottery A system of picking names from a container so that each person has an equal chance of being chosen

Jury A group who listens to court cases and decides the outcome

Lesson 4
Architecture The art of building

Enslave To force people to become slaves

Helot A slave in Sparta

Patriotic Being loyal toward one's country

Lesson 5
Fleet A group of ships

Independence Being free; being able to govern one's self

Maneuver To move around easily

Lesson 6
Goddess A female god

Column A tall post used to support a building

Philosopher A person who tries to find truth by asking questions

Astronomy The study of the stars

Biology The study of living things

Ethics The study of what is right and wrong

Logic The science of thinking

Physics The science of matter and energy

Politics The work of government

Lesson 7
Hellenism The blend of Western and Eastern cultures made possible by Alexander the Great

Geometry The study of the measurement of flat and round things

Hellenistic Age The time between 323 B.C. and 31 B.C., when Greek culture influenced the world

Heroic

Being brave and bold

Unlike Mesopotamia, Egypt, India, and China, the Greek civilization did not develop around river valleys. Greece is a peninsula. Its mainland reaches out into the Mediterranean Sea like the fingers of a hand. One ancient Greek teacher said that the Greeks lived on the shores of the sea "like frogs around a pond."

What Was the Minoan Civilization?

The first people to develop a civilization in this area lived on the island of Crete. In 1900, Sir Arthur Evans discovered the ruins of this island civilization. One town he dug up was Knossos. It probably had a population of 100,000 people in ancient times. Evans named this island civilization Minoan because a legend said that a king named Minos once ruled it.

Who Were the Mycenaeans?

The Greek civilization came after the Minoan. About 2000 B.C., people from the north moved southward into the peninsula of Greece. Historians call these people the Achaeans. They built walled cities in the southern part of Greece. Warrior kings ruled these cities. Their most important city was Mycenae. Because of this city, historians call the Achaeans by a second name—the Mycenaeans.

These warlike people sailed to other cities around the Aegean Sea and suddenly attacked them. Their most famous attack was on the city of Troy around 1200 B.C. Hundreds of years later, Greeks saw this time in their history as an age of heroes. The Trojan War became a symbol of **heroic,** or brave and bold, actions.

The Lion's Gate at Mycenae and similar ruins show what Mycenaean buildings were like.

How Do We Know About the Trojan War?

We remember the Trojan War because of two long poems—the *Iliad* and the *Odyssey*. A blind poet named Homer probably wrote them about 500 years after the war ended. He spoke or sang the stories. For centuries, the Greeks continued to sing these poems. In this way, they remembered the story of the war. Then, many years after Homer died, someone wrote them down.

Why Did the Mycenaeans Fight the War?

According to Homer, the Mycenaeans fought the Trojans because of a beautiful woman named Helen. She was the wife of the Achaean king. Paris, a son of the king of Troy, took her back to Troy. The Mycenaeans fought the Trojan War to win Helen back.

How Did the Mycenaeans Win the War?

The two sides fought for 10 years. Finally, the Mycenaeans defeated Troy with a clever trick. They pretended to sail away from Troy. But they left behind a giant wooden horse. The Trojans thought that they had won the war and that the Mycenaeans had left behind a victory gift. They opened their gates and brought the wooden horse within the city's thick, protective walls. Then they closed their gates. They thought they had locked the enemy out. Instead, they had locked the enemy in! Mycenaean warriors hid inside the wooden horse! During the night, these warriors silently left the horse and opened the gates of Troy. The rest of the Mycenaean army poured into the city and destroyed it.

Word Bank
Crete
Helen
Mycenaean
Odyssey
Trojan War

Lesson 1 Review On a sheet of paper, use the words from the Word Bank to complete each sentence correctly.

1. The _____ civilization came after the Minoan civilization.

2. The Minoan civilization was located on the island of _____.

3. The Mycenaeans fought a 10-year war called the _____.

4. They fought the war because Paris, a son of the king of Troy, had stolen the beautiful _____.

5. We can read the story of the Trojan War in the *Iliad* and the _____.

What do you think ?

Do you think the Mycenaeans won the Trojan War fairly?

Objectives

◆ To identify early forms of government in Greece

◆ To understand the meaning of democracy and why it developed in Athens

Polis

The Greek name for a city-state

Acropolis

A hill on which the people in a Greek city built their main temple

Aristocrat

A member of the powerful ruling class

Tyrant

A leader who rules by force and not by law

Greece is rocky and mountainous. In ancient times, the mountains kept the people isolated from one another. So the Greeks had many small settlements or city-states. They called each city-state a "**polis.**" Each polis was independent, or self-governing. A Greek was a citizen of the polis, or city-state.

The Greeks built their polis around a hill called an **acropolis.** On this high ground stood their main temple. Below the acropolis, they built homes and a marketplace. They also built theaters where they enjoyed plays and meeting places for the government.

What Kinds of Government Did the Greeks Try?

Over a period of time, the Greek city-states tried several different forms of government. In 800 B.C., kings ruled and passed their power to their sons. By 700 B.C., a small group of families with large amounts of land had taken over. We call members of these powerful families **aristocrats.** They also passed the right to rule from father to son. In about 600 B.C., strong leaders began to use force to take over the government of several city-states. We call such a person a **tyrant.** At first, tyrants kept the peace and passed fair laws. They also helped trade grow. Then some tyrants became cruel and unjust. Today, the word *tyrant* means anyone who uses power in a cruel and unfair way.

The acropolis was a hill overlooking the city where temples were built. This photo shows the acropolis at Athens—the most magnificent of all in the Greek city-states.

Word Bank

acropolis

Athenians

democracy

polis

Solon

What Is the Greatest Contribution of the Greeks?

A leader named Solon helped create **democracy,** or rule by the people, in Athens. In 594 B.C., the Athenian leaders were fighting among themselves. Solon set out to improve the government. Because of his improvements, the average citizens of Athens had political power for the first time. Democracy has become the most important contribution the ancient Greeks made to civilization.

Lesson 2 Review On a sheet of paper, use the words from the Word Bank to complete each sentence correctly.

1. A _____ is a Greek city-state.

2. On the _____ in each city-state, the people built their main temple.

3. The form of government known as _____ is the most important contribution the ancient Greeks made to civilization.

4. The _____ were the first Greeks to develop a democratic government.

5. A leader named _____ helped to create the democratic form of government.

What do you think ?

Why do you think the Greek people built their main temple on a hill in each city-state?

Objectives

◆ To define direct democracy

◆ To explain who could be a citizen

◆ To describe the responsibilities of citizenship

Direct democracy

A type of government in which each citizen votes on everything

Assembly

A meeting

Lottery

A system of picking names from a container so that each person has an equal chance of being chosen

Reading Strategy:
Inferencing

After reading this section, what inference can you make about the fairness of democracy in Athens?

Athenian democracy meant rule by only some people, not all. Only 40,000 of the 300,000 Athenians had the right to vote, or choose leaders and pass laws. Only citizens had this right, and only Athenian men could be citizens. Women, the more than 100,000 slaves, and Greeks from other city-states could not be citizens.

An Athenian leader expected three things of each citizen. He had to be loyal to Athens. He had to take part in the government. He also had to defend the city when necessary.

Why Did the Athenians Change Their Direct Democracy?

At first, each Athenian citizen voted on every law. We call this type of government a **direct democracy.** Soon, however, the number of citizens at the city **assembly,** or meeting, became too large. The government created a council of 500 citizens.

The government chose the members of this council by **lottery.** That is, they picked names from a container. In that way, each citizen had an equal chance of being chosen. The council members served for one year. During that time, they carried out the day-to-day business of Athens.

A Greek legend says that the goddess Athena named Athens after herself. This is the "Contemplating Athena" sculpture.

Jury

A group who listens to court cases and decides the outcome

Reading Strategy:
Inferencing

After reading this lesson, what inference can you make about the people of ancient Athens? What words helped you make your inference?

How Large Was an Athenian Jury?

Athenian courts did not use judges, but they did use large **juries.** A jury is a group who listens to a case in court and decides the outcome. Each year, the Athenians chose 6,000 citizens by lottery to serve on juries.

Between 201 and 501 people made up each jury. (In the United States, juries usually have 12 members.) When a court case was serious, 1,000 citizens might serve on the jury. Athenians believed that no one could bribe, or pay, a large jury to make a certain decision.

Why Did People Come to Athens?

Athens was near a seaport. Its sea trade helped this city-state grow in wealth and power. Because the citizens had money to pay artists, writers, and teachers, many of them came to Athens. They created beautiful art and built beautiful buildings. They started schools that lasted for centuries.

Lesson 3 Review On a sheet of paper, write the answer to each question. Use complete sentences.

1. How many slaves lived in ancient Athens?

2. Which people were not allowed to vote in Athens?

3. What is a direct democracy?

4. Why did the Athenian citizens begin to use a lottery for their government meetings?

5. How did Athenian juries differ from American juries?

What do you think ?

Do you think large juries are better than small ones? Why or why not?

Objectives

◆ To describe how men, women, children, and slaves were treated in Sparta

◆ To identify how Sparta is different from Athens

Enslave

To force people to become slaves

Helot

A slave in Sparta

Sparta, another city-state, was located on a peninsula in southern Greece called the Peloponnesus. Around 1100 B.C., people settled in the area. They built the city of Sparta and became known as Spartans. They **enslaved** the farmers who already lived there. That is, they forced the farmers to become slaves. They called these new slaves **helots.** The helots farmed the land surrounding the city.

What Was Sparta's "Wall of Men"?

For every Spartan, there were seven helots. This many slaves was a danger to the Spartans. What if the helots rebelled? Yet the leaders built no protective wall around their city. They thought that their military skills would protect them. According to one leader, they had a wall of men instead of bricks.

About 600 B.C., the helots did rebel. The Spartans defeated them, but the event frightened the Spartans. They sent people to spy on the helots. They also killed any helot who started to make trouble.

What Was Life Like for a Spartan Man?

In Sparta, government officials examined each newborn baby. They left sick children on hills to die. When a boy was seven, the government took him from his parents. It kept him hungry and expected him to steal food. But if he got caught, he was punished severely. At the age of 20, he became a citizen. At 30, he married. Until age 60, he lived in a military camp with all the other soldiers.

Writing About History

Imagine that you are an Athenian visiting Sparta or a Spartan visiting Athens. In your notebook, write a letter home. Describe what you have seen. Tell what you think of this city-state.

Reading Strategy: Inferencing

After reading this lesson, what can you infer about the Spartans' attitude toward life? What words helped you make your inference?

What Did Spartan Women Say to the Men?

Spartan women were independent and **patriotic,** or loyal, to their city-state. When a husband went off to war, his wife told him two things: Come home as a victor carrying your shield, or come home dead, being carried on your shield. He was to do one or the other, nothing else.

What Price Did the Spartans Pay for Being Warriors?

Art or **architecture,** which is the art of building, did not interest the Spartans. They did not trade with others, and they feared new ideas. Yet many people thought that they were the best soldiers in Greece and maybe in the whole world!

Lesson 4 Review On a sheet of paper, write the letter of the answer that correctly completes each sentence.

1. Sparta was located on the _____ peninsula.

    A Athenian   **B** Indian   **C** Sinai   **D** Peloponnesus

2. The helots were Spartan _____.

    A citizens   **B** slaves   **C** traders   **D** officials

3. For every Spartan citizen there were _____ helots.

    A 7   **B** 10   **C** 20   **D** 100

4. Spartan boys began training to be soldiers at the age of _____.

    A 7   **B** 20   **C** 30   **D** 60

5. A Spartan woman wanted her warrior husband to come home carrying his _____ or to be carried home on it.

    A horse   **B** shield   **C** spear   **D** chariot

What do you think ?

Why do you think the Spartans wanted boys to steal and then punished them if they got caught?

War Tests the Greeks

Objectives

◆ To describe the battles at Marathon, Thermopylae, and Salamis

◆ To explain the causes and results of the Peloponnesian War

Fleet

A group of ships

Between 500 and 400 B.C., the Greeks fought several wars. They fought the first two against the huge and powerful Persian Empire. It lay to the east of Greece. These wars united the city-states and made the Greeks proud. In the next war, the city-states of Athens and Sparta battled. We call this the Peloponnesian War. It lasted for 27 years.

Why Did the Persians Invade Greece?

Around 545 B.C., the Persians conquered a group of people called the Ionian Greeks who lived in Asia Minor. Forty-six years later, in 499 B.C., they asked the mainland Greeks to help them remove the Persians. Athens sent warships, but the Ionian Greeks could not win their freedom.

All this made King Darius of Persia angry. He wanted to punish Athens. In 490 B.C., Darius sent 600 ships and thousands of soldiers to invade Greece. According to legend, Athens sent the runner Pheidippides to ask the Spartans for help. He ran 150 miles in two days. When he arrived, the Spartans were celebrating a religious feast and refused to help until the next full moon.

Who Won the Battle of Marathon?

The Persian **fleet,** or group of ships, landed at the Bay of Marathon, about 25 miles northeast of Athens. The Persian army had more soldiers and weapons than the Athenians. The Athenians had no one to help them.

The Persians decided to attack Athens by sea. While they were loading their ships, the Athenians attacked and defeated them. A Greek legend says that Pheidippides ran 25 miles from Marathon to Athens to announce the victory. When he arrived, he yelled, "Nike!" or victory. Then he fell dead, worn out by his run. Today, we remember what Pheidippides did in the modern-day 26-mile marathon run. The Battle of Marathon may be the most important battle in Greek history.

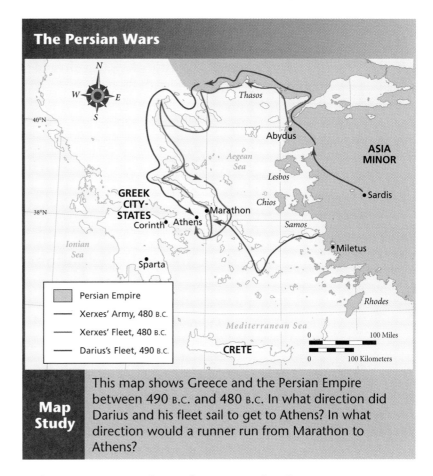

The Persian Wars

Persian Empire
Xerxes' Army, 480 B.C.
Xerxes' Fleet, 480 B.C.
Darius's Fleet, 490 B.C.

Map Study This map shows Greece and the Persian Empire between 490 B.C. and 480 B.C. In what direction did Darius and his fleet sail to get to Athens? In what direction would a runner run from Marathon to Athens?

What Happened at Thermopylae?

Ten years later in 480 B.C., Xerxes, the son of Darius, sent 150,000 soldiers and nearly 600 ships against the Greeks. This time, 31 Greek city-states joined together to meet the Persian invaders. The Spartans took charge of the army; Athens supplied the navy.

The great Persian army had little trouble as it moved through northern Greece. Then it came to a narrow mountain pass called Thermopylae. There, 7,000 Spartans waited for the Persians. For several days, they stopped the Persian army from moving forward.

Then a Greek traitor led the Persians behind the Greek army. The Spartan soldiers began to retreat to their ships. As the Persians marched forward, 300 Spartan warriors faced them. To protect the retreat of the others, they gave up their lives.

Who Won at Salamis?

The Persians marched almost 100 miles south and destroyed Athens. The Athenians had already moved to Salamis, a small island nearby. Hundreds of Persian ships attacked the Athenian navy near this island. Yet the Athenians defeated the powerful empire. How? The large Persian ships could not **maneuver,** or move around easily, in the water. The smaller Greek ships destroyed them by poking holes in them with their battering rams. Historians call this one of history's great sea battles. Defeated, King Xerxes returned to Persia. The Greeks had won the battle with a wooden wall of Athenian ships.

What Caused the Peloponnesian War?

In 477 B.C., more than 100 Greek city-states formed a military alliance called the Delian League. Each city-state agreed to give money or ships to be used to defend all of them. Athens led the alliance. During the next 30 years, the Athenians used the alliance money to rebuild Athens. As Athens became rich and powerful, Sparta and other city-states became jealous and angry.

In 431 B.C., war broke out between Athens and Sparta. We call it the Peloponnesian War because Sparta was located on the Peloponnesian peninsula. Sparta had the stronger army, but Athens had the better navy. The war lasted 27 years and ended in 404 B.C. Sparta destroyed Athens. The war divided and weakened the other Greek city-states. They were unable to form a new alliance. Sparta tried to rule all of them.

The Peloponnesian War weakened all the city-states. They were no longer as rich and powerful. In 338 B.C., King Philip II of Macedon, a small kingdom just north of Greece, led his army from the north and conquered Greece. His dream was to control all of Greece. The Greeks lost their **independence,** or freedom. They no longer governed themselves. However, their ideas continued to influence the world.

Spartan soldiers were trained to be fighters from a very early age.

Herodotus: c. 480–430 B.C.

The Greek writer Herodotus was born in Asia Minor. He had enough money to travel widely, so he toured Egypt and the Middle East. He is known as "the father of history" because he wrote the first history of the ancient world. Herodotus wrote about events he saw. He also included stories and legends.

His book *History* has two main parts. The first describes the people of the huge Persian Empire. It is a travel guide to customs and geography. The other part tells about the wars between Persia and Greece. Much of what we know about this period comes from his books.

Lesson 5 Review On a sheet of paper, write the answer to each question. Use complete sentences.

1. Who were the Ionian Greeks?

2. What was the Battle of Marathon?

3. What did Xerxes do?

4. How did the Greeks win at Salamis?

5. Why did Athens and Sparta fight the Peloponnesian War?

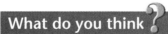

What do you think

Why do you think the Spartans won the Peloponnesian War?

On the Athenian acropolis stand the ruins of a temple to Athena—a female god, or **goddess.** We call the temple the Parthenon. Many people think it is one of the most beautiful buildings ever built. The Athenians built it after the Persian Wars ended. We call this period of time the "Golden Age of Athens."

Their love of beauty led the Greeks to create beautiful works of art. Besides making beautiful things with their hands, they used their minds. They asked questions about nature, society, and themselves. Their art and their search for truth are two of Greece's greatest contributions to civilization.

How Did Greek Architecture Please the Eye?

The Athenians built many beautiful public buildings and decorated them with fine works of art. Their Parthenon has 46 **columns,** or tall posts used for support. It is 237 feet long and 110 feet wide. The builders knew that columns seem to bend when seen from a distance. They made each column curve a little. Because of this, the columns seem to be perfectly straight when someone sees them from a distance.

The Parthenon, built in the 400s B.C. in Athens, is considered by many to be the most perfect building ever made.

What Are the Two Kinds of Greek Plays?

The Greeks were the first people to perform plays in outdoor theaters. A group of actors, called the chorus, stood on stage and talked about what was happening in the play. Only men could act in a Greek play.

Greek play writers wrote tragedies and comedies. In a tragedy, the gods defeat the hero. The hero is always smart and he always has courage. He also has too much pride. He tries to achieve more than the gods want him to. After seeing a tragedy, the Greeks felt both sad and happy. They were sad because the hero met defeat. They were happy because the hero had shown courage and strength.

Greek comedies made fun of important people or ideas. A writer named Aristophanes wrote many famous comedies. In his play *The Clouds*, he made fun of Socrates, a famous **philosopher.** Philosophers try to understand the basic nature of knowledge and reality.

History in Your Life

A Gift from the Muses

Ancient Greeks believed music was a gift from the gods. Their word for music meant "arts of the Muses." The Muses were nine goddesses. They looked after music (songs and dances), poetry, history, drama, and astronomy. Musical instruments also came from the gods. The lyre and the pipes were two popular instruments. A lyre is a small stringed instrument.

Some special humans also had the gift of music. The most famous was Orpheus. It was believed that even wild animals stopped to hear him play and sing.

Early Greek poets sang or chanted their verses. They played along on the lyre. Music was part of most special occasions. Some poets wrote lyrics for a chorus to sing. These songs often honored winners of athletic games. Music and dancing went with them. Greek drama used music, too. A chorus danced and sang between scenes in a play.

Some ancient Greek theaters are still standing today. Greek plays were performed outdoors.

What Do Philosophers Want to Prove?

In Greek, the word *philosopher* means "a lover of wisdom."
Most philosophers ask questions to lead them to wisdom. They
want to find truth. In fact, they want proof of the truth. They
do not stop asking questions until they have this proof. Greece
produced three of the greatest philosophers in history: Socrates,
Plato, and Aristotle.

Why Did the Athenians Want to Get Rid of Socrates?

By asking questions, the philosopher Socrates forced people
to examine what they believed. This great teacher always
said, "Know thyself." He meant that people need to know why
and what they believe. They need to look at why they think
something is true, beautiful, just, or good.

Socrates questioned everything, even Athenian democracy.
Many Athenians did not trust him. They had just lost the
Peloponnesian War, and they thought that anyone who asked
questions was unpatriotic.

Reading Strategy:
Inferencing

After reading this lesson, what can you infer about the teachings of Greek philosophers?

In 399 B.C., when Socrates was 70 years old, the Athenian citizens spoke out against him. They said that his teachings hurt the young people of Athens. More than half of the 501 members of the jury voted against him. They said that he must kill himself by drinking poison. His friends and pupils arranged for his escape from Athens, but Socrates refused. He chose to obey the Athenian law, and was put to death.

What Was Plato's Republic?

Plato, a pupil of Socrates, was 28 years old when his teacher died. What the Athenians had done upset Plato. He wrote a book called *The Republic* about a made-up society. It was perfect, orderly, and just. In this society, three classes of people lived: workers, soldiers, and philosophers.

Plato's make-believe society was not a democracy. He thought that only the wisest men and women—philosophers—should rule. Why? Because they would decide things with their brains, not with their feelings. A fine teacher, Plato began a school in Greece that lasted for 900 years. We still study his ideas today.

What Did Aristotle Write About?

Plato's most famous pupil was Aristotle. He wrote important works on **astronomy** (the study of the stars); **biology** (the study of living things); **ethics** (the study of what is right and wrong); **logic** (the science of thinking); **physics** (the science of matter and energy); and **politics** (the work of government).

In his book *Politics,* Aristotle wrote about different kinds of governments. He said that no government was perfect. Just as we still study Plato's writings today, so we study what Aristotle had to say about government.

Today, we can only imagine what the death of Socrates looked like. This is one artist's version.

The Olympic Games

Today's Olympic Games come from ancient Greece. The Greeks loved sports. At that time, sporting contests were part of religious festivals. The Olympic Games began about 776 B.C. They were held at Olympia, a place sacred to the god Zeus.

Ancient Olympic athletes hoped to win glory for themselves and their city. Contests included foot races, boxing, the broad jump, and the discus throw. Unlike now, women could not compete. Nor were there any team sports.

The first modern Olympics took place in 1896 in Athens, Greece. They were the idea of a Frenchman, Pierre de Coubertin. Today, there are Olympic Games every two years. The winter games alternate with the summer games. They take place in different countries. The games include many new sports.

Word Bank

Aristophanes

Aristotle

Parthenon

Plato

Socrates

Lesson 6 Review On a sheet of paper, use the words from the Word Bank to complete each sentence correctly.

1. The _____ was built for the goddess Athena.

2. One Athenian writer of comedies was _____.

3. The philosopher _____ had to drink poison because the Athenians thought he was unpatriotic.

4. The philosopher _____ wrote a book about a government ruled by philosophers.

5. The philosopher _____ thought that no government was perfect.

What do you think ?

Do you think philosophers would make the best leaders of a country? Why or why not?

Objectives

◆ To identify the lands that Alexander the Great conquered

◆ To identify the Hellenistic Age

Aristotle's most famous pupil was Alexander, the son of Philip II of Macedon. After Philip II conquered the Greeks in 338 B.C., he planned to conquer Persia too. He died before he could make that happen, so his son set out to conquer the world. Soon people would call him Alexander the Great.

What Did Alexander Conquer?

When Philip II died in 336 B.C., Alexander was 20. Two years later, Alexander marched eastward with 35,000 soldiers. They quickly conquered Asia Minor. At the eastern end of the Mediterranean, they defeated the armies of Darius III, the Persian king. Swinging south, Alexander freed Egypt from Persian rule. At the mouth of the Nile River, he built the city of Alexandria.

How Far Did Alexander's Army March?

Reading Strategy:
Inferencing

What can you infer about Alexander's abilities as a leader?

Next, Alexander moved east again and conquered Babylon. He continued to move eastward, deeper into the Persian Empire. By 330 B.C., Alexander had defeated all the Persian armies. He was now king of Persia and dreamed of uniting the known world under one government.

Alexander the Great conquered many lands at a very young age.

For four more years, Alexander's tired army moved eastward. They went as far as the Indus River. For the Greeks, this was the end of the known world. Alexander wanted to push on, but his men begged him to turn back.

In 323 B.C., Alexander developed a fever in Babylon. Within a few days, the 32-year-old leader was dead. For 13 years, Alexander ruled. During that time he had changed the world.

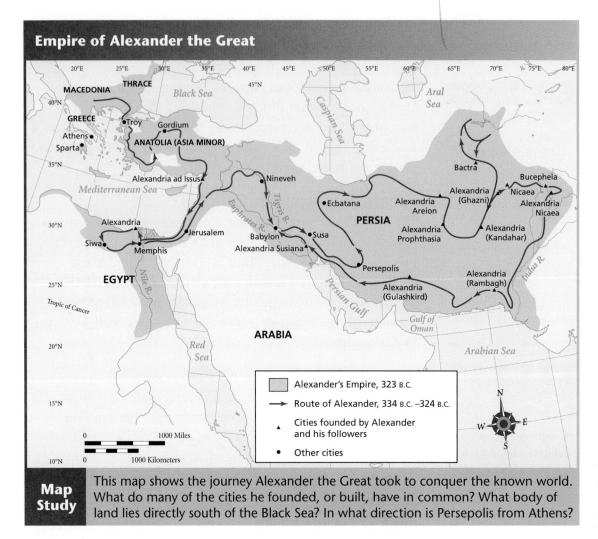

Empire of Alexander the Great

Map Study

This map shows the journey Alexander the Great took to conquer the known world. What do many of the cities he founded, or built, have in common? What body of land lies directly south of the Black Sea? In what direction is Persepolis from Athens?

What Is the Hellenistic Culture?

Alexander's huge empire fell apart after his death. His three generals divided the empire into three kingdoms—Macedon, Egypt, and Syria. These three kingdoms often fought each other. But one thing held them together—their Greek culture.

Throughout the Middle East, people adopted Greek customs. They spoke Greek, they built their buildings as the Greeks did, and they gave themselves Greek names. At the same time, many Greeks married Persian women. Some began to dress like the Persians. Some Persians joined the Greek army. Soon Greek culture and Persian culture blended into what is called **Hellenism.**

What Made Alexandria Famous?

The **Hellenistic Age** was the time between 323 and 31 B.C., when Greek culture influenced the world. The people built great cities. Antioch, in Syria, had lighted streets, which the builders paved to make them smooth and level. However, Alexandria in Egypt was the greatest city in the Hellenistic Age. Its harbor had ships from every Mediterranean country. It had a lighthouse 35 feet tall. It had wide streets with many statues. It also had a museum, a zoo, and an art gallery. More than 500,000 people lived in this center of learning. Its library had nearly 500,000 works for them to read.

What Did the Hellenistic Age Contribute to Civilization?

During this time, Euclid of Alexandria put together everything people knew about **geometry.** It's the study of the measurement of flat and round things. Some schools in the 20th century still used his book. Archimedes was Euclid's student. He used mathematics to explain how to lift heavy things with levers and pulleys. (A pulley is a wheel for a rope to pass over.) Archimedes said, "Give me a place to stand, and a lever long enough, and I will move the Earth."

Other important people during the Hellenistic Age included Eratosthenes and Hippocrates. The scientist Eratosthenes is thought to be the first man to calculate the distance around the earth. Hippocrates was a great physician during this time. He is known as the founder of medicine.

Hellenistic culture influenced the Mediterranean world for nearly 300 years. However, Alexander's dream did not come true during this time. He hoped to create an empire ruled by one government. The Greeks did not do this, but the Romans did. Their homeland lay to the northwest of Greece.

Lesson 7 Review On a sheet of paper, write the answer to each question. Use complete sentences.

1. How far eastward did the empire of Alexander the Great go?

2. What city did Alexander build in Egypt?

3. For how many years did Alexander rule the known world?

4. What word describes the blend of Eastern and Western cultures after Alexander's death?

5. What mathematical information did Euclid organize?

What do you think ?

How did Alexander help Greek culture spread far and wide?

History in Your Life

Math—and Music, Too

The famous scholar Pythagoras was born on the Greek island of Samos in 580 B.C.

He is best known for his study of math. Pythagoras found that a diagonal line through a square was longer than any side of the square. He and his followers created formulas for this and other math questions. Pythagoras also believed that people could use numbers to understand everything in the world. This would include many sciences, even astronomy.

Pythagoras experimented with strings, bells, and hammers to learn about music. He used numbers to explain changes in musical tones. He created scales and the idea of the octave in music. Many people feel that his work was the basis for music as we know it today. After Pythagoras' death in about 500 B.C., his many students continued his work.

Pericles Praises Athens

Pericles was a great leader of Athens. In about 431 B.C., he made a famous speech. It honored Athenians who had died in the war with Sparta. It is known as "Pericles' Funeral Oration." In the speech, Pericles explains why Athens is great.

Thucydides was the greatest Athenian historian. This speech is in his History of the Peloponnesian War. *Thucydides probably heard Pericles give the speech. This is the way Thucydides remembered it.*

Pericles: c. 495–425 B.C.

Our form of government does not enter into rivalry with the institutions of others. We do not copy our neighbors, but are an example to them. It is true that we are called a democracy, for government is in the hands of the many and not of the few. But while the law secures equal justice to all alike in their private disputes, the claim of excellence is also recognized; and when a citizen is in any way distinguished, he is elected to the public service, not as a matter of privilege, but as the reward of merit. Neither is poverty a bar, but a man may benefit his country whatever may be the obscurity of his condition.

And we have not forgotten to provide for our weary spirits many relaxations from toil; we have regular games and sacrifices throughout the year; at home the style of our life is refined; and the delight which we daily feel in all these things helps to banish melancholy. Because of the greatness of our city, the fruits of the whole earth flow in upon us, so that we enjoy the goods of other countries as freely as of our own.

And in the matter of education, whereas the Spartans from early youth are always undergoing laborious exercises which are to make them brave, we live at ease, and yet are equally ready to face the perils which they face.

. . . For we are lovers of the beautiful, yet simple in our tastes, and we cultivate the mind without loss of manliness. . . . An Athenian citizen does not neglect the state because he takes care of his own household; and even those of us who are engaged in business have a very fair idea of politics. We alone regard a man who takes no interest in public affairs, not as a harmless, but as a useless character. . . .

Document-Based Questions

1. According to Pericles, why is Athens a democracy?

2. Why is a person elected to public service?

3. How do Athenians relax?

4. According to Pericles, how are the Athenians different from the Spartans?

5. How important are public affairs to Athenians? How can you tell this from the speech you just read?

Greek Mythology

Have you ever admired the strength of Hercules? He is a famous person in Greek mythology. Myths are stories that try to answer questions about natural events. Why does the sun move across the sky? Why do the seasons change? What causes thunder and lightning?

The Greeks believed in many gods. The chief family included twelve gods and goddesses. They lived on Mount Olympus. These gods were powerful, but not perfect. They acted like the Greeks themselves. They had quarrels. They got angry. Often they took part in people's lives. Many Greek poems and plays retold myths about the gods.

Zeus was the father of the gods. He was lord of the sky. When he was angry, he threw lightning bolts. His brother, Poseidon, ruled the sea. His other brother, Hades, ruled the underworld. One of his sons was Apollo, god of the sun. The Greeks believed that every morning he drove his fiery chariot across the sky. Apollo was also the god of music and medicine. Artemis was his twin sister. She was the goddess of the moon. Artemis protected the young, wild animals, and women. Zeus's favorite child was Athena. She protected city life, especially Athens.

Myths also tell about giants and heroes. Atlas was a giant. He and other giants went to war against the Olympians. They lost. Zeus punished Atlas harshly. He would have to hold the world on his shoulders forever. A book of maps, an atlas, gets its name from this giant.

Some Greek heroes were part god. Others were human beings with special gifts. The greatest hero was Hercules. He was brave and strong. He also had a quick temper. One story

tells how he had to perform 12 difficult tasks. Then he would be forgiven for a terrible crime.

The story of the Trojan War has many heroes. Achilles was the greatest Greek warrior. When he was a child, his mother dipped him in a magic river. Its water would always protect him. She did not notice that the heel she held stayed dry. His "Achilles' heel" was the one place where he could be hurt. At Troy an arrow struck his heel, and he died.

The hero Odysseus was both brave and clever. He thought of the idea for the Trojan horse. That trick helped the Greeks capture Troy. After the war, it took him many years to get home. Homer's *Odyssey* tells of his adventures on the way.

Wrap-Up

1. What is a myth?

2. Where did the main Greek gods live?

3. Who was the father of the gods?

4. What was Atlas's punishment?

5. Who are two heroes of the Trojan War?

- Greece is on a hilly peninsula in the Mediterranean Sea. The Minoan civilization started on the island of Crete. About 2000 B.C., the Achaeans built walled cities in southern Greece. Their main city was Mycenae.

- The Mycenaeans fought a 10-year war with Troy. Two long poems by Homer, the *Iliad* and the *Odyssey,* tell about heroes of the Trojan War.

- The Greeks lived in small city-states. Each was a polis. At the center was a hill, or acropolis, and a temple.

- The city-state of Athens began the first democracy. Its citizens ran the government. Only Athenian men were citizens. Women, slaves, and foreign residents were not citizens.

- Sparta was a city-state on a peninsula called the Peloponnesus. Slaves called helots farmed the land.

- Spartan men were soldiers all their lives. Spartan women expected them to fight heroically. Unlike Athenians, Spartans did not care about trade or the arts.

- The Greek city-states united to fight the Persian Empire twice. In 490 B.C., King Darius of Persia tried to invade Greece. The Greeks defeated the Persians at Marathon.

- Persians under Xerxes invaded Greece again in 480 B.C. Spartan soldiers held off the Persians at Thermopylae. The Athenian navy defeated them at Salamis.

- In 431 B.C., Athens and Sparta went to war against each other. This was the Peloponnesian War. Sparta won. The war weakened all the city-states. In 338 B.C., Philip II of Macedon conquered Greece.

- The "Golden Age" of Athens followed the Persian Wars. Greek writers invented two kinds of drama—tragedy and comedy. Socrates, Plato, and Aristotle were Greek philosophers who explored ideas.

- Alexander the Great was the son of Philip II of Macedon. Alexander had studied with Aristotle. He became ruler of Greece in 336 B.C. Alexander's army conquered the Persian Empire.

- Alexander died in 323 B.C. His conquests helped spread Greek culture. A new culture, Hellenism, began. Alexandria, Egypt, was a center of Hellenistic culture.

Chapter 6   R E V I E W

Word Bank

Alexander

Aristophanes

Aristotle

Homer

Minos

Parthenon

Philip II

Plato

Socrates

Xerxes

On a sheet of paper, use the words from the Word Bank to complete each sentence correctly.

1. The Minoan civilization is named after King _____.

2. _____ was a blind poet who wrote the *Iliad*.

3. In 480 B.C., the Greeks defeated the Persian Army of King _____.

4. _____ wrote a play called *The Clouds,* which made fun of the philosopher Socrates.

5. The name of the temple of Athena in Athens is the _____.

6. In 399 B.C., the Athenians found the philosopher _____ guilty of teaching things that hurt the young people of Athens.

7. The philosopher _____ wrote *The Republic* about a perfect society.

8. The philosopher _____ wrote a book about the different kinds of governments.

9. Alexander the Great was the son of _____ of Macedon.

10. The conquering army of _____ spread Greek culture into Asia.

On a sheet of paper, write the letter of the answer that correctly completes each sentence.

11. The Greek city-state that trained all its citizens to be soldiers was _____.

    A Persia   C Sparta
    B Athens   D Alexandria

12. The philosopher Aristotle wrote books on _____.

    A ethics   C astronomy
    B biology   D all of the above

13. The Athenians defeated the Persian fleet at the battle of
_____ in 480 B.C.

   A Marathon   **C** Thermopylae
   B Salamis   **D** Babylon

14. Alexander the Great's army fought against the _____
Empire.

   A Persian   **C** Mycenaean
   B Roman   **D** Minoan

15. The _____ civilization developed on the island of Crete.

   A Mycenaean   **B** Persian   **C** Minoan   **D** Greek

On a sheet of paper, write the answer to each question. Use
complete sentences.

16. Greece is on a peninsula and has many rocky mountains.
What effect did this geography have on its history?

17. Why did the Greeks want to defeat the Persian Empire?

18. What are three contributions the Greek civilization made
to the world? Give three details of each contribution.

Critical Thinking On a sheet of paper, write your response to
each question. Use complete sentences.

19. Which ancient Greek city-state would you want to live
in—Athens or Sparta? Give three reasons why.

20. Does Alexander deserve to be called "the Great"? Why or
why not?

Test-Taking Tip

Do not wait until the night before a test to study. Plan your
study time so that you can get a good night's sleep the night
before a test.

7

The Roman Republic

The ancient Romans had a legend that twin brothers named Romulus and Remus founded Rome in 753 B.C. Cruel leaders ruled the Romans until 509 B.C. In that year, the people rebelled and created a republic. In this chapter, you will learn about the patricians who ruled this republic. You will also learn about the plebeians who fought as citizen-soldiers for the republic. Finally, you will learn what happened to bring the Roman Republic to an end.

Goals for Learning

◆ To describe the early history of the Roman peninsula

◆ To define the term *republic* and explain the organization of the Roman republican form of government

◆ To explain the causes of the Punic Wars

◆ To explain how Rome lost its republican form of government

◆ To identify Julius Caesar and Octavian and explain their importance to Roman history

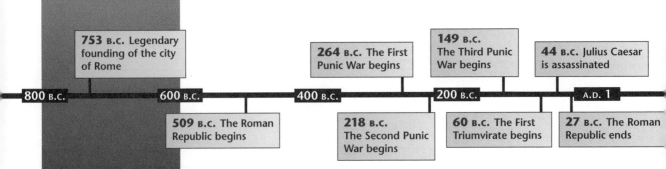

753 B.C. Legendary founding of the city of Rome

264 B.C. The First Punic War begins

149 B.C. The Third Punic War begins

44 B.C. Julius Caesar is assassinated

800 B.C.　　600 B.C.　　400 B.C.　　200 B.C.　　A.D. 1

509 B.C. The Roman Republic begins

218 B.C. The Second Punic War begins

60 B.C. The First Triumvirate begins

27 B.C. The Roman Republic ends

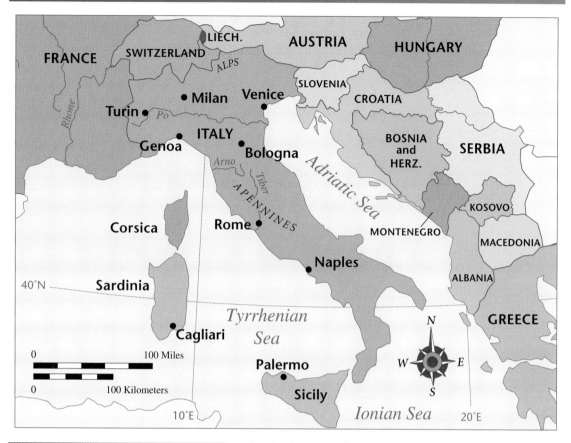

Map Skills

Italy is a boot-shaped peninsula in southern Europe. It has two mountain ranges. One of these—the Alps—forms the northern border of Italy. This is an important natural barrier, or wall, between Italy and other nations. Three important rivers flow through Italy. Its capital city sits next to one of them—the Tiber.

Study the map, then answer the following questions:

1. What is the name of the mountain range that lies northeast of the city of Rome?

2. What are the names of three rivers in Italy?

3. What is the name of the large island that lies near the southern tip of Italy?

4. What is the name of the sea along Italy's east coast?

5. What European country lies to the far northwest of Italy?

Reading Strategy:
Metacognition

Metacognition means "thinking about your thinking." Use metacognition to become a better reader:

♦ Preview the text.

♦ Make predictions and ask yourself what you already know about the topic.

♦ Write the main idea, details, and any questions you have.

♦ Visualize what is happening in the text. If something does not make sense, go back and read it again.

♦ Summarize what you have read and make inferences about the meaning.

Key Vocabulary Words

Lesson 1

Founded To have begun a country or city

Advanced Beyond the beginning stage

Senate A governing body

Patrician A Roman who owned land and helped a ruler govern

Lesson 2

Republic A type of government with no king in which a few people represent, or speak for, everyone

Representative A person who speaks and governs for others

Consul A Roman leader who served a one-year term in the government

Veto To say no to a decision

Dictator A leader who has full control of laws and rules with force

Laborer A person who does hard work with his or her hands

Plebeian A common person in Rome who was not wealthy

Tribune A representative who protected the rights of the plebeian class

Political Having to do with governing

Lesson 3

Ally A friend; a country or person who helps another

Lesson 4

Senator A member of a senate

Reform To make something better through change

Politician A government leader

Triumvirate Rule by three people

Lesson 5

Assassinate To kill someone important

Retire To give up one's job

Emperor A person who is ruler of an empire

Objectives

◆ To tell the legend of how Rome was founded

◆ To describe how the Etruscans governed Rome

Reading Strategy:
Metacognition

Before you read the rest of this lesson, think about what you can do that will help you understand the Latins and Etruscans.

Founded

To have begun a country or city

Advanced

Beyond the beginning stage

Senate

A governing body

Patrician

A Roman who owned land and helped a ruler govern

Rome sits on the western side of the boot-shaped peninsula of Italy. It is 20 miles inland on the Tiber River. No one really knows how or when Rome began. An ancient legend says that the twin brothers Romulus and Remus **founded,** or began, the city in 753 B.C. According to this legend, the baby twins were left to die on the banks of the Tiber River. A she-wolf found them and cared for them. Then a shepherd killed the wolf and raised the twins as his sons. As men, Romulus and Remus built a city. They fought over who should rule. Romulus killed his brother, became king, and named the city Rome.

Who Were the Latins and the Etruscans?

A group of people called Latins lived on a plain called Latium. This plain was located south of the Tiber River. This tribe spoke Latin. Because they could not write, they have left us no written records. However, they did build small villages on hills near the Tiber. Rome grew from these settlements.

People from Greece built several city-states on the southern coast of the Italian peninsula. They brought their Greek culture with them. The Latin people learned many things from their Greek neighbors.

The Etruscans were a tribe of people who lived north of the Tiber. Like the Greeks, they were **advanced,** or beyond the beginning stage. They had a written language and made pottery and fine clothing. They were also expert sailors and traded throughout the Mediterranean. By 600 B.C., the Etruscans had conquered Rome and the plain of Latium. They drained the marshes around Rome to create more living space.

Etruscan kings ruled the Romans for more than a century. The king appointed men to a **senate.** This governing body helped him make decisions. The senate members, or **patricians,** also controlled large amounts of land. Since *patrician* is related to *pater,* the Latin word for father, they were thought to be the "fathers of the state."

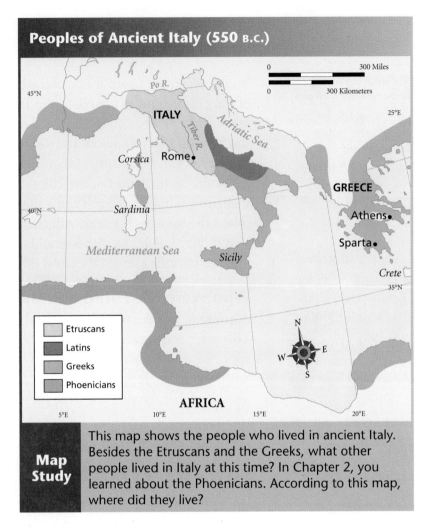

Peoples of Ancient Italy (550 B.C.)

0 — 300 Miles
0 — 300 Kilometers

45°N

ITALY

Po R.

Tiber R.

Adriatic Sea

25°E

Corsica

Rome●

GREECE

40°N

Sardinia

Athens●

Sparta●

Mediterranean Sea

Sicily

Crete

35°N

N
W E
S

Etruscans
Latins
Greeks
Phoenicians

AFRICA

5°E   10°E   15°E   20°E

Map Study This map shows the people who lived in ancient Italy. Besides the Etruscans and the Greeks, what other people lived in Italy at this time? In Chapter 2, you learned about the Phoenicians. According to this map, where did they live?

Lesson 1 Review On a sheet of paper, write the answer to each question. Use complete sentences.

1. According to Roman legend, who founded Rome?

2. What tribe lived to the south of the Tiber River and built settlements on the surrounding hills?

3. What people ruled the Romans for a century?

4. What does the word *patrician* mean in Latin?

5. Why did the Romans call wealthy landowners patricians?

What do you think ❓

Do you think the legend about Romulus and Remus is at all true? Why or why not?

◆ To compare the patrician and plebeian classes

◆ To identify the Law of the Twelve Tables

Republic

A type of government with no king in which a few people represent everyone

Representative

A person who speaks and governs for others

Consul

A Roman leader who served a one-year term in the government

Veto

To say no to a decision

Dictator

A leader who has full control of laws and rules with force

In 509 B.C., the patricians rebelled against the cruel Etruscan king. They defeated the king and set up a different kind of government—a republic. In a **republic,** citizens vote to elect **representatives,** or people who will speak and govern for them. (In a republic, rule does not pass from parent to child.) This Roman Republic lasted from 509 B.C. to 27 B.C.—almost 500 years.

Who Governed the Roman Republic?

The Romans replaced the Etruscan king with two **consuls.** These leaders served the government for a one-year term. Each consul could **veto,** or say no to, a decision by the other consul. Serving only one year and the threat of the veto kept the consuls from becoming too powerful.

The Roman senate, made up of 300 patricians, helped the consuls rule. It had the power to pass laws. In times of war, it could choose a **dictator** for six months. This kind of leader had full control of laws and ruled with force.

What Class Ruled Rome?

The Roman Republic was not a democracy, because it allowed only patricians to vote. They were from the oldest and the richest families in Rome. This wealthy patrician class made up only 10 percent of the population, or all the people, of Rome. Yet patricians ran government. They thought of themselves as the ruling class.

The Roman senate was made up of 300 patricians.

Laborer

A person who does hard work with his or her hands

Plebeian

A common person in Rome who was not wealthy

Tribune

A representative who protected the rights of the plebeian class

Who Were the Plebeians?

Most Romans were not wealthy. They were small farmers, merchants, and **laborers**—people who did hard work with their hands. Yet they were citizens of Rome. The Romans called them **plebeians,** which means "from the common people."

As citizens, the plebeians paid taxes and served in the army. They could not marry out of their class. Also, the patricians could sell plebeians into slavery if they did not pay their debts. They had little power alone, but as a group they were powerful. There were more plebeians than there were patricians. The upper classes tried to keep the plebeians happy with "bread and circuses." In other words, the plebeians were given food and entertainment.

How Did the Plebeians Gain Political Rights?

The plebeians had one important power. They were citizen-soldiers. The patricians needed them to defend Rome against its enemies. In 494 B.C., the Roman Republic gave the plebeians the right to elect, or choose by voting, two **tribunes.** These two representatives protected the rights of the plebeian class.

As time passed, the number of tribunes increased from two to ten. They sat outside the door of the senate and shouted "Veto!" when they did not like a law that a patrician wanted. By 350 B.C., the senate could pass only those laws to which the tribunes said yes.

What Is the "Law of the Twelve Tables"?

In the beginning of the republic, the senate did not write down the laws it passed. The plebeians were not sure what the laws were. As a result, patrician judges were unfair to plebeians. Soon, they demanded that the senate write the laws down. Around 450 B.C., the senate wrote their laws on 12 bronze tablets. Then they put them in the marketplace. Every school child had to learn these laws.

Reading Strategy:
Metacognition

Note the main idea and important details of this lesson. After each section, summarize what you have read.

When Did the Republic Become More Democratic?

By 280 B.C., Rome had become more democratic. Plebeians could hold **political,** or governing, offices. They could also serve in the senate. In fact, one consul could come from the plebeian class. Still, problems continued between the patricians and the plebeians. This struggle became an important part of Roman history for several centuries.

Lesson 2 Review On a sheet of paper, use the words from the Word Bank to complete each sentence correctly.

Word Bank

Etruscan

patricians

plebeians

republic

tribune

1. In 509 B.C. some Romans rebelled against the _____ king.

2. After defeating him, they set up a _____, or representative form of government.

3. At first, only _____ sat in the senate and made laws.

4. As time passed, the _____, or common people, got some power in the Roman government.

5. A _____ was a person who represented the plebeians in the Roman Republic.

Writing About History

You are running for the office of tribune in the Roman Republic. In your notebook, write a speech. In it, tell the plebeians what you will do for them. Explain why they should choose you.

What do you think ?

What can happen when laws are not written down?

Then and Now

Echoes of Roman Rule

At one time, Rome ruled most of Western Europe. Many modern governments have taken ideas from Rome. For instance, in 509 B.C. the Romans rebelled against their kings. They set up a republic. In a republic, the people elect others to represent them. For example, the United States is a republic.

The senate was the main governing body in ancient Rome. The word comes from *senex,* or "old." The United States also has a law-making group called the Senate, but senators are elected. Some Roman officials could *veto* a law. This Latin word means "I forbid." Today, the American president has veto power.

Objectives

♦ To describe the three Punic Wars

♦ To describe the expansion of Rome

During the years of the republic, Rome was often at war with its neighbors. First, the Romans defeated the Etruscans to the north. By 275 B.C., they had conquered the Greeks in southern Italy.

What Caused the Punic Wars?

To the south of Rome, on the northern coast of Africa, lay Carthage. The Phoenicians had settled Carthage, and it had a powerful navy. It controlled Northern Africa, Spain, and several islands close to Italy. Then in 264 B.C., Carthage tried to take control of all of Sicily, an island at the southern tip of Italy. This led to war. In fact, Rome and Carthage fought three wars that lasted over 100 years. The Romans called them the Punic Wars, because *Punici* is the Latin word for "Phoenician."

How Did the Romans Win the First Punic War?

The First Punic War lasted 23 years—from 264 B.C. to 241 B.C. Carthage had a mighty, or powerful, navy. Also, its population of 250,000 was three times the size of Rome. Rome had a fine army, but no navy. How could Rome defeat Carthage?

The Romans added a plank, or long, wide, flat piece of wood, to their ships. When they got close enough to a Carthaginian ship, the plank hooked it and linked the two ships together. Then Roman soldiers ran across the plank and jumped down into their enemy's ship. In this clever way, the Roman army defeated the Carthaginian navy. In 241 B.C., Carthage asked for peace. Rome took control of Sicily and the other islands off its coast.

What Did Hannibal Do in the Second Punic War?

In 218 B.C., Hannibal, a great Carthaginian soldier, planned a bold attack on Rome. His army of 60,000 soldiers, 38 elephants, and many horses marched across Spain, over the Pyrenees, to the foot of the Alps. The Romans thought that these mountains would protect them from attack.

Hannibal's bold attack on Rome surprised the Romans.

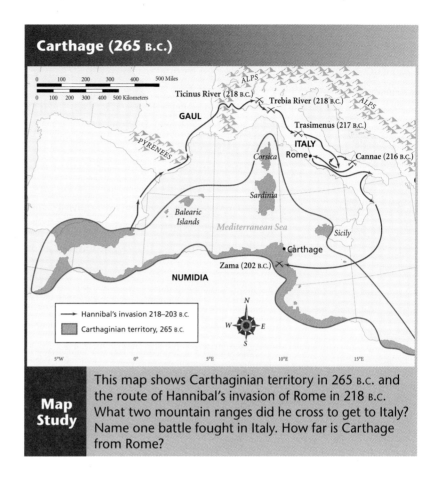

Carthage (265 B.C.)

This map shows Carthaginian territory in 265 B.C. and the route of Hannibal's invasion of Rome in 218 B.C. What two mountain ranges did he cross to get to Italy? Name one battle fought in Italy. How far is Carthage from Rome?

Map Study

Reading Strategy:
Metacognition

Remember to ask yourself questions as you read. This will help you make sure that you understand what you are reading.

For two weeks, his soldiers, elephants, and horses moved through narrow, snow-covered mountain paths. They faced snowstorms and bitter cold. Half of his men and most of the elephants died.

Finally, Hannibal's army came down onto the northern plain of Italy. It attacked and defeated the surprised Romans. In less than two years, Hannibal defeated three more Roman armies. Filled with fear, the Romans retreated behind the strong walls of Rome. Even Hannibal could not knock them down.

For 15 years, Hannibal's army moved up and down the Italian peninsula. It destroyed towns and farmland. Then, in a surprise move, the Romans crossed the Mediterranean and attacked Carthage in North Africa. Hannibal had to rush home to defend the city.

Ally

A friend; a country or person who helps another

Word Bank

Carthage

Punic

Romans

Second

Zama

What do you think

Do you think Hannibal was a great general? Why or why not?

In 202 B.C., the Roman general Scipio defeated Hannibal's army at Zama. This ended the Second Punic War. Rome forced Carthage to destroy most of its navy and took control of Spain.

What Happened in the Third Punic War?

The Third Punic War began in 149 B.C. Carthage attacked an **ally,** or friend, of Rome. Rome then invaded Carthage. When the Romans cut off food supplies to the city, many Carthaginians starved to death. The Romans burned Carthage to the ground and sold its people into slavery. A legend says that the Romans covered the farmland outside the city with salt so that nothing would grow. Carthage was no more.

Lesson 3 Review On a sheet of paper, use the words from the Word Bank to complete each sentence correctly.

1. The _____ Wars were fought between Rome and Carthage.

2. The _____ won the First Punic War.

3. Hannibal fought the Romans in the _____ Punic War.

4. Hannibal lost the war at the battle of _____.

5. The Romans destroyed _____ around 150 B.C. and won the Third Punic War.

History in Your Life

What Year Is It?

What year is it? That depends on when you start to count. Julius Caesar set up the Julian calendar about 46 B.C. It had a 365-day year of 12 months, plus a leap year. For the Romans, Year One was the legendary founding of Rome. By our counting, that was 753 B.C. (What year is it now by the Roman calendar?)

There were small errors in the Julian calendar. Pope Gregory XIII, therefore, set up a new one in 1582. His calendar starts on the date that people thought Jesus was born. Countries gradually began to use it. Today most people in the world use the Gregorian calendar, at least for business.

Some calendars count in still other ways. The Chinese calendar begins at 2637 B.C. on our calendar. The Hebrew calendar starts 3,760 years earlier than the Gregorian. That is considered by the Hebrews as the date of the creation of Earth.

Senator

A member of a senate, a governing body

By 133 B.C., Rome controlled the Greek city-states and Asia Minor. It was the most powerful state in the Mediterranean area. The Romans even called this sea *Mare Nostrum,* which means "Our Sea."

Why Did the Roman Poor Grow Poorer?

The early Roman Republic depended on its soldiers, who were free citizens. These citizen-soldiers worked as farmers, laborers, and merchants when they were not fighting a war. Before Rome expanded, its citizen-soldiers fought only in Italy. When a battle ended, they returned home.

But as Rome grew more powerful, it had more territory to defend. Soldiers traveled overseas for long periods of time to fight. Citizens had to pay taxes to support the government. Many soldiers returned home to nothing, because the government had sold their farms for unpaid taxes.

Having no land, the farmers moved to the city. Jobs were hard to find because slaves were doing most of them. With no land and no jobs, many plebeians lost hope. To get a little money, they sold their votes to people running for political office. In this way, the rich became richer; the poor became poorer.

Reading Strategy:
Metacognition

Remember to look at the photographs, illustrations, and maps. Note the descriptive words. This will help you visualize what you are reading.

What Happened to Those Who Helped the Poor?

In 134 B.C., a tribune named Tiberius Gracchus tried to give public land to the poor. He said that soldiers, who fought to protect the wealthy, got nothing in return. The plebeians liked Gracchus, but the patrician **senators,** or members of the senate, feared him. They started a riot, and Gracchus and his followers were killed.

One third of the Roman population were slaves.

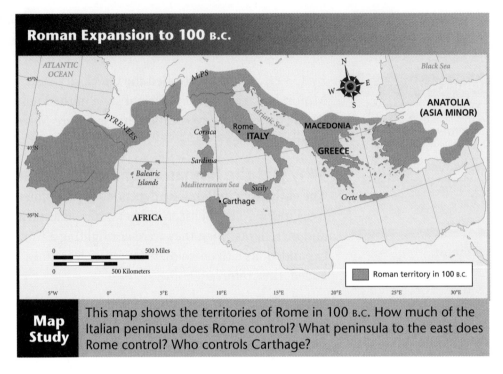

Roman Expansion to 100 B.C.

ATLANTIC OCEAN
45°N
ALPS
Black Sea
PYRENEES
Adriatic Sea
ANATOLIA (ASIA MINOR)
Corsica
Rome • **ITALY**
MACEDONIA
40°N
GREECE
Sardinia
• Balearic Islands
Mediterranean Sea
Sicily
Crete
35°N
• Carthage
AFRICA

0   500 Miles
0   500 Kilometers

Roman territory in 100 B.C.

5°W   0°   5°E   10°E   15°E   20°E   25°E   30°E

Map Study This map shows the territories of Rome in 100 B.C. How much of the Italian peninsula does Rome control? What peninsula to the east does Rome control? Who controls Carthage?

Reading Strategy:
Metacognition

Before you read the next section, think about what you can do that will help you understand more about military leaders in Rome.

Reform

To make something better through change

When Tiberius's brother Gaius was elected tribune in 123 B.C., he too helped the poor plebeians. He was able to lower the price of grain for the poor. He also helped more people in Italy become citizens. But once again, the patrician senators stopped the **reform** movement. They did not want change that would make things better for the plebeians. Gaius Gracchus and several thousand of his followers were killed.

How Did Military Leaders Gain Power?

The plebeians and the tribunes wanted reform. The patrician senators hated it. What happened? Military generals took power. In 110 B.C., Marius, a popular army general, formed an army from the poor who had no land. He promised them a share of the money made from conquering other people. His army won victories in North Africa and Gaul. His soldiers were more loyal to him than to the republic.

In 88 B.C., Lucius Sulla, another powerful general, challenged the power of Marius. War between followers of the two men began. Thousands of people died before Sulla defeated Marius and made himself dictator.

Politician

A government leader

Triumvirate

Rule by three people

By law, dictators had power for only six months. Sulla threw out this law so he could rule longer. Military generals continued to rule Rome until 27 B.C.

What Was the First Triumvirate?

In 60 B.C., three men agreed to rule Rome together: Crassus, a wealthy **politician,** or government leader, and two generals—Pompey the Great and Julius Caesar. Caesar was elected consul. We call the rule by these men the First **Triumvirate.** It lasted less than 10 years.

Lesson 4 Review On a sheet of paper, write the letter of the answer that correctly completes each sentence.

1. The Roman Republic depended on its _____.

    A navy   **C** citizen-soldiers

    B dictators   **D** enemies

2. A tribune named _____ tried to give land to the poor.

    A Pompey the Great   **C** Tiberius Gracchus

    B Julius Caesar   **D** Crassus

3. The citizen-soldiers became loyal to _____.

    A senators   **C** laws

    B Carthaginians   **D** generals

4. _____, a military general, threw out the Roman law that allowed a dictator for only six months.

    A Tiberius Gracchus   **C** Marius

    B Gaius Gracchus   **D** Lucius Sulla

5. We call the rule of three Romans in 60 B.C. the _____.

    A Mare Nostrum   **C** senate

    B tax   **D** First Triumvirate

What do you think ?

Imagine that you are a citizen of a republic. Why would selling your vote to someone hurt the republic?

Objectives

◆ To explain how Julius Caesar used his power

◆ To identify who assassinated Julius Caesar

◆ To explain how Octavian became Rome's first emperor

Assassinate

To kill someone important

Reading Strategy:
Metacognition

Notice the structure of this lesson. Look at the titles, headings, and boldfaced words.

Pompey feared Julius Caesar. He got the senate to limit Caesar's power. In 49 B.C., the senate ordered Caesar to return to Rome without his army. He challenged their power by marching his army to the Rubicon River between Gaul and Italy, crossing it, and marching on to Rome. Pompey fled. Caesar's army defeated Pompey's troops in Greece, Spain, and Egypt. Caesar had broken Roman law, but he had won power.

How Did Caesar Use His Power?

Now Caesar had more power than the senate. He gave jobs to the poor. He told the rich to stop wearing pearls and other signs of their wealth. He passed tougher laws against crime. He also forgave his old enemies and made them government officials. He also made the Roman calendar more accurate, or correct. People in Europe used his calendar for the next 1,500 years.

Who Assassinated Julius Caesar?

In 44 B.C., the senate made Caesar a dictator for life. Many artists carved statues of him, and people could see these everywhere in Rome. The government even stamped his face on Roman coins. Because of all this, some senators feared that they would lose their power. This would end the republic. Some senators **assassinated,** or killed, him on March 15, 44 B.C. These senators, some of them his friends, said that they had killed Caesar to save the republic.

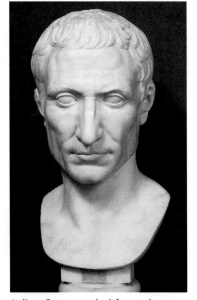

Julius Caesar ruled for a short time before he was assassinated.

Who Formed the Second Triumvirate?

After Caesar's death, fighting broke out. His 19-year-old son, Octavian, and two of his supporters—Mark Antony and Marcus Lepidus—formed the Second Triumvirate. They divided the Roman Empire into three areas. Octavian ruled the West; Antony ruled the East; and Lepidus ruled North Africa. Each shared power over Italy. After Lepidus **retired,** or gave up his job, Octavian and Mark Antony fought for complete power.

How Did Octavian Become Rome's First Emperor?

Mark Antony formed an alliance with Cleopatra, the queen of Egypt. This upset Octavian, because he feared that Antony and Cleopatra would create their own empire. Octavian asked the senate to take away Antony's power. Then Octavian declared war on Antony and Cleopatra. In 31 B.C., at the battle of Actium, the Romans defeated the Egyptians. After learning of their defeat, Antony and Cleopatra killed themselves.

Four years later, in 27 B.C., the Roman Republic ended. The senate made Octavian the **emperor.** For the next 500 years, emperors ruled Rome.

Retire

To give up one's job

Emperor

A person who is ruler of an empire

Reading Strategy:
Metacognition

Note the main idea and important details of this lesson. After each section, summarize what you have read to make sure you understand how the Roman Republic ended.

Biography

Cleopatra: 69–30 B.C.

Cleopatra is famous for her charm. She was also brave and ambitious. She became queen of Egypt at age 17. Her family was Greek. They had ruled Egypt for almost 300 years.

Cleopatra and her brother were at war. Julius Caesar helped her win. After his death, she turned to Mark Antony, a Roman general. He helped her keep Egypt independent. They married and had three children.

Then Rome declared war on Antony and Cleopatra. Octavian's fleet defeated them, so Antony killed himself. Cleopatra could not bear to be Octavian's prisoner, so she also killed herself. She and Antony were buried together.

Lesson 5 Review On a sheet of paper, write the answer to each question. Use complete sentences.

1. How did Julius Caesar disobey the senate?

2. Why was Caesar assassinated?

3. What was the Second Triumvirate?

4. Who was Cleopatra?

5. Who became the first emperor of Rome?

What do you think ?

Do you think the senators who assassinated Julius Caesar did so for the good of the republic? Why or why not?

Communication in History

Our Legacy from Latin

Is Latin a "dead language"? Has anyone used it since the ancient Romans? In fact, Latin lives on. For many years, educated people in Europe learned it. Scientists still use Latin for plant and animal names. The French, Spanish, and Romanian languages are partly based on Latin.

The English language has two main sources. One is German. The other is Latin. In fact, the word language comes from the Latin word *lingua*. School, library, table—all of these words have Latin roots.

Latin came into English in two ways. At first, many people in England spoke the language of the Angles, Saxons, and Jutes. These were Germanic languages. Then, in 1066, Normans from France conquered England. They added many French words to the language. Other Latin words came from scholars and scientists. For a while, ordinary people used Saxon words. People of higher rank used Latin-based words. Over time, the two blended to form our modern English language.

How to Get Elected in Rome

Ancient Rome was a republic. It did not have a king, and it was not a democracy. Only patricians held office. For many years, ordinary people tried to get some voice in government. They won some rights, but power stayed with just a few.

However, Roman officials did need the people's support. Like modern politicians, they tried different ways to get it. This reading is from a letter written in 63 B.C. In it, Quintus Cicero tells his brother how to get elected.

Whoever gives any sign of liking you, or regularly visits your house, you must put down in the category of friends. . . . You must take great pains that these men should love you and desire your highest honor as, for example, your tribesmen, neighbors, clients, and finally your freedmen, yes even your slaves; for nearly all the gossip that forms public opinion emanates from your own servants' quarters.

In a word, you must secure friends of every class, magistrates, consuls and their tribunes to win you the vote of the centuries [that elect the consuls]: men of wide popular influence. . . .

So you see that you will have the votes of all the centuries secured for you by the number and variety of your friends. . . . After that, review the entire city, all guilds, districts, neighborhoods. If you can attach yourself to the leading men in these, you will by their means easily keep a hold upon the multitude.

And you should be strenuous in seeing as many people as possible every day of every possible class and order, for from the mere numbers of these who greet you, you can make a guess of the amount of support you will get on the balloting. It often happens that people, when they visit a number of candidates, and observe the one that pays special heed to their attentions, leave off visiting the others, and little by little become real supporters of the man.

Document-Based Questions

1. Whom does Cicero say a candidate should consider as friends?

2. Why should a candidate make sure that his servants think highly of him?

3. How can a candidate get support throughout Rome?

4. Why do people often vote for a candidate?

5. Would Cicero's advice be useful to someone running for political office today? Why or why not?

Life in Rome

Rome was the largest city in the Roman Empire. By about A.D. 100, it had nearly one million people. The city was busy and crowded. At the heart of Rome was the Forum. It had great temples, theaters, and markets. The public baths were also important buildings. They were popular meeting places.

Romans also loved games and races. The city had several huge public arenas. People watched chariot races in the huge Circus Maximus. Gladiators and wild animals fought in the Colosseum. (You can still see the ruins of this stadium in present-day Rome.)

In town, wealthy patricians lived in comfortable townhouses. They had gardens and fountains. These nobles also owned large country homes called *villas*. Most ordinary Romans rented small apartments in buildings with four or five floors. Small shops took up the first floor. These wooden buildings were dark and crowded. Fire was a constant danger.

Crime was also a problem in Rome. Wealthy people avoided certain parts of the city. They might walk there only with armed slaves.

The family was the center of Roman life. In early Rome, the father had total control over his household. Later, fathers became less strict. They still made major family decisions. They held religious ceremonies to honor household gods. The goddess Vesta was the spirit of the hearth. The god Janus guarded the doorway. Each family also had its own spirits to protect it.

A Roman father took charge of his sons' education. Tutors were often Greek slaves. Young boys learned to read, write, and do arithmetic. Later they studied Greek and Latin literature. Public speaking was also important. Girls were taught cooking and sewing at home. Young women in patrician families got more education. They learned literature, music, and dance. Poorer women often worked in a shop or laundry.

Like people today, Romans cared about their looks. They wore jewelry. Women had elaborate hairstyles. Men wore a simple short-sleeved garment that fell to the knees. Women wore a similar, but longer, tunic. Their robes were wool, linen, or silk. Men who were Roman citizens could wear a toga. This was a long piece of cloth that was wrapped around the body. Different styles of togas had special meaning. Senators, for example, wore white togas with a purple border. It was hard to move while wearing a toga. Workers and soldiers usually wore just the tunic.

Wrap-Up

1. What kinds of buildings would you see in ancient Rome?

2. What did Romans do for fun?

3. Where did most ordinary Romans live?

4. What was the father's role in the Roman family?

5. What was Roman clothing like?

- Legends say that Romulus and Remus founded Rome in 753 B.C.

- The Latins lived on the plains south of the Tiber River. Greek settlers lived in city-states nearby. The Latins learned from the Greeks.

- The Etruscans lived north of the Tiber River. They were more advanced than the Latins. By about 600 B.C., they conquered Rome. Etruscan kings ruled Rome. Wealthy landowners, called patricians, ran the government.

- In 509 B.C., the Romans overthrew the Etruscan kings. They set up a republic. Two officials called consuls ran the republic. A senate of patricians made laws.

- Most ordinary Romans were plebeians. They paid taxes and served as soldiers. The plebeians wanted political power. Two officials—tribunes—were named to represent them. Tribunes and consuls could veto laws.

- In about 450 B.C., Roman laws were written down on 12 bronze tablets. Plebeians gradually got more power.

- The Roman Republic fought its neighbors. Rome's land and power grew. Three wars were fought with Carthage, a powerful Phoenician city. The First Punic War lasted 23 years, from 264 to 241 B.C. Rome won. In the Second Punic War, Hannibal crossed the Alps. He invaded Rome itself. A Roman general finally defeated him at Zama in 202 B.C. Rome won the Third Punic War as well. The Romans destroyed Carthage about 149 B.C.

- By 133 B.C., Rome ruled the Mediterranean. But the plebeians were getting poorer. Two brothers named Gracchus tried to help. Both were killed along with many followers.

- Military leaders took power in Rome. Two popular generals were Marius and Sulla. In 60 B.C., three leaders agreed to rule together as the First Triumvirate. Two were generals—Pompey and Julius Caesar. The other was a wealthy politician, Crassus.

- The senate made Caesar dictator for life. Some senators thought that would end the Republic, so they killed Caesar in 44 B.C.

- The Second Triumvirate formed. It included Caesar's adopted son, Octavian, and another general, Mark Antony. A third man, Lepidus, retired. Antony made an alliance with Cleopatra, queen of Egypt. Octavian declared war on them and defeated them. The Senate named him emperor.

Word Bank

Cleopatra

Gaius Gracchus

Hannibal

Julius Caesar

Lucius Sulla

Mark Antony

Octavian

Pompey the Great

Scipio

Tiberius Gracchus

On a sheet of paper, use the words from the Word Bank to complete each sentence correctly.

1. _____ defeated Hannibal at Carthage.

2. _____ got rid of the law about dictators governing only six months.

3. _____, a great general from Carthage, won many victories against the Romans.

4. As a tribune, _____ gave land to poor plebeians.

5. Along with Crassus and Julius Caesar, _____ was a member of the First Triumvirate.

6. _____ took power by disobeying the Roman senate and marching his army across the Rubicon River.

7. As queen of Egypt, _____ formed an alliance against Rome with Mark Antony.

8. Along with Octavian and Marcus Lepidus, _____ was a member of the Second Triumvirate.

9. _____, the adopted son of Julius Caesar, became the first emperor of Rome.

10. As a tribune, _____ was able to lower the price of grain so that the poor could buy it.

On a sheet of paper, write the letter of the answer that correctly completes each sentence.

11. The word _____ comes from the Latin word for father.

    A plebeian   **C** patrician

    B senate   **D** republic

12. A _____ is a form of government in which citizens elect representatives to govern them.

    A dictatorship   **C** patrician

    B senate   **D** republic

13. To _____ something is to say no to it.

    A veto   **C** term

    B accurate   **D** elect

14. In times of war, the Romans would appoint a _____ to rule for six months.

    A senate   **C** dictator

    B senator   **D** emperor

15. _____ means "from the common people."

    A Plebeian   **C** Senate

    B Patrician   **D** Triumvirate

On a sheet of paper, write the answer to each question. Use complete sentences.

16. Explain how each of the following was important for the Roman Republic: two consuls; the senate; the veto; the tribunes; the Law of the Twelve Tables.

17. What was one difference between the patricians and the plebeians?

18. Why did the Roman patricians need the Roman plebeians?

Critical Thinking On a sheet of paper, write your response to each question. Use complete sentences.

19. The Roman Republic lasted 500 years. Why do you think it lasted so long?

20. Why do you think the Roman Republic finally ended?

Test-Taking Tip

Look over a test before you begin answering questions. See how many parts there are. See what you are being asked to do on each part.

The Roman Empire

I n 27 B.C., Rome began the second great period of its history. It became an empire that lasted for 500 years. People of different races, customs, and religions lived in the Roman Empire. In this chapter, you will learn about the Pax Romana, which Octavian began. You will also learn about the rise of Christianity and about the fall of the Roman Empire in A.D. 476.

Goals for Learning

◆ To describe the reign of Octavian, who was known as Augustus Caesar

◆ To distinguish between Rome's good and bad emperors

◆ To describe the rise of Christianity and the conflicts between Rome and Christianity

◆ To list at least three reasons for the fall of the Roman Empire

◆ To recognize the practical gifts of the Romans to world civilization

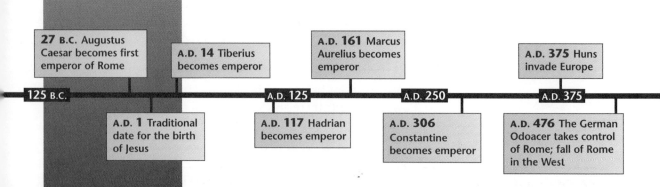

27 B.C. Augustus Caesar becomes first emperor of Rome

A.D. 14 Tiberius becomes emperor

A.D. 161 Marcus Aurelius becomes emperor

A.D. 375 Huns invade Europe

125 B.C.   A.D. 125   A.D. 250   A.D. 375

A.D. 1 Traditional date for the birth of Jesus

A.D. 117 Hadrian becomes emperor

A.D. 306 Constantine becomes emperor

A.D. 476 The German Odoacer takes control of Rome; fall of Rome in the West

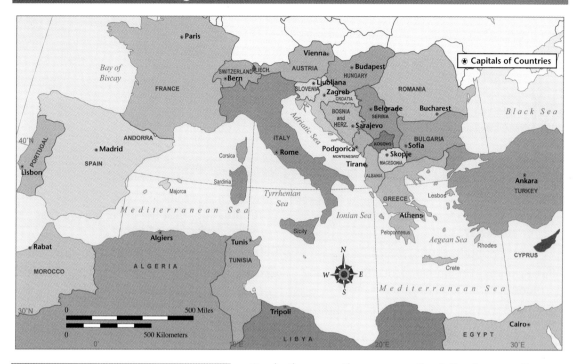

Map Skills

By 27 B.C., Rome controlled most of the known world. The Roman Empire was very large. Much of the empire included what we now call the Mediterranean Region. The Romans called the Mediterranean Sea *Mare Nostrum.* This means "Our Sea."

Study the map, then answer the following questions:

1. What is the capital of Greece?

2. Which country lies directly west of Italy and what is its capital?

3. What countries in northern Africa lie to the south of Italy?

4. What sea touches the coastline of Italy on its east?

5. How many miles does the Mediterranean Sea stretch from east to west?

Reading Strategy:
Summarizing

As you read the text in this chapter, you will want to ask yourself questions to help you understand what you read.

◆ What is the chapter about?

◆ What new ideas am I being introduced to?

◆ Why is it important that I remember these ideas?

Key Vocabulary Words

Lesson 1

Aqueduct A structure that carries water from far away

Eternal Lasting forever

Pax Romana The Roman peace that began during the reign of Augustus Caesar

Civilized Having good government and the things that make life easier

Lesson 2

Decline To lose power

Plague A disease that spreads from person to person and kills many people

Lesson 3

Christianity The religion based on the teachings of Jesus Christ

Prophet A person who speaks for God

Homeland The land that belongs to a people

Messiah A person sent by God to save people

Gospel One of four books of the New Testament part of the Bible; a word that means "good news"

Betray To stop being loyal to someone

Crucify To hang someone on a cross to die

Disciple A follower of someone

Gentile A non-Jew

Lesson 4

Co-emperor A person who rules part of an empire while another person rules the other part

Lesson 5

Vaulted A ceiling that is high, arched, and covers a large space

Sanitation The act of keeping something clean and free from disease

Imperfection Something that makes an object or person less than perfect

Objectives

◆ To explain why Augustus Caesar's reign is called the "Golden Age of Rome"

◆ To describe the Pax Romana

Aqueduct

A structure that carries water from far away

Eternal

Lasting forever

Augustus Caesar

In 27 B.C., Octavian, now known as Augustus Caesar, began the second great period of Roman history. Rome was no longer a republic; it had become an empire. This empire lasted for 500 years—from 27 B.C. to A.D. 476.

The empire stretched northwest to Britain and as far north as the Rhine and Danube Rivers. Rome controlled the Mediterranean Sea, much of North Africa, and Egypt. It reached the Euphrates River in the East and the Atlantic Ocean in the West. Nearly 100 million people lived under its rule.

Who Ruled During Rome's Golden Age?

We call Augustus Caesar's 41-year reign the "Golden Age of Rome." He wanted to bring back the old customs of the republic. He slept on a plain bed and wore the same clothes that common people wore. Augustus brought new things to the empire too.

Augustus built new temples, theaters, public buildings, and roads. He also built a large **aqueduct**—a structure that carried water to Rome. He said, "I found Rome a city of brick and left it a city of marble." The Romans were proud of their beautiful city, which was hundreds of years old. They thought it would last forever; it was the "**eternal** city."

More than 50,000 people could attend sporting events in the Roman Colosseum. It was completed in A.D. 80.

What Kept Government Officials Honest?

The Romans called the lands outside of Italy the provinces. The people in these provinces paid heavy taxes. But some officials were not honest. Much of this money never reached Rome. What could Augustus do to change this?

He divided the provinces into two groups. The senate controlled the older provinces. The emperor controlled the newer provinces on the frontier. Two government officials took care of the business of each province. One official took care of military and governmental things. The other official took care of everything that had to do with money. Each official watched the other. This kept them honest.

What Is the Pax Romana?

With these changes, Augustus brought peace to Rome and order to the empire. This period of peace lasted for 200 years—from 27 B.C. to A.D. 180. We call it the **Pax Romana,** or the Roman peace. During this time, each province could trade with every other province, and the people lived **civilized** lives. That is, the people had good government and the things that make life easier and more beautiful.

Reading Strategy:
Summarizing

What process is this section about?

Pax Romana

The Roman peace that began during the reign of Augustus Caesar

Civilized

Having good government and the things that make life easier

Biography

Claudius Ptolemy: c. A.D. 100–165

Ptolemy was a famous scientist. He lived and worked in Alexandria, Egypt. We know little else about his life.

Ptolemy observed the sun and stars. He studied Greek geometry. His writings on these topics are in 13 books. They are called the *Almagest.* That means "the greatest." Ptolemy said the earth was the center of the universe. It stood still. The sun and stars moved around it. For about 1,400 years, almost everyone believed this. Ptolemy was also a geographer. In his *Geography,* he corrected the mistakes of earlier geographers. He drew a map of the world that everyone accepted.

Reading Strategy:
Summarizing

What did you learn about Rome's Golden Age in this lesson?

Lesson 1 Review On a sheet of paper, write the answer to each question. Use complete sentences.

1. What do we call the reign of Augustus Caesar?

2. About how many people lived under the rule of the Roman Empire?

3. How did Augustus change the city of Rome?

4. Why did Romans call their city the "eternal city"?

5. What do we call the period of peace that began during the reign of Augustus?

What do you think ?

How could having two government officials in each province keep them both honest?

History in Your Life

The Buried City of Pompeii

The year was A.D. 79. The day was August 24, a day just like any other day in the Roman city of Pompeii. Then the volcano Mount Vesuvius exploded! Fiery lava, or hot melted rock, lit the sky. Ash and cinders—small pieces of burnt rock—rained down on everyone and everything. They made the sky dark as night for three days.

Thousands of frightened people tried to run from the city. They tied pillows on their heads for protection from the rain of fire. Within days, 30 feet of ash and cinders buried Pompeii. Poison gas killed the people who had not gotten away. Some fell dead in the streets; others died in their homes. One merchant died next to a stack of coins. Pets died with their masters.

Then the rain of fire ended. Only the tops of walls and a few columns stood above the blanket of ash and cinders. The city of Pompeii had disappeared! Over time, it was completely buried and forgotten. Then in 1748, a man hit a wall while digging one day. He had discovered Pompeii after more than 1,600 years!

For many years, archaeologists have been digging up the ruins of Pompeii. They have discovered that mud had covered and hardened on many dead bodies. When the bodies decayed, they left their shape, or mold, behind in the hardened mud.

The archaeologists have also discovered nuts, bread, figs, eggs on dinner tables, furniture, and children's toys that still work! Today, visitors can see the Pompeii of 1,900 years ago. Its ruins stand frozen in time.

Objectives

◆ To list three good and three bad Roman emperors

◆ To identify at least three reasons why the Roman Empire began to decline

Writing About History

Augustus Caesar had the Latin poet Virgil write a poem about Rome's greatness. Think about what you have read about the Roman Empire. In your notebook, write a poem about ancient Rome.

Augustus did good things for the people in his empire. After his death in A.D. 14, however, some emperors did well, while others did poorly. Because these emperors served for life, people had to accept them. Sometimes, when citizens did not want to accept the bad emperors, they murdered them! Between A.D. 180 and 284, there were 29 emperors; 25 of them were murdered.

Who Were Some Bad Emperors?

After the death of Augustus in A.D. 14, his son, Tiberius, became Rome's second emperor. He knew how to lead, but he was not popular. He was intelligent, but he suffered from depression. In his last years, he became a cruel tyrant.

In A.D. 37, Caligula became emperor. He was mentally ill. Some say he made his favorite horse a senator and demanded that people call him a god. He spent all the government's money on foolish things. Because of this, his own guards killed him.

How Did Claudius Become Emperor?

After Caligula's death, the senate tried to decide who should be the next emperor. While they talked about this problem, the guards picked Claudius, the 50-year-old uncle of Caligula. Most senators thought he was a fool. However, Claudius surprised everyone by becoming a fine ruler.

Claudius helped Rome to be orderly and peaceful. In A.D. 54, his second wife poisoned him. Nero, her 16-year-old son from another marriage, became emperor.

What Kind of Emperor Was Nero?

Most historians think that Nero was one of Rome's worst emperors. He sang and played the lyre, a small musical instrument with strings. People were forced to listen to him. Even the senators and the soldiers thought he played poorly.

Decline

To lose power

Plague

A disease that spreads from person to person and kills many people

In A.D. 64, a fire lasting nine days destroyed half of Rome. Some said that Nero not only started the fire, he played his lyre while Rome burned! In A.D. 68, some powerful army generals rebelled against Nero. The senate sentenced him to death. Rather than be executed by the government, Nero took his own life.

How Did Good Leaders Improve the Empire?

For 80 years—from A.D. 98 to 180—three good leaders ruled Rome. Under Trajan, the first of the three, Rome reached its greatest size. He gave grain to the poor and let farmers borrow money at low cost.

Hadrian, who followed Trajan as emperor, passed laws that protected women, children, and slaves. He built new buildings, lowered taxes, and built a wall across England.

Marcus Aurelius spent much of his time as emperor in the field with soldiers.

Marcus Aurelius, the last of the three, took direct command of the Roman army. He did this because Germanic tribes from the north wanted to settle within the empire.

As the empire grew, Rome needed many soldiers to defend and protect it. All these soldiers cost the government a lot of money. Aurelius wanted peace. Rather than fight the Germanic invaders, he let them settle inside the borders of the empire. The empire lasted for another 300 years, but it had already started to **decline,** or lose its power. A Roman historian wrote that Rome had changed "from a kingdom of gold to one of iron and rust."

Reading Strategy:
Summarizing

What event is this section about?

Why Did the Empire Decline?

The Roman Empire began to weaken for several reasons. First, its government never found a simple way to choose a new emperor. Too often when an emperor died, civil war broke out. Often, military generals fought each other for power. Sometimes, as with Claudius, soldiers chose the new leader.

Second, because of its wars, taxes were high. The government had little money. Third, a **plague,** a deadly disease that spreads from person to person, hit. All this weakened the empire.

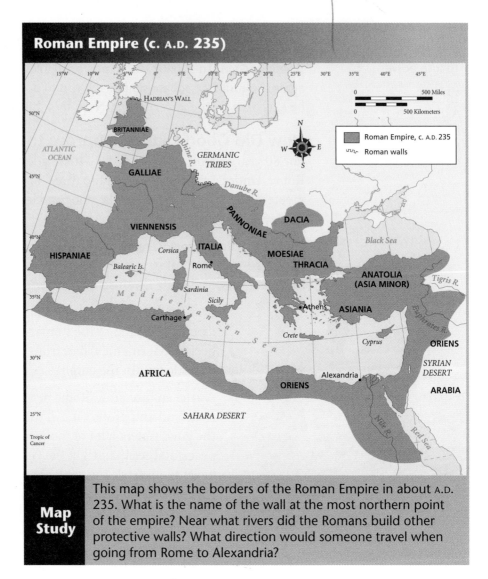

Roman Empire (c. A.D. 235)

Map Study

This map shows the borders of the Roman Empire in about A.D. 235. What is the name of the wall at the most northern point of the empire? Near what rivers did the Romans build other protective walls? What direction would someone travel when going from Rome to Alexandria?

Lesson 2 Review On a sheet of paper, write the answer to each question. Use complete sentences.

1. Who chose Claudius to be emperor?

2. How did Trajan help the empire?

3. What did Hadrian do to help people?

4. Why did Marcus Aurelius allow German invaders to settle inside the empire?

5. What were three reasons the Roman Empire declined?

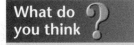

What do you think

How would a plague weaken a country or an empire?

Objectives

◆ To explain who Jesus of Nazareth was and what he did to spread Christianity

◆ To identify the major conflicts between Rome and Christians

Christianity

The religion based on the teachings of Jesus Christ

Prophet

A person who speaks for God

Homeland

The land that belongs to a people

Messiah

A king sent by God to save people

Gospel

One of four books of the New Testament part of the Bible; a word that means "good news"

While Augustus Caesar was emperor, Jesus of Nazareth was born. His home was in the far eastern section of the Roman Empire called Judea, part of Palestine. Jesus preached a new message to the poor. Out of his preaching grew a new religion— **Christianity.** It changed the Roman Empire and became one of the world's great religions.

Why Did the Jewish People Want a Messiah?

Rome allowed the people in its empire to believe in their own gods. However, the Jews did not have political freedom. For centuries their **prophets**—people who speak for God—said that the Jews would one day rule their own **homeland.** (Homeland is the land that belongs to a people.) Palestine was their homeland. They felt it belonged to them, not to Rome. The Jews believed that their god would send a **messiah,** or savior, to lead them to political freedom. Some people thought that Jesus of Nazareth was this messiah.

What Did Jesus of Nazareth Teach?

Four books called the **Gospels** tell about Jesus. *Gospel* means "good news." The Gospels are the first four books of the New Testament of the Bible. Jesus' followers wrote these books after his death.

Jesus grew up as a Jew in the small town of Nazareth. He earned his living as a carpenter. When he was 30, he began to preach a new message—God loved all people equally. Jesus asked his followers to love all people, just as God did. They were to show this love through service. Finally, he asked them to love even their enemies. Jesus showed a special interest in people others thought were less important: sick people, women, and foreigners.

Reading Strategy:
Summarizing

What details help
you understand the
teachings of Jesus?

Betray

To stop being loyal to
someone

Crucify

To hang someone on
a cross to die

Disciple

A follower of
someone

Gentile

A non-Jew

Jesus said that God had sent him to preach this good news to the poor. The poor in Palestine liked his message. Large crowds gathered to hear him speak. The Gospels report that he healed the sick, gave sight to the blind, and performed other miracles. Because of this, many people began to follow him.

Why Did Some People Fear Jesus of Nazareth?

For three years, Jesus preached God's love. Then some Jewish leaders turned against him. They feared that his followers would rebel against Rome. Then one of the followers of Jesus **betrayed** Jesus, or stopped being loyal to him. He turned Jesus over to his enemies. Roman soldiers arrested Jesus. Pontius Pilate, the Roman governor, charged him with being a rebel. Then soldiers **crucified** Jesus, or hung him on a cross to die.

Why Did His Followers Call Jesus, the Christ?

The New Testament says the followers of Jesus believed that God raised him from the dead. They also believed that Jesus was the son of God and that he had returned to his father in heaven. These followers, or **disciples,** carried on his teachings. They called him the Christ, or *Christos,* which is the Greek word for "messiah." Those who believed he had risen from the dead became known as Christians, or followers of Christ.

How Did the Gospel Spread?

At first, Jesus' disciples preached their good news only to Jews. Then Saul, who now took the Roman name Paul, became a follower of Jesus. For 30 years, he traveled from Palestine to Greece to Italy. He preached that God had raised Jesus from the dead, and people should love and serve others. He preached to Jews and **gentiles,** or non-Jews. He helped Christianity take its first steps in becoming a world religion.

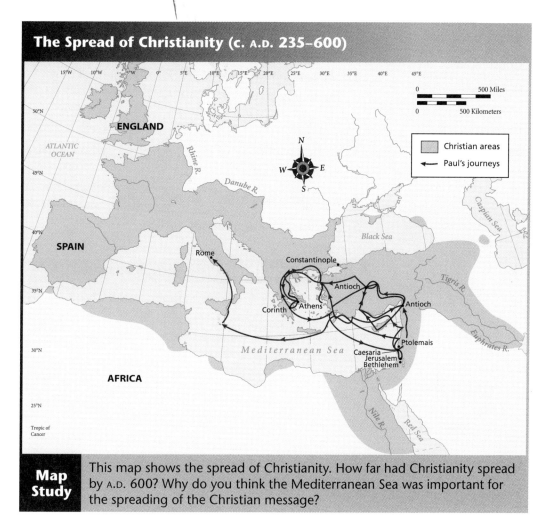

The Spread of Christianity (c. A.D. 235–600)

Map Study This map shows the spread of Christianity. How far had Christianity spread by A.D. 600? Why do you think the Mediterranean Sea was important for the spreading of the Christian message?

Reading Strategy:
Summarizing

What process does this section describe?

How Did Christianity Affect Rome?

Roman law said that everyone must honor the emperor as a god. Christians refused to follow this law. Because of this and some other Christian beliefs, the Romans killed many of them.

Over the next three centuries, the Roman Empire grew weaker, but Christianity grew stronger. Many people, especially the poor, saw Christianity as an answer to their problems. Jesus had preached that God loved all people equally. He had promised eternal life to those who believed in him. By A.D. 337, Rome had its first Christian emperor—Constantine. In A.D. 395, the emperor Theodosius I made Christianity the official religion of the Roman Empire.

Word Bank

Constantine

gentiles

Gospels

messiah

Saul

Lesson 3 Review On a sheet of paper, use the words from the Word Bank to complete each sentence correctly.

1. We learn about Jesus of Nazareth from the four _____ that his followers wrote.

2. Many Jews believed Jesus was the _____.

3. Another follower of Jesus was _____, who later became known as Paul.

4. Paul preached to Jews and _____.

5. The first Christian emperor was _____.

What do you think ?

Why do you think the Roman Empire feared Christianity and its message?

In A.D. 284, Diocletian, a general, became the Roman emperor. He thought that the empire was too large for one person to govern, so he divided it into two parts. The dividing line between the two parts lay west of Greece. Diocletian ruled the eastern part. Another person ruled the western part. This person was the **co-emperor,** or person who ruled one part of an empire while another person ruled the other part.

Who Moved the Capital to Byzantium?

In A.D. 306, Constantine became emperor. By this time, the western part of the empire—the part in which Rome was located—was weak. Constantine moved the capital to Byzantium. This old Greek city stood on the western edge of Asia Minor. He named his new capital Constantinople after himself.

Who Were the Huns and Visigoths?

For hundreds of years, German tribes had fought the Roman army. In battle, they were skilled warriors. By A.D. 200, many Germans lived within the empire. Some of them even became Roman soldiers.

Around A.D. 375, a non-Germanic tribe called the Huns invaded Eastern Europe. They came from central Asia and were expert horsemen and fierce warriors. Their most famous leader was Attila the Hun.

For many years, the Huns rode across Europe, defeating every tribe they met in battle. One German tribe, the Visigoths, feared them. Rome let the Visigoths move within the Roman Empire. The Visigoths promised not to bring weapons with them. Rome promised to give them land. Neither side kept its promise.

Co-emperor

A person who rules part of an empire while another person rules the other part

Reading Strategy:
Summarizing

What groups of people are being introduced in this section?

As king of the Huns, Attila led his warriors on several raids on the Roman Empire.

What Year Did the Roman Empire Fall?

The Visigoths began to attack Roman towns. In A.D. 378, Rome sent an army against them. But the Visigoths defeated the Romans at the Battle of Adrianople. This was one of the most important events in world history. For the first time in hundreds of years, Rome could not defend itself!

In A.D. 410, the Visigoths sacked Rome. In A.D. 455, another German tribe, the Vandals, came into Rome and destroyed much of its beauty. (To this day, we call people who destroy property vandals.)

Reading Strategy:
Summarizing

What are some important details that help you understand the fall of the Roman Empire?

Then in A.D. 476, Odoacer, a German leader, took control of Rome. Roman rule—as a republic and as an empire—had lasted for 1,000 years, but now it was no more. The western part of the empire had collapsed. However, the eastern part survived.

Lesson 4 Review On a sheet of paper, write the letter of the answer that correctly completes each sentence.

1. Emperor _____ divided the Roman Empire into two parts.

   A Marcus Aurelius   **C** Diocletian
   B Constantine   **D** Visigoth

2. Emperor _____ moved the capital of the empire from Rome to Byzantium.

   A Marcus Aurelius   **C** Diocletian
   B Constantine   **D** Attila

3. The name of the new capital was _____.

   A Adrianople   **C** Odoacer
   B Hun   **D** Constantinople

4. The best known leader of the Huns was _____.

   A Attila   **C** Diocletian
   B Odoacer   **D** Visigoth

What do you think ❓

How do you think the Germanic tribes were able to take over the Roman Empire?

5. Historians give the date of A.D. _____ for the fall of Rome.

   A 378   **B** 410   **C** 455   **D** 476

Vaulted

A ceiling that is high, arched, and covers a large space

Reading Strategy:
Summarizing

What is the main idea of this paragraph?

The fall of Rome did not end its influence. Roman culture influenced the German invaders. Its influence continues to this day, because Rome gave many gifts to world civilization. These gifts were useful for the Romans, who were a practical people. They liked useful things.

Why Is Roman Law a Gift to Civilization?

In many ways, Roman law made the empire a success for a thousand years. Romans respected the law. They thought that a law should be fair, just, and reasonable. They thought that law should do two things. First, it should protect people's lives and property. Second, it should punish those who do wrong. Law codes based on Roman ideas are still used in some countries of Europe. Roman law stated that all people are equal before the law.

What Useful Things Did the Romans Build?

The Romans became the greatest road builders before modern times. (People in some countries still use Roman-built roads today!) They also built fine bridges and large aqueducts.

The Romans developed a kind of concrete with which to build. (Concrete is a mixture of sand, water, and other materials. It hardens to become rocklike.) To add beauty to their concrete buildings, they covered them with thin, flat, wide pieces of marble. To make the buildings larger, they built high **vaulted** ceilings. A vaulted ceiling has an arch to it and can support a roof that covers a large space.

Imperfection

Something that makes an object or person less than perfect

What Is the Pantheon?

Emperor Hadrian built the Pantheon, which is still standing today. It is a temple for all the Roman gods. With its vaulted ceiling, the Pantheon is 142 feet wide. Some Roman buildings could hold 3,000 people. In fact, the Colosseum, where the Romans went for entertainment, could seat 50,000 people! The practical Romans built their roads and their buildings to last. People still use a few of them today.

Reading Strategy:
Summarizing

What important details help you understand the wonders of Roman art and architecture?

How Were Roman Art and Science Practical?

The Romans wanted to find a good use for art and science. This made them different from the Greeks, who wanted perfect beauty and knowledge. For example, Greeks made their statues perfect. Roman artists showed **imperfections,** such as broken noses and wrinkles. These imperfections made an object or person more realistic.

One practical thing the Romans did was build aqueducts like this one. These were used to transport water.

Romans also used their knowledge of science in a practical way. They set up the first health-care system. Government doctors cared for the poor. The Romans built sewers to improve public **sanitation.** Sewers, which are usually underground pipes, carry away dirty water and human waste. This helps sanitation. That is, it helps keep people clean and free from disease.

Galen, who was a Greek, practiced medicine in Rome around A.D. 180. He wrote a book in which he wrote down everything anyone knew about medicine. We now know that the book has many mistakes. Still, it influenced medicine for more than a thousand years.

Then and Now

Roman Technology

Roman engineers could build large structures. Two advances helped them. One was the round arch. The arch was not new. The Greeks, for example, had built arched gates. The Romans learned how to use it in new ways, however. The Roman arch was a half circle. Side columns supported it. It could hold up heavy loads. The Romans built arched stone bridges across rivers. They also used round arches to build great aqueducts. They brought freshwater to Roman cities everywhere. The Romans also built arched roofs over large indoor spaces.

The other advance was concrete. Concrete was a Roman invention. It let them build strong walls and arched roofs. Concrete also made Roman roads strong and lasting. Modern builders still use this Roman technology.

Lesson 5 Review On a sheet of paper, write the answer to each question. Use complete sentences.

1. What did the Romans believe laws should do?

2. What was the basic principle of Roman law?

3. Why did Emperor Hadrian build the Pantheon?

4. How did Roman art differ from Greek art?

5. Describe three contributions the Romans made to civilization.

What do you think ?

The book of medicine that Galen wrote had mistakes in it. Do you think it still helped people after his time? Why or why not?

The Battle of Adrianople

Ammianus Marcellinus was a professional Greek soldier. He was born about 330; the date of his death is not known. He wrote a history of the Roman Empire that includes a description of the Battle of Adrianople, which happened in A.D. 378. This battle is considered to be a turning point in Roman history. Marcellinus was living at the time of the battle, but he was not there. He refers to written sources and also talked to people who were there. The following excerpt gives us an idea of how horrible the war was.

By this time such great clouds of dust arose that it was hardly possible to see the sky. The air resounded with terrible cries. The darts, which brought death on every side, reached their mark and fell with deadly effect, for no one could see them quickly enough to place himself on guard. The barbarians, rushing on with their enormous army, beat down our horses and men and gave us no open spaces where we could fall back to operate. They were so closely packed that it became impossible for us to escape by forcing a path through them. Our men finally began to despise the thought of death and, again taking their swords, slew all they encountered. Helmets and breastplates were smashed in pieces by mutual blows of battle-axes. . . .

The plain was covered with corpses, showing the mutual ruin of the combatants. The groans of the dying, or of men horribly wounded, were intense and caused much dismay on all sides. Amidst all this great tumult and confusion, our infantry were exhausted by toil and danger, until at last they had neither the strength left to fight nor the spirit to plan anything. Their spears were broken by the frequent collisions, so that they were forced to content themselves with their drawn swords, which they thrust into the dense battalions of the enemy, disregarding their own safety, and seeing that every possibility of escape was cut off. . . .

Document-Based Questions

1. What details does Marcellinus give that make it sound like he fought in the battle?

2. How did his experience as a soldier help him write this account of the battle?

3. Later historians thought his descriptions of the battle were accurate. Do you think it is possible for a writer to give a balanced report of an event?

4. This work was written to be read in public. What details might Marcellinus have added just to make the account more interesting?

5. How do you think he felt about war?

Source: Charles D. Yonge. The Roman History of Ammianus Marcellinus During the Reigns of the Emperors Constantius, Julian, Jovianus, Valentinian, and Valens. (London: 1862), book XXXI, chapters 12-14.

Women in Greek and Roman History

Women in ancient Greece and Rome led limited lives. Few got an education. Still, we know of some women who did influence history.

Sappho was a Greek poet. She was born around 630 B.C. She married and had a daughter, Cleis. One of her poems says, "I have a beautiful child who looks like golden flowers." Sappho wrote many poems about feelings and friendship. Only one complete poem exists today. Others have only a few lines.

All Roman emperors were men. But sometimes the real rulers were their wives or mothers. Julia Domna was the wife of the emperor about A.D. 200. She was known as Julia the Philosopher. She invited scholars and artists to court. They discussed art and ideas. Julia's son Caracalla became emperor in A.D. 211. While he went to war, she ruled the empire. A few years later, in A.D. 222, the teenage Alexander Severus became emperor. His mother, Julia Mamaea, ruled the empire for 13 years.

In the early 300s A.D., Constantine became emperor of the eastern part of the Roman Empire. The most powerful woman in this empire was Empress Theodora (A.D. 497–548). Her family was poor. Her father worked in a circus. She was an actress. Then she met and married Justinian, the emperor's nephew. Justinian became emperor in A.D. 527. She became empress and co-ruler.

Empress Theodora and her court.

Theodora was smart and ambitious. She was also brave. In A.D. 532, the rulers faced dangerous riots. Justinian was ready to flee. Theodora changed his mind. She spoke to his advisers. "I'll never see the day," she said, "when I am not hailed as Empress. Caesar [Justinian's title], if you wish to flee, well and good. You have the money. The ships are ready. The sea is clear. But I shall stay!" Justinian stayed. Then the riots ended.

Wrap-Up

1. For what was Sappho famous?

2. What did all Roman emperors have in common?

3. How did Julia Domna influence Rome?

4. Where did Justinian and Theodora rule?

5. How did Theodora show she was brave?

- Rome became a great empire during the reign of Augustus Caesar. The empire lasted from 27 B.C. to A.D. 476.

- Augustus ruled for 41 years. This time is called the Golden Age. He built many new buildings in Rome. He reformed government in the provinces. Roman rule brought peace and order to the empire. Pax Romana, the Roman peace, lasted from 27 B.C. to A.D. 180.

- Good and bad emperors followed Augustus. His stepson Tiberius ruled cruelly. The next emperor, Caligula, was insane. The imperial guards killed him. They then picked Claudius to be emperor. He ruled well, but was poisoned by his wife. Her son Nero became emperor. In A.D. 64, while Nero ruled, a fire destroyed much of Rome.

- From A.D. 98 to 180, Rome had three good emperors. They were Trajan, Hadrian, and Marcus Aurelius. To avoid war, Aurelius let German tribes settle inside the empire.

- The Roman Empire began to decline. Soldiers fought over who would become emperor. Diseases and the cost of wars made the empire weak.

- Jesus was born in Palestine during the reign of Augustus. Jews had religious freedom under Roman rule. Jesus preached about God's love. He made enemies among both Jewish leaders and Romans. He was crucified under Roman law. After his death, his followers wrote the Gospels to tell about his life and work.

- Followers of Jesus believed he was the son of God. His disciples, called Christians, spread his teachings. Paul helped spread Christianity.

- Some Roman rulers harmed Christians. In A.D. 337, however, Emperor Constantine became a Christian. Christianity later became the official religion.

- Emperor Diocletian wanted to make the empire easier to rule. He divided it into eastern and western parts.

- In A.D. 306, Emperor Constantine moved the capital to Byzantium. He renamed the city Constantinople.

- The Huns invaded Eastern Europe around A.D. 375. The Visigoths feared the Huns, so they moved into the Roman Empire. Then they attacked Roman towns. They beat a Roman army at Adrianople. The Visigoths and the Vandals attacked Rome. The western empire fell in A.D. 476. Odoacer, a German, took control.

- Roman law was one important Roman contribution. Other gifts were in art, building, language, and medicine.

Chapter 8   REVIEW

Word Bank

Attila
Augustus Caesar
Christianity
Constantine
Diocletian
Jesus
Odoacer
Paul
Theodosius I
Visigoths

On a sheet of paper, use the words from the Word Bank to complete each sentence correctly.

1. Historians call the reign of _____ the "Golden Age of Rome."

2. When _____ was 30 years old, he began to preach good news to the poor in Palestine.

3. _____ was a follower of Jesus who preached to Jews and gentiles.

4. The new religion that came from Jesus's teaching was called _____.

5. Rome could not defend itself for the first time in history when the _____ attacked.

6. _____, king of the Huns, led his tribe of warriors across Europe.

7. Emperor _____ divided the Roman Empire into two parts.

8. _____ was the first Christian emperor.

9. _____ made Christianity the official religion of the Roman Empire.

10. A German leader, _____, took control of Rome in A.D. 476 and ended the Roman Empire.

On a sheet of paper, write the letter of the answer that correctly completes each sentence.

11. The Pax Romana was a period of peace in Rome that lasted for _____ years.

    A 41   B 100   C 200   D 1,000

12. _____ was an unpopular emperor because in his last years, he was a cruel tyrant.

    A Augustus Caesar   C Caligula
    B Tiberius   D Claudius

13. The Romans gave Jewish people _____ freedom.

    A political   **C** worldwide

    B religious   **D** none of the above

14. The Roman Empire declined because of _____.

    A a plague

    B lack of money

    C no system to pick an emperor

    D all of the above

15. The _____ and the Vandals invaded Rome in A.D. 410 and 455.

    A Visigoths   **C** Carthaginians

    B Huns   **D** Greeks

On a sheet of paper, write the answer to each question. Use complete sentences.

16. In what ways were the Romans a practical people?

17. Why did the Roman Empire decline and then fall?

18. In what ways did Augustus Caesar make Rome better?

Critical Thinking On a sheet of paper, write your response to each question. Use complete sentences.

19. Rome never found a good way to pick a new emperor. What happened because of this?

20. Why do you think Christianity spread easily throughout Europe?

Test-Taking Tip

On the day of the test, try to arrive at class early. Sometimes teachers give helpful information about the test at that time.

9

Civilizations of the Americas

The first Stone Age humans set foot in what is now the Americas as early as 20,000 B.C. They had no idea that they were the first people to walk on this land. They did not know that the land consisted of two huge continents that we call North and South America. Within these two regions lies a cultural region we call Mesoamerica. It is made up of Mexico and Central America. Some of the earliest civilizations in the Americas developed here.

Goals for Learning

◆ To explain how the first Americans may have come to the Americas

◆ To identify three important early Southwestern cultures

◆ To explain characteristics of four regional Indian cultures

◆ To identify the cultures of early Mesoamerica and South America

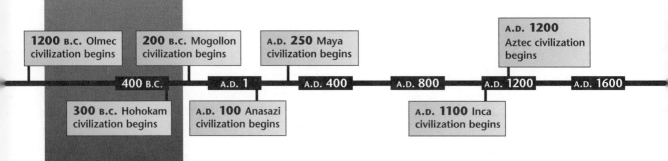

1200 B.C. Olmec civilization begins

200 B.C. Mogollon civilization begins

A.D. 250 Maya civilization begins

A.D. 1200 Aztec civilization begins

400 B.C.   A.D. 1   A.D. 400   A.D. 800   A.D. 1200   A.D. 1600

300 B.C. Hohokam civilization begins

A.D. 100 Anasazi civilization begins

A.D. 1100 Inca civilization begins

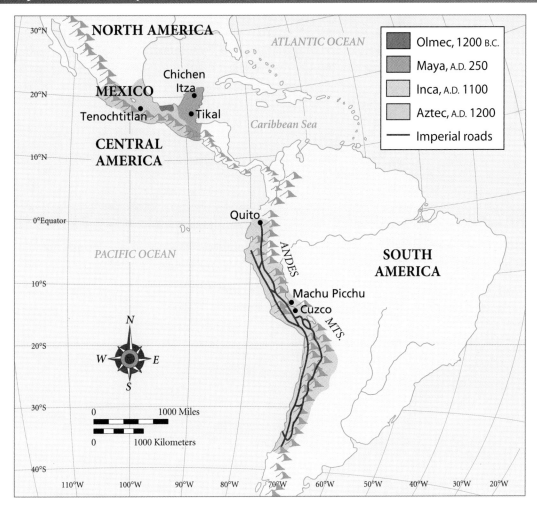

Map Skills

The land that connects the continents of North America and South America is called Mesoamerica. It is made up of Mexico and Central America.

This map shows four early American empires—the Olmecs, the Mayas, the Aztecs, and the Incas. The dates show about when those empires began. It also shows the roads in the Incan Empire.

Study the map, then answer the following questions:

1. Why did the Incan roads run mostly north and south instead of east and west?

2. Which empire seems to have been the biggest?

3. Which empire was the smallest?

4. What mountain range runs along the west coast of South America, within the Incan empire?

5. Which empire is the oldest?

Reading Strategy:
Questioning

As you read, ask yourself questions. This will help you understand more of the information. You'll also become a more active reader. Questioning the text will also help you to be a more active reader. Ask yourself:

◆ What do I hope to learn from this text?

◆ What do the facts and details in this text tell me?

◆ Are there any people or situations in this text that make connections with my life?

Key Vocabulary Words

Lesson 1 ————————————
Glacier a thick sheet of ice

Lesson 2 ————————————
Kiva a small underground building used for ceremonies

Geometric Having simple designs made up of straight lines and circles

Lesson 3 ————————————
Palisade a wooden fence

Objectives

◆ To explain how people may have first come to the Americas

◆ To describe an important discovery in New Mexico

◆ To explain the importance of the Folsom Point and the Clovis Point

Reading Strategy:
Questioning
_____

What details are important to understanding the first Americans?

Glacier
_____

A thick sheet of ice

Archaeologists want to learn when the first Americans reached the Americas. They also want to learn where the people came from and what their lives were like. These people lived so long ago that archaeologists have found only a few artifacts. Archaeologists will continue to search for new evidence to help them better understand these people.

How Did the First Americans Come to the Americas?

The first Americans came to the Americas during the last Ice Age. Thick sheets of ice called **glaciers** covered the upper third of North America. Life during the Ice Age was hard, bitter cold, and very dangerous. People were nomads, surviving by hunting. A nomad is a person who moves from place to place. Eventually, they walked from Asia over a frozen body of water now called the Bering Strait. In search of food, they probably were following herds of animals. Others would follow them over thousands of years. When the Ice Age ended, the land grew warmer. Slowly, the people we now call American Indians settled in communities all over North and South America. They created different cultures. Some created ways of living that were simple. Other cultures created complex societies like those in Europe, Asia, and Africa.

How Long Have Indians Lived in North America?

At one time, scientists thought that American Indians had lived in North America for no more than 4,000 years. Then, in 1908, George McJunkin, an African American cowboy, made a discovery. He was riding his horse in Folsom, New Mexico. Heavy rain had flooded the area. McJunkin noticed that the floodwaters had washed away many layers of dirt. The water had uncovered many very large animal bones. He called it his "bone pit." He knew that the bones were important because of how big they were and how deep they were buried.

Reading Strategy:
Questioning

Think beyond the
text. Consider your
own thoughts and
experiences as you
read about important
discoveries.

**Writing About
History**

Imagine you have
just made a discovery
like the one George
McJunkin made.
Write two paragraphs
in your notebook
describing the first
thing you would do.

Although self taught, McJunkin had collected ancient bones,
rocks, minerals, and old arrowheads. He owned books on
geology and natural history. McJunkin wrote to scientists
asking them to come and see what he had discovered. At first,
scientists were not interested. It was only after McJunkin died
in 1922 that scientists decided to take his advice and examine
his "bone pit."

What Did Scientists Learn from the "Bone Pit"?

In 1926, the animal bones were dug up and brought to the
Colorado Museum of Natural History. They turned out to
be important evidence about how long American Indians
had lived in North America. The bones were those of ancient
buffaloes. Radiocarbon dating of the bones showed them to
be about 9,000 years old. Scientists also discovered a piece of
flint stuck in the ribs of one of the animals. It had been shaped
by a human into a sharp spear point. Scientists named the
sharpened flint piece the Folsom Point. The Folsom Point had
been buried at the same time as the bones. That meant that
American Indians had been living in the New Mexico area
for at least 9,000 years. George McJunkin had made a major
scientific discovery. Anthropologists now wondered if those
who made the Folsom Point were really the oldest people. Were
there even more ancient people who lived before the makers of
the Folsom Point?

The Clovis Point was found in Clovis, New Mexico, in the 1930s.

Were the Clovis People the First Americans?

In Clovis, New Mexico, a new spear point was found in the 1930s. The Clovis Point was more than 4,000 years older than the spear point found in Folsom. Many anthropologists believe that the Clovis people entered the Americas about 13,000 years ago. For many years, anthropologists thought that the Clovis people were the first Americans. However, new evidence changed that belief. It is now thought that other groups entered the Americas at about the same time.

Lesson 1 Review On a sheet of paper, write the answer to each question. Use complete sentences.

1. How do we think the first people got to the Americas? Why did they come here?

2. What was George McJunkin's discovery?

3. How did scientists determine the age of the bones in the pit?

4. Why are the Folsom Point and the Clovis Point important?

5. Why did many anthropologists think that the Clovis people were the first Americans?

What do you think ?

George McJunkin knew that his discovery was important. Why do you think that scientists were not interested in it until after he died?

Objectives

◆ To identify the cultures of the Hohokam, the Mogollon, and the Anasazi

◆ To explain the environment in which each of these cultures lived

---

Reading Strategy:
Questioning

What do you think you will learn about early Southwestern cultures?

In what is now the Southwestern United States, archaeologists discovered the remains of three important societies of ancient Indians. These Indians—the Hohokam, the Mogollon, and the Anasazi—shared a similar background. Each had changed from hunting and gathering their food to growing their food. However, the environments where they lived were very different.

Where Did Each of the Southwestern Cultures Live?

The Hohokam lived in a dry desert area in what is now Arizona. The Mogollon lived among tree-lined mountain ranges and a river valley in southeastern Arizona and southern New Mexico. The Anasazi lived in the canyons and the flat-topped mesas where Arizona, New Mexico, Utah, and Colorado meet. Because of the different environments, the cultures developed different methods of farming, building shelters, and showing their artistic ideas.

Why Did the Hohokam Build Canals?

Anthropologists believe that the Hohokam developed from a combination of local people in Arizona and Mesoamericans who had moved from the south. Their civilization began about 300 B.C. The Hohokam lived in a desert area. They had to figure out how to bring water to their land. Their solution was to build irrigation canals using simple hand tools. From A.D. 800 until 1000, they built hundreds of miles of canals. The network of canals provided the Hohokam with more than just water for their crops. The canals provided water for drinking, cooking, and washing. The Hohokam grew cotton that was woven into cloth. They used canal water to create painted pottery. The Hohokam also made beautiful jewelry using seashells.

Kiva

A small underground building used for ceremonies

Geometric

Having simple designs made up of straight lines and circles

What Was Snaketown?

Snaketown was an important place for the Hohokam. This settlement ruled smaller villages by controlling their canals. The Hohokam built ball courts in Snaketown for sports and rituals. Mounds found within the remains of Hohokam villages may have been dance platforms or places where their leaders lived. By about 1450, most people had abandoned the Hohokam area. This most likely was caused by a lack of water and a failed irrigation system. The Pima Indians later lived in the same area. They named the earlier people *Hohokam,* meaning "the vanished ones."

Why Are the Mogollons Known for Their Artwork?

We do not know what ancient peoples called themselves. For example, Mogollons were given their name by anthropologists because they lived among the Mogollon mountain ranges. These mountains were named after Don Juan Mogollon, a Spanish governor of New Mexico in the early 1700s. It is believed that the Mogollon people began farming this area about 200 B.C. The Mogollon created shelters both on high ground and underground. These unusual **kivas,** or small underground buildings, were used for religious ceremonies and councils.

The Mogollon people are especially known for their artwork. They created a new form of pottery. Between A.D. 900 and 1200, they created beautiful clay bowls. These had black and white **geometric** designs and animal images. Geometric designs are created with circles and straight lines. The most important art that the Mogollons are known for is their rock art. Over a wide geographic area, the Mogollon people carved thousands of mysterious images into the surfaces of rocks. There are images of insects, fish, reptiles, birds, and mammals. There are also human faces and masks. No other people anywhere in the world created so many artistic images.

How Do We Know the Anasazi Were Master Builders?

The Anasazi are known as the master builders of the Southwestern ancient Indian cultures. Their "Golden Age" was between A.D. 850 and 1150. During these 300 years, the Anasazi constructed a planned community. This community contained a massive complex of ceremonial buildings and roads. This building project was shaped like a wagon wheel (which the ancient Indian people did not use). The center of the "wheel" was in Chaco Canyon in New Mexico. It was here that huge ceremonial buildings, known as great houses or cliff dwellings, were built. The style of the stone buildings is called pueblo.

It is estimated that more than 100,000 pieces of timber had to be carried from the mountains to create floors and roofs. They had no work animals, such as horses, to help them. The timber had to be carried about 50 miles on the backs of workers. Roads were built from the center like the spokes of a wheel. The roads led to villages lying along the rim of the wheel. The villages

could be as far as 10 miles away from the center. The leaders of the Anasazi communicated from the central great houses to these villages with signal fires. They used obsidian glass like a mirror to reflect the message being signaled by the firelight.

This is an example of Anasazi petroglyphs, or rock art.

What Was the Chaco Canyon Settlement?

There may have been more than 100,000 people living in the Chaco Canyon Anasazi settlement. It became a major center for trade, crafts, and religious ceremonies. There is evidence that it was also a place to carefully study the stars and planets. It was a place of wealth and power. Eventually, around A.D. 1150, the "Golden Age" ended. The people left the area for unknown reasons. Maybe there was not enough rain. There may have been too many people and not enough resources. Leaders may have lost their ability to lead such a complex community.

Word Bank
Anasazi
Chaco Canyon
Hohokam
Mogollon
Snaketown

Lesson 2 Review On a sheet of paper, use the words from the Word Bank to complete each sentence correctly.

1. The _____ built canals to bring water to their land.

2. The _____ were known as "master builders" because of their buildings and roads.

3. The _____ were known for their beautiful pottery.

4. The _____ settlement ruled the canals of smaller villages.

5. The _____ planned settlement became a major center for trade.

What do you think ?

Why do you think the Chaco Canyon settlement disappeared?

History in Your Life

Visiting Anasazi Treasures

Explorers of the 2000s are lucky to be able to visit places built by the Anasazis.

Archaeologists have found the ruins of numerous Anasazi creations. Most of these can be found in the Four Corners area, where Colorado, Utah, Arizona, and New Mexico meet.

Mesa Verde National Park and the nearby Ute Mountain Tribal Park are located in southwestern Colorado. Both parks feature Anasazi cliff dwellings and rock art. Mesa Verde Park features Cliff Palace, the largest known cliff home. Other attractions include mesa-top pueblos and pit houses.

Reading Strategy:
Questioning

What do you think you will learn about by reading this lesson?

Objectives

◆ To describe where the Woodland Indians lived

◆ To describe Mississippian civilizations

◆ To describe a Plains Indian settlement

◆ To explain one way the Indians of the Pacific Northwest were different from other cultures

Indian cultures differ from one region to another. Anthropologists divide these cultures into four basic groups. These groups are Woodland, Mississippi River (Mississippian), Great Plains, and Pacific Northwest. Adena and Hopewell were early Woodland cultures. Mississippian Indian settlements were in what is now the Midwestern and Southeastern states in the United States. The Indians of the Great Plains lived west of the Mississippi River. Their way of life was very different from the Woodland and Mississippian Indians. On the West Coast, the Indians of the Pacific Northwest had a way of life different from all the others.

What Is Known About the Woodland Indians and the Adena Burial Mounds?

Woodland Indians lived east of the Mississippi River. They could be found on the East Coast and around the Great Lakes. They lived in forest areas near streams and lakes. The Adena and Hopewell were Woodland Indians. They were also hunter-gatherers and mound builders. In Ohio, on private property called Adena, burial mounds were discovered. The Adena burial mounds measured 300 feet wide. Inside the burial mounds were small log rooms in which the dead were buried. The burial rooms also contained tobacco and pipes. Adena pipes were beautifully made and are considered works of art. The Adena people lived in villages of less than 500 people. This culture survived from 700 B.C. to A.D. 100.

What Was the Hopewell People's Snake Mound?

The Hopewell people followed the Adena in the Ohio area. Hopewell mounds were found in the 1840s on the Hopewell farm in Ohio. The largest mound was over 30 feet high. By A.D. 100, the Hopewell people had become farmers. They planted barley, sunflowers, and squash. By concentrating on farming, they took an important step to control their food supply.

One of the most interesting creations in this area is a very large earthen Snake Mound. The jaw of the Snake Mound is 17 feet long. Its mouth is swallowing a huge egg. The Snake Mound curves over the land for more than a quarter mile. Some archaeologists believe the Snake Mound is an Indian symbol of growth and change. There is evidence that Indian cultures believed this because snakes grow and change by shedding their skin.

Reading Strategy:
Questioning

As you read, notice the details in the text. What questions can you ask yourself about these early cultures?

Where Was the Poverty Point Culture?

In the 1950s, archaeologists discovered an old aerial photograph of what looked like a 19th-century Louisiana cotton plantation. The plantation, named Poverty Point, was located in the lower Mississippi River Valley. The photograph showed the outlines of a large earthwork made by humans. It was more than 4,000 years old. This great structure is evidence of the existence of another highly developed ancient American Indian culture. This group of Mississippians was named the Poverty Point people.

The Poverty Point culture was unusual because it appeared to be made up of hunter-gatherers, not farmers. Hunter-gatherers must get their food by hunting, fishing, and gathering wild plants. They move from place to place. This way of life does not usually produce extra food for workers. It took many workers hundreds of years to create and enlarge the earthwork. It was completed around 1000 B.C. After that, the Poverty Point culture declined and eventually ended.

Where Was the City of Cahokia?

The city of Cahokia was located in the present state of Illinois. By 1200, the city of Cahokia had a population of more than 20,000 people. At the time it was the largest settlement of Mississippians in North America, covering six square miles. Cahokia was located where three rivers come together: the Missouri, Illinois, and Mississippi Rivers.

Cahokia was a planned city with many public buildings. A wooden fence called a **palisade** surrounded the city. The people of Cahokia were also mound builders. They built 120 mounds. One mound, called Monk's Mound, is the largest mound in North America. Monk's Mound was named after a French monk who found it in the early 1800s. Over the years, the population of the city declined. It is not known why this happened. It could be because the weather changed and they were unable to produce enough food. Disease may have played a part, or wars may have caused a decline. By 1500, the people of Cahokia had vanished.

Where Was the City of Moundville?

The city of Moundville was located in present-day Alabama. Second only to Cahokia, it had the largest population between 1000 and 1400. This Mississippian settlement was built on a high bluff overlooking the Black Warrior River. In the center of the settlement were 26 earthen mounds located on a large plaza. A major agricultural center, Moundville had large supplies of Indian maize, or corn. The people of Moundville were known for their artistic achievements. They made excellent pottery, copper pieces, and stonework. By 1350, Moundville began to decline. By the 1500s, it had been abandoned.

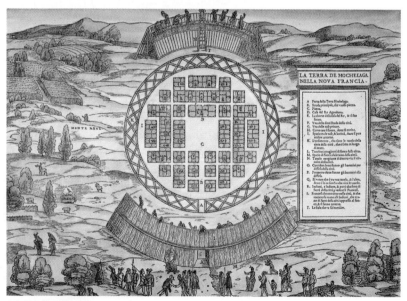

Iroquois Village

Why Were the Iroquois Important?

Between 1200 and 1400, a powerful Woodland culture in Upper New York developed. These people are believed to have descended from the Mississippian Indians. Six tribes called the Iroquois created a peace treaty called the "Great Law of Peace." They organized themselves into a democracy. Their great leaders, Hiawatha and Seneca, are still remembered today for their important speeches. When Europeans arrived, the Iroquois were the most powerful Indians in North America.

What Was the Culture of the Great Plains Indians Like?

The Great Plains is an area located between the Mississippi River and the Rocky Mountains. The Great Plains is a place of flat grasslands, rivers, streams and a few mountains. There are not many trees. Summers are hot and dry, and winters are very cold. The Plains Indian tribes living in the 1800s were the Sioux, Cheyenne, Comanche, and Blackfoot. These Indians rode horses while hunting buffalo. But their way of life was not always like this. Before the 1500s, there were no horses in the Americas. The horse arrived later, with Spanish explorers.

Indian settlements before the 1500s were mostly found on the borders of the Great Plains near rivers and streams. From about 850, settlements grew up along the Missouri River. The Mandan tribe lived along this river in present-day North Dakota. Each Mandan village contained only a few hundred people. They lived in dome-shaped buildings. This type of building was made of large logs covered with earth and straw. These Indians were farmers.

How Were the Pacific Coast Indians Different from the Plains Indians?

The abundant supply of many natural resources made the way of life of the Pacific Coast Indians different from that of the Plains Indians. The Pacific Coast Indians lived in Puget Sound in what is now Washington State. Puget Sound is a large body of water surrounded on three sides by land. It is an area rich in seafood, especially salmon. The Indians were experts at fishing. Besides an endless supply of seafood, the woods were filled with wildlife, nuts, berries, and root vegetables.

Even in winter there was enough food. In winter, they ate stored food that they had preserved by drying. The woods were filled with cedar trees. The Indians used cedar to build their shelters. These buildings were called longhouses, because they could be up to 100 feet long. They shaped cedar into shoes, clothing, rope, and mats. They carved it into tools and shaped it into bows and arrows. Even their canoes were made of cedar.

The Pacific Coast Indians showed their wealth with a custom called a potlatch. The word *potlatch* means "to throw through the air." The host of the potlatch gave the guests many gifts. The potlatch custom appears to be something only the Pacific Coast Indians did.

Who Are the Inuit?

In the Arctic in present-day Alaska and northern Canada, north of the Pacific Northwest Indians, live the people that others call Eskimo. The word *Eskimo* means "eaters of raw meat." They call themselves *Inuit,* meaning "real people." Their lives were hard. They lived in a harsh, frozen environment for most of the year. They built shelters out of blocks of snow. The shelter is called an igloo, which means "home." They hunted sea mammals and caribou for food. Their possessions were simple. They are known for their delicate carvings of ivory and soapstone.

Lesson 3 Review On a sheet of paper, write the letter of the answer that correctly completes each sentence.

1. The Adena and _____ were early Woodland cultures.

   A Hopewell   **C** Poverty Point
   B Seneca   **D** Cahokia

2. Mound builders buried _____ in the mounds along with people who had died.

   A weapons   **C** tobacco and pipes
   B extra food   **D** barley, sunflowers, and squash

3. The _____ culture was probably made up of hunter-gatherers, not farmers.

   A Hopewell   **C** Poverty Point
   B Seneca   **D** Cahokia

4. Plains Indians of the Mandan tribe lived in _____ buildings

   A low, flat   **C** square
   B dome-shaped   **D** log

5. The abundant supply of seafood, wildlife, nuts, berries, and vegetables made the lives of the _____ Indians unusual.

   A Woodland   **C** Great Plains
   B Mississippian   **D** Pacific Northwest

What do you think ?

Great leaders of this time, such as Hiawatha and Seneca, are remembered for their speeches. Who do you think will be remembered for their speeches 100 years from now?

Objectives

◆ To identify the area known as Mesoamerica

◆ To identify five cultures of Mesoamerica and South America

Reading Strategy: Questioning

Study the photographs and artwork in this lesson. Ask yourself how they relate to what you are reading.

More than 10,000 years ago, in a valley in what is now Mexico, an ancient hunter walked in the mud for 30 feet. In 2006, archaeologists discovered 13 of his footprints preserved in solid rock. Today, we call the area where he walked Mesoamerica. *Mesoamerica* means "middle America." It is the name given to the land between the continents of North and South America. It is in Mesoamerica that American Indians reached their highest level of cultural development. The Olmecs, the Mayas, the Toltecs, and the Aztecs created these advanced Mesoamerican civilizations. The Inca Empire on the continent of South America is another important example of a highly advanced civilization in the Americas.

What Were the Cultural Contributions of the Olmecs?

The Olmecs were ancient people living in the heart of Mesoamerica between 1200 B.C. and 400 B.C. During this time, the Olmecs developed the first important civilization in this area. The Olmecs created the first system of writing in America. They were good mathematicians and astronomers. They used the zero many centuries before the Greeks. They developed a calendar of 365 days and a special 260-day religious calendar. The best example of Olmec art is 10-foot-tall stone heads. The purpose of the giant stone heads is a mystery.

What Were Olmec Settlements Like?

Olmec settlements contained up to 1,000 people. They lived in a rich agricultural area and grew maize, squash, and beans. Around 900 B.C. they built a very tall earthen mound shaped like a pyramid with a flat top. Some anthropologists believe that the Olmecs were the "mother culture" of Mesoamerica. This means that the Olmecs' cultural developments laid the foundation for the achievements of the Mayas, the Toltecs, and the Aztecs.

Reading Strategy:
Questioning

What do you already
know about the
Mayas?

Why Are the Mayas Considered the Most Advanced Culture in Mesoamerica?

Maya civilization is considered the most advanced in Mesoamerica. It started around A.D. 250. The Mayas developed an excellent written language. It equaled the complex written languages of the Europeans and Chinese. The Mayas were scientists, master mathematicians, and excellent astronomers. These skills allowed them to keep track of time in the past and into the future. The Maya calendar began in 3114 B.C. It was based on 13 cycles of 400 years each. The Mayas thought that this calendar would end in 2012. After this date, a brand-new calendar cycle would begin.

Maya civilization was a complex agricultural society. The Mayas farmed an area for up to five years. Then they planted nothing there for five to 10 years, allowing the soil to recover. Their favorite drink was chocolate. Chocolate was so special it was reserved for political and religious leaders.

A large, stone temple stood in the center of each Maya city. This photo shows the temple and surrounding areas of the Maya city of Chichén Itzá in Yucatán, Mexico.

The Mayas were skilled engineers. They cleared jungles and built large cities throughout the area. These cities contained impressive buildings and boulevards. The Mayas were also known for their beautiful artwork, especially their colorful murals. Ancient artists in other cultures were not identified. However, Maya artists added their names to their art work. Today, the descendants of the Mayas still live in the land of their ancestors.

What Kind of Political System Did the Mayas Have?

A king ruled the Mayas. A central council headed by the king ruled on very important matters. There was a court system with local judges. Taxes were paid to tax collectors. To keep expanding their teritory, the Mayas had a well-organized army. The army conquered other people who were then brought into the Maya civilization.

How Was the Toltec Civilization Different from the Olmecs and Mayas?

Around A.D. 900, the Toltecs moved into the Valley of Mexico. There they found a city called Tula. The city of Tula became the center of a great Toltec Empire. The Toltec culture was different from the Olmecs and the Mayas. Political and religious leaders were most important in those cultures. But in the Toltec culture, a special class of warriors gained power. Warriors of the Jaguar, the Coyote, and the Eagle were names for organized military units. For 200 years, the Toltecs' military might made them the strongest culture in Mesoamerica. By A.D. 1200, a less advanced invader destroyed the Toltec Empire. Eventually the city of Tula was destroyed. However, for another 200 years, Toltec influence could be seen throughout the area. The ideas and achievements of the Toltecs heavily influenced the Aztec civilization.

What Caused the Aztecs to Settle on an Island in Mexico?

Around A.D. 1200, the Aztecs began moving into the Valley of Mexico. Their culture was a simple one. They were not a powerful people. In fact, other groups looked down upon them. At this time, the Aztecs had no written records. But they told a story of how, around A.D. 1300, a god spoke to their leader. The god told their leader, Tenoch, to take his people to an island in Lake Texcoco. On the island he should look for an eagle eating a snake. The eagle would be sitting on a cactus growing from a rock. It was on that spot that Tenoch was told to build a great city. They named the city *Tenochtitlán,* or "the city of Tenoch." The island was not a good building site. Large buildings gradually sank into the wet land. The Aztecs kept building new buildings on top of those that sank below ground. Eventually, the wet land was filled in. Tenochtitlán became a magnificent city. To connect the island to the mainland, the Aztecs built raised stone roads.

How Did the Aztecs Become an Empire?

In 1376, they selected their first emperor. Their leader's ancestors were the Toltecs. The Aztecs sought to recreate the influential Toltec civilization. Like the Toltecs, the Aztecs began

to conquer other groups by military force. They forced these conquered people to pay part of their food or other valuables to them. By the early 1500s, the Aztecs had built a large empire and had become a harsh military power.

This is a sun stone or a calendar from the temple at Tenochtitlán, the Aztec capital city.

Reading Strategy:
Questioning

What details are
important to
understanding the
Incas' problems?

Who Were the Incas?

The empire of the Inca was located in the valleys of the Andes
Mountains in South America. Their capital city of Cuzco
was built high in the mountains of what is now Peru. Around
A.D. 1100, the Incas began conquering tribes from the
surrounding lands. By 1453, the Inca Empire covered a large
area containing more than six million people. The Inca Empire
included parts of five modern nations: Ecuador, Peru, Chile,
Argentina, and Bolivia. It was the largest empire in North and
South America.

The Inca Empire faced more difficult problems than the
empires in Mesoamerica. One of the problems was how to
govern such a large area with so many different kinds of people.
First, the Incas divided the empire into four geographic areas.
They call their empire the "Land of the Four Quarters." *Inca*
was the name they gave their emperor. Second, once a tribe
was conquered by military force, they asked the tribal leaders
to become partners in the empire. The Incas set up rules that
the tribal leaders had to follow. In this way, local leaders could
make many decisions for their own tribes but still remain loyal
to the Inca Empire.

Biography

Pachacutec Inca Yupanqui: died 1471

The year of Pachacutec's birth is not known.
His name means "he who changes the world."
He became emperor of the Inca people in
1438. Pachacutec proved himself to be a brave
warrior and a good ruler. He also served as the
religious leader of his empire. During his rule,
Inca territory expanded, and the Incas built
a system of roads. He developed an effective
government and economy. Pachacutec was responsible for many
building projects. It is thought that he built Machu Picchu as
a place to go to relax. Machu Picchu, also known as the "Lost
City," is high in the Andes Mountains. Many historians consider
Pachacutec to be one of the greatest rulers of all time.

Why Were Roads So Important to the Incas?

The empire covered about 2,500 miles from the northern to the southern end. Cuzco was the capital city. From Cuzco, the Inca emperor needed to communicate with the rest of the empire. The Incas were skilled engineers. They built more than 14,000 miles of roads. The network of roads connected the coastal areas and the valleys. In the mountains, roads rose to heights of 5,000 feet. Using the network of roads, the Incas created a fast communication system by using relay runners along the roads. There were rest areas that contained food and water.

Machu Picchu, in Peru, is an important archaeological site.

How About a Game of Basketball?

In the center of Maya cities near the temples and palaces, you might have found a large court. Its shape was like today's basketball court. Tall stone walls stood on the two long sides of the court.

High in the middle of each wall was a stone ring, or hoop. Often, it was 30 feet above the ground! The Mayas put the hoop straight up and down instead of parallel to the ground. The Mayas used the court to play a game with a ball made of solid rubber. The ball weighed about five pounds. Players were not allowed to use their hands or feet to get the ball through the hoop. They passed the ball back and forth with their hips, knees, and forearms.

Some people believe that for the Mayas, the game represented the battle between life and death. The rubber ball may have been a symbol of the sun. What do you think the game of basketball represents today?

Lesson 4 Review On a sheet of paper, write the answer to each question. Use complete sentences.

1. What is Mesoamerica?

2. What was the culture of the Mayas like?

3. Why do some anthropologists think that the Olmecs may be the "mother culture" of Mesoamerica?

4. Why did the Aztecs build their city on an island in a lake in Mexico?

5. Why did the Incas build so many miles of roads?

What do you think ?

What is the most important thing you have learned by studying these ancient Mesoamerican cultures?

Knighthood for the Incas

In the Inca empire, it was a great honor for a boy to become a knight. He had to be over 16 years old to take part in this test. His whole family shared his honor—or his disgrace, if he failed. Here is an account of the difficult test faced by one group.

The candidates were required to observe a very strict fast for six days, receiving only a handful of raw sara (their corn) apiece and a jug of plain water, without anything else. . . .

Such a rigorous fast was not usually permitted for more than three days, but this period was doubled for the initiates undergoing their ordeal, in order to show if they were men enough to suffer any hunger or thirst to which they might be exposed in time of war. The fathers, brothers, and other close relatives of the candidates underwent a less rigorous, but none the less strictly observed, fast, praying their father the Sun to strengthen and encourage the youths so that they might come through the ordeal with honor. Anyone who showed weakness or distress or asked for more food was failed and eliminated from the test. After the fast they were allowed some victuals

[food] to restore their strength and then tried for bodily agility. As a test they were made to run from the hill called Huanacauri, which they regarded as sacred, to the fortress of the city . . . at the fortress a pennant or banner was set up as a finishing post, and whoever reached it first was elected captain over the rest. Those who arrived second, third, fourth, and down to the tenth fastest were also held in great honor, while those who flagged or fainted on the course were disgraced and eliminated. . . .

The next day they were divided into two equal bands . . . and they were required to fight one against the other . . . so that they could all display their agility and skill . . . In such struggles the weapons were blunted so that they were less formidable than in real warfare; nevertheless there were severe casualties which were sometimes fatal. . . .

Document-Based Questions

1. How do you know that this event is important in the lives of young men in Peru?

2. Why do you think that family members of the candidates also fasted?

3. Why is showing hunger or thirst considered a sign of weakness?

4. Do you think that this custom is a fair test of a man's strength? Explain.

5. From the last sentence, how do you know that this custom could be very dangerous?

Source: Royal Commentaries of the Incas and General History of Peru, by Garcilaso de la Vega, El Inca.

The Lady of the Lines

Before the Great Incan Empire existed, the Nascan people lived near Peru's southern coast from 200 B.C. to A.D. 650. Today, because of the work of Maria Reiche, we now know that the Nascans created mysterious, gigantic drawings in one of the world's driest deserts. Nasca means a "hard place to live." Each of the more than 70 drawings was created by a single line. The drawings are known as the Nasca Lines of Peru.

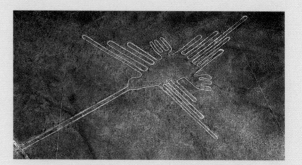

Maria Reiche was born in Germany in 1903. In 1940, although a mathematician, she became an assistant to an archaeologist studying the Nasca Lines. Most of the drawings are of animals or geometric designs. They are so large that they can be seen only from an aircraft. What one can see on the ground are straight paths with dark rocks lining the sides.

Maria made the study of the Nasca Lines her life's work. The work was physically difficult. The wind continually covered the lines with pebbles. She had to sweep the pebbles away. The people in the area called her the "crazy woman sweeping the desert." Maria said, "What compelled me on this quest was my curiosity."

Maria Reiche especially wanted to know how and why the drawings were made. She thought that the Nascans created the drawings by first drawing crisscrossed parallel lines, called a grid, on cloth. They then drew a picture on the grid to use as a model. Next, they drew a larger grid on the desert floor. They then copied the smaller cloth drawing onto the larger desert grid. By doing this they were able to create enormous drawings.

Maria noticed that at different times of the year many of the lines directly pointed to the rising and setting of the sun and the moon. She thought the Nascans used the drawings to determine when to plant seeds to assure a good harvest. The drawings, she thought, were a sky calendar.

Maria Reiche, the Lady of the Lines, died at age 95. She said that the Nasca Lines "should be treated like a very fragile manuscript that is guarded in a special room in a library." Because of her work, in 1995 the United Nations declared that the location of the Nasca Lines was a World Heritage Site.

Wrap-Up

1. Why did Maria Reiche want to study the Nasca Lines?

2. What did the people in the area think of her?

3. How could her background as a mathematician help Reiche in her study of the Nasca Lines?

4. Why don't we know exactly why the ancient society in Peru created the Nasca Lines?

5. Why is it important to preserve historical sites like this one?

Chapter 9   S U M M A R Y

- The first Americans arrived during the last Ice Age. They walked from Asia over the Bering Strait. Clues about how and when this happened are still being discovered.

- Bones found in Folsom, New Mexico, proved that American Indians had been living in the area for at least 9,000 years.

- The Clovis Point was more than 4,000 years older than the Folsom Point. Scientists believe that the Clovis people were the first Americans.

- The Hohokam civilization began about 300 B.C. in what is now Arizona. They built irrigation canals and created beautiful pottery and jewelry.

- Beginning about 200 B.C., the Mogollon lived in what is now southeastern Arizona and southern New Mexico. They created more artistic images than any other people in the world.

- The Anasazi are known as master builders. Their civilization began in about 100 A.D. They lived where Arizona, New Mexico, Utah, and Colorado meet.

- The Adena (beginning about 700 B.C.) and Hopewell (beginning about A.D. 100) were early Woodland cultures. They were both mound builders.

- Beginning around A.D. 1200, the Iroquois, a group of six different tribes, were a powerful Woodland culture in Upper New York.

- The Plains Indians lived between the Mississippi River and the Rocky Mountains. They were Sioux, Cheyenne, Comanche, and Blackfoot Indians. The Mandans lived in what is now North Dakota.

- The Pacific Coast Indians lived in what is now Washington State. They were experts at fishing.

- Eskimos, or Inuits, lived a hard life in a frozen environment. They are known for their ivory and soapstone carvings.

- Mesoamerica is the land between North and South America. The Olmecs developed the first important civilization in this area around 1200 B.C.

- The Mayas developed an excellent written language. Their most important cultural and artistic achievements took place between A.D. 300 and 900.

- Around A.D. 900, the Toltecs moved into the Valley of Mexico. In this culture, warriors gained power.

- The Aztecs moved into the Valley of Mexico around A.D. 1200. In 1521, the Aztec Empire ended.

- The Inca Empire was in the Andes Mountains in South America. The empire lasted about 100 years, ending in 1532.

Chapter 9   R E V I E W

Word Bank

Anasazi

Aztec

Clovis

Hohokam

Incas

Inuit

Mayas

Mogollons

Olmecs

Toltecs

On a sheet of paper, use the words from the Word Bank to complete each sentence correctly.

1. Scientists think the _____ people were among the first Americans.

2. The _____ are known for their rock art—images of insects, fish, reptiles, birds, and mammals.

3. The _____ built cliff dwellings in the rock near where Arizona, New Mexico, Utah, and Colorado meet.

4. Because they lived in the desert, the _____ had to build irrigation canals to water their crops.

5. The _____ created the first system of writing in the Americas.

6. The _____ are known for their calendar, which was based on 400-year cycles.

7. By the early 1500s, the _____ people had become a harsh military power.

8. The _____ built more than 14,000 miles of roads to connect people in their large empire.

9. _____ civilization was different from others because of the importance of their military.

10. The _____, or Eskimo, people built shelters out of blocks of snow.

On a sheet of paper, write the letter of the answer that correctly completes each sentence.

11. The settlement of _____ was an important place for the Hohokam.

    A Clovis   **B** Folsom   **C** Snaketown   **D** Cahokia

12. Archaeologists named the _____ after the mountain ranges in which they lived.

    A Hohokam   **B** Mogollan   **C** Anasazi   **D** Adena

13. The _____ people created a very large earthen Snake Mound.

    A Hohokam **B** Mogollan **C** Iroquois   **D** Hopewell

14. The _____ culture was unusual because even though they were not farmers, they had the resources to build large earthen structures.

    A Anasazi   **B** Adena   **C** Poverty Point **D** Cahokia

15. The _____ tribes lived in Puget Sound, a large body of water surrounded on three sides by land.

    A Pacific Coast   **C** Inuit
    B Plains Indian   **D** Iroquois

On a sheet of paper, write the answer to each question. Use complete sentences.

16. Choose one of the cultures you have just studied. How did the environment determine what kinds of shelters they built and how they farmed?

17. How did George McJunkin know that the bones he discovered in 1908 were an important scientific discovery?

18. Besides water for their crops, how did the Hohokam use the water from their canals?

Critical Thinking On a sheet of paper, write your response to each question. Use complete sentences.

19. After the Incas conquered a tribe by military force, they asked the tribal leaders to become partners in their empire. How did this make the Incan Empire stronger?

20. Why do you think archaeologists have found so few artifacts from the earliest Americans?

Test-Taking Tip

Try to answer all questions as completely as possible. When asked to explain your answer, do so in complete sentences.

Unit 1

Skill Builder

Timelines

Timelines show dates and events on a line, or scale. They may span thousands of years or only a few months. A timeline may show key events in a region. It may list events in one person's lifetime. It may show events of a certain kind, such as scientific discoveries. In reading a timeline, always look at the beginning and ending dates.

Timelines show the time relationships between events. They help you think about events in the order they occurred. You see when an event happened. Then you can see what happened before and after it.

Each chapter in this book begins with a timeline. Those timelines will help you focus on key events and ideas in the chapter. As you read a chapter, create your own timeline of events. That will help you study those events.

This timeline gives the dates of some important events in the first half of the 20th century. Study it. Then answer the questions.

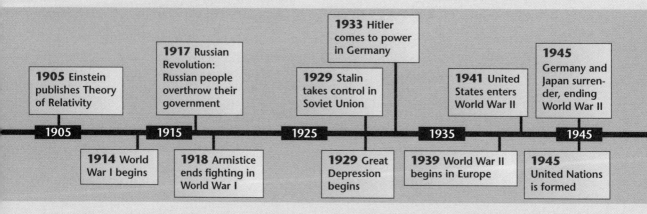

1905 Einstein publishes Theory of Relativity

1917 Russian Revolution: Russian people overthrow their government

1933 Hitler comes to power in Germany

1929 Stalin takes control in Soviet Union

1941 United States enters World War II

1945 Germany and Japan surrender, ending World War II

1905 — 1915 — 1925 — 1935 — 1945

1914 World War I begins

1918 Armistice ends fighting in World War I

1929 Great Depression begins

1939 World War II begins in Europe

1945 United Nations is formed

1. What are the beginning and ending dates on this timeline?

2. Did Einstein publish the Theory of Relativity before or after World War I?

3. In what year did World War I begin?

4. What event on this timeline happened during World War I?

5. What two events on this timeline happened in 1929?

6. Who came to power first—Hitler or Stalin?

7. How many years after Hitler came to power did World War II begin?

8. How long did World War II go on before the United States entered the war?

9. When was the United Nations formed?

10. Create a timeline showing key events in your life during the last school year.

- The discovery of fire and the beginning of farming were among the most important events in human history.

- The time before humans left written records is called prehistory.

- Civilizations began in Mesopotamia about 7,000 years ago.

- Sumerians invented a system of writing called cuneiform.

- The Assyrians were a warrior tribe in Mesopotamia.

- The teachings of Zoroaster influenced Judaism and Christianity.

- Egyptian civilizations developed in the valley of the Nile River in Africa.

- Pharaohs in Egypt built pyramids for tombs. People filled them with things the ruler would need in the afterlife.

- The first Indian civilization began in the Indus River Valley.

- Hinduism is based on castes, or classes. Everyone is born into a caste.

- Siddhartha Gautama became the Buddha. Buddhism spread from India into Asia.

- The Yangtze is the longest river in China; the first cities were built along this river about 2000 B.C.

- Socrates, Plato, and Aristotle were Greek philosophers during the "Golden Age" of Athens.

- In 60 B.C., Pompey, Julius Caesar, and Crassus ruled together as the First Triumvirate.

- Jesus was born in Palestine during the reign of Augustus. Followers of Jesus believed he was the Son of God.

- The Roman Empire fell in A.D. 476.

- Mesoamerica is the land between North and South America.

- The Olmecs developed the first system of writing in the Americas. They were mathematicians and astronomers.

- The Mayas are considered the most advanced culture in Mesoamerica. They influenced other great civilizations of Mesoamerica.

- The Aztecs moved into the Valley of Mexico about A.D. 900. Their capitol was the magnificent city of Tenochtitlán.

- The Incan Empire grew up in the Peruvian Andes Mountains. It ended in A.D. 1532.

"It is impossible for one person, however intelligent and capable, to be able to make wise decisions by himself. Acting alone, he may be able, if he is fortunate, to make five right decisions out of ten each day. . . . Instead he should delegate authority to the most able and virtuous men he can find and supervise their work from above most diligently."

~Taizong, emperor of China (A.D. 626–649), from "On the Art of Government"

Unit 2

Regional Civilizations

By A.D. 500, the Roman Empire had fallen apart. Historians call the 1,000 years following the fall of Rome the Middle Ages. These years are in the middle between the fall of Rome and the rebirth of learning in Europe in the 1500s.

In this unit you will learn about the lives of serfs, peasants, and knights. You will visit a castle of the Middle Ages, learn about Gothic architecture, and go on the Crusades. You will meet Muhammad and journey to Ghana and Mali. Then you will sail back to India to meet Buddha, follow Genghis Khan into China, and travel into Japan.

Chapters in Unit 2

The High and Late Middle Ages

After the Roman Empire fell, the Germanic tribes made war on one another for many years. During this time, the monks and nuns of the Roman Catholic Church tried to keep learning alive. Some members of the church also tried to take control of the Holy Land. In this chapter, you will join the Crusades and travel to Palestine. Then you will return to your castle and the manor and learn about the life of a serf, a peasant, a page, a squire, a knight, a vassal, and a lord. While doing this, you will learn about feudalism.

Goals for Learning

◆ To explain the role of the Roman Catholic Church in the Middle Ages in Europe and recognize the causes and effects of the Crusades

◆ To describe European feudalism

◆ To describe life on a manor

◆ To describe improvements in culture during the Middle Ages

1066 Normans conquer England

1154 Henry II begins to rule in England

1291 Muslims conquer the last Christian city in the Holy Land; Crusades to Holy Land end

1000   1250   1500

1095 Pope Urban II calls for the First Crusade

1348 Plague breaks out in Europe

The Crusades

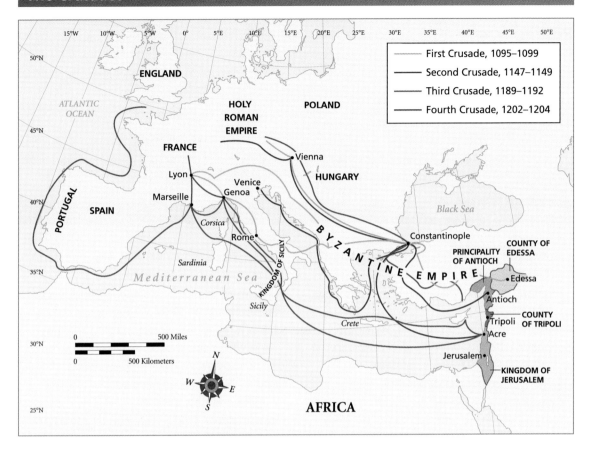

Map Skills

In A.D. 1095, the Europeans of the western world began a series of military journeys called the Crusades. They traveled to Palestine, which they called the Holy Land because Jesus had lived there. But by 1095, people of the Muslim faith lived in Palestine. The Europeans thought that God wanted them to rescue the Holy Land from the Muslims. For almost 200 years, European Christians went on the Crusades to win back Palestine.

Trace the routes these Christian warriors took, then answer the following questions:

1. From what countries did the four biggest Crusades begin?

2. On which crusade did Europeans go by land from Constantinople to Jerusalem?

3. Which crusade went to the Holy Land by a water route only?

4. In which crusade did the English take part?

5. Why do you think that each of these four Crusades took so long?

Reading Strategy:
Predicting

As you read a text, you can make predictions about what will happen next. It helps to preview the text and think about what you already know about the topic. As you make predictions, keep these things in mind.

◆ Make your best guess about what happens next.

◆ Use what you know to predict what will be next.

◆ Check your predictions. As you learn more information, you may find you need to change your predictions.

Key Vocabulary Words

Lesson 1

Holy Land Palestine; the area where Jesus of Nazareth lived

Pilgrim A person who travels to visit a holy place

Muslim A follower of Islam, the religion that Muhammad founded in Arabia in the seventh century

Schism A permanent separation

Crusade Any of the military journeys taken by Christians to win the Holy Land from the Muslims

Lesson 2

Feudalism A political and military system based on the holding of land

Lord A king or a noble who gave land to someone else

Vassal A person who received land from a king or noble

Fief The land and peasants who farmed it, which a lord gave to a vassal

Page A young noble who learned certain behaviors to become a knight

Squire A 15-year-old page who learned how to ride a horse and use weapons to become a knight

Knighted To be made a knight

Lesson 3

Manor The part of a fief that peasants farm to support the lord's family

Blacksmith A person who works with iron and makes tools and weapons

Serf A peasant who was bound to the land and whose life was controlled by the lord of the manor

Moat A dug-out area filled with water that circles a castle

Drawbridge A bridge that can be raised or lowered over a moat

Courtyard A large open area inside the castle walls

Joust A contest between two knights carrying lances and riding horses

Lesson 4

Bishop A priest who is in charge of other priests and a number of churches

Romanesque A style of building that was like what the Romans built with thick walls and arches

Gothic A style of architecture with thin walls, pointed arches, many windows, and flying buttresses

Parliament The English council or lawmaking assembly

Objectives

◆ To identify the Benedictines

◆ To explain why Christian pilgrims traveled to Palestine

◆ To describe those who joined the Crusades

The Roman Empire fell apart in A.D. 476. Soon Europe broke up into hundreds of small governments. But the Church remained strong. Its officials did things that the Roman government had done before. For example, the church set up courts and collected taxes.

By the year 1050, Western Europe had settled down. For years, Germanic tribes had fought wars. Now farming and trade expanded again. We call the years from 1050 to about 1500 the late Middle Ages. The word *medieval* refers to this period between ancient and modern times.

What Did Religious Groups Do?

Some Christian men left the world behind and became monks. Some Christian women also gave up material things and became nuns. Both monks and nuns joined together in religious groups to serve God.

The monks lived and worked in monasteries; the nuns lived in convents. In the early sixth century, a monk named Benedict wrote a rule for monks and nuns. They promised never to marry, never to own property, and never to disobey the head of the monastery or convent.

The Benedictines spent their lives praying and working. Some took care of the sick and the homeless. Some learned new things about farming and taught the farmers who lived nearby. Some welcomed travelers. (They had no place else to stay because there were no hotels at this time.) Religious groups also supplied teachers to the new towns that were springing up.

Mont St. Michel is a famous old monastery in Normandy, France.

How Did the Church Keep Learning Alive?

Monks and nuns copied books from the past by hand. No one in Europe had invented a machine to copy words. They decorated these books with bright colors and pictures. Over time, the largest monasteries and convents became centers of learning. They kept alive the learning from ancient Greek and Rome.

Where Did Christian Pilgrims Go?

Reading Strategy:
Predicting

Read the title of the next section. What do you think the people of the church did to advance learning?

Holy Land

Palestine; the area where Jesus of Nazareth lived

Pilgrim

A person who travels to visit a holy place

Muslim

A follower of the religion that Muhammad founded in Arabia in the 7th century

During the Middle Ages, Christians called Palestine the **Holy Land** because Jesus of Nazareth had lived there. Many Christians traveled there to see places that Jesus had visited. We call such a trip a pilgrimage. People who go on a pilgrimage are **pilgrims.**

In the 7th century, **Muslims** conquered Palestine. (The Muslims were members of a religion founded by a man named Muhammad.) For nearly 400 years, the Muslims let Christian pilgrims visit the Holy Land. Then another group of Muslims took control of Palestine. According to some reports, this group killed Christians and destroyed churches.

What Caused the Leadership Crisis in the Christian Churches?

Reading Strategy:
Predicting

Think about your prediction. What details can you now add to make your prediction more specific?

At about the same time, the Christian church faced a leadership crisis. For many centuries the Christian church had been divided into the Western and Eastern Churches. In the West, in the city of Rome, the pope was the leader of the Roman Catholic Church. There was a different leader in the East, nearly 900 miles away, in the city of Constantinople. Here, the patriarch was the leader of the Greek Orthodox Church. The two churches developed different beliefs and practices. Latin, not Greek, was the language of the Roman Catholic Church. Unlike the Roman Catholic Church, the Greek Orthodox Church allowed priests to marry. (*Orthodox* refers to religious groups who follow well-known customs and traditions.)

Schism

A permanent separation

Crusade

Any of the military journeys taken by Christians to win the Holy Land from the Muslims

There were differences in the celebration of holy days. The pope asserted that he alone was leader of all Christians. In 1054, religious differences led to a **schism,** or permanent separation, between the Greek Orthodox and the Roman Catholic Church. This is known as the Great Schism of 1054.

What Were the Crusades?

In 1095, Pope Urban II, the head of the Roman Catholic Church, called for a **crusade,** or war, against the Muslims. He wanted to free Palestine from their control. The pope promised heaven to those who died on the crusade. Historians believe that about 5,000 men on horseback, and 25,000 foot soldiers, fought in this First Crusade. A large number of common people also joined the crusade. We call all these people crusaders.

Why Did People Volunteer for the Crusades?

Many people became crusaders. Some felt that they were following God's orders. Others wanted adventure. Still others wanted to escape hard work at home. Kings and nobles joined the Crusades to get more power. The pope encouraged them to do this by forgiving their debts and by letting them pay fewer taxes.

For almost 200 years—from 1096 to 1291—European crusaders went to the Holy Land. They fought four big Crusades and many small ones. But they did not get control of the Holy Land. In 1291, the Muslims conquered Acre, the last Christian city. After that, the Muslims controlled Palestine until modern times.

What Were the Results of the Crusades?

The Crusades did not win control of the Holy Land for Christians. However, the pope and European kings ended up with more power. Also, because Europe began to trade with the Middle East, Europeans could buy things like sugar, lemons, and spices. The crusaders also learned about Arab art, architecture, medicine, and mathematics. The Crusades brought other changes too. During the Crusades, Europeans traveled to Palestine, which was far away from their homeland. When they returned home, their small villages in Europe seemed less interesting. They wanted to see more faraway lands. Many people began to explore Africa, Asia, and America.

Many bad things happened during the Crusades, too. Christians began to kill Jews simply because they were not Christians. During the 200 years of the Crusades, Muslims killed thousands of Christians, and Christians killed thousands of Muslims. In fact, some European Christians killed eastern Christians simply because they dressed like the Muslims. Before the Crusades, most Muslims had accepted Christians. After all the killing and violence, they thought Christians were uncivilized. They viewed the Christians as enemies.

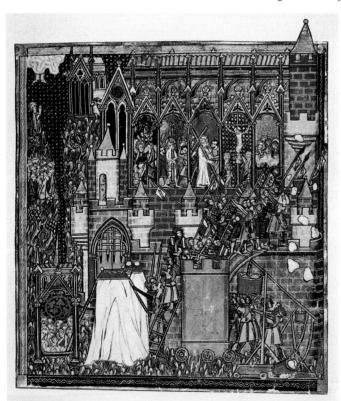

This painting shows crusaders storming Jerusalem during the Crusades.

Biography

Saladin: 1138–1193

Saladin was a Muslim leader. He became the ruler of Egypt and Syria. Saladin built schools and mosques there. He was so brave and honorable that even crusaders admired him.

For years, the crusaders held Palestine. Saladin wanted those Muslim lands back. He united Muslims against the crusaders. His forces captured Jerusalem in 1187. Then they took back most of Palestine.

As a result, the Third Crusade began. It ended Saladin's two-year siege of the crusaders at Acre. But they never won back Jerusalem. Finally, Saladin and crusade leader Richard the Lion-hearted met. Their truce let Christian pilgrims visit Jerusalem.

Lesson 1 Review On a sheet of paper, write the answer to each question. Use complete sentences.

1. According to Benedict, how were monks and nuns supposed to live?

2. Why did monks and nuns copy books?

3. What was the Holy Land?

4. Why did Pope Urban II start the First Crusade?

5. Describe one good and one bad outcome of the Crusades.

What do you think ?

Were the Crusades good or bad for the people of Europe and the Middle East? Explain your answer.

Feudalism

A political and military system based on holding land

Lord

A king or a noble who gave land to someone

Vassal

A noble who received land from a king or noble

Fief

The land and peasants to farm it

Page

A young noble who learned to become a knight

Squire

A 15-year-old page who learned to ride a horse and use weapons to become a knight

The Roman Empire had laws to govern people and armies to protect them. But during the Middle Ages, there was no one power in Europe. A new political and military system arose. We call this system **feudalism.** It was based on the holding of land.

How Did Feudalism Work?

Under the feudal system, the king owned all the land. But he needed loyal nobles to serve him. How could he win their loyalty? He could give them land. The nobles could then give land to other people and ask for their loyalty.

What Were the Titles of the Nobles?

We call the powerful kings and nobles who gave land **lords.** We call the nobles who received land **vassals.** When lords gave land, they did so in a special ceremony. The vassal knelt down before the lord and promised loyalty. He would serve the lord and help him in battle.

In return, the lord gave the vassal a **fief,** or piece of land, and peasants to farm it. To protect his fief, each vassal needed his own soldiers. He had much land, but little money. He offered land to men who agreed to be his vassals. The lords and vassals kept dividing the land into smaller and smaller pieces.

How Many Years Did Someone Train to Become a Knight?

The Middle Ages was a time of thousands of small wars. Knights, or soldiers who fought for a lord, did most of the fighting. Only the son of a noble could become a knight. A young noble started training to be a knight by first becoming a **page.** He learned religion, manners, obedience, and loyalty. When he was about 15 years old, the page became a **squire.** Then he learned to ride a horse and use weapons. At age 21, most squires became knights.

During the Middle Ages, knights fought each other for sport on horseback.

Armor of the Middle Ages

During the Middle Ages, knights, lords, and even kings rode to their many battles in armor. Armor changed as weapons and ways of fighting changed.

In 1066, when William the Conqueror invaded England, his knights wore simple cone-shaped helmets and suits of mail. To make this mail, an iron worker heated and then hammered out a small iron bar. When it was long and thin, he wound it around another rod. Next, he cut rings from the thinned iron. Finally, he linked them together so that they overlapped, or partly covered, one another. He spent many months making a complete mail suit. It looked like a mesh suit of iron.

The knights wore padded coats underneath the mail. Because the sun makes metal hot, the knights often wore a loose-fitting cloth coat over their mail suit.

By the 1200s, knights wore a helmet that covered their face. As time passed, they began to protect their whole body with armor. A breast plate protected their chest. Other pieces of armor protected their shoulders, hands, and legs. The knight wore spurs on his armored heels. He used these spiked wheels to make his horse obey.

On his clothes, each knight painted his coat of arms. This was a design in the shape of a shield. Each man wore a different coat of arms. It showed everyone who he was. Some coats of arms were simple. Others contained trees, birds, and animals.

Reading Strategy:
Predicting

Based on what you just read about the training of a knight, what do you predict will be expected of him?

Knighted

To be made a knight

Word Bank

feudalism

fief

knight

lord

peasant

What Did Lords Expect from Their Knights?

A lord **knighted** a squire, or made him a knight, in a special ceremony. The lord commanded the new knight to be brave, polite, and loyal. The knight promised to defend the church, be loyal to the lord, protect the weak, and be polite to women.

Each knight had to be strong. He wore heavy armor and carried a lance, or steel-tipped spear; a two-edged sword; a dagger, or sharp-pointed knife; and a broad ax called a battle ax. His armor and weapons could weigh as much as 100 pounds.

Every knight hoped to become a lord and have a great amount of land to give to vassals some day. However, many knights never became lords. They spent their entire lives fighting one war after another.

Lesson 2 Review On a sheet of paper, use the words from the Word Bank to complete each sentence correctly.

1. The _____ of the Middle Ages was a political and military system based on the holding of land.

2. A _____ gave land to a vassal and asked for his loyalty.

3. A _____ is the name of the land the vassal received.

4. A _____, or poor farmer, worked the land.

5. A _____ was a soldier who was loyal to a noble and fought for him.

What do you think ?

What would be one good thing and one bad thing about being a knight?

Objectives

◆ To explain changes in farming

◆ To explain why nobles built castles and what life was like in them

Manor

The part of a fief that peasants farm to support the lord's family

Blacksmith

A person who works with iron and makes tools and weapons

Serf

A peasant who was bound to the land and whose life was controlled by the lord of the manor

The whole feudal system was based on the control of land. A **manor** was that part of the fief that peasants farmed to support a lord's family.

What Made the Manor Self-Sufficient?

A manor was self-sufficient because the people who lived on it grew, raised, or made nearly everything that they needed without help. They made clothing from the wool of the sheep they raised. They cut wood for building from the manor's forests. They grew or raised all the food they ate. The **blacksmith** worked with iron to make tools and weapons. The lord of the manor bought only a few things—like salt and iron—from the outside world.

Who Were Serfs?

About 90 percent of the people who lived during the Middle Ages were peasants. A few peasants were free, but most were **serfs.** They had to stay on the manor on which they had been born. A serf's life was controlled by the lord of the manor.

Serfs worked on the manor farms from early in the morning until late at night. They did the farmwork, cut wood, and built fences. Women serfs worked in the fields, cooked, made clothing, and cared for the house. About 60 percent of what each serf raised went to the lord of the manor and to the church.

Women of the Middle Ages spent much of their time spinning wool and weaving cloth.

Moat

A dug-out area filled with water that circles a castle

Drawbridge

A bridge that can be raised or lowered over a moat

Reading Strategy:
Predicting

How do you think these improvements in farming affected the farmers in the Middle Ages?

What Improved Farming?

During the Middle Ages, farming changed because of five inventions: the three-field system, the horseshoe, a better plow, the waterwheel, and the windmill.

Under the three-field system, a lord left one-third of his fields unplanted each year. This allowed the soil to rest. Then the field produced more food when the serfs planted it a year later. Up to this time, people had used the slow-moving ox to do heavy work. With horseshoes, they could plow with the faster-moving horse.

With a better plow, a tool used to dig up soil before planting seeds, serfs could farm the heavy soil of northern Europe. The newly invented waterwheel used the power of running water to make more power. With this new power, serfs could grind grain, like wheat, into flour. Windmills, invented in Holland around 1170, used wind power for the same purpose.

How Did Better Farming Change the Population?

Because of these new inventions, farmers began to grow their crops in better ways. This meant that they produced more food. More food meant that the population grew. In 300 years—from 1000 to 1300—the number of people living in Western Europe got three times as big. Because they had more food than they needed, some people had time to do other things. This led to a rebirth of learning.

Why Did Nobles Build Castles?

Many nobles lived in huge stone castles to protect themselves from their enemies. Most castles had high walls. A **moat,** or dug-out area filled with water, made a circle around the castle. To enter the castle, visitors crossed the moat by using a **drawbridge.** The people inside the castle lowered and raised it over the moat.

The nobles often built their castles on hilltops or by river bends. This made the castle easier to protect and defend. Some castles were big enough to include the noble's house and his household—all the people who lived and worked inside the castle. The fields and the homes of the serfs were outside the castle walls. In times of war, they moved inside the walls for protection.

Inside the castle walls was a large open area called a **courtyard.** In good weather, the lord held his court there. The courtyard also contained many small buildings and sheds: the blacksmith's workshop; the bakery; the kitchen; the stable for the knight's horses; and rooms to store weapons and extra food. An attack against the castle could last many months. The lord of the manor had to store plenty of weapons and food.

Castles were designed for protection. This castle is from 15th century France.

What Was Life Like in a Castle?

Castles were dark, damp, and cold. Their tiny windows let in little light. Straw covered the floor of the dining area. The straw was usually dirty because the lord and his household threw garbage on the floor for the dogs to eat! The serfs cooked the food in the courtyard. It was often cold by the time the lord and his family ate it.

But not everything was dull in a castle. During the long winter nights, the lord and his guests drank and sang. They played board games like chess and backgammon. In better weather, the nobles held tournaments, or contests between knights. In these tournaments, two knights in armor would **joust.** They would carry lances and ride horses toward each other at full speed. Each would try to knock the other off his horse!

Writing About History

Imagine that you live on a feudal manor. Be the lord or lady of the manor, a peasant, a serf, a page, or a knight. In your notebook, write about your daily life.

Then and Now

Chess, the Game of Kings

Have you ever played chess? It was a popular game in the Middle Ages, too. Even then, it was centuries old. Like silk and spices, it came to Europe from the East. It was played in Asia as early as 550 B.C. The Arabs brought it to Spain in the 700s.

Chess pieces changed during the Middle Ages to reflect life at that time. Kings, queens, knights, and bishops moved around the board. There were even foot-soldiers (pawns) and castles (rooks). As in medieval warfare, pawns had the least value. In the language of the game, players "capture" pieces, such as castles. The object of the game is to capture your opponent's king. Playing chess is indeed like looking back into the Middle Ages.

Lesson 3 Review On a sheet of paper, write the letter of the answer that correctly completes each sentence.

1. Most of the peasants were _____.

    A serfs   **B** free   **C** knights   **D** slaves

2. Serfs gave _____ percent of what they raised to the lord of the manor and to the church.

    A 30   **B** 60   **C** 90   **D** 100

3. Farming improved during the Middle Ages because of the invention of the _____.

    A three-field system   **C** horseshoe
    B waterwheel   **D** all of the above

4. A _____, which was a dug-out area filled with water, made a circle around a castle.

    A manor   **B** fief   **C** moat   **D** drawbridge

5. Castles were _____.

    A dark   **B** damp   **C** cold   **D** all of the above

What do you think ?

How does having more food lead to more time to learn?

Reading Strategy:
Predicting

Preview the lesson title. Predict what you will learn about culture in the Middle Ages.

Objectives

◆ To identify changes in education, art, architecture, literature, and law

◆ To describe the influence of the Church in each area of culture

Bishop

A priest who is in charge of other priests and a number of churches

When the Roman Empire fell, education stopped. But then monasteries opened schools to prepare boys to become monks or priests. From about 1000 to 1100, **bishops** set up schools in their cathedrals. Bishops are priests who are in charge of other priests and a number of churches. A cathedral is the church where the bishop is the main priest. These cathedral schools were located in towns that later became centers of learning.

What Did Students Study?

Classes at cathedral schools lasted 10 hours a day. In addition to religion, they studied seven subjects: Latin; rhetoric (speaking and writing correctly); arithmetic; geometry; astronomy; logic (figuring things out); and music. The teachers often beat lazy students. As years passed, the number of subjects increased. This led to the first universities.

What Did Art Teach the People?

Artists and artisans during the Middle Ages built beautiful churches and cathedrals. They made beautiful windows out of colored glass. They carved life-like statues and created colorful wall paintings to show the life of Jesus, the saints, and people from the Bible. Most people did not know how to read or write. They learned about Christianity from these windows and statues and paintings.

The first schools in the Middle Ages were set up to prepare boys to become monks or priests.

What Is Gothic Architecture?

Until about 1100, most churches looked like Roman buildings. We call this style of architecture **Romanesque.** The churches had rounded arches. To hold up the heavy roof, the builders built thick walls with narrow openings for windows. Because of this, Romanesque churches were dark and gloomy.

Around 1200, church builders began building in a new style. We call it **Gothic.** Narrow, heavy ribs of stone supported the roof. To keep these thin walls from collapsing, the builders used flying buttresses. The buttresses held up the thin walls. Finally, they used pointed arches, which drew the eyes upward.

Artists and artisans built hundreds of churches and cathedrals in the Gothic style. Some were so large that builders worked on them for many years. For example, the beautiful cathedral of Notre Dame in Paris took 150 years to finish. It can hold 9,000 people.

This gothic church is Rheims Cathedral in France.

Romanesque

A style of building that was like what the Romans built with thick walls and arches

Gothic

A style of architecture with thin walls, pointed arches, many windows, and flying buttresses

What Was Literature Like in the Middle Ages?

People wrote two kinds of literature in the Middle Ages. Some wrote in Latin. Others wrote in the language of the common people.

The Latin works included important writings on Christianity. Thomas Aquinas wrote a book called *Summa Theologica*. In it, he explained that faith and reason are both gifts from God. He tried to bring the two together. He helped to keep alive much of the learning of the ancient world.

Some people wrote stories in the language of the common people. They usually retold an old story. People had passed these stories down in song. Storytellers had told them long before anyone wrote them down.

One well-known story was the *Song of Roland*. It is the oldest and greatest French medieval poem. The *Nibelungenlied* puts together several German legends. The first great work in English is *Beowulf*. Like the two other stories, it tells about the heroic deeds of a warrior.

What Changes Took Place in Law?

Important developments in law took place during the Middle Ages. Henry II, an English king who ruled from 1154 to 1189, introduced the use of the jury in English courts.

The English jury was a group of 12 people who helped the judge. The jury asked questions to discover the truth. Then it could decide whether a person accused of doing something wrong was guilty or innocent. Today, we call this a grand jury.

If the jury thought that a crime might have been committed, a judge held a trial with another jury. This jury examined all the information and the facts in court. The jury decided if the person had done wrong. Today, we call this a petit jury.

What Is a Parliament?

During the Middle Ages, kings began to ask nobles for ideas about government. Soon councils of nobles and church leaders formed in most of Western Europe. The English called their council, or lawmaking assembly, **Parliament.** The French called their council the Estates General. Nobles organized assemblies in other countries during the Middle Ages, but these rarely lasted.

Lesson 4 Review On a sheet of paper, write the answer to each question. Use complete sentences.

1. What were the seven subjects studied in the cathedral schools of the Middle Ages?

2. How did church buildings help the people of the Middle Ages learn about their faith?

3. What are two differences between Romanesque and Gothic architecture?

4. What is one thing that is the same about the *Song of Roland,* the *Nibelungenlied,* and *Beowulf?*

5. What changes did Henry II introduce into English law during the Middle Ages?

What do you think ❓

Would you have liked going to school during the Middle Ages? Explain your answer.

History in Your Life

Learning the Latin Language

Why could educated people from different lands understand each other during the early Middle Ages? They spoke Latin. It was the international language of Europe. Knowledge from the past was written in Latin. Any new learning or information, such as a law, would also be in Latin.

But Latin was a foreign language. It was different than what students spoke every day. In English, you say, "I know" but "he knows." The -*s* is a verb ending. In Latin,

there is a different ending for each person— *I, he, we, you, they.* Other kinds of words, such as nouns and adjectives, also have endings. Take, for example, the words *boys, ball, big,* and *hit.* In Latin, endings would tell if the sentence meant:

The big boys hit the ball or *The big ball hit the boys.*

Latin was the key to knowledge. Grammar schools, therefore, became very important.

A Crusader's Letter

Thousands of people joined the First Crusade in 1096. Many were princes and nobles. Much of what we know about the Crusades comes from letters. This letter is from Stephen, count of Blois in France. His wife, Adele, was the daughter of William the Conqueror.

Count Stephen to Adele, his . . . wife, to his dear children, and to all his vassals of all ranks—his greeting and blessing:

You may be very sure, dearest, that the messenger whom I sent to you left me before Antioch safe and unharmed and, through God's grace, in the greatest prosperity. And already at that time, together with all the chosen army of Christ . . . , we had been continuously advancing for twenty-three weeks toward the home of our Lord Jesus. You may know for certain, my beloved, that of gold, silver, and many other kinds of riches, I now have twice as much as you, my love, supposed me to have when I left you. For all our princes, with the common consent of the whole army, though against my own wishes, have made me, up to the present time, the leader, chief, and director of their whole expedition.

You have . . . heard that after the capture of the city of Nicaea we fought a great battle with the Turks and, by God's aid, conquered them. Next we conquered for the Lord all Romania. . . .

We besieged it [Antioch] and had many conflicts there with the Turks. Seven times we fought with the citizens of Antioch and with the troops coming to their aid; we rushed to meet them and we fought with the fiercest courage under the leadership of Christ; and in all these seven battles, by the aid of the Lord God, we conquered, and . . . killed . . . [many] of them. In those battles, indeed, and in very many attacks made upon the city, many of our followers were killed, and their souls were borne to the joys of paradise. . . .

I can write to you only a few, dearest, of the many things which we have done. Although I am not able to tell you all that is in my mind, I trust that all is going well with you, and urge you to watch over your possessions and to treat as you ought your children and your vassals. You will certainly see me as soon as I can possibly return to you. Farewell.

Document-Based Questions

1. What is the "army of Christ"?

2. When Stephen sent the messenger to Adele, how long had he been away?

3. What honor did the other nobles give Stephen?

4. Name two cities where Stephen fought in battles.

5. Reread the advice Stephen gave Adele. What can you tell about her duties at home?

Unlucky King John and the Magna Carta

In all of English history, there has been only one King John. He was so unpopular that no other English king has used the name. John was not just unpopular. He was unlucky too.

John's older brother was Richard I, the Lionhearted. Richard was a well-loved hero. While he was on the Third Crusade, John tried to make himself king. When Richard came home in 1199, he banished his brother from England.

After Richard died in 1199, John became king. He was actually able and clever, but things never went right. The French beat him in a war. That defeat cost him money and influence. He lost English lands in France, too. Next, John had a serious disagreement with the pope. The pope cut him off from the Church. John had to agree to be the pope's vassal.

Then the king demanded more services from his vassals. He placed new taxes on the Church. Both the nobles and church leaders got angry at John. Many members from both groups felt that the king had too much power. By the spring of 1215, there was a war going on inside England. Some nobles backed John. Some wanted to get rid of him. A large army marched toward London.

To avoid losing his throne, John gave the rebel leaders new rights. The event took place on June 15, 1215, in a large open field called Runnymede. The leaders and churchmen met King John. They told him the terms that they wanted him to sign, and John agreed to them. Then he put his royal seal on the document that Church leaders had written.

The paper that King John signed is called the Magna Carta, or Great Charter. It gave specific rights to the feudal nobles and to the towns. It also promised church leaders some freedoms. Most importantly, the Magna Carta meant that even the king had to obey the law.

King John signing the Magna Carta in 1215.

At first, the Magna Carta protected mainly the rights of nobles. Gradually these rights were extended. Finally, every Englishman would claim them. English settlers brought these ideas to America.

Wrap-Up

1. Why has there only been one King John in English history?

2. What caused John's disagreement with his brother Richard?

3. What actions made leaders angry with John?

4. What is the most important principle in the Magna Carta?

5. How has the importance of the Magna Carta changed since 1215?

- After 1050, Western Europe was again at peace. Farming and trade began to grow again.

- The Catholic Church was important in the Middle Ages. Monks and nuns were members of religious groups. Some cared for the sick or studied farming methods. Others taught students and supplied places for travelers to stay. The Catholic Church kept learning alive.

- Christian pilgrims visited Palestine, or the Holy Land. In about 1095, one group of Muslims stopped pilgrimages. The pope then called for a holy war, or crusade, to regain control of Palestine.

- Europeans fought four major Crusades between 1096 and 1291. Both nobles and common people were crusaders. In the end, Muslims kept control of Palestine.

- The Crusades had three results. These included increased trade with the Middle East and curiosity about distant lands. Unfortunately, they were also the beginning of harsh treatment toward Jews and Orthodox Christians.

- Feudalism began in Europe in the Middle Ages because there was no central government. It was based on an exchange of a lord's land for a vassal's service.

- Knights were medieval soldiers who came from noble families. They trained for knighthood first as pages and then as squires.

- Feudal manors were self-sufficient. Most people were peasants; some were serfs who could not leave the land.

- Five inventions changed farming. They were the three-field system, the horseshoe, an improved plow, the waterwheel, and the windmill. With better crops and more food, the population of Europe grew larger.

- Nobles built strong castles for protection. Sometimes knights practiced their skills in tournaments on castle grounds.

- In the Middle Ages, boys began attending school in monasteries and cathedral schools. Classes were conducted in Latin.

- Early medieval churches were Romanesque. They had thick walls with rounded arches. The later Gothic style had pointed arches and tall, thin walls. The stained glass windows taught people religious stories.

- There were two kinds of medieval literature. Religious works were written in Latin and traditional stories in local languages.

- English law introduced the jury system and Parliament.

Chapter 10   R E V I E W

Word Bank
convent
fief
knight
lance
lord
manor
moat
page
pilgrim
serf

On a sheet of paper, use the words from the Word Bank to complete each sentence correctly.

1. The land given to a vassal by his lord is a _____.

2. A _____ was a young nobleman training to be a knight.

3. A _____ was a peasant bound to the land on which he or she was born.

4. Nuns live in a _____.

5. A _____ visited the Holy Land to see the place where Jesus had lived.

6. A _____ is a steel-tipped spear.

7. A _____ is a dug-out place filled with water that circles a castle.

8. A _____ is a self-sufficient area of land on which the peasants grew or raised almost everything that the lord and they needed.

9. A _____ is a king or noble who gives land to someone else in return for loyalty.

10. A _____ is a soldier who gives loyalty to his lord.

On a sheet of paper, write the letter of the answer that correctly completes each sentence.

11. The military journeys to the Holy Land that lasted for nearly 200 years are the _____.

    A Muslims   **C** Crusades

    B Vassals   **D** Romanesque

12. _____ was a political and military system used in the Middle Ages that was based on the holding of land.

    A Gothic   **C** Monastery

    B Feudalism   **D** Buttress

13. Gothic architecture had _____.

    A pointed arches   **C** flying buttresses

    B thin walls   **D** all of the above

14. Many castles had _____.

    A courtyards   **C** drawbridges

    B moats   **D** all of the above

15. The oldest and greatest French medieval poem is the _____.

    A *Song of Roland*   **C** *Beowulf*

    B *Nibelungenlied*   **D** none of the above

On a sheet of paper, write the answer to each question. Use complete sentences.

16. What is one good thing and one bad thing that resulted from the Crusades?

17. What was feudalism?

18. What did the church have to do with education, art, and architecture during the Middle Ages?

Critical Thinking On a sheet of paper, write your response to each question. Use complete sentences.

19. Why do you think the people living on manors welcomed travelers, actors, and musicians? Describe how this tells about what life was like living on a manor.

20. If you were a crusader, what reasons would you give for being one? List at least three reasons.

Test-Taking Tip

After you have completed a test, reread each question and answer. Ask yourself: Have I answered the question that I was asked? Have I answered it completely?

11

The Byzantine Empire, Russia, and Eastern Europe

During the Middle Ages, the eastern part of the old Roman Empire grew strong. But the western part broke into many parts and fell into decay. In this chapter, you will learn about the Byzantine Empire and its greatest emperor. You will discover the ways this empire influenced the Slavic people of Eastern Europe. You will follow the Germanic tribes as they invade Western Europe. You will sail with the Vikings and find new lands! Finally, you will witness a battle that changed England forever.

Goals for Learning

◆ To compare the Byzantine and the Roman Empires

◆ To describe the influence of the Byzantine Empire on the people of Eastern Europe, especially Russia

◆ To list several reasons why some historians call this period the "Dark Ages" and explain the importance of Charlemagne to European history

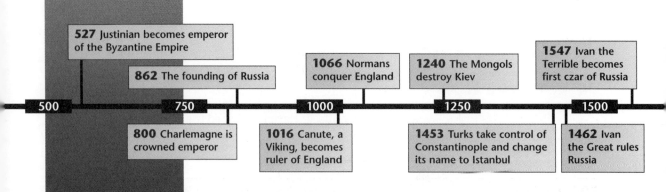

527 Justinian becomes emperor of the Byzantine Empire

862 The founding of Russia

1066 Normans conquer England

1240 The Mongols destroy Kiev

1547 Ivan the Terrible becomes first czar of Russia

| 500 | 750 | 1000 | 1250 | 1500 |

800 Charlemagne is crowned emperor

1016 Canute, a Viking, becomes ruler of England

1453 Turks take control of Constantinople and change its name to Istanbul

1462 Ivan the Great rules Russia

Charlemagne's Empire

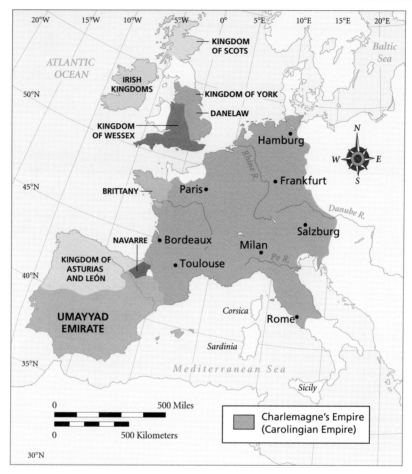

Map Skills

After the fall of the Roman Empire in A.D. 476, Europe broke into many small kingdoms. Cities disappeared. More than 300 years passed before a strong king united all of Western Europe again. His name was Charlemagne, or Charles the Great. This map shows his empire. It was located where the countries of France, Italy, Spain, Switzerland, Austria, the Czech Republic, and Germany are now located.

Study the map, then answer the following questions:

1. What are the names of three rivers in Charlemagne's empire?

2. What are the names of five cities in his empire?

3. What sea lies to the south of the empire?

4. How many miles did this empire stretch from east to west at its widest point? from north to south at its widest point?

5. Between what two lines of latitude was much of Charlemagne's empire?

Reading Strategy:
Text Structure

Before you begin reading this chapter, look at how it is organized. Look at the title, headings, boldfaced words, and photographs. Ask yourself:

◆ Is the text a description or sequence?

◆ Is it compare and contrast or cause and effect?

Key Vocabulary Words

Lesson 1 —————————————

Relic A holy object

Saint A person who follows God's ways

Barbaric Not civilized

Patriarch A leader of the church

Icon A small picture of a saint or Jesus

Lesson 2 —————————————

Monk A member of a religious order

Cyrillic alphabet The alphabet invented by Cyril and Methodius and used to translate the Bible into Slavic languages

Boyar A Russian noble who owned land

Veche The Russian assembly that represented all free, adult male citizens

Kremlin The center of the Russian church and the Russian government

Czar The ruler of Russia; a Russian title that means "caesar"

Lesson 3 —————————————

Literature The written works that have lasting influence

Pope The head of the Roman Catholic Church

Objectives

◆ To list the accomplishments of the Byzantine Empire

◆ To identify the greatest Byzantine emperor

◆ To explain the disagreement that divided Christians

Reading Strategy:
Text Structure

Preview the first two headings. How do you know that they will compare and contrast two things?

Relic

A holy object from the past

Saint

A person who follows God's ways

Remember when Emperor Diocletian divided the Roman Empire into two parts in A.D. 284? The eastern part became the Byzantine Empire. Constantine founded the city of Constantinople there in A.D. 330. He made his new city the capital of the Byzantine Empire.

How Was the Byzantine Empire Like Rome?

Constantine called his capital city the "new Rome." He built as the emperors had in Rome. One building—the Hippodrome—was like Rome's Colosseum. Constantine held chariot races in it.

An army of officials helped the emperor rule. They took charge of building and repairing roads. As in Rome, there was a senate, but the emperor held all the power. He organized the army along Roman lines. In the early years of the empire, all the Byzantine emperors were Roman and spoke Latin.

But Constantinople was not Rome. Most of its people were Greek and spoke the Greek language. Many had come there from other lands. Constantinople was located on one of the most important trade routes between Asia and Europe. Jews, Turks, Persians, Slavs, and Italians lived there.

How Did Rome and Constantinople Differ?

Constantinople was a Christian city. Emperor Constantine built many beautiful Christian churches there. Often, these churches were the most beautiful buildings in the city. He collected **relics** for them. These relics were holy objects from the past. That is, they had something to do with God or with **saints**—people who followed God's ways. People came from all parts of the empire to pray in these churches.

Barbaric

Not civilized

Who Was the Greatest of the Byzantine Emperors?

In 527, a man named Justinian became emperor. Most historians call him the greatest of the Byzantine emperors. We remember him for three reasons. First, he tried to win back the Roman lands in the West. Second, he put together a code of laws. Third, he made Constantinople more beautiful.

Reading Strategy:
Text Structure

Notice that the section headings are written as questions. After you read each section, try to answer the question asked in the heading.

What Land Did Justinian Win Back?

Justinian tried to win back all the western lands that Rome had lost the century before. One of his armies won back much of Italy and North Africa. Another army threw back the Persians. During this time, several different Germanic tribes took over Rome. Finally, Justinian's armies won control of Rome. But the **barbaric** tribes, which were not civilized, had left it in ruins.

What Was Good About Justinian's Code of Laws?

Justinian asked a group of Greek and Latin scholars to collect and organize the laws of his empire. They published their code of laws in 533. Historians call this the greatest thing Justinian did.

The code was a complete record of Roman legal customs. It listed the rights that the empire gave to each person. For 900 years, this code was the basis for Byzantine law. The main ideas of the code later shaped the legal systems of Europe and the United States.

How Did Justinian Make Constantinople More Beautiful?

Justinian built a government building in which 20,000 people worked. Across from it, he built one of the world's most beautiful churches—the Hagia Sophia. Its ceiling rises 180 feet

Justinian (center) is considered to be one of the best emperors of the Byzantine Empire.

Patriarch

A leader of the church

Icon

A small picture of a saint or Jesus

from the floor. He used beautifully colored marble for the walls, floors, and pillars. Justinian also built three walls to protect Constantinople. A marketplace on its main street offered goods from Africa, Asia, and Europe.

What Caused a Split in the Christian Church?

Justinian's motto was "one empire, one church, one law." He became the head of the church within the lands he controlled. Priests and **patriarchs,** or leaders of the church, became government officials. But some Christians did not want an emperor to control the church. They fought over this.

They also fought over the use of **icons**—small pictures of the saints and Jesus. Several emperors wanted to get rid of them. They thought people were worshipping the icons instead of God.

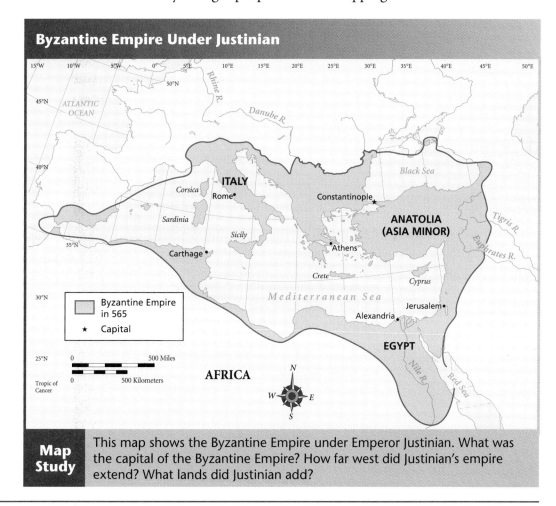

Byzantine Empire Under Justinian

Map Study This map shows the Byzantine Empire under Emperor Justinian. What was the capital of the Byzantine Empire? How far west did Justinian's empire extend? What lands did Justinian add?

Soon, riots broke out. Christians in the eastern part of the old Roman Empire and Christians in the western part began to think differently. This caused a split in the church. In 1054, the church in the West became known as the Roman Catholic Church. The church in the East became the Eastern Orthodox Church.

Why Did the Byzantine Empire Decline?

The death of Justinian in 565 marked the beginning of the end for the Byzantine Empire. Garbage filled Constantinople's narrow streets. Civil war broke out. People fought to decide who should become the next emperor. In the centuries after Justinian, the empire faced attacks by Persians, Slavs, Vikings, Mongols, and Turks. In 1453, the Turks took control of Constantinople and changed its name to Istanbul. It became the capital of the Ottoman Empire.

Lesson 1 Review On a sheet of paper, use the words from the Word Bank to complete each sentence correctly.

1. Constantine tried to build his capital like _____.

2. The _____ was like Rome's Colosseum.

3. Historians think that _____ was the greatest emperor of the Byzantine Empire.

4. Justinian built the beautiful church known as the _____.

5. People in the Byzantine Empire began to fight over the use of icons, or small pictures of saints and _____.

Word Bank

Hagia Sophia

Hippodrome

Jesus

Justinian

Rome

What do you think ?

A plague weakened both the western Roman Empire and the eastern Byzantine Empire. Why do you think that the people at that time had such trouble with plagues?

Objectives

◆ To explain the relationship between Russia and the Byzantine Empire

◆ To describe the formation of an independent Russia

Monk

A member of a religious order

Cyrillic alphabet

The alphabet invented by Cyril and Methodius and used to translate the Bible into Slavic languages

The Byzantine Empire greatly influenced the people of Eastern Europe. We call these people Slavs. They moved from central Asia into the countries we now call Russia, Ukraine, Slovakia, Bulgaria, the Czech Republic, Slovenia, Croatia, and Poland.

The Slavs included many groups. Each group had its own culture and language, but they were alike in some ways. The largest group was the Russians.

What Happened When the Slavs Became Christians?

The Slavs admired the Byzantine civilization. Around 900, two **monks,** or members of a religious group, began to preach to the Slavs. Cyril and Methodius helped many Slavs give up their old religions and become Christians.

The Slavs had no written language. The monks invented an alphabet for their spoken language. We call this the **Cyrillic alphabet.** Some Slavic countries still use it today. Then the monks translated the church's Bible, songs, and ceremonies into Slavic languages. Because of this, the Slavs could read the Bible and understand the songs and ceremonies.

Two monks named Cyril and Methodius helped Slavs become Christians.

Byzantine Christianity helped unite the people of Eastern Europe. The Slavs accepted the Eastern Orthodox Church. However, most of the rest of Europe belonged to the Roman Catholic Church. This difference isolated the Slavs. For nearly 300 years, they knew little of the discoveries and inventions that were changing civilization in Western Europe.

Reading Strategy:
Text Structure

Notice that the section headings are written as questions. After you read this section, answer the question asked in the heading.

What Ties Did Russia Have with the Byzantine Empire?

In 989, Eastern Orthodoxy became the official religion of Russia. Now Russians felt closer to the Byzantine Empire. For example, Vladimir, an early Russian king, married the sister of the Byzantine emperor. The empire and Russia traded with one another. Also, the Russians built their churches to look like the ones in the Byzantine Empire. The beautiful church of Saint Sophia in Kiev is one example of this. By 1050, Russian civilization was the most advanced in Europe.

Early Russia (c. A.D. 1000)

Russia

Paying tribute to Russia

Major trade routes

★ Capital

Map Study This map shows Russia in about A.D. 1000. Along what river did traders travel north from Constantinople? What city was both a capital and a trade center?

Olga: c. A.D. 890–969

Olga, Grand Princess of Kiev, was Russia's first woman ruler. Her husband, Prince Igor, was murdered in 945. In response to this, Olga had hundreds of people executed. Since her son was young, Olga ruled Kiev for him. Then the young prince came of age. But he was more interested in war than in ruling. While he was away, Olga ruled Kiev.

Most people in Kiev still worshipped the old gods. Olga, however, became a Christian in 957. She went to Constantinople and invited Byzantine missionaries to Russia. Kiev became Christian under her grandson Vladimir.

Boyar

A Russian noble who owned land

Veche

The Russian assembly that represented all free, adult male citizens

What Made Kiev So Important?

Historians give 862 as the date Russia was founded. In that year, Prince Rurik became ruler. His capital was Kiev. It is located on the Dnieper River—one of the main north-south water trade routes. Whoever controlled Kiev controlled Russia's trade with Constantinople.

Kiev was also at the center of two other trading routes: one between Europe and Asia and one between Scandinavia and the Middle East. By 1000, Kiev was the biggest city in Europe. It was larger than London or Paris.

At this time, Russia was a group of small territories. The Grand Prince of Kiev ruled these territories. He shared power with other princes and with **boyars**—Russian nobles who owned land. A **Veche,** or assembly, represented all free, adult male citizens. It could accept or remove a prince. It also handled business and government.

Why Did Kiev Fall?

Kievan Russia reached its peak between 1000 and 1050. Its ruler unified Russia. However, when he died, his sons fought each other for control. This weakened the kingdom. Trade with Constantinople was cut off. In 1240, fierce Mongol armies from central Asia completely destroyed Kiev.

Kremlin

The center of the
Russian church
and the Russian
government

Czar

The ruler of Russia;
a Russian title that
means "caesar"

When Did Moscow Become Important?

To escape the invaders, many Russians headed north. In that same year, Alexander, a Russian prince, defeated the Swedes at the Neva River. The Swedes had tried to force the Russians to become Catholics. The Russians gave Alexander the title *Nevsky* or "of the Neva."

In 1294, Nevsky's youngest son, Daniel, became ruler of Muscovy, or Moscow. (It is the capital of Russia today.) At that time, Moscow was a small, rich town located on an important trade route. Later, the princes of Moscow took the title, or name, of "Grand Prince of All Russia."

Who Was the Founder of Modern Russia?

By the late 1400s, Moscow was the most powerful city in Russia. It became the center of the Russian church. Historians call Ivan III, or Ivan the Great, the founder of modern Russia. He ruled from 1462 to 1505. This great leader freed Russia from foreign rule and set up a government.

Ivan's wife, Sophia, was related to the last Byzantine emperor. She got him to adopt the double-headed eagle as his symbol. (It had been the symbol of Byzantine emperors.) Sophia also encouraged Ivan to take complete power of both the church and the government. Ivan the Great rebuilt the **Kremlin.** It became the center of the Russian church and the Russian government.

Reading Strategy:
Text Structure

Read the heading
of the next section.
What does it tell you
about the rule of
Ivan IV?

Who Was Ivan the Terrible?

In 1533, Ivan IV, just three years old, became the ruler of Russia. He was the grandson of Ivan the Great. Ivan IV began to govern when he was 14. During his reign, he made the kingdom three times larger. He believed that the Roman emperor Augustus Caesar was one of his ancestors. So in 1547, he crowned himself the first **czar** of Russia. This title means the same as the Roman title "caesar."

Ivan IV was a good military leader, but he was also cruel. He ordered thousands of Russians and enemy soldiers killed. Because he was so cruel, historians call him Ivan the Terrible.

Lesson 2 Review On a sheet of paper, use the words from the Word Bank to complete each sentence correctly.

1. Methodius and _____, both monks, created an alphabet for the Slavic languages and used it to translate the Bible.

2. _____, an early Russian king, married the sister of the Byzantine emperor.

3. Historians date the founding of Russia to A.D. 862 when Prince _____ became ruler.

4. Prince Alexander became a hero to the Russians, and they called him _____ because of where he won a great battle.

5. Ivan the Great rebuilt the _____ as the center for church and government.

Word Bank

Cyril

Kremlin

Nevsky

Rurik

Vladimir

What do you think ?

Would creating an alphabet for a spoken language be hard? Explain your answer.

History in Your Life

The Kremlin

The Kremlin is more than the center of Russian government. It contains beautiful churches and palaces. They stand inside a walled area more than a mile around. Impressive brick towers guard the entrance gates.

The first Kremlin was a wooden fort on the Moscow River. The Mongols burned it several times. By the late 1400s, however, Moscow was the most powerful city in Russia. Its ruler, Ivan the Great, hired Italian and Russian architects to build a new Kremlin. Inside its thick walls, they built three beautiful cathedrals with gold domes. Rulers were crowned in one church. They married in another. Their funerals were in the third. Later rulers added palaces and other buildings.

Today some buildings in the Kremlin are museums. There you can see the czars' crown jewels and other treasures.

Objectives

◆ To describe some Germanic tribal kingdoms that replaced the Roman Empire

◆ To identify some groups that invaded Britain and influenced its language and culture

Literature

The written works that have lasting influence

Reading Strategy:
Text Structure

As you read the next section, notice the sequence of events that led to the Dark Ages.

The fall of Rome brought important changes to Western Europe. Germanic tribes slowly moved south and took over Roman lands. People did not obey Roman laws any longer. Roman soldiers could not keep order.

For 500 years there had been one Roman Empire. Now hundreds of little kingdoms took its place. These kingdoms had no system for collecting taxes. Rulers had little money for a government.

What Happened in Europe During the Middle Ages?

These little kingdoms were always at war with one another. This made doing business almost impossible. Also, along each road, robbers waited to attack travelers. Merchants were afraid to take their goods from city to city. There were no governments to repair roads and bridges. These fell into ruin. Towns and villages did, too.

As time passed, people lost interest in learning. Many useful books and artwork were lost in wars. People no longer learned about art, architecture, and **literature**, or written works that have lasting influence. The schools closed and the people had only enough time to take care of their day-to-day needs. Civilization lost its knowledge of the past.

Think of what life was like then. All the tribes fought, people were afraid to travel, they had no schools, few could read or write—the world was falling down around them. Historians call this period of history the "Dark Ages." The early Middle Ages was a difficult time for people in Western Europe.

Pope

The head of the Roman Catholic Church

Who Were the Franks?

The Franks were one of the largest of the German tribes. They began a civilization that later developed into the modern countries of France, Germany, and Italy. In 481, a warrior named Clovis united the Franks and became their king. He made Paris his capital. He was the first Germanic king to become a Roman Catholic.

Clovis united the Franks. He ruled for more than 20 years.

Who United All of Western Europe?

In 800, one king became strong enough to unite all of Western Europe. His name was Charlemagne, or Charles the Great. First, Charlemagne defeated the other Germanic tribes. Then he united them into one kingdom, with one religion—Roman Catholic. Next, Charlemagne fought against the enemies of the Roman Catholic Church. **Pope** Leo III, the head of the Roman Catholic Church, crowned him "Emperor of the Romans."

Then and Now

I Didn't Know There Was a God Named Tuesday

Have you ever wondered where the names for the days of the week come from? At one time, they were all named for Roman gods. Then Germanic peoples invaded Western Europe and beat the Romans. This fact may surprise you, but the English language comes from theirs. As a result, most English names for days honor Germanic gods.

Woden was the chief Germanic god. His son Thor's magic hammer made the sound of thunder. Tiw was god of war. Tuesday (Tiw), Wednesday (Woden), and Thursday (Thor) are named after them. Friday belongs to Frigg. She was the goddess of love. What about the other days? Sunday and Monday belong to the sun and moon. Saturday is named after the Roman god Saturn.

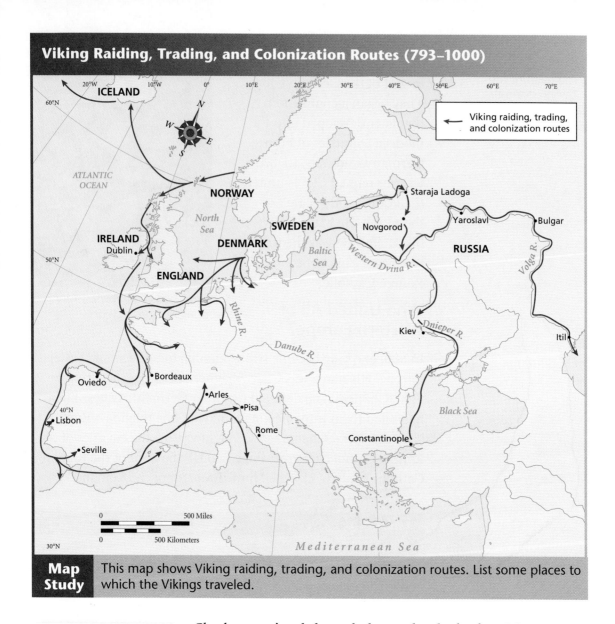

Viking Raiding, Trading, and Colonization Routes (793–1000)

Viking raiding, trading, and colonization routes

ICELAND
ATLANTIC OCEAN
NORWAY
North Sea
SWEDEN
IRELAND
Dublin
DENMARK
Baltic Sea
ENGLAND
Rhine R.
Staraja Ladoga
Novgorod
Yaroslavl
Bulgar
RUSSIA
Western Dvina R.
Volga R.
Oviedo
Bordeaux
Danube R.
Arles
Pisa
Lisbon
Rome
Seville
Kiev
Dnieper R.
Itil
Black Sea
Constantinople
Mediterranean Sea

0   500 Miles
0   500 Kilometers

Map Study This map shows Viking raiding, trading, and colonization routes. List some places to which the Vikings traveled.

Reading Strategy: Text Structure

Study the map on this page. How does it help you understand how widely the Vikings traveled?

Charlemagne's rule brought law and order back to Western Europe. However, less than 30 years after his death, his empire broke apart. Civil war began. New invaders threatened his kingdom.

Writing About History

Imagine you are a news reporter. You have been assigned to report on the Viking voyages. In your notebook, write what you would say in your report.

How Far Did the Vikings Travel?

One group of invaders that attacked Charlemagne's empire was the Vikings. They came from Northern Europe—from the present-day countries of Denmark, Sweden, and Norway. The Vikings were fine sailors who built excellent ships. They could sail them on shallow rivers and in deep oceans. These ships had both sails and long oars. The largest ship held up to 100 men, but as few as 15 men could sail a Viking ship.

Viking explorers traveled to Russia, all across Europe, and to America. They set up colonies on the islands of Iceland and Greenland. A Viking named Leif Eriksson landed on an island on the northeast coast of North America. He called it Vinland. Today, we call this area Newfoundland. It is part of Canada.

What Viking Became King of England?

After the Romans left Britain in the fifth century, different Germanic tribes invaded the island. Historians know little about the tribes called Angles, Saxons, and Jutes. What they do know is that they destroyed as they invaded. Beginning in 835 and continuing for over 100 years, the Vikings invaded Britain too. In 1016, a Viking named Canute became the ruler of England. In 1042, Edward the Confessor, an Anglo-Saxon, became king.

How Did the Normans Begin to Rule England?

When Edward died, his brother-in-law Harold was chosen to rule. William, Duke of Normandy, also claimed the throne. (Normandy is a peninsula in present-day France.) At the Battle of Hastings in 1066, William defeated Harold. William the Conqueror, as he was now known, became king of England. The year 1066 is an important date in English history. William's victory meant that the Normans, rather than the Anglo-Saxons, would rule England. This has had a lasting influence on the English language and on the culture of England.

Lesson 3 Review On a sheet of paper, write the letter of the answer that correctly completes each sentence.

1. Historians call the period of time after the fall of Rome the "Dark Ages" because _____.

   A there were no governments in Western Europe
   B schools closed
   C the people lost the learning of the past
   D all of the above

2. _____ brought the Franks together and made Paris his capital.

   A Charlemagne   **C** Clovis
   B William of Normandy   **D** Leif Eriksson

3. In 800, Pope Leo III named _____ as the "Emperor of the Romans."

   A Charlemagne   **C** Clovis
   B William of Normandy   **D** Leif Eriksson

4. The Vikings visited _____.

   A Iceland   **C** Newfoundland
   B Greenland   **D** all of the above

5. The Battle of _____ took place in 1066.

   A Charlemagne   **C** Hastings
   B Normandy   **D** Newfoundland

What do you think ?

What would the world be like today if we lost all books and Internet learning from the past?

Technology Connection

The Byzantine Dromon

Byzantine craftspeople of around A.D. 500 believed they could build a better ship. They improved upon the Greek galley most commonly used up until that time. The dromon was a faster, lighter ship used for war as well as for the ample trade within the Byzantine Empire.

Dromons used as warships were built with a tower in the center. From this tower, warriors could fire arrows or hurl spears at enemies. From the large flat deck below, others could use catapults or rams during sea battles. Dromons used for trade provided faster delivery of goods. Dromons were powered by rowers and by sail. They could carry large amounts of cargo or up to 300 passengers.

Life Among the Germans

Tacitus was a Roman historian. He did not like the way that Romans lived during his lifetime—he thought people lived in sin. Tacitus served as an official in several parts of the empire. As a result, he learned about different barbarians—people who were not Romans.

Many Germanic tribes lived on the northern borders of the empire. Tacitus admired their strength and simple life. He thought the Germans stood for an older, simpler way of life. After Rome fell, Germanic tribes conquered much of the empire. They soon controlled Europe.

This reading comes from Tacitus's history of the German tribes. He wrote it in A.D. 98.

The same make and form is found in all [men], eyes stern and blue, yellow hair, huge bodies, but vigorous only in the first onset. Of pains and labour they are not equally patient, nor can they at all endure thirst and heat. To bear hunger and cold they are hardened by their climate and soil. . . .

Their lands . . . consist of gloomy Forests, or nasty Marshes; . . . very apt to bear Grain, but altogether unkindly to fruit Trees; abounding in Flocks and Herds, but generally small of growth. . . .

They who live more remote are more primitive and simple in their dealings . . . The money which they like is the old and long known . . .

that impressed with a chariot and two horses. Silver too is what they seek more than gold . . . because small silver pieces are more ready in purchasing things cheap and common.

In the choice of Kings they are determined by the splendor of their race, in that of Generals by their bravery . . . their Generals procure obedience not so much by the force of their authority, as by that of their example. . . .

The moment they rise from sleep, which they generally prolong till late in the day, they bathe, most frequently in warm water, as in a country where the Winter is very long and severe. From bathing they sit down to meat, every man apart, upon a particular seat, and at a separate table.

Upon the funeral pile they accumulate neither apparel nor perfumes. Into the fire are always thrown the arms of the dead, and sometimes his horse.

This is what in general we have learnt of the original and customs of the whole people of Germany.

Document-Based Questions

1. What did Tacitus think were Germanic weaknesses?

2. How did the Germans choose their rulers and generals?

3. How did the Germans govern themselves?

4. Where did Germans eat? Why might this seem odd to Romans?

5. Describe a typical day for German men.

How the Russians Became Christians

The early Russian state was a mixture of two cultures. It was both Slavic and Viking. Rurik was the first ruler. He was probably a Viking chief and trader from Scandinavia. The people were mostly Slavs. They worshipped the old Slavic gods. In about 900, some people became Christians. Missionaries from the Byzantine Empire came to Kiev around 950. Olga, the Grand Princess, became a Christian in 957. Her grandson, Vladimir I, made Russia a Christian country.

St. George and the Dragon is the oldest religious icon in Russia.

An old Russian document says that several religions sent groups to Vladimir. He was still a pagan. Each pointed out the advantages of their faith. A group of Muslims came from Bulgaria. Vladimir rejected them because Muslims may not drink wine. "Drink," said Vladimir, "is the joy of the Russians." He also rejected the Jews. He saw that Jews were scattered throughout the world. Vladimir felt that their god had not protected them.

Vladimir still had two choices to consider. There was the Roman Catholic Church, the Christian church in the West. In addition, there was the Byzantine Church, the Christian church in the East.

Vladimir then sent his own men to investigate. They watched people worshipping. From Germany, they wrote, "We beheld no glory there!" German Catholic churches seemed too simple and plain. Another group went to Constantinople. That city was the center of the Byzantine Church. They visited the beautiful cathedral of Hagia Sophia. They were amazed. The church had mosaics of gold. Thousands of candles lit the soaring interior. They wrote, "We knew not whether we were in heaven or on earth. . . . We know only that God dwells there among men."

Two other things about the Byzantine Church appealed to Vladimir. First, the Russians could use their own language in church. He preferred this choice. In contrast, the Western Christian Church insisted that people worship in Latin. Second, the emperor was the head of the Byzantine Church. He had some control over it. The pope in Rome was head of the Western Church. In matters relating to religious faith, the pope could tell rulers what to do. Vladimir kept his independence. He chose the Byzantine Church. He ordered his people to be baptized. It was several hundred years, however, before most Russians accepted this new religion.

Wrap-Up

1. What religion did most Russians follow before 900?

2. Who was the first Christian Russian ruler?

3. Why did Vladimir reject the Muslims? the Jews?

4. How did Vladimir's team feel about Hagia Sophia?

5. For what other reasons did Vladimir join the Byzantine Church?

- Constantine founded the Byzantine capital Constantinople in 330. It was a beautiful Christian city with many churches.

- Justinian, the greatest Byzantine emperor, began to rule in 527. He won back Roman lands from the Germans and made a code of laws. He also built the Church of Hagia Sophia.

- The Byzantine emperor was head of the church. Church leaders ran the government. People disagreed over church rule and the use of icons. In 1054, the Christian church split in two. It became the Eastern Orthodox Church and the Roman Catholic Church.

- The Byzantine Empire declined and civil war broke out. In 1453, Turks captured Constantinople and changed its name to Istanbul.

- Many people in Eastern Europe were Slavs. The Russians were the largest Slavic group. Byzantine missionaries converted many Slavs to Christianity. To be able to write Slavic languages, two monks invented the Cyrillic alphabet.

- The Russian state began about 862 in Kiev, a trading center. Kiev was ruled by a Grand Prince and nobles, the boyars. Byzantine culture influenced early Russia.

- Mongols from Asia destroyed Kiev in 1240. Swedes also invaded Russia, but were held off by Alexander Nevsky. Power then shifted to the princes of Moscow.

- Ivan the Great founded modern Russia. He rebuilt the Kremlin, a walled city of palaces and churches. Ivan the Terrible, his grandson, made Russia larger. He became the "czar."

- The period after the fall of Rome is called the "Dark Ages." Western Europe split into many kingdoms and wars were frequent. Learning also declined.

- The Franks were a Germanic tribe. They lived in what are now France, Germany, and Italy. Clovis became their king in 481, and he made Paris their capital.

- A Frankish king, Charlemagne, united Western Europe in 800. The Pope crowned him "Emperor of the Romans." However, his empire collapsed after his death.

- Vikings attacked various parts of Europe. They also established colonies in Iceland and North America.

- Germanic tribes—Angles, Saxons, Jutes—settled in Britain. Vikings also invaded it. In 1066, William of Normandy invaded and conquered Britain, bringing French influence to England.

Word Bank

Charlemagne

Constantine

Franks

Hagia Sophia

Ivan the Great

Justinian

Leo III

Methodius

Rurik

Vikings

On a sheet of paper, use the words from the Word Bank to complete each sentence correctly.

1. _____, Rome's first Christian emperor, built Constantinople.

2. The Byzantine emperor _____ ordered a code of all Roman laws.

3. Cyril and _____, both monks, invented an alphabet so that the Slavic people could read the Bible.

4. Justinian built a great church called the _____.

5. Russia was founded in 862, which was the year that Prince _____ became ruler.

6. _____ of Russia rebuilt the Kremlin.

7. The _____ were one of the largest of the German tribes.

8. In 800, _____ united all of Western Europe.

9. Pope _____ crowned Charlemagne "Emperor of the Romans."

10. The _____, who were excellent sailors, came from northern Europe.

On a sheet of paper, write the letter of the answer that correctly completes each sentence.

11. The name for the leaders of the Russian church is _____.

    A relic   **C** patriarchs
    B icons   **D** boyars

12. A _____ is a holy object from the past that has something to do with God or the saints.

    A relic   **C** Veche
    B patriarch   **D** czar

13. The nobles in Russia who owned land are _____.

   A icons   **C** czars

   B patriarchs   **D** boyars

14. Small religious pictures of saints and Jesus are _____.

   A relics   **C** boyars

   B icons   **D** titles

15. _____ is written works that have a lasting influence.

   A Literature   **C** Principle

   B Ceremony   **D** Icons

On a sheet of paper, write the answer to each question. Use complete sentences.

16. Why did Constantine call Constantinople the "new Rome"?

17. Why was the development of the Cyrillic alphabet important to the Slavic people?

18. Give three reasons why some historians call the Middle Ages in Europe the "Dark Ages."

Critical Thinking On a sheet of paper, write your response to each question. Use complete sentences.

19. Charlemagne's empire fell apart 30 years after his death. How might world history be different if his empire had stayed together until the present time?

20. Imagine that you are a Viking. Describe the ship you travel on. Name and describe the foreign lands you visit. Describe what you like best about your life.

Test-Taking Tip

Wear a watch to the test and use it to pace yourself as you work through the test questions.

12

Africa and the Spread of Islam

Things changed in Europe between 500 and 1500. Things also changed in Africa. In Arabia, the prophet Muhammad founded a new religion called Islam. From about 1150 to 1200, the Islamic world was the center of world civilization. In Africa, powerful kingdoms arose during the "Golden Age." In this chapter, you will travel and trade with the people of Arabia, Ghana, Mali, and Songhai.

Goals for Learning

◆ To recognize that Islam is one of the great religions of the world

◆ To identify contributions Arabs have made in science, mathematics, and literature

◆ To compare three West African civilizations

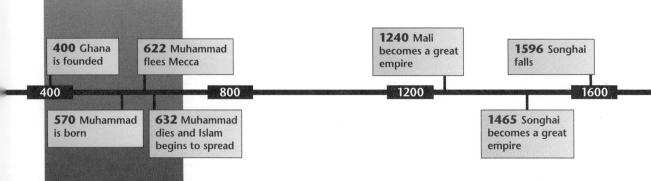

400 Ghana is founded

622 Muhammad flees Mecca

1240 Mali becomes a great empire

1596 Songhai falls

400   800   1200   1600

570 Muhammad is born

632 Muhammad dies and Islam begins to spread

1465 Songhai becomes a great empire

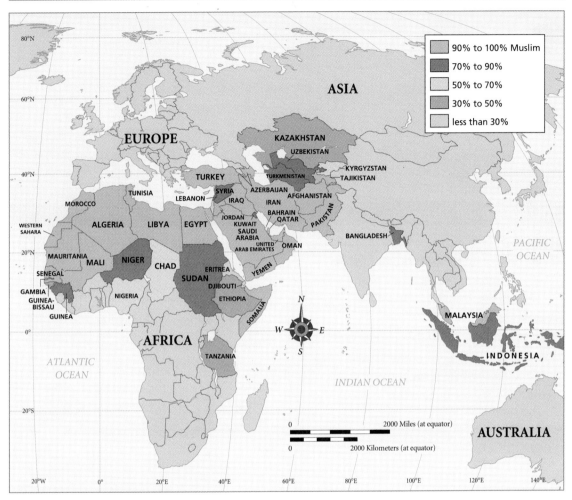

Map Skills

This map shows the percentage of Muslims in Africa and Asia today. About one in every five people on the earth today is of the Islam faith. More than 50 countries have populations with a majority of Muslims. Most Muslims are Sunnis. About 10 to 15 percent are Shi'ites.

Study the map carefully, then answer the following questions:

1. Which part of Africa, north or south, has the most Muslims?

2. What percent of Muslims is there in Chad?

3. What percent of Muslims is there in Tanzania?

4. Name three countries that are 90 to 100 percent Muslim.

5. Name three countries that are between 70 and 90 percent Muslim.

Reading Strategy:
Visualizing

Visualizing is like creating a movie in your mind. It will help you understand what you are reading. Use the following ways to visualize a text:

◆ Think about the order in which things are happening. That may be a clue to what will happen next.

◆ Look at the photographs, illustrations, and descriptive words.

◆ Think about experiences in your own life that may add to the images.

Key Vocabulary Words

Lesson 1 ————————————

Fast To give up eating food for a while

Hegira Muhammad's journey from Mecca to Medina; his flight from danger

Vision A visit from God's angel

Idol A statue of a god that people worship

Qur'an The holy book of the Muslims that contains the teachings of Islam

Alms The money or care that one gives to the poor and needy

Hajj The pilgrimage to Mecca that is a religious duty of all Muslims

Lesson 2 ————————————

Jihad A holy war fought by Muslims to spread Muhammad's teachings

Mosque A Muslim place of worship

Lesson 3 ————————————

Infidel One who does not believe in the religion of another person

Objectives

◆ To describe how the prophet Muhammad founded and spread Islam

◆ To list the five basic duties each Muslim must accept

Fast

To give up eating food for a while

Vision

A visit from God's angel

Hegira

Muhammad's journey from Mecca to Medina; his flight from danger

In 570, a man named Muhammad was born in Mecca in Arabia. When he was young, he saw nomads fighting and suffering as they moved from one oasis to another.

Who Visited Muhammad in a Vision?

Once a year, Muhammad went to a desert cave to pray and to **fast,** or give up eating food for a while. One year, the angel Gabriel came to him in this cave. Gabriel said, "O, Muhammad, you are the messenger of Allah." Muhammad was to be God's prophet.

In the beginning, Muhammad told only a few people about his **vision,** or visit from God's angel. Soon, he began to preach, but he had little success. The people of Mecca worshipped hundreds of gods. They did not like the idea of only one god—Allah. Life became dangerous for Muhammad and his followers in Mecca, so they had to flee the city.

What Was the Hegira?

In 622, the people in Yathrib invited Muhammad to come and preach. They accepted his teachings and renamed their city Medina to honor Muhammad. (Medina means "City of the Prophet.") Historians call Muhammad's journey from Mecca to Medina the **Hegira.** This word means a journey, or flight, from danger.

Muhammad's teachings started a new religion—Islam. This Arabic word means to give oneself to God. Those who surrender themselves to Allah are Muslims. The Hegira, or Muhammad's flight, is an important event for Muslims. The year of his journey is the first year of the Islamic calendar.

Why Did Muhammad Return to Mecca?

Muhammad began to gather around him an army of 10,000 followers. In 630, he returned to Mecca with his army and took over the city. He went to the center of the city. In a temple there, called the Kaaba, people of Mecca worshipped statues, or **idols,** of their many gods. Muhammad destroyed these idols and told the people, "There is but one God, and Allah is his name."

What Is the Holy Book of Islam?

Do you remember that the Bible contains the holy teachings of the Jews and Christians? The holy book of the Muslims is the **Qur'an** (also spelled *Koran*). It contains the teachings of Islam. That is, it contains the words God spoke to Muhammad through the angel Gabriel.

The Qur'an says that God spoke to earlier prophets of the Jews and the Christians. Muslims recognize the teachings of Judaism and Christianity. They believe that Jesus was born of the spirit of God and did many wonderful things.

Muslims must pray five times a day, no matter where they are. They kneel and face toward Mecca, their holy city.

The angel Gabriel gave the Qur'an to the prophet Muhammad in the Arabic language. Because of this, Muslims always study their holy book in Arabic. Translations could be wrong or the reader might not understand them. As Islam spread across the world, so did the Arabic language. Muslims still use Arabic for their religious services, even in non-Arab countries.

What Are the Five Pillars of Islam?

The Qur'an lists five duties, or pillars, for each Muslim. The first pillar is the statement of faith. A person becomes a Muslim by announcing, "There is no God but Allah, and Muhammad is His Prophet."

The second pillar is prayer. Muslims must pray five times a day wherever they are—in a field, at home, or in an office. As they begin to pray, they face Mecca, their holy city. Then they go through the motions of washing their heads, hands, and feet. To show their surrender to God, they kneel, bow, and touch their foreheads to the ground.

The third pillar of Islam is the giving of **alms.** That is, Muslims are expected to help the poor and needy by giving money to them or by caring for them.

The fourth pillar includes a fast. During the holy month of Ramadan, healthy adult Muslims stop eating and drinking from sunrise to sunset. At the end of Ramadan, they celebrate with a large meal and then give presents.

The fifth pillar of Islam is the **Hajj,** or the pilgrimage to Mecca. At least once in their lifetime, all Muslims who are able to travel must visit Mecca. It is their religious duty. Visiting Mecca, the birthplace of Muhammad, is often the high point of a devout Muslim's life. All the pilgrims to Mecca wear the same simple clothes. This shows their belief that all people are the same before God, whether rich or poor. The pilgrims follow special rules about what to do and say. Those who make the trip add the title "hajji" to their name. This means "someone who will go to heaven when he or she dies."

Lesson 1 Review On a sheet of paper, write the answer to each question. Use complete sentences.

1. Who was Muhammad?

2. Why is Mecca an important city to Muslims?

3. What is the Qur'an?

4. Why is the Qur'an written in Arabic?

5. Identify three of the five pillars of Islam.

What do you think ?

Why do you think that visiting Mecca is the high point of a Muslim's life?

Objectives

◆ To identify the two groups of Muslims

◆ To describe life in Islamic cities

◆ To explain how Arabs treated conquered peoples of different religions

Muhammad died in 632. His death raised the question of who should succeed him. Different answers to that question led to the creation of two groups of Muslims—the Sunnis and the Shia. The Sunnis believe that Muhammad did not appoint a successor. Therefore, a new religious leader could be chosen by a vote. The new leader did not have to be a relative of Muhammad. Shi'ites believe that Muhammad appointed Ali as his successor. Ali was married to Muhammed's daughter. Shi'ites believe that a new religious leader should be related to Muhammad. Eventually, these two groups developed different laws and religious practices. Today, it's believed that about 90% of Muslims are Sunnis.

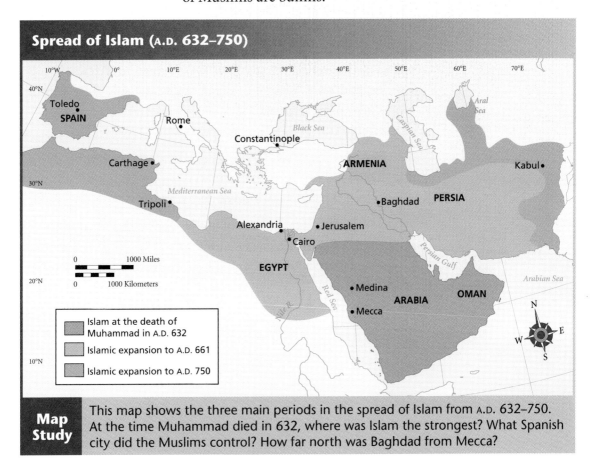

Spread of Islam (A.D. 632–750)

Islam at the death of Muhammad in A.D. 632

Islamic expansion to A.D. 661

Islamic expansion to A.D. 750

Map Study

This map shows the three main periods in the spread of Islam from A.D. 632–750. At the time Muhammad died in 632, where was Islam the strongest? What Spanish city did the Muslims control? How far north was Baghdad from Mecca?

How Did the Muslim Leaders Spread Islam?

Muslim leaders carried Muhammad's teachings to others by means of holy wars, or **jihads.** Islam spread across North Africa and into Europe. West and northward, it spread across the Persian Empire and the Byzantine Empire to parts of India, Southeast Asia, and China.

What Were Islamic Cities Like?

In 750, the Abbasid dynasty became rulers of the Arabian Empire. The rulers built a new capital—Baghdad—on the banks of the Tigris River. It became, and still is, an important center of trade. Thousands of people worked for four years to build Baghdad. It had many large public buildings, including libraries, hospitals, and gardens.

How Did Arabs Treat Others?

The Islamic Empire became rich because of its trade, farming, and respect for others. It controlled the most important trade routes in the world. These routes linked together Africa, Europe, and Asia. Islamic traders bought and sold things from all parts of Africa, China, India, and Russia. Arab artisans made many things to sell to people in other places.

The Muslims improved farming. The lands of Mesopotamia and the Nile Valley produced more than enough food. Farmers were able to feed the people who lived in the many large Arab cities.

Arabs respected the cultures of people they conquered in their holy wars. They allowed Jews and Christians to keep their own religions. Islamic culture blended the cultures of many people with the Arab culture.

What Made Arab Medicine a Science?

The Muslims built hospitals to care for the sick. In these hospitals, doctors studied why people got sick. Muslims became the first people to make a science of medicine. They studied it carefully and they trained their doctors carefully. From their study, they discovered that some sicknesses are able to spread from one person to another.

One Arab doctor named Al-Razi wrote books about two diseases—smallpox and measles. He also wrote a set of 25 books about medicine. Students in both the East and the West used these until the 1400s. Al-Razi may have been the first doctor to sew up cuts and to put casts on broken arms and legs.

What Did Muslim Scientists Figure Out About the Earth?

Arab astronomers figured out that the earth is round. They correctly guessed that it was about 25,000 miles around. An Arab geographer was the first to put a map on a ball to show the right shape of the earth.

Other Arab scientists studied light and were the first to learn that it travels in a straight line. They also learned that the curving of a lens makes things appear larger. The greatest Muslim scholar was an Arab named Jabir. His discoveries led to the science of chemistry. Chemists study the makeup of substances. He may have been the first person to carefully record the results of an experiment. Other Arab scientists invented much of the equipment we use today in chemistry.

Reading Strategy:
Visualizing

How could this paragraph be written differently to create a stronger picture in your mind?

Writing About History

Some amazing discoveries are described here. Research one of them--how light travels, why a curved lens makes things appear larger, different kinds of chemistry equipment—or something else that is mentioned in this section--and draw it in your notebook. Be sure to label parts of the item you are drawing.

What Mathematical Gifts Did the Muslims Give Us?

In mathematics, Muslim scholars expanded on what they learned from other people. From India, they borrowed the nine numbers that we still use today. We call these "Arabic numbers" even though they came from India.

From the Hindus, the Arabs borrowed the decimal system. This is a number system based on the number 10. It includes the idea of zero. This was a good system because it was much easier to use than the Babylonian system based on 60.

What Is Islamic Art Like?

Islamic art never shows people or animals. Artists decorate **mosques,** or Muslim places of worship, with beautiful designs and writing. Islamic art also appears on their world-famous rugs, on leather goods, and on swords.

Muslim scholars studied medicine, the heavens, chemistry, and mathematics.

Many Arab artists wrote poems about the beauty of nature and love. The best known Muslim poet was Omar Khayyam, who wrote *The Rubaiyat.* Westerners know another collection of Arab stories called the *Arabian Nights.* In it are the stories "Ali Baba and the Forty Thieves" and "Aladdin and His Lamp."

Al-Razi

Baghdad

Jabir

jihads

Khayyam

Lesson 2 Review On a sheet of paper, use the words from the Word Bank to complete each sentence correctly.

1. The Arabs spread their religion through a series of _____, or holy wars.

2. The Abbasid dynasty ruled the Islamic Empire in A.D. 750 and built the city of _____.

3. _____ may have been the first doctor to put casts on broken arms and legs.

4. The greatest Arab scholar was _____, whose work led to the science of chemistry.

5. Omar _____ wrote the poem *The Rubaiyat*, which is about love and nature.

What do you think ?

What do you think is the best gift the Arab people of the Middle Ages gave the world? Explain your answer.

Communication in History

Borrowed Words

Have you eaten *sherbet*? Are you studying *algebra*? We borrowed these words from the Arabic language. We got some from the Muslims who lived in Spain. Others were the names of products from the Middle East—*sugar, alcohol,* and *syrup.* Traders also brought the *lime, orange,* and *artichoke* to Europe. *Mohair* and *cotton* are Arabic, too.

Muslim scholars studied chemistry and astronomy. The words *alkali* and *zenith* resulted from their knowledge. They gave us the names for stars, such as *Aldebaran.* From Arab mathematicians came *tariff* and *zero.* We use Arab words that describe how people live or the world around us. People sit on a *sofa.* A *sultan* and a *sheik* are kinds of rulers. The commander of a fleet is an *admiral.* English is indeed a richer language because of these Arabic words.

The crusaders first set out to capture the Holy Land in 1095.
About that time, a series of empires developed in West Africa.
Arab geographers called this grassland area the Sudan. It is
very different from the dry Sahara to the north and the wet
tropical rain forest to the south.

How Did Ghana Become Powerful?

Ghana was founded about 400. Within 400 years, it had
become an important center of trade. In fact, Ghana controlled
all the important trade routes from the Sudan to North Africa.

Early stories about Ghana call it "the land of gold." Ghana
never owned any gold fields, but it controlled the trade in gold.
With gold came power.

The gold came from a region near the Senegal River. People
there had much gold, but no salt, and they needed salt to live.
Arab traders on camel caravans carried their goods to the
people near the Senegal River in the south. Then they traded
salt for gold. Next, the caravan turned north again to trade
with their gold. On both trips, they traveled through Kumbi,
the largest city in Ghana. The government of Ghana taxed the
caravan each way. Both the Arabs from the north and the forest
people from the south paid tribute to the king of Ghana.

How Did Ghana's Army Create Peace?

By 1070, Ghana was one of the most powerful empires in the
world. Taxes from trade filled the king's treasury. With all this
money, he could keep as many as 200,000 warriors. (At this
same time, William the Conqueror could raise an army of only
15,000 soldiers to invade England.)

Ghana's large army gave it great power. With this power, Ghana
created peace in West Africa and made trade safe. Ghana could
easily have conquered its weaker neighbors, but it did not.
Instead, it took tribute from these neighbors.

What Made Ghana Fall?

The kings of Ghana invited Muslim teachers to begin schools in Kumbi and other cities. The rulers of Ghana did not become Muslims, but many of the people of Ghana did. This helped improve the connection between the two areas and brought money to the empire.

In 1076, Arabs from North Africa, called Almoravids, invaded Ghana. They began a holy war against the **infidels,** or non-Muslims, of Ghana. (An infidel does not believe in the religion of another person.) They destroyed Kumbi. During this time, people stopped paying tribute to Ghana. In time, Ghana defeated the Almoravids. However, the country was never again as powerful as it had once been.

How Did Mali Become Powerful?

Mali existed as early as 1000. When Ghana lost its power, Mali was able to form a new empire. It, too, took control of the trade routes.

The man most responsible for Mali's rise to greatness was Sundiata Keita. He took control of the gold fields. His armies swept across Africa, and his empire included large areas of the Sahara. Keita divided his kingdom into provinces. Then he put one general in charge of each province. Each general was responsible for keeping law and order in his province.

Timbuktu was a great center of learning and trade in West Africa.

Which Famous Mali King Became a Muslim?

Mansa Musa was king of Mali when it was most powerful. Unlike the rulers of Ghana, Mansa Musa became a Muslim. He brought many Arab scholars to his capital. He set up a great center of Islamic learning in Timbuktu. Scholars came from all over the world to study there.

Mansa Musa ran his kingdom well. Arab visitors wrote about the peace and safety of Mali. The visitors saw how the people of Mali obeyed the Five Pillars of Islam. In fact, one writer said that Mali parents wanted their children to learn the Qur'an by heart. If the children did not do this, they were put in chains until they memorized the holy book.

What Was Mansa Musa's Pilgrimage?

Mansa Musa was famous for building a university, being a Muslim, and visiting the holy city of Mecca. Some historians think that 60,000 people made the pilgrimage with Mansa Musa. (About 12,000 of them were his servants.) They loaded 80 camels with bags of gold dust to pay for the 3,000-mile trip from Mali to Mecca. Imagine all the food and supplies 60,000 people would need!

History in Your Life

African Metalworking

Learning to work with iron was a big step forward in technology. Iron made stronger farming tools and weapons. Ironworking in Africa probably began at Meroë, in the kingdom of Kush along the Nile. Artisans in Kush began to work with iron about 500 B.C. Iron ore came from local mines. Forests supplied wood for hot fires. These craftspeople worked with gold, too.

Another tribe, the Nok, lived in West Africa. They worked with iron, gold, and tin. The Bantu people learned these skills. Then the Bantu moved south. They carried this knowledge to others.

Africa was rich in many metals, such as copper. This beautiful metal was used for jewelry and pots. People combined copper with other metals to make bronze. The kingdom of Benin was famous for its bronze sculptures. Artists made them by pouring melted bronze into molds.

The pilgrimage began in 1324 and took more than a year. Everywhere Mansa Musa went he gave away gold to rulers and government officials. When he reached Mecca, Mansa Musa gave that city gold, too.

Mansa Musa's gifts of gold made news even in Europe. In 1375, someone in Spain drew a map that shows Mansa Musa. He holds a large gold ball in his hand. The artist wrote on the map. The writing says that Mansa Musa has so much gold that "he is the richest and most noble king of all the land."

After Mansa Musa died, civil war broke out in Mali. Within 150 years, the great empire fell. Then the last great empire of this golden age arose—Songhai.

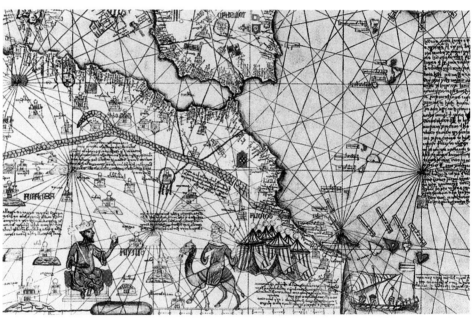

This map shows Mansa Musa holding a gold ball.

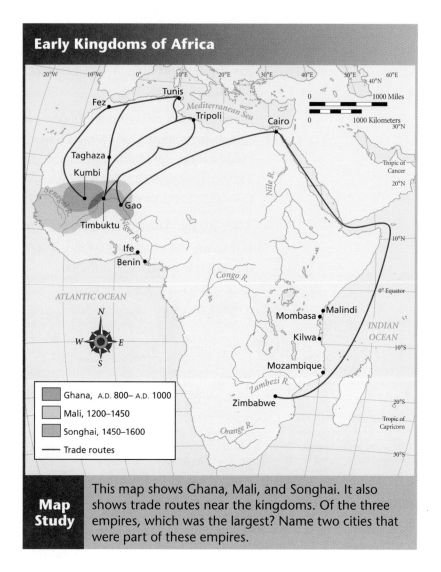

Early Kingdoms of Africa

Legend	
Ghana, A.D. 800– A.D. 1000	
Mali, 1200–1450	
Songhai, 1450–1600	
Trade routes	

Map Study

This map shows Ghana, Mali, and Songhai. It also shows trade routes near the kingdoms. Of the three empires, which was the largest? Name two cities that were part of these empires.

How Did Songhai Become Powerful?

The third and last of the great empires of West Africa was Songhai. Songhai already existed in the 800s, but it did not become powerful until the 1400s. Like Ghana and Mali before it, Songhai grew powerful by controlling the gold and salt trade.

Songhai's greatest king was Sonni Ali. From 1464 until 1492, he never lost a battle. King Sonni Ali made Songhai the largest empire that West Africa ever had. His army captured the university city of Timbuktu. Ali's empire stretched from the Atlantic Ocean eastward nearly 1,800 miles.

Ali divided Songhai into provinces. Then he chose officials to carry out the laws. He also made sure that all weights and measures were the same in his empire.

Other countries wanted Songhai's riches and attacked it. At first, Songhai's army easily defeated its neighbors. Then, in 1590, the Arab ruler of Morocco in North Africa sent an army to conquer Songhai. The Arab army had only 2,000 soldiers, but it had a new, powerful weapon—the gun. In 1596, Songhai fell. The empire broke apart, and West Africa was never united again.

Biography

Sonni Ali: died 1492

King Sonni Ali made Songhai a powerful empire. He took lands from the old Mali empire. It was weak when he became king in 1464. First, he captured Timbuktu in 1468. It was a center of Muslim learning. Later, he captured Jenne, a wealthy trade center. Sonni Ali won many victories partly because he used cavalry well.

Sonni Ali was a harsh ruler, however. He had scholars in Timbuktu killed. He executed many people, even close friends. His death in 1492 was a mystery. Some stories said he drowned. Others said he was murdered.

Lesson 3 Review On a sheet of paper, write the letter of the answer that correctly completes each sentence.

1. The first empire to develop in West Africa was _____.

   A Ghana   **C** Songhai

   B Mali   **D** Timbuktu

2. King Mansa Musa of Mali founded a university at _____.

   A Kumbi   **C** Paris

   B Songhai   **D** Timbuktu

3. _____ controlled trade in West Africa.

   A Ghana   **C** Songhai

   B Mali   **D** all of the above

4. Traders from the north brought _____ to trade for gold.

   A horses   **C** guns

   B salt   **D** fish

5. The Arab ruler of Morocco defeated the last great empire of West Africa because he had _____.

   A camels   **C** gold

   B guns   **D** a large army

What do you think ?

Why does control of a trade route lead to power?

The Qur'an

The Qur'an (also spelled Koran) is the holy book of Islam. It contains 114 chapters, which are divided into verses. Muslims believe that the Qur'an is the word of God as given to Muhammad. The following excerpt tells Muslims how to be righteous and faithful.

It is not righteousness
That ye turn your faces
Towards East or West;
But it is righteousness—
To believe in Allah
And the Last Day,
And the Angels,
And the Book,
And the Messengers;
To spend of your substance,
Out of love for Him,
For your kin,
For orphans,
For the needy,
For the wayfarer,
For those who ask,
And for the ransom of slaves;
To be steadfast in prayer,
And practice regular charity,
To fulfil the contracts
Which ye have made;
And to be firm and patient,
In pain (or suffering)
And adversity,
And throughout
All periods of panic.
Such are the people
Of truth, the God-fearing.
2:177

Document-Based Questions

1. What is righteousness?

2. What should believers do for the needy?

3. What other behavior should a righteous person have?

4. To which Pillars of Islam does this excerpt refer?

5. What should Muslims do when they are suffering?

Farming in Africa and Oceania

Most early societies depended on farming. People ate whatever they could grow. They also fished or hunted. Bringing food from other places was not practical. In Africa south of the Sahara, the economy has always centered on farming. That is also true of the islands in the Pacific Ocean. Both those places have warm climates. They grow some of the same foods. The history of their economies is quite different, though.

Africa is a huge continent. Farming varies greatly from place to place. In the rain forests, people grow small gardens. For thousands of years, yams have been a favorite crop. So has palm oil. Some of its oils are used in cooking. Others make soaps and other products. People also grow several kinds of nuts, including peanuts. Plantains are another popular food.

The grasslands areas of Africa are drier. People here planted fields of grain.These grains can be pounded or ground into flour. Flour is used in porridges, puddings, and flat breads. About 2,000 years ago, people began using iron tools. Iron hoes and knives made farming easier. Farming villages became more stable.

Farming in the Pacific Islands has a different history. In Africa, people have farmed for about 7,000 years. The Pacific Islands were settled only recently. Polynesians reached the islands of Hawaii between about A.D. 300 and 500. By about A.D. 1000, they had settled New Zealand. The first settlers brought yams, taro, and sweet potatoes. They also brought pigs, dogs, and chickens. They grew flax to make cloth. In some places, they built terraces or ponds to grow taro. People eat the starchy root of this plant. Islanders also planted coconut palms, bananas, and breadfruit trees. These trees grew around fields and gardens.

People used the coconut palm tree in many ways. They ate its meat and drank the liquid inside. The hard shell became a cup or bowl. Palm leaves could be woven into baskets. They were also used for roofs.

Farming is still important in Africa and the Pacific. Some crops have changed, though. Trade brought new foods to Africa. From the Americas came sweet potatoes, chili peppers, and tomatoes. From Asia came taro. Europeans also took new crops to the Pacific Islands when they settled there.

Wrap-Up

1. How is farming in Africa and in the Pacific Islands similar?

2. What kinds of crops did people plant in Africa's grasslands?

3. What major change in technology influenced farming in Africa?

4. Who first settled Hawaii and New Zealand? About when did they arrive?

5. What crops were grown in the Pacific Islands?

- Muhammad was born in Arabia in 570. He preached a new religion, Islam, with one god, Allah. Its followers are called Muslims.

- In 622, Muhammad and his followers fled from Mecca to Medina. This event is called the Hegira.

- Muhammad died in 632. After his death, two branches of Islam developed—the Sunnis and the Shi'ites. They have different laws and religious practices.

- The holy book of Islam is the Qur'an, written in the Arabic language. Muslims regard Muhammad as God's prophet. They also recognize Jewish and Christian prophets.

- Islam has five duties, or pillars. They must state their faith, pray five times a day, give alms, and fast. If possible, they make a pilgrimage, or Hajj, to Mecca.

- Holy wars, or jihads, helped Islam grow. It spread across North Africa, into Europe, and to parts of Asia.

- The Abbasid dynasty began in 750. Its capital was Baghdad. The Islamic Empire excelled in trade and farming. It let Jews and Christians keep their customs.

- Muslims made important advances in medicine; science, especially chemistry; and mathematics. Islamic art shows beautiful patterns, not people or animals.

- Ghana became rich by taxing the trade in gold and salt. By 1070, Ghana had built a powerful army to keep peace. Muslim Arabs from North Africa invaded it in 1076.

- Mali followed Ghana as the most powerful empire. Its king Sundiata Keita made Mali great. Another king, Mansa Musa, became a Muslim. He made Timbuktu a center for Islamic scholars.

- The greatest king of Songhai was Sonni Ali. His empire fell to an Arab army armed with guns in 1596.

Chapter 12 REVIEW

Word Bank

Abbasid

Allah

Al-Razi

Ghana

Islam

Jabir

Mansa Musa

Medina

Muhammad

Songhai

On a sheet of paper, use the words from the Word Bank to complete each sentence correctly.

1. The prophet _____ was born in 570.

2. He started a religion known as _____.

3. The Muslims call God _____.

4. People in the city of Yathrib renamed their city _____ in 622.

5. In 750, the _____ dynasty ruled the Arabian Empire.

6. The Arab doctor _____ wrote many books about medicine.

7. The greatest Arab scholar was _____.

8. People called _____ "the land of gold."

9. The ruler _____ founded a university in Mali.

10. People from Morocco attacked the empire of _____ with guns.

On a sheet of paper, write the letter of the answer that correctly completes each sentence.

11. Islam was spread through holy wars, or _____.

    A mosques   **C** causeways
    B jihads   **D** infidels

12. Muslims accept five duties, or _____, of their religion.

    A languages   **C** pillars
    B visions   **D** caravans

13. The holy book of the Muslims is the _____.

    A Qur'an   **C** Rubaiyat
    B Arabian Nights **D** Song of Roland

14. _____ grew powerful because of trade.

   A Ghana   **C** Songhai

   B Mali   **D** all of the above

15. Mansa Musa's pilgrimage took him from Mali to _____.

   A Timbuktu   **C** Mecca

   B South Africa   **D** all of the above

On a sheet of paper, write the answer to each question. Use complete sentences.

16. What are the five basic duties each Muslim must accept?

17. What was the key to power for the three empires of West Africa?

18. Why did the religion of Islam break into two groups, the Sunnis and the Shi'ites?

**Critical Thinking** On a sheet of paper, write your response to each question. Use complete sentences.

19. Which one of the following people would you like to have met and why? Sundiata Keita, Mansa Musa, Sonni Ali

20. In this chapter, you learned about many wonderful cities—Mecca, Medina, Baghdad, Kumbi, Timbuktu. Which one of these cities would you like to have visited and why?

Test-Taking Tip

When studying for a test, use the titles and subtitles in the chapter to help you recall information.

13

The Spread of Civilization in East and Southeast Asia

The continent of Asia also experienced many changes. In this chapter, you will learn about India and the Mongol invaders. Then you will find out about China and its many wonderful inventions. Finally, you will discover the religion called Shintoism that was born in Japan. In all these places, you will meet rulers and scholars, scientists and artists, inventors and warriors.

Goals for Learning

◆ To identify some inventions that made ancient China the richest and most powerful country in the world

◆ To describe life in China under Mongol rule

◆ To explain how geography has influenced Japan's history

◆ To explain why the Shinto religion is unique

◆ To compare Japanese and European feudalism

◆ To list the reasons why Japan and China turned to isolationism

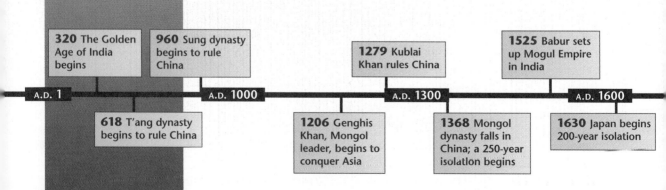

320 The Golden Age of India begins

960 Sung dynasty begins to rule China

1279 Kublai Khan rules China

1525 Babur sets up Mogul Empire in India

A.D. 1

A.D. 1000

A.D. 1300

A.D. 1600

618 T'ang dynasty begins to rule China

1206 Genghis Khan, Mongol leader, begins to conquer Asia

1368 Mongol dynasty falls in China; a 250-year isolation begins

1630 Japan begins 200-year isolation

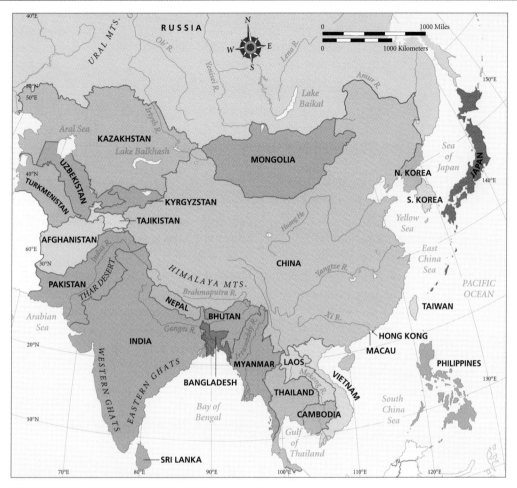

Map Skills

Asia is the largest of the world's continents. China and India—Asia's two largest countries—have a population of well over two billion people. Out of every five people on the earth, two are either Chinese or Indian. Both in population and in land area, Japan is smaller than China and India. But it has many people for its size.

Study the map, then answer the following questions:

1. Which of the three nations—Japan, China, or India—is located farthest south?

2. Which of the three is an island nation?

3. Find the mouth of the Yangtze River at the East China Sea. Then find the mouth of the Indus River at the Arabian Sea. What is the distance—by the most direct route—from one river mouth to the other?

4. What mountains separate India, Nepal, and Bhutan from China?

5. In what direction is Vietnam from China? from India? from Japan?

Reading Strategy:
Inferencing

Sometimes you have to make an inference to figure out what the text means. You have to make an inference because the meaning of a text is not directly stated.

◆ What You Know + What You Read = Inference

You can make inferences by thinking "beyond the text." Add what you already know to what you read in the text. This is a helpful strategy for making inferences.

Key Vocabulary Words

Lesson 1 ———————

Stupa A large building in which a monk is buried

Civilian A person who is not in the military

Civil service A system of government run by civilians

Lesson 2 ———————

Abacus A tool that helps people add and do other things with numbers

Masterpiece A piece of art that seems almost perfect

Lesson 3 ———————

Barbarian An uncivilized person

Lesson 4 ———————

Shinto The Japanese religion that involves a love of nature and worship of spirits

Kami Spirits of the Shinto religion

Lesson 5 ———————

Shogun A Japanese word that means "great general"; a military dictator

Daimyo The highest nobles next to the shogun

Estate A large piece of land with a house on it

Samurai A Japanese warrior who received land from a daimyo and fought for him

Calligraphy The art of beautiful handwriting

Bushido The Samurai code of honor in Japan

Hari-kari The act of killing oneself with a knife

Lesson 6 ———————

Ikebana One Japanese art of arranging flowers

Noh drama A Japanese play with only two actors

Kabuki A Japanese play with exaggerated actions

Objectives

◆ To describe India's Golden Age

◆ To explain what happened during the Mogul Empire and what led up to it

Stupa

A large building in which a monk is buried

The Golden Age of India lasted from 320 to 535. The Gupta dynasty ruled India at this time. The Gupta rulers and most Indian people were Hindus, not Buddhists. The four major castes of Hinduism had divided into smaller groups. In time, nearly 3,000 castes developed.

How Was Indian Art Unique?

Most Indian art during this time had something to do with religion. Indian artists decorated large, rounded buildings called **stupas,** in which monks were buried. They also decorated temples with carved animals, flowers, and pictures of the Hindu gods.

For centuries, Greek art influenced Indian artists. During the Golden Age, Indian art became unique. It was like no other art anywhere. Wall drawings in the Ajanta caves tell us about ancient India. These colorful paintings show hunting parties, dancing women, and the life of Indian nobles.

Some of the oldest Indian art can be seen at the Ajanta caves in central India.

What Did Indian Scientists Discover?

During the Golden Age, scientists in India made many discoveries. They figured out the size of the moon. They also understood gravity many years before Europeans did.

Indian mathematicians made important discoveries too. They were the first people to use a system of numbers based on 10. We still use their symbols for 1 to 9. They were also among the first mathematicians to use zero. The Arabs later adopted the Indian decimal and number system.

Reading Strategy:
Inferencing

After reading about Indian doctors and scientists, what can you infer about the abilities of some Indians at this time?

What Were Indian Doctors Able to Do?

Indian doctors learned to inoculate people against disease. They put a small amount of the disease into a person's body to keep the person from getting the disease. (Europeans first tried inoculations about 1,000 years later.) These doctors performed many different types of surgery. The Indians invented hundreds of different medical tools. They set broken bones and made medicine from plants.

What Happened to the Gupta Empire?

The Huns—nomads from central Asia—attacked the Gupta Empire. The empire slowly got smaller until it disappeared during the 600s. From 600 until 1300, India became a land of small kingdoms. Warriors invaded it again and again. The Indian Muslims and Hindus also fought one another.

Who Were the Mongols?

In 1398, the Mongols invaded India. These fierce warriors had already conquered Persia and Mesopotamia. Their leader's name was Timur the Lame. (Later, he became known as Tamerlane.) Timur and his armies attacked India, killing thousands of Hindus and Muslims. When he marched away from a conquered village, Tamerlane left behind pyramids of human skulls.

How Did Akbar Keep Peace?

In 1525, another conqueror from central Asia named Babur attacked India. Babur set up the Mogul Empire there. (The name *Mogul* probably comes from the word *Mongol*.) The most famous Mogul ruler was Babur's grandson, Akbar. He ruled the empire from 1556 to 1605. Some of his soldiers rode elephants. More than 12,000 soldiers rode horses. His army helped Akbar add new lands to his empire.

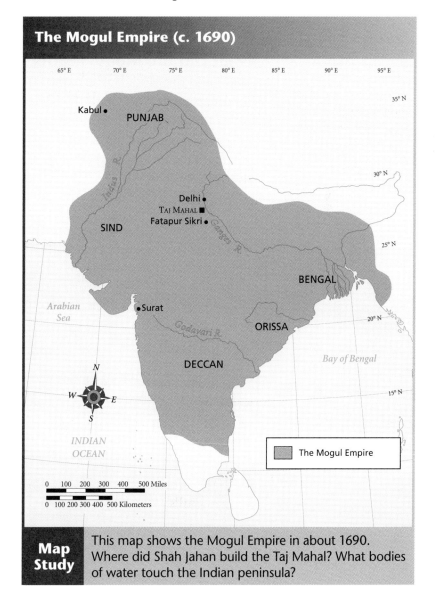

The Mogul Empire (c. 1690)

Map Study This map shows the Mogul Empire in about 1690. Where did Shah Jahan build the Taj Mahal? What bodies of water touch the Indian peninsula?

Akbar divided his empire into 12 provinces. He appointed nonmilitary, or **civilian,** officials to run the day-to-day business of each province. This system is called **civil service** because civilians run the government. These officials figured out how much food each province should produce. Then Akbar used their findings to work out fair taxes.

Like all the Mogul rulers, Akbar was a Muslim. To keep peace, he married a Hindu princess and appointed Hindus to important positions in the government. He tried to give everyone religious freedom and to treat them all fairly.

What Did the Mogul Leaders Build?

Akbar and the Moguls who came after him built beautiful buildings. Shah Jahan built the beautiful Taj Mahal as a tomb for his favorite wife. In addition, Mogul rulers built three royal palaces that contained thousands of jewels from all over Asia. The Red Fort in Agra had ceilings of solid gold. Even today, visitors say that no words can describe the beauty of these buildings.

Lesson 1 Review On a sheet of paper, use the words from the Word Bank to complete each sentence correctly.

Word Bank

Akbar

Hindus

Huns

Mongols

Tamerlane

1. The Gupta rulers during India's Golden Age were _____.

2. Toward the end of this Golden Age, the _____ invaded the Gupta Empire.

3. In 1398, the _____ invaded India.

4. _____, the leader of the Mongols, left behind skull pyramids as he marched through India.

5. _____, who ruled India from 1556 to 1605, was a great ruler.

What do you think ?

Why do you think that Greek ideas influenced Indian artists? (Hint: Remember Chapter 6 and Alexander the Great.)

Objectives

◆ To describe accomplishments of the T'ang and Sung dynasties

◆ To explain what it meant to be educated in the T'ang dynasty

From 618 to 907, the T'ang dynasty ruled China. During this period, China became the richest and most powerful country in the world. Civil servants governed T'ang China. They got their jobs after taking difficult tests on law, mathematics, and events happening in the world. Any Chinese man could take the test. However, those who passed it always had a good education. China soon had a ruling class of scholars.

With Whom Did T'ang China Trade?

T'ang China welcomed traders from other lands. These traders brought goods into China from Persia, the Middle East, Korea, and Southeast Asia. They carried silk and porcelain out of China to the Middle East and the West. This exchange of goods also led to an exchange of ideas. A large number of foreigners worked side-by-side with the Chinese within the capital city.

What Could Educated People Do in T'ang China?

Every educated person in T'ang China could read, write, and create poems. (During this time, someone said that "whoever was a gentleman was a poet.") Chinese poems were about nature or about the problems ordinary people face in everyday life. During the T'ang dynasty, the artists painted mostly in black and a few other colors. Usually their paintings were about nature.

Reading Strategy:
Inferencing

What do you already know about inventions in China during this time?

Why Was the Invention of Printing Important?

Around 1040, the Chinese invented printing. An artisan carved Chinese characters on a block of wood. Then a printer covered the wooden surface with ink and pressed sheets of paper against it. (The Chinese began printing books nearly 400 years before Europeans.)

Before the development of printing, people copied books by hand. Copying took time, so there were few books. But a printer could make more books faster. Since people learn by reading, printing led to the spread of knowledge.

Biography

Taizong: 600–649

Emperor Taizong made the T'ang dynasty great. He helped his father Kao-tsu defeat the Sui dynasty. In 626, Taizong became emperor.

Years of civil war had destroyed most local government. Taizong restored it. He set up local schools. There, students studied the teachings of Confucius. Interested students could take civil service exams. Until then, nobles had held most government jobs. Over time, civil servants took power away from the nobles.

Taizong also fought off the Turks. He also began to gain control over many other kingdoms by controlling trade routes.

Reading Strategy: Inferencing

After reading this section, what inference can you make about life in the Sung dynasty?

What Was the Sung Dynasty?

The Sung dynasty ruled China from 960 to 1279. After 1126, the center of Chinese civilization shifted south, from the Huang He Valley to the Yangtze River Valley.

Sung China was rich. Its capital city, Hangzhou, was one of the most modern cities of the world. At this time, European cities had dirty, dark, narrow, and crowded streets. Hangzhou had wide streets with streetlights. People cleaned these streets every day. Hangzhou even had a fire department.

What Things Did Sung China Create?

The Chinese invented many things that helped change world history. By the 800s, they had invented gunpowder. At first, they used it only for fireworks. Some think they may have used it later as a weapon.

An Arab trader in China learned how to make gunpowder and introduced it to Europe. Sung rulers were not interested in expanding their borders, so they made little use of gunpowder. However, Europeans developed guns and cannons. This changed the way soldiers fought wars.

Abacus

A tool that helps people add and do other things with numbers

Masterpiece

A piece of art that seems almost perfect

Someone in the Sung dynasty also invented the compass. This is a tool for finding direction by the use of a magnet. The magnetic needle of this compass always points north-south. The compass allowed Chinese ships to travel far away.

The Chinese invented the **abacus.** This tool helps people add and do other things with numbers. They also invented the clock and a machine to detect, or discover, earthquakes.

What Did Sung Artisans Create?

The artists of Sung China painted pictures that people today call **masterpieces.** That is, the paintings seem almost perfect. Sung artists painted on paper or silk scrolls. Most Sung artists tried to show the mood of what they saw. Their paintings show people as small and unimportant. Nature—trees, mountains, and water—are most important.

Nature was often the theme for Sung artists. This scroll painting shows a temple in front of mountain peaks.

History in Your Life

Gunpowder

It is the Fourth of July. You watch as brilliant fireworks burst in the sky. Whom can you thank for these exciting displays? The chemists of ancient China.

Fireworks are made mainly of gunpowder. Other materials add color. About 1,000 years ago, the Chinese discovered the formula for gunpowder. It was the first explosive. Gunpowder has three ingredients: charcoal, sulfur, and saltpeter. Charcoal is made from burned wood. Sulfur and saltpeter are mined.

In the 1200s, Muslim armies learned the secret of gunpowder from the Chinese. This knowledge reached Europe in the 1300s. Explosives changed warfare and history. Medieval castles could no longer protect the people inside. Bombs and cannons could knock down their walls.

Artisans of Sung China created beautiful porcelain. This is a shiny pottery made from a baked white clay. Sung artisans made thin porcelain bowls and vases. When Europeans came to China, they studied the making of porcelain. They used the word *china* to describe the beautiful porcelain.

Lesson 2 Review On a sheet of paper, write the answer to each question. Use complete sentences.

1. Who governed T'ang China?
2. What did trading lead to in T'ang China?
3. Why was the invention of printing important?
4. What was the capital of Sung China like?
5. What are three important inventions of Sung China?

What do you think?

Why do you think artisans of the Sung period showed human beings as small and nature as large?

Objectives

◆ To describe life in China under Mongol rule

◆ To explain the results of China's isolation after Mongol rule fell

The Mongols rode out of central Asia and conquered Russia, India, and China. Their greatest leader was Genghis Khan. Between 1206 and 1227, he conquered most of Asia.

What Did Kublai Khan Build?

In 1279, Kublai Khan, a grandson of Genghis Khan, conquered China. He adopted the Chinese name Yuan for his dynasty. Kublai Khan spent almost all his life in China. In time, the Mongol rulers adopted many Chinese ways. Kublai Khan built a new Chinese capital city. (Today we call this city Beijing.) At its center was his palace. It was the largest empire the world had ever seen.

How Did the Mongol Rulers Make Trade Easier?

The Mongol rulers built great highways and protected merchants and travelers. Travel and trade increased. Traders from the Middle East, Russia, and Europe came to China. Some Chinese and Mongols settled in Russia and Europe.

All this was important to world history. The Arabs and the Europeans learned from the Chinese. The Europeans got paper, porcelain, printing, gunpowder, and other inventions from the Chinese. The Chinese got glass, clothes, cotton, silver, carpets, honey, and slaves in return.

How Did Chinese Opera Begin?

Mongol rulers did not allow the Chinese to become high government officials. They gave these jobs to Mongols or to foreigners. Chinese scholars who had been officials began to write plays and operas. (An opera is a play in which people sing all the words.) The actors, who were all men, acted, sang, and danced while the musicians sat on stage and played music.

Kublai Khan (center), grandson of Genghis Khan, was a Mongol who ruled China under the Yuan dynasty.

Barbarian

An uncivilized person

Reading Strategy:
Inferencing

After reading this section, what can you infer about life in China during this time?

Why Did China Begin to Isolate Itself?

In 1368, the Mongol dynasty fell. Afterward, the Chinese did not see as many foreigners. The Ming emperors gained power. They thought the people who lived in all other countries were **barbarians,** or uncivilized. In the 1500s, these emperors began to isolate China from other countries. They kept foreigners out and the Chinese in.

Isolation kept the Chinese from learning the exciting new things happening elsewhere. For the next 250 years, the Chinese did little trading or traveling, so China changed. It had been ahead of other civilizations, but isolation caused it to fall behind.

Lesson 3 Review On a sheet of paper, write the answer to each question. Use complete sentences.

1. Who was Kublai Khan?

2. What was the capital of the Yuan dynasty?

3. What are two ways the Mongol rulers protected travelers and merchants?

4. Why was Chinese trade important to the Europeans?

5. Why did the Chinese begin to write operas?

What do you think ?

Why did the Ming dynasty begin to isolate China?

Objectives

◆ To explain how geography has shaped Japan's history

◆ To explain why the Shinto religion is like no other

Shinto

The Japanese religion that involves a love of nature and worship of spirits

Kami

The spirits of the Shinto religion

Reading Strategy:
Inferencing

Based on what you just read, what can you infer about the importance of geography to Japan?

Japan is a country spread over more than 3,000 islands. The islands stretch for more than 1,200 miles. People have lived on them for thousands of years, perhaps as far back as 30,000 B.C. These Stone-Age people probably came from nearby China and Korea.

How Has Geography Shaped Japan's History?

The waters that surround Japan have protected it from invaders. Unlike China and India, Japan has never been conquered by foreign armies. Yet these same waters brought ideas to Japan from Korea and China. The Japanese changed these ideas to fit their own way of life. This resulted in a unique Japanese culture.

For example, the Japanese adopted the Chinese system of writing. This allowed them to read Chinese books about medicine, mathematics, and science. The Japanese copied Chinese art and literature, wore Chinese clothing, and used the Chinese calendar. For a time, the Japanese adopted the Chinese civil service. Later, they changed this system so that nobles, rather than scholars, ran the government.

What Makes the Shinto Religion Unique?

The religion born in Japan is **Shinto.** Historians do not know who founded it. It has no holy books like the Vedas, the Bible, or the Qur'an. Shinto followers love nature and worship **kami,** or spirits. They believe that these kami control the forces of nature.

The word *Shinto* means "the way of the gods." The Japanese people worship thousands of gods and spirits. The goddess of the sun is the most important Shinto god. In fact, the Japanese call their country Nippon, which means "source of the sun."

The royal family of Japan traces its ancestors back to Jimmu. According to myth, Jimmu was the founder of Japan. The Japanese believe that he was connected in some way to the sun goddess. Until the end of World War II, they thought that their emperor was a god.

In 600, a Japanese prince sent a large group of young men to China to study. Many became Buddhists. Later, they returned to Japan. There they tried to get the Japanese to change their religion from Shintoism to Buddhism.

Buddhist missionaries came to Japan from Korea. Soon, Japanese rulers and warriors accepted many Buddhist ideas. Many artists and writers became Buddhist monks.

This image shows Amaterasu, the Shinto sun goddess.

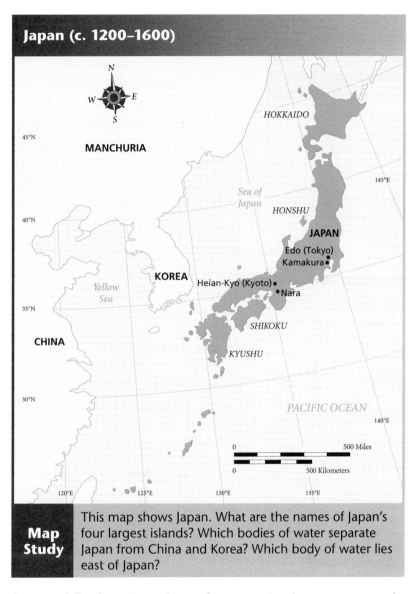

Japan (c. 1200–1600)

HOKKAIDO

MANCHURIA

45°N

145°E

Sea of Japan

HONSHU

40°N

JAPAN
Edo (Tokyo)●
Kamakura●

KOREA

Heian-Kyo (Kyoto)●
●Nara

35°N

Yellow Sea

SHIKOKU

CHINA

KYUSHU

30°N

PACIFIC OCEAN

140°E

0   500 Miles

0   500 Kilometers

120°E   125°E   130°E   135°E

Map Study This map shows Japan. What are the names of Japan's four largest islands? Which bodies of water separate Japan from China and Korea? Which body of water lies east of Japan?

Lesson 4 Review On a sheet of paper, write the answer to each question. Use complete sentences.

1. Why did no one invade Japan during its Middle Ages?

2. What did Japan borrow from China?

3. What does the word *Shinto* mean?

4. What is unique about the Shinto religion?

5. From what two countries did Buddhism come to Japan?

What do you think ?

Why do you think the Japanese call their country Nippon, or the "source of the sun"?

Objectives

◆ To describe the culture that developed in Japan during the Heian era

◆ To compare the feudal systems of Japan and Europe

Shogun

A Japanese word that means "great general"; a military dictator

Writing About History

Using what you have just learned about haiku and tanka, write your own haiku or tanka in your notebook. Remember, these poems usually show a mood or a feeling, and haiku is often about nature.

Japan had borrowed from the Chinese and Korean cultures. Then between 800 and 1200, it began to develop its own culture. This period of Japanese history is called the Heian era. The life of the Japanese ruling class was different from that of the common people. The common people were mostly farmers and fishermen who lived in small villages. The ruling class was made up of nobles who stayed in the cities.

The nobles played music and games and wrote poetry, especially the tanka and the haiku. The tanka is a five-line poem with 31 syllables. The three-line haiku has 17 syllables. It has five in its first line, seven in its second, and five in its third. Haiku is often about nature. Both poems usually show a mood or a feeling. The nobles wrote them for special times and put them in letters.

What Was Japanese Feudalism?

During this time, the emperor was the head of the government. But noble families held the real power. Because they refused to pay taxes, they grew rich and bought much land.

To keep their power, these lords gave away some of their land to other people. These people promised to be loyal to the lords. Soon Japan was divided into many pieces of land by different nobles.

In the late 1100s, one noble family grew more powerful than any other. The leader of this family forced the emperor to appoint him **shogun.** This word means "great general." For the next 700 years, powerful shoguns governed Japan. They said that they ruled in the emperor's name. In fact, the shogun was a military dictator who controlled officials, judges, and armies.

Daimyos

The highest nobles next to the shogun

Estate

A large piece of land with a house on it

Samurai

A Japanese warrior who received land from a daimyo and fought for him

Calligraphy

The art of beautiful handwriting

Bushido

The Samurai code of honor in Japan

Hari-kari

The act of killing oneself with a knife

Reading Strategy:
Inferencing

After reading this section, what inference can you make about the samurai? What words helped you make your inference?

The highest nobles next to the shogun were the **daimyos.** They controlled large **estates.** An estate is a large piece of land with a house. An army of warriors fought for each daimyo. The daimyos gave land to these warriors who were known as **samurai,** which means "one who serves." The samurai were fearless soldiers who carried sharp swords. They believed that to die in battle was an honor.

When the samurai were not fighting, they developed strength through sports. They practiced judo and karate, which are martial arts. These are ways of fighting or defending oneself. Sumo wrestling was also popular.

The samurai were also artists. They painted beautiful scroll pictures, wrote poetry, and perfected the Japanese tea ceremony. When they were not using swords, the samurai used brushes to do **calligraphy**—the art of beautiful handwriting.

What Was Bushido?

A samurai had a code of honor called **bushido.** It demanded that he be brave and loyal to his lord. He had to obey orders and practice self-discipline, or control over one's feelings and actions. Honor was the most important thing in his life. If he lost his honor, a samurai committed **hari-kari,** or *seppuku.* That is, he killed himself with a knife. The nobles believed that hari-kari brought back honor.

This is what a Samurai warrior looked like.

How Did Japanese and European Feudalism Differ?

Japanese and European feudalism differed in four ways. First, the connection between the European lord and his vassal was a kind of legal arrangement. However, the Japanese based their connection on morality instead of law. A samurai obeyed because he believed that his daimyo had the right to rule.

Second, when a vassal died in Europe, his property was given to the oldest son. Or it was divided among all his sons. This often led to civil war. In Japan, a man chose the son who could best take care of the land. If a daimyo had no son, he adopted one.

FEUDAL SOCIETY IN JAPAN

EMPEROR
Held the highest rank in society, but had no political power

↑

SHOGUN
Actual ruler

↑

DAIMYOS
Great landowners

↑

VASSALS AND SAMURAI SOLDIERS
Held land granted by daimyo or shogun

↑

LANDLESS SAMURAI SOLDIERS
Fought for daimyo, but held no land

↑

PEASANTS AND ARTISANS
Provided food and weapons for samurai class

↑

MERCHANTS
Held low social status, but gradually gained influence

After reading this section, what can you infer about the effect of feudalism in Japan and Europe?

Third, in Europe, lords and vassals thought women were not equal to men, but they still respected women. Japanese warriors expected women to be tough and self-disciplined. They had to accept bad times—even death or hari-kari—without complaining.

Fourth, a European knight did not think that education was important. However, a Japanese samurai took pride in his poetry and calligraphy.

Anyone for Tea?

The Japanese began to practice tea ceremonies in the 1400s. Since then, they have made rules about how to prepare and serve tea. The ceremony takes place in a small room with a water container, flowers, and a hanging scroll.

To begin the ceremony, the host carefully prepares the tea. Then the host places the tea bowl in front of the most honored guest. The guest takes a sip and praises the tea maker on the flavor of the tea. Next, the guest takes another sip or two and passes the bowl.

This continues until the bowl comes back to the host. The tea maker carefully wipes the rim of the bowl with a special piece of paper.

Four things are important in a tea ceremony: harmony, respect, purity, and peace. Harmony comes from the plain tools the host uses in making the tea, the sounds of the wind and water, and the flowers. The host respects the guests; the guests respect the host. Their minds are pure and clear. When the ceremony is over, the tea maker and the guests are at peace with themselves and nature.

Lesson 5 Review On a sheet of paper, use the words from the Word Bank to complete each sentence correctly.

1. A _____ is a three-line poem with 17 syllables.

2. A _____ is a five-line poem with 31 syllables.

3. The military dictator of Japan was the _____.

4. The great landowners of Japan were the _____.

5. The _____ were Japanese warriors.

What do you think ?

How did calligraphy and poetry help the samurai win control of his feelings and actions?

Communication in History

A Romantic Novel from Japan

Literature was important in Heian Japan. Many women at court kept diaries. They described their elegant life. One lady of the court wrote the world's first novel. We know only her court name, Murasaki Shikibu. She came from a noble family. She married and had a daughter. A few years later, her husband died. Lady Murasaki then went to court to serve the empress. Her novel grew out of her diary of court life.

Her novel is called *The Tale of Genji*. Its hero is Prince Genji, the "shining Prince." Genji has many adventures and romances.

The Japanese used many Chinese characters in their writing. There were, however, some Japanese sounds that these characters could not express. As a result, a new way of writing Japanese developed around 1000. It is called kana. *The Tale of Genji* is written in kana.

Objectives

◆ To explain how geography helped Japan become isolated

◆ To describe some arts of Japan

Reading Strategy:
Inferencing

After reading this section, what can you infer about the power of shoguns in Japan?

In 1603, the Tokugawa family took control of Japan. The shogun forced the daimyos to move to Edo, a small town on the coast. He could keep his eye on them there. (Today, Edo is the city of Tokyo, one of the world's largest cities.) A daimyo could visit his estate only if he left his wife and oldest son in Edo.

Why Did Japan Isolate Itself?

In the 1600s, many foreigners—merchants and missionaries—visited Japan. But the shoguns thought that Western influence could hurt their power. Beginning in 1623, they began to isolate Japan. They killed all foreign missionaries or forced them to leave. In 1614, the shogun said that no one could be a Christian. In the next 20 years, thousands of Christian Japanese were killed.

The Japanese could not leave Japan. If they did, they could not return. By 1639, only the city of Nagasaki was open to foreigners. The shogun let some Chinese and Dutch traders live there. For the next 200 years, Japan shut itself off from the world.

The Japanese still have beautiful gardens, as they had hundreds of years ago.

What Arts Did Japan Develop?

Japanese paintings usually show the beauty of Japan. Some samurai painters drew pictures of war. The most famous painter of ancient Japan was Sesshu, a Buddhist monk. In the late 1400s, he painted a beautiful silk scroll that is 52 feet long. It shows the land of Japan as it changes over the four seasons of the year.

In their gardens, the Japanese copy nature in a small way. They carefully choose and place rocks in the garden. They also make hills and ponds that look natural.

Ikebana

One Japanese art of arranging flowers

Noh drama

A Japanese play with only two actors

Kabuki

A Japanese play with exaggerated actions

Japan still developed a rich culture. Among its arts are arranging flowers, writing and acting in plays, painting, and gardening. The Japanese call one art of arranging flowers **ikebana.** This art uses only a few flowers.

Noh dramas began in 1325. A Noh play uses only two actors, who wear masks. A storyteller tells the story while musicians play and the two actors act. In 1586, **kabuki** developed. A kabuki play uses song and dance to show strong feelings. Actors tell the story with exaggerated movements that are larger than in real life.

Lesson 6 Review On a sheet of paper, write the letter of the answer that correctly completes each sentence.

1. The Tokugawa shogun moved the capital of Japan to _____.

   A Edo   **C** Hangzhou
   B Beijing   **D** Nagasaki

2. Noh dramas use only _____ actors.

   A five   **B** four   **C** three   **D** two

3. Kabuki plays developed _____ Noh plays.

   A earlier than   **C** at the same time as
   B later than   **D** 200 years later than

4. The Japanese call one art of flower arranging _____.

   A shogun   **C** ikebana
   B exaggerate   **D** hari-kari

5. _____ was the name of the family that began to isolate Japan.

   A Shogun   **C** Samurai
   B Daimyo   **D** Tokugawa

What do you think ?

What do you like best about the Japanese arts discussed in this lesson? Explain your answer.

Marco Polo in China

Marco Polo wrote a book about China in the late 1200s.

Marco Polo's father and uncle were merchants in Venice, Italy. In 1271, they left Venice for the court of Kublai Khan in China. Marco Polo was 17 years old.

Polo worked as an official for the Khan. When he returned to Europe in 1295, he wrote The Travels of Marco Polo. *This reading from that book describes the Khan's palace.*

For three months every year Kublai Khan lives in the capital of Cathay . . . where he has a great palace. It is surrounded by a square wall, each side of which is a mile long. The wall is very thick and ten paces high. . . . At each of the four corners of the square there is a splendid and beautiful palace where the Great Khan's arms are stored. Halfway along each side of the square there is another similar palace, making eight in all. Every palace houses different equipment. For example, in one there is harness for the horses; in another there are bows, ropes, arrows, quivers and all the implements for archery; in a third there are breastplates and armour made of boiled leather; and so it goes on.

There are five gates in the south side of the wall. The central one is only opened for the Great Khan himself. Two small gates on either side of the main gate and two large ones near the corners of the wall are for citizens and other people.

Inside this wall is another one, slightly longer than it is wide. . . .

Within the second wall is the Great Khan's palace—the biggest palace ever to be seen. It abuts onto the northern wall, but to the south is a wide open space where barons and soldiers parade. It is built on only one floor, with a very high roof. . . .

The walls inside are covered with silver and gold and there are paintings of horsemen, dragons, and every kind of bird and animal. The vaulted ceiling is also entirely covered with paintings and gold ornamentation. The main reception room can seat more than 6,000 people. There is an overwhelming number of rooms; no architect in the world could have designed the palace better. The roof is beautifully painted in many colors—vermilion, green, blue, yellow, and so forth—so that it shines like a jewel and can be seen from afar. . . .

Document-Based Questions

1. The Khan's palace was well protected. Describe the area around it.

2. How were the eight palaces on the outer wall used?

3. Why was the central gate special?

4. How were the palace walls and ceilings decorated?

5. How many people could the main reception room hold?

The Taj Mahal— A Monument of Love

The Taj Mahal is one of the most beautiful buildings in the world. It is also a love story in stone.

Shah Jahan was one of the last Mogul emperors. He was the grandson of Akbar. In 1631, Shah Jahan's favorite wife died. They had been close companions for 19 years of marriage. The broken-hearted shah built this tomb to show their great love. The queen's name was Mumtaz Mahal. It means "Chosen One of the Palace." The building's name comes from her name.

Workers brought materials from all over Asia. White marble was brought up the Jumna River to the town of Agra. More than 20,000 workers worked for 22 years to complete it.

The Taj Mahal itself is a four-sided marble building. It sits on a raised square platform. Each side has a huge central arch and small domes. Both the inside and outside walls are delicately carved. At each corner stands a slender tower, or minaret. Gardens surround the tomb. Nearby are a mosque and other buildings.

Here is one visitor's reaction: "With its minarets rising at each corner, its dome and tapering spire, it creates a sense of airy, almost floating lightness. Looking at it, I decided [that] I had never known what perfect proportions were before."

The burial room is eight-sided, with a marble screen around it. The screen is carved so delicately that it looks like lace. At first it was decorated with jewels. A blanket of pearls covered the queen's coffin. Gold and silver decorated the walls. Blue sapphires and red

The Taj Mahal was built for Shah Jahan's favorite wife.

rubies gave color to carved marble flowers. Over time, the pearls and other treasures were stolen.

Shah Jahan planned to build a copy of the Taj Mahal for himself. It would be in black marble. A bridge of silver would join the two tombs. The black tomb, however, was never built. Shah Jahan lost power in 1658. He died in 1666. He was buried next to his beloved queen in the Taj Mahal.

Wrap-Up

1. Why did Shah Jahan build the Taj Mahal?

2. What material was used for the Taj Mahal?

3. How long did the construction take?

4. How was the inside of the building decorated?

5. What were Shah Jahan's plans for his own burial? What happened?

- The Gupta dynasty ruled India during its Golden Age (320 to 535). Indian religious artists developed a unique style. Scientists made many discoveries. Mathematicians used zero and the numerals 1 through 9.

- In 1398, Mongols led by Tamerlane attacked India. In 1525, another Mongol leader began the Mogul empire. Akbar was its best-known ruler. Mogul architects built beautiful buildings.

- China was rich and powerful during the T'ang dynasty (618 to 907). Scholars ran the government, and trading brought foreign visitors and new ideas.

- In the Sung dynasty (960 to 1279), the center of culture shifted south to the Yangtze River Valley. Chinese inventions included gunpowder, the compass, the abacus, the clock, and porcelain.

- In the 1200s, Mongols conquered China, India, and Russia. Later, Kublai Khan established the Yuan dynasty. Mongol rulers encouraged trade with the Arabs and Europeans. Scholars wrote and performed in plays and operas.

- After the fall of the Mongols in 1368, China began to isolate itself.

- The Japanese adapted many ideas from Korea and China. Japan's native religion, Shinto, worships many nature spirits. Many Japanese also became Buddhists.

- During the Heian era (800 to 1200), Japanese nobles wrote haiku and tanka poetry. Noble families took power from the emperor. The shoguns were the real rulers.

- In Japan's feudal system, the daimyos were powerful lords. Samurai were warrior knights. The samurai practiced martial arts and were artists. They followed a code of honor called bushido. Women were also expected to be brave.

- Shoguns from the Tokugawa family took control of Japan in 1603. They moved the capital to Edo. They tried to end foreign influence, including Christianity.

- Flower-arranging, plays, painting, and gardening are important arts in Japanese culture. Noh and kabuki are forms of drama.

Chapter 13 REVIEW

Word Bank

Ajanta

Genghis Khan

Gupta

Mongols

Sesshu

Shinto

Shoguns

Sung

T'ang

Tokugawa

On a sheet of paper, use the words from the Word Bank to complete each sentence correctly.

1. Wall drawings in the _____ caves tell us about life in ancient India.

2. The _____ dynasty ruled India during its Golden Age.

3. The _____ invaded India in 1398.

4. In the _____ dynasty, scholars ruled China.

5. The artists of the _____ dynasty painted masterpieces.

6. The greatest Mongol conqueror was _____.

7. _____ is the religion born in Japan.

8. _____ ruled Japan in the name of the emperor.

9. The _____ shoguns isolated Japan from the rest of the world.

10. _____ was the most famous painter of ancient Japan.

On a sheet of paper, write the letter of the answer that correctly completes each sentence.

11. During the Golden Age, scientists in India figured out the _____ of the moon.

    A size   **C** craters

    B shape   **D** weight

12. Indian doctors learned about _____ 1,000 years before Europeans did.

    A Shinto   **C** inoculation

    B compass   **D** abacus

13. The Chinese invented _____.

    A gunpowder   **C** clocks

    B compasses   **D** all of the above

14. The real ruler of Japan during the Heian era was the _____.

A shogun   **C** samurai
B daimyo   **D** tanka

15. The Japanese wrote _____.

A haiku   **C** kabuki
B tanka   **D** all of the above

On a sheet of paper, write the answer to each question. Use complete sentences.

16. What is one gift India has given to world civilization?

17. What is one gift China has given to world civilization?

18. What is one thing that is the same and one thing that is different between Japanese and European feudalism?

Critical Thinking On a sheet of paper, write your response to each question. Use complete sentences.

19. Imagine that you are a European merchant in the Middle Ages. Which country would you choose to visit: India, China, or Japan? Explain why.

20. Chinese and Japanese artists usually paint nature—trees, mountains, and flowers. Western artists often draw people. What does this tell you about the different cultures?

Test-Taking Tip

Save tests and quizzes you take. Use them to study for future tests.

Unit 2

Fact and Opinion

As you study history, you will read many facts. Sometimes people write books about history in which they state their opinions. You need to be able to tell the difference between fact and opinion.

A fact can be proved true or false.

> Mansa Musa ruled Mali in the 1300s.

An opinion is someone's judgment, belief, or way of thinking about something. To identify an opinion, look for words that tell how someone felt. An opinion is more than just a fact.

> Mansa Musa was a rich and noble ruler.
>
> Mansa Musa was generous to everyone.

Read each pair of sentences in items 1–4. Decide which sentence in each pair is fact and which is opinion. Explain your answer.

1. Justinian had Roman laws collected and organized into a code. Justinian was a wise and able ruler.

2. William the Conqueror's victory was a great step in English history. William the Conqueror's victory made him king of England.

3. The pope called for the First Crusade to free Palestine. The crusades were necessary to defend Christianity.

4. The kings of Ghana invited Muslim teachers to begin schools in Kumbi. This helped improve the connection between the two areas.

5. Write a fact and an opinion about the Middle Ages.

Unit 2 SUMMARY

- Farming and trade revived in the late Middle Ages. Between 1095 and 1291, Europeans went on Crusades to take Palestine from the Muslims.

- Under feudalism, a lord granted land to a vassal in exchange for service. Knights fought frequent wars. Peasants and serfs worked the farm on a manor.

- Romanesque churches were dark and heavy with rounded arches. Gothic buildings had pointed arches; tall, thin walls; and stained-glass windows.

- The eastern Roman Empire became the Byzantine Empire. Its greatest ruler, Justinian, organized a code of laws. The empire fell to the Turks, however, in 1453.

- In 1054, the Christian Church split into Roman Catholic and Eastern Orthodox.

- Russia began in Kiev about 862. Then power shifted to Moscow. Modern Russia began in the 1400s when Ivan the Great drove out Mongol invaders.

- Charlemagne, a Frankish king, united Western Europe in 800. Later, Vikings attacked parts of Europe. William of Normandy invaded Britain in 1066.

- Muhammad was born in Arabia in 570. He preached a new religion, Islam, with one god, Allah. Its followers are called Muslims.

- The holy book of Islam is the Qur'an, written in Arabic. Muslims regard Muhammad as God's prophet.

- Muslims have five duties, or pillars. They must state their faith, pray five times a day, give alms, and fast. If possible, they make a pilgrimage, or Hajj, to Mecca.

- Ghana, Mali, and Songhai were great trading kingdoms in West Africa. Their wealth came from the gold-salt trade.

- The Gupta dynasty (320 to 535) brought a Golden Age to India. Mathematicians invented zero and the numerals 1 through 9. The Mogul empire in India began in 1525.

- China was rich and powerful in the T'ang and Sung dynasties. Trade was important. Chinese inventions included printing, gunpowder, the compass, and porcelain. Mongols led by Genghis Khan conquered China, India, and Russia in the 1200s.

- The Heian era (800 to 1200) was important in Japanese culture.

- In Japan's feudal system, the daimyos were land-owning lords. Samurai, or warrior knights, followed a code of honor and discipline. Military leaders, called shoguns, ruled Japan instead of the emperor. After 1603, the Tokugawa shoguns ended foreign influence.

"I do not know what I may appear to the world, but to myself I seem to have been only like a boy playing on the seashore . . . now and then finding a smoother pebble or a prettier shell than ordinary, whilst the great ocean of truth lay all undiscovered before me."

~Sir Isaac Newton, *shortly before his death in 1727*

Unit 3

Early Modern Times

After the Middle Ages in Europe, change began to creep across the land. In this unit, you will settle in Rome, where great artists create masterpieces. You will be there for the Renaissance, or rebirth of learning. You will travel to Germany and learn about the Reformation. Then you will journey to many parts of Europe to see how scientists used the new scientific method to question old beliefs.

Later in the unit, you will meet kings and queens, explorers and conquistadors, emperors and warriors as you sail back and forth across the Atlantic Ocean.

Chapters in Unit 3

14

The Renaissance

Between the years 1348 and 1600, change came to Europe. During this period, people questioned old beliefs. They also took a new interest in learning, creativity, and independent thinking. Historians call this the Renaissance. It ended the Middle Ages. In this chapter, you will see how the Black Death affected Europe. You will travel to Florence and visit Lorenzo the Magnificent. Then you will journey to England to meet the playwright William Shakespeare. Finally, you will sail back to Italy and watch Leonardo da Vinci, Michelangelo, and Raphael create art masterpieces.

Goals for Learning

◆ To describe the changes the Black Death brought to Europe and explain why historians use the term *renaissance* for this period

◆ To describe the beliefs of humanism

◆ To describe the beginning of the Renaissance in Italy

◆ To list some Renaissance writers and their works

◆ To describe the work of Renaissance artists

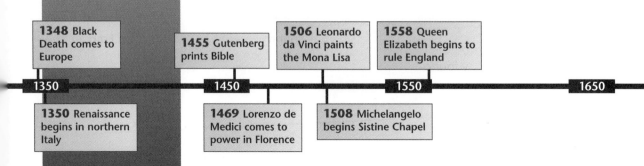

1348 Black Death comes to Europe

1455 Gutenberg prints Bible

1506 Leonardo da Vinci paints the Mona Lisa

1558 Queen Elizabeth begins to rule England

1350   1450   1550   1650

1350 Renaissance begins in northern Italy

1469 Lorenzo de Medici comes to power in Florence

1508 Michelangelo begins Sistine Chapel

Renaissance Europe

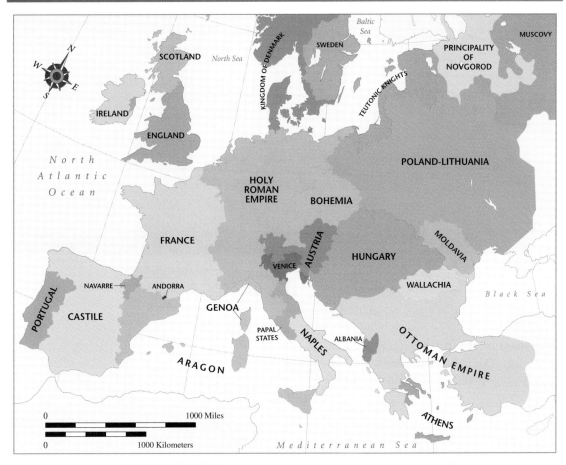

Map Skills

During the Renaissance, many of today's nations began to develop. As you look at the map, you will see names you know, such as England, France, and Sweden. However, two large empires existed during this period that no longer exist now. In addition, the city-states and kingdoms of Italy during the Renaissance took nearly four centuries to unite.

Study the map, then answer the following questions:

1. What sea separates England from the Kingdom of Denmark?

2. What sea is northeast of the Holy Roman Empire?

3. What country borders Castile on the west?

4. In what direction are the Papal States from England?

5. What country borders the Holy Roman Empire on the west?

Reading Strategy:
Metacognition

Metacognition means being aware of the way you learn. Use metacognition to become a better reader.

◆ Write the main idea, details, and any questions you have.

◆ Make predictions and ask yourself what you already know about the topic.

◆ Visualize what is happening in the text. If something doesn't make sense, go back and read it again.

◆ Summarize what you have read and make inferences about the meaning.

Key Vocabulary Words

Lesson 1

Clergy Leaders of religious groups

Rebellion A fight by people against a government; a struggle for change

Renaissance Rebirth; a period in European history that focused on being an individual and expanding creative thoughts and ideas

Lesson 2

Humanism A belief that human actions, ideas, and works are important

Tutor A teacher who teaches one person at a time

Lesson 3

Architect A person who draws plans for buildings

Sculptor A person who carves statues

Worldly Having nothing to do with religion

Lesson 4

Drama A story that is acted out on stage

Sonnet A 14-line poem about one idea

Lesson 5

Portrait A drawing of a person

Fresco A painting done in wet plaster on a wall

Patron A person who supports an artist with money

Chapel A small church

Vatican The home of the pope

Reading Strategy:
Metacognition

Before you read this lesson, think what you can do that will help you understand the impact of the Black Death.

Objectives

◆ To describe the effects of the Black Death on Europe

◆ To explain why people looked to Greece and Rome for ideas

Clergy

Leaders of religious groups

During the 1300s, troubled times came to Western Europe. Workers had little money, and the cost of food was high. Early in the century, when many people had no food, nearly 10 percent of them died.

Then, in 1348, a plague hit Western Europe. This deadly disease made ugly black spots on people's skin, so they called it the Black Death. People got this disease from fleas. These small, wingless insects live on the bodies of people and animals. In the 1300s, the fleas on sick rats spread the Black Death from one person to the next. Between 1348 and 1400, millions of people died. England alone lost nearly one-third of its population.

What Did a Smaller Population Mean for Europe?

When the Black Death attacked Europe, people left the towns and cities and fled to the country. Millions died. Because fewer people were left alive to pay taxes, governments had less money. Fewer people were left to work, so employers had to pay their workers more money. Also, less food was needed for a smaller population. The price of food dropped, and farmers made less money. Because of this, many serfs wanted to leave the manor farms and work somewhere else.

How Did the Black Death Change Society?

During the Middle Ages, nobles and **clergy**—the leaders of religious groups—stood at the top of society. At the bottom stood peasants, or serfs. The law did not let them leave the land on which they worked. But as death marched through Europe, some peasants demanded change.

The Black Death killed millions of people in Europe. This image shows the burying of plague victims in Tournai, Belgium.

Rebellion

A fight by people against a government; a struggle for change

Renaissance

Rebirth; a period in European history that focused on being an individual and expanding on creative thoughts and ideas

These peasants began to question old beliefs. In 1381, English peasants started a **rebellion** against King Richard II. They began to fight for their rights. The king and his nobles stopped it. But the rebellion was a clear warning: change marched with the Black Death!

Why Did People Look Back to Greece and Rome?

Now people wanted to use their imaginations to make things. They looked back to ancient Greece and Rome where people had done this. They studied the art, literature, science, and philosophy of Greece and Rome.

Historians call this new creative period the **Renaissance.** This French word means "rebirth." This period focused on being an individual and expanding on creative thoughts and ideas. With the beginning of the Renaissance, the Middle Ages in Europe ended.

What do you think ?

Why did people leave the cities and flee to the country when the Black Death attacked Europe?

Lesson 1 Review On a sheet of paper, write the answer to each question. Use complete sentences.

1. What was the Black Death?

2. How did the Black Death affect Europe's population?

3. How did the Black Death affect the peasants?

4. What was another name for the Black Death?

5. What is the period after the Black Death called?

History in Your Life

The Bubonic Plague

The first recorded cases of the Black Death were on the Black Sea in Russia. Starting in 1347, the Black Death, or bubonic plague, spread west along trade routes. It attacked seaports, then inland cities, and finally rural areas. At first, people thought poisoned air or water caused the Black Death. They fled from areas where others were sick.

The Black Death spread very easily. It spread by infected fleas on rats, coughing, and sneezing. By fleeing from the disease, people protected themselves somewhat. As of 1352, the plague had killed over 25 million people in Europe. Over the next 300 years, the sickness broke out over and over again.

The last great outbreak of the Black Death took place in China in 1894. There were two small outbreaks in India in 1994. Modern medicine can control the disease. Today, finding and treating the sickness quickly can save 90 to 95 percent of its victims.

Objectives

◆ To explain what people during the Renaissance thought of people in the Middle Ages

◆ To list the qualities of Renaissance men and women

Humanism

A belief that human actions, ideas, and works are important

Reading Strategy:
Metacognition

Remember to ask yourself questions as you read. This will help you make sure that you understand the Renaissance period in history.

The Renaissance dominated Europe for 250 years. It began around 1350 in a few city-states in northern Italy and spread to other countries.

Renaissance people thought that the people of the Middle Ages were ignorant, meaning they had little knowledge or education. One Renaissance writer called the Middle Ages the "Dark Ages." He thought that the "light of learning" had gone out in Europe when Rome fell in A.D. 476. Renaissance people believed that progress in art, literature, and science had stopped in the Middle Ages.

What Is Humanism?

The Renaissance produced **humanism.** It is the belief that human actions, ideas, and works are important. During the Middle Ages, people wanted to get ready for life after death. That was their reason for living. They believed that happiness came only after death. Humanists said that people should be happy while alive.

Humanists discovered that the Greeks and Romans had felt the same way they did. They searched libraries and monasteries for writings from ancient Greece and Rome. Then they studied the Greek and Latin languages to read these writings. All this led to a rebirth, or renaissance, of learning.

What Could a Renaissance Man Do?

Renaissance thinkers loved learning. They wanted to know many different things. A Renaissance man could read and talk about the writings of ancient Greece and Rome. Art and science interested him, too. However, book learning was not enough. He had to have fine manners and be interesting and funny when he talked. He had to play music, dance, and write poetry. He had to be strong and good at games. He also had to ride a horse and use a sword well.

Tutor

A teacher who teaches one person at a time

What Could a Renaissance Woman Do?

During the Renaissance, many women from wealthy families were also well educated. **Tutors,** teachers who taught one person at a time, came to their homes to teach these women. One of the most famous women during the Italian Renaissance was Isabella d'Este. Isabella was born in 1474. When she grew up, she married a wealthy man. Later, however, an enemy captured her husband in a war. Isabella then became the ruler of Mantua, a small territory in Italy.

Isabella d'Este had political power. She was also a well-educated woman. She studied Greek and Latin, and she collected many books for her home. She also sang beautifully and gave money to artists who created great works. At the time, some called her "the first lady to the world."

Isabella d'Este was a Renaissance woman of many talents and interests.

Biography

Niccolò Machiavelli: 1469–1527

Machiavelli was a famous writer and historian. He had a job as secretary to a government council that traveled throughout Italy. During these trips, Machiavelli met many rulers. He wondered how they got and kept power. As a result, he watched how they acted.

Based on what he saw, Machiavelli set up his own ideas about how to rule. He stated them in his book *The Prince*. He believed that for a ruler, the end justifies the means. He said that the usual rules for behavior do not apply to rulers. He believed they should focus on power and success.

Word Bank

Greece

Humanism

Italy

Mantua

Renaissance

Lesson 2 Review On a sheet of paper, use the words from the Word Bank to complete each sentence correctly.

1. _____ is the belief that human actions, ideas, and works are important.

2. The Renaissance began in northern _____.

3. People of the Renaissance studied the writings of ancient Rome and _____.

4. A _____ man was interested in learning to do many things well.

5. Isabella d'Este became the ruler of _____, Italy.

What do you think ?

Who do you think had better ideas about the way to live life—the people of the Middle Ages or the people of the Renaissance? Explain your answer.

At the beginning of the Renaissance, Italy was made up of more than 200 separate city-states. Many of these city-states had less than 10,000 people. However, as time passed, several cities in northern Italy grew to a population of 100,000. Outside Italy, only Paris had more people.

How Did Italian City-States Become Wealthy?

These city-states grew wealthy and powerful by controlling trade. Most of the trade routes from the East passed through the eastern end of the Mediterranean Sea. Goods then went to the northern Italian city-states of Venice, Milan, Florence, and Genoa.

Because northern Italy was not united, each city-state had its own ruler. At times, these city-states fought each other. In the 14th century, Venice defeated Genoa and gained control of Mediterranean trade. Because Venice was by the Adriatic Sea, people called it the "Queen of the Adriatic."

What Type of Government Did Florence Have?

The city-state of Florence showed the creative spirit of the Renaissance. The city became wealthy because it produced wool cloth. As many as 30,000 workers made this cloth.

Florence was an exciting city during the Renaissance. Scholars and artists came to this city from all over Europe.

Florence had a republican form of government. However, several hundred wealthy families controlled the election of government leaders. These leaders were usually bankers and merchants. One of the most important of these ruling families in Florence was the Medici.

Who Was Lorenzo the Magnificent?

In 1469, the most famous ruler of Florence came to power. His name was Lorenzo de Medici. He used his family's wealth to help artists and scholars. Florence came alive with new ideas, holidays, and beautiful art. **Architects**—people who draw plans for buildings—built wonderful buildings. **Sculptors** carved statues and put them outside so everyone could enjoy them.

Every year on the birthday of the Greek philosopher Plato, Lorenzo held a party. The best scholars in Italy came to it. They ate, drank, listened to music, and talked about new ideas. The ancient Athenians had done this, too. With his yearly party and his support for the arts, Lorenzo made Florence the "Athens of Italy."

Because of all this, people called Lorenzo "the Magnificent." He died in 1492, the year Christopher Columbus sailed west into unknown waters. The king and queen of Spain wanted him to find a new trade route to the East. If Columbus could find this route, the Italian city-states would no longer control trade with the East. Spain would.

Lorenzo de Medici was called Lorenzo "the Magnificent" for his leadership in Florence.

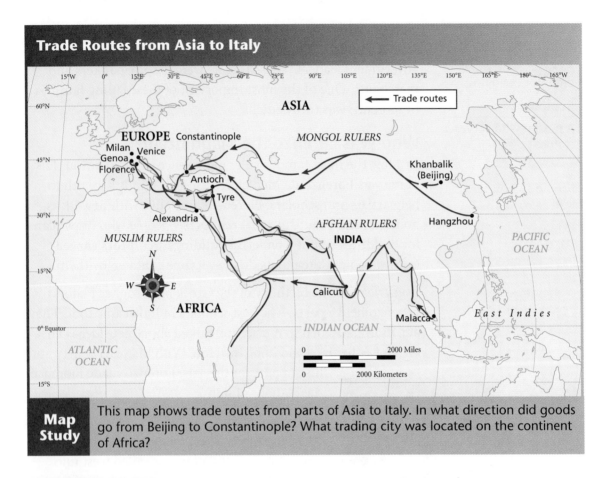

Trade Routes from Asia to Italy

Map Study: This map shows trade routes from parts of Asia to Italy. In what direction did goods go from Beijing to Constantinople? What trading city was located on the continent of Africa?

Worldly

Having nothing to do with religion

Why Did People Give Up Their Worldly Possessions?

Near the end of Lorenzo's life, the economy of Florence began to decline. People grew poorer. Food was scarce. Then a monk named Savonarola began to preach against the Renaissance. He said that the people of Florence thought too much about themselves and not enough about religion.

All over Italy, religious leaders warned people about the dangers of dancing, poetry, and nonreligious music. They asked everyone to throw their nonreligious books, artwork, beautiful clothing, and other goods into a bonfire. All these possessions were **worldly.** That is, they had nothing to do with religion.

How Did Savonarola Gain Power?

Savonarola called Lorenzo Medici a tyrant. Then in 1494, the French attacked Florence. The Medici family gave up the city without a fight. When this happened, the people of Florence thought Savonarola had been right. They forced the Medici family out of power. Then Savonarola became the leader of Florence.

What Happened to Savonarola?

For four years, Savonarola tried to force the people of Florence to change their lives. But soon the people of Florence became tired of Savonarola and his hard ways. Then he began to say bad things about the pope. The people did not like this. They arrested him and put him on trial. Then they executed him in the city square.

Florence continued to decline. However, it remained a powerful symbol of the spirit of the Renaissance.

Lesson 3 Review On a sheet of paper, write the answer to each question. Use complete sentences.

1. Where did the Renaissance begin?

2. Who was Lorenzo the Magnificent?

3. Which city-state was called the "Athens of Italy"?

4. Why did the spirit of the Renaissance upset some religious leaders?

5. What religious leader gained political power in Florence?

Reading Strategy:
Metacognition

Before you read this section, make a prediction about what will happen to Savonarola. Check your prediction as you continue reading.

What do you think ?

Why do you think the people of Florence tired of Savonarola's hard ways?

Objectives

- To identify the language writers used during the Renaissance
- To identify great writers from Italy, England, and Spain
- To explain who printed the first book in Europe

Drama

A story that is acted out on stage

Sonnet

A 14-line poem about one idea

Reading Strategy:
Metacognition

Before you read this lesson, think about what you can do that will help you understand the text.

During most of the Middle Ages, people wrote books in Latin—the language of educated people. Then, near the end of the Middle Ages, writers and poets began to write in their own languages. The great Italian poets Petrarch and Dante wrote in Italian. In England, Geoffrey Chaucer wrote stories in Old English. Even today, people still read the works of these great writers.

Who Was a Great Writer of the Elizabethan Age?

Between 1558 and 1603, Queen Elizabeth I ruled England. She was one of England's greatest rulers. Today, historians call the time of her reign the Elizabethan Age. During these years, England gained new political power and economic wealth.

The Elizabethan Age produced some of the finest writers in English history. William Shakespeare, one of the greatest writers in the English language, lived during this time. Between 1590 and 1613, he wrote many works, including **dramas,** or stories acted out on stage. He also wrote beautiful **sonnets.** This type of poem is 14 lines about one idea.

Who Was a Great Renaissance Writer from Spain?

Another leading writer of the Renaissance was Miguel de Cervantes, a Spanish writer. He created the wonderful character of Don Quixote. Cervantes published the first part of his novel, *Don Quixote de la Mancha*, in 1605.

Quixote sees himself as a knight who must right the wrongs of the world. With his servant, Sancho Panza, he rides throughout Spain. They have one adventure after another. Don Quixote is a funny character. People have loved Don Quixote for over 400 years.

What Was the First Book Printed in Europe?

You already learned that in 1040 the Chinese invented a printing press that used wood blocks. Historians believe that in the 1400s, Johann Gutenberg from Germany invented the first printing press that used moveable metal type.

In 1455, Gutenberg printed a Bible. The Gutenberg Bible was one of the first books printed in Europe. Soon printers were printing books in Italy, France, England, and 15 other countries. By the 1500s, they had printed thousands of books. Learning began to spread as books became part of education.

Then and Now

William Shakespeare

William Shakespeare (1564–1616) wrote 39 plays. *Romeo and Juliet* is about two teenagers from warring familes who fall in love. In *Macbeth*, the main character is too ambitious. *Hamlet* is the story of a prince who seeks revenge for his father's murder. Although his plays are over 400 years old, many are still performed today. Perhaps you have seen one done as a movie.

Many of Shakespeare's plays were first produced in London's Globe Theatre. It has been rebuilt and once again his plays are being performed there. Works by Shakespeare are often seen in major London and New York theaters, too. There are also many Shakespeare festivals. Stratford-upon-Avon, his birthplace, has hosted such an event since 1769.

Newspapers Are Born

When Gutenberg invented movable metal type in the 15th century, printing became easier and cheaper. As a result, newspapers were born. Their purpose was to report news and information to people.

Early newspapers were small, usually one page. They looked like newsletters. They were published weekly, not daily.

The first known newspaper started in Germany in 1609. It told about events in other countries. The first London paper began in 1622. Then in 1665, *The London News Gazette* started. It was published on a regular basis in newspaper format. *The Boston News-Letter* was the first continuously published American newspaper. It began in 1704. Like papers today, it had financial and

Gutenberg's press allowed people to publish books and newspapers for the first time.

foreign news. It also recorded births, deaths, and social events.

Lesson 4 Review On a sheet of paper, write the letter of the answer that correctly completes each sentence.

1. During most of the Middle Ages, people wrote books in the _____ language.

   A English **B** Italian **C** French **D** Latin

2. One of the greatest English writers of plays and sonnets was _____.

   A Petrarch **B** Dante **C** Chaucer **D** Shakespeare

3. The English writer _____ wrote stories in the English language.

   A Petrarch **B** Dante **C** Chaucer **D** Shakespeare

4. The Italian poet _____ wrote in his country's language.

   A Dante **B** Chaucer **C** Gutenberg **D** de Cervantes

5. The first book that _____ printed was the Bible.

   A Dante **B** Chaucer **C** Gutenberg **D** de Cervantes

What do you think

Why would having books in one's own language lead to more learning?

During the Renaissance, artists wanted to make their paintings and sculptures look just as good as those of Greek artists. In fact, someone once heard the great Renaissance sculptor Donatello say to one of his sculptures, "Speak then! Why will you not speak!"

But artists also wanted the people in their paintings and sculptures to look even better than they did in real life. By doing this—with paint, bronze, and marble—they created masterpieces. During the Renaissance, people called a gifted artist a genius. That is, the artist had been born with special skills and was different from ordinary people. Many artists produced important works of art during the Renaissance. However, few of them produced masterpieces like those of da Vinci, Michelangelo, and Raphael Santi.

Portrait

A drawing of a person

Reading Strategy:
Metacognition

Remember to look at the photographs and illustrations, and to note the descriptive words. This will help you visualize Renaissance art.

What Is Leonardo da Vinci Remembered For?

Leonardo da Vinci was a true Renaissance man. Born in the small Italian village of Vinci in 1452, he had many interests and much skill. His curiosity drove him to explore many fields of study. Leonardo was an artist, a scientist, an engineer, and a clever inventor.

Leonardo left us only a few paintings. He completed his most famous painting in 1503. It is the **portrait,** or drawing, of a 24-year-old woman from Florence.

Leonardo da Vinci was a very skilled Renaissance man. This drawing is a self-portrait.

She looks at us with a mysterious smile. The painting, called the *Mona Lisa,* is one of the most famous paintings in the world.

Another important painting of Leonardo's is the *Last Supper.* It shows Jesus of Nazareth eating with his disciples on the night before he died. Leonardo painted it in wet plaster on a wall. Plaster is a mixture of sand, water, and lime. It gives a smooth finish to a wall. Leonardo used his own way of doing this **fresco.**

Like all Renaissance artists, Leonardo needed **patrons.** These people supported artists by giving them money. One of Leonardo's patrons was Beatrice d'Este, the wife of the duke of Milan. Another was the king of France, Francis I. Leonardo's work in France helped spread Renaissance ideas to countries beyond Italy. Leonardo da Vinci died in 1519 at the age of 67.

The *Mona Lisa is one of da Vinci's most famous portraits.*

Fresco

A painting done in wet plaster on a wall

Patron

A person who supports an artist with money

What Are Two Sculptures by Michelangelo?

Michelangelo was born near Florence in 1475. As a young man, he wanted to be a sculptor, and Lorenzo de Medici helped him in his studies. At the age of 23, Michelangelo became famous for carving the Pietà, which means "pity." The sculpture shows Mary, the mother of Jesus, holding his dead body. In 1504, Michelangelo completed a statue of David. (In a Bible story, David killed the giant Goliath with a stone thrown from a slingshot.) Michelangelo loved being a sculptor. But he also became famous as a painter.

Michelangelo was an artistic genius. He thought of himself as a sculptor, but he was also a painter.

Chapel

A small church

Vatican

The home of the
pope

*Michelangelo painted
this fresco in the Sistine
Chapel. It is titled* The
Last Judgement.

Reading Strategy:
Metacognition

Note the important
details about
Michelangelo.
Summarize what you
have read about him.

What Ceiling Did Michelangelo Paint?

In 1508, Pope Julius II asked 33-year-old Michelangelo to come
to Rome. The pope wanted him to paint frescoes on the ceiling
of the Sistine **Chapel** in the **Vatican.** The chapel was a small
church in the Vatican. The Vatican is the home of the pope.

Michelangelo did not want the job. He insisted that he was
a sculptor and not a painter. But the pope held firm, and
Michelangelo finally accepted.

The pope told Michelangelo that he could paint what he
wanted. So on the wet plaster of the ceiling, Michelangelo
painted pictures from Bible stories. He started with the
creation, or the making of the world, and ended with the
great flood.

Raphael Santi painted mostly religious paintings during the Renaissance.

For four years, Michelangelo painted the ceiling while lying on his back, 80 feet above the floor. Paint dropped into his eyes. At night he painted by candlelight. He felt tired, gloomy, and anxious. Only his genius and physical strength enabled Michelangelo to complete the ceiling. He painted more than 300 people and pictures on that ceiling! Some were ten feet tall. Most historians think that the ceiling of the Sistine Chapel is one of the greatest masterpieces in the history of art. Michelangelo died in 1564.

What Is Raphael Remembered For?

Raphael Santi was born in Italy in 1483. He painted mostly religious pictures. People remember him for his paintings of Mary and the baby Jesus. Art historians call these his Madonna paintings. (*Madonna* is Italian for "my lady.") One of Raphael's most famous paintings is the *School of Athens*. At the center of the painting, Raphael placed the Greek philosophers Plato and Aristotle. He surrounded them with other Greek scholars. The painting shows that the learning and culture of ancient Greece influenced the Renaissance. Raphael, another genius of the Renaissance, died in 1520 at the age of 37.

Lesson 5 Review On a sheet of paper, write the answer to each question. Use complete sentences.

1. What is the name of Leonardo's most famous painting?

2. Why did Renaissance artists need patrons?

3. What are two statues Michelangelo carved?

4. Why was working on the Sistine Chapel hard for Michelangelo?

5. What painting of Raphael's showed the Renaissance interest in ancient Greek culture?

What do you think ❓

Why do you think being a sculptor was more important to Michelangelo than being a painter?

The Making of a Renaissance Gentleman

In 1528, Baldassare Castiglione published The Book of the Courtier. *A courtier was a person who visited a royal court. This book told young gentlemen what the rules were for visiting the court. Gentlemen followed its rules for several centuries.*

Besides his noble birth, then I would have the Courtier [show] a certain grace and (as we say) air that shall make him at first sight pleasing and agreeable to all who see him. . . .

[The Courtier should] know how to swim, to leap, to run, to throw stones, for besides the use that may be made of this in war, a man often has occasion to show what he can do in such matters; whence good esteem is to be won, especially with the multitude. . . . Another admirable exercise, and one very befitting at court, is the game of tennis. . . .

I would have him more than passably accomplished in letters, at least in those studies that are called the humanities. . . . Let him be versed in the poets, and not less in the orators and historians, and also proficient in writing verse and prose, especially in [speech] . . . for besides the enjoyment he will find in it, he will by this means never lack agreeable

entertainment with ladies, who are usually fond of such things. . . .

I am not content with the Courtier unless he be also a musician and unless, besides understanding and being able to read notes, he can play . . . instruments. For if we consider rightly, there is to be found no rest from toil or medicine for the troubled spirit more becoming and praiseworthy in time of leisure, than this; and especially in courts, where . . . many things are done to please the ladies, whose tender and gentle spirit is easily penetrated by harmony and filled with sweetness. . . .

When dancing in the presence of many and in a place full of people, it seems to me that he should preserve a certain dignity, . . . and airy grace of movement.

Document-Based Questions

1. What is a courtier?

2. Why was *The Book of the Courtier* written?

3. What athletic abilities should a courtier have?

4. According to the author, in what two ways may a courtier please the ladies?

5. How may the knowledge of music help a courtier in his personal life?

The Hundred Years' War

The Hundred Years' War extended over the reigns of five English and five French kings. From 1337 to 1453, they fought for control of France. This struggle was actually a series of battles broken by truces and treaties.

The war had several causes. The French kings wanted to control the English province of Gascony in southwest France. Gascony was a valuable wine-producing region. The French supported the Scots against the English. These actions angered the English. English and French sailors and fishermen fought over rights in the English Channel. The wool trade in Flanders was also a point of disagreement. In addition, in 1337, the English king, Edward III, claimed the throne of France. His uncle, the French king, had died without a male heir. When Edward III landed an army in Normandy, the Hundred Years' War began.

In the fighting that followed, the English won many battles. But the French won the war. The French had three times the resources—soldiers, supplies, and wealth—of the English. Several events also hindered the warfare. The Black Death, the deadliest plague ever known, killed millions of people. There was also a peasant revolt in England.

During the war, new military tactics developed. English archers used the newly developed longbow. With that weapon, they won the war's greatest victory in the Battle of Crecy (1346). The English also won the Battle of Poitiers (1356). Then the Treaty of Bretigny in 1360 began a brief period of peace. Henry V of England renewed the fighting, though. He won the Battle of Agincourt (1415). The Treaty of Troyes in 1420 gave him the French crown.

The Battle of Crecy.

The peace was short-lived, however. Henry V died in 1422 and the French reclaimed the throne. War flared up again. By 1428, the English controlled northern France. They laid siege to Orléans, an important city in central France. Then Joan of Arc, an unknown peasant girl, led a French army to save Orléans. She claimed to have had visions from heaven. In them, saints told her to lead a French army against the English. Joan was victorious in Orléans, Patay, and Reims. Later, the English took her prisoner and burned her as a witch.

The French kept winning battles and the English retreated. At the end of the war in 1453, they controlled only the city of Calais. The French took over this port in 1558.

Wrap-Up

1. What two countries fought the Hundred Years' War?

2. What were five causes of the war?

3. Why did England's Edward III claim a right to the French throne?

4. What problems inside France and England interrupted the war?

5. Who was a French hero during the war?

- A deadly plague, the Black Death, struck Europe in 1348. Millions of people died. As a result, society changed. There were fewer workers, so workers and serfs could demand more rights.

- The Renaissance began about 1350, ending the Middle Ages. It was a time of creativity and learning. People studied the classical learning of ancient Greece and Rome.

- Men and women of the Renaissance valued education, art, and science. They also valued good manners and skills such as music, dance, and swordplay.

- The Renaissance began in the city-states of Italy. City-states such as Venice, Milan, Florence, and Genoa grew rich from trade with the East. Each had its own ruler. In the 1300s, Venice, on the Adriatic Sea, defeated Genoa. It gained control of trade in the Mediterranean.

- The Medici were the leaders of Florence, the "Athens of Italy." Lorenzo de Medici encouraged artists and scholars.

- Florence began to decline in the late 1400s. The monk Savonarola led a religious movement against the Renaissance. The Medicis lost power. Savonarola tried to establish a more religious way of life in Florence. After a few years, people rebelled against him.

- Renaissance artists made lifelike paintings and sculptures. Artists depended on wealthy patrons, such as Isabella d'Este and the pope.

- Late medieval writers wrote in their native languages, not Latin. Renaissance writers also used local languages. In England, Shakespeare wrote plays and sonnets. In Spain, Cervantes created the character Don Quixote. In Germany, Gutenberg used moveable metal type to print a Bible in 1455. Printed books spread learning.

- Leonardo da Vinci was an artist, scientist, and inventor. His most famous paintings are the *Mona Lisa* and the *Last Supper*. When Leonardo worked in France for King Francis I, Renaissance ideas spread.

- Michelangelo was a sculptor in Florence. He is famous for statues, such as *David*. He also painted the ceiling of the Sistine Chapel.

- Raphael made many religious paintings. He was influenced by the learning and culture of ancient Greece.

Chapter 14   R E V I E W

Word Bank

Beatrice d'Este

Cervantes

Gutenberg

Isabella d'Este

Leonardo da Vinci

Lorenzo de Medici

Michelangelo

Raphael

Savonarola

Shakespeare

On a sheet of paper, use the words from the Word Bank to complete each sentence correctly.

1. People called _____ "the Magnificent" because he worked to make Florence into a great city.

2. The monk _____ criticized the people of Florence because they liked worldly possessions.

3. _____, the ruler of Mantua, was a true Renaissance woman.

4. People call _____ one of the greatest writers in the English language.

5. _____ wrote a funny novel about a Spaniard who wanted to be a knight so he could right the wrongs of the world.

6. _____ invented the first printing press to use moveable metal type.

7. _____ was an artist, scientist, engineer, and inventor.

8. _____ painted the ceiling of the Sistine Chapel.

9. People remember _____ for his paintings of the Madonna.

10. One of Leonardo da Vinci's patrons was _____.

On a sheet of paper, write the letter of the answer that correctly completes each sentence.

11. During the Renaissance, many people believed in _____, which said that the actions, ideas, and works of human beings were important.

   A architect   **C** humanism
   B sculptor   **D** philosophy

12. It is the job of _____ to design buildings and other structures.

   A philosophers   **C** humanists
   B frescoes   **D** architects

13. A 14-line poem is a(n) _____.

A sonnet   **C** tanka
B haiku   **D** opera

14. A _____ is a person who supports an artist.

A portrait   **C** sonnet
B patron   **D** tutor

15. A _____ is a drawing of a person.

A portrait   **C** plaster
B patron   **D** sonnet

On a sheet of paper, write the answer to each question. Use complete sentences.

16. How did the Black Death change Europe?

17. Why was Leonardo da Vinci a Renaissance man?

18. Renaissance men and women were skilled and smart. What would a Renaissance person be like today? Write down three people living today who could be called "renaissance" people.

Critical Thinking On a sheet of paper, write your response to each question. Use complete sentences.

19. During the Renaissance, some religious leaders asked people to give up their worldly possessions. Imagine that these leaders are alive today. What possessions might they want you to give up?

20. Before the Renaissance, writers wrote in Latin. But few people could read this language. Describe your life if all web sites, books, television shows, and movies were in a language you did not know or understand.

Test-Taking Tip

For open-book tests, write short summaries of every chapter or section.

15

The Reformation

In Chapter 14, you read about the Renaissance. Much of this took place in Italy. This chapter takes you north to Germany. There you will see how a monk named Luther began the religious reform movement. From Germany, you will cross the English Channel and meet Henry VIII, who also led reform. Next, you will travel to Geneva to learn about John Calvin and his beliefs. Finally, you will journey back to Italy. There you will see how the Catholic Church decided to fight the other reformers—the Protestants.

Goals for Learning

◆ To define the term *Reformation*

◆ To explain the importance of Martin Luther in the Reformation

◆ To list the three basic reforms Martin Luther made

◆ To explain how the Anglican Church was founded

◆ To describe the beliefs of Calvinism

◆ To describe the Catholic Reformation

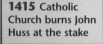

1415 Catholic Church burns John Huss at the stake

1534 Henry VIII begins Anglican Church

1545 The Council of Trent begins

1450   1500   1550   1600

1517 Luther writes his 95 theses and starts the Reformation

1536 Calvin publishes *Institutes of the Christian Religion,* begins Calvinist Church

1572 French Catholics kill Huguenots in St. Bartholomew's Day Massacre

Reformation Europe (1550)

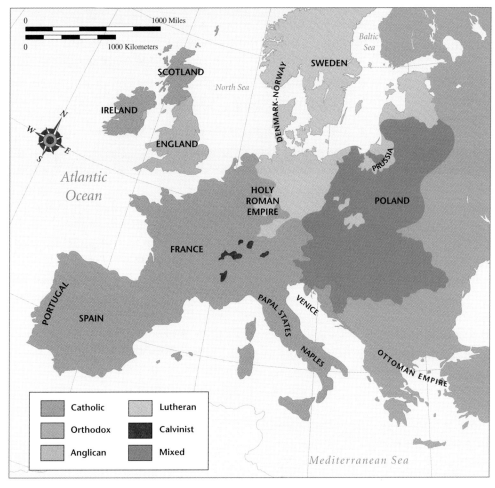

0 — 1000 Miles

0 — 1000 Kilometers

SCOTLAND

IRELAND

ENGLAND

North Sea

DENMARK-NORWAY

Baltic Sea

SWEDEN

Atlantic Ocean

PRUSSIA

HOLY ROMAN EMPIRE

POLAND

FRANCE

PORTUGAL

SPAIN

PAPAL STATES

VENICE

NAPLES

OTTOMAN EMPIRE

Mediterranean Sea

Legend:
- Catholic
- Orthodox
- Anglican
- Lutheran
- Calvinist
- Mixed

Map Skills

Before the Protestant Reformation, the Catholic Church had great power in most of Western Europe. However, people began to challenge this power. New religions began. This map shows where different religions had developed by 1550.

Study the map, then answer the following questions:

1. What religion was practiced in England at this time?

2. What religions were practiced in the Holy Roman Empire?

3. Where was the Catholic religion still practiced?

4. Where did the Calvinist religion develop?

5. What religion dominated Western Europe at this time?

Reading Strategy:
Summarizing

When you summarize, you ask questions about what you are reading. That way you can review what you have just read. As you read the text in this chapter, ask yourself these questions:

◆ What details are most important to the person or period in history?

◆ What is the main thing being said about the person?

◆ What events are pointed out about this period in history?

Key Vocabulary Words

Lesson 1 ————————————

Authority Power

Reformer A person who tries to change something

Heretic A person who holds a belief that a religious authority thinks is false

Lesson 2 ————————————

Reformation A movement that challenged and changed the Catholic religion in Europe

Salvation Eternal happiness for one's soul

Indulgence A church paper that says that a person will not be punished after death for their sins

Purgatory A place of suffering after death

Thesis A statement that people argue about or try to prove

Lesson 3 ————————————

Excommunicate To say that someone can no longer be a member of a church

Lutheran Church The church established by Martin Luther

Minister A person who can lead a religious ceremony in a Lutheran church

Ritual A ceremony

Baptism A ritual by which a person becomes a Christian

Communion A ritual by which Christians grow in their faith

Protestant A reformer who protested against the Catholic Church

Lesson 4 ————————————

Annul To announce that a marriage never existed between two people

Archbishop The top religious leader in a church province

Anglican Church The Church of England

Compromise An agreement in which both sides give up something

Puritan An English Protestant who wanted to purify the Anglican Church

Purify To make clean

Lesson 5 ————————————

Calvinism The religious movement founded by John Calvin

Elect A Calvinist term for those whom God has chosen to save

Elder An experienced, older person

Huguenot A French Calvinist

Massacre The act of killing many people who are often defenseless

Lesson 6 ————————————

Catholic Reformation The Catholic Church's reforms that attempted to fight Protestant beliefs

Censor To prevent someone from reading or viewing something

Roman Inquisition A Catholic court that inquired into people's religious beliefs

Jesuit A member of the Catholic religious order known as the Society of Jesus

Objectives

◆ To describe how the king of France challenged the pope and Rome

◆ To define the word *reformer* as used in this chapter

◆ To understand the threat that the reformers posed to the Catholic Church

Authority

Power

Reformer

A person who tries to change something

In Unit 2, you studied the Middle Ages. Historians also call this period the Age of Faith. The Catholic Church had great religious and political power. In fact, the pope could command kings. Beginning in the 1300s, some people challenged the **authority,** or power, of the church.

Who Challenged the Church's Political Authority?

In 1294, King Philip IV of France tried to tax church officials. The pope told the French clergy not to pay the tax. In 1303, the king arrested Pope Boniface VIII, an Italian. Six years later, the king helped to elect a French pope, Clement V. The new pope moved from the Vatican in Rome to Avignon in France.

Seventy years passed before a pope lived in Rome again. But problems continued. At different times, more than one person claimed to be pope. Some church leaders suggested that a council should take the place of the pope. All this weakened the church's power.

Who Challenged the Church's Religious Authority?

Other people challenged the religious authority of the church. We call them **reformers** because they believed that the church needed to be reformed, or changed, for the better.

One reformer in the 1300s was the Englishman John Wycliffe. He said that the church had too much power and wealth. He also said that the Bible, and not leaders of the church, should be the authority for Christians. To allow people to read the Bible, Wycliffe translated the Latin Bible into English.

John Wycliffe was an early church reformer.

Word Bank

Avignon

Bible

Huss

King Philip IV

Wycliffe

People called Wycliffe's followers the "Poor Preachers." They had no interest in money. All they wanted to do was to teach religion to people in their own language instead of in Latin.

Why Did John Huss Criticize the Church?

The ideas of John Wycliffe influenced John Huss. He was a well-known scholar at the University of Prague in Bohemia. (Bohemia was part of the Holy Roman Empire. It is now part of the Czech Republic.) Huss thought that the church's clergy were too worldly and that the church should remove them from office.

When Huss and his followers criticized the church, both religious and political leaders feared a rebellion. Church leaders said that Huss was a **heretic**. A heretic teaches a belief that a religious authority thinks is false. In 1415, they arrested Huss and burned him at the stake.

Lesson 1 Review On a sheet of paper, use the words from the Word Bank to complete each sentence correctly.

1. _____ of France challenged the authority of the pope in 1294.

2. In 1309, Pope Clement V moved from the Vatican to _____.

3. John _____ said that the church had too much money and power.

4. Wycliffe translated the _____ from Latin to English.

5. The church burned John _____ as a heretic.

What do you think ?

Why did the church not want to lose its political and religious authority?

Objectives

◆ To explain Martin Luther's disagreements with the Catholic Church

◆ To describe the way Luther spread the word about his disagreements

Reformation

A movement that challenged and changed the Catholic religion in Europe

Salvation

Eternal happiness for one's soul

Indulgence

A church paper that says that a person will not be punished after death for their sins

Reading Strategy:
Summarizing

What reformer is being introduced in this lesson?

Just over 100 years after Huss was executed, Martin Luther challenged the church's religious authority. What he did began a new period of European history—the **Reformation.** This movement challenged and changed Christianity in Europe.

What Troubled Luther?

Martin Luther was born in Germany in 1483. His father wanted him to become a lawyer. But when Luther studied law, he did not like it. Then, in 1505, Luther was caught in a summer storm and lightning nearly hit him. Fearing for his life, Luther promised to become a monk if he lived. In 1507, he kept his promise.

In 1512, Luther began to teach religion at the University of Wittenberg in Saxony. Questions about **salvation,** or eternal happiness for his soul, troubled him. How, he asked, should he act to save his soul? Luther struggled for a long time with this problem. Then, while reading the Bible, he found his answer.

Luther came to believe that he could win salvation by faith alone. He said that fasting, prayer, and religious ceremonies could not guarantee, or promise, salvation. But the Catholic Church said that people needed to do these good works to save their souls. Luther said that his discovery made him feel as though he were "born again."

Why Did the Church Begin to Sell Indulgences?

In 1517, Luther and the church leadership began to struggle with one another because Pope Leo X started to sell **indulgences.** These are papers the church gives people that say they will not be punished after death for their sins. People bought indulgences for themselves and for loved ones who were already dead. The church said that doing this was a good deed. The pope sold indulgences because he needed more money to build St. Peter's Church, a big church in Rome.

In 1517, a monk named John Tetzel began selling indulgences near Luther's university. Tetzel told people to buy an indulgence to free a friend's soul from **purgatory.** This is what is believed to be a place of suffering after death. Tetzel said that the person who bought the indulgence could be sure of salvation. He raised a great deal of money and sent it back to Rome for St. Peter's Church.

What Are Luther's 95 Theses?

Someone asked Luther what he thought about the selling of indulgences. He said that it was wrong because people could not buy forgiveness for sins. On hearing this, Tetzel criticized Luther.

Martin Luther started the Reformation by disagreeing with the Catholic Church.

Luther began to write a series of 95 **theses,** or statements, against indulgences and other actions of the church. He nailed these statements on the door of a church. He wanted to argue the theses with church officials. On October 31, 1517, he let other people read his ideas. Printers printed Luther's 95 statements. People sent them to other countries. Because of this, the sale of indulgences went down, and the church lost money. The church decided to take steps to stop Luther's influence in Europe.

Then and Now

Origins of the Lutheran and Presbyterian Churches

Many Protestant churches began during the Reformation. Martin Luther formed the Lutheran Church and John Calvin's ideas shaped the Presbyterian Church. Both churches rejected the power of the pope and stressed the authority of the Bible. Their members believed in the importance of individual faith.

Both churches are still thriving today in the United States. The Evangelical Lutheran Church has just over 5 million members. The Presbyterian Church has almost 4 million members. There are many other Protestant churches as well.

History in Your Life

Disks for the Eyes

When were eyeglasses invented? The Chinese claim to have used them before A.D. 300. Marco Polo wrote in 1275 that he saw many Chinese wearing glasses. The scientist Roger Bacon mentioned eyeglasses in his writings in 1268. History, however, has no record of their invention.

We do know that by the 1300s, eyeglasses were popular among Europe's upper classes. However, people could use them only for seeing at a distance. What about glasses for seeing objects that were close? It took another hundred years to learn how to make them.

Venice became the chief producer of eyeglasses. However, people did not call them glasses. They called them "disks for the eyes."

In the 1500s, the demand for eyeglasses increased. The printing presses were producing more books and more people were reading. Some scholars needed glasses to be able to read.

Lesson 2 Review On a sheet of paper, write the letter of the answer that correctly completes each sentence.

1. Martin Luther was born in _____.

    A England   **C** Italy

    B Germany   **D** France

2. As a monk and teacher, Luther struggled with the idea of _____.

    A salvation   **C** confrontations

    B vows   **D** translations

3. Luther believed that people could be saved by _____ alone.

    A the Bible   **C** faith

    B good works   **D** indulgences

4. Pope Leo X began to sell _____ to pay for the building of St. Peter's Church.

    A theses   **C** frescoes

    B portraits   **D** indulgences

5. Luther wrote _____ theses, or statements, about church actions that he did not agree with.

    A 85   **B** 95   **C** 105   **D** 1500

What do you think

Do you think that Luther had trouble with more than just indulgences? Explain your answer.

Excommunicate

To say that someone can no longer be a member of a church

Lutheran Church

The church established by Martin Luther

Minister

A person who can lead a religious ceremony in a Lutheran church

Ritual

A ceremony

Baptism

A ritual by which a person becomes a Christian

Communion

A ritual by which Christians grow in their faith

When Luther called for reform, the church ordered him to stop. Luther said he could not go against his beliefs. He said, "Here I stand. I cannot do otherwise."

What Did the Church Do to Luther?

In 1521, Pope Leo X said that Luther's beliefs were wrong and **excommunicated** him. That is, the pope said that Luther was no longer a member of the Catholic Church. The ruler of the Holy Roman Empire—a Catholic—signed the Edict of Worms. This decree said that anyone could kill Luther without being punished. But several German princes protected Luther from this.

What Did Luther Want to Change?

Luther called for three reforms. First, he said that only faith in Jesus Christ could save people. Good works alone would not save them. Second, he taught that religious truth came from the Bible. People should read the Bible and decide for themselves what it meant. Third, Luther said that people did not need the clergy to tell them what the Bible means. To help people read the Bible, Luther translated it into German.

What Church Did Luther Begin?

In the beginning, Martin Luther did not want to break away from the Catholic Church. All he wanted was to debate his 95 theses and reform the church. However, in time, he started the **Lutheran Church.** His church had some differences from the Catholic Church. Catholic priests were not allowed to marry, but Lutheran **ministers** could. (Ministers are the leaders of religious ceremonies.) The job of a minister was to help people find or strengthen their faith in Jesus Christ.

Luther also got rid of some of the **rituals,** or ceremonies, of the Catholic Church. Luther did, however, keep two rituals—**Baptism,** by which people become Christians, and **Communion,** by which Christians grow in their faith.

Why Did German Princes Become Lutherans?

Many German princes liked Luther's ideas. They began to protest the ways of the Catholic Church. Because of this, people called them **Protestants.** In the 1530s, war broke out between the armies of the Protestant Lutheran princes and Charles V, a Catholic ruler.

In 1546, Martin Luther died. Nine years after his death, a treaty was signed to stop the fighting. According to this treaty, each German prince could pick his own church. All the people in his area had to follow his religion. Called the Peace of Augsburg, the treaty kept the German princes from fighting for more than 50 years.

Lesson 3 Review On a sheet of paper, write the answer to each question. Use complete sentences.

1. What does the term *excommunication* mean?

2. Why did the Catholic Church excommunicate Martin Luther?

3. According to Luther, where could people find religious truth?

4. What is one difference between a Catholic priest and a Lutheran minister?

5. Why did people call religious reformers Protestants?

What do you think ?

What might have kept Luther from starting a new church?

Objectives

◆ To explain how a
political problem
started the
Reformation in
England

◆ To describe the
influence of Queen
Mary and Queen
Elizabeth I on the
church

Reading Strategy:
Summarizing

What important
person is introduced
in this section?

Annul

To announce that
a marriage never
existed between two
people

Luther's religious reform movement quickly spread beyond
Germany. By 1534, it reached England, where Henry VIII ruled.
Just 13 years before, Henry had attacked Luther's ideas. To
thank him, Pope Leo X called the king "Defender of the Faith."

Why Did Henry VIII Break with the Pope?

A political problem started the Reformation in England. Henry
VIII became king there in 1509. He married a Spanish princess,
Catherine of Aragon. They had a daughter named Mary. In
1527, Henry VIII tried to end his marriage to Catherine. He
wanted a son, but Catherine could not have more children.
However, the Catholic Church did not allow divorce. Henry
asked Pope Clement VII to **annul** the marriage. That is, to
announce that the marriage had never existed.

Catherine refused to
accept this. She asked
her nephew, Charles
V, who was the Holy
Roman emperor, to
influence the pope's
decision. Charles
had an army in Italy,
so Catherine won
the pope's support.
He refused to annul
the marriage. But
by then, Henry had
secretly married
another woman,
Anne Boleyn.

*King Henry VIII of England was a powerful
ruler who helped start the Anglican Church.*

What Was the Name of Henry's New Church?

In order to divorce Catherine, Henry VIII appointed a new **archbishop** of Canterbury. An archbishop is the top religious leader in a church province. This archbishop said that Henry's marriage to Catherine was not legal. In 1534, Parliament made the king the head of the Church of England, or **Anglican Church.** Henry took control of all lands the Catholic Church owned in England.

What Did Edward Do as King?

Henry and Anne had a daughter they named Elizabeth. But three years after their marriage, Henry said that Anne was not faithful to him and executed her. Then he married Jane Seymour and they had a son named Edward. When Henry died in 1547, his nine-year-old son became King Edward VI. The young king accepted several Protestant reforms. During his reign, Protestant bishops created the *Book of Common Prayer* for Anglican religious services.

Who Tried to Change the Protestant Reforms?

Edward ruled for only six years and died in 1553. Then Mary—Henry's first child—became queen of England. She was a Catholic and used her power to make England a Catholic nation once again. To strengthen her power, she married the Catholic king of Spain, Philip II. But the English Protestants hated Mary and refused to become Catholics again.

Word Bank

Anglican

Edward VI

Elizabeth I

Henry VIII

Puritans

What Compromise Did Elizabeth Make?

When Mary died in 1558, her half-sister became Queen Elizabeth I. She tried to join together the Protestants and Catholics into the Anglican Church. The king or queen of England was still the head of the Anglican Church. But Anglican bishops ran the day-to-day church business. Many Anglican rituals became a blend of Catholic and Protestant ceremonies.

Not all Protestants liked this **compromise,** or agreement in which both sides give up something to stop an argument. Some wanted to rid the Anglican Church of Catholic rituals. Historians call this group of English Protestants the **Puritans** because they wanted to **purify** the church, or make it clean. In the 1600s, some Puritans left England and settled in North America.

Lesson 4 Review On a sheet of paper, use the words from the Word Bank to complete each sentence correctly.

1. Pope Leo X gave _____ the name "Defender of the Faith."

2. Henry VIII of England began the _____ Church.

3. During the reign of _____, the Anglican clergy produced the *Book of Common Prayer.*

4. _____ tried to work out a compromise between the English Protestants and Catholics.

5. The _____ were English Protestants who did not like the compromise and wanted to purify the church.

What do you think ?

What do you think Charles V's army might have done if the pope had let Henry divorce Catherine of Aragon?

Calvinism

The religious movement founded by John Calvin

Elect

A Calvinist term for those whom God has chosen to save

Elder

An experienced, older person

Reading Strategy:
Summarizing

What religious movement is being described in this lesson?

Martin Luther had sparked the religious Reformation in 1517. Almost 20 years later, another man created an organized set of Protestant beliefs. Because his name was John Calvin, we call his religious movement **Calvinism.** He greatly influenced the Protestant Reformation.

What Did Calvin Teach?

John Calvin was born in France in 1509. During his life, his body was weak, but his will was strong. In 1536, he published his most important book—*Institutes of the Christian Religion.* This book contained what he thought each person should believe about religious questions.

First, Calvin taught that people are full of sin when they are born. Next, he said that few people would be saved from sin. Finally, Calvin told his followers that God had already chosen who would be saved. He called these special people the **"elect."** Calvin believed that the elect of God had a political mission. They were to rule Christian society.

Why was Calvin's book important? Because for the first time, the Protestant movement had a fully organized set of beliefs. However, not all Protestants accepted Calvin's ideas. In fact, the Lutherans in northern Germany accepted none of his ideas. The Anglicans in England accepted some and refused to accept others.

How Big Was Calvin's Religious Community?

John Calvin's teaching quickly spread. In 1541, the city officials of Geneva, Switzerland, asked him to organize their city into a religious community. (Geneva's population was 20,000.) Calvin started a school there to train ministers. Then he set up a council of 12 **elders.** These men were older and experienced.

John Calvin started his own Protestant religion called Calvinism. This religion was the first Protestant religion with a fully organized set of beliefs. Calvin lived from 1509 to 1564.

Huguenot

A French Calvinist

Massacre

The act of killing many people who are often defenseless

Next, Calvin gave these elders the power to make laws that said what was right and what was wrong. The elders said that playing cards, betting money on something, drinking alcohol, singing, and dancing were wrong, or sinful.

Finally, Calvin said that citizens had to go to church services several times a week. Members of the council even visited people's homes once a year to make sure that people were leading good lives. The council put people in prison if they did not live the Calvinist way. Sometimes, the council forced people to leave the city. In time, Calvinists began to call Geneva a "city of saints."

What Happened on St. Bartholomew's Day?

Calvinism soon spread to the Catholic country of France. By 1560, about 15 percent of the French population was Calvinist. These French Calvinists became known as **Huguenots.** Many Catholics and Huguenots hated one another.

On August 24, 1572, the hate exploded. On that day, the Catholic Church was celebrating St. Bartholomew's Day. At daybreak, in the city of Paris, Catholics began attacking and killing Huguenots. Historians call the attack the St. Bartholomew's Day **Massacre.** A massacre is the act of killing many people who are often defenseless.

For a month, in the towns and cities of France, Catholics murdered Protestants. More than 12,000 Huguenots lost their lives. But people still continued to become Calvinists. Finally in 1598, the king of France issued the Edict of Nantes. This gave the Protestant Huguenots more political and religious rights. It also protected Catholics by discouraging the building of Protestant churches in Catholic areas. Tension continued between Catholics and Protestants. In 1685, King Louis XIV ended the Edict of Nantes by making Protestantism illegal in France. Hundreds of thousands of Protestants fled France. The loss of so many skilled workers hurt the economy of France for many years.

Lesson 5 Review On a sheet of paper, write the letter of the answer that correctly completes each sentence.

1. John Calvin organized a set of _____ beliefs.

   A Catholic   **C** Protestant
   B Anglican   **D** Lutheran

2. Calvin taught that people are born _____.

   A sinful   **C** educated
   B holy   **D** strong

3. The city of _____ was organized into a religious community.

   A Paris   **C** Canterbury
   B Rome   **D** Geneva

4. Calvin gave the _____ power to make laws.

   A kings   **C** peasants
   B elders   **D** elect

5. St. _____ Day Massacre led to the death of many Huguenots.

   A Peter's   **C** Luther's
   B Bartholomew's   **D** John's

What do you think ❓

Calvin said that people are sinful and that God has already chosen those to be saved. Why do you think so many people accepted these ideas?

Objectives

◆ To describe the purpose of the Council of Trent

◆ To identify Ignatius of Loyola and his work

Catholic Reformation

The Catholic Church's reforms that attempted to fight Protestant beliefs

Censor

To prevent someone from reading or viewing something

Roman Inquisition

A Catholic court that inquired into people's religious beliefs

In the mid-1500s, the Catholic Church began its own reform—the **Catholic Reformation.** (This is sometimes called the Counter-Reformation.) It had three goals. The first was to reform the church itself. The second was to convert non-Christians into Catholics. The third goal was to stop the spread of Protestant beliefs.

What Did the Catholic Church Do First?

Popes Paul III and Paul IV tried to fix problems within the church itself. They appointed new church officials who were well educated. They also began to **censor** books. That is, they prevented people from reading certain books. Finally, they set up a special court—the **Roman Inquisition.** It looked into the religious beliefs of people. It could execute heretics.

What Did the Council of Trent Do?

In 1545, the church called for a council of church officials to meet at the Italian city of Trent. This council lasted 18 years. It wrote down the most important beliefs of the Catholic Church and stopped the sale of indulgences. It refused to accept the teachings of Luther and Calvin on salvation. The council said that people found salvation only through the Catholic Church.

The council also said that to be saved people had to go to church and do good deeds. They also had to accept the pope as the only leader of the Christian Church. Finally, Catholics had to agree with the church's interpretation of the Bible. To counter Protestant translations of the Bible, the council ordered its own new translation.

Who Were the Jesuits?

Ignatius of Loyola was born in Spain in 1491. He played a big part in the Counter-Reformation. Like Luther and Calvin, he asked questions about salvation. But his answers were different from theirs. Ignatius thought that self-discipline and good actions saved people.

The Council of Trent wrote down the most important beliefs of the Catholic Church.

Ignatius created a new Catholic religious order called the Society of Jesus. Members of this order are called **Jesuits.** They had to be smart, strong, and holy, because they wanted to help Catholics stay in the Catholic Church. They also wanted to help Protestants return to it. Over the next 200 years, Jesuit missionaries spread their faith to non-Christians in Africa, Asia, and North and South America.

What Countries Stayed Catholic?

Europe now had two groups of Christian churches—Catholic and Protestant. Many people in northern Germany, Norway, Sweden, the Netherlands, Switzerland, England, and Scotland became Protestants. Most of the people in Italy, France, Spain, and southern Germany stayed Catholic. Soon these different religious beliefs caused wars. Between 1550 and 1650, Europeans fought over their different religious beliefs.

Lesson 6 Review On a sheet of paper, write the answer to each question. Use complete sentences.

1. What did the Catholic Reformation try to do?

2. What was the name of the court that Pope Paul III created to inquire into people's beliefs?

3. What council wrote down the most important beliefs of the Catholic Church?

4. What religious group did Ignatius of Loyola start?

5. What were the two jobs of Jesuits?

What do you think ?

What kind of books do you think Pope Paul III censored during the Catholic Reformation?

Biography

Jacob Amman: late 17th century

Jacob Amman was a Swiss man who belonged to a Protestant group called Mennonites. However, he and others disagreed with some of the church's practices. They thought the church rules were not strict enough. Amman led a group away from the church in the 1690s. They became known as the Amish. Following his directions, they shunned, or completely avoided, excommunicated members.

The Amish first came to America in the 1720s. Today they still live in farm communities. They teach separation from the world. Members must not go to war, swear oaths, or hold public office. Their personal life must be simple. They do not use electricity or telephones. They limit education to the eighth grade.

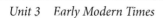

John Calvin's Strict Code of Conduct

John Calvin believed in a very strict moral code of conduct. He published his beliefs in the Institutes of the Christian Religion *in 1536. Later, this code was called puritanical. The English who settled in Plymouth, Massachusetts, in 1620 followed Calvin's rules. They were called Puritans.*

Whoever shall have blasphemed, swearing by the body or by the blood of our Lord, or in similar manner, he shall be made to kiss the earth for the first offense; for the second to pay five sous, and for third six sous, and for the last offense be put in the pillory for one hour.

If anyone sings immoral, dissolute, or outrageous songs, or dances the virollet or other dance, he shall be put in prison for three days and then sent to the consistory [church court].

That no one shall take upon interest or profit more than five percent upon penalty of confiscation of the principal and of being condemned to make restitution, as the case may demand.

That no one shall play at any game whatsoever it may be, neither for gold nor silver nor for any excessive stake, upon penalty of five sous and forfeiture of stake played for.

No one who wishes to be thought religious dares simply deny predestination, by which God adopts some to hope of life and sentences others to eternal death. When we attribute foreknowledge to God, we mean that all things always were, and perpetually remain, under his eyes, so that to his knowledge there is nothing future or past but all things are present. Therefore, as any man has been created to one or the other of these ends, we speak of him as predestined to life or to death.

He has appointed duties for every man in his particular way of life. And that no one may thoughtlessly transgress his limits, he has named these various kinds of living "callings." Therefore each individual has his own kind of living assigned to him by the Lord as a sort of sentry post, so that he may not heedlessly wander about throughout life.

Document-Based Questions

1. What was the punishment for singing outrageous songs?

2. How much profit should a person be allowed to earn?

3. What is Calvin's position on gambling?

4. What does the term *predestination* mean?

5. In your opinion, what parts of the moral code would help business people be successful?

The Harsh Life of the German Peasants

In 1524, German peasants revolted against the princes who ruled them. Peasants were protesting the poor conditions in which they lived. They expected Martin Luther to support their rebellion. Luther had challenged the authority of the Catholic Church. To them, their revolt against the nobles seemed similar to his.

As the revolt spread, however, Luther sided with the German princes. He feared the mob violence that it had caused. Luther condemned the revolt. He wrote, "Let every soul be subject unto the higher powers. Peasants should be obedient." Because of Luther's actions, he lost peasant support.

The Peasants' War, as the revolt is known, was a bloody event. More than 100,000 peasants were killed. Homes and farmlands were destroyed. People starved. Disease spread from one area to another. Children wandered the countryside. They had no parents or means to take care of themselves. Bands of soldiers attacked defenseless villages. Bandits roamed about, attacking the weak and helpless.

Before the revolt, some peasants worked in towns as paid laborers. Some were skilled craftsmen. Serfs, however, could not leave a noble's land. By the 1500s, some peasants were free, but many still worked the nobles' lands. Many were heavily in debt to the landowners.

During the Reformation, the life of a peasant was harsh. Peasants were not allowed to keep or sell all of the crops they raised. The church, for example, got 10 percent of their crops. This rule also applied to their farm animals. Twice a year, a percentage of their crops went to the lord of the manor. In addition, they

had to work for him for two months a year. A landowner could use peasants any way he wished.

Food was often in short supply. Peasants sometimes risked hunting animals, or poaching, in the manor woods. This activity was strictly forbidden. Peasants caught poaching were severely punished.

Peasants could not even get married without permission from their lords. In addition, they had to pay a marriage tax.

Wrap-Up

1. Why did German peasants revolt in 1524?

2. What did Martin Luther say about this revolt?

3. How did the Peasants' War affect the common people in Germany?

4. What are two examples of the harsh conditions in which German peasants lived?

5. Do you agree or disagree with the position that Luther took on the revolt? Why?

■ Beginning in the 1300s, reformers challenged the authority of the Catholic Church. Wycliffe translated the Bible into English so ordinary people could read it. John Huss in Bohemia criticized the clergy.

■ Martin Luther, a German monk, questioned Church teachings about salvation. In 1517, he wrote 95 theses, or statements. His actions led to the Reformation.

■ The pope punished Luther with excommunication. The Holy Roman Emperor agreed that he could be killed. However, some German princes protected Luther.

■ Luther taught that people could be saved only by faith. He also translated the Bible into German.

■ Luther eventually started his own church. The Lutheran Church kept two Catholic rituals—baptism and communion. Unlike priests, Lutheran ministers could marry.

■ Some German princes agreed with Luther. They were called Protestants. In the 1530s, war broke out between Catholic and Protestant rulers. A peace treaty let each prince decide the religion in his lands.

■ King Henry VIII of England wanted to divorce Catherine of Aragon. The pope refused to allow a divorce, so Henry broke with the church and started a new church, the Anglican Church.

■ Henry VIII married several more wives. He had three children: Mary, Elizabeth, and Edward VI. During Edward's reign, Anglican bishops wrote the *Book of Common Prayer.*

■ As queen, Mary tried to make England Catholic again. After her death in 1558, Elizabeth became queen. She compromised with some Catholic beliefs. But strict Protestants, called Puritans, wanted to rid the church of all Catholic rituals.

■ John Calvin wrote a book organizing Protestant beliefs. He taught that God had already chosen those who would be saved. Angry Catholics killed French Calvinists, or Huguenots, in the St. Bartholomew's Day Massacre of 1572.

■ The Catholic Church began the Catholic Reformation. The pope reformed the clergy. He began the Roman Inquisition. The Council of Trent restated Catholic beliefs.

■ Ignatius of Loyola began the Society of Jesus to strengthen the church.

■ The Reformation split Europe into Catholic and Protestant areas. Wars of religion went on between 1550 and 1650.

Chapter 15   REVIEW

Word Bank

Calvin

Elizabeth I

Henry VIII

Huss

Ignatius of Loyola

Luther

Mary

Pope Leo X

Pope Paul III

Wycliffe

On a sheet of paper, use the words from the Word Bank to complete each sentence correctly.

1. The "Poor Preachers" were the religious followers of _____.

2. The Catholic Church burned _____ at the stake in 1415 for his religious beliefs.

3. _____ ordered the Catholic Church to sell indulgences to help build St. Peter's Church.

4. _____ wrote 95 theses to show what he thought about the sale of indulgences.

5. Pope Leo X called _____ the "Defender of the Faith."

6. _____ tried to make England a Catholic nation again.

7. _____ of England tried to talk Catholics and Protestants into a compromise.

8. _____ believed that God had already chosen the people who would be saved.

9. _____ tried to reform the Catholic Church and called a special council to do this.

10. _____ began the Jesuit order to help in the Catholic Reformation.

On a sheet of paper, write the letter of the answer that correctly completes each sentence.

11. A(n) _____ is a person who teaches a belief that a religious authority thinks is false.

   A elder   **C** thesis
   B salvation   **D** heretic

12. A(n) _____ is a member of the Society of Jesus.

   A Jesuit   **C** Anglican
   B Calvinist   **D** Lutheran

13. _____ were French Calvinists.

   A Jesuits   **C** Huguenots

   B Archbishops   **D** Censors

14. The _____ were Anglicans who wanted to purify their church.

   A Jesuits   **C** Huguenots

   B Puritans   **D** Calvinists

15. The Catholic Church sold _____ that were supposed to take away punishment for sins.

   A indulgences   **C** salvation

   B heretics   **D** theses

On a sheet of paper, write the answer to each question. Use complete sentences.

16. What was one cause of the Reformation?

17. How did Calvin's reforms differ from Luther's and King Henry VIII's?

18. What was one thing the Catholic Church did during the Catholic Reformation?

Critical Thinking On a sheet of paper, write your response to each question. Use complete sentences.

19. What part do you think the printing press played in the Reformation?

20. Luther, Calvin, and Ignatius of Loyola all asked questions about salvation. Which of their answers do you like best and why?

Test-Taking Tip

Look for multiple-choice answers that are opposites. Often, one of them is correct.

16

The New Science

During the 1500s and 1600s, a new method of learning about the physical world developed. Scientists challenged beliefs from the past. Instead, they began to use experiments to find truth for themselves. In this chapter, you will meet many of these scientists, and you will learn what they studied.

Goals for Learning

◆ To list the five steps of the scientific method

◆ To describe early theories of the universe

◆ To describe Galileo's discoveries about the universe and gravity

◆ To describe the role Isaac Newton played in the history of science

◆ To list the inventions and contributions of a number of early scientists

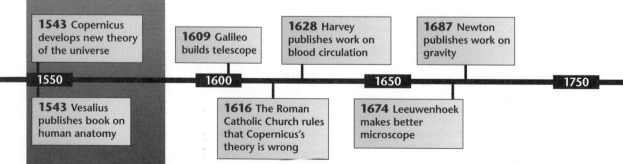

1543 Copernicus develops new theory of the universe

1609 Galileo builds telescope

1628 Harvey publishes work on blood circulation

1687 Newton publishes work on gravity

1550   1600   1650   1750

1543 Vesalius publishes book on human anatomy

1616 The Roman Catholic Church rules that Copernicus's theory is wrong

1674 Leeuwenhoek makes better microscope

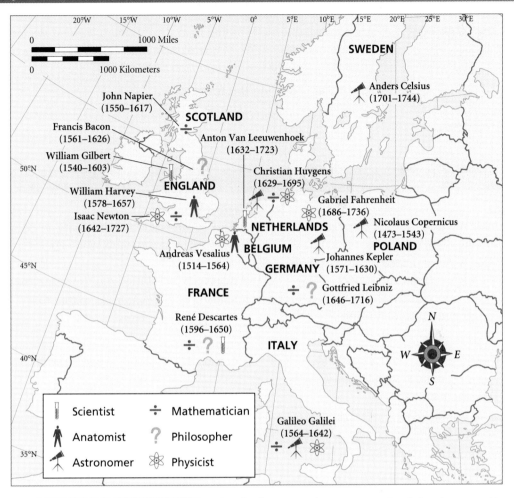

Map Skills

A great number of scientists of all kinds worked in Europe during the 1500s, 1600s, and early 1700s. Some of them invented new ways to solve mathematical problems. Others looked at the sky above them. Some made discoveries about the physical world. This was an exciting time, but a frightening one as well. These scientists found that many things that people had believed for centuries were wrong.

Study the map, then answer the following questions:

1. In what country did Galileo work?

2. How long did Francis Bacon live?

3. In what country did Andreas Vesalius do his work?

4. How many great scientists does the map show in England during this time?

5. What is the name of the French mathematician, scientist, and philosopher from this period?

Reading Strategy:
Questioning

Ask yourself questions as you read. Questioning the text will help you to be a more active reader. You will remember more of what you read if you do this. As you read, ask yourself:

◆ Why am I reading this text?

◆ What connections can I make between this text and my own life?

◆ What decisions can I make about the facts and details in this text?

Key Vocabulary Words

Lesson 1

Scientific method A set of steps scientists follow for study

Hypothesis An educated guess based on what a scientist already knows

Conclusion An answer; a decision reached through step-by-step thinking

Lesson 2

Revolve To move around something

Theory A statement that explains why or how something happens

Universe All the planets and stars that exist in space

Conclude To decide by using facts

Ellipse The shape of an egg

Lesson 3

Experimental science The science that begins with and depends on careful experiments and measurements

Lesson 4

Prism A three-sided object that can be seen through and separates white light into colors

Attract To pull something toward oneself

Scientific law A pattern in nature that someone can predict

Lesson 5

Community A group of people with something in common

Anatomy The structure of a human or animal body

Core The center of something

Amber The hard, yellowish remains of a liquid that comes out of trees

Static electricity The electricity that builds up in something and is produced when one object rubs up against another

Objectives

- To describe how people learned about the natural world before the scientific method was developed
- To identify who worked out the scientific method

Scientific method

A set of steps scientists follow for study

Hypothesis

An educated guess based on what a scientist already knows

Conclusion

An answer; a decision reached through step-by-step thinking

Reading Strategy:
Questioning

Ask yourself: Did I understand the five steps of the Scientific Method? If not, read the section again.

Before 1500, most scholars decided what was true or false in two ways: they read the Bible and they read ancient Greek and Roman writers. During the Middle Ages, they believed that the writings of Aristotle were true. Only the Bible was a higher authority than this great Greek philosopher. The word *science* comes from a Latin word that means "to know." As time passed, science became a popular way to find truth.

What Is the Scientific Method?

During the 1500s and 1600s, a new way of learning about the natural world developed. Scientists based their new way of doing things on a few important steps. They called these steps the **scientific method.**

At the heart of the scientific method is the experiment. When scientists experiment, they carefully control a test. The test helps them discover truth for themselves. They no longer depend on authorities who say that something is true or false. Leonardo da Vinci wrote that science should be "born from experiment, the mother of all certainty." In the 1500s, this idea was new.

What Are the Five Steps of the Scientific Method?

In the 1620s, Francis Bacon, an Englishman, worked out the five steps of the scientific method. First, a scientist picks a problem or question. Second, the scientist makes a guess about the answer. This is an educated guess, based on what he or she already knows. We call such a guess a **hypothesis.** Third, the scientist does an experiment and carefully controls it. Fourth, the scientist observes what is happening during the experiment and makes notes. Fifth, the scientist draws a **conclusion,** or answer, from these notes. Then the scientist decides if the hypothesis was right.

Bacon's five steps still influence science today. Scientists still conduct experiments using these ideas.

Then and Now

The Scientific Method

The scientific method is a well-defined series of steps. Accurate measurement is very important at each step. Scientists began to use this method in the 1500s. However, they did not have today's instruments and techniques.

New technologies have changed what scientists can do. Computers quickly count and compare data. In the past it would take people years to do the same jobs. More powerful microscopes see much smaller objects. Telescopes look farther. Unlike in the 1500s, scientists can look inside living beings and materials.

Today there is also an increasing number of highly trained scientists. In the 1500s, one person might investigate a problem. Today an army of scientists attacks an issue. There has been a tremendous growth in scientific knowledge in the last 100 years.

Lesson 1 Review On a sheet of paper, write the letter of the answer that correctly completes each sentence.

1. Before the 1500s, scholars often decided what was true or false by reading _____.

   A the Bible
   B ancient German writers
   C ancient French writers
   D the Vedas

2. The name of the steps that scientists use to discover the truth is the _____.

   A experiment
   B scientific method
   C hypothesis
   D conclusion

3. At the heart of the scientific method is the _____.

   A experiment
   B Bible
   C tool
   D Aristotle's teaching

4. The _____ is an educated guess in the scientific method.

   A experiment
   B hypothesis
   C mathematics
   D note

5. The scientific method has _____ steps.

   A three   **B** four   **C** five   **D** six

What do you think ?

How could an experiment prove that a hypothesis is wrong? Explain your answer.

Objectives

◆ To describe Copernicus's new theory of the universe

◆ To explain why many people thought Copernicus was wrong

For thousands of years, humans have looked up at the night sky. They have wondered about the movement of the stars and planets. In the daylight hours, they watched as the sun climbed slowly into the eastern sky, traveled overhead, then disappeared into the west. People could see all of this, but they could not explain it. One question they asked was "Does the sun **revolve,** or move around, a nonmoving Earth?" Most people thought the answer was yes.

What Were Some Early Theories About Earth?

About 150, Ptolemy, an Egyptian scientist, developed a **theory** about heavenly movement. A theory is a statement that explains why or how something happens. His theory said that the earth is the center of the **universe.** The universe is all the planets and stars that exist in space. Ptolemy believed that the sun and the five known planets revolved around the earth. This theory lasted for 1,400 years.

Revolve

To move around something

Theory

A statement that explains why or how something happens

Universe

All the planets and stars that exist in space

Reading Strategy:
Questioning

What do the details about these theories tell you about their outcome?

Nicolaus Copernicus was the first to think that the earth traveled around the sun.

A Polish churchman named Nicolaus Copernicus did not accept Ptolemy's theory. In 1543, he published a book that said that the sun was the center of the universe. The earth, he said, traveled around the sun. His theory was a simple explanation for what he saw happening in the skies.

How did he explain the rising and the setting of the sun? Copernicus said that the earth spun like a top. Many people laughed at this idea. They asked why things did not fly off into space if the earth spins. Later, Isaac Newton, another scientist, answered that question. He was the first to outline the laws of gravity.

Johannes Kepler proved that Copernicus was right—the earth does orbit the sun.

Who Proved Copernicus's Theory?

Johannes Kepler proved that Copernicus was right. In the early 1600s, Kepler carefully observed the planet Mars. He **concluded,** or decided by using facts, that the earth and other planets did move around the sun.

Using mathematics, Kepler even showed the shape of a planet's orbit around the sun. He proved that a planet did not orbit in a circle. It orbited in an **ellipse,** which is the shape of an egg. With this discovery, Kepler proved Aristotle wrong too. Almost 1,900 years before, Aristotle had written that all movement in the heavens had to be in a circle. A circle is perfect, and the heavens were a perfect place.

Lesson 2 Review On a sheet of paper, use the words from the Word Bank to complete each sentence correctly.

1. In 1543, _____ said that the sun was at the center of the universe.

2. _____ concluded that the earth's orbit around the sun was in the shape of an ellipse.

3. _____ was the Egyptian scientist who developed a theory about heavenly movement that was accepted for 1,400 years.

4. The new discoveries about the planets challenged _____'s theories.

5. The Law of Gravity was _____'s most important discovery.

What do you think

Why would a person need courage to announce a new scientific theory at this time?

Technology Connection

The Men Who Made Temperatures

Gabriel Fahrenheit was a German physicist. He invented the alcohol thermometer in 1709. Then in 1714 he introduced the mercury thermometer, the same type in use today. He developed the Fahrenheit temperature scale. Water boils at 212 degrees and freezes at 32 degrees. Anders Celsius, a Swedish inventor and astronomer, presented the Celsius, or centigrade scale, in 1742. On the Celsius scale, water boils at 100 degrees and freezes at 0 degrees.

Objectives

♦ To explain why the Roman Catholic Church condemned the teachings of Galileo

♦ To describe why Galileo is called the father of experimental science

Writing About History

Galileo conducted an experiment with a one-pound and a ten-pound ball. Do a similar experiment with a tennis ball and a basketball. Drop them from a high place and time their falls. Then write about what you observed.

Galileo Galilei became the most important supporter of Copernicus's theory of a sun-centered universe. He was born in Italy in 1564. When he was a young man, a Dutch lens maker put glass lenses at the ends of a tube to make a simple telescope. This new tool excited Galileo. In 1609, he greatly improved the telescope and used it to look at the night sky.

What Did Galileo Galilei Discover with a Telescope?

Galileo Galilei was born in Italy in 1564. He was a mathematics teacher at the University of Padua until 1610. He became the most important supporter of Copernicus's theory of a sun-centered universe. Galileo used the telescope to look at the heavens. He saw the rough surface of the moon and that the moon reflected light from the sun. He discovered the dark spots on the sun and the four moons of Jupiter. From his observations, Galileo concluded that Copernicus was right. The earth was not the center of the universe; the sun was.

Why Did Galileo's Work Cause Problems?

Many scholars and church officials refused to accept Galileo's discoveries. The Catholic Church said that this theory challenged the Bible. The church even censored Copernicus's work. They said that people could not read it.

However, Galileo did not give up. In 1632, he published a book to debate the theories of the universe. Church authorities said Galileo's book was an attack on Catholic teachings and put him on trial for heresy. He was forced to admit he was wrong. He was ordered to stop writing about the theory of Copernicus.

The Roman Inquisition found Galileo guilty of heresy. He was then imprisoned in his own home, but he continued his work.

Reading Strategy:
Questioning

As you read, notice the details of Galileo's experiment. What questions can you ask yourself about these details?

Experimental science

The science that begins with and depends on careful experiments and measurements

During his imprisonment, Galileo wrote about his earlier discoveries. By experimenting and measuring with iron balls, he found that the ten-pound ball fell at the same rate of speed as the one-pound ball. His findings contradicted, or went against, the teachings of Aristotle. Galileo showed that gravity makes all objects on the earth fall at the same rate of speed. Today, many scientists call Galileo the father of **experimental science.** That is, he started the science that begins with careful experiments and measurements.

Lesson 3 Review On a sheet of paper, write the answer to each question. Use complete sentences.

1. What instrument did Galileo use to prove Copernicus's theory?

2. Why did Galileo's scientific discoveries cause problems for the Roman Catholic Church?

3. What were some of Galileo's discoveries?

4. How did the church punish Galileo for his support of Copernicus's theory?

5. What discovery did Galileo make concerning falling objects?

What do you think ?

What things did Galileo do that show he was a great scientist?

Objectives

◆ To describe Newton's explanation for why objects appear in certain colors

◆ To explain Newton's Universal Law of Gravitation

Prism

A three-sided object that can be seen through

Attract

To pull something toward oneself

What Discoveries Did Isaac Newton Make?

When Isaac Newton was a 23-year-old mathematician at Cambridge University, a plague broke out in London. Newton left Cambridge to protect his health. In the next two years, he made important discoveries.

First, Newton discovered that white sunlight is a mixture of all colors. Second, Newton discovered why objects appear to be a certain color. He said that a red object appears red because it reflects red light and absorbs all the other colors in sunlight. When an object reflects a color, the other sunlight colors bounce off the object. When the object absorbs colors, it soaks them up so that they disappear from our sight. Newton proved this with an experiment. He passed light through a **prism,** or a three-sided object that can be seen through.

What Was Newton's Most Important Discovery?

Newton built on the work of Copernicus, Kepler, and Galileo. They showed that the planets orbit the sun. Now Newton began to think that Galileo's idea of gravity went as far as the orbit of the moon.

Newton used a falling apple to explain his theory. He said that because of gravity, the earth **attracts** a falling apple. (That is, earth pulls a falling object toward itself.) Then he said that a force exists in the universe. This force causes everything in the universe to attract every other thing. This force is gravity. It increases as objects move close to each other. Big objects have a greater attractive force than smaller objects. Newton said that the sun's strong gravity kept planets traveling in their orbits.

Isaac Newton used a falling apple to explain gravity.

Scientific law

A pattern in nature that someone can predict

Newton showed that we can predict the pattern for all objects in the universe. We call a predictable pattern a **scientific law.** Historians call Newton's discovery the Universal Law of Gravitation. (Universal means that his law about gravity applies to the whole universe.)

In 1687, Newton published a book about his work. His ideas excited scientists. His law showed that the universe was orderly and logical. Scientists began to look for other natural laws. Mathematics, the scientific method, and human reason became powerful tools for unlocking nature's secrets.

Lesson 4 Review On a sheet of paper, write the answers to the following questions. Use complete sentences.

1. What two discoveries did Newton make when he was a young man?

2. What did Newton prove by using a prism?

3. What was the force Newton discovered that keeps planets in orbit around the sun?

4. What did Newton call the predictable pattern for all objects in the universe? What did it show?

5. How did the book Newton published in 1687 affect other scientists?

What do you think

Do you think Newton was a genius? Explain your answer.

History in Your Life

The Original Mother Goose

Isaac Newton's work affected people's lives. Charles Perrault's did, too, but in a different way.

Perrault became a lawyer in 1651, but the work bored him. He became a French government official, but that was not satisfying. Then he found work that gave him pleasure. He recorded fairy tales that he was fond of telling to his children.

In 1697, Perrault published a book called *Histories or Tales of Times Passed with Morals.* Its stories were timeless tales that most of us have heard many times. They included "Little Red Riding Hood," "Sleeping Beauty," "Puss in Boots," and "Cinderella." Perrault wrote them in a simple, charming style.

On the front of the book was a picture of an old woman sitting by a fireplace. A sign on the wall read: "Tales of Mother Goose." For this reason, some people believe Perrault was the original Mother Goose.

Objectives

♦ To explain what is meant by *scientific community*

♦ To describe how advances in mathematics and tools helped scientists

Community

A group of people with something in common

Anatomy

The structure of a human or animal body

Reading Strategy:
Questioning

What do you think you will learn about by reading this lesson?

During this period, scientists developed new ways of doing mathematics. They also invented new scientific tools. By the end of the 1600s, a scientific **community** had developed. A community is a group of people with something in common. This community studied science. Isaac Newton had said that all scientists were friends because they were all seeking truth.

What Did Vesalius Study?

Andreas Vesalius, a Belgian doctor, studied the **anatomy,** or structure, of the human body. Up to his time, people knew little about anatomy. What they did know, they had learned from studying animals and from reading Galen, an ancient Greek doctor. Vesalius wanted more than this. He wanted to see for himself.

The Catholic Church said that cutting up the human body was wrong. Vesalius went against church law and began to study the anatomy of dead human bodies. In 1543, he published his findings. His book contained thousands of careful drawings of the parts of the human body.

Many of Vesalius's drawings showed that Galen was wrong. (For example, Vesalius discovered that the heart had no bone in it.) Today, historians call Vesalius's work the beginning of the modern study of anatomy.

What Did Harvey Describe?

In the early 1600s, William Harvey, an English doctor, also studied human anatomy. He performed many experiments on the hearts and blood vessels of animals. A blood vessel is a tube in the body through which blood passes. He discovered that the heart works as a pump. It circulates, or moves in a pattern, blood through the vessels of the body. (At that time, doctors thought that the blood did not move.) Harvey published his findings in 1628.

What Did Gilbert Study?

William Gilbert, another Englishman, studied the compass.
He wanted to know why a compass needle always points
north. After much study, he explained that the earth is a large
magnet. A compass needle points to the magnetic **core,** or
center, of the earth.

Next, Gilbert explored **amber**—the hard, yellowish remains
of a liquid that comes out of trees. Like the ancient Greeks,
he wondered why amber attracted other objects when he
rubbed it. Gilbert experimented and discovered that glass
behaved in the same way. Gilbert called these objects
"electric." He got the word from the Greek word *elektron*,
which means "amber."

What Did Franklin Prove?

Gilbert's work became the basis for the study of electricity.
In 1752, American Benjamin Franklin proved that lightning
was a form of **static electricity.** Static electricity builds up in
something. When one object rubs up against another, the static
electricity escapes. To prove this, Franklin did a dangerous
experiment. He tied a metal key to a kite and flew it in a
thunderstorm. Lightning struck the kite and traveled down
the string. This made the metal key spark. Franklin proved
his theory, but he was lucky that he was not harmed from his
experiment. His work led to the invention of the lightning rod
to protect buildings and tall trees from lightning.

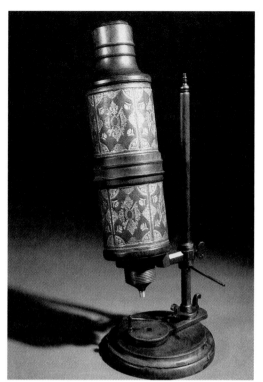
Early microscopes looked different from those used today. This one is from the 1600s.

What Advances in Mathematics Helped Scientists?

New scientific tools and advances in mathematics helped early scientists make important discoveries about nature. One advance was the use of symbols to represent addition (+), subtraction (–), multiplication (×), division (÷), and equality (=). In Scotland, John Napier discovered a way to make mathematics easier. He turned multiplication and division problems into addition and subtraction problems. René Descartes, a great French mathematician, found a way to represent points in space. We call his discovery analytic geometry. Both Isaac Newton in England and Gottfried Leibniz in Germany developed a new way to calculate forces that change all the time. We call their method calculus.

What New Tools Helped Scientists?

Early in the 1590s, a Dutch maker of eyeglasses invented the microscope. In 1674, Anton van Leeuwenhoek, also from the Netherlands, made a lens that magnified an object 270 times. The object appeared much larger than it really was.

Looking at water, Leeuwenhoek was the first person to see one-celled animals. He proved that fleas and flies hatch from eggs. (At the time, people thought that fleas came from sand and flies from spoiled meat.)

Three scientists who gave us scientific tools that we use in our homes were Christian Huygens, Gabriel Fahrenheit, and Anders Celsius. In 1656, Huygens gave us a new kind of clock. Fahrenheit and Celsius gave us the thermometer.

In many ways, the modern world began with the investigations of scientists in the 1500s and 1600s. The scientific method became the way to search for truth.

Margaret Cavendish: 1623–1673

When you look at Margaret Cavendish's background, she seems like any English noblewoman. She was educated by tutors. She married a noble—William Cavendish, Duke of Newcastle. But Cavendish was an unusual woman. For one thing, she was one of the first females to write a biography. It was about her husband. For another, she was not afraid to speak her mind in the company of men.

Her brother-in-law Charles was a scientist and a member of the Newcastle Circle. She spent many hours in discussion with these scientists and philosophers. She argued in person and in books.

Lesson 5 Review On a sheet of paper, write the answer to each question. Use complete sentences.

1. What did the scientist Andreas Vesalius study?

2. Which English scientist discovered that the blood circulates through the body?

3. How did William Gilbert answer the question of why a compass needle always points north?

4. Where did the term *electric* come from?

5. What were some advances in mathematics that helped scientists study the natural world?

What do you think ?

Why would it be exciting to be a scientist during the 1500s and 1600s?

True Directions Concerning the Interpretation of Nature

In 1620, Francis Bacon set down the scientific method. It told scientists what they should do to discover how nature worked. Bacon said to ignore all existing ideas on a topic. Scientists should experiment and observe the results. As they worked, scientists should carefully record what they did and saw. New ideas should only come from what they observed. These principles are in his Novum Organum, or True Directions Concerning the Interpretation of Nature. *The following is a passage from that writing.*

Francis Bacon

Those who have taken upon them to lay down the law of nature as a thing already searched out and understood whether they have spoken in simple assurance or professional affectation have therein done philosophy and the sciences great injury. . . . For as they have been successful in inducing belief, so they have been effective in quenching and stopping inquiry; and have done more harm by spoiling and putting an end to other men's efforts than good by their own.

Now my method, though hard to practice, is easy to explain. I propose to establish progressive stages of certainty. . . . I open and lay out a new and certain path for the mind to proceed in, starting directly from the simple . . . perception. . . . Namely, that the entire work of the understanding be commenced afresh, and the mind itself be from the very outset not left to take its own course, but guided at every step; and the business be done as if by machinery.

[First there is] simple experience, which, if taken as it comes, is called an accident. If [experience] is sought for, [it is called] an experiment. [A good] experiment [is like] lighting a candle. Then by means of the candle, [it] lights the way [to the truth about nature.]

Let men, therefore, cease to wonder that the course of science is not yet wholly run [its course]. The [scientific] method rightly ordered leads by an unbroken route through the woods of experience to the open ground of [natural laws].

And therefore there are [some] things which [scientists] should be warned [against]. First then, . . . [fancy writing], let it be utterly dismissed. [Next,] all superstitious stories and experiments of ceremonial magic should be altogether rejected.

Document-Based Questions

1. According to the reading, what was Bacon's main contribution to science?

2. What does Bacon think his system can do?

3. In your opinion, why did Bacon call simple experience an accident?

4. Why does Bacon compare a good experiment to a candle?

5. According to Bacon, what should scientists do with superstitions and magic?

The Importance of the Clock

The work of Newton and other scientists showed that the universe was very orderly. People began to think that there were rules to explain everything in nature. In the 1700s, it seemed that the universe operated like a giant mechanical clock. The idea that the universe was like a machine was very powerful. The idea lasted into the 1900s.

Why did people living in the 1700s compare the world to a clock? For them, the clock was a marvelous device. Before its invention, people used many methods to tell time. None of them were very accurate, however.

The ancient Egyptians, Greeks, and Romans used sundials, or "shadow clocks." A sundial was a flat surface with a standing piece of wood or metal. As the sun traveled through the sky, it cast a shadow off this piece. The shadow's length told the time. At night or on cloudy days, water clocks were popular. They had two parts—a large bucket and a pan with measurement lines. Water dripped through a tiny hole in the bucket into the pan. By checking the level of the water in the pan, people could tell the time. Sand glasses were also popular with the Romans. They looked like the egg timers we use today. Sand flowed through a small hole in the top container into the bottom one.

The first mechanical clocks were so large they needed to be in towers. They worked by allowing gravity to gradually pull heavy weights connected to ropes to the ground. These weights were hooked up to a device that struck the hour.

Then in the early 1500s, there was a new development. A German locksmith built a small clock that used a tightened spring. The spring gradually released its energy to turn an hour hand. In 1656, Christian Huygens

This clock is from the 1660s England.

invented the pendulum clock. It stood upright and had hour and second hands. Falling weights drove the pendulum. In time, this type of clock became the famous grandfather clock.

The mechanical clock changed our concept of time. It became very precise. Now, people could ask the time in the late afternoon. They would get an exact answer, such as "ten minutes after four." The mechanical clock changed people's relationship to each other and to their work. For the first time in history, being "on time" was measured to the minute!

Wrap-Up

1. What role did Newton play in improving the measurement of time?

2. In the 1700s, what was the universe compared to?

3. What were three early methods of telling time?

4. Who invented the pendulum clock? When?

5. How did the mechanical clock change people's idea of time?

- During the 1500s and 1600s, scholars no longer accepted answers given by the Bible or ancient writers. They used experiments to investigate the natural world.

- In the 1620s, Francis Bacon worked out the five steps of the scientific method. It begins with a problem and an educated guess, or hypothesis, about its answer. The next steps are to experiment, to observe, and to make conclusions. Scientists still follow this method.

- From ancient times, most people thought Earth was the center of the universe. Ptolemy wrote that the sun and planets revolve around the earth.

- In 1543, Copernicus published a new theory. He said that the earth traveled around the sun. Kepler used mathematics to prove the theory of a sun-centered universe. He showed that planets travel in elliptical, or egg-shaped, orbits, not circles.

- Galileo, an Italian scientist, built a telescope to study the sky. He discovered the moons of Jupiter. He concluded that Copernicus was right about a sun-centered universe. The Catholic Church tried to stop Galileo's work. They forced him to say he was wrong.

- Isaac Newton was an English mathematician of the late 1600s. He studied light and color. He also demonstrated the earth's gravity and how gravity keeps the planets in orbit. He showed that the Universal Law of Gravitation applies throughout the universe.

- By the end of the 1600s, a community of scientists was at work in Europe.

- Belgian Andreas Vesalius studied human anatomy. His work showed that Galen, an ancient Greek doctor, was wrong. William Harvey, an English doctor, showed how blood circulates in the body.

- William Gilbert showed that the earth acts like a magnet. He also discovered electricity. Benjamin Franklin, an American, showed that lightning is a form of electricity.

- Mathematics was an important tool of the new science. Napier made multiplication and division easier. Descartes discovered analytic geometry. Newton and Leibniz developed calculus.

- New scientific tools included the microscope and the thermometer. Leeuwenhoek used magnifying lenses to observe one-celled animals.

Chapter 16   R E V I E W

Word Bank

Bacon

Copernicus

Galileo

Gilbert

Harvey

Kepler

Leeuwenhoek

Napier

Newton

Vesalius

On a sheet of paper, use the words from the Word Bank to complete each sentence correctly.

1. _____ worked out the basic steps of the scientific method.

2. In 1543, a book by _____ challenged the belief that the sun travels around the earth.

3. Using mathematics, _____ discovered that the planets revolve around the sun in an orbit shaped like an ellipse.

4. The Catholic Church put _____ on trial because he said that the earth travels around the sun.

5. _____ discovered the Law of Universal Gravitation.

6. In 1543, _____ wrote a book about human anatomy.

7. After many experiments, _____ discovered that the heart was a pump.

8. _____ used the new word *electric* to describe materials, like amber, that attract feathers and bits of dust.

9. Thanks to _____, multiplying and dividing numbers is easier today.

10. _____ invented a powerful microscope to see one-celled animals for the first time.

On a sheet of paper, write the letter of the answer that correctly completes each sentence.

11. To _____ something is to make it appear larger than it really is.

    A magnify   C theory
    B revolve   D hypothesis

12. The _____ is a set of steps scientists follow for study.

    A theory   C scientific method
    B hypothesis   D prism

13. A _____ is an educated guess.

    A theory   **C** method

    B basic   **D** hypothesis

14. A _____ is a statement that explains how or why something happens.

    A logical   **B** theory   **C** univers   **D** heresy

15. Benjamin Franklin proved that lightning is a form of _____.

    A static electricity   **C** steam

    B amber   **D** gravity

On a sheet of paper, write the answer to each question. Use complete sentences.

16. What are the five steps of the scientific method?

17. Before Copernicus, what did most scholars believe about the earth and the heavens?

18. How did Newton build on the work of Copernicus, Kepler, and Galileo?

Critical Thinking On a sheet of paper, write your response to each question. Use complete sentences.

19. You read in Chapter 14 about the rebirth of learning during the Renaissance. Why do you think the scientists in this chapter went against some of that learning?

20. Isaac Newton said, "I seem to have been only like a boy playing on the seashore . . . finding a smoother pebble . . . whilst the great ocean of truth lay all undiscovered before me." In your own words, explain what Newton meant.

Test-Taking Tip

If an essay question asks for facts, give facts and not opinions.

17

Beginnings of Our Global Age

In the 1400s, European explorers set sail to find a water route to China and India. Portugal began the search, but soon explorers from other countries took to the seas. In this chapter, you will learn about Columbus and other explorers. You will witness how cruel Europeans were to the native people they found. Then you will study the African slave trade. All of this was part of the settling of the Americas by the Europeans.

Goals for Learning

◆ To explain why some European nations searched for an all-water route to China and India

◆ To list three reasons why Spaniards came to the Americas

◆ To describe what Spanish conquest did to the American Indian population

◆ To describe how Spain established colonies in America

◆ To explain why Portugal introduced African slavery into the New World

◆ To describe the growth of European colonies in the Americas

1487 Bartholomeu Dias sails around the tip of Africa

1518 Portuguese bring African slaves to the Americas

1607 English settle Jamestown in Virginia

1620 Pilgrims settle Plymouth in Massachusetts

1425

1525

1625

1498 Vasco da Gama sails around Africa to India

1532 Francisco Pizarro conquers Incas in Peru

1608 Champlain settles Quebec in Canada

CATHAYA–China

MANGI AND CIAMPA–Provinces of China, according to a letter Toscanelli wrote to Columbus

CAMBALUC–Chinese city of Peking

ZAITON–Chinese city of Zhengzhou, visited by Marco Polo

JAVA–Islands off coast of Southeast Asia

CIPANGO–Japan

AZORES–Group of islands off Portugal

ANTILIA–An island described in medieval legends

ST. BRANDAN– A mythical land described in medieval tales

HIBERNIA–Ireland

MADEIRA–Islands off Africa

CANAROS–Islands off Africa

SIERRA LEONE–Region on African Coast

Map Skills

Paolo Toscanelli made a map similar to the above map in 1474. Christopher Columbus used a copy to find a water route to China. As the map shows, a good sailor could do this by sailing west. Clearly, Toscanelli did not know about North or South America!

Study the map, then answer the following questions:

1. Near what continent are the Madeira Islands?

2. What is the name of a group of islands that lie north of the equator and west of Spain?

3. What was Ireland's name during Columbus's time?

4. On what continent do you find Sierra Leone?

5. Cipango is another name for what country?

Reading Strategy:
Predicting

Preview the text. Think about what you already know about a subject. Look for new information. These things will help you predict what will happen next.

Check your predictions as you read. As you learn more information, you may find you need to change your predictions.

Key Vocabulary Words

Lesson 1 ————————————
Navigation The science of planning and directing a ship's journey

Lesson 2 ————————————
Exploration The act of looking around some unknown place

Strait A narrow strip of water that connects two bigger bodies of water

Lesson 3 ————————————
Conquistador A Spanish conqueror

Lesson 4 ————————————
Viceroy An official who governs land for the king or queen

Plantation A large area of farmland

Encomienda The Spanish system of forced physical labor

Lesson 5 ————————————
Slavery The owning of human beings as property

Abolish To get rid of something

Lesson 6 ————————————
Colonist A person who settles in a new place

Majority More than half of a group of people or group of things

Mayflower Compact The agreement made by the Pilgrims that set up a form of government for their new colony

Economic Having to do with money

Objectives

◆ To explain why Portugal sought a new route to China and India

◆ To identify a technical advance that helped sailors improve their travel

Navigation

The science of planning and directing a ship's journey

Reading Strategy:
Predicting

Preview the lesson title. Predict what you will learn about trade routes in this lesson.

During the 1300s and 1400s, Arab merchants bought goods like silks and spices in China and India. (People wanted spices because they helped preserve food. They also covered up the taste and smell of spoiled food.) Then they carried these goods overland to the eastern end of the Mediterranean Sea. There, they loaded the goods on Italian ships and took them to the Italian city-states.

The overland journey was slow and hard. But once on the sea, the journey was fast and easy. Soon, the goods arrived in the Italian city-states. Then Italian merchants sold the goods at high prices to other European states. Italian city-states like Venice grew wealthy from this eastern trade.

For many years, these city-states controlled the trade routes to the East. Other countries wanted to become wealthy too. They began to look for new trade routes. During the 1400s, Portugal began its search for a new route to the East.

How Did Prince Henry Help Portugal?

Prince Henry the Navigator helped the Portuguese prepare for their search. Around 1416, he established a school where geographers, astronomers, and mapmakers helped sea captains improve their **navigation.** That is, they learned how to plan and direct a ship's journey.

Prince Henry the Navigator established a school in Portugal to teach sea captains navigation and other skills.

Word Bank

Africa
Bartholomeu Dias
Italian city-states
Prince Henry
western

What do you think ?

Why do you think King John of Portugal did not want sea captains to be scared by the name "Cape of Storms"?

With this learning, Portuguese captains sailed south to explore the western coast of Africa. There the Portuguese set up trading centers. Merchants in Africa traded gold and ivory for goods from Portugal. Soon, people began calling the western coast of Africa the Gold Coast.

What Did Bartholomeu Dias Do for Portugal?

In 1481, King John II of Portugal had his sea captains begin to look for a water route to India and China. Such a route would make Portugal rich and powerful. They carefully sailed south along the western coast of Africa. Each captain went a little farther south. Then mapmakers made maps of the coastline.

In 1487, Bartholomeu Dias sailed around the southern tip of Africa. If the Portuguese could do that, they could also sail eastward to India and China. The weather at the tip of Africa was bad. Dias named it the Cape of Storms. But King John II renamed it the Cape of Good Hope. He did not want the other sea captains to be scared off by the name.

Lesson 1 Review On a sheet of paper, use the words from the Word Bank to complete each sentence correctly.

1. _____ controlled the trade routes to India and China during the 1300s.

2. _____ established a school for sailors in Portugal.

3. Portuguese sailors first explored the _____ coast of Africa.

4. The Portuguese were the first Europeans to sail around the southern tip of _____.

5. _____ named the southern tip of Africa the Cape of Storms.

Objectives

◆ To describe the journeys of Columbus, da Gama, and Magellan

◆ To explain how the pope controlled exploration

There were two problems in trying to reach India and China by sailing around Africa. First, the weather at the southern tip of Africa made the voyage dangerous. Second, reaching the southern tip of Africa took a long time. Sailing on to India took even longer.

Christopher Columbus thought that he had a better way to reach the East. He would sail west across the Atlantic Ocean. At the time, his idea seemed strange. How could a sailor reach the Indies by sailing west?

What Did Columbus Find When He Sailed West?

For many years, Columbus tried to get an important person interested in his idea. Then, in 1492, he convinced Queen Isabella of Spain to provide the money for his voyage. On August 3, 1492, Columbus, his officers, and his crew sailed from Spain. They sailed in three ships: the *Niña*, the *Pinta*, and the *Santa Maria*.

First, the ships headed south. Then they caught a wind that blew them west into the unknown waters of the Atlantic Ocean. Early on the morning of October 12, 1492, a sailor

sighted land! Columbus thought that he had reached the islands of the East Indies, so he called the people he met "Indians." He was sure that China and Japan were nearby.

In 1493, Columbus returned to Spain. He made three more voyages across the Atlantic Ocean. In 1506, Columbus died, still believing that he had discovered a new route to Asia.

Columbus convinced Queen Isabella of Spain to pay for his voyage across the Atlantic.

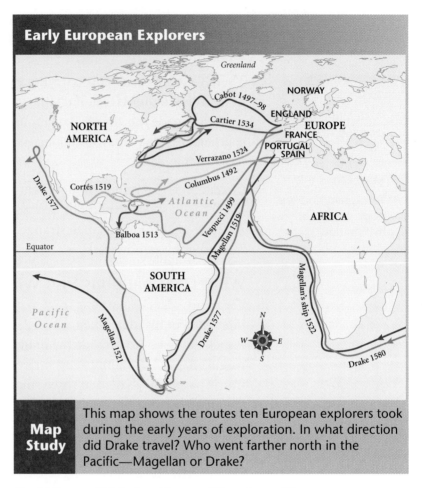

Early European Explorers

Greenland

NORWAY

Cabot 1497–98

Cartier 1534

ENGLAND

EUROPE

FRANCE

NORTH
AMERICA

Verrazano 1524

PORTUGAL
SPAIN

Columbus 1492

Cortés 1519

*Atlantic
Ocean*

Vespucci 1499

AFRICA

Drake 1577

Balboa 1513

Magellan 1519

Equator

Magellan's ship 1522

SOUTH
AMERICA

*Pacific
Ocean*

Drake 1577

N

Magellan 1521

W   E

S

Drake 1580

Map Study

This map shows the routes ten European explorers took during the early years of exploration. In what direction did Drake travel? Who went farther north in the Pacific—Magellan or Drake?

To Whom Did the Pope Give Land?

Exploration

The act of looking around some unknown place

As early as the 1450s, the pope gave Portugal control over all African trade and **exploration.** Exploration is the act of looking around some unknown place. Then, 30 years later, the pope gave Portugal the right to explore and trade as far as the East Indies. After the first journey by Columbus, Spain asked the pope what non-Christian areas it might claim.

In 1493, the pope drew a line down a map and divided the world into two parts. He said that Spain could control all new land discovered west of the line. Portugal could control all new land east of the line: Africa and India. But Portugal did not like this decision. In 1494, officials from Spain and Portugal met to settle the problem. They agreed to move the line farther west. This let Portugal control Brazil in the Americas.

Predict what da
Gama will find on this
voyage.

What Direction Did da Gama Sail to Reach India?

Columbus reached land by sailing west. The Portuguese still wanted to reach India by sailing south and then eastward. In the summer of 1497, Vasco da Gama left Portugal with four ships. Three months later, he rounded the Cape of Good Hope. In May 1498, da Gama reached Calicut, India.

Da Gama and his men returned to Portugal in September 1499. He proved that an all-water route to India existed. Now the Italian city-states would no longer control trade with India and China.

Da Gama's ships came back to Portugal with spices like pepper and cinnamon, along with jewels and other goods. When they sold this cargo, it brought 60 times the cost of the trip! That was an enormous profit. But of the 170 men who left with da Gama, only 54 were left alive to return to Portugal.

History in Your Life

Pass the Pepper, Please

Why did European explorers try so hard to reach the Indies? One answer is in your kitchen—pepper. Ordinary black pepper was not ordinary at all in Europe. Meat was often eaten half-spoiled. Pepper made it taste better. Sailors on long voyages even carried small sacks of peppercorns. But pepper grew only in India and Java.

Italian merchants got rich importing spices, which they sold to the rest of Europe. Then, about 1300, the Turks cut off trade to these eastern lands. So explorers looked for new routes to Asia. Some went south around Africa. Others sailed west . . . and found the Americas.

Europeans did not find the black pepper they were looking for in the Americas. Rather, a new kind of pepper grew there. In 1493, Columbus brought red peppers from Haiti to Spain. Their spicy taste quickly became popular. The use of red pepper then spread to Africa and Asia.

What European Countries Traded With China and Japan?

For most of the 1500s, the Portuguese controlled the spice trade in the East Indies. As the years passed, their ships reached China and Japan too. The Chinese and Japanese did not trust Europeans, so the Chinese allowed the Portuguese to trade only in one off-shore island, Macau. Later the Chinese allowed the Dutch and the Spanish to open a trading center in the city of Canton.

Who Was the First to Sail Around the World?

In September 1519, Ferdinand Magellan, a Portuguese captain, set sail from Spain with five ships and about 265 crewmen. King Charles I of Spain asked him to find the western route to India that Columbus had failed to find.

First, Magellan sailed south. Then he turned westward and explored the coast of South America. The trip was so long that some sailors rebelled, and Magellan lost one ship. The four remaining ships slowly moved through a **strait** at the tip of South America. A strait is a narrow strip of water that connects two bigger bodies of water. This strait connected the Atlantic Ocean with the Pacific Ocean, but Magellan did not know that. (Geographers now call it the Strait of Magellan.)

What Did Magellan Find Beyond the Strait?

After passing through the strait, the three remaining ships reached the calm, open water of the Pacific Ocean. But as they journeyed for three months across this peaceful ocean, conditions for the crew worsened. They had to eat wormy food, rats, and cooked leather. Their water turned yellow and tasted bad.

Finally the three ships reached the Philippine Islands. Here, in a fight with the native people, Magellan was killed. (A native is someone who was born in a particular place.) Soon, two more ships were lost. All alone, the last ship sailed across the Indian Ocean, down the eastern coast of Africa, around the Cape of Good Hope, and up the western coast of Africa.

Strait

A narrow strip of water that connects two bigger bodies of water

Reading Strategy:
Predicting

Based on what you have just read, predict what Magellan finds.

In September 1522—three years after leaving Spain—this one ship, with 18 sailors, reached home port. The voyage covered about 44,000 miles. It had sailed around the world and proved two things: First, the world is round. Second, the earth contains much more water than land.

Lesson 2 Review On a sheet of paper, write the answer to each question. Use complete sentences.

1. What was one problem that sailors faced in traveling around the southern tip of Africa?

2. Who thought that he could reach the East by sailing across the Atlantic Ocean?

3. Who was the first European to reach India by sailing around Africa?

4. What are the names of three countries that sent ships to China to trade?

5. Who led the expedition that proved the world was round?

What do you think ?

How do you think the Arab and Italian merchants felt when Vasco da Gama's ships sailed into Calicut? Explain your answer.

Then and Now

Navigating at Sea

How did sailors long ago know where they were? On a clear night, they could spot the North Star. The sun's position was also a guide. But the compass was the first navigational instrument. Its magnetized needle points north.

By the 1400s, sailors were making longer voyages and needed better tools. One such tool was the astrolabe. It could measure the angle of the sun or the North Star with the horizon. From that, a navigator could determine latitude, or the distance north or south of the equator.

Today's instruments would amaze Columbus! The newest method is GPS, or global positioning system. It uses signals from 24 satellites orbiting the earth to determine position. Ships, planes, and cars can use GPS. It has made travel much easier.

Conquistador

A Spanish conqueror

Reading Strategy:
Predicting

Preview the lesson title. Predict what empires the Spanish conquer.

Writing About History

What did the Spaniards and the Aztecs say on meeting for the very first time? In your notebook, write a conversation that happened then. One person is a Spanish soldier. The other is an Aztec.

Some Spaniards liked to explore and discover new places. Others—the **conquistadores,** or conquerors—wanted gold and glory. Jesuit missionaries wanted the Indians to change their religion and become Catholics. These missionaries and the conquistadores came to Central and South America for "God, Gold, and Glory."

What Aztec Legend Helped Cortés?

In 1519 Hernando Cortés sailed with 11 ships to the coast of Mexico. Some 500 soldiers and 16 horses sailed with him. The fleet landed on the Mexican coast in an area that the Aztecs ruled.

Before this time, the Aztecs had conquered other tribes in the area to create an empire. Montezuma was the Aztec ruler. When he heard that Cortés had landed, the emperor thought of an ancient Aztec legend. According to this legend, the Aztec god Quetzalcoatl had sailed from Mexico toward the East. The legend said that the great feathered god would one day return. According to the legend, Quetzalcoatl was to return in 1519! The Aztecs at first believed that Cortéz and his men were gods.

Why Did Montezuma Send Cortés Gifts?

Montezuma had more than 200,000 warriors, but he did not march against the Spanish invaders. Thinking they were gods, he sent golden gifts to them. This was a mistake. The gifts made the Spanish want more gold.

Soon, Cortés met a woman who spoke several native languages. She helped Cortés speak with the other tribes that the Aztecs had conquered. Many of these tribes hated their Aztec rulers, so they became allies of Cortés.

How Did the Spanish Treat Montezuma?

Cortés and his 500 men marched to Tenochtitlan, the Aztec city where the emperor lived. When they reached it, Montezuma allowed them to enter. That was his second mistake. Once inside the city, Cortés made Montezuma a prisoner. The Aztecs quickly rebelled and forced the Europeans out of Tenochtitlan. At that point, Cortés asked his Indian allies for help. With the Spaniards, they surrounded the city for three months. Finally, the Aztecs surrendered. Spain had broken the power of the Aztec Empire.

What Did the Conquistadores Do to the Incas?

To the south of Mexico, in the mountains of Peru, the Spanish conquered another empire, the Incas. In 1532, fewer than 200 Spanish conquistadores landed in South America. Francisco Pizarro led them. King Charles V of Spain had told him to conquer South America.

Pizarro and his men marched toward the Inca capital. They came at a time when Atahualpa, the Inca emperor, was fighting a civil war with his brother. Atahualpa heard that the Spanish were coming, so he went out to meet them with many of his people. When they met, Pizarro and his men attacked. The Incas carried no weapons, so the Spanish killed many of them and captured Atahualpa.

The Inca emperor offered to fill a large room with gold if Pizarro would release him. Pizarro agreed. From all parts of the Incan Empire, gold poured into the room until it was full.

Atahualpa was emperor of the Incas in 1532. Pizarro captured and executed him. The Spanish then took control of the Inca Empire.

Reading Strategy:
Predicting

Think about your prediction. What details can you now add to make your prediction more specific?

How Did Pizarro Treat the Inca Emperor?

The emperor had kept his promise. Now the time had come for Pizarro to keep his. But Pizarro had heard an untrue story that Inca warriors were going to attack. He put Atahualpa on trial and executed him.

The Inca emperor was dead, and his warriors had no guns and no will to fight, so they accepted Spanish rule. By 1535, the Spanish controlled much of the Incan Empire. In time, Pizarro and his men argued over the gold, and they killed him.

Why Did the Empires in the Americas Fall?

In less than 20 years, small groups of Spaniards conquered two large empires in the Americas. How was this possible? Historians give five reasons.

First, they came at the right time. Montezuma believed an Aztec legend was coming true. Pizarro arrived when a civil war was going on. Second, tribes that did not like the Aztecs or Incas joined the Spanish to fight against them. Third, the Spanish had cannons and guns. The American Indians had never seen weapons like these. Fourth, the Spanish had horses. They were new too. At first, the Indians thought that each horse and its rider was a two-headed god. When a rider got off his horse, the god seemed to divide itself into two parts. Fifth, the Spanish brought smallpox and measles to the Americas. The Indians had no natural protection against these diseases. This killed millions of Indians.

The Incan Empire

One problem facing the Incan Empire was that it stretched thousands of miles through the rugged Andes Mountains. At the time, communication was difficult over such a distance. However, to connect its different parts, the Incas built an excellent system of roads. Some ran along the coast. Others crossed the mountains. Woven bridges allowed people to cross rivers and canyons. These roads allowed merchants and officials to travel safely throughout the empire. In addition, they enabled relays of runners to quickly deliver messages.

The Incan Empire faced two other communications problems. Its people spoke several different languages, and there was no system of writing. As a result, the Incas developed an unusual way to keep records—the quipu. It was a long cord that had other strings tied to it. The cords were knotted in different ways. Knots and spaces represented different numbers—ones, tens, hundreds. The colors of the cords represented different items. One color meant taxes. Another was used to keep track of food in storehouses.

Word Bank
Atahualpa
Aztecs
God
Montezuma
Pizarro

Lesson 3 Review On a sheet of paper, use the words from the Word Bank to complete each sentence correctly.

1. Many Spaniards came to the Americas in the 1500s for _____, Gold, and Glory.

2. The _____ built a great civilization in present-day Mexico.

3. The Aztec ruler _____ thought that Cortés was a god.

4. _____ was the leader of the Inca Empire in Peru.

5. _____ put the Inca emperor on trial and executed him.

What do you think ?

Could the Incas and the Aztecs have defeated the Spaniards? Explain your answer.

Objectives

◆ To explain how Spain governed its colonial lands in the Americas

◆ To describe the relationship between Spanish landowners and the people who worked for them

Viceroy

An official who governs land for the king or queen

Plantation

A large area of farmland

Encomienda

The Spanish system of forced physical labor

For many years, the Spanish explored the Americas. Hernando de Soto—one of Pizarro's men—went north and explored Florida. Then he turned west. By 1541, he reached the Mississippi River. Another Spaniard, Francisco de Coronado, led an expedition into the southwest of North America. Spain claimed control of this area in 1560 and called it "New Mexico."

Who Ruled New Spain?

Spain also had a name for the land that had once been the Aztec and Inca Empires. These became New Spain. Soon the king of Spain created five provinces in New Spain and sent a **viceroy,** or official, to govern each province. To encourage Spanish settlement, the king gave large areas of land to Spanish conquistadores. Their descendants formed a class of wealthy landowners.

Why Did the Encomienda Lead to Death?

Spain had a lot of land in the Americas. Spanish landowners wanted to make money on it. To do that, they needed millions of farmworkers. They also needed miners for the silver mines in Mexico. Bringing millions of workers from Spain was not practical. The Spanish forced the native people to work for them. The Spanish landowners were cruel to these workers.

Often a Spanish landowner forced a whole village of natives to work on **plantations,** or large areas of farmland. The Spanish called this system of forced physical labor the **encomienda.** Under this system, a Spanish landowner had two duties. First, he had to care for the needs of the natives. Second, he wanted to change their religion so that they became Catholics. Often, the landowner paid little attention to the first duty.

The Spanish forced American Indians to work in silver mines. This dangerous work killed many Indians.

Because of the encomienda, thousands of native people suffered and died. More than 25 million lived in Latin America when the Spanish first came there. Within 100 years, the native population was down to 4 million because of European diseases and hard, dangerous work in the silver mines. The Spanish refused to allow them to practice their customs and traditions. They had to accept new and strange ways of doing things. Because of all this, many native people lost hope.

How Did las Casas Try to Help?

A Spanish priest named Bartolomé de las Casas tried to end the cruel treatment of the natives by the Spanish. He wrote to King Charles V and explained that the natives were dying in great numbers. Something had to be done.

But the plantation owners needed workers, so las Casas suggested that Spain use African workers. Soon Spain began to import Africans to the Americas. Las Casas quickly felt sorry that he had ever suggested this. He had solved one problem, but caused another.

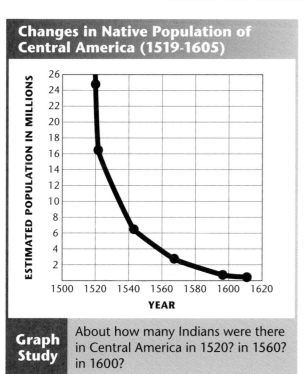

Changes in Native Population of Central America (1519-1605)

ESTIMATED POPULATION IN MILLIONS

YEAR

Graph Study About how many Indians were there in Central America in 1520? in 1560? in 1600?

Lesson 4 Review On a sheet of paper, write the letter of the answer that correctly completes each sentence.

1. For the Spanish, the former Aztec and Inca Empires became _____.

   A New Mexico   **C** India
   B New Spain   **D** China

2. The Spanish explorer _____ traveled as far west as the Mississippi River.

   A Hernando de Soto   **C** Cortés
   B Francisco de Coronado   **D** Pizarro

3. _____ was a Spanish priest who tried to help the native people.

   A Hernando de Soto   **C** Francisco de Coronado
   B Pizarro   **D** Bartolomé de las Casas

4. Bartolomé de las Casas suggested to the Spanish king that _____ workers could take the place of the native workers.

   A Spanish   **C** African
   B Italian   **D** Chinese

5. The Spanish used a system of forced physical labor that they called the _____.

   A viceroy   **C** encomienda
   B plantation   **D** conquistador

What do you think ?

Why did the Spanish treat the Indians in such a cruel way?

Objectives

◆ To explain why African slavery was introduced into the New World

◆ To describe how slaves were brought to the Americas

Slavery

The owning of human beings as property

Reading Strategy: **Predicting**

Preview the lesson title. Predict what you will learn about the beginning of slavery.

A slave is a person who is forced to work without pay or rights and is treated as property. Slaves built the Egyptian pyramids. Slaves labored in Greece and Rome. In the ancient world, people became slaves in different ways. Many were captured in wars. Others may not have been able to pay a debt, so they became property of the person they owed.

What European Country Began to Buy and Sell Slaves?

In a small way, **slavery,** or the owning of human beings as property, had existed in Africa for many centuries. But in Africa, slaves had rights. The owner was not allowed to overwork them. The owner had to let slaves earn money. The slaves could then buy their freedom.

In the 1440s, the Portuguese started buying slaves. They set up slave trading centers along the Gold Coast of Africa and the Gulf of Guinea. In 1518, Spain let Portugal bring African slaves to the Americas. This solved the Spanish labor problem in their American colonies.

What Was the Journey to the Americas Like for Slaves?

Europeans took away the rights the slaves had in Africa. European slave traders and owners were cruel. The traders packed African men and women into dirty ships and locked them in chains. The chained slaves spent most of the voyage to the Americas below deck. Their food was unfit to eat, they never had enough water, and slave traders whipped them.

Why Did the Slave Trade Grow?

For over 300 years, slave traders captured and sold into slavery more than 20 million Africans. Of these, 5 million, or one-fourth, never reached the Americas. They died on ship, and the slave traders threw their bodies into the sea.

The slave trade became popular when colonization began in the Americas. For hundreds of years, African slaves were taken to the Americas. Many died on the way; those who survived had to endure harsh treatment.

Abolish

To get rid of something

Soon European colonies expanded from South and Central America to North America. As Europe settled more colonies, the slave trade grew. Slaves worked the Spanish sugar plantations in the Caribbean Islands of Cuba and Haiti. They also worked the Portuguese sugar plantations in Brazil.

The English forced slaves to work in the colonies of North America. (In 1713, England took control of the slave trade from Spain.) On southern plantations, slaves worked long hours to raise rice, tobacco, and cotton for their owners. In all these places, slaves had no freedom. Cruel owners sometimes beat and killed them.

How Long Did Slavery Last in the Americas?

Slavery in the Americas lasted for almost 400 years. During that time, a number of slaves rebelled. Most of these rebellions failed, but some slaves did gain freedom.

In the 1790s, slaves on the island of Haiti led a successful rebellion. Haiti had the first government in the Americas led by the free Africans. Many years passed before the United States **abolished,** or got rid of, slavery. This happened in 1865, after a civil war. In 1888, slavery ended in all of the Americas. In that year, Brazil abolished it.

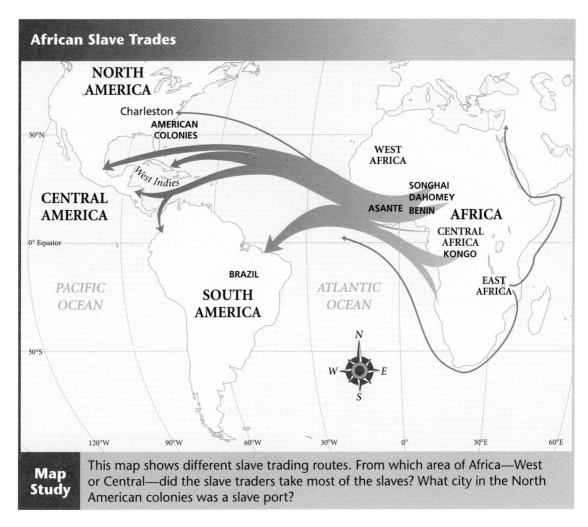

African Slave Trades

NORTH AMERICA

Charleston
AMERICAN COLONIES

30°N

West Indies

CENTRAL AMERICA

0° Equator

PACIFIC OCEAN

30°S

SOUTH AMERICA

BRAZIL

ATLANTIC OCEAN

WEST AFRICA

SONGHAI
DAHOMEY
ASANTE BENIN

AFRICA

CENTRAL AFRICA
KONGO

EAST AFRICA

N
W   E
S

120°W   90°W   60°W   30°W   0°   30°E   60°E

Map Study This map shows different slave trading routes. From which area of Africa—West or Central—did the slave traders take most of the slaves? What city in the North American colonies was a slave port?

Lesson 5 Review On a sheet of paper, write the answer to each question. Use complete sentences.

1. Who were the first Europeans to begin buying and selling African slaves?

2. How did the lives of slaves in Africa and in Europe differ?

3. Over a period of almost 300 years, how many African men and women did traders capture?

4. Who took control of the slave trade in 1713?

5. What was the first country in the Americas in which African slaves rebelled and won their freedom?

What do you think ❓

Why did slave traders begin to buy and sell slaves?

The Results of Exploring and Establishing Colonies

Colonist

A person who settles in a new place

Majority

More than half of a group of people or group of things

Spain, Portugal, the Netherlands, England, and France explored and set up colonies in the Americas. They brought change with them. Some changes were good. Other change destroyed whole civilizations in the Americas. In Africa, the slave trade destroyed African life and cultures.

What Was the First English Colony in North America?

Spain was the first country to send explorers to the Americas. It also set up colonies. Then England and France did the same. In 1585, Sir Walter Raleigh established an English colony on Roanoke Island, off the coast of North Carolina. Within three years, all the **colonists**—the people who had settled in this new place—disappeared. No one knows what happened to them.

In 1607, the English established another colony in Virginia. They named it Jamestown after King James I. It became the first permanent English colony in America.

Who Helped the English Pilgrims?

In 1620, the Pilgrims, who wanted religious freedom, came to North America on the *Mayflower*. On board ship, they agreed to base their government on the rule of the **majority** of men settlers. A majority means

The Mayflower Compact was based on the idea of rule by the majority. It was the beginning of democracy in America.

that more than half of them had to agree on something to make it a law. Historians call the agreement made by the Pilgrims the **Mayflower Compact.** The Pilgrims named their colony Plymouth.

Half of the Plymouth colonists died during the first winter. However, American Indians helped them, and the Pilgrims soon did well in their new settlement, or colony. In time, English settlements grew. By 1733, there were 13 English colonies on the Atlantic coast of North America.

Where Did the French Settle?

French fishing boats sailed off the Newfoundland coast. In 1535 Jacques Cartier claimed for France the land that is now eastern Canada. The first French colony in North America was Quebec, in present-day Canada. Samuel de Champlain founded it in 1608. The French also founded settlements along the Great Lakes and the Mississippi River. (The French mostly trapped animals and traded their furs.) In the 1680s, the French claimed Louisiana in the lower Mississippi Valley. They named this rich land after King Louis XIV. Like the Spanish, the French gave their land in North America a name—New France.

European trade ships brought goods to and from the Americas and Europe.

Amerigo Vespucci: 1454–1512

Amerigo Vespucci was not the first European to find the Americas. Still, these continents are named for him.

In 1491, this Italian worked for a bank in Spain. It lent money for voyages of exploration. Later, Vespucci became a navigator. He made several voyages, including two that reached and explored Brazil.

Unlike Columbus, Vespucci thought he had seen a new continent. Around 1503, he wrote a letter about his travels. It was published under the title "New World." Many people read it, including a German mapmaker. He then named these new lands "America" on his maps.

France and England tried to outdo one another in North America. Both wanted money and power. After a number of wars, France lost its lands in North America. The French and Indian War was a nine-year war between France and England. When it ended in 1763, French lands in Canada went to Britain. French territory west of the Mississippi River went to Spain.

How Did Plants from the Americas Help Others?

Reading Strategy: Predicting

Preview the title of the next section. Predict what plants will be new to the Europeans.

When European ships came to the Americas, they carried animals, plants, and goods. The American Indians had never seen horses, pigs, and chickens. They had never grown plants like wheat, oats, rice, apples, bananas, coffee, and sugar cane.

These same ships carried corn and potatoes back to Europe. These became important foods for the whole world. Corn and potatoes were easy to grow. With more food to eat, fewer Europeans starved, and the population grew.

The Indians grew other crops that were new to people in the rest of the world. Some of these were tomatoes; cacao, for making chocolate; lima beans; and tobacco. Indians were the first to use tobacco, smoking it in pipes. At first, the Europeans used tobacco as medicine. Then they also began to smoke it.

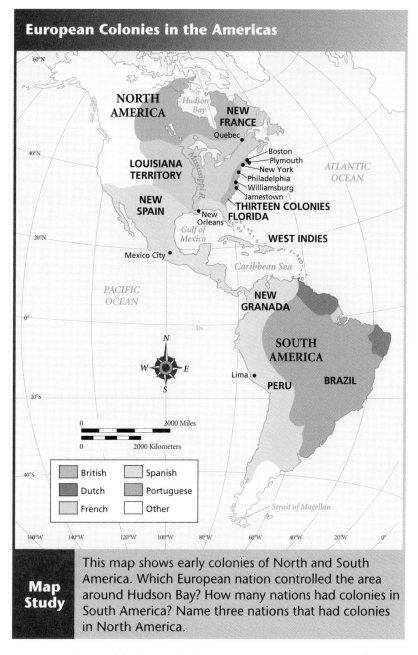

European Colonies in the Americas

NORTH AMERICA

Hudson Bay

NEW FRANCE

Quebec

LOUISIANA TERRITORY

Mississippi R.

Boston
Plymouth
New York
Philadelphia
Williamsburg
Jamestown

THIRTEEN COLONIES

NEW SPAIN

New Orleans

FLORIDA

Gulf of Mexico

ATLANTIC OCEAN

WEST INDIES

Mexico City

Caribbean Sea

NEW GRANADA

PACIFIC OCEAN

SOUTH AMERICA

Lima

PERU

BRAZIL

N
W E
S

0   2000 Miles

0   2000 Kilometers

Strait of Magellan

	British		Spanish
	Dutch		Portuguese
	French		Other

60°N
40°N
20°N
0°
20°S
40°S

160°W 140°W 120°W 100°W 80°W 60°W 40°W 20°W 0°

Map Study

This map shows early colonies of North and South America. Which European nation controlled the area around Hudson Bay? How many nations had colonies in South America? Name three nations that had colonies in North America.

In 1612, John Rolfe planted tobacco in Jamestown. Englishmen were willing to pay high prices for it. Tobacco became an important cash crop for colonists in Virginia and Maryland.

Who Controlled the World at the End of the 1800s?

The Europeans explored the Americas for more than two centuries. During this time, they took control of the rich lands of North America and Latin America. The Spanish, Dutch, English, and French set up colonies in North America. As the years passed, European power grew stronger throughout the world. By the late 1800s, European nations had gained political and **economic** control of India, parts of the Middle East, and most of Africa and Asia. That is, Europe controlled the government and money matters in these places.

Lesson 6 Review On a sheet of paper, write the answer to each question. Use complete sentences.

1. What two American vegetables became an important food for the world?

2. What English colony became the first permanent English colony in North America?

3. What was the Mayflower Compact?

4. Where did the French establish colonies in North America?

5. Which European nation came to dominate half of the North American continent by 1763?

What do you think

What do you think happened to the "Lost Colony" at Roanoke?

A Warm Welcome for Cortés

Spanish settlers in the Americas treated the natives cruelly. One of these conquistadores was Hernando Cortés. In search of riches, Cortés sailed to the coast of Mexico. When the Aztec emperor Montezuma (here spelled Moctezuma) heard of the arrival, he thought that Cortés and his men were gods. In this excerpt, Moctezuma welcomes Cortés to Tenochtitlán, the capital of the Aztec empire. Within months of the meeting, Cortés killed Montezuma and destroyed the Aztec Empire.

Then Cortés addressed Moctezuma: "Is this indeed you? Are you not Moctezuma?"

"Yes," Moctezuma answered; "I am he."

On this, he rose, to stand facing Cortés. He bowed deeply, drew him close, and stood firmly. Then he said,

"O our lord, you have tired yourself; you are weary. At last you have come to earth; you have come to govern your city of Mexico, to take your position of authority, which for a short time I have been keeping and guarding for you. Your former deputy governors have departed—the rulers Itzcoatl, Moctezuma the Elder, Axayacatl, Tizoc, Auizotl, who also had come to keep watch, to govern the city of

Cortés and Montezuma meet in peace in 1519.

Mexico for you a short time ago and keep your people under their protection. Do the former rulers know what is happening in their absence? O that any of them might see, might wonder at what has befallen me—at what I am seeing now that they have gone. For I cannot be dreaming.

"For some time now I have been afflicted; I have gazed at the clouds, the mists, out of which you have come. And now this has come to pass. The departed rulers said as they left us that you would revisit your city, would return to your position of authority, and now it has so happened. You have come; you have tired yourself; you are weary. Rest yourself. Go into the palace; rest. Peace be with our lords."

Document-Based Questions

1. Why did Cortés go to Mexico?

2. Why did Montezuma think that Cortés was a god?

3. Why do you think Montezuma is so friendly toward Cortés when they first meet?

4. What does Montezuma tell Cortés to do?

5. The word *afflicted* means "worried." Why was Montezuma worried?

Source: The War of Conquest: How It Was Waged Here in Mexico, *by Arthur J. O. Anderson and Charles E. Dibble.*

Diseases in Human History

Cortés and his army came to Mexico in 1519. At that time, about 11 million natives lived in central Mexico. By about 1650, fewer than 2 million remained. Cruel treatment and hard work had killed some. But diseases from Europe had been the main killer.

In Europe, diseases such as measles were common. Over time, many Europeans had built up a natural immunity, or resistance, to these illnesses. To understand how immunity develops, take a look at measles. For centuries, people in Europe caught measles when they were young. There were no modern medicines. Some children died. Many survived, though. They were now immune to measles. Mothers passed on some of their immunity to their children. They might get measles, but they would recover. This happened generation after generation. Finally, fewer people died from measles.

What made smallpox, chickenpox, measles, and mumps so deadly in America? The native people had never been exposed to them. They, therefore, had no immunity.

Epidemics of these diseases broke out among the native people. An epidemic is a sickness that spreads quickly through a group of people. It affects most of them. The first smallpox epidemic in Mexico began in 1520. It helped the Spaniards defeat the Aztecs. Other smallpox epidemics happened later in the 1500s. Measles and flu were also serious. These diseases swept through villages, killing people of all ages. When adults died, there were fewer people to bear children. The native population fell each year. Whole cultures disappeared. Later, the same thing happened to natives in North America.

Today, modern medicine can make people immune to some diseases. In the 1700s, smallpox was a dangerous disease. About 20 percent of those who caught it died. Smallpox also left bad scars on people's skin. About 1790, Edward Jenner, a British physician, noticed that milkmaids did not get smallpox. They got a similar, milder illness called cowpox. Jenner made a vaccine using the cowpox virus and gave it to a boy. When tested, the boy was immune to smallpox. Soon many doctors were giving vaccinations or "shots." In 1980, world health officials said that smallpox had been wiped out everywhere.

Scientists have since made vaccines against other diseases. These include measles, mumps, chicken pox, and polio. Most children in the United States now get these shots and others. Many developing countries do not have these health services for their children.

Wrap-Up

1. Why did the native population in Mexico fall after 1519?

2. How do people become naturally immune to a disease?

3. What diseases did Europeans bring to the Americas?

4. What is an epidemic?

5. How did Edward Jenner help wipe out smallpox?

Chapter 17   SUMMARY

- Arab merchants and Italian city-states traded in spices and other goods from Asia. In the 1400s, other countries looked for new trade routes.

- Prince Henry of Portugal began a school that taught navigation. In 1487, Dias sailed around the tip of Africa, the Cape of Good Hope.

- Columbus believed he could reach Asia by sailing west. Queen Isabella of Spain provided money for his voyage in 1492.

- In 1493, the pope said that newly discovered eastern lands belonged to Portugal and western ones to Spain.

- Da Gama sailed around Africa to reach India in 1498. Eventually, the Portuguese, Spanish, and Dutch traded at certain ports in China.

- Magellan's expedition sailed west around the world in 1519–1522, exploring the Pacific Ocean. The trip proved that the world is round and that the earth contains more water than land.

- Cortés conquered the Aztecs of Mexico in 1519. In 1532, Pizarro's men defeated the Incan Empire.

- Guns and horses gave the Spanish an advantage over the native people. Many were also killed by European diseases.

- De Soto explored Florida and reached the Mississippi River. Coronado explored the American Southwest.

- Aztec and Inca lands became the colony of New Spain. Under the encomienda system, Spanish landowners used native workers.

- Spanish landowners in the Americas began to use African slaves instead of the native people. The slave trade was cruel and inhuman. Millions of Africans died. African slaves worked in the Caribbean, Brazil, and the English colonies in North America. Slaves in Haiti rebelled successfully in the 1790s.

- England and France wanted colonies in North America. The English settled Jamestown, Virginia, in 1607. In 1620, English Pilgrims settled Plymouth colony. They signed the Mayflower Compact.

- Champlain founded Quebec in 1608. The French had fur-trading posts around the Great Lakes. They claimed Louisiana of the lower Mississippi valley. France lost its North American lands in 1763.

- Europeans brought new plants and animals, such as horses, to the Americas. Corn, potatoes, tomatoes, chocolate, and other products from the Americas were introduced to Europe.

Chapter 17 R E V I E W

Word Bank

Columbus
Cortés
da Gama
Dias
Las Casas
Magellan
Montezuma
Pizarro
Prince Henry
Sir Walter Raleigh

On a sheet of paper, use the words from the Word Bank to complete each sentence correctly.

1. _____ established a school in Portugal to help sea captains get better at navigation.

2. In 1487, _____ sailed around the tip of Africa.

3. In 1492, _____ sailed west across the Atlantic Ocean to reach Asia.

4. In 1498, _____ left Portugal with four ships and reached India.

5. In 1519, _____ began a three-year trip around the world.

6. In 1519, _____ sailed to Mexico and conquered the Aztec Empire.

7. _____ led the Aztec Empire when the Spanish landed in Mexico.

8. In 1532, _____ marched up the mountains of Peru and conquered the Incan Empire.

9. _____ was a priest who tried to help American Indians in New Spain.

10. In 1585, _____ established an English colony that later disappeared.

On a sheet of paper, write the letter of the answer that correctly completes each sentence.

11. Europeans from _____ explored the Americas.

   A Spain   **C** France
   B England   **D** all of the above

12. The first French settlement in North America was _____.

   A Quebec   **C** Jamestown
   B Roanoke   **D** Plymouth

13. The English Pilgrims settled at _____.

   A Roanoke   **C** Plymouth

   B Jamestown   **D** Quebec

14. In 100 years, the American Indian population went from 20 million to _____ million.

   A 10   **B** 8   **C** 6   **D** 4

15. In 300 years, traders captured and sold into slavery more than _____ million Africans.

   A 60   **B** 40   **C** 20   **D** 1

On a sheet of paper, write the answer to each question. Use complete sentences.

16. Why did Portugal and Spain want to find a water route to China and India?

17. Why did so many native people die under Spanish rule?

18. What new plants did the Europeans find in the Americas and how did these change European civilization?

Critical Thinking On a sheet of paper, write your response to each question. Use complete sentences.

19. Historians give five reasons why the Spanish defeated the Aztecs and the Incas. Which of these reasons seems the most important to you and why?

20. The Spanish conquistadores said they came to the Americas for "God, Glory, and Gold." Which of these do you think was the most important to them? Explain your answer.

Test-Taking Tip

Write your answers neatly on essay questions. Neat papers are easier for the teacher to read and grade.

18

The Age of Kings

In Chapter 10, you read about feudalism. It was the political organization of the Middle Ages. Now you will learn about nationalism. As you watch nations develop, you will study many different kings and queens. Some thought that God gave them the right to rule. Many thought that everything revolved around them.

You will do more than learn about kings and queens in this chapter. You will sail in an armada, learn about a beautiful capital in St. Petersburg, Russia, and see a civil war in England. You will also learn about Prussia and Russia.

Goals for Learning

◆ To explain nationalism and explain how nations developed

◆ To describe the rise and fall of Spain as a powerful nation

◆ To explain rule by "divine right"

◆ To describe England's constitutional monarchy

◆ To explain how Louis XIV help France become powerful

◆ To explain why historians call two Russian monarchs "Great" and explain how Prussia became powerful

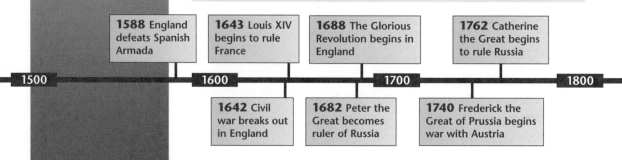

1588 England defeats Spanish Armada

1643 Louis XIV begins to rule France

1688 The Glorious Revolution begins in England

1762 Catherine the Great begins to rule Russia

1500   1600   1700   1800

1642 Civil war breaks out in England

1682 Peter the Great becomes ruler of Russia

1740 Frederick the Great of Prussia begins war with Austria

Map Skills

Spain became the most powerful nation in Europe during the 1500s. During this time, Spain sent explorers to the Americas. This brought money into the Spanish treasury. Spain used some of this money to build a great navy. Its navy brought Spain more power. Madrid, located in central Spain, was its capital city.

Study the map carefully, then answer the following questions:

1. What strait do ships pass through to get from the Mediterranean Sea to the Atlantic Ocean?

2. What mountains separate Spain from France?

3. What bay is directly north of Spain?

4. What river flows through Seville?

5. What are the names of two seaports in Spain?

Reading Strategy:
Text Structure

Understanding how text is organized helps you decide which information is most important. Before you begin reading this chapter, do these things:

- ◆ Look at how it is organized.
- ◆ Look at the title, headings, boldfaced words, and photographs.
- ◆ Ask yourself: Is the text a problem and solution, description, or sequence? Is it compare and contrast or cause and effect?
- ◆ Summarize the text by thinking about its structure.

Key Vocabulary Words

Lesson 1

Nationalism Loyalty to one's country or nation

Boundary Dividing line

Tradition A custom, idea, or belief handed down from one person to the next

Monarch A king or a queen

Absolute monarch A king or queen who had complete and unlimited power over his or her people

Lesson 2

Inherit To receive money, land, or a title from someone who has died

Armada A large fleet of warships

Formation A shape or pattern

Lesson 3

Divine right The belief that God chooses the ruler of a nation

Petition of Right An English document that brought about more democracy

Resolution A formal statement that a governmental body writes

Treason The act of turning against the laws and people of your own country

Lesson 4

Cavalier A person who fought for the king in the English Civil War

Roundhead A Puritan who fought for Parliament in the English Civil War

Restoration The period that saw monarchy return to England in 1660

Habeas Corpus A law that says that the government has to charge someone with a crime before putting the person in prison

Tory A person who supported a strong monarchy in England

Whig A person who supported the English Parliament

Glorious Revolution The overthrow of James II and the crowning of William and Mary as monarchs of England

Constitutional monarchy A form of government in which a king or queen rules, but there are laws of a democracy to protect the people

Lesson 5

Cardinal A high official of the Roman Catholic Church

Advisor A person who gives advice

Lesson 6

Constitution A body of laws that states the rights of the people and the power of the government

Military state A place in which a leader rules through the military

Objectives

◆ To compare feudalism and nationalism

◆ To identify what "absolute power" meant during this time

Nationalism

Loyalty to one's country or nation

Boundary

Dividing line

Tradition

A custom, idea, or belief handed down from one person to the next

Monarch

A king or a queen

Reading Strategy:
Text Structure

Preview this lesson. Notice the headings, features, and boldfaced words.

The Renaissance, the Reformation, and new scientific discoveries brought great change to European societies. Each challenged the way people had lived since the Middle Ages. Another challenge came when Europe began to develop into nations.

What Is Nationalism?

Feudalism was a political and military system based on the holding of land. In the feudal system, many people might share the same language and customs. But they were loyal to different nobles, because the nobles controlled the land they lived on. People did not think of themselves as English, French, or Spanish. When did they begin to think of themselves that way? When **nationalism**—loyalty to one's country—developed.

Nationalism began in Europe in the 11th century when England became a nation. France soon followed. People in these new countries shared the same geographic **boundaries,** or dividing lines.

In these new nations, people shared the same language and history. They also shared the same **traditions,** or customs, ideas, and beliefs that had been handed down from one person to the next. The nation became part of who a person was. When someone asked "Who are you?" a person could answer: "I am English" or "I am French." (Nationalism continues to be an important force today.)

What Is Absolute Power?

All new nations had to answer one question: what form of government shall we have? Different groups wanted power—city governments, the nobility, church officials. The English philosopher Thomas Hobbes wrote in the 1600s that a powerful **monarch,** or king or queen, was the best way to unify a nation. Gradually, some monarchs in Europe gained great power.

Louis XIV was a powerful French monarch. This painting shows him unveiling a statue in France.

For some rulers, this power was so great that it had no limits. These monarchs had so much power that historians call them **absolute monarchs.** An absolute monarch had complete, unlimited power over his or her people.

But why give all this power to one person? Doing this was one early answer to the question of how to govern a new nation. Historians call this period of absolute monarchs the Age of Kings.

How Absolute Was a Monarch's Power?

How powerful did these monarchs become? There was a humorous story told about Philip III, for example. Early in the 1600s, Philip III, the king of Spain, fell asleep before a blazing fire. Earlier the king had ordered that only one person could move his chair. But this one person was no longer in the room. Seeing that the fire was going to burn the king, his servants searched the castle. No one found the man who had permission to move the king's chair, so the servants stood there and did nothing. They let the fire burn the king! If they had moved the chair, they would have gone against a royal order. That is absolute power! The story, however, is not true.

Then and Now

Modern Monarchs

Rulers had absolute, or total, power in the Age of Kings. People often believed this power came from God. Such a monarch ruled by "divine right." During the 1700s and 1800s, some people rebelled against their rulers. World War I ended other monarchies.

Some countries, however, still have a king or queen. They include Great Britain, Spain, Holland, and Sweden. Present-day monarchs wear rich robes and jeweled crowns for important events. They live in castles and their children inherit the throne. But today's monarchs are only symbols. They stand for a country's tradition and history. In all these countries, a constitution severely limits a monarch's powers. The parliament and prime minister actually make the laws.

Lesson 1 Review On a sheet of paper, write the letter of the answer that correctly completes each sentence.

1. _____ is rule by a king or queen.

   A Crusades   **C** Feudalism

   B Nationalism   **D** Monarchy

2. During the Age of Kings, _____, or loyalty to one's country, developed.

   A nationalism   **C** monarchy

   B feudalism   **D** none of the above

3. _____ developed into a nation before France did.

   A The United States   **C** North America

   B Italy   **D** England

4. During this period many monarchs had absolute, or _____, power.

   A limited   **C** little

   B unlimited   **D** some

5. Philip III of _____ was a king with absolute power.

   A France   **C** Spain

   B England   **D** Italy

What do you think ?

What might happen to someone who questioned a monarch's absolute power?

Both England and France became nations before Spain. However, Spain was the first to become truly powerful. During most of the 1500s, its political and economic power was much greater than that of England and France. Spain's story begins with the Moors.

Where Did the Moors Settle?

The Moors were nomads in northern Africa. In the eighth century, they accepted Islam—the religion of Muhammad. They invaded Spain and brought with them their new religion. The Moors pushed through Spain and over the Pyrenees Mountains to Tours. The Franks defeated them there in 732. The Moors settled in southern Spain. There, they built a civilization that lasted for almost 800 years.

Reading Strategy:
Text Structure

Notice that the section headings are written as questions. After you read each section, try to answer the question asked in the heading.

What Was the City of Córdoba Like?

At that time, civilization was in decline in Europe. But the Moors in Spain built Córdoba. More than a million people lived there. Lamps lit the streets. The library contained thousands of books from all over the world. In fact, the Moors helped to reintroduce ancient Greek and Roman learning into Europe. They studied geometry, astronomy, medicine, and philosophy. Christian scholars came from all over Europe to study in Moorish Spain.

How Did Spain Become a Nation?

Reading Strategy:
Text Structure

As you read, look for words like *first, then, next, afterward,* and *finally.* These words will help you understand the order of the events in the rise and fall of Spain.

Slowly, four Christian kingdoms developed in Spain. Castile and Aragon were the strongest. In 1469, Ferdinand, the king of Aragon, married Isabella of Castile. Their marriage united much of Spain under two strong rulers. They forced Spanish nobles to accept their rule. Ferdinand said that he should make all important decisions because "one head is better than a thousand."

Why Did Isabella Go to War?

Isabella wanted to make all of Spain into a Catholic nation. In 1482, she went to war against Granada—the last Moorish kingdom in Spain. In 1492, Granada surrendered. Then Isabella said everyone in Spain had to be Catholic. Any Moor or Jew who refused to become a Catholic had to leave Spain. A few months after conquering Granada, the two rulers provided Christopher Columbus with three ships. He sailed west and found great wealth in the Americas.

What Empire Did Charles V Rule?

King Ferdinand died in 1516. Then his grandson Charles became the second king of Spain. Charles I was also the grandson of the Holy Roman Emperor. When the emperor died in 1519, Charles became Charles V, emperor of the Holy Roman Empire. He was only 19, but he ruled one of the largest empires in history and was the most powerful king in Europe.

Queen Isabella and her husband, King Ferdinand, united Spain, and made the nation Catholic. They paid for Christopher Columbus's voyages to the Americas.

Inherit

To receive money, land, or a title from someone who has died

What Countries Made Up Charles V's Empire?

Charles V was a member of the powerful Hapsburg family. It held power for more than 700 years—from the 1200s to 1918. Charles V **inherited** lands in France from his father. To inherit is to receive money, land, or a title from someone who has died. Through his grandfather, he became ruler of Austria. He also ruled half of Italy and all of the Netherlands, Germany, and Belgium. Charles also controlled all the lands that Columbus and other Spanish explorers discovered. The gold and silver from the Americas made Charles's empire rich.

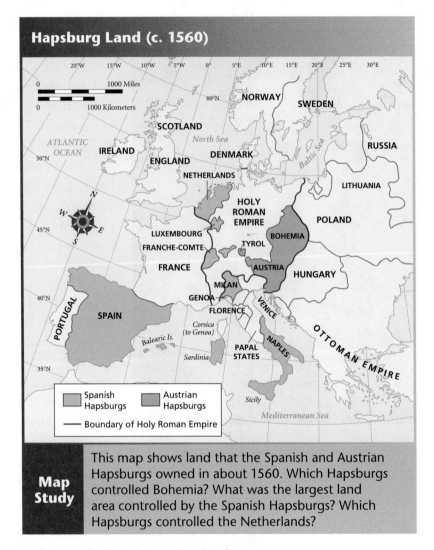

Hapsburg Land (c. 1560)

20°W 15°W 10°W 5°W 0° 5°E 10°E 15°E 20°E 25°E 30°E

0   1000 Miles

0   1000 Kilometers

NORWAY SWEDEN 60°N

SCOTLAND *North Sea* *Baltic Sea* RUSSIA

ATLANTIC OCEAN IRELAND 50°N

ENGLAND DENMARK

NETHERLANDS LITHUANIA

HOLY ROMAN EMPIRE POLAND

45°N LUXEMBOURG BOHEMIA

FRANCHE-COMTE TYROL

FRANCE AUSTRIA HUNGARY

MILAN

GENOA 40°N

PORTUGAL SPAIN FLORENCE VENICE

Corsica (to Genoa) OTTOMAN EMPIRE

Balearic Is. PAPAL STATES NAPLES

Sardinia 35°N

☐ Spanish Hapsburgs ☐ Austrian Hapsburgs
— Boundary of Holy Roman Empire

Sicily

Mediterranean Sea

Map Study   This map shows land that the Spanish and Austrian Hapsburgs owned in about 1560. Which Hapsburgs controlled Bohemia? What was the largest land area controlled by the Spanish Hapsburgs? Which Hapsburgs controlled the Netherlands?

Why Did Charles V Retire?

Charles V was one of the most powerful rulers in history. His large empire kept him busy. He fought religious wars in Germany. He fought against France over lands in Italy. In fact, Charles spent most of his life traveling throughout his empire fighting one enemy after another.

Armada

A large fleet of warships

Finally, when he was 56, Charles V had had enough. In 1556, he gave up his power. He gave control of the Holy Roman Empire to his brother, Ferdinand I. He gave his lands in Italy, the Netherlands, and Spain to his son, Philip II. Afterward, Charles went to a monastery and stayed there until his death.

Why Did Philip II Build an Armada?

As a Roman Catholic, Philip II wanted to stop the spread of Protestantism. Elizabeth I of England had made her country into a leading Protestant nation. Philip II wanted to defeat Elizabeth I and England. He thought that Europe would then become Catholic again.

Philip II decided to invade England. To do this, he built a naval **armada,** or large fleet of warships. In the spring of 1588, the Spanish Armada of 130 ships sailed for England with 1,100 cannons and 30,000 soldiers.

The English navy defeated the Spanish Armada in 1588. Only half of the Spanish Armada ships made it back to Spain. The loss put an end to Spain's status as a sea power.

History in Your Life

Sailing Ships

Explorers in the 1400s used the new full-rigged ships. They had three masts and multiple sails. Such a ship moved under sail power. It did not rely on rowers. The Portuguese developed a full-rigged ship called a caravel to explore the African coast. It was small and very fast. Explorers used it to explore other places too.

In comparison, galleons were heavier and larger. They were first built in the 1500s.

They could carry bulky cargoes or heavy guns. Spanish galleons, for example, brought gold and silver from the Americas to Spain. About one-third of the Spanish Armada in 1588 were galleons. These craft relied on boarding an enemy ship and using soldiers to capture it. English galleons, however, were faster and easier to maneuver. They relied on firepower, which could disable an enemy ship from a distance. This ability defeated the Spanish Armada

---

Formation

A shape or pattern

How Did England Defeat the Armada?

The Spanish fleet sailed north and anchored off the coast of England. Next, the captains put the ships into a protective **formation,** or shape. But then they broke their formation. The English captains sent three burning ships into the Spanish fleet. This scattered all the Spanish ships.

The Spanish Armada ships also had a weakness: they were too big and too slow. The smaller and faster English ships attacked the scattered Spanish ships. One by one, they sank.

Knowing that the English had defeated them, the Spanish captains tried to sail home. A sudden storm sank many more of their ships. Only half of them returned to Spain. In 1598, Philip II died. In the next two centuries, England and France replaced Spain as the most powerful nations in Europe.

Lesson 2 Review On a sheet of paper, write the answer to each question. Use complete sentences.

1. From what area of Africa did the Moors come?

2. What important city did the Moors build in Spain?

3. What are the names of the king and queen who first unified Spain?

4. In 1519, who became the most powerful ruler in Europe?

5. What country defeated the Spanish Armada?

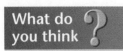

What do you think

Where do you think Philip II got the money to build the Spanish Armada?

Objectives

◆ To explain how King James I used his power

◆ To identify the "Petition of Right"

Divine Right

The belief that God chooses the ruler of a nation

Petition of Right

An English document that brought about more democracy

Reading Strategy:
Text Structure

This lesson tells about a problem and the solution. Ask yourself: What is the problem? What is the solution?

Elizabeth I was a strong monarch in England. She shared power with the English Parliament. For example, Elizabeth took care of business with other countries. Parliament made laws and taxed people.

What Is Divine Right?

When Elizabeth died in 1603, King James of Scotland became James I of England and Scotland. He refused to share power with Parliament. Instead, he said that he ruled by **divine right.** That is, James thought that God had chosen him to rule. He thought no one had the right to question him and his decisions.

A simple story shows how divine right worked. In 1603, a man accused of stealing was brought before James. James ordered that the man be hanged without a trial. He believed that, as king, he was both judge and jury.

What Made Parliament and the People Angry?

James I died in 1625. His son, Charles I, also believed in divine right. But Parliament did not. Soon after becoming king, Charles asked Parliament for money to fight a war with Spain. Parliament said no. Because of this, the king did not have money to pay for a place for his soldiers to stay. Charles forced people to house the soldiers. The people and Parliament did not like this. They decided to do something to limit the king's power.

When Did Parliament Limit the King's Power?

In 1628, the king again asked Parliament for money. Once again, Parliament refused. Parliament said that it would give money only if the king signed the **Petition of Right**. This important paper was a big step in the growth of English democracy. By signing it, the king agreed to three things.

King James I believed that God had given him the right to rule England as he pleased.

1. Only Parliament can collect taxes.

2. The king can send no one to prison without a trial.

3. No one, not even the king, can force citizens to house soldiers unless these citizens want to.

The next year, Charles again asked for money. This time, Parliament passed a **resolution,** or formal statement, that said three things.

1. The king cannot change English Protestantism.

2. The king cannot tax the English people unless Parliament says he can.

3. If the king does these things, he commits the crime of **treason.** That is, he turns on his country and its laws.

Charles was forced to accept these limits. Slowly, power shifted from monarchs to Parliament.

Resolution

A formal statement that a governmental body writes

Treason

The act of turning against the laws and people of your own country

Lesson 3 Review On a sheet of paper, write the answer to each question. Use complete sentences.

1. In England, which government group makes the laws?

2. How did James I rule England?

3. How did Charles I anger Parliament?

4. What was the Petition of Right?

5. What are two things Parliament said in its resolution?

What do you think ?

Should Parliament have limited the power of Charles I? Explain your answer.

Objectives

◆ To describe the period known as the Restoration

◆ To explain how political groups brought about the Glorious Revolution

Reading Strategy:
Text Structure

Study the map on page 440. How does it help you understand the causes of the civil war in England?

What Led to Civil War in England?

In 1639, Charles was again out of money. He needed it to put down a rebellion in Scotland. The people of Scotland refused to become members of the Church of England.

Once again Charles asked Parliament for money. And once again, Parliament worked to limit the king's power. Then, in 1642, the king tried to arrest the leaders of Parliament. This was too much for the English people. They became so angry that Charles had to leave London. Civil war broke out between two groups: the people who supported the king and the people who supported Parliament.

The English Parliament (above) and the Puritans fought the king and his supporters in the English Civil War.

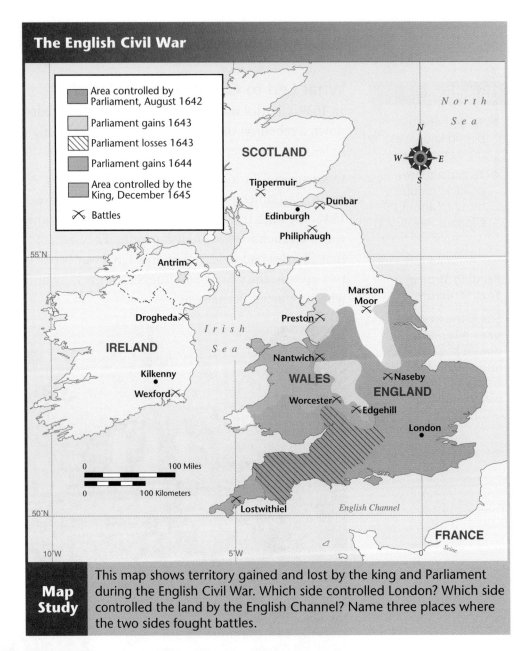

The English Civil War

Legend:
- Area controlled by Parliament, August 1642
- Parliament gains 1643
- Parliament losses 1643
- Parliament gains 1644
- Area controlled by the King, December 1645
- ✕ Battles

SCOTLAND

North Sea

Tippermuir ✕

Dunbar ✕

• Edinburgh

Philiphaugh ✕

55°N

Antrim ✕

Marston Moor ✕

Preston ✕

Drogheda ✕

Irish Sea

IRELAND

Nantwich ✕

WALES

Kilkenny •

Wexford ✕

✕ Naseby

ENGLAND

Worcester ✕

✕ Edgehill

• London

0   100 Miles

0   100 Kilometers

Lostwithiel ✕

English Channel

50°N

FRANCE

Seine

10°W   5°W

Map Study

This map shows territory gained and lost by the king and Parliament during the English Civil War. Which side controlled London? Which side controlled the land by the English Channel? Name three places where the two sides fought battles.

Who Fought the English Civil War?

The two groups who fought the war were different. They had different religions and they dressed differently. **Cavaliers** fought for the king. They were mostly Anglicans or Catholics. They dressed in fancy clothes and wore wigs with long curls.

Reading Strategy:
Text Structure

As you read the lesson, use a graphic organizer to compare and contrast the Cavaliers and the Roundheads.

Puritans fought for Parliament. They were English Protestants who wanted to purify the Anglican Church. The Puritans dressed simply. Because they wore their hair so short, people called them **Roundheads.** Oliver Cromwell led the Roundheads. His army was better than the king's Cavaliers. In 1643, the Roundheads defeated the Cavaliers.

What Did the Puritans Do to Charles I?

The Roundheads put King Charles I on trial. They found him guilty of treason. That is, he had turned against England and its laws. Charles was then beheaded in 1649. Never before had a king been put on trial and then put to death before a crowd of people.

What happened next? In 1653, Cromwell took control of the English government. He became a military dictator. The Puritans began to change English society. They closed the theaters; they said no one could play sports. All this lasted until Cromwell's death in 1658.

What Is the Restoration?

The English grew tired of Puritan rule. In 1659, Parliament voted to bring back the monarchy to England. In the spring of 1660, the oldest son of Charles I returned to England. He was crowned Charles II. Historians call his 25-year reign the **Restoration.**

Charles II rejected the idea of the divine right of kings. He tried to avoid religious problems by asking Catholics and Puritans to be tolerant toward one another. That is, they should respect one another's beliefs and customs.

Oliver Cromwell led the Roundheads during the English Civil War. He ruled England after defeating the king in the war.

The English people liked Charles II. He encouraged the theater, sports, and other entertainment. He loved to have fun, so people called him the "Merry Monarch."

What New Law Did Parliament Pass?

In 1679, Parliament passed the **Habeas Corpus** Act. This law said that the government has to charge someone with a crime before putting the person in prison. *Habeas corpus* is Latin for "you should have the body." The Habeas Corpus Act is an important protection of a citizen's rights. Now, not even the king could take away a person's freedom without a trial.

What Is the Glorious Revolution?

When Charles II died in 1685, his brother, James, became king. Like Charles, James II was a Catholic. But James wanted the monarchy to have more power.

At the time, two political groups held power in England. The **Tories** supported a strong monarchy; the **Whigs** supported a strong Parliament. Both sides agreed on one thing—they did not want a Catholic king. However, James was old and his two daughters were Protestant. The Tories and the Whigs believed that after the king's death, they would have a Protestant ruler. Then, in 1688, James II's wife gave birth to a son.

This son would grow up and become a Catholic king. The Tories and the Whigs joined together. They said that Mary, who was James II's older daughter, should become queen. In the fall of 1688, Mary and her husband, William, left the Netherlands and arrived in England with an army.

James II had no support, so he fled to France. Parliament then said that William and Mary were the king and queen of England and Scotland. The English had rebelled against their king without anyone being killed. Historians call this the **Glorious Revolution.**

What Is a Constitutional Monarchy?

Before William and Mary could become monarchs, they had to sign the English Bill of Rights. This document said that only Parliament can make laws. It also said that the king must obey the laws Parliament passes.

The document also gave the members of Parliament freedom of speech. Now the king could not arrest them if he did not like what they said.

Between 1628 and 1689, Parliament passed the Petition of Right, the Habeas Corpus Act, and the English Bill of Rights. These documents showed that England did not want an absolute monarch.

England wanted both a democracy and a king. We call this form of government a **constitutional monarchy.** That is, England has a monarchy, plus a body of laws and elected officials to protect the rights of the people.

Constitutional monarchy

A form of government in which a king or queen rules, but there are laws of a democracy to protect the people

Lesson 4 Review On a sheet of paper, use the words from the Word Bank to complete each sentence correctly.

Word Bank

Cavalier

Charles I

Cromwell

Roundhead

William and Mary

1. _____ was the king of England when civil war broke out.

2. A _____ was a person who supported the king in the civil war.

3. A _____ was a person who supported Parliament in the civil war.

4. _____ was the leader of the group that fought against the king.

5. _____ were the first English monarchs who ruled under a form of government called a constitutional monarchy.

What do you think ?

Why did the English get tired of Puritan rule?

Objectives

◆ To explain the problems that Louis XIV faced

◆ To describe how his love of beautiful things caused a problem

Cardinal

A high official of the Roman Catholic Church

Advisor

A person who gives advice

Reading Strategy:
Text Structure

As you read, look for the words *but, that is,* and *however.* These words often introduce important information to help you understand what you are reading.

Much was happening in England during the seventeenth century. But much was also happening across the English Channel in France. In 1643, Louis XIII of France died. His son, who was only five, then became king. He ruled as Louis XIV.

Who Helped the Young King Rule?

Louis XIII had been a weak king. He had turned over much of his power to a **cardinal,** or high official, in the Catholic Church. From 1624 to 1642, Cardinal Richelieu served as the king's **advisor.** That is, he gave advice to the king. Richelieu was against any form of democratic government.

By the time Louis XIV became king, the French monarchy had a lot of power. For many years, however, Louis XIV was too young to make decisions. Another church official, Cardinal Mazarin, really ruled France. Under the leadership of these two cardinals, France became the strongest nation in Europe.

When Cardinal Mazarin died, people wanted to know who would be the king's next advisor. Louis was now 23. He decided then and there that he alone would rule France. He ruled France alone for 54 years. Louis became one of the most powerful monarchs in history.

Louis XIV faced many problems when he decided to rule France alone, but he soon became a powerful king.

Reading Strategy:
Text Structure

Notice that the section headings are questions. After you read each section, try to answer the question.

What Problems Did Louis XIV Face?

Louis wanted to rule France alone. But many problems stood in his way. The nobles often paid little attention to what he wanted. He had a hard time collecting taxes. Each noble had his own army, but he had no national army that he could control. Sometimes the nobles and their armies fought against him.

How Did Louis XIV Centralize France's Government?

All these problems existed because France had no central, or main, government that was more powerful than the nobles. Louis wanted to force these nobles to obey his wishes. He thought that he alone should decide what was best for the people of France, so he began to centralize the government.

Louis XIV built a grand palace at Versailles as a symbol of his power. Some historians estimate that he spent $100 million to build it.

First, Louis XIV appointed officials to collect taxes. They ruled over different areas of France in the name of the king. Next, Louis reorganized the French army. He gave uniforms to the soldiers to show that they belonged to his army. Then he increased the size of the army from 100,000 to 400,000. This large army made Louis XIV powerful.

What Other Things Did Louis XIV Do As King?

Louis XIV lived in a palace in Paris called the Louvre. He built a second great palace at Versailles, which was 10 miles away. Versailles took 30 years to complete. More than 30,000 people worked to build this dream palace. His love of beautiful things was a problem for the French taxpayers. They had to pay for all of this. They also had to pay for the wars Louis XIV fought. Between 1667 to 1714, he fought many wars to get more land. These wars drained the French treasury. At the end of his life, Louis XIV was sorry that he had fought so much. Before he died in 1715, he advised his grandson, the future king, to keep peace. Louis said, "I have been too fond of war."

The long reign of Louis XIV was a great time for France. Beautiful churches and palaces were built. Art and music spread. The French nobility was weakened. People called Louis XIV the "Sun King" because all of France seemed to revolve around him like planets around the sun.

Lesson 5 Review On a sheet of paper, write the answer to each question. Use complete sentences.

1. What two cardinals advised Louis XIII and Louis XIV of France?

2. What are five problems Louis XIV faced when he decided to rule alone?

3. What steps did Louis XIV take to improve the army of France?

4. Where did Louis XIV build his second great palace?

5. What advice did Louis XIV give his grandson?

What do you think ?

What could happen to a country like France if an absolute monarch puts too great a burden on the people?

Biography

Cardinal Richelieu: 1585–1642

Armand Richelieu was often called the true power behind the throne of King Louis XIII. He started studying religion when he was a teenager. In 1622, he was made a cardinal in the Roman Catholic Church. He advised the king on government matters from 1624 to 1642.

Henry IV had issued the Edict of Nantes in 1598 to give religious freedom to the Huguenots. Richelieu was against participation in state affairs by any Huguenots. He wanted to make the monarchy stronger. After King Louis died, Richelieu changed the Edict of Nantes to limit the Huguenots' freedoms.

Richelieu chose Cardinal Mazarin to take his place when he died. During the reign of Louis XIV, Mazarin continued to work toward a stronger monarchy.

Objectives

◆ To describe what Peter the Great did for Russia

◆ To describe what Catherine the Great did for Russia

◆ To explain how Prussia expanded its territory

Reading Strategy: **Text Structure**

As you read this lesson, use a graphic organizer to keep track of facts about the two countries Russia and Prussia.

Russia and Prussia also had strong absolute monarchs. In 1613, a young noble was chosen to lead Russia. His name was Mikhail Romanov. His family ruled Russia for the next 300 years, until the Russian Revolution of 1917. One of Russia's most powerful leaders was his grandson, Peter the Great. He became king in 1682 and believed in his absolute power.

What Was Peter's "Window on the Sea"?

Peter the Great wanted to make Russia into a modern nation. To improve his nation's culture, he invited scholars and artists to his country. He also wanted to increase trade with the nations in Western Europe. Russia's ports were frozen during the winter, so he went to war to gain warm water seaports.

To do this, Peter fought to gain control of Swedish territory on the Baltic Sea to the north and Turkish territory on the Black Sea to the south. Peter wanted these ports to give his nation a "window on the sea." On the Baltic Sea, Peter built a new, modern capital called St. Petersburg. He said that it was the perfect "window for Russia to look at Europe."

What Did Catherine the Great Do for Russia?

In 1762, Catherine the Great became queen of Russia. She was a strong leader. She improved education and allowed more religious freedom in Russia. In 1767, she tried to have a **constitution** written for her nation. A constitution is a body of laws that states the rights of the people and the power of the government. However, this effort failed.

For a time, Catherine favored freedom for Russian serfs. When the serfs rebelled against the nobles, she no longer supported the idea.

When Did Prussia Become a Military State?

Until the late 1600s, the German states were small and weak. This changed with the rise to power of Prussia—one of the German states. Frederick William came to power as an absolute ruler in 1713. He increased the size of the Prussian army and made Prussia into a **military state.** A military state is one in which a leader rules through the military.

How Did Prussia Expand Its Territory?

In 1740, Frederick William's great-grandson became Frederick II. He wanted to increase the size and power of Prussia. He invaded the Austrian territory of Silesia, which was south of Prussia.

At that time, Maria Theresa—a strong leader—ruled Austria. She decided to fight the Prussian army. But she had to battle more than one army. Both France and Spain wanted more power too. They invaded Austria. Then England, the Netherlands, and Russia entered the war and supported Maria Theresa. The war lasted on and off for many years.

When all the fighting ended, Maria Theresa lost Silesia to Prussia, which doubled its size. Because of his success, the Prussian people called their king Frederick the Great. By the 1790s, Prussia had become a powerful military force in Europe.

Catherine the Great of Russia was a strong ruler. She improved education and granted more religious freedom to her people.

Lesson 6 Review On a sheet of paper, write the letter of the answer that correctly completes each sentence.

1. Peter the Great built the new Russian capital _____.

    A St. Petersburg   **C** Prussia

    B Romanov   **D** Silesia

2. _____ wanted to have warm water seaports so (s)he could trade with other European nations.

    A Catherine the Great   **C** Maria Theresa

    B Peter the Great   **D** Frederick II

3. For a while, _____ wanted to free the serfs.

    A Catherine the Great   **C** Peter the Great

    B Frederick William I   **D** Frederick II

4. _____ invaded the Austrian territory of Silesia.

    A Catherine the Great   **C** Maria Theresa

    B Peter the Great   **D** Frederick II

5. Austria's monarch, _____, had a long reign marked by many wars.

    A Frederick William I   **C** Maria Theresa

    B Frederick II   **D** Peter the Great

What do you think ?

Why did England and Russia support Maria Theresa in her war with Prussia and Spain?

The English Bill of Rights

As you read in Lesson 4 of this chapter, the English Parliament passed the English Bill of Rights in 1689. It gave members of Parliament more authority than kings and queens. It also said that Roman Catholics could not become kings or queens. In addition, it said that the people of England also had rights. The ideas in the English Bill of Rights spread to the colonies. These ideas helped to shape the Constitution of the United States. Here are some excerpts.

[Members of Parliament declared]

That the pretended [claimed] power of dispensing with [setting aside of] laws or the execution of laws by regal authority, as it hath been assumed and exercised of late, is illegal;

That levying [collecting] money for or to the use of the Crown by pretence of prerogative [power] without grant of Parliament, for longer time or in other manner than the same is or shall be granted, is illegal;

That it is the right of the subject to petition [request from] the king, and all commitments and prosecutions for such petitioning are illegal;

That the raising or keeping a standing army within the kingdom in time of peace, unless it be with consent of Parliament, is against law;

That election of members of Parliament ought to be free;

That the freedom of speech and debates or proceedings in Parliament ought not to be impeached [doubted] or questioned in any court or place out of Parliament;

That excessive bail ought not to be required, nor excessive fines imposed, or cruel and unusual punishments inflicted; . . .

And that, for redress [setting right] of all grievances and for the amending, strengthening, and preserving of the laws, Parliaments ought to be held frequently.

Document-Based Questions

1. How did kings and queens rule before the English Bill of Rights was passed?

2. The Magna Carta, written in 1215, limited the power of kings and queens. Why do you think the kings and queens ignored it?

3. What is one way the United States Declaration of Independence was like the English Bill of Rights?

4. Do you think that the rights demanded in the English Bill of Rights were reasonable? Why or why not?

5. Why is a document identifying the rights of its citizens important to a country?

Playing the Fool

Clowns make us laugh. So do other comic actors. They poke fun at people. They get away with pointing out people's faults. Historically, that has been their job.

Playing the fool has a long history. In earlier times, clowns were called fools or jesters. The pharaohs of ancient Egypt had fools, as did the ancient Romans.

Fools were very popular from the Middle Ages to the 1600s. Often they lived at the court of a ruler or wealthy noble. A jester sometimes seemed like a family member. He shared meals and celebrations, played with the children, and heard family secrets.

The jester's costume was a checked coat of many colors. A fool wore bright-colored hose, pointed shoes, and a tight jacket with a pointed hood. Bells jingled on his toes and coat.

Most court jesters acted silly and foolish. They danced and tumbled. They also made up clever songs and verses. They used their wit and sharp tongues to tease.

Jesters held a special place at court. They could say almost anything. Sometimes their purpose was amusement. At other times, they pointed out unwise actions. Fools could have a lot of influence. Richard Tarlton was a famous English comic actor. He was also a jester for Queen Elizabeth I. He was the only person who could criticize her. Louis XIV's court jester was called

L'Angely. Nobles were afraid of his sharp wit.

Archie Armstrong was the fool for King James I of England. He was known as Count Archie. The king sent him to Spain with his ambassadors and he insulted the Spanish. Then Archie wrote the king to tell him what a good job he had done. Eventually, this jester went too far. He insulted church officials and had to leave the court, but he was already wealthy.

Even the powerful Catholic Church could not avoid foolishness. The Feast of Fools was a popular holiday, especially in France. People chose a mock pope or bishop and made fun of church ceremonies.

Court jesters lost their popularity in the 1700s. Today, clowns are only entertainers, but some comedians still carry on the jester's tradition. They say what no one else dares.

Wrap-Up

1. How long have there been jesters?

2. How was a jester like a part of a noble family?

3. What did a court jester usually wear?

4. What has been the role of court jesters and fools in history?

5. What used to happen on the Feast of Fools?

- As European nations developed, nationalist feelings grew. Absolute monarchs had total power over their subjects.

- Moors from North Africa occupied southern Spain in the 700s. They made Córdoba a center for learning.

- Christian kingdoms in Spain fought the Moors. Ferdinand of Aragon and Isabella of Castile united Spain. By 1492, they had conquered Granada, the last Moorish kingdom. Jews and Moors had to become Catholic or leave Spain.

- In the 1500s, Spain was more powerful than England or France. King Charles I of Spain, a Hapsburg, became the Holy Roman Emperor Charles V. This family ruled large parts of Europe. Charles defended the Catholic faith.

- Philip II, the son of Charles V, ruled Spain, part of Italy, and the Netherlands. In 1588, he sent the Spanish Armada against England to make it Catholic again. Philip failed when fast English ships and a storm sank Spanish ships.

- King James of Scotland followed Elizabeth I as England's ruler and ruled by divine right. His son Charles I fought with Parliament over money and power. Parliament made Charles sign the Petition of Right.

- Civil war broke out in England. The Cavaliers, on the king's side, were mostly Anglican or Catholic. Puritans, or "Roundheads," were Protestant. Their leader was Oliver Cromwell.

- The Puritans won the English Civil War in 1643. Charles I was tried for treason and beheaded. Cromwell set up a strict military government. In 1659, Parliament voted to restore the monarchy under King Charles II.

- In the Glorious Revolution (1688), Parliament rebelled against James II, a Catholic king. His Protestant daughter Mary and her husband, William, ruled next. They agreed to a Bill of Rights.

- Louis XIV of France became Europe's most powerful ruler. Louis fought many wars and made the central government stronger.

- Peter the Great wanted to make Russia more like Europe. He built a new capital at St. Petersburg. Later, Catherine the Great supported education and the idea of a constitution.

- Prussia, in Germany, became a military state. Its ruler Frederick II went to war against Maria Theresa, the ruler of Austria. Prussia became a powerful military force in Europe.

Word Bank

Catherine

Charles I

Charles V

Cromwell

Hobbes

Isabella

James I

Louis XIV

Peter

Philip II

On a sheet of paper, use the words from the Word Bank to complete each sentence correctly.

1. _____ was a philosopher who believed that a powerful king should rule a nation.

2. The marriage of Ferdinand and _____ united Spain into one kingdom.

3. _____, a powerful emperor and the king of Spain, gave up his power and went to live in a monastery.

4. _____ sent a powerful Armada to invade England in 1588.

5. The English king from Scotland who believed that he ruled by divine right was _____.

6. During the English Civil War, _____ led the Roundheads.

7. _____ was the first English king to be put to death by his own people.

8. The French called _____ the "Sun King."

9. _____ the Great tried to improve his country's culture by inviting artists and scholars to Russia.

10. _____ the Great tried to have a constitution written for Russia.

On a sheet of paper, write the letter of the answer that correctly completes each sentence.

11. During the English Civil War, the _____ supported the king.

    A Cavaliers   **C** Parliament

    B Roundheads   **D** Whigs

12. During the Glorious Revolution, the _____ supported a strong Parliament.

    A Cavaliers   **C** Whigs

    B Roundheads   **D** Tories

13. The _____ caused problems for Louis XIV of France.

    A nobles with armies   **C** lack of a national army

    B collection of taxes   **D** all of the above

14. Prussia doubled its territory under the leadership of _____.

    A Peter the Great   **C** Catherine the Great

    B Frederick the Great   **D** Isabella of Castile

15. The queen of Austria when Prussia attacked was _____.

    A Maria Theresa   **C** Isabella of Castile

    B Catherine the Great   **D** Elizabeth I

On a sheet of paper, write the answer to each question. Use complete sentences.

16. What is the difference between feudalism and nationalism?

17. What does ruling by "divine right" mean?

18. What is the difference between an absolute monarchy and a constitutional monarchy?

Critical Thinking On a sheet of paper, write your response to each question. Use complete sentences.

19. Do you think that the name "Sun King" was a good description of King Louis XIV? Explain your answer.

20. King Philip II said, "When Spain stirs, the earth trembles." After the defeat of his navy in 1588, what do you think Queen Elizabeth I might have said about his boast?

Test-Taking Tip

Pace yourself. If you are unsure about a question, put a check next to it and move on. If you have time left, go back and try to answer the checked questions.

Unit 3

Cause and Effect

Looking for causes and effects will help you better understand what you read. An effect is something that happens as a result of a cause. One cause may have several effects. To determine causes and effects, ask these questions:

Why did the event happen? (cause)

What made the event happen? (cause)

What triggered an event? (cause)

What happened as a result of the event? (effect)

What happened because of that event? (effect)

Here is an example of one cause and effect related to the Hundred Years' War:

Cause: The French wanted control of the English province of Gascony.

Effect: The English fought to keep their control of Gascony.

In the next column are more causes and effects related to the Hundred Years' War. Read each pair of sentences. Decide which statement is the cause and which is the effect. Rewrite each sentence on your paper. Label it with "cause" or "effect."

1. France's king died without a male heir.

   Edward III of England was the French king's nephew. He thought the French throne should go to him.

2. Edward III landed an army in Normandy. It was part of his plan to get the French throne.

   Edward III decided to take the French throne by force.

3. The English developed the longbow.

   The English beat the French in battle.

4. Joan of Arc beat the English at Orléans, Patay, and Reims.

   Joan of Arc said that she saw visions from heaven. They told her to lead the French against the English. French soldiers believed what she told them.

5. England had to give up all its land in France except for Calais.

   The French won many battles and the Hundred Years' War.

- The Renaissance began about 1350. It was a time of creativity and learning.

- Education, art, and science were important during the Renaissance.

- Great Renaissance writers include Shakespeare and Cervantes. Important artists include da Vinci, Michelangelo, and Raphael.

- The Protestant Reformation began in the 1400s.

- Martin Luther questioned the teachings of the church. His actions led to the Reformation. Luther started the Lutheran Church in about 1530.

- King Henry VIII of England began the Anglican Church after the pope refused to allow his divorce.

- The Catholic Church began a Catholic Reformation, which led to the Roman Inquisition.

- The Reformation split Europe into Catholic and Protestant areas.

- During the 1500s, scholars began to investigate the natural world. Francis Bacon worked out the scientific method in the 1620s.

- In 1543, Copernicus said the earth traveled around the sun. Galileo built a telescope and concluded that Copernicus was right. The Catholic Church tried to stop Galileo's work.

- Isaac Newton studied light and color; he also discovered how gravity works.

- Advances were made in the study of the human body. Magnetism and electricity were discovered.

- Mathematics, geometry, and calculus, along with the microscope and thermometer, were important scientific tools.

- In the 1400s, explorers from many European countries began to look for new trade routes.

- Columbus and da Gama tried to reach Asia. Magellan proved that the world is round during his trip of 1519 to 1522.

- Cortés and Pizzaro destroyed Indian empires in Mexico and South America. The land became the colony of New Spain.

- The English founded the colonies of Jamestown in 1607 and Plymouth in 1620. Champlain founded Quebec in 1608.

- In the 1500s, Spain was more powerful than England or France.

- Civil war broke out between the Catholics and Protestant Puritans in England; the Puritans won in 1643.

- In France, Louis XIV became Europe's most powerful ruler.

"You cannot hope to build a better world without improving the individuals. To that end each of us must work for his own improvement, and . . . share a general responsibility for all humanity, our particular duty being to aid those to whom we think we can be most useful."

~ *Marie Curie, from her* Autobiographical Notes, *1891*

Unit 4

Enlightenment and Revolution

I n this unit, you will meet thinkers who wanted to use reason to improve society. These enlightened people include rulers, writers, and composers. You will march with revolutionaries in search of freedom. You will learn about factories and how the industrial revolution changed the lives of workers. And you will read about revolutions that changed the face of Europe and Latin America.

459

The Age of Reason

In 1687, Isaac Newton published an important scientific book. It changed the way people thought about the universe and about society. His scientific reasoning led to the Age of Reason. In this chapter, you will learn about people like Locke and Voltaire who had theories about people and government. You will spend time with enlightened rulers like Maria Theresa of Austria. You will experience the wonder of the music of Mozart—a musical genius. They will all help you understand the belief that order and balance rule the universe.

Goals for Learning

◆ To explain how Isaac Newton's work influenced the Age of Reason and why historians call this historical period the Age of Reason

◆ To explain the views of three important philosophers of this time

◆ To describe the period called the Enlightenment

◆ To name enlightened thinkers, rulers, musicians, and writers

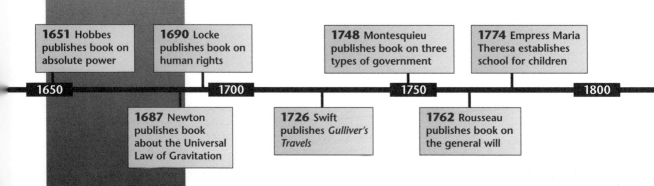

1651 Hobbes publishes book on absolute power

1690 Locke publishes book on human rights

1748 Montesquieu publishes book on three types of government

1774 Empress Maria Theresa establishes school for children

1650   1700   1750   1800

1687 Newton publishes book about the Universal Law of Gravitation

1726 Swift publishes *Gulliver's Travels*

1762 Rousseau publishes book on the general will

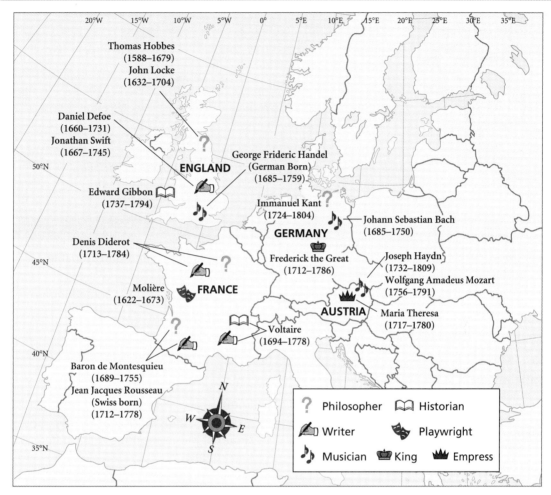

Notable People, 1687-1789

Thomas Hobbes
(1588–1679)
John Locke
(1632–1704)

Daniel Defoe
(1660–1731)
Jonathan Swift
(1667–1745)

50°N   ENGLAND

George Frideric Handel
(German Born)
(1685–1759)

Edward Gibbon
(1737–1794)

Immanuel Kant
(1724–1804)

GERMANY

Johann Sebastian Bach
(1685–1750)

Denis Diderot
(1713–1784)

45°N   FRANCE

Frederick the Great
(1712–1786)

Joseph Haydn
(1732–1809)
Wolfgang Amadeus Mozart
(1756–1791)

Molière
(1622–1673)

AUSTRIA

Maria Theresa
(1717–1780)

Voltaire
(1694–1778)

40°N

Baron de Montesquieu
(1689–1755)
Jean Jacques Rousseau
(Swiss born)
(1712–1778)

35°N

? Philosopher	📖 Historian
🖊 Writer	🎭 Playwright
🎵 Musician	👑 King	👑 Empress

Map Skills

During the Age of Reason—from about 1687 to 1789—many famous people tried to think reasonably about government, the arts, and society. They made important contributions to history, philosophy, and culture. We remember some of them for their novels and plays. We remember others for the music they wrote. We remember many of them for the way they changed people's ways of thinking.

Study the map, then answer the following questions:

1. In what country did Bach write his music?

2. In what year did the philosopher John Locke die?

3. In what year was Maria Theresa of Austria born?

4. For what is Molière famous?

5. In what country did the historian Edward Gibbon live?

Reading Strategy:
Visualizing

Visualizing is like creating a movie in your mind. It is also a strategy to help you understand what you are reading. These are some ways you can visualize a text:

◆ As you read this chapter, notice the images of people from this time in history. How does this help you visualize the events described in the chapter?

◆ Think about experiences in your own life that may add to the images. For example, does a salon sound like an early online "chat room"?

Key Vocabulary Words

Lesson 1

Enlightened Having a belief in reasoning; moving away from ignorance

Lesson 2

Contract A legal agreement

Lesson 3

Enlightenment A time in European history when thinkers and writers tried to solve the problems of society by using reason

Salon A meeting of artists, writers, and thinkers in a Paris home during the Enlightenment

Prejudice An unfair and unreasonable opinion

Ban To get rid of; to make something not legal

Lesson 4

Classical A type of music from the 1700s and early 1800s that is orderly and balanced; in the style of ancient Greece or Rome

Symphony A long musical work played by a group of musicians using many different instruments

---

In Chapter 16, you learned about Isaac Newton and his Universal Law of Gravitation. In 1687, he published his law in a book. In it, he showed how this law applied to the universe. He also showed how to use mathematics to describe the law.

How Did Newton Make His Discoveries?

Newton discovered these things using reason, or thinking in a logical way. He did not experiment. Instead, by reason alone, he discovered a mathematical law that controls the movement of planets and other objects in space.

How Did Newton's Reasoning Influence People?

After reading Newton's book, people began to think of the universe as a kind of huge clock. A clock ticks off the minutes of the day in a predictable, orderly way. They believed that the universe works this way too. It is predictable. That is, people can discover what will happen in the universe.

Reading Strategy:
Visualizing

Visualize the clock mentioned in this paragraph. How does this image help you understand the way people began to view the universe?

Newton influenced many scientists. They decided to use careful, scientific reasoning to find the truth about how nature worked. He influenced nonscientists too. They now knew that nature followed natural laws. Perhaps other natural laws controlled the actions of human beings. If so, then scientific reasoning was a tool. They could use this tool to solve the problems of society.

Enlightened

Having a belief in reasoning; moving away from ignorance

What Was an Enlightened Thinker?

People who believed in scientific reasoning called themselves **enlightened** thinkers. They had found the light! No longer did they walk in the darkness of ignorance, or lack of knowledge. Enlightened thinkers asked difficult questions. They searched for the truth about how nature and human societies really work.

History in Your Life

Fake Science and Miracle Cures

Even in the Age of Reason, people could be fooled. They bought "miracle cures" from "quacks." Quacks were individuals who offered fake cures for illnesses. The name *quack* came from their loud sales talk. Quacks often used scientific-sounding explanations and names for their cures.

One quack treated patients with tools called "Metallic Tractors." He said the tractor could draw a sickness out of someone. This idea fooled even great thinkers such as Benjamin Franklin.

The German Franz Mesmer used a mysterious force called "animal magnetism."

In this treatment, patients sat around a tub of water and held hands. Animal magnetism was then supposed to flow through them. Mesmer also used a kind of hypnotism, which put people into a trancelike state. Later, doctors used this technique.

In England, many people were convinced that a woman named Mary Tofts could give birth to rabbits! She became so popular, the king of England was willing to support her. However, it was found out that she was a fake. She was secretly buying rabbits at a local market. She and many others had fooled everyone during a time when science and careful thinking were popular.

Reading Strategy:
Visualizing

Draw a picture to help you remember the three goals of enlightened thinkers.

What Is the Age of Reason?

Newton's ideas helped begin the Age of Reason. During this age, many enlightened thinkers had three goals:

1. They wanted to improve how people live.

2. They wanted to think clearly and logically, without letting their feelings guide them.

3. They wanted to use scientific reasoning to examine every part of society—education, religion, economics, law, and government.

Lesson 1 Review On a sheet of paper, write the answer to each question. Use complete sentences.

What do you think ?

Are there natural laws that can help us predict how people will act? Explain your answer.

1. How did Newton discover natural laws?

2. In what way are Newton's ideas of the universe like a clock?

3. Why did people who believed in scientific reasoning think of themselves as enlightened?

4. How did enlightened thinkers search for the truth?

5. During the Age of Reason, enlightened thinkers had three goals. What were they?

Objectives

Objectives

- ◆ To compare the views of Thomas Hobbes and John Locke
- ◆ To understand Baron de Montesquieu's idea of balance of powers
- ◆ To explain Jean Rousseau's views concerning the general will

Contract

A legal agreement

The enlightened thinkers of the Age of Reason asked questions about government. What was the best form of government? Are there natural laws that people should follow in setting up a government? These thinkers used logic and reason to find answers.

What Did Thomas Hobbes Say About Government?

In 1651, English philosopher Thomas Hobbes published a book on government. According to Hobbes, at one time people lived without any government. Their lives were short and unhappy. At some point, people agreed to give up their freedom to a ruler to gain order and safety.

Hobbes thought that an agreement existed between the ruler and the ruled. Under this agreement, people agreed to obey the rulers even if they ruled poorly. Hobbes said that monarchs needed absolute power to keep people from fighting among themselves. For Hobbes, order was more important than freedom.

What Rights Did Locke Believe People Were Born With?

In 1690, Englishman John Locke published another book on government. Like Hobbes, Locke thought that government should keep order in a society. He also thought that government was a **contract,** or legal agreement, between the ruler and those who are ruled. But the two men had different ideas too. For example, Locke believed that people were reasonable. Given the chance, they would act in an orderly manner.

John Locke said every person has the right to life, property, and liberty. He thought government should protect these rights.

Unlike Hobbes, Locke believed that people had rights. He believed that they were born with three rights: the right to life; property; and liberty. The job of government was to protect these rights. Locke said that people kept these rights even when they agreed to be governed. He believed that people had a right to rebel when the ruler or government did not protect their rights.

In France, Baron de Montesquieu believed that the government must have separate branches to divide the power.

What Did Montesquieu Say About Government?

Across the English Channel in France, two enlightened thinkers also published books about government. One of them was Baron de Montesquieu. He studied the government of ancient Rome and governments in his own time. Then, in 1748, he published a book about his studies.

Montesquieu thought that the best monarchs used their wealth and power for the good of everyone. Virtue, or goodness to one another, held a republic together. Montesquieu said that people in a republic needed to elect people who would serve the good of the community.

What Are Separate Powers?

Montesquieu admired the English government of the 1700s. It divided power into three branches.

1. Parliament made the laws.

2. The king enforced the laws.

3. The courts interpreted the laws.

Reading Strategy:
Visualizing

Make a chart showing the three branches of the English government of the 1700s. How did this division keep any one branch from becoming too powerful?

Montesquieu said that separating these powers kept each of the three branches from becoming too powerful. Each branch checked and balanced the powers of the two other branches.

How Did Rousseau Differ from Hobbes?

The other French thinker and writer of this time was Jean Jacques Rousseau. Rousseau said that people had once done only good things. They began to do bad things when civilizations developed.

This was just the opposite of what Hobbes had said. The English philosopher believed that people were born greedy and selfish. Civilization made them responsible and orderly.

Rousseau turned Hobbes's idea upside down. He said that people were born good and that civilization made them do bad things. "Man is born free," he wrote, "but everywhere he is in chains."

Rousseau strongly believed that peasants were just as good as kings and nobles. He said that no one was better than anyone else, so no one should have any special privileges, or rights. All were equal.

Reading Strategy:
Visualizing

Create a graphic organizer that shows how the views of Montesquieu and Rousseau are alike and different.

What Did Rousseau Mean by "General Will"?

In 1762, Rousseau published his book on government. In it, he disagreed with Hobbes and Locke and their idea of a contract between the ruler and the ruled. Rousseau said that in order to get along, people made a contract with each other, not with a ruler. He thought that shared customs, traditions, and values held together a community of people.

Rousseau called these shared customs, traditions, and values the "general will." According to Rousseau, a community expressed what it wanted through its general will. Because of this, Rousseau favored rule by the majority.

Then and Now

An Enlightened Government

Montesquieu thought that a government should have three parts. If political power were split, no one group would have too much power. Each branch would balance the other. This idea has become a driving force for many governments today.

These ideas were put to practice in England first; then they spread to America. Americans such as Thomas Jefferson and James Madison had studied Locke and Montesquieu. In 1787, Americans who believed in these ideas designed a government based on "separation of powers." It had three branches. The legislative branch made laws, the executive branch carried them out, and the judicial branch decided what the laws mean. The United States government and other governments still use this system.

Lesson 2 Review On a sheet of paper, write the answer to each question. Use complete sentences.

1. According to Thomas Hobbes, who should rule a government?

2. With what rights did John Locke believe people were born?

3. Why did Montesquieu believe that powers should be separated into several branches of government?

4. What did Rousseau say about people that was different from what Hobbes said?

5. What does Rousseau's term "general will" mean?

What do you think

Why might Locke's theory of rights appeal to people today?

Objectives

◆ To explain how the Paris salons helped advance the Enlightenment

◆ To describe the importance of Diderot's encyclopedia

Enlightenment

A time in European history when thinkers and writers tried to solve the problems of society by using reason

Salon

A meeting of artists, writers, and thinkers in a Paris home during the Enlightenment

Reading Strategy:
Visualizing

Study the image on this page. Does this help you visualize how a gathering might have looked?

Enlightened thinkers wanted to improve government. They also wanted to change or reform unreasonable customs and traditions. They asked society to allow people to have political, economic, and religious freedom. In fact, they thought that more liberty could improve the lives of everyone.

What Is the Enlightenment?

During the middle 1700s, many French writers and artists criticized their society. They wanted to use reason to solve society's problems. Their writings began a movement that historians call the **Enlightenment.** Enlightened thinkers lived all over Europe, but Paris became the center of the Enlightenment.

What Was a Salon?

Enlightened people met to talk about new ideas. In Paris, wealthy women invited writers, artists, and educated nobles to gather in their homes. They called these meetings **salons.** During the evening, a guest might read a poem aloud. Another guest might play some music. The guests talked about new books, plays, and the latest scientific ideas. They loved to talk and share their opinions.

People used salons during the Enlightenment to share new ideas, poetry, and music.

What Rights Did Voltaire Think People Had?

Voltaire was an enlightened French thinker who influenced many people. He wrote histories, poetry, and over 50 plays. In these, he criticized the wealth and privileges of French kings and nobles. Twice, King Louis XV put Voltaire in jail to keep him from criticizing the French monarchy.

Free speech, free press, and religious freedom are important human rights, according to Voltaire.

Voltaire defended a person's right to think and to say anything. He is reported to have said, "I do not agree with a word you say, but I will defend to the death your right to say it." Voltaire also supported freedom of religion. Free speech, free press, and religious freedom seemed to him to be rights that belonged to every person. According to Voltaire, governments had to respect these rights.

Why Did Diderot Publish an Encyclopedia?

During the Age of Reason, scientists and other people discovered many new things. Frenchman Denis Diderot decided to publish a set of books containing all this new knowledge. He wanted to put together all this knowledge so that everyone could learn it.

How Long Did Diderot Work on His Encyclopedia?

Beginning in the 1740s, Diderot spent 30 years working on his encyclopedia. More than 200 important thinkers—such as Rousseau and Voltaire—wrote articles for the encyclopedia. Madame Geoffrin, famous for her salon, helped finance Diderot's work.

Diderot's encyclopedia was a collection of articles that explored new learning. It also questioned people in authority in every field of learning. Diderot published the first volume of his encyclopedia in 1751. For 21 years, he worked to complete his encyclopedia. Finally, in 1772, he published the final book. Publishers sold thousands of this 28-volume set in France and other countries in Europe. The work of Diderot helped spread the ideas of the Enlightenment.

What Enlightened Things Did Frederick the Great Do?

The Enlightenment influenced several monarchs in Europe. These enlightened monarchs accepted reason as important in governing. Two of these monarchs were Frederick the Great of Prussia and Empress Maria Theresa of Austria.

Frederick the Great rejected the divine right of a king to rule. He thought that the idea was unreasonable. The Prussian ruler said that he was king because he was the person most able to lead. Frederick wanted to fight the ignorance and the **prejudices** in Prussia. A prejudice is an unfair and unreasonable opinion. People who are prejudiced form an opinion without having all the facts.

Frederick the Great wanted to enlighten his people and reform his country. He made the court system more fair. During this time, governments often used torture to get people to confess to a crime. Frederick **banned,** or got rid of, torture, except for the crimes of murder and treason.

Frederick asked people to be more tolerant of different Christian religions. He improved the lives of German farmers by giving them seed and rebuilding homes and barns. Frederick so impressed Voltaire that the French thinker called him "Frederick the Great." Voltaire was the first person to give the Prussian ruler that name.

What Enlightened Thing Did Empress Maria Theresa Do?

The Enlightenment also influenced other European rulers. Many of them tried to change old customs and traditions. They tried to improve the lives of their people. In 1774, Empress Maria Theresa of Austria used government money for an enlightened cause. She established schools for all children between the ages of 6 and 13.

Biography

Maria Theresa: 1717–1780

Empress Maria Theresa had to fight for her throne because she was a woman. Her father was the Holy Roman Emperor. When he died, other rulers denied her right to become empress. In the war that followed, she lost one province to Frederick the Great. Her husband, Francis Stephen, became Holy Roman Emperor. They had 16 children. Her daughter, Marie Antoinette, became queen of France.

Maria Theresa was a wise ruler who followed Enlightenment ideas. She established public education in Austria. Its goal was a better-educated workforce. Maria Theresa also made the lives of Hungarian serfs better.

Word Bank
Diderot
Frederick
Geoffrin
Paris
Voltaire

Lesson 3 Review On a sheet of paper, use the words from the Word Bank to complete each sentence correctly.

1. The center of the Enlightenment was the city of _____.

2. Madame _____ held famous parties, or salons, for enlightened thinkers.

3. _____ was an enlightened thinker who favored free speech, free press, and religious freedom.

4. The encyclopedia by _____ spread the learning of the Enlightenment.

5. The enlightened ruler _____ the Great urged his people to be more tolerant of different Christian religions.

What do you think ?

Are free speech, free press, and religious freedom important? Explain your answer.

Objectives

◆ To explain how music was influenced by enlightened thinking

◆ To describe the kinds of books that were written during the Age of Reason

Enlightenment ideas influenced scientists, philosophers, reformers, and rulers. But the idea of an orderly universe governed by natural laws also influenced musicians, writers, and painters.

What Is Baroque Music?

The Age of Reason produced important new musical forms. At the end of the 1600s and during the early 1700s, baroque music became popular. (The French word *baroque* means "strange.") Renaissance music had sounded simple; baroque music sounded more complex.

During this time, composers—people who make up music for musicians to play—wrote fugues. In a fugue, the composer uses different musical instruments to repeat a melody. Perhaps the composer has the flute play the melody first. Then the composer changes the melody a little and repeats it on a trumpet. Sometimes, the composer uses two or three melodies in one fugue. Johann Sebastian Bach and George Friderick Handel were great baroque composers.

Reading Strategy:
Visualizing

Examine the details in this drawing of people dancing a minuet. Does this help you visualize the slow and careful way people danced during this period?

What Is Classical Music?

By the mid-1700s, another type of music appeared. Following the ideas of the Enlightenment, this new music was orderly and balanced. Musicians called it **classical** music. Historians used the word classical to describe the order and balance of ancient Greek art. The musicians of the Age of Reason used the same word to describe their music.

Dancing during the Age of Reason followed a precise pattern of movement. The minuet was a popular dance. It involved slow movements, bowing, and toe pointing.

Classical

A type of music from the 1700s and early 1800s that is orderly and balanced; in the style of ancient Greece or Rome

Symphony

A long musical work played by a group of musicians using many different instruments

The classical period of European music lasted from 1750 to 1820. Classical musicians developed forms of music that are still popular today. One of the most important of these new forms was the **symphony.** It is a long musical work played by a group of musicians using many different instruments.

Why Is Haydn the "Father of the Symphony"?

Joseph Haydn and Wolfgang Amadeus Mozart were two of the most important classical composers. Historians call Haydn the "father of the symphony." He was the first European to compose a complete symphony using string and woodwind musical instruments. A woodwind instrument is one that a musician plays by blowing into it. During this time, artisans made these instruments out of wood.

One of the most famous composers of classical music was Wolfgang Amadeus Mozart of Austria. As a young boy, he shocked people with his musical talent. He died young and poor, but he left behind some of the world's most beautiful music.

How Did Mozart Show He Was a Musical Genius?

Wolfgang Amadeus Mozart was a musical genius. Haydn's student, Mozart began to compose music at age 5 and played the piano for European nobles at age 8. By age 13, he had written his first opera. He wrote more than 600 musical works before he died at age 35. However, he died a poor man. Today, his music is more popular than when he was alive. Singers and musicians perform his operas *The Magic Flute* and *The Marriage of Figaro* around the world.

Which Writers Examined Human Nature?

During the Age of Reason, writers carefully observed what was going on around them. They often wrote books about the foolish actions they had seen. In 1726, Englishman Jonathan Swift published *Gulliver's Travels*. In this book, Swift made his readers laugh at the foolish things people do. Writers observed foolish actions in France too. It was there that Molière wrote plays. His plays made fun of the behavior of French nobles and middle-class people.

Other books were written based on real events. In the novel *Robinson Crusoe,* English author Daniel Defoe told the story of a shipwrecked man named Robinson Crusoe. Living on a deserted island, Crusoe had to find a way to continue his life without civilization.

What Kind of History Did People Study?

The study of history also became popular during the Age of Reason. Historians studied the civilization of ancient Greece and Rome. Edward Gibbon wrote an important book called *The Decline and Fall of the Roman Empire.*

Lesson 4 Review On a sheet of paper, write the letter of the answer that correctly completes each sentence.

1. During the Enlightenment, baroque musicians developed the _____, a new form of music.

   A classical **C** fugue
   B symphony **D** melody

2. Classical musicians developed the _____, a new form of music.

   A opera **C** baroque
   B symphony **D** flute

3. _____ was a great baroque musician.

   A Bach **B** Mozart **C** Haydn **D** Defoe

4. _____ was a great classical musician.

   A Bach **B** Defoe **C** Molière **D** Mozart

5. _____ wrote plays during the Enlightenment.

   A Mozart **B** Haydn **C** Molière **D** Bach

What do you think ?

How might the Enlightenment have influenced painters? Hint: Think about order and balance!

What Is the Enlightenment?

Immanuel Kant

Immanuel Kant was a German philosopher (1724–1804). He believed in using reason to solve human problems. People who did so were called "enlightened." This excerpt is from an essay Kant wrote in 1784. In it, he explains the term "enlightenment."

Enlightenment is man's leaving his self-caused immaturity. Immaturity is the incapacity to use one's intelligence without the guidance of another. Such immaturity is self-caused if it is not caused by lack of intelligence, but by lack of determination and courage to use one's own intelligence without being guided by another. . . . Have the courage to use your own intelligence! is therefore the motto of the enlightenment.

Through laziness and cowardice a large part of mankind . . . gladly remain immature. It is because of laziness and cowardice that it is so easy for others to usurp the role of guardians. It is so comfortable to be a minor! If I have a book which provides meaning for me, a pastor who has conscience for me, a doctor who will judge my diet for me and so on, then I do not need to exert myself. I do not have any need to think; if I can pay, others will take over the tedious job for me. The guardians who have kindly undertaken the supervision will see to it that by far the largest part of mankind, including the

entire "beautiful sex," should consider the step into maturity, not only as difficult but as very dangerous. . . .

But it is more nearly possible for a public to enlighten itself: this is even inescapable if only the public is given its freedom. . . .

All that is required for this enlightenment is *freedom;* and particularly the least harmful of all that may be called freedom, namely, the freedom for man to make *public use* of his reason in all matters. . . .

The question may now be put: Do we live at present in an enlightened age? The answer is: No, but in an age of enlightenment. Much still prevents men from being placed in a position . . . to use their own minds securely and well in matters of religion. But we do have very definite indications that this field of endeavor is being opened up for men to work freely and reduce gradually the hindrances preventing a general enlightenment and an escape from self-caused immaturity. In this sense, this age is the age of enlightenment. . . .

Document-Based Questions

1. How does Kant define immaturity?

2. For Kant, what is the motto of the enlightenment?

3. According to Kant, how do people avoid becoming mature?

4. What does the public need to become enlightened?

5. Did Kant think that he lived in an enlightened age? Why or why not?

In Defense of Women's Rights

Enlightenment thinkers often wrote about the rights of men. Nearly all ignored the rights of women. Mary Wollstonecraft tried to change that attitude. In the 1700s, women had few rights. They could not own property. If they worked, their pay went to their fathers or husbands. A husband could divorce his wife and take the children. A woman could not do the same.

Mary Wollstonecraft was born in London in 1759. As was typical, her brother Edward was sent away to a good school. Mary went to a day school where she learned French and composition. Years later, she and her sisters started a school for small children. From this experience, she wrote her first book. It was called *Thoughts on the Education of Daughters*. It contained ideas that she would develop in the future.

Finally, her luck changed. She began working for a publisher. In 1792, she went to France where the French Revolution was under way. There she wrote two more books. One was a collection of original stories for children. The other book defended the ideals of the French Revolution.

French political ideas led to Mary's most important book. Published in 1792, it was called *A Vindication of the Rights of Women.* Vindication means "defense." She wrote, "I wish to see women as neither heroines nor brutes; but reasonable creatures." Women, she argued, should have the same rights as men. They should be entitled to a good education to develop their minds. Her book is still important in the history of women's rights.

Mary Wollstonecraft

Her book became popular. Mary became famous throughout Europe. She met other people who held similar ideas. One was William Godwin, a free-thinking political writer, whom she married. In August 1797, their daughter was born. Mary died a few days later at the age of 38.

Her daughter, Mary Godwin, also became a writer. She married the poet Percy Bysshe Shelley. In 1818, Mary Wollstonecraft Shelley wrote a book that is still famous. It tells about a scientist who created a monster. The scientist's name is the title of the book: *Frankenstein!*

Wrap-Up

1. In the 1700s, men had many rights that women did not. What were some of them?

2. What was Mary Wollstonecraft's most important book?

3. What were her views about education?

4. Who was William Godwin?

5. Why is Mary Wollstonecraft's daughter famous today?

- The Age of Reason changed the way people thought about the universe. Ideas of order and balance influenced ideas about government.

- Newton's scientific discoveries introduced the ideas of natural, universal laws that could predict natural events. People began to look for natural laws in human behavior and society. Believers in reason were enlightened thinkers. They wanted to use reason to improve people's lives and all parts of society. This movement is called the Enlightenment.

- Thomas Hobbes, an English philosopher, believed strong rulers were needed to keep peace in society. John Locke thought that people and their government made a contract, or agreement. He wrote that people had rights to life, liberty, and property. Government was to protect those rights.

- Montesquieu and Rousseau were enlightened French thinkers. Montesquieu thought that government powers should be divided among separate branches. Rousseau believed that people were naturally good, but that civilization made them evil. He wrote that people made a contract with each other. Their shared values, the general will, created a community.

- During the Enlightenment, people met to discuss ideas. In Paris, these meetings were known as salons.

- Voltaire was a French philosopher and writer. He defended people's right to free speech, a free press, and religious freedom.

- Denis Diderot in France wrote a many-volume encyclopedia including the knowledge of the Age of Reason.

- Some European monarchs adopted Enlightenment ideas. Frederick the Great of Prussia rejected the idea of the "divine right" of kings. He believed in religious tolerance and made the court system more just. Maria Theresa of Austria set up schools for children.

- Enlightenment ideas influenced artists as well as scientists and rulers. In baroque music, composers such as Bach and Handel wrote complex pieces such as fugues.

- Classical music was balanced and orderly. Joseph Haydn developed the symphony form. Wolfgang Amadeus Mozart, his student, wrote hundreds of works in his short lifetime.

- Enlightenment writers used reason to examine society and history. These writers included Swift, Defoe, and Gibbon in England, and Molière in France.

Chapter 19   R E V I E W

Word Bank

Handel

Diderot

Frederick the Great

Hobbes

Locke

Maria Theresa

Montesquieu

Newton

Rousseau

Voltaire

On a sheet of paper, use the words from the Word Bank to complete each sentence correctly.

1. _____ discovered a law that made Europeans begin to use scientific reasoning.

2. _____ believed that rulers should have absolute power.

3. _____ believed that people had the right to life, liberty, and property.

4. _____ believed in separation of powers in government.

5. _____ said that all people were born good.

6. _____ rejected the divine right of a king to rule.

7. _____ criticized the French government and the king put him in jail.

8. _____ published the first encyclopedia.

9. Empress _____ of Austria was an enlightened ruler.

10. _____ was a famous baroque composer.

On a sheet of paper, write the letter of the answer that correctly completes each sentence.

11. Enlightened thinkers believed that _____ could lead them to truth.

    A feeling   **C** traditions
    B reason   **D** government

12. According to Montesquieu, _____ held a republic together.

    A virtue   **B** fear   **C** honor   **D** rebellion

13. Hobbes thought that order was more important than _____ in a society.

    A government   **B** writing   **C** freedom   **D** virtue

14. _____ composed music during the Age of Reason.

    A Handel   **C** Bach

    B Mozart   **D** all of the above

15. Many enlightened thinkers thought that reason could solve the problems of _____.

    A society   **B** fugue   **C** woodwind   **D** privilege

On a sheet of paper, write the answer to each question. Use complete sentences.

16. Why do historians call the years 1687 to 1789 the Age of Reason?

17. Why do historians also call these years the Enlightenment?

18. What did Hobbes and Locke agree and disagree about with regard to government?

Critical Thinking On a sheet of paper, write your response to each question. Use complete sentences.

19. The enlightened thinkers during the Age of Reason believed that they could make societies and people better by using reason. Do you agree with this belief?

20. According to Rousseau, people are born good. Society creates people who do bad things. What do you think of this theory? If possible, give examples to explain your answer.

Test-Taking Tip

If you do not know a word in a question, read the question again but leave out the word. Then see if you can figure out the word from its use in the sentence.

20 Revolutions and Napoleon

Economic and political revolutions bring change. In this chapter, you will become part of the American Revolution. This change brought about a new nation—the United States. Across the ocean, the French watched this revolution and learned from it. You will see how they too revolted. Then you will meet Napoleon, a military leader. With him, you will march into a Russian winter and end up on a rocky island in the Atlantic. This chapter will help you understand how revolution changed Europe and America.

Goals for Learning

◆ To list the causes of the American Revolution

◆ To explain how the American Revolution changed the world

◆ To describe the causes of the French Revolution

◆ To describe the Reign of Terror in France

◆ To list the accomplishments and failures of Napoleon

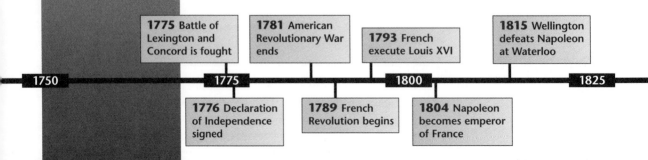

1775 Battle of Lexington and Concord is fought

1781 American Revolutionary War ends

1793 French execute Louis XVI

1815 Wellington defeats Napoleon at Waterloo

1750   1775   1800   1825

1776 Declaration of Independence signed

1789 French Revolution begins

1804 Napoleon becomes emperor of France

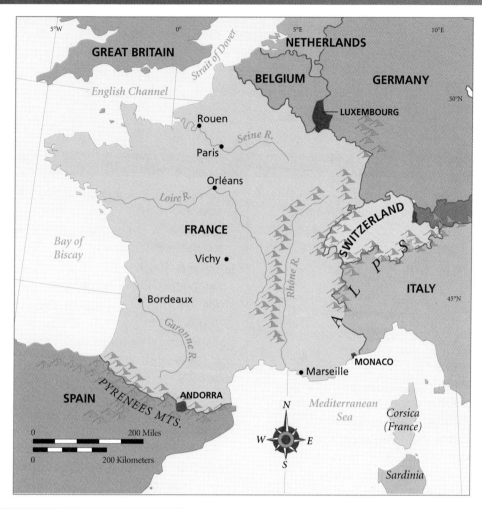

Map Skills

During this time, revolution started in America, then spread to France. Great changes took place in this European country. The common people revolted and took power away from the nobles and the king. Their cry was "Liberty, equality, and fraternity!" They wanted everyone to be part of a brotherhood in which all were free and equal.

Study the map and answer the following questions:

1. What city in France is near the Mediterranean?

2. What island in the Mediterranean did France hold?

3. What are the names of four rivers in France?

4. What mountains separate France from Spain?

5. What mountains form the boundary between Italy and France?

Reading Strategy:
Inferencing

Sometimes the meaning of a text is not directly stated. You have to "read between the lines" to understand what is really being said.

◆ What You Know + What You Read = Inference

◆ As you read, look for clues that help you understand what is happening.

Key Vocabulary Words

Lesson 1
Quarter To provide soldiers with a place to live

Violate To go against

Repeal To do away with a law

Lesson 2
Boycott To refuse to buy something

Minutemen Colonial soldiers in the Revolutionary War who were ready to fight at any time

Declaration of Independence A document the American colonists signed declaring their freedom from Great Britain

Complaint A statement about something that that tells why a person is unhappy

American Revolution The American struggle against Great Britain for independence

Lesson 3
Estate A class of people in France

Estates-General The French governmental body made up of representatives from the three estates

Bastille A prison in Paris

French Revolution The war that the common people of France fought to achieve freedom

Lesson 4
Equality The same rights for everyone

Enforce To make sure that people follow the laws and rules

Convention A group of people who meet to get something done

Émigré A French noble who fled France during the French Revolution

Moderate One who wants to change things little by little

Radical One who wants to change things all at once

Jacobin A radical leader during the French Revolution

Reign of Terror The one-year period in French history when radical leaders put many people to death

Guillotine A machine used to execute people by chopping off their head

Legislature The lawmaking body of government

Executive The branch of government that enforces laws

Lesson 5
Tactic A plan that helps someone win a game or a battle

Neutral Not choosing either side in a war

Exile To send someone away from his or her own country

Code of Napoleon A code of law Napoleon passed that made all men equal in France

Objectives

- To identify the Stamp Act and the Townshend Acts
- To identify the cause of the Boston Massacre
- To explain what happened at the Boston Tea Party

Quarter

To provide soldiers with a place to live

Violate

To go against

Geography Note

Beginning in the late 1700s, many American settlers moved westward on the Wilderness Road. Daniel Boone, on behalf of the Transylvania Company, had blazed a trail through the wilderness. The road began in Virginia and spanned the Appalachian Mountains.

Between 1607 and 1733, England established 13 colonies in North America. For the people living in America, the colonists, life was different from life in England. Land was cheap. People could earn money and not be poor anymore. For more than 150 years, England pretty much left the colonists alone. Then, in 1763, England changed the way it treated the colonies.

What Law Took Away the Colonists' Rights?

From 1754 to 1763, the English and the French fought to control North America. The war cost a lot of money. After it ended, England left British soldiers in the colonies to protect the colonists. But Great Britain needed money to pay these soldiers and to pay off the bills from the war.

To raise money, the British government tried for the first time to make the colonists obey the Navigation Acts. These laws said that the colonists had to ship their trading goods on British ships. The money England got from the colonists would pay for the cost of protecting them. The colonists said that they did not need British protection.

Then, in 1765, the British government passed the Quartering Act. This law said that the colonists had to let British soldiers **quarter** in their homes. That is, colonists had to provide the soldiers with a place to live. The colonists also had to feed these soldiers. The colonists said that this law **violated,** or went against, their rights.

Why Did the Colonists Dislike the Stamp Act?

In 1765, the English Parliament also passed the Stamp Act to raise money. This law put a tax on colonial newspapers, playing cards, and legal documents. In England, this type of tax was common.

Before the Stamp Act, the price of everything included a British tax. But most colonists did not know this, so they thought that the Stamp Act was new. They thought that it was the first direct tax England had placed on them.

The colonists did not like the Quartering Act. They also did not like the Stamp Act, even though it was a small tax. They said that Great Britain had not asked them if they wanted this tax. The colonists believed that England had no right to tax them unless they agreed to taxation. They refused to pay the tax, and in 1766, the British Parliament **repealed,** or did away with it.

What Did Angry Colonists Do in Boston?

In 1767, the British Parliament passed a new group of laws called the Townshend Acts. These laws placed a tax on common products, such as paper, paint, glass, and tea. Once again, the colonists said that England could not tax them without their consent.

The bad feelings between Great Britain and the colonists got worse. Then, in 1770, British soldiers in Boston fired into a crowd that had tossed sticks and snowballs at them. Historians call this event the Boston Massacre.

In 1773, some colonists in Boston dressed up as American Indians. Then they climbed on board a British merchant ship that was carrying tea. The colonists threw the tea into the harbor. Historians call this event the Boston Tea Party.

The Boston Tea Party was a protest against Britain's unfair control of the tea trade. Colonists dumped over 300 chests of tea into Boston Harbor.

Reading Strategy:
Inferencing

How does what you already know about the Boston Tea Party add to what you have just read?

Word Bank

Boston Tea Party

Navigation Acts

Quartering Act

Stamp Act

Townshend Acts

Why did the colonists do this? Before this, British companies had sold tea to merchants in the colonies. Then these merchants had sold tea to the colonists. In that way, the colonial merchants ran a business and made money. But Parliament had now given a British company the right to sell tea directly to colonists. This cut out colonial merchants. Clearly, the colonists and the British were not getting along.

Lesson 1 Review On a sheet of paper, use the words from the Word Bank to complete each sentence correctly.

1. The _____ made colonists ship goods on British ships.

2. The _____ put a tax on items such as paper and glass.

3. The _____ required colonists to let British soldiers live in the colonists' homes.

4. The _____ put a tax on colonial newspapers, playing cards, and legal documents.

5. The _____ was some colonists' response to the Townshend Acts.

What do you think

Do you think that England had the right to tax the colonists to pay for the soldiers' protection? Explain your answer.

Biography

Abigail Adams: 1774–1818

Abigail Smith Adams was the wife of one American president (John Adams) and the mother of another (John Quincy Adams). She was very active in her husband's career. Abigail was also one of the most influential women of her day. She supported equal education for women. She often spoke out against slavery.

We know a great deal about Abigail from her letters. She wrote to her husband while he was attending Congress during the American Revolution. There are also letters from when he was a diplomat in Europe. Still more letters present a clear picture of Washington, D.C., up to 1800.

Objectives

- To identify the minutemen
- To identify the writer of the Declaration of Independence
- To describe how the Revolutionary War ended

Boycott

To refuse to buy something; to refuse to deal with a person, business, or country

Minutemen

Colonial soldiers in the Revolutionary War who were ready to fight at any time

Because of the Boston Tea Party, Parliament closed the port of Boston. It also forced the colony of Massachusetts to accept military rule. This upset the colonists. In 1774, representatives from 12 colonies met in Philadelphia. They agreed to **boycott**— or refuse to buy—any British goods; to send a protest to King George III in England; and to meet again.

What Was the "Shot Heard 'Round the World"?

Before the representatives could meet again, something happened. In April 1775, British soldiers marched to Concord, Massachusetts, to seize colonial weapons. At Lexington, some colonial soldiers called **minutemen** met the British soldiers. (These soldiers were ready to fight at any time.) Someone fired a gun. This started a small battle. An American poet later wrote that this was the "shot heard 'round the world."

The British soldiers began to march back toward Boston. But their bright red uniforms were easy to see. As they retreated, the minutemen fired on them from behind trees and rocks. By the time the British "redcoats" reached Boston, the colonists had killed a third of them.

The first shots of the American Revolutionary War were fired at Lexington and Concord in 1775.

Declaration of Independence

A document the American colonists signed in which they declared their freedom from Great Britain

Complaint

A statement about something that tells why a person is unhappy

American Revolution

The American struggle against Great Britain for independence

Who Wrote the Declaration of Independence?

In May 1775, the colonial representatives met again. They agreed to pay for an army that George Washington would command. On July 4, 1776, they signed the **Declaration of Independence.** In this document, they declared that the colonies were free states. They were no longer part of the British Empire. The Declaration of Independence also listed more than 20 **complaints** against King George III. That is, it told why the colonists were unhappy.

Thomas Jefferson wrote most of the document. He accepted the political ideas of John Locke. Jefferson wrote that people could change their government if that government no longer protected their rights of life and liberty. Jefferson also said that people had the right to try to find happiness.

Who Helped the Colonists Fight the War?

The struggle against Great Britain—the **American Revolution**—lasted from 1776 to 1781. The battles fought during this war did not go well for the colonists at first. George Washington's soldiers had little training and lacked supplies, but they managed to win some battles.

George Washington commanded the colonial forces in the Revolutionary War.

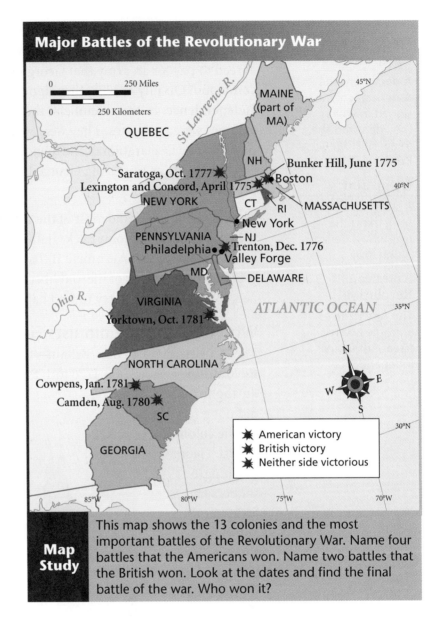

Major Battles of the Revolutionary War

QUEBEC

St. Lawrence R.

45°N

MAINE (part of MA)

NH

Saratoga, Oct. 1777

Bunker Hill, June 1775

Boston

Lexington and Concord, April 1775

NEW YORK

CT

RI

MASSACHUSETTS

40°N

New York

PENNSYLVANIA

NJ

Philadelphia

Trenton, Dec. 1776

Valley Forge

MD

DELAWARE

Ohio R.

VIRGINIA

Yorktown, Oct. 1781

ATLANTIC OCEAN

35°N

NORTH CAROLINA

Cowpens, Jan. 1781

Camden, Aug. 1780

SC

30°N

GEORGIA

* American victory
* British victory
* Neither side victorious

N E W S

0   250 Miles
0   250 Kilometers

85°W   80°W   75°W   70°W

Map Study

This map shows the 13 colonies and the most important battles of the Revolutionary War. Name four battles that the Americans won. Name two battles that the British won. Look at the dates and find the final battle of the war. Who won it?

In 1777, the colonists won an important victory at Saratoga. Because of this, France sent soldiers to help the colonists defeat Great Britain. In 1779, Spain declared war on Great Britain. In 1780, the Netherlands joined the American fight. Great Britain was now at war with the colonies and with France, Spain, and the Netherlands.

What Brought an End to the War?

Finally, in 1781, the colonial army rushed southward to Yorktown, Virginia. Here, the British army, led by General Cornwallis, was trapped. In front, it faced the colonial army. At its back was the sea and the French fleet.

Reading Strategy:
Inferencing

What can you infer about the ability of the colonial army?

Because of these French ships, the British navy could not rescue Cornwallis and his soldiers. Cornwallis surrendered. Some political leaders in Great Britain began to oppose the war. Two years later, the colonists and England signed a peace treaty in Paris, France. Great Britain accepted the independence of the 13 American colonies. The American Revolution had ended.

How Did the American Revolution Affect Europe?

The British soldiers marched out of Yorktown in 1781. As they did so, their band played the song "The World Turned Upside Down." And the world had turned upside down. The American Revolution brought change for Americans and for Europeans.

The Declaration of Independence said that "all men are created equal." The declaration also said that people had a right to choose their own form of government. In 1789, the people of France followed the lead of the Americans. The French also turned their world upside down.

Lesson 2 Review On a sheet of paper, write the answer to each question. Use complete sentences.

1. Who were the minutemen?

2. In what place did the American Revolutionary War begin?

3. When did the colonial representatives sign the Declaration of Independence?

4. What European countries helped the colonists win the war?

5. Where and when did the fighting in the American Revolution end?

What do you think

What do you think life would be like in America today if the American Revolution had been a failure?

Then and Now

Independence Day

The Fourth of July is the anniversary of American independence. It celebrates the signing of the Declaration of Independence. This national holiday first took place in Philadelphia on July 8, 1776. The Declaration was read aloud, city bells rang, and bands played. Independence is now celebrated with parades, picnics, and fireworks. In 1976, the United States was 200 years old. During the whole year, cities and towns held special events to remember independence.

Other countries also have independence days. Mexico marks its independence from Spain on September 16. Ghana celebrates independence from Great Britain on March 6.

Objectives

◆ To identify the three estates
◆ To explain the importance of the Bastille

Estate

A class of people in France

In the early 1770s, France probably had more money than any other nation in Europe. Throughout Europe, most educated people spoke French. Many of the most important ideas of the Enlightenment came from French thinkers. However, France had two big problems. First, French society was still like the feudal societies of the Middle Ages. Second, the king—an absolute monarch—was a weak ruler.

What Were the Three Estates?

French society was divided into three **estates,** or classes. The clergy—1 percent of the population—made up the First Estate. These religious leaders owned 10 percent of the land. The nobles—5 percent of the population—made up the Second Estate. They held all the important jobs in the government. They also controlled most of the money and property in their country. The Third Estate included three different groups of common people. At the top were doctors, teachers, bankers, business people, and lawyers. In the middle were city workers. At the bottom were farmers, who made up more than 80 percent of the population.

Who Paid Taxes in France?

The clergy and the nobility paid no taxes to the government. But the three groups of the Third Estate had to pay taxes on the money they made and on their land. They also had to pay taxes when they bought salt, tobacco, and soap.

The farmers paid about half of their money in taxes. They also had to work once a year on government projects without pay. The members of the Third Estate paid a lot of taxes, but they had little or no political power.

Why Did the French Government Need Money in 1789?

In 1789, the French treasury was empty. France had spent a lot of money helping the American colonies revolt against Great Britain. To raise money, the government decided to find a way to tax the nobles. They did not like this and demanded that the king call a meeting of the **Estates-General.** This was a government body made up of the representatives from the three estates. The last time the Estates-General had met was in 1614.

Louis XVI agreed. The Estates-General met at Versailles on May 5, 1789. At this meeting, the representatives would decide if the nobles had to pay taxes. But each of the three estates had only one vote. So, the First and Second Estates—the clergy and the nobles—could defeat the Third Estate, which was already paying all the taxes.

What Did the Third Estate Do in 1789?

The 610 representatives of the Third Estate wanted everyone at the meeting to have a vote. They could then outvote the 591 representatives of the other two estates. But the king said that the meeting would follow the old rule of three votes.

The representatives of the Third Estate declared that they were a National Assembly that represented the French people. The king locked them out of the meeting hall. But they simply marched outside and decided to write a constitution. They called for an end to absolute monarchy. Under pressure, Louis XVI ended the meeting of the Estates-General. He told the clergy and the nobles to join the National Assembly.

The storming of the Bastille, a prison in France, became a symbol of the French Revolution.

What Did Mobs Do in Paris in 1789?

In the 1780s, many poor people lived in Paris. Mostly, they ate bread. If the price of bread increased, they starved. Sometimes, mobs—large groups of people—seized carts of grain and bread because of their hunger.

In 1788, the grain harvest in France was poor, so bread doubled in price. In the spring of 1789, the starving people in Paris got mad. Angry mobs rioted in the streets. On July 14, 1789, these mobs attacked a city prison called the **Bastille.** The government kept a few political prisoners there as well as gunpowder. When the French soldiers joined the mob, the Bastille fell!

A noble woke Louis XVI from his sleep and told him what had happened. The angry king said, "Why, this is a revolt!" "No," the noble said. "It is a revolution." It was the beginning of the **French Revolution.** The common people of France fought against the king, nobles, and one another to achieve freedom.

Lesson 3 Review On a sheet of paper, write the letter of the answer that correctly completes each sentence.

1. In the early 1770s, France probably had more _____ than any other nation in Europe.

   A bread   **B** grain   **C** money   **D** population

2. The Third Estate was made up of _____.

   A clergy   **C** nobles
   B kings   **D** common people

3. Members of the Third Estate wanted to end France's _____.

   A clergy   **C** grain harvest
   B absolute monarchy   **D** Bastille

4. The Bastille in Paris is a _____.

   A prison   **B** palace   **C** castle   **D** navy yard

5. The French Revolution began in _____.

   A 1775   **B** 1780   **C** 1789   **D** 1791

Objectives

◆ To identify the government formed by the National Assembly

◆ To describe what the Jacobins wanted

◆ To identify the Directory

Equality

The same rights for everyone

Enforce

To make sure that people follow the laws and rules

The National Assembly quickly started to reform French government. On August 4, 1789, it ended the feudal privileges of the clergy and the nobles. It also adopted a document that gave citizens three rights—free speech, freedom of religion, and **equality** under the law. Equality means that everyone shares the same rights.

Why Did the King Leave Versailles?

In October 1789, thousands of women rioted over the cost of bread. They marched on Versailles, which was ten miles from Paris. When they got to Versailles, the women broke into the palace and killed several guards. Then they demanded that the king and queen move to Paris. Frightened, the rulers agreed to do so. In June 1790, Louis XVI and his family tried to escape from France. But someone recognized the king. He and his family had to return to Paris.

What Type of Government Did the Assembly Form?

The National Assembly continued to make changes. By 1791, it had created a new form of government. Members of the assembly wrote a constitution that limited the king's power. This new government was a constitutional monarchy.

According to the constitution, the new Legislative Assembly had the power to make laws. The king had the power to **enforce** the laws, or make sure people follow them. The new constitution said that all men were equal before the law. However, only property owners—less than 1 percent of the population—could be elected to the government.

Reading Strategy:
Inferencing

After reading about the unstable governments, what can you infer about life in France at this time?

What Was the Next Government of France?

The new constitutional government lasted only 11 months. In September 1792, the French abolished it. Then they elected a National Constitutional **Convention.** A convention is a group of people who meet to get something done. The Constitutional Convention met to form a new, more democratic government for France—a republic.

The new government took away all of Louis XVI's power. It gave all French men the right to vote and to hold political office. The government also decided to fight to bring freedom to all the common people in Europe.

Which Nations Tried to Stop the French Revolution?

Many French nobles, called **émigrés,** had fled France. They asked Leopold II of Austria to overthrow the new French government. In August 1791, Leopold and the king of Prussia said that all kings had the duty to "restore order to France." The armies of Great Britain, Austria, Prussia, and Spain joined together to try and defeat the French and end the French Revolution.

What Happened to Louis XVI?

The French no longer thought of Louis XVI as king. He was just a common citizen. In June 1790, he had written a letter condemning the revolution. In December 1792, the government put him on trial for treason. On January 21, 1793, it executed him. That same year, France raised a citizen army of 300,000 men. Many French women went to war with the men.

The French created a horrible way to put people to death: the guillotine. This picture shows Louis XVI before his execution by the guillotine.

Queen of France Marie Antoinette was one of the first to be sent to the guillotine in France.

Who Were the Jacobins?

After the king was executed, the French peasants rebelled. Then, **moderate** and **radical** leaders in the government began to fight one another for power. Moderates wanted to bring about reform little by little. Radicals wanted to change everything at once.

In Paris, a mob rushed into the Convention and arrested all the moderate leaders. Then the radicals—called **Jacobins**—controlled the government. The Convention formed a Committee of Public Safety. Maximilien Robespierre led the committee. He wanted to kill anyone who opposed the revolution.

Moderate

One who wants to change things little by little

Radical

One who wants to change things all at once

Jacobin

A radical leader during the French Revolution

What can you infer about this period from the title of the section? What words helped you make your inference?

Reign of Terror

The one-year period in French history when radical leaders put many people to death

Guillotine

The machine used to execute people by chopping off their head

Legislature

The lawmaking body of government

Executive

The branch of government that enforces laws

Word Bank

Leopold

Louis XVI

Marie Antoinette

Robespierre

Versailles

What Was the Reign of Terror?

Between July 1793 and July 1794, the Jacobins executed thousands of people by chopping off their heads. Historians call this the **Reign of Terror.** One of the first people to lose her head was the woman who had been queen—Marie Antoinette. The radicals executed many nobles, but mostly they put common people to death.

For one year, Robespierre was a dictator. But the Reign of Terror ended on July 28, 1794, when the radicals sent Robespierre himself to the **guillotine.** (This was the machine the French used to execute someone by chopping off their head.)

What Was the Directory?

During the next five years, the National Convention drew up another new constitution. (This was the third one since 1789.) They divided the **legislature,** or lawmaking body, into two houses. They established an **executive** branch—the Directory—made up of five people. (The executive branch enforced the laws.)

For a time, the Directory brought order to France. Then, in November 1799, it also fell from power. Three men took control of the government. One of them was a 30-year-old military officer named Napoleon Bonaparte.

Lesson 4 Review On a sheet of paper, use the words from the Word Bank to complete each sentence correctly.

1. In 1789, women marched on _____ and demanded that their rulers return to Paris.

2. The king of France at this time was _____.

3. The queen of France was _____.

4. _____ led the Reign of Terror for a year.

5. _____ of Austria called all kings to bring order to France.

What do you think

Why do you think the kings of other nations opposed the French Revolution?

Objectives

◆ To explain why soldiers supported Napoleon

◆ To describe how Napoleon was crowned emperor

◆ To explain what happened when Napoleon invaded Russia

◆ To identify ways that Napoleon affected history

Tactic

A plan that helps someone win a game or a battle

Reading Strategy:
Inferencing

After reading this section, what can you infer about the kind of person Napoleon was?

Napoleon Bonaparte was born in 1769 on the small island of Corsica. As a boy, he went to a military school in France. When he was 16, he joined the king's army. The French Revolution began in 1789. At that time, Napoleon was a little-known, low-level military officer. But he developed a new military **tactic,** or plan that would help him win. He moved his soldiers quickly, then put most of them at the weakest point of the enemy line.

Soldiers liked to fight for Napoleon. He was a natural leader and helped them win battles against stronger armies. Within four years, he became a general. (He was only 24.) Six years later, Napoleon took control of the disorganized government of France. Later, he said, "I found the crown of France lying on the ground, and I picked it up with a sword."

For the next 15 years, Napoleon ruled France as a military dictator. As time passed, he conquered most of Europe. His actions dominated European history from 1800 to 1815. Historians call those years the Age of Napoleon.

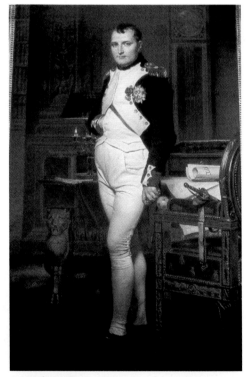

Napoleon Bonaparte saw himself as a conqueror like Alexander the Great. He became emperor of France in 1804.

When Did Napoleon Become First Consul?

Napoleon dreamed of making France into a mighty empire like that of ancient Rome. He saw himself as a modern-day Alexander the Great. When Napoleon first came to power, he acted as if he was the elected leader of a democratic republic. Then, in 1800, he asked the people of France to approve a new constitution. It gave him the title of First Consul. (Consuls led the ancient Roman republic.) As First Consul, Napoleon had more power than any other French official.

Who Crowned Napoleon As the Emperor?

In 1802, the French people elected Napoleon their First Consul for life. More than 3 million people voted, and only 9,000 of them voted against Napoleon. Then, on December 2, 1804, Pope Pius VII came to Paris. He waited at the Cathedral of Notre Dame to crown Napoleon emperor of France. Napoleon, dressed in purple, entered the cathedral. He walked up to the pope, took the crown from him, and placed it on his own head! Through his own military skill, he had risen to power. Now, by his own hand, he made himself Emperor Napoleon I.

History in Your Life

A Song for the Revolution

In 1792, more than 500 soldiers marched from Marseilles to Paris. They were all volunteers, caught up in the spirit of the Revolution. On the way, they sang "The War Song of the Rhine Army." This emotional song of liberty had captured the feeling of hope and revolutionary change. It was written by Claude-Joseph Rouget de L'isle, a young French army captain.

The song was renamed "The Marseillaise." In 1795, it became the national anthem of France. When France became an empire,

Napoleon banned "The Marseillaise." He feared it would continue to rouse the French to revolution. However, in 1875 France, once again, adopted "The Marseillaise" as its national anthem.

Arise, ye sons of France!
Your day of glory has arrived!
Oh army of citizens!
Form your battalions.
March on, march on!
All hearts dedicated
to liberty or death!

What Was the Confederation of the Rhine?

In 1805, Britain, Austria, and Russia formed a military alliance against France. Napoleon quickly defeated the armies of Austria and Russia. From 1806 to 1812, his power increased in Europe. He took control of Italy and made himself king there. Then he ended the Holy Roman Empire. (This empire had lasted for many centuries.) In its place, he created a loose alliance of German states. He called this alliance the Confederation of the Rhine.

Napoleon let his brothers rule some of this conquered land. Louis Bonaparte became king of Holland. Jerome Bonaparte ruled over the Kingdom of Westphalia in Germany. Joseph Bonaparte ruled over the Kingdom of Naples and Sicily and later became the king of Spain.

What Mistakes Did Napoleon Make?

Only Great Britain stood against the spreading French power. In 1805, England destroyed the French fleet off the coast of Spain. In 1806, Napoleon decided to ruin the British economy by ordering other European countries to stop trading with Great Britain. He called his plan the Continental System.

But Napoleon misjudged the power of the British navy. It prevented trading ships from entering French and other European ports. The successful actions of the British navy hurt the economy of France and these other countries.

Because of their lost trade, the **neutral** European nations quickly turned against France. (A neutral country is one that does not choose either side in a war.) Napoleon's mistake had weakened French power. In 1812, he made a second mistake—a bigger one. He invaded Russia.

Why Did Napoleon Invade Russia?

In 1807, Czar Alexander I of Russia had agreed to support the Continental System. But lack of trade hurt the Russian economy. In 1812, Alexander began to trade with Britain once again. His decision made Napoleon angry.

Napoleon was a natural military leader. This painting shows him at the Battle of Eylau in 1807. Perhaps his greatest mistake was invading Russia in 1812.

To punish Russia, Napoleon organized the largest army in history up to that time. His Grand Army of 500,000 was made up of soldiers from all parts of the French Empire. In May 1812, this army set out to invade Russia.

How Did the Russian Army Fight?

Napoleon thought that he could defeat Russia in a few months. But the Russian army did not want to fight one big battle. Instead, it kept retreating. As the French army followed, the Russian soldiers retreated eastward, deeper and deeper into Russia. As they pulled back, the soldiers destroyed anything that could help Napoleon's invading army. The Russians left behind only burned fields and houses.

Near Moscow, the French and Russian armies finally met. The French won the battle. But when the soldiers entered the capital, they found only a burned-out and deserted city. Once again the Russians had destroyed food and shelter that Napoleon's army needed.

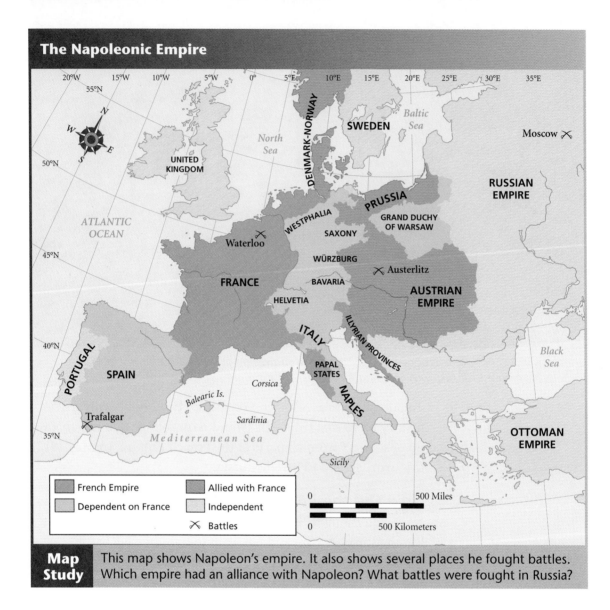

The Napoleonic Empire

Map Study This map shows Napoleon's empire. It also shows several places he fought battles. Which empire had an alliance with Napoleon? What battles were fought in Russia?

What Happened When Napoleon Left Russia?

Napoleon sent several messages of peace. However, he heard nothing from the Russians. In October 1812—after five weeks of waiting—Napoleon ordered his army to return to France. The Grand Army had already lost thousands of soldiers. Many had died of disease. Now the soldiers faced a cold Russian winter without food and warm clothing.

The Russian winter was a hard enemy. As the French army moved slowly westward, thousands of soldiers died of starvation. Many froze to death. Over 500,000 soldiers had marched boldly into Russia. Only 40,000—tired and beaten—returned to France. And only 10,000 of them were still able to fight. Napoleon's retreat from Russia was a military disaster.

Who Defeated Napoleon the First Time?

Seeing the weakened French army, Napoleon's enemies attacked. In March 1814, the British, Russian, Prussian, and Austrian armies captured Paris. The leaders removed Napoleon from power and sent him to Elba, an island off the coast of Italy. Then they restored the monarchy to France. (The brother of the executed Louis XVI became king.)

In February 1815, Napoleon escaped from Elba and returned to France. First, he declared himself emperor. Then he began to raise an army. The French king quickly sent his soldiers to stop Napoleon. When Napoleon met the king's soldiers, he asked if any one of them wished "to kill his emperor." They all cried, "Long live the emperor!"

Who Defeated Napoleon the Second Time?

For the next three months, Napoleon was once again the hero of France. During that time, he organized an army of 125,000 men. On June 18, 1815, his new army met the combined armies of Britain and Prussia at Waterloo in present-day Belgium.

Writing About History

In your notebook, write an epitaph, or writing on a tombstone, for Napoleon. What were his dreams? his accomplishments? Why did he capture the French imagination? Why did Napoleon fall from power?

The Duke of Wellington led the British and Prussian troops. On the battlefield at Waterloo, these troops finally defeated Napoleon. Once again, he was **exiled,** or sent away, to a lonely island, this time in the South Atlantic. He was ordered not to come back to France.

In 1821, six years after the Battle of Waterloo, Napoleon Bonaparte died at the age of 52 on the rocky island of St. Helena. For a few years, his dream of a French empire came true. No one could stop his army. Then he met a Russian winter and Waterloo.

How Did Napoleon Affect History?

Napoleon's leadership had many important effects. In France, he achieved one important goal of the French Revolution—he made every man equal before the law. He did this with a new code of laws called the **Code of Napoleon.**

Napoleon's success as a military conqueror changed the political boundaries of Europe. The leaders of the French Revolution had wanted liberty and equality. Napoleon's success spread these ideas throughout Europe.

These ideas changed people. Napoleon had conquered many people. Many of them now wanted their own nation. This rising spirit of nationalism helped to shape European history throughout the 19th century.

Lesson 5 Review On a sheet of paper, write the answer to each question. Use complete sentences.

1. What years in French history do historians call the Age of Napoleon?

2. What did Napoleon do before he came to power in France?

3. When did Napoleon become the emperor of France?

4. How successful was Napoleon's invasion of Russia?

5. At which battle did Napoleon meet his final defeat?

What do you think ?

Why do you think the Russians did not answer Napoleon's messages of peace near Moscow?

Declaration of the Rights of Man and of the Citizen

The National Assembly of France approved this document in 1789. It was based on two other important documents: the English Bill of Rights and the American Declaration of Independence. The basic principles of the French declaration, such as freedom and equality of all male citizens, helped start the revolution. The declaration also presumed that women were inferior. In response to this, a woman named Olympe de Gouges wrote the Declaration of the Rights of Women in 1791. It began, "Woman is born free and lives equal to man in her rights…" For writing that document, de Gouges was executed by guillotine!

Here are some excerpts from the 1789 document.

1. Men are born and remain free and equal in rights. Social distinctions may be founded only upon the general good.

4. Liberty consists in the freedom to do everything which injures no one else. . . .

5. Law can only prohibit such actions as are hurtful to society. Nothing may be prevented which is not forbidden by law, and no one may be forced to do anything not provided for by law.

6. Law is the expression of the general will. Every citizen has a right to participate personally, or through his representative, in its foundation. . . .

11. The free communication of ideas and opinions is one of the most precious of the rights of man. Every citizen may, accordingly, speak, write, and print with freedom, but shall be responsible for such abuses of this freedom as shall be defined by law.

16. A society in which the observance of the law is not assured, nor the separation of powers defined, has no constitution at all.

Document-Based Questions

1. Why do you think the Declaration of the Rights of Man did not include any reference to the rights of women?

2. Would you describe liberty the same way that it is described in number 4 above?

3. Number 6 says that every citizen has the right to participate in making laws. Do you think that every citizen did this?

4. What rights are listed in number 11?

5. According to number 16, what is important for a society to have?

Another Kind of Hero

During the French Revolution and the Age of Napoleon, many people were heroes. However, not all heroes are political or military leaders. There is another kind of hero. In spite of great problems, this person reaches for worthy goals. One such hero was a musician named Ludwig van Beethoven.

He was born in Bonn, Germany, in 1770. He was trained in classical music. When he was 12, he became the assistant organist to the royal court in Bonn. Then at age 22, Beethoven went to Vienna to study with Joseph Haydn. Haydn was Europe's greatest classical composer.

Near the end of the 1700s, Beethoven began to compose a new style of music. It was based on his own feelings.

Then a terrible thing happened to him. He started losing his hearing. In 1802, Beethoven wrote, "I was soon compelled to withdraw myself, to live life alone. If at times I try to forget all this . . . I am flung back by the doubly sad experience of my bad hearing. Yet, it is impossible for me to say to people, 'Speak louder, shout, for I am deaf.'" Fate had played a horrible trick on him. He was a great composer. But he was less and less able to hear the beautiful sounds that he created.

Beethoven did not give up. In 1808, he wrote his *Fifth Symphony.* It opens with Fate knocking on the door: *Dah-Dah-Dah Daaaaaaah!* In the end, Music wins the battle with Fate.

Beethoven was going deaf, but his deafness did not stop him from creating music.

In 1824, Beethoven conducted his *Ninth Symphony,* his last work for a large orchestra. In the last movement, a chorus sings the "Ode

Ludwig van Beethoven

to Joy." It calls for brotherhood among people throughout the world. It also states that the human struggle against Fate can end in peace and joy. When the *Ninth Symphony* ended, Beethoven stood staring at the orchestra. He could not hear the audience's thunderous applause! A musician made Beethoven turn around and face them. Then he saw what he could not hear.

Beethoven died on March 26, 1827. More than 20,000 people attended his funeral in Vienna. What did Beethoven think about his talent as a composer? In a letter years before, Beethoven had written a possible answer to that question. "There will always be thousands of princes, but there is only one Beethoven." And so there was.

Wrap-Up

1. Where was Beethoven born?

2. How was Beethoven's music different from composers before him?

3. What terrible thing happened to Beethoven?

4. What feeling did Beethoven try to express in his *Ninth Symphony?*

5. Do you think that Beethoven was a hero? Explain your answer.

■ After 1763, Britain wanted its North American colonies to pay for the war against France. Britain used the Navigation Acts, the Quartering Act, the Stamp Act, and the Townshend Acts to raise money. The colonists protested. The Boston Massacre and the Boston Tea Party followed. Representatives of the 12 colonies met in Philadelphia in 1775. They agreed to boycott British goods. Then minutemen fought British soldiers at Lexington and Concord.

■ Jefferson wrote most of the Declaration of Independence. It stated people could change their government if it did not protect their rights. Colonial representatives signed it on July 4, 1776.

■ The American victory at Saratoga earned French help. The Revolutionary War ended in 1781. An American army and French ships forced the British under Cornwallis to surrender.

■ France in the 1770s consisted of three estates—the clergy, the nobles, and the common people. The Third Estate paid all the taxes. This group wanted each representative in the Estates-General to have a vote. The other estates and Louis XVI refused. The Third Estate established a constitutional monarchy. It gave everyone freedom of speech and religion and equality under the law. Mobs stormed the Bastille, and the French Revolution began.

■ During the Revolution, there were several governments. In 1792, the National Constitutional Convention created a republic. It wanted to spread the revolution to other countries. Other European countries united to stop France.

■ After an attempted escape, the king was executed and peasants rebelled. Moderates and radicals fought to control the government. The Jacobins under Robespierre came to power and began the Reign of Terror. Then came the Directory and the Consulate. Napoleon became First Consul and then First Consul for life. In 1804 he crowned himself emperor.

■ Napoleon's victories increased French power, but he made two mistakes. The Continental System turned countries against France instead of ruining the British economy. His Russian invasion destroyed his army. Britain, Prussia, Russia, and Austria defeated Napoleon in 1814 and exiled him. He returned and was defeated at Waterloo.

■ In France, the Code of Napoleon made every man equal under the law. Napoleon's conquests spread the ideas of the French Revolution.

Chapter 20   R E V I E W

Word Bank

Alexander I

Antoinette

Bonaparte

Cornwallis

George III

Jefferson

Locke

Louis XVI

Washington

Wellington

On a sheet of paper, use the words from the Word Bank to complete each sentence correctly.

1. _____ was the British king when the colonists rebelled.

2. Thomas _____ was the main writer of the Declaration of Independence.

3. The Declaration of Independence is based on many of the ideas of John _____.

4. George _____ commanded the colonial army.

5. General _____ surrendered the British army at Yorktown.

6. During the reign of _____, the French Revolution began.

7. The French executed Marie _____, the queen of France.

8. Napoleon _____ became the emperor of France.

9. Czar _____ of Russia decided to trade with England, so Napoleon invaded Russia.

10. The Duke of _____ defeated Napoleon at Waterloo.

On a sheet of paper, write the letter of the answer that correctly completes each sentence.

11. England enforced the _____ that said that colonists had to ship their trading goods on British ships.

    A Stamp Act   **C** Navigation Acts

    B Townshend Acts   **D** Quartering Act

12. _____ helped the colonists win the Revolutionary War.

    A France   **C** The Netherlands

    B Spain   **D** all of the above

13. At this time, French society was divided into _____ classes, or estates.

    A 3   **B** 6   **C** 9   **D** 19

14. The French wanted liberty and _____ for all people.

A constitutions   **C** equality

B consuls   **D** boycotts

15. The leader of the French Reign of Terror was _____.

A Antoinette   **C** Cornwallis

B Robespierre   **D** Wellington

On a sheet of paper, write the answer to each question. Use complete sentences.

16. What were the colonists rebelling against during the American Revolution?

17. What were the French rebelling against during the French Revolution?

18. What is one way in which the American Revolution changed Europe and one way in which the French Revolution changed Europe?

Critical Thinking On a sheet of paper, write your response to each question. Use complete sentences.

19. Which revolution—the American or the French—would you like to have been part of and why?

20. Pretend that Napoleon's army is marching across Russia and that you are advising the czar. What would you tell him to do?

Test-Taking Tip

Read test questions carefully to identify those that require more than one answer.

21 The Industrial Revolution Begins

Beginning in the 1750s, workers left farms and moved to cities. There, they labored in factories instead of at home. In this chapter, you will learn more about these factories. You will meet inventors who changed the way people worked and lived. You will discover inventions such as the flying shuttle, the steam locomotive, the light bulb, and the telephone. These inventions and other great changes were all part of the Industrial Revolution.

Goals for Learning

◆ To name the economic conditions needed for industrialization to take place

◆ To explain what was revolutionary about the economic changes that took place in England during the Industrial Revolution

◆ To identify improvements in transportation that helped industrialization

◆ To describe the benefits and problems of industrialization

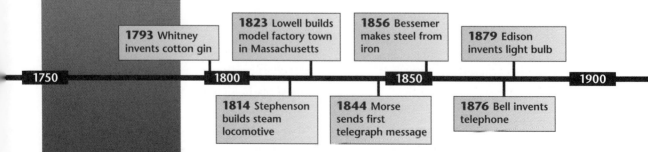

1793 Whitney invents cotton gin

1823 Lowell builds model factory town in Massachusetts

1856 Bessemer makes steel from iron

1879 Edison invents light bulb

1750 1800 1850 1900

1814 Stephenson builds steam locomotive

1844 Morse sends first telegraph message

1876 Bell invents telephone

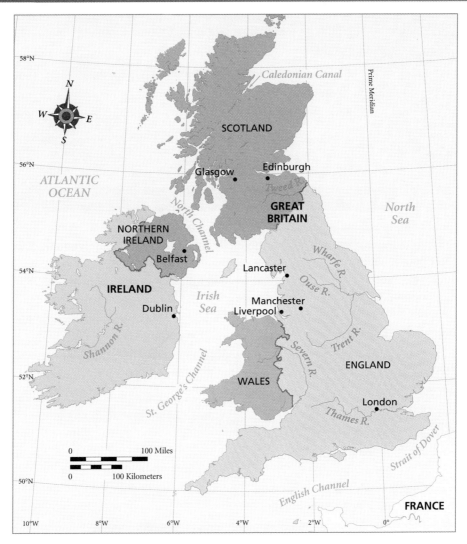

Map Skills

The British Isles consists of two large islands and many smaller ones. Scotland, Wales, and England are on the larger island that we call Great Britain. Between 1750 and 1850, Great Britain became the center of the Industrial Revolution. Industry changed the way people worked and where they lived.

Study the map, then answer the following questions:

1. What channels separate Ireland from Great Britain?

2. What are the names of three cities in England?

3. What is the major river of Ireland?

4. In what area of Great Britain is the Caledonian Canal located?

5. What sea is to the east of Great Britain?

Reading Strategy:
Metacognition

Metacognition means being aware of the way you learn. It will help you become a better reader.

◆ Preview the text, noting the main idea, details, and any questions you have.

◆ If you don't understand something, go back and read it again.

◆ Summarize what you have read. Make inferences about the meaning.

Key Vocabulary Words

Lesson 1

Industrial Revolution An important change in the way people work

Natural resources Things—such as coal, ore, and water—that come from nature and help humans

Capital Money used to start a business

Industrialization The process of getting machines to do work

Economist A person who studies money

Lesson 2

Manufacturer A person who hires people to work with machines to make something to sell

Mass production A way of making large amounts of the same thing in a factory

Lesson 3

Transportation The movement of people and things from one place to another

Locomotive A self-propelled vehicle that runs on rails

Efficient Working well with little loss of time or energy

Raw materials The materials that are used to make things

Lesson 4

Labor union An organized group of workers who try to improve their working conditions

Internal combustion engine An engine that burns gasoline to produce power

Objectives

◆ To list three things that helped England industrialize

◆ To explain how the Industrial Revolution spread beyond England

◆ To explain the difference between industrialized nations and developing nations

Reading Strategy:
Metacognition

Before you read this section, think about what you can do that will help you understand the text.

Industrial Revolution

An important change in the way people work

Natural resources

Things—such as coal, ore, and water—that come from nature and help humans

Capital

Money used to start a business

Beginning in the 1750s, quick economic change came to England. Before then, workers made things by hand in their homes. Now they began to work in factories and use machines to produce goods. Before this time, people had used their own strength or the strength of animals to provide power. Now they used the steam engine.

What Is an Industrial Revolution?

We call all these changes the **Industrial Revolution.** What does this term mean? *Industrial* means related to work or labor. *Revolution* means an important change in the way something is done. So the term *Industrial Revolution* means an important change in the way people work. During the Industrial Revolution, people stopped making goods by hand. They began to use machines to produce goods.

In the mid-1700s, England had three things that helped it industrialize: **natural resources,** plenty of workers, and **capital** to build factories and machines. (Natural resources are things that come from nature and help humans. Capital is money used to start a business.)

What Are Natural Resources?

Factory owners need power to run machines. In the 1750s, England could industrialize because it had a source of power. In fact, it had three: coal, iron ore—a rock that contains metal— and rivers. The heat from burning coal turned water into steam power. The iron ore in rocks was made into iron tools and machines. Fast-moving rivers provided power for machines. Nature supplied the coal, the ore, and the rivers. We call these things natural resources. They come from nature, so they are natural. They help us, so they are resources.

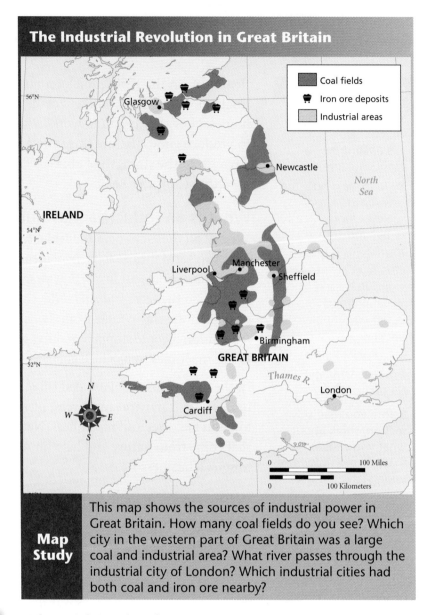

The Industrial Revolution in Great Britain

Coal fields

Iron ore deposits

Industrial areas

56°N

Glasgow

Newcastle

North Sea

IRELAND

54°N

Liverpool • Manchester
• Sheffield

Birmingham

GREAT BRITAIN

52°N

Thames R.

London

N
W   E
S

Cardiff

0   100 Miles

0   100 Kilometers

Map Study

This map shows the sources of industrial power in Great Britain. How many coal fields do you see? Which city in the western part of Great Britain was a large coal and industrial area? What river passes through the industrial city of London? Which industrial cities had both coal and iron ore nearby?

Reading Strategy:
Metacognition

Make a prediction about why England had so many workers in the 1850s. Check your prediction as you continue reading and revise if needed.

Why Did England Have So Many Workers?

Factory owners need workers to run their machines. In the 1850s, England had a large group of workers. Between 1750 and 1800, the population of England increased by 50 percent because there was a new food source from the Americas—the potato.

Biography

Adam Smith: 1723–1790

In 1776, Adam Smith published one of the most important books on economics. It was called *An Inquiry into the Nature and Causes of the Wealth of Nations.* Smith thought that people should be free to produce and sell products at a profit. Government should not interfere in this process. Competition would produce the best goods at the lowest prices.

Smith's ideas are called "capitalism." Capital is money that is used to produce more money. In a capitalist system, individuals and private businesses own and control most of the capital. Today, the United States is the most powerful capitalist nation in the world.

Industrialization

The process of getting machines to do work

At the same time, the English government forced farmworkers off the land. How did they do this? The government passed a law that allowed rich landowners to fence in open fields. For hundreds of years, poor families had farmed these unfenced lands. Now they had no land to farm. So factory owners now had two work sources—an increased population and farmers who had no land to farm.

What Is Capital Used For?

Factory owners need power to run machines and people to work these machines. But where do the machines and the factories come from? The factory owners must buy and build them. Owners do this with capital to start a business and to make more money.

Did the Industrial Revolution Spread Beyond England?

This change in the way people worked began in England, but it soon spread to other countries. By 1860, Germany was industrialized. By the 1870s, the United States became a powerful industrial nation. Today, the process of **industrialization,** or getting machines to do work, is still going on.

Economist

A person who studies money

Economists, or people who study money, often divide the people of the world into two groups. One group lives in industrialized nations that have factories to produce goods. The second group lives in developing nations that do not have an industrial economy. Nations need these things to industrialize: capital to buy machines and start up factories, a source of power to make machines work, and workers to run the machines.

Word Bank

developing nations
England
Germany
industrialized nations
United States

Lesson 1 Review On a sheet of paper, use the words from the Word Bank to complete each sentence correctly.

1. Important economic changes beginning in the 1750s took place mainly in _____.

2. By 1860, _____ was industrialized.

3. By the 1870s, the _____ became an industrial nation.

4. Nations that have factories to produce goods are called _____.

5. Nations that do not have an industrial economy are called _____.

What do you think ?

What are some new sources of power that factory owners use today as they industrialize?

Technology Connection

Marc Seguin and the Bridge

French engineer Marc Seguin built the first wire-cable suspension bridge in 1825. The bridge spanned the Rhone River near Lyons, in eastern France. A suspension bridge uses bearing cables attached to towers at either end. Suspender cables, connected to the bridge platform, are attached vertically to those bearing cables. Suspension bridges had been around since ancient times. However, the cables of those bridges were most often made of hemp rope. The rope could not support all that much weight and it did wear out.

Marc Seguin initiated or supervised the construction of 186 bridges throughout France.

Objectives

◆ To list the inventions that helped the textile industry

◆ To explain the advantages of mass production

◆ To describe how iron is made into steel

Reading Strategy:
Metacognition

Before you read this lesson, think about what you can do that will help you understand how industries began.

For industry, people had to invent new machines and discover new sources of power. In the 1700s, English inventors made several new machines for the textile industry. A textile is a cloth that workers weave from cotton, silk, or wool.

What Inventions Helped the Textile Industry?

In 1733, an English weaver named John Kay invented a "flying shuttle." A shuttle is the part of a weaving machine that carries the thread from one side to the other. The flying shuttle did this more quickly than the human hand could. Because of the flying shuttle, workers could weave twice as much cloth.

To weave more cloth, workers needed more yarn. At that time, people working at home used a spinning wheel to spin yarn. Each spinning wheel had only one spindle. (A spindle twists thread into yarn.) But all the spinning wheels in England could not produce all the yarn the weavers needed.

Then, in 1764, James Hargreaves invented a machine to spin wool or cotton yarn. He called his machine the "spinning jenny." It was a spinning wheel with eight spindles instead of one. In the same year, Richard Arkwright invented a large machine that produced tighter cotton yarn than the spinning jenny.

Manufacturers built large textile mills like this one in Lancashire, England. These mills could produce large amounts of textiles quickly.

In 1778, Samuel Crompton combined the spinning jenny and Arkwright's invention into the "spinning mule." This machine could spin a thread 150 miles long from a single pound of cotton!

Why Did Manufacturers Build Factories?

Before this time, people spun yarn at home and wove it into cloth. Textile **manufacturers** brought wool, cotton, and silk to the workers' homes. (A manufacturer hires people to work with machines to make something to sell.) But hand work at home was slow and costly, and manufacturers wanted to save time and money. They built factories, and workers then left their homes and came to the factory to work. The factory system brought workers, machines, and a source of power together to produce a product.

This system changed the way people worked. The worker now had to work when and where the manufacturer said. The worker had to work the hours the manufacturer wanted. And the worker had to do the amount of work the manufacturer demanded.

The cotton gin allowed workers to separate seeds from cotton faster than doing it by hand. It made cotton, which is used to make cloth, a much more valuable material.

A way of making large amounts of the same thing in a factory

What Problem Did Cotton Growers Have?

Textile workers in factories now needed more cotton to spin into yarn and to weave into cloth. Getting cotton from the field to the factory was hard work. Natural cotton contains sticky, tightly-held seeds. In the 1700s, people had to remove these seeds by hand. This took a lot of time.

Then, in 1793, Eli Whitney invented a machine that solved the problem. While fixing other machines in Georgia, Whitney invented the cotton gin. His invention was a wooden box with a wire brush and grille, or screen. Workers placed cotton on one side of the grille. Then the revolving brush grabbed the cotton and pushed it through the grille. The seeds were too large to pass through the screen, so the machine separated the seeds from the cotton thread.

With the cotton gin, workers could clean cotton 50 times faster than by hand. Within 20 years, cotton became the most important export from the southern United States. Cotton farmers exported most of this cotton to the textile factories in Great Britain.

Reading Strategy:
Metacognition

Note the main idea and important details of this paragraph. Summarize what you have read to make sure you understand the importance of mass production.

What Is Mass Production?

Whitney made little money from his invention of the cotton gin. But he became wealthy as a gun manufacturer. Before Whitney, workers made guns one at a time. Each part of a gun was a little different from the same part on another gun. Whitney had workers make gun parts that were identical, or exactly alike.

Then the workers assembled, or put together, these identical parts to make identical guns. The guns were alike in every way. If a part from one gun needed to be replaced, that same part from another gun of the same kind could be used. We call this **mass production.** It is a way of making large amounts of the same thing in a factory. It greatly cuts the time workers need to make something, so they can produce more.

Henry Bessemer developed a low-cost way to make steel. Steel became an important building material after it was invented. This picture shows a steel mill.

Who Found a Way to Make Steel?

Manufacturers built their new industrial machines from iron. In 1709, Englishman Abraham Darby found a way of making iron with coke, or purified coal. However, making iron was still a problem because iron ore had impurities, or materials in it that made it not pure and made iron products break easily. In the late 1700s, it was discovered that stirring hot iron helped burn off the impurities.

In 1856, Englishman Henry Bessemer found a way to get rid of more impurities in iron. He discovered that air forced into melted iron burned away these impurities. His process produced a new product—steel. It was stronger than iron and did not break as easily. Soon, steel manufacturing became an important industry in many industrial countries. Those countries that had large amounts of coal and iron ore built steel mills.

The English built their steel mills in the north. In Germany, the Ruhr Valley became a great steel center. In the United States, Pittsburgh, Pennsylvania, became an important steel-producing city.

Lesson 2 Review On a sheet of paper, write the letter of the answer that correctly completes each sentence.

1. The _____ industry became more profitable with the invention of the flying shuttle, spinning jenny, and spinning mule.

   A steel   **C** cotton
   B iron   **D** textile

2. The factory system brought together _____ to produce a product.

   A workers   **C** a source of power
   B machines   **D** all of the above

3. _____ invented the cotton gin.

   A Whitney   **C** Hargreaves
   B Kay   **D** Bessemer

4. The term _____ means producing identical products in great number.

   A spinning jenny   **C** textile
   B mass production   **D** industry

5. _____ discovered a way to make steel from iron.

   A Whitney   **C** Bessemer
   B Kay   **D** Hargreaves

What do you think ?

What is good and what is bad about the factory system?

Objectives

◆ To explain how improvements in the construction of roads and canals helped industrialization

◆ To describe how the steam engine led to the development of railroads

Transportation

The movement of people and things from one place to another

Reading Strategy: **Metacognition**

Notice the structure of this chapter. Look at the titles, headings, and boldfaced words.

Improved **transportation** also helped industrialization. Transportation is the movement of people and things from one place to another. Industry needs good transportation.

The problem with transportation in the early 1700s was that people had to travel on dirt roads. When rain fell, the dirt turned into thick mud into which horses and carriages sunk. In 1770, two Scotsmen—Thomas Telford and John McAdam— developed better road-building methods. Telford built roads in two layers, so water quickly ran off. McAdam built roads of crushed stone.

How Did Canals Help Industry?

For many years, manufacturers used roads to move products that were not so heavy. Then, in the 1760s, workers dug the first modern canal in England. (The United States built its first canal in 1825.) The seven-mile-long canal stretched from Manchester to a coal mining area nearby. Now, manufacturers could easily move large amounts of coal from mines to cities, so coal became cheaper.

On a canal, manufacturers could ship heavy products like coal. Canals cost a lot of money to dig, and they needed a source of water. Good roads were a faster means of transportation for moving light products from place to place. But no one could travel fast on them in rainy weather.

English manufacturers had a problem. They needed to quickly move large amounts of products—light or heavy—to different places in any type of weather. But roads got muddy and canals needed water. What could these manufacturers do?

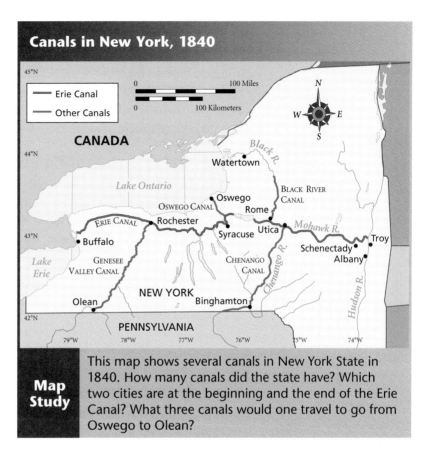

Canals in New York, 1840

—— Erie Canal	
—— Other Canals	

0 — 100 Miles

0 — 100 Kilometers

CANADA

Lake Ontario

Watertown

Oswego

Rome

BLACK RIVER CANAL

OSWEGO CANAL

Rochester

ERIE CANAL

Syracuse

Utica

Mohawk R.

Troy

Buffalo

GENESEE VALLEY CANAL

Schenectady

Albany

Lake Erie

CHENANGO CANAL

NEW YORK

Olean

Binghamton

PENNSYLVANIA

Map Study This map shows several canals in New York State in 1840. How many canals did the state have? Which two cities are at the beginning and the end of the Erie Canal? What three canals would one travel to go from Oswego to Olean?

How Did the Steam Engine Change the Textile Industry?

The answer to the manufacturers' transportation problem was a steam **locomotive.** This is a self-propelled vehicle that runs on rails. But before learning about that, you need to know about steam engines. In 1705, the simple steam engine was invented. Workers used it to pump water out of coal mines.

In 1763, James Watt began to look for a way to improve the steam engine and make it more **efficient,** or work better with little time or energy wasted. In 1773, Watt developed a steam engine that turned wheels. Textile machines had wheels, so this new engine could operate those machines.

Locomotive

A self-propelled vehicle that runs on rails

Efficient

Working well with little loss of time or energy

Up to that time, swiftly falling water produced the power to run textile machines. Manufacturers had to build textile factories next to fast-moving streams. Now manufacturers could power their textile machines with steam engines. They could build their factories anywhere. By 1800, more than 500 steam engines were powering machinery in British factories.

Who Is the Founder of Railroads?

Early in the 1800s, workers used a little steam engine on wheels to pull small carts of coal out of mines. This steam engine did the work of one or two horses. Then, in 1814, George Stephenson—a mining engineer—built a steam locomotive. It moved along iron rails, or bars, on the ground. These rails went on and on and became a kind of road, so the locomotive traveled on a road of rails, or a railroad.

Stephenson called his locomotive *Blucher.* He had discovered a way to increase the heat in the boiler. (A boiler is the tank that heats water.) By increasing the heat, Stephenson produced steam under higher pressure. *Blucher* could pull almost 30 tons of coal at a speed of four miles per hour.

George Stephenson's Rocket could reach a top speed of 30 miles per hour.

Raw materials

The materials that are used to make things

How Fast Could Stephenson's Next Locomotive Go?

In 1829, Stephenson built the *Rocket*—a faster locomotive. At that time, some businessmen wanted to build a railroad between Liverpool and Manchester. They had a contest to find a locomotive to quickly go this distance. Stephenson entered the contest and won.

Stephenson's *Rocket* pulled a train of cars for more than 30 miles. It reached a speed of 30 miles per hour. This meant that the *Rocket* was more powerful than 80 horses pulling together. Stephenson went on to design railroad bridges, tunnels, and the roadbed for the Liverpool and Manchester Railway. Today, historians call him the "founder of the railways."

Why Did Railroads Become Important?

Railroads became the most important form of transportation in the 19th century. During the 1840s and 1850s, they went back and forth across England. They greatly helped factory owners. How? By providing them with a fast and inexpensive way to move **raw materials** and finished products. (Raw materials are the materials such as cotton, wood, iron, and oil that workers use to make things.)

Railroads needed metal rails, cars, and locomotives. The iron and steel industry grew quickly. Railroad owners hired thousands of workers to clear land and lay railroad tracks. Other European countries also built railroad lines. In 1869, the United States completed the transcontinental railroad. It ran from one side of the continent to the other and linked the Atlantic and Pacific coasts together.

Then and Now

Railroads

Stephenson's invention of the steam locomotive started a race. Who could develop the fastest, most efficient transportation for people and goods? After the steam locomotive came the diesel, and then the even faster electric locomotive. The first trains traveled about four miles per hour. Today, Japan and France have high-speed trains that travel more than 200 miles per hour.

Countries also began to build miles and miles of tracks. The world's longest railroad line is the Trans-Siberian Railroad. It runs 5,700 miles—from Moscow to Vladivostock, Russia.

The United States has over 140,000 miles of rail in use today. About 40 percent of goods are still shipped by rail. But less than 1 percent of city passenger transportation is by rail.

Lesson 3 Review On a sheet of paper, write the answer to each question. Use complete sentences.

1. Why is good transportation needed for the growth of industry?

2. What was one big problem with transportation in the 1770s?

3. Why were canals not the best type of transportation for industry?

4. Who found a way of making the steam engine more efficient?

5. Why is George Stephenson important in the history of transportation?

What do you think

How would cheap coal help industry grow?

Objectives

◆ To explain why cities grew during the Industrial Revolution

◆ To describe the problems factory workers faced

◆ To identify two new sources of power

Reading Strategy:
Metacognition

Look at the photographs and illustrations, and note the descriptive words. This will help you visualize the inventors and inventions named in this lesson.

Before the 1750s, most people worked as farmers in small villages. Each family grew its own food and made its own clothing. Many people never traveled more than 10 miles from where they were born.

Industrialization changed all this. People in Great Britain were the first to experience these changes. In the 1800s, industrialization also changed Europe and the United States. However, British textile factories still made more than half of the world's cotton cloth. In fact, British factories produced so many goods that people called Great Britain the "workshop of the world."

What Laws Stopped the Spread of Industrialization?

For many years, Great Britain tried to keep other countries from learning the lessons of industrialization. In fact, Britain passed laws so that merchants could not sell new machines to other countries. Up until the 1840s, Britain also refused to let skilled workers leave the country. People feared that these workers could design or make tools and machinery that would help other countries industrialize.

How Did A British Worker Help the United States?

In 1789, Samuel Slater—a British factory worker—memorized plans for building a spinning machine. Then he dressed himself as a simple farmer and got on a ship sailing to the United States. (British officials would have stopped him if they had known he could build a spinning machine.) Once in the United States, Slater met Moses Brown—a Rhode Island businessman. In 1793, Brown built the first thread-making factory in the United States. He used spinning machines that Slater built.

The Population Growth of Five British Cities

Population (Thousands)

	1685	1760	1881
Liverpool	4,000	35,000	555,425
Manchester	6,000	45,000	393,676
Birmingham	4,000	30,000	400,757
Sheffield	4,000	20,000	284,410
Bristol	29,000	100,000	206,503

■ Liverpool ■ Birmingham ■ Bristol
■ Manchester ■ Sheffield

Graph Study Which city had the largest population in 1685? Which city had the largest population in 1881? How many people did it have?

What Did Lowell Do for His Factory Workers?

In 1823, Francis Lowell built a factory town in Massachusetts and named it after himself. He hired young farm women to work in his factory. First, he taught them how to work the textile machines. Then he set up a school to teach them how to read and write. Finally, he gave them a clean place to live. Soon, textile mills spread throughout the New England states. However, few factory owners followed Lowell's ideas.

History in Your Life

Child Labor Laws

As industry increased, factory owners began to hire children. They could pay them much lower wages than men. Children might work as many as 14 hours a day. Their working conditions were often dangerous as well. Some British orphans were treated almost like slaves.

Reformers began to force governments to stop the evils of the factory system. Reformers wanted to protect children and give them a chance to go to school. Early laws failed to correct these evils. Later laws carried more power. Today, Europe, North America, Australia, Japan, and New Zealand enforce child labor laws. In the United States, the minimum age for employment is 14. The work must be done outside of school hours, and it cannot be in manufacturing.

In less developed countries, however, millions of children still work. Some as young as seven years old work in quarries, mines, and factories.

What Did Industrialization Do to Cities?

Industrialization changed the way people worked. It also changed where they lived. Before the Industrial Revolution, most people lived on farms, not in cities. Then manufacturers began to build factories near cities. People from the country then moved to the cities to get work.

Industry greatly changed many cities. This picture shows the crowded living conditions and soot-filled air of Manchester, England, in 1876.

Industrialization caused city populations to grow quickly. For example, in 1750, the English town of Manchester had less than 16,000 people. By 1850, it had become a major textile center with a population of more than 300,000. From 1800 to 1850, the number of European cities with a population of more than 100,000 doubled to nearly 50.

But bigger cities created problems. People lived in unhealthy conditions. Garbage filled the streets. Bad water and sanitation caused disease. Still, people moved to the cities to find jobs. In fact, by 1900, almost 75 percent of the people of Great Britain lived in cities.

What Problems Did Factory Workers Have?

As you know, during the Industrial Revolution, unskilled workers came to cities for work. Whole families labored in factories. Children as young as six years old worked 8 to 14 hours a day. They worked among dangerous machines. But factory owners refused to pay for doctors to help workers hurt by these machines. Also, owners refused to pay workers if they were hurt or sick and could not work for a while.

Writing About History

There were so many inventions in the 1800s—the train, steamboat, telegraph, and telephone, for example. They all affected people's lives. Research one such invention. Then write a paragraph in your notebook describing the changes it caused.

Telegraph Provides Instant Communication

Samuel F. B. Morse, an artist and inventor, invented the telegraph in the United States in the 1830s. Two British men, Charles Wheatstone and William Cooke, also made a telegraph machine.

The telegraph freed communication from the problems of long distance transportation. In the United States, the Pony Express

service was the fastest way to communicate. However, it was discontinued in 1861 because the telegraph was much faster.

The telegraph also solved a traffic control problem for railroads. Using the telegraph, railroad workers could keep track of trains. This helped them avoid accidents. Railroads also used the telegraph to check on schedules, passengers, and freight shipments.

Labor union

An organized group of workers who try to improve their working conditions

Workers wanted safer factories, more pay, and shorter hours. They could not get what they wanted because the law did not let them form **labor unions.** A labor union is an organized group of workers who try to improve their working conditions.

The workers could not change the law because they had no political power. In England, only people who owned property could vote. But most factory workers owned no property, so they could not vote. Without a vote, they could not change the laws that kept them from forming unions.

What Two New Sources of Power Changed the World?

As you know, coal and steam provided power for the Industrial Revolution. But in the late 19th century, inventors discovered two new sources of power—electricity and oil.

Reading Strategy:
Metacognition

Remember to ask yourself questions as you read. This will help you make sure that you understand what you are reading.

The use of electricity began in the 1840s when Samuel F. B. Morse invented the telegraph. With this machine, he could send messages over long distances by making and breaking an electric current. In 1844, Morse sent his first message from Washington, D.C., to Baltimore, Maryland. For the message, he used a code he had created. In this code, a different pattern of long or short electrical signals represented each letter of the alphabet. This was called Morse code.

Alexander Graham Bell demonstrates how to use his telephone, which he invented in 1876.

In 1866, workers laid a cable on the floor of the Atlantic Ocean to carry electrical messages between the United States and Europe. Before this, messages took days to deliver; now they took minutes.

In 1876, Alexander Graham Bell invented the telephone. For the first time, a human being could hear another person's voice over an electrical wire. In 1879, Thomas Edison invented the light bulb. It provided safe light to homes, businesses, and factories.

Internal combustion engine

An engine that burns gasoline to produce power

Why Was the Discovery of Gasoline Important?

Oil was another important new source of power. Before the 1860s, people mostly used oil to grease wheels. Now, they began to use it to provide heat and to power machinery.

People learned that they could make gasoline from oil. Gasoline ran the **internal combustion engine** that Gottlieb Daimler invented in 1885. The internal combustion engine burned gasoline to produce power. It made the automobile possible.

Thomas Edison poses with perhaps his greatest invention, the light bulb. He invented it in 1879.

In 1903, Wilbur and Orville Wright—two American men who liked to work with machines—were the first to fly an airplane successfully. They used a gasoline engine.

The Wright brothers were the first people to fly an airplane successfully.

Word Bank

Bell

Daimler

Lowell

Morse

Slater

Lesson 4 Review On a sheet of paper, use the words from the Word Bank to complete each sentence correctly.

1. In 1789, Samuel _____ left England and came to the United States to build spinning machines.

2. In 1823, Francis _____ built a model factory town in Massachusetts.

3. In 1844, Samuel F. B. _____ sent the first telegraph message.

4. In 1876, Alexander _____ invented the telephone.

5. In 1885, Gottlieb _____ built the internal combustion engine.

What do you think ?

Do you think industrialized nations should let workers form labor unions? Explain your answer.

A Manchester Housewife's Weekly Budget in 1833

Living and working conditions were terrible in manufacturing areas during the early 1800s in England. As a result, Parliament formed committees in the 1830s to see if workers earned enough to feed, clothe, and house themselves. This report discusses the weekly budget of a housewife in Manchester, a manufacturing city.

A word about English money: the "s" after a number stands for shilling. A "d" means pence. One shilling contains 12 pence. At this time, 20 shillings were equal to $5.

Mrs. B., Manchester. This witness was accidentally met with, 13th May, 1833. She was waiting for Dr. Hawkins, to consult him about her niece's health. I took her into a room, and examined her about the customs and comforts of operative families. . . .

Her husband is a fine spinner, at Mr. M's, where he has been from 1816, has five children. Her eldest daughter, now going on 14, has been her father's helper for three years. At present her husband's earnings and her daughter's together amount to about 25s a week.

Breakfast is generally porridge, bread, and milk, lined with flour or oatmeal. On Sunday, a cup of tea and bread and butter. Dinner, on weekdays, potatoes and bacon, and bread, which is generally white. On a Sunday, a little fresh meat, no butter, egg, or pudding. Tea time every day, tea, and bread and butter; nothing extra on Sunday at tea. Supper,

oatmeal porridge and milk; sometimes potatoes and milk. Sunday, sometimes a little bread and cheese for supper; never have this on a weekday. Now and then buys eggs when they are as low as a halfpenny apiece, and fries them with bacon.

They never taste any other vegetable than potatoes; never use any beer or spirits; now and then may take a gill of beer when ill, which costs a penny. . . .

The house consists of four rooms, two on each floor; the furniture consists of two beds in the same room, one for themselves and the other for the children; have four chairs, one table in the house, boxes to put clothes in, no chest of drawers, two pans and a tea kettle for boiling, a gridiron and frying pan, half a dozen large and small plates, four pair of knives and forks, several pewter spoons.

Document-Based Questions

1. What kind of work does the husband in this family do?

2. How much money does the family make in a week?

3. How many people are in this family?

4. Do you think this family's diet is a healthy one? Why or why not?

5. Do you think that the family's housing is adequate? Why or why not?

Hard Times and Charles Dickens

"Now what I want is, Facts. Teach these boys and girls nothing but Facts. Facts alone are wanted in life. Plant nothing else, and root out everything else. . . . This is the principle on which I bring up my own children, and this is the principle on which I bring up these children. Stick to the Facts, Sir!"

So wrote Charles Dickens in *Hard Times,* one of his many novels. *Hard Times* is a story about the difficult lives of textile workers. Through Dickens's novels, a reader can relive the world of 19th-century England. He was the greatest observer of his times. And, like the schoolmaster in *Hard Times,* Dickens gathered the facts of his world. He used actual people, places, and social groups in England in his writings. But unlike the schoolmaster, Dickens's mind took "a fanciful photograph" of a person or place. He turned facts into unforgettable stories. The schoolroom and master in *Hard Times* are only examples of this ability. Dickens had a gift for describing places and creating memorable characters. As a result, he is called "the greatest master of English character since Shakespeare."

Dickens's novels captured the sights and sounds of a world that no longer exists. Today, there are no debtors' prisons. But Dickens helps the reader picture these terrible places. There are no more stagecoaches, but he makes you feel their bumpy ride. There are no more workhouses for poor orphaned children. But Dickens shows you the children. You see the poverty, hopelessness, and hard work that ages them beyond their years.

When he was a young man in the 1830s, Dickens found work as a journalist. In 1836, he published his first novel *The Pickwick Papers.*

Then he wrote *Oliver Twist.* Oliver is a boy caught in a world of crime and workhouses for the poor. The novel appeared in parts in a monthly magazine. *A Christmas Carol* came later. It is the story of Ebenezer Scrooge, a greedy man with a heart of stone. In the end, Scrooge comes to a new understanding about life. He learns that joy can come from kindness to others.

Charles Dickens

Dickens's stories are a time machine to the past. Through them, we travel through time and experience a different world.

Wrap-Up

1. Who was Charles Dickens?

2. Dickens said that he would take a "fanciful photograph" of a person or place. What did he mean?

3. What kind of work did Dickens do when he was young?

4. How did readers first experience the story of Oliver Twist?

5. Why are Dickens's novels valuable for historical purposes?

- The Industrial Revolution began in England in the 1750s. England could industrialize because it had coal, iron ore, and rivers as natural resources. A growing population and farmers looking for work increased the workforce. There was capital to build factories and buy machinery.

- By 1860, Germany was industrialized. By the 1870s, so was the United States. The world became divided into industrialized and developing nations.

- The English invented new machines, making textile manufacturing possible. Kay invented the flying shuttle to make weaving faster. Hargreaves developed the spinning jenny to spin yarn faster. Crompton invented the spinning mule to spin thread faster.

- The factory system brought workers, machines, and power together to make a product. Manufacturers built factories to save time and money.

- Whitney's cotton gin removed cotton seeds from the fiber faster. He also developed mass production to speed up the assembly of goods.

- Darby developed an improved way of making iron with coke. In 1856, Bessemer discovered how to make steel.

- Manufacturers could use roads for light-weight loads, but not when they were muddy. In the 1760s, manufacturers started using canals for heavy loads, but canals needed water.

- Watt improved the steam engine, so it could power factories. Stephenson built the first steam locomotive. Railroads were the most important means of transportation in the nineteenth century. They were a fast and cheap way to move raw materials and finished goods.

- England kept information about industrialization secret. However, in 1789, Slater built the first spinning machine in the United States.

- Industrialization caused the growth of cities. Workers moved to cities for jobs in factories.

- Workers wanted better working conditions and wages. Laws kept them from forming unions. Most workers could not vote because they did not own land.

- In the late 19th century, electricity and oil were new sources of power. Morse invented the telegraph. Bell developed the telephone. Edison invented the electric light. Daimler invented the internal combustion engine. The Wright Brothers made the first successful airplane flight.

Word Bank

Bessemer

Daimler

Hargreaves

Kay

McAdam

Morse

Slater

Stephenson

Watt

Whitney

On a sheet of paper, use the words from the Word Bank to complete each sentence correctly.

1. In 1733, the English weaver John _____ invented the flying shuttle.

2. In 1764, James _____ invented a machine that increased the amount of yarn that one person could spin.

3. In 1770, John _____ built roads of crushed rock and improved transportation.

4. In 1773, James _____ developed a way to make the steam engine turn wheels.

5. In 1793, Eli _____ invented a simple machine that separated the seeds from cotton.

6. In 1814, George _____ built a steam locomotive called Blucher.

7. In 1789, Samuel _____ brought plans for a spinning machine to the United States.

8. In 1844, Samuel F. B. _____ sent the first telegraph message.

9. In 1856, Henry _____ invented a way to remove impurities from iron to make steel.

10. In 1885, Gottlieb _____ invented the internal combustion engine.

On a sheet of paper, write the letter of the answer that correctly completes each sentence.

11. Something from nature that people use is called a(n) ____.

    A mass production   **C** capital
    B industrial revolution   **D** natural resource

12. New machinery first helped the _____ industry.

    A steel   **B** textile   **C** gasoline   **D** electric

13. The automobile was made possible by the _____ engine.

A internal combustion   **C** iron
B steel   **D** steam

14. A(n) _____ is a person who hires people to work with machines to make something to sell.

A economist   **C** manufacturer
B capital   **D** labor union

15. _____ is a way of making large amounts of the same, or identical, thing in a factory.

A Mass production   **C** Natural resource
B Raw material   **D** Capital

On a sheet of paper, write the answer to each question. Use complete sentences.

16. Why do historians use the word *revolution* to describe the industrial changes that took place in England during the 1700s?

17. What three conditions are necessary for an industrial revolution to take place in a country?

18. Why is a good transportation system needed for the growth of industry?

Critical Thinking On a sheet of paper, write your response to each question. Use complete sentences.

19. Which invention from the Industrial Revolution was the most important and why?

20. During this period, would you have moved from the farm to the city to work in a factory? Explain your answer.

Test-Taking Tip

Make flash cards to study vocabulary. Write the word on the front of the card. Write the definition on the back. Use the flash cards in a game to test your vocabulary skills.

22 Revolutions in Europe and Latin America

The French Revolution changed Europe. The leaders of Austria, Britain, Prussia, and Russia did not like change. They feared nationalism, so they met in Vienna to stop it. In this chapter, you will see how they divided the map of Europe. Then you will find out how people rebelled—first in Greece, then in the Spanish colonies of Latin America. You will see how Simón Bolívar and José San Martín liberated South America. You will sail to Europe and learn about Metternich and Marx. Finally, you will witness 1848, when nearly 50 rebellions broke out in Europe.

Goals for Learning

◆ To state the purpose and outcome of the Congress of Vienna

◆ To explain the idea of nationalism

◆ To describe the wars of national liberation in Latin America

◆ To explain the difference between radicals, conservatives, and liberals

◆ To explain the ideas of the socialists

1804 Haiti wins independence

1821 Mexico wins independence

1822 Brazil wins independence

1800   1810   1820   1830   1840   1850

1816 Argentina gains independence

1821 Santo Domingo wins independence

1829 Greece wins independence

1848 Revolutions break out in Europe

Map Skills

This is a map of modern South America. Portugal and Spain once controlled all this land of high mountains, dry deserts, and steamy tropical rain forests. The largest river system in the world flows through South America.

Study the map, then answer the following questions:

1. What are the names of four cities in South America?

2. What are the names of five rivers in South America?

3. On which coast of South America do the Andes Mountains stand?

4. What sea is on the north coast of South America?

5. What two oceans touch the shores of South America?

Reading Strategy:
Summarizing

When readers summarize, they look for key ideas and phrases. Then they rewrite them in their own words, using as few words as possible. A summary of key points will help you remember the important ideas you have read. As you read the text, ask yourself these questions:

◆ What are some important ideas or phrases in the text?

◆ How can I write these ideas or phrases in just a few words?

◆ How will this remind me of the main idea in the section or the lesson?

Key Vocabulary Words

Lesson 1

Congress of Vienna An important meeting in 1814 and 1815 in which leaders restructured Europe

Influential Having the power to change things or to affect what happens

Foreign minister A person who handles one country's dealings with other nations

Balance of power The condition that exists when all countries or all sections of government have equal strength

Confederation A union, or group, of states or nations

Lesson 2

Nationality A group of people who share the same language, culture, and history

Lesson 3

Peninsular A person who came to South America from Spain and held an important office in the colonial government

Creole A wealthy landowner who had been born in a Spanish colony in the Americas but whose ancestors came from Spain

Lesson 4

Conservative A person who likes the old political order and is against revolution or change

Liberal A person who wants change; a person who wants to limit the absolute power of kings and nobles and give power to the middle class

Ordinance A law set forth by someone in government

Lesson 5

Socialist A person who wants to end private ownership of land and factories

Utopia A type of society in which everyone works peacefully together for the good of all

Proletariat The working class, according to Marx

Reading Strategy:
Summarizing

What is the main idea of this paragraph?

Congress of Vienna

An important meeting in 1814 and 1815 in which leaders restructured Europe

Influential

Having the power to change things or to affect what happens

Foreign Minister

A person who handles one country's dealings with other nations

The French Revolution, which began in 1789, changed France. Ten years later, Napoleon Bonaparte seized power. The wars he fought changed Europe because he conquered other countries and gathered them into his empire.

In 1814 and 1815, four European countries—Austria, Prussia, Great Britain, and Russia—defeated Napoleon and sent him into exile. Then the leaders of these countries met in Vienna, Austria. Historians call this meeting the **Congress of Vienna.** Leaders restructured Europe during this meeting.

Who Influenced the Meeting?

Many powerful leaders attended the meeting. Two were kings—William III of Prussia and Czar Alexander of Russia. The Duke of Wellington and Lord Castlereagh represented Great Britain. Charles Talleyrand came for France. But Prince Metternich of Austria was the most **influential.** He had the power to affect what happened.

Prince Metternich was Austria's **foreign minister.** That is, he handled his country's dealings with other nations. He hated the democratic goals of the French Revolution. In fact, he thought that they had made Europe weak. The Congress of Vienna had to cure Europe of this disease called revolution.

What Plan Did Metternich Offer?

Metternich had a plan to make Europe what it had been before the French Revolution. His plan had three main parts. First, Metternich wanted to make sure that France could not threaten other nations again. Second, he wanted a **balance of power** in Europe. That is, he wanted the major nations to have equal strength so as to keep peace. Third, Metternich wanted to return royal families to power.

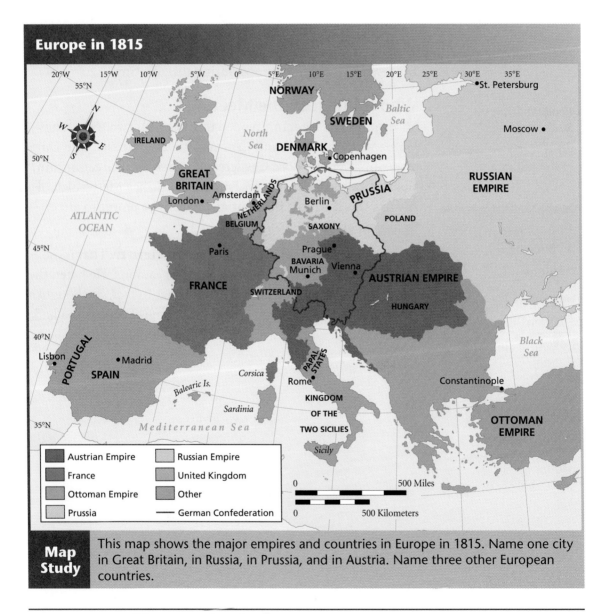

Europe in 1815

Legend:
- Austrian Empire
- France
- Ottoman Empire
- Prussia
- Russian Empire
- United Kingdom
- Other
- German Confederation

Map Study

This map shows the major empires and countries in Europe in 1815. Name one city in Great Britain, in Russia, in Prussia, and in Austria. Name three other European countries.

The Congress decided to restore all the kings whom Napoleon had driven from power. But what if some of them had died? Then relatives, or family members, would take their place on the throne. The Congress placed kings on the thrones of France, Spain, Portugal, and Sardinia in Italy.

Who Redrew the Map of Europe?

During Napoleon's reign, several nations had lost land to France. (This land became part of his empire.) The Congress gave land to the nations that had lost land to France and that had fought against Napoleon.

The Congress gave Finland and most of Poland to Russia. It gave part of northern Italy to Austria. Great Britain got the island of Ceylon, some of South Africa, and Malta in the Mediterranean Sea. Sweden gained control of Norway. Then the Congress organized the many German states into a German **Confederation.** A confederation is a union, or group, of states or countries. Austria would lead this group.

What about the people in Finland, Ceylon, South Africa, and other places? What they wanted did not matter to the leaders of the Congress of Vienna. The Congress felt that this nationalism was part of the "disease" of the French Revolution.

Lesson 1 Review On a sheet of paper, write the answer to each question. Use complete sentences.

1. Which four large nations were against the goals of the French Revolution?

2. What was the name of the meeting that these four nations held after the defeat of Napoleon?

3. Who was the most influential leader at the Congress of Vienna?

4. What were the three major parts of Metternich's plan to cure Europe of the disease of nationalism?

5. What is one way that the Congress of Vienna changed the map of Europe?

Objectives

◆ To explain how nationalism remained a strong movement in Europe
◆ To describe how nationalism affected Greece's independence

Nationality

A group of people who share the same language, culture, and history

Reading Strategy:
Summarizing

What event is described in this section?

Through all of history, people have organized themselves into groups. In the 19th century, nationalism became an important way to organize. (Nationalism is loyalty to one's country.) People who shared the same history, traditions, customs, and language wanted to unite under one government. They wanted to become a nation. They would then be loyal to this huge family.

Why Did Metternich Fear Nationalism?

The French Revolution and the Age of Napoleon helped nationalism develop. Before the French Revolution, European armies fought for money or for kings. But the army of revolutionary France fought for the nation of France. This citizen army was loyal to, and willing to die for, their homeland.

Metternich feared nationalism. He believed that it would lead to war. He also thought that nationalism threatened the Austrian Empire. People of different **nationalities** made up the empire. (A nationality is a group of people who share the same language, culture, and history.)

Allowing each nationality to have its own nation would end the Austrian Empire. The leaders of the Congress of Vienna tried to stop nationalism. But nationalists continued to meet in secret. They published books and planned revolutions to set up national governments.

How Did Greece Gain Its Independence?

The first successful national revolution in Europe began in Greece in 1821. For several centuries, Greece had been part of the Ottoman Empire. Now the Greeks wanted independence. They fought long and hard for it. But Greek nationalists needed help to break away from the Ottoman Empire. They got that help in 1827 when France, Britain, and Russia entered the war. These three nations sent a fleet of ships to defeat the Ottoman navy. Finally, after eight years of fighting, Greece became an independent nation.

Who Wanted Greece to Be Independent?

Even though some leaders feared nationalism, many educated people throughout Europe favored Greek nationalism. They respected the Greeks for their ancient civilization. In fact, the art, literature, and philosophy of classical Greece had become an important part of Western civilization.

Lesson 2 Review On a sheet of paper, write the answer to each question. Use complete sentences.

1. Describe nationalism in your own words.

2. Why did Metternich fear nationalism?

3. Why did Metternich think nationalism threatened the Austrian Empire?

4. How did Greece gain its independence?

5. Why was Greek independence important to the rest of Europe?

What do you think ?

Why would people of different nationalities want to form different countries?

History in Your Life

Romanticism

Romanticism became important during the first half of the 19th century. It affected all the arts—literature, art, and music. Romanticism contained four basic ideas. First, feeling was as important as thinking. Second, it stressed the importance of the individual. It was especially interested in heroes. Third, it viewed nature as powerful and mysterious. Fourth, it focused on the past.

Romanticists wrote many novels and poems that people still read today. *The Three Musketeers* by Alexander Dumas is about 17th-century France. Victor Hugo wrote *The Hunchback of Notre Dame.* Sir Walter Scott's *Ivanhoe* tells about the adventures of a knight during the Middle Ages.

Objectives

◆ To describe the liberation of South America and Mexico

◆ To identify key figures in Latin America's fight for independence

Reading Strategy:
Summarizing

What character is being introduced in this section?

Nationalism became a force in Latin America. This geographic region includes Mexico, Central America, the islands of the Caribbean Sea, and the continent of South America. In the early 19th century, Spain, France, and Portugal ruled most of this large area.

Which Latin American Colony Revolted First?

The first successful revolt in Latin America took place on the island of Hispaniola in the Caribbean Sea. France controlled the western half of the island. Spain controlled the eastern half. African slaves worked the island's sugar plantations. In 1794, a former slave named Toussaint L'Ouverture led a revolt of free blacks and slaves. They forced the French to leave the island. L'Ouverture became the first governor of the western half of the island.

However, in 1802, the French put L'Ouverture in prison, where he died. Then Napoleon tried to retake the island, but he failed. In 1804, black rebels established the independent country of Haiti

Toussaint L'Ouverture led a revolt of free blacks and slaves against the French in Hispaniola in 1794.

on the western half of the island. It was the first independent country in Latin America. Santo Domingo—the eastern half of the island—gained its independence from Spain in 1821.

Who Rejected Spanish Rule in South America?

Napoleon conquered Spain in 1808. To keep control of Spain, Napoleon made his brother king. That meant a Frenchman ruled Spain and the Spanish colonies. Some people in the colonies did not want a French ruler.

Two groups of people dominated the Spanish colonies in South America. The most important group was the **peninsulars.** They had been born in Spain, and they held the most important offices in the colonial government. The second group was the **creoles.** These wealthy landowners had been born in South America, but their ancestors had come from Spain. When Napoleon's French brother became king of Spain, many peninsulars became loyal to him. But many creoles did not.

Two creole leaders rejected Spanish rule. One was Simón Bolívar in New Granada, the northern area of South America. The other was José San Martín in the southern area. Together they freed much of South America from Spanish rule.

When Did Bolívar Free New Granada?

Simón Bolívar was born into a wealthy family in Venezuela. In 1810, he led a revolution to free this colony from Spanish control. At first, he had little success. Then in 1819, his army defeated the Spanish in Colombia.

Simón Bolívar came from a wealthy creole family. His army defeated the Spanish in Colombia in 1819.

Father Miguel Hidalgo y Costilla: 1753–1811

As a priest, Father Hidalgo worked to improve the lives of his people. He taught them farming. He helped them operate small industries such as brick making. Father Hidalgo believed that Mexicans would be better off without Spanish control. On September 16, 1810, he led a revolt against the Spanish. Thousands joined him.

Father Hidalgo was defeated, but many Mexicans consider him a saint for the revolution he started. The Mexican state of Hidalgo is named for him. His parish, Dolores, was renamed Dolores Hidalgo. In his honor, Mexicans celebrate September 16 as Independence Day.

Bolívar became president of the new nation of Great Colombia. He dreamed of uniting all the colonies of South America into one great nation. But his dream did not come true. Great Colombia became the nations of Colombia, Ecuador, and Venezuela.

What Colonies Did San Martín Free?

José San Martín's native land was Argentina. Argentina had gained its independence in 1816, and San Martín wanted it to remain free.

But San Martín feared that Argentina would lose its freedom. Spain still controlled Chile and Peru, Argentina's neighbors, in the southern part of South America. San Martín organized an army. It crossed the Andes Mountains and captured Santiago, Chile, in 1817.

In 1821, San Martín moved his army by sea to Lima, Peru. The Spanish forces retreated into the mountains. San Martín now needed a larger army to force the Spanish out of the mountains, so he met with Simón Bolívar.

No one knows what the two men said to each other during their historic meeting. After the meeting, Bolívar took command of San Martín's army. San Martín left South America and sailed to Europe. He never returned, and died there in 1850.

Reading Strategy:
Summarizing

What are some
important details that
help you understand
this section?

Bolívar led his army and San Martín's up into the Andes
Mountains. In December 1824, they defeated the Spanish
army. The last of the Spanish colonies in South America were
now free.

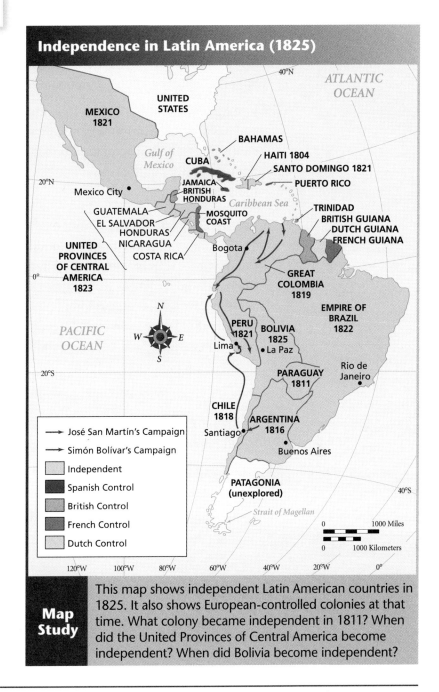

Independence in Latin America (1825)

This map shows independent Latin American countries in
1825. It also shows European-controlled colonies at that
time. What colony became independent in 1811? When
did the United Provinces of Central America become
independent? When did Bolivia become independent?

Map Study

Who Led Mexico to Independence?

In 1821, Mexico freed itself from Spanish control after an 11-year struggle. The Indians played an important role in the revolution. It began when Miguel Hidalgo, a poor Mexican priest, challenged the Indian peasants to rebel against their Spanish landowners. Quickly, they formed an army and began a 200-mile march to Mexico City. By the time it got there, the army had 60,000 men. When they met the Spanish army, the Spanish captured and executed Hidalgo.

José Morelos, another priest, took Hidalgo's place. Morelos and his army of peasant rebels were successful. By 1813, they controlled most Mexican land outside of the major cities. Representatives of the peasants met and declared Mexico an independent republic.

What Did Mexican Creoles Fear?

The Indians in Mexico wanted independence from Spain. Wealthy Mexican creoles wanted it, too. However, they feared that a new government would give their land to the landless peasants. In 1815, creole soldiers captured and executed Morelos. Six years later, in 1821, creole leaders successfully revolted against Spain and achieved independence.

Brazil, the largest colony in South America, won its independence from Portugal peacefully in 1822.

Lesson 3 Review On a sheet of paper, use the words from the Word Bank to complete each sentence correctly.

1. Toussaint _____ led slaves on the island of Hispaniola to independence.

2. Simón _____ led the people of New Granada, in the northern part of South America, to independence.

3. The armies of José _____ freed Chile and Peru.

4. Miguel _____, a priest, began a revolution in Mexico.

5. José _____, another priest, also led the Mexican peasants in their revolt.

Word Bank

Bolívar

Hidalgo

Morelos

L'Ouverture

San Martín

What do you think ?

What might San Martín and Bolívar have said to one another at their famous meeting?

Objectives

◆ To understand the political views that divided Europeans

◆ To explain France's struggle with various leaders and governments after Napoleon's defeat

The French Revolution promoted the ideas of nationalism, liberty, and equality. These ideas and the events of the French Revolution brought into being three political groups—conservatives, liberals, and radicals.

What Is a Conservative?

Conservatives were mainly rich landowners and nobles. They formed the upper class of most societies. As a group, they liked the old political order. In fact, conservatives thought that revolution was dangerous. They thought that it brought only disorder and pain. Because of this, they supported the absolute power of kings.

What Is a Liberal?

Usually, **liberals** were wealthy businessmen and merchants. As such, they belonged to the upper middle class. But many people in the middle class had no political power. The liberals wanted to limit the absolute power of kings and nobles and give power to the middle class. How did they plan on doing this? They would write a constitution and elect a parliament.

Most liberals wanted only some people to have the right to vote. They feared democracy because they did not trust that the uneducated working class and the poor would vote reasonably.

Conservative

A person who likes the old political order and is against revolution or change

Liberal

A person who wants change; a person who wants to limit the absolute power of kings and nobles and give power to the middle class

What Is a Radical?

The word *radical* means "root." Radicals wanted to change society down to its very roots. They wanted monarchies to become democracies in which every man had the right to vote.

Many radicals were willing to use violence, or great physical force, to bring about change in society. The French Reign of Terror had frightened conservatives and liberals. It did not frighten radicals. They saw it as necessary to make France into a true democracy.

Reading Strategy:
Summarizing

What is the main idea of this paragraph? What key words help you identify it?

The condition of the poor in Paris in 1831 was a reminder why radicals were calling for reforms.

Who Ruled France From 1814 to 1824?

In 1793, the French had executed Louis XVI for treason. The monarchy ended. Then, after Napoleon's defeat in 1814, the monarchy was restored to France. The king's brother became King Louis XVIII. He ruled from 1814 to 1824.

Reading Strategy:
Summarizing

Summarize the conflict that Louis XVIII faced in this section.

Louis XVIII tried to please both the conservatives and the liberals. Conservatives wanted him to support the right of nobles to rule. Liberals wanted him to give more people in the middle class the right to vote. The king could not please both groups, so neither group was happy with him.

What Kind of Power Did Charles X Want?

When Louis XVIII died in 1824, his brother became King Charles X. He wanted to be an absolute monarch. He asked the French legislature to pass laws that limited the rights of many people. When the legislature refused to do this, Charles X closed it down.

Next, Charles X called for an election to get representatives for a new legislature. He thought it would be a conservative one. However, the election results surprised him. The French people voted for liberals.

How Did Charles X Bring About a Rebellion?

Charles wanted to end the power of this new liberal legislature. In July 1830, he issued new laws. These laws abolished the legislature, limited voting rights, and ended freedom of the press. Historians call these laws the July **Ordinances.** An ordinance is a law set forth by someone in government. French newspapers encouraged their readers to ignore the king's laws.

On July 28, 1830, middle-class liberals, workers, and students took to the streets of Paris in protest. They built barriers in the streets. The king then sent his soldiers to break up the riots. But many soldiers refused to shoot the rioters. In fact, some troops joined the protest movement. When Charles X saw this, he fled to England. Once again, the French had forced a king from his throne.

Who Became the "Citizen King"?

Many of the working-class rebels thought that the July Revolution, as it was called, would make France a republic. They wanted this to happen because in a republic, every man could vote. Middle-class leaders wanted a constitutional monarchy instead of a republican form of government.

With middle-class support, Louis Philippe (the cousin of Charles X) became king. Historians call him the "citizen king" because he dressed like a middle-class businessman. He often walked through Paris and spoke to the people he met there.

Louis Philippe was known as the "citizen king" because he sided with the middle class.

What Other European Nationalists Rebelled?

Between 1830 and 1848, France influenced rebels in other countries. People in Belgium rebelled against the Netherlands in 1830 and won their independence. Polish people also tried to rebel and win their independence from Russia. But the Russian army defeated them. Nationalists in Italy and Germany also rebelled. Austrian troops put down the revolt in Italy. The Confederation of German States used force to end the rebellion in Germany.

Lesson 4 Review On a sheet of paper, write the answer to each question. Use complete sentences.

1. What three political groups came out of the French Revolution?
2. Who followed Louis XVIII as king of France?
3. In what year did the July Revolution in France take place?
4. Who was known as the "citizen king"?
5. When did Belgium free itself from rule by the Netherlands?

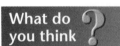

What do you think

Why would Charles X want a conservative legislature?

Then and Now

Photography

Did you know that you probably see more than 1,000 camera images a day? Yet the photograph was unknown before 1827!

French inventor Joseph Niepce made the first photograph from nature that year. It showed the courtyard of his house. In 1844, the first book of photographs was published in Paris. It contained photos of the Egyptian countryside.

Photographs have become popular for several reasons. They tell the truth. Photographs of the United States Civil War first showed what war is really like. Scientists use photos to record information about whatever they are studying—humans, animals, space. People have used them to win support for causes, such as helping the poor. Photographs also record important personal events. Museums even consider photography an art form.

Objectives

◆ To describe how socialism changed Europe

◆ To explain what the utopian socialists thought

◆ To describe the kind of society that Karl Marx wanted

In 1848, revolutions swept through Europe. Once again, the French rebelled against their government. This time, French radicals demanded that workers be given the right to vote. Louis Philippe, the citizen king, said, "There will be no reform. I do not wish it."

In February 1848, the people of Paris took to the streets in a protest against their government. The king sent troops to restore order. Then a mob marched on the king's palace. After he fled to England, revolutionary leaders set up a Second French Republic to govern the nation. (The French established the First Republic during the French Revolution of 1789.)

What Did Socialists Want?

The new republican government had trouble because the radical leaders were divided into two groups. One group wanted to reform only the French political system. The second group wanted both political and economic reform.

Revolutions swept through Europe in 1848.

Louis Blanc—a **socialist**—led the second group. Socialists wanted to end the private ownership of land and factories. In Chapter 21, you read about the Industrial Revolution. In that chapter, you learned that a nation needs three things to industrialize—natural resources, plenty of workers, and capital. In France, as in most countries, only a few people owned land and had the capital to build factories and machines.

How Did Socialists Frighten the Middle Class?

The socialists believed that private ownership caused the poor economic conditions of the working class. They wanted the state to control the land and the factories. This radical idea frightened the middle class.

Blanc demanded that the government establish workshops to give jobs to people who had none. For a time, the government did this, but then it closed the workshops. This angered the workers, so they rioted.

Before the riots ended, government soldiers had killed thousands of workers. This violence upset the French people. They blamed the radical socialists for these riots and disorder. The French then wrote a new constitution. It called for the election of a parliament and a powerful president.

Louis Blanc, a French socialist, set up workshops to give jobs to people who had none.

Reading Strategy:
Summarizing

Summarize the idea
of a Utopian society.

Who Brought Peace to France?

In December 1848, the French voters elected Louis Napoleon
Bonaparte (Napoleon III) as their new president. (Napoleon
Bonaparte was his uncle.) Louis Napoleon brought order to
France. Soon after his election, he set aside the republican
form of government.

In 1851, Louis Napoleon declared that he was the only ruler of
France. Many French people liked this change. In an election,
more than 90 percent of the voters supported Napoleon III
as a single powerful leader. France achieved peace, but lost
democracy. Napoleon III ruled France for nearly 20 years.

What Did Utopian Socialists Think?

Not all socialists agreed on the best way to improve the lives
of the working class. One group—the **utopian** socialists—
thought that they could reform society peacefully. The word
utopian comes from a book Thomas More, an Englishman,
wrote in 1516. It was about a future society where everyone
worked together peacefully for the good of all. Utopia was
a perfect society. No one was poor, no one committed any
crimes, and no one fought. Utopian socialists believed that
people could live and work together peacefully if they had the
chance to do so.

What Did Marx Think About Factory Owners?

A German named Karl Marx thought that the utopian
socialists were dreamers. Marx said that all societies were
made up of the "haves" and the "have-nots." The "haves" have
power and wealth. The "have-nots" have nothing. They have
no money and no power.

Marx said that powerful leaders would never willingly give
up their power. He thought workers would always fight with
factory and landowners. Marx believed that all of history was a
class struggle between the rich (the "haves") and the poor (the
"have-nots"). He thought that factory owners grew rich from
the labor of the workers. Factory owners paid workers low
wages and kept the profit from the business for themselves.

What Kind of Society Did Marx See in the Future?

Marx believed that workers could improve their lives and gain power only by violent revolution. In a pamphlet called *The Communist Manifesto,* written by Marx and Friedrich Engels, we read, "Workers of the world, unite!" Marx believed that workers had ". . . nothing to lose . . . but their chains." Marx called these industrial workers the **proletariat.**

In the future, Marx saw a society that had no need for government. Each member of this society would be equal. There would be no rich or poor. The ideas of Karl Marx influenced history from the last years of the 19th century to the present.

Karl Marx believed that only violent revolution could improve workers' lives.

Look for important details in this section. Why did these revolutions fail?

What Ended the Old Ways of Government?

Throughout 1848, violent revolutions occurred in the Italian states, in Prussia, and in the Austrian Empire. Nearly 50 rebellions broke out in different areas of Europe. Some revolutionaries wanted national independence. Others wanted more say in who governed them. Some rebellions combined both goals. In the end, all these revolutions failed.

However, the rebellions ended the system that the Congress of Vienna established in 1814. When a revolt broke out in Austria, Prince Metternich fled to England. The old ruling order was finished. Nationalism had become the most important organizing force for societies.

As time passed, noble families lost their power and privilege. Like all members of the royal class, Czar Nicholas of Russia was nervous. He said, "What remains standing in Europe?"

Communication in History

Reading with Fingertips

The Frenchman Louis Braille was a blind teacher of blind children and teenagers. In 1824, he invented a reading system that enables blind people to read. He based it on Charles Barbier's night reading principle. Barbier developed it so that the military could read messages at night. His system was made up of dots pressed into paper.

Braille's system uses six raised dots arranged in cells, or letter spaces. Each cell contains three rows and two columns. Each letter, number, and punctuation mark has its own layout of larger and smaller dots. Braille taught people how to read these dots with their fingertips.

Braille was first printed by hand. A sharp, pointed tool raised small dots on heavy paper. In 1892, the stereotyping machine made it possible to transfer dots to printing plates. For today's books, computer programs translate print into Braille. The blind can also write Braille. They use a Braillewriter, which resembles a typewriter.

Lesson 5 Review On a sheet of paper, write the letter of the answer that correctly completes each sentence.

1. The "Year of Revolutions" is _____.

    A 1776   **C** 1815

    B 1789   **D** 1848

2. Louis Blanc, a(n) _____, wanted to end the private ownership of land and factories.

    A absolute monarch   **C** conservative

    B socialist   **D** liberal

3. The _____ socialists believed that they could peacefully bring about a perfect society.

    A utopian   **C** conservative

    B communist   **D** radical

4. _____ called industrial workers the "proletariat."

    A Louis Philippe

    B Louis Napoleon Bonaparte

    C Karl Marx

    D Prince Metternich

5. The authors of *The Communist Manifesto* said that society is made up of _____.

    A the "haves"   **C** class struggle

    B the "have-nots"   **D** all of the above

What do you think ?

Why did the radicals want the state to control land and factories?

The Communist Manifesto

Karl Marx and Friedrich Engels were the leaders of a new social movement. They believed that a workers' revolution would take place in England. They were wrong, however. Then in 1848, the two men published a pamphlet. This Communist Manifesto *stated their beliefs. Marx and Engels argued that workers (proletariat) would overthrow the owners of business (bourgeoisie). Marx and Engels called themselves Communists. Their revolutionary ideas would become an important force in the 20th century.*

Karl Marx and Friedrich Engels

In the earlier times of history, we find almost everywhere a complicated arrangement of society into various orders of social rank. In ancient Rome, we have patricians, knights, plebeians, slaves; in the Middle Ages, feudal lords, vassals, guild-masters, journeymen, apprentices, serfs.

The modern bourgeois society [middle class factory owners] that has sprouted from the ruins of feudal society . . . has but established new classes, new conditions of oppression, new forms of struggle in place of the old ones. . . .

The modern labourer . . . instead of rising with the progress of industry, sinks deeper and deeper below the conditions of existence of his own class. He becomes a pauper [poor person]. . . . And here it becomes evident that the bourgeoisie is unfit any longer to be the ruling class in society. What the bourgeoisie therefore produces, above all, are its own grave diggers. Its fall and the victory of the proletariat are equally inevitable. . . .

The Communists turn their attention chiefly to Germany, because that country is on the eve of a bourgeois revolution that . . . will be but the prelude to an immediately following proletarian revolution. . . .

The Communists openly declare that their ends can be attained only by the forcible overthrow of all existing social conditions. Let the ruling classes tremble at a Communist revolution. The proletarians have nothing to lose but their chains. They have a world to win.

Working men of all countries, unite!

Document-Based Questions

1. According to this writing, what two classes made up society in his day?

2. Who were the bourgeoisie?

3. The authors said that workers were sinking "deeper and deeper below the conditions of existence." What did they mean?

4. Why might non-Communists fear the Communists?

5. Why did the authors believe that workers should rebel?

Dressing for Success

Throughout history, clothes have been a symbol of success, social status, and wealth. Fashions change for many reasons. For example, during the Middle Ages in Europe, both men and women wore long gowns. They only had buckles to hold their clothing together. Clothing, therefore, had to be large enough to pull over the head. Then in the 1200s, the crusaders returned from the Middle East, bringing back buttons. Buttons could make clothes fit closer to the body.

People wore fancy, elaborate clothing in Europe during the 1700s.

In the 1400s, women still dressed mostly in floor-length gowns. Men began to wear tight-fitting jackets though. They also wore hose to show off the shape of their legs. Over the years, the dress of upper class men became more fancy and colorful. This trend continued for the next three centuries.

Benjamin Franklin's arrival at the French court in 1779 showed how men's clothing would change. Franklin decided not to wear the fancy, colorful clothes in style at the time. He wore a simple black coat and matching knee breeches. Franklin's dress caused a new fashion trend. His clothes were thought to be the perfect symbol of the "natural man" of the middle class.

In 1789, the French-Estates General met. Members of the Third Estate, or common people, could not wear colors or decorated ornaments. After the French Revolution swept the upper class from power, their fashion-setting days ended. Instead, the clothing of the middle class became the acceptable style of dress. Men dressed in dark-colored jackets and trousers. Men's fashion kept this same basic suit well into the 20th century.

Here is an interesting fact from the history of clothing styles. The upper classes often passed clothing styles down to the working class. In the 1700s, the upper class wore powdered wigs, colorful jackets, and knee breeches. In the 1800s, household servants dressed this way. To get dressed up, gentlemen of the 19th century wore a tuxedo. In the 20th century, waiters in fancy restaurants sported tuxedos.

Wrap-Up

1. Besides modesty and warmth, why do people dress as they do?

2. How did the button change men's clothing in Europe?

3. Why was Benjamin Franklin's clothing the talk of the French court?

4. What impact did the French Revolution have on clothing styles?

5. In your opinion, how are fashion styles set today?

- Britain, Prussia, Austria, and Russia defeated and exiled Napoleon in 1814. They met at the Congress of Vienna to decide France's fate.

- Metternich had three goals. France should never threaten other nations again. Major European nations should have equal strength. This balance of power would keep the peace. Royal families should return to power and end nationalism.

- The Congress of Vienna divided the French empire among European countries and established a German Confederation. It also put royal families back on their thrones.

- The ancient Greeks contributed much to Western civilization. Many Europeans supported Greek independence for this reason.

- Nationalism spread to Latin America. Led by L'Ouverture, Haiti gained its independence from France. Later Santo Domingo won independence from Spain.

- In northern South America, Bolívar freed Colombia, Ecuador, and Venezuela. San Martín freed Chile and Peru. Later Brazil got its freedom from Portugal peacefully.

- Fathers Hidalgo and Morelos led Mexican peasants successfully against the Spanish. But Mexican creoles wanted power for themselves. This struggle delayed Mexican independence until 1821.

- In France, conservatives were mainly rich landowners and nobles. They supported absolute royal power. Liberals were usually wealthy businessmen and merchants. They wanted a say in the government. Radicals wanted to change monarchies to democracies and were willing to use force.

- A series of kings ruled France. Charles X's desire to be an absolute ruler caused the Revolution of 1830. Between 1830 and 1848 other people revolted: Belgians, Poles, Italians, and Germans.

- Europe was torn by revolutions in 1848, but they all failed. In France, revolution founded a republic. The revolutionaries, however, were divided. Liberals wanted to reform the political system. Socialists wanted to end the private ownership of land and factories. Louis Napoleon was elected president and declared himself Napoleon III.

- Karl Marx and Friedrich Engels wrote *The Communist Manifesto.* They believed only violent revolution could improve workers' lives.

Chapter 22   R E V I E W

Word Bank
Alexander
Blanc
Bolívar
Hidalgo
L'Ouverture
Marx
Metternich
Ottoman
Philippe
San Martín

On a sheet of paper, use the words from the Word Bank to complete each sentence correctly.

1. Prince _____ of Austria was the most influential leader at the Congress of Vienna.

2. Czar _____ of Russia represented his nation at the Congress of Vienna.

3. Before it won its independence, Greece was part of the _____ Empire.

4. Toussaint _____ led the slave revolt against the French in Haiti.

5. Simón _____ liberated New Granada from Spain.

6. José _____ led an army into Chile to free it from Spanish control.

7. The Mexican priest Miguel _____ challenged the Indian peasants to rebel against the Spanish.

8. Louis _____ became the "citizen king" of France in 1830.

9. Louis _____ led one group of French socialists.

10. Karl _____ and Friedrich Engels wrote *The Communist Manifesto*.

On a sheet of paper, write the letter of the answer that correctly completes each sentence.

11. The French Revolution promoted the idea(s) of _____.

    A nationalism   **C** equality

    B liberty   **D** all of the above

12. _____ led revolts against the Spanish in Latin America.

    A Byron   **C** Metternich

    B Blanc   **D** San Martín

13. At the Congress of Vienna, _____ said that nationalism was a disease and that he had the cure for it.

   A Metternich   **C** Louis Philippe
   B Marx   **D** Byron

14. A _____ is a person who likes the old order of things.

   A liberal   **B** radical   **C** conservative   **D** socialist

15. A _____ is a person who wants to end the private ownership of land and factories.

   A conservative   **C** monarch
   B socialist   **D** peninsular

On a sheet of paper, write the answer to each question. Use complete sentences.

16. What is nationalism?

17. Why did the leaders at the Congress of Vienna fear nationalism?

18. How did events in France in the 19th century influence other European and colonial revolutionaries?

Critical Thinking On a sheet of paper, write your response to each question. Use complete sentences.

19. Prince Metternich believed nationalism was like a disease. He said, "When France sneezes, Europe catches cold." What did Metternich mean? If possible, use an example of a "sneeze" and a "cold" in your answer.

20. The political group called the conservatives thought that revolution was a danger to society. Do you agree with them? Why or why not?

Test-Taking Tip

When taking a matching test, first match the items you know belong together. Cross these items out. Then try to match the items that are left.

Unit 4

Using Reference Materials

Reference materials are sources for finding different kinds of information. Here are some examples of reference materials and the kinds of information you can find in them.

General information almanac — Book of recent and historical facts and figures about many subjects

Atlas — Book of maps of countries, states, and some cities

Encyclopedia — One book or a set of books with summaries and histories of many different subjects

Gazetteer — Dictionary of geographic place names and information

Newspaper — Daily or weekly publication with national, local, sports, and business news and regular features

Periodical index — Listing of magazine articles by subject and the publication in which they appear

Internet — Worldwide computer network with information on a variety of subjects; includes on-line encyclopedias, newspapers, and periodicals

Here is a list of research questions. You could probably find the answers to all of them somewhere on the Internet. Name at least one other listed source that you could use to answer each question.

1. Where could you find a short biography of Queen Isabella of Spain?

2. What kind of government does Austria have today?

3. You remember seeing a magazine article about foods and dishes brought from Africa by slaves. Where can you find the date and name of the publication in which it appeared?

4. Where could you find a map of Spain with an inset of Madrid?

5. Where could you find information about the Andes Mountains?

6. Where could you find information about instruments used for navigation in modern submarines?

7. Where could you look for results of a vote taken in Congress yesterday?

8. What are the names of some compositions by Joseph Haydn?

9. In what part of England is Plymouth located?

10. Who is the present king of Spain?

Unit 4 S U M M A R Y

- Newton's discovery of natural, universal laws introduced the Age of Reason.

- Enlightenment thinkers wanted to use reason to improve society. Hobbes, Locke, Montesquieu, Rousseau, and Voltaire wrote about government. Locke said people had natural rights to life, liberty, and property.

- Handel and Bach were baroque composers. Haydn and Mozart were classical composers. The Age of Reason influenced writers such as Swift and Molière.

- After 1763, Britain wanted its North American colonies to pay for the war against France. The colonists protested. Then colonial representatives signed the Declaration of Independence. The French helped Americans win a revolution against Britain.

- France in the 1770s consisted of three estates—the clergy, the nobles, and the common people. The Third Estate paid all the taxes. This group established a constitutional monarchy in 1789. In 1792, the National Constitutional Convention created a republic. The Jacobins under Robespierre began the Reign of Terror. Then came the Directory and the Consulate. In 1804, Napoleon crowned himself emperor.

- Napoleon's victories increased French power, but he made two mistakes. The Continental System turned countries against France. His Russian invasion destroyed his army. The allies defeated Napoleon in 1814 and again at Waterloo. In France, the Code of Napoleon made every man equal under the law. Napoleon's conquests spread the ideas of the French Revolution.

- The Industrial Revolution began in England in the 1750s. England could industrialize because it had natural resources, workers, and capital.

- The English invented new machinery. The factory system brought workers, machines, and power together.

- Under Metternich's lead, the Congress of Vienna reorganized Europe. It promoted the balance of powers.

- Nationalism was a major force. Bolívar and San Martín freed South American countries from Spain. Father Hidalgo began the Mexican fight for independence.

- Conservatives supported absolute royal power. Liberals favored a constitutional monarchy. Radicals wanted to change monarchies to democracies. In 1848, there were revolutions throughout Europe. None succeeded. In France, Napoleon III became emperor. Marx believed only violent revolution could improve workers' lives.

"[Germany had once been admired as a] nation of thinkers and philosophers, poets and artists, idealists and enthusiasts . . . [but now the world saw Germany as] a nation of conquerors and destroyers, to which no pledged word, no treaty, is sacred. . . . We are neither loved nor respected, but only feared."

~*Crown Prince Friedrich of Germany, in his 1870 diary*

TO AND FROM
GIBRALTAR EGYPT AND INDIA

Unit
5

A New Global Age

European leaders fought to create strong nations, and nationalism spread. In Italy, revolts exploded between 1820 and 1848. Germany was brought together as one nation by the Franco-Prussian War.

Imperialism also swept across the world during the 19th century. European nations established colonies in Africa and Asia.

In this unit, you will meet nationalism and imperialism face to face. First you will read about the ways nationalism can bring people together. You will learn why Europeans thought that imperialism helped the colonized nations. You will also learn why the people in those colonized nations did not think that imperialism was a good thing.

Chapters in Unit 5

23

Nationalism

As you have read, nationalism is the loyalty people have for their country. This became a powerful force for change in the world during the 1800s. In this chapter, you will meet Giuseppe Mazzini, who led a rebellion in 1848. You will meet Camillo di Cavour, who united most of Italy. You will also meet Giuseppe Garibaldi, known for his military ability. Then you will see how Germany was brought together as one nation.

Goals for Learning

◆ To explain nationalism

◆ To identify the leaders of Italian unification

◆ To explain how Germany became a unified nation

1848 Mazzini leads unsuccessful revolt in Italy

1871 Prussia defeats France; Germany becomes one country

1840　　　　　　　　　　1860　　　　　　　　　　1880

1848 Sardinia declares war on Austria

1860 Garibaldi unites most of Italy

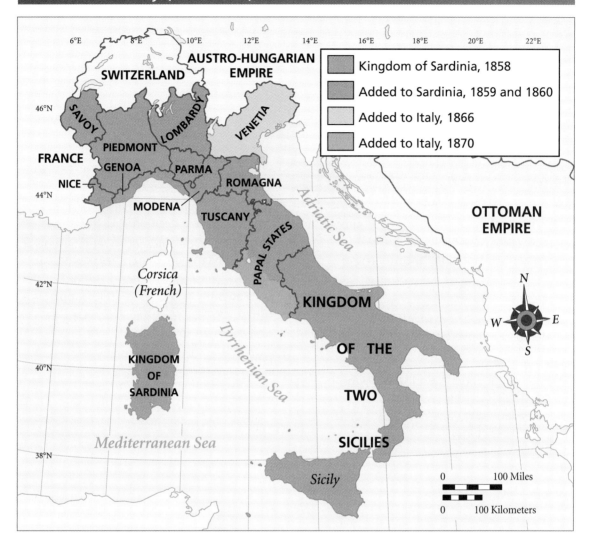

Map Skills

This map shows how Italy became unified as one country by adding territory between 1858 and 1870. In 1870, the last independent state became part of Italy. Rome became the capital of Italy.

Study the map, then answer the following questions:

1. What states became part of the Kingdom of Sardinia in 1859 and 1860?

2. What state was added to Italy in 1866?

3. When did the last independent state become part of Italy?

4. What sea separates Italy from the Ottoman Empire?

5. Which sea lies to the west of Italy?

Reading Strategy:
Questioning

As you read this chapter, ask yourself questions. You will understand and remember more information if you ask yourself questions as you read. As you read, ask yourself:

◆ What is my reason for reading this text?

◆ What connections can I make between this text and my own life, or something I have read before?

Key Vocabulary Words

Lesson 1

Multilingual A society in which a number of languages are spoken

Heritage The traditions ancestors have passed down

Lesson 2

Prime minister The leader in some democratic government systems

Lesson 3

Militarism A nation's warlike policy or practice

Policy A plan that helps a person or a country make a decision

Ambassador A person sent to represent his or her government in another country

Siege The act of surrounding a city or fort with an army and cutting off its supplies

Negotiate To talk together, make bargains, and agree on something

Kaiser The emperor of Germany

Reich The German word for empire

Objectives

◆ To identify how language and culture affect nationalism

◆ To explain how foreign invaders, government, and history affect nationalism

Multilingual

A society in which a number of languages are spoken

Reading Strategy: Questioning

What do you think you will learn about by reading this lesson?

Nationalism swept across Europe in the 1800s and early 1900s. As you have already learned, nationalism is loyalty to one's country. But there are many other things that make up nationalism.

How Does Language Affect Nationalism?

A common language is an important part of nationalism. Usually the people of one country speak the same language. This unites them. In some countries, however, people speak more than one language. This kind of society is **multilingual.** However, they are still loyal to their country.

How Does Culture Affect Nationalism?

A common culture is another part of nationalism. The people of a nation often share the same beliefs, customs, religion, music, and way of life. A belief in freedom, democracy, and equality unites Americans. A common religion unites people in nations such as Israel or Iran. Both Japan and China have a culture that is different from other countries. In any country, the citizens may be different from one another. But they all love their country and feel loyal to it.

How Do Foreign Invaders Affect Nationalism?

Sometimes people lose their land. Foreign invaders (people from other countries) might take it over. For example, powerful neighbors have taken over Poland over the years. Also, for many years, non-Chinese leaders ruled China.

But nationalism can remain even if people lose their land or government. In fact, being invaded often makes people have more nationalism. For example, today many Palestinians are scattered throughout the Middle East. They are now fighting for a land of their own.

Heritage

The traditions ancestors have passed down to their descendants

Geography Note

Not all people in European countries felt a sense of nationalism. Many traveled to the United States to find a better life. Ellis Island, in New York Bay, was the first stop for most. It was the main U.S. immigration station beginning in 1892. By the time it closed in 1954, more than 20 million people had passed through its gates.

How Do Government and History Affect Nationalism?

Having only one government is another part of nationalism. For example, people who live in the 50 states of the United States follow the laws in the Constitution. They also follow the laws made by the government in Washington, D.C.

A common history is another part of nationalism. In American schools, students study the history of the United States. They feel pride in their shared history. The flag, the symbol of Uncle Sam, and the "Star-Spangled Banner" mean something special to all Americans.

Students in other countries also study their history so they will love their country, be loyal to it, and value their **heritage.** Heritage is made up of all the traditions our ancestors have passed down to us.

Lesson 1 Review On a sheet of paper, write the answer to each question. Use complete sentences.

1. Why is a common language an important part of nationalism?

2. What three things do the people of a nation often share?

3. How can nationalism remain even when people lose their land?

4. How does having one government unite people in different parts of a country?

5. Why do students in other countries study the history of their country?

What do you think ?

What do you think is the most important symbol of your country? Why?

Objectives

◆ To identify three important leaders in Italy and what they did

◆ To identify the first king of Italy

Prime minister

The leader in some democratic government systems

Reading Strategy: Questioning

What details are important to understanding nationalism in Italy?

The Napoleonic Wars gave birth to nationalism in Italy. In Chapter 21, you read about the Congress of Vienna, which met in 1814 after Napoleon's defeat. The leaders of this meeting divided Italy into about 30 states and provinces. Austria, France, and Spain controlled these provinces.

What Did Giuseppe Mazzini Do?

Many people in Italy had strong nationalist feelings. In 1848, revolts broke out in many states. Giuseppe Mazzini led the rebellion. Historians call him the "soul" of Italian unity because he stood for its spirit of freedom. But Mazzini's rebellion failed. Thousands of soldiers from Austria and France marched into Italy and put down the revolt. For the next 20 years, French troops controlled Rome.

What Did Camillo di Cavour Do?

Count Camillo di Cavour then stepped forward to lead the fight for unity. He was the **prime minister** of the Kingdom of Sardinia. A prime minister is the leader in some democratic government systems.

Sardinia was the only Italian state that an Italian king ruled. (Remember that France, Austria, and Spain ruled all the other Italian states.)

Cavour was a skilled politician, and he figured out a way to free the Italian states from outside rule. First, he made a secret agreement with France. Together, they declared war against Austria in 1859. The combined French-Sardinian army defeated Austria. This action won the respect of people in all the states of Italy.

Next, nationalist revolts broke out in the northern provinces that Austria controlled. By 1860, all these provinces had become part of the Kingdom of Sardinia. Cavour planned how to get two major powers to fight one another and leave Italy alone. Historians call him the "brain" of Italian unity.

What Did Giuseppe Garibaldi Do?

Cavour united the northern states of Italy, while secretly helping nationalists in the southern states. In May 1860, a small army of Italian nationalists invaded the island of Sicily. Giuseppe Garibaldi led them.

Garibaldi always wore a red shirt in battle. His supporters imitated him, and the red shirt became their uniform. The "Red Shirts" swept through Sicily and marched northward toward Rome. There, Garibaldi's army met up with Sardinian troops. Together, they had united almost all of Italy. Because of his great military feats, historians call Garibaldi the "sword" of the revolution.

Giuseppe Garibaldi, the "sword" of Italian unity, united most of Italy.

Who Became Italy's First King?

In March 1861, a parliament representing most of the Italian states chose a ruler. King Victor Emmanuel II of Sardinia became the first king of a unified Italy. In 1870, the last independent state became part of Italy. Rome became the capital. The parliament set aside part of Rome for the pope's use. Vatican City is still the home of the pope and the center of the Roman Catholic Church.

Communication in History

The Wireless Telegraph

The Italian engineer Guglielmo Marconi invented the wireless telegraph in 1895. He performed his first experiment near his home in Bologna, Italy. There he transmitted signals on radio waves across a mile of countryside. In 1901, he sent messages by telegraph a much longer distance, across the Atlantic Ocean from England to Newfoundland. Marconi went on to build communication products for ships at sea. A few years later, Canadian Reginald Fessenden and American Ernst Alexanderson learned how to send speech and music on the same radio waves. Another American, Lee de Forest, created a device to make these radio messages louder.

Vatican City

From 756 to 1870, the pope ruled much of central Italy. However, with the unification of Italy, the pope's rule was reduced to one city-state, Vatican City. Established in 1929, Vatican City is the world's smallest independent country. Located in northwestern Rome, it has an area of 110 acres.

Medieval and Renaissance walls surround the city. The most important building is Saint Peter's Church. The Vatican, the pope's palace, is also within these walls. The Sistine Chapel is part of this palace. Michelangelo painted its ceiling. The government offices of the Roman Catholic Church are also found here.

Vatican City has its own currency, postal system, and telephone and telegraph services. It also has a railroad station and a radio station. Its population is less than 1,000.

Lesson 2 Review On a sheet of paper, write the letter of the answer that correctly completes each sentence.

1. After 1814, _____ controlled most of the 30 states in Italy.

   A Austria   **C** Spain

   B France   **D** all of the above

2. The "soul" of Italian unity was _____.

   A Mazzini   **C** Cavour

   B Garibaldi   **D** Victor Emmanuel II

3. The "brain" of Italian unity was _____.

   A Mazzini   **C** Cavour

   B Garibaldi   **D** Victor Emmanuel II

4. The "sword" of Italian unity was _____.

   A Mazzini   **C** Cavour

   B Garibaldi   **D** Victor Emmanuel II

5. The first king of Italy was _____.

   A Mazzini   **C** Cavour

   B Garibaldi   **D** Victor Emmanuel II

What do you think ?

Red is an easy color to shoot at. Why would Garibaldi wear red in battle?

Objectives

♦ To explain how the failed German Revolution of 1848 affected Germany

♦ To identify the role Otto von Bismarck played in German unification

♦ To identify the first ruler of Germany

Reading Strategy:
Summarizing

What do you think you will learn by reading about the 1848 German Revolution?

The Napoleonic Wars also gave birth to nationalism in Germany. Germany had many independent states. From 1814 to 1815, the Congress of Vienna organized the German Confederation. It included 38 German states and their rulers. But the confederation was weak.

Soon, the idea of unifying Germany became popular. The people in all the German states spoke German. They also had the same culture and shared the same land.

Why Did the 1848 German Revolution Fail?

The revolts that swept over Europe in 1848 affected Germany. In April 1849, representatives of the German states met in a parliament and issued a constitution. The parliament asked the Prussian king, Frederick Wilhelm IV, to become king of all the German states. (Prussia was the largest German state.)

The king refused the offer because the people of Germany, and not the princes of all the states, had offered him the crown. He wanted the nobles, not the common people, to choose him.

Soon, fighting broke out between the liberals and the conservatives. The liberals wanted gradual change and a democratic government; the conservatives wanted none of this. Then King Wilhelm sent his Prussian army to break up the parliament. When the liberal leaders fled, the conservatives once again controlled the German states.

How Did Bismarck Plan to Unite the German States?

After the 1848 revolution failed, most German nationalists thought that only Prussia could unite Germany. Prussia was the strongest German state and had the best army. In 1862, Otto von Bismarck became prime minister of Prussia. Bismarck, a member of the rich landlord class, was loyal to the Prussian king. He wanted to unite all the German states under Prussia's leadership.

Bismarck, who was a conservative, did not believe in democratic rule. In his first speech as prime minister, he told the Prussian parliament that the only way to solve problems was "by blood and iron." For him, "blood" meant war and "iron" meant a king with absolute power.

What Is Militarism?

Bismarck wanted to make Prussia into a great military power. He forced the Prussian parliament to give him money to build a strong army. He believed that war would unite the German states. Historians have a name for this belief: **militarism.** For such a country, nothing is more important than the military.

Who Won the Austro-Prussian War?

In 1864, Bismarck's army defeated Germany's northern neighbor, Denmark. Then, in 1866, his army defeated Austria in just seven weeks. To do this, Bismarck used Prussia's new railroads and better weapons. After Austria's defeat, Bismarck forced its neighbor to give up some of its German land.

Austria gave Hungary more independence. Austria and Hungary each had its own parliament and officials. However, the Austrian emperor was still the king of Hungary. Also, the two countries had one **policy,** or plan, toward other countries. They also shared one army. Historians call this new empire Austria-Hungary.

How Did Bismarck Start the Franco-Prussian War?

Next, Bismarck and Prussia went to war with France. It started when the French **ambassador,** a representative of the French government, came to Prussia. He wanted to talk to the king about who should become the next king of Spain.

Bismarck then lied to the newspapers about what the two men said to one another. His lie made the French think that the Prussian king had said something rude to their ambassador. It made the Germans think that the French ambassador had threatened them. Nationalists in both countries felt that they had to go to war. Only then could they defend their national honor.

Who Won the Franco-Prussian War?

The well-trained Prussian army moved quickly. In 1870, German soldiers poured into northern France. At the Battle of Sedan, the Prussian army defeated the French and captured about 100,000 French soldiers. Included among them was the French ruler, Napoleon III.

The Prussian army surrounded Paris and cut off its supplies. After this four-month **siege**, Paris surrendered. Bismarck forced the French to sign a treaty called the Treaty of Frankfurt. According to the treaty, France had to pay Prussia a huge sum of money. It also had to give up two important territories, Alsace and Lorraine. These provinces, which lay on the border with Germany, contained France's richest coal and iron fields.

What Was the Second Reich?

The Franco-Prussian War brought all the German states together. After the Austro-Prussian War, Prussia took control of northern Germany. Then it formed the North German Confederation. After the Franco-Prussian War, the people in the four southern states joined the rest of Germany.

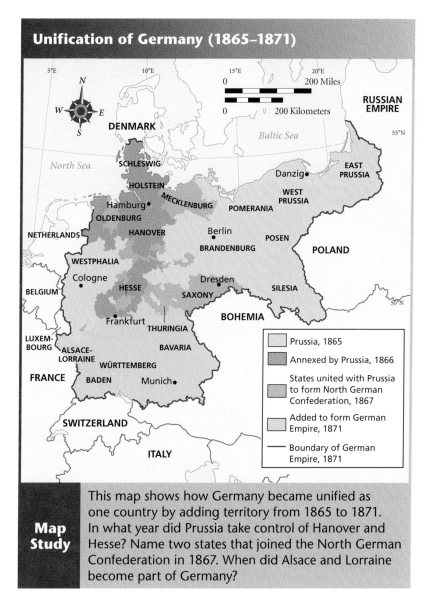

Unification of Germany (1865–1871)

Legend:
- Prussia, 1865
- Annexed by Prussia, 1866
- States united with Prussia to form North German Confederation, 1867
- Added to form German Empire, 1871
- Boundary of German Empire, 1871

Map Study This map shows how Germany became unified as one country by adding territory from 1865 to 1871. In what year did Prussia take control of Hanover and Hesse? Name two states that joined the North German Confederation in 1867. When did Alsace and Lorraine become part of Germany?

Wilhelm I agreed to become the first **kaiser,** or emperor, of Germany. He was crowned in January 1871 at the French palace of Versailles. Historians call this new German empire the Second **Reich.** The German word *reich* means empire or nation. The Holy Roman Empire was the First Reich in that part of Europe.

Word Bank

Bismarck

Prussia

Sedan

Wilhelm I

Wilhelm IV

Lesson 3 Review On a sheet of paper, use the words from the Word Bank to complete each sentence correctly.

1. Germans looked to _____ for leadership in unifying Germany.

2. _____ refused the offer to become king of all the German states.

3. In 1862, _____ became prime minister of Prussia.

4. In the Battle of _____, the Prussian army defeated the French army.

5. _____ became the first kaiser of Germany.

What do you think

Why do you think the Treaty of Frankfurt probably made the French feel ashamed?

Biography

Marie Curie: 1867–1934

Marie Curie was a Polish-born French chemist. She and her husband, Pierre, studied radioactivity, which is the energy in atoms. Marie received the Nobel Prize in physics in 1903 and in chemistry in 1911.

The Curies wanted everyone to benefit from their studies. During World War I, Marie helped equip ambulances with X-ray equipment to help wounded soldiers. She even drove ambulances to the front lines. She also taught others how to use the equipment.

Her work meant that she was often near radioactive materials. Its dangers were not known at the time. Radiation gave her cancer. In a twist of fate, today we use controlled radiation to treat cancer.

A Lady's Glimpse of the Late War in Bohemia

Little is known about Lizzie Selina Eden, who wrote this account in 1867. She was traveling in Europe when the Austro-Prussian War broke out in 1866. The Prussian army defeated Austria in seven weeks.

"Love oft since this strange world began,

Walking his path of awe and wonder,

Has brought a better age to man

In blood, and fire, and battle thunder.

Angels, that with the evening star

Looked down upon the field of doom,

Wept – but serenely, for they saw

Beyond the veil the good to come."

We went over to Tetschen in the evening, but a gloomy distrust seemed on every face – a dim foreshadowing of the dismal tidings that burst on us next morning, when the sad fact could no longer be withheld, and we learnt the melancholy truth that Austria had been beaten – utterly and completely beaten. . . .

It was piteous this evening, and on many succeeding days, to see . . . raftsmen and wood-cutters out of employ, and many other sturdy-looking Bohemians who had nothing to do, for there was no work to be had – standing the whole day on the banks of the Elbe, watching for the first sight of the victorious Prussian army.

The weather even seemed now to share in the general depression, and changed from the intense heat of the previous week to cold, chilly days. A melancholy little robin, too, used to come and perch itself close to my window, and sing its dreary song all day, so that I felt in my room as melancholy as if I were in a churchyard. I quite longed to be told some day with a grin by our cheery-looking little waiter . . . that there were robins for dinner, among which this one might be included, so that henceforth we should be rid of its doleful song.

Scarcely anyone in England will ever know the extent of the misery and beggary which that fatal six weeks has brought on Bohemia. Many who were rich and prosperous are now fearfully reduced, and thousands are literally beggars. All, however, bear their hard doom with wonderful resignation, and make the best of their sad fate.

Document-Based Questions

1. What event is Eden describing?

2. Why is there such sadness around her?

3. Why does Eden mention the weather?

4. Why does she want the robin to go away?

5. Why are the rich people now beggars?

Source: A Lady's Glimpse of the Late War in Bohemia, *by Lizzie Selina Eden, 1867.*

Bismarck's *Kulturkampf*

For centuries the Roman Catholic pope has exercised power over European land owned by the church. Many of those properties were in Germany. Otto von Bismarck wanted to reduce the power of the Roman Catholic Church in his empire.

Bismarck was a devoted Protestant. He was afraid that the Catholics in Germany would not be loyal to his empire. He believed that their only real loyalty was to Rome. In 1871 he began a program called *Kulturkampf,* or "struggle for the minds controlling civilization."

Bismarck led the German parliament to pass laws limiting the power of the church. The Jesuits, an important order of teaching priests, had to leave Germany. Other clergy members had to obey strict rules about what they could teach. Those who did not agree to these rules were imprisoned. Catholics were banned from all jobs connected to government. In 1872 Germany ended all ties with the Vatican.

Bismarck's government had a very hard time enforcing these rules. In many cases, the government authorities were secretly working for the Catholic Church. Reaction to the *Kulturkampf* brought new support for the Roman Catholic Center Party. Even many non-Catholics who opposed the chancellor's actions joined the new party. A growing contempt for the *Kulturkampf* had become widespread within a very short time. One angry Catholic even tried to assassinate Bismarck!

Bismarck had encouraged free trade with other countries. This was weakening the Germany economy, as the country became flooded with foreign goods. People throughout the empire began to blame Bismarck for their money problems.

The groups that had previously supported Bismarck also favored free trade. He needed to find backing from more conservative voters. Many of those voters were the very Catholics he was trying to control. The Catholic political party members agreed to support Bismarck if he agreed to end his *Kulturkampf.*

Bismarck began to repeal the laws against Catholics. He reestablished ties with the Vatican. By 1887 he had completely ended the *Kulturkampf.* Otto von Bismarck knew he had made a mistake and he worked to correct it. However, he never regained the support of many people in the growing German middle class.

Wrap-Up

1. What was the *Kulturkampf?*

2. What laws were enacted under the *Kulturkampf?*

3. How could the Catholics help Bismarck?

4. Why did Bismarck end the *Kulturkampf?*

5. For how long did the *Kulturkampf* last?

- Nationalism grows stronger when a group of people have one language, one culture, one government, and a common history. They share the same customs, music, way of life, and religion. Nationalism can remain even if people lose their land or their government.

- Giuseppe Mazzini was called the soul of Italian independence because he stood for its spirit of freedom. He led a failed revolt in 1848.

- Count Camillo di Cavour was known as the brain of Italian unity. He got French support for Sardinia's war against Austria. The war won independence for several Italian provinces.

- Giuseppe Garibaldi was called the sword of Italian independence because of his military accomplishments. He and his Red Shirts freed Sicily. They joined Sardinian troops near Rome and united Italy.

- Victor Emmanuel II became Italy's first king. The parliament set aside part of Rome for the pope. It became Vatican City.

- The German Revolution of 1848 failed. The Prussian ruler refused to become king of all the German states. German nationalists believed only Prussia, the strongest German state, could unite Germany.

- In 1862, Otto von Bismarck became Prussia's prime minister. Prussia was the largest German state. Bismarck did not believe in democratic rule.

- Bismarck used militarism to conquer the German states. He defeated Austria in just seven weeks. A new empire, Austria-Hungary, was formed.

- In the Franco-Prussian War of 1870, Prussia defeated France and won French territory. The remaining independent German states joined Prussia to become a united Germany. Wilhelm I became its first kaiser in 1871.

Chapter 23 REVIEW

Word Bank

Bismarck
Cavour
Garibaldi
Mazzini
Napoleon III
Napoleonic Wars
Prussia
Red Shirts
Victor Emmanuel II
Wilhelm I

On a sheet of paper, use the words from the Word Bank to complete each sentence correctly.

1. The _____ started nationalism in Italy.

2. The _____ were supporters of Giuseppe Garibaldi.

3. Italy's first king, chosen in 1861, was _____.

4. _____ was an Italian nationalist and the "soul" of Italian unity.

5. _____ was a skilled politician and the "brain" of Italian unity.

6. _____ was a fine soldier and the "sword" of Italian unity.

7. _____ was the Prussian prime minister who wanted to unite all the German states under Prussia's leadership.

8. The strongest German state was _____.

9. In the Battle of Sedan, Prussian soldiers captured _____ and 100,000 other prisoners.

10. The first kaiser of a united Germany was _____.

On a sheet of paper, write the letter of the answer that correctly completes each sentence.

11. The love people have for their country is _____.

    A nationalism   **C** colonialism
    B militarism   **D** protectorate

12. Another name for a German emperor is _____.

    A conservative   **C** kaiser
    B liberal   **D** protectorate

13. Bismarck believed in _____ for Germany.

    A imperialism   **C** militarism
    B nationalism   **D** all of the above

14. After the Franco-Prussian War, Bismarck forced the French to sign the Treaty of _____.

    A France   **C** Frankfurt

    B Prussia   **D** Lorraine

15. Prussian King Frederick Wilhelm IV refused to become king because he wanted the _____ to choose him.

    A nobles   **C** Germans

    B common people   **D** liberals

On a sheet of paper, write the answer to each question. Use complete sentences.

16. Why did the 1848 German Revolution fail?

17. How can an invasion of their land make people have more nationalism?

18. Why is a common language an important part of nationalism?

Critical Thinking On a sheet of paper, write your response to each question. Use complete sentences.

19. Do you agree or disagree with Bismarck that leaders must decide problems with "blood and iron"? Explain your answer.

20. Do you think that nationalism is always a good thing? Explain your answer.

Test-Taking Tip

Read multiple-choice questions completely before reading the answer choices.

24

Imperialism

In this chapter you will learn about imperialism, when European powers took control of Asia and Africa. There were several reasons for this. Manufacturers in Europe needed new natural resources. Some missionaries and doctors were concerned for the well being of people in these countries. Another reason was that many Europeans thought they were superior to everyone else. They thought it was up to them to "improve" life for the people in these countries. The results were often violent.

Goals for Learning

◆ To explain imperialism

◆ To describe the effects of imperialism on Asia

◆ To describe the effects of imperialism on Africa

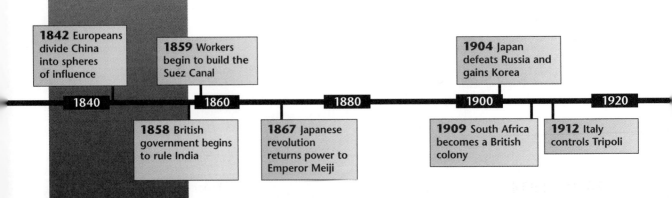

1842 Europeans divide China into spheres of influence

1859 Workers begin to build the Suez Canal

1904 Japan defeats Russia and gains Korea

| 1840 | 1860 | 1880 | 1900 | 1920 |

1858 British government begins to rule India

1867 Japanese revolution returns power to Emperor Meiji

1909 South Africa becomes a British colony

1912 Italy controls Tripoli

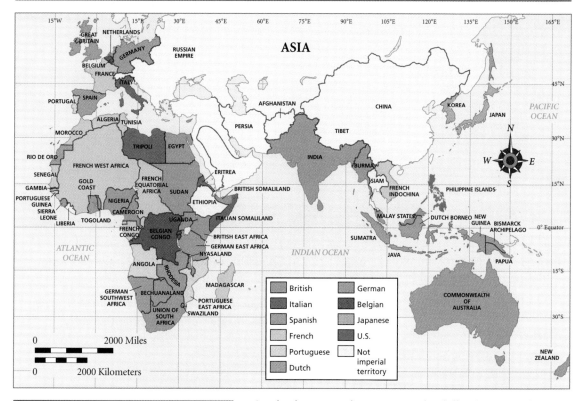

Map Skills

Between 1850 and 1900, the world went through great change. By 1900, a few powerful nations dominated the map. Many countries in Europe had huge empires in Africa and Asia. The European powers divided nearly all of Africa among themselves. Outsiders also controlled much of Asia. This map shows European and American imperialism in Africa, Europe, and Asia.

Study the map, then answer the following questions:

1. Which European power controlled the largest empire?

2. What country controlled the island of Madagascar, off the east African coast?

3. What are the names of three African colonies that Portugal controlled?

4. What were the major Dutch colonies in Asia?

5. What country controlled Australia?

Reading Strategy:
Predicting

Previewing a text helps prepare readers to look for new information—to predict what will come next. A prediction is your best guess about what might happen next:

◆ As you read the text, notice details that could help you make predictions.

◆ While you read, check your predictions.

◆ You may have to change your predictions as you learn more information.

Key Vocabulary Words

Lesson 1 ——————————————

Imperialism Control or influence a powerful nation has over a weaker nation

Colonialism The controlling of colonies; another name for imperialism

Market A place to sell goods

Mother country A nation that controls a colony

Lesson 2 ——————————————

Sphere of influence An area in which only one foreign country can trade

Lesson 3 ——————————————

Protectorate An independent country whose foreign policy is controlled by a major power

Objectives

- ◆ To explain how industrialization and nationalism helped spread imperialism
- ◆ To describe how people's attitudes and the quest for military power helped imperialism

Reading Strategy:
Predicting

Preview the lesson title. Predict what you will learn in this lesson.

Imperialism

Control or influence a powerful nation has over a weaker nation

Colonialism

The controlling of colonies; another name for imperialism

Market

A place to sell goods

Mother country

A nation that controls a colony

Imperialism occurs when a powerful nation controls a weaker nation. During the 1500s, many European countries set up colonies in the Americas. Spain controlled most of Latin America and England controlled most of North America. **Colonialism**, or the controlling of colonies, is another name for imperialism.

By the beginning of the 1800s, however, wars like the American Revolutionary War had changed Europe's opinion about colonialism. Colonies seemed to cause more trouble than they were worth. However, by 1900, the industrialized countries of Europe, Japan, and the United States controlled nearly the whole world. How did this happen? There are many reasons.

How Did Industrialism Help Imperialism?

The Industrial Revolution was one reason why imperialism spread. Factory owners in industrialized nations needed the natural resources and raw materials of other countries. To keep their factories running, they needed coal, iron ore, gold, silver, tin, and copper. They could get these from colonies.

These same nations needed places to sell their manufactured goods. That is, they needed markets. By taking over colonies, they could control **markets.** Each major nation let its colonies buy only those goods manufactured in the **mother country**—the nation that controls a colony.

How Did Nationalism Help Imperialism?

Some countries thought that an empire would make them look important in the eyes of the world. Italy, Germany, Japan, and the United States thought colonies would make them as powerful as England and France. Many countries agreed with the statement that "there has never been a great power without great colonies."

Queen Victoria of England rides on top of an elephant in Delhi, India, in this picture.

Reading Strategy:
Predicting

Think about what you predicted earlier. Was your prediction correct, or do you need to change your prediction?

How Did Militarism Help Imperialism?

In the late 1800s, many countries built up their military power. Sea power was especially important, because it helped nations control trade routes. Mother countries could use their colonies as military bases. Ships from these mother countries could stop at colonial ports to get supplies for the military.

What Attitudes Helped Promote Imperialism?

Many people in Europe and the United States thought that they were better than people from the East. They thought that these people—especially Africans and Asians—were ignorant and uncivilized. Westerners believed that they should bring Christianity and western civilization to these countries.

Lesson 1 Review On a sheet of paper, write the answer to each question. Use complete sentences.

1. What is imperialism?

2. Why did many countries lose interest in imperialism at the beginning of the 1800s?

3. What is the connection between the Industrial Revolution and imperialism?

4. What is the connection between nationalism and imperialism?

5. Why do you think Europeans and Americans thought of themselves as better than people from Africa and Asia?

What do you think ?

Was imperialism a good thing? Explain your answer.

Then and Now

The Color Khaki

During the American Revolution, British soldiers wore white pants, a shiny black hat, and a bright red coat. Because of these bright coats, people called them "redcoats" or "lobster backs." Their uniforms looked great in a parade, but an enemy could easily see these red coats.

Years later, while fighting in India, the British soldiers decided to make the enemy's job harder. They covered their uniforms with brown dirt in the dry season and with mud in the wet season. In time, the British adopted the dull yellowish-brown color of Indian dirt for their battle uniforms. Today, we call this "khaki." It comes from the Indian word for dust.

Objectives

◆ To explain why India was important to Britain

◆ To explain why Southeast Asia was important to Europe

◆ To describe how Japan became imperialistic

By the 1600s, Britain was the greatest sea power in the world. It was also the most industrialized country and the country that did the most trading. Because of all this, Britain wanted colonies in Asia. Soon, the British would brag that "the sun never sets on the British empire."

Why Was India Important to Britain?

The Mogul Empire ruled most of India in the 1500s and 1600s, but it collapsed in 1707. India was then divided into many weak, independent states. By the mid-1700s, France and Britain were fighting each other for control of India. Britain won. At first, the British ruled India through a privately owned company— the British East India Company. However, in 1858, the British government took over direct rule of India.

India won its independence in 1947. But for nearly 100 years, India was very important to Britain. It provided Britain with natural resources and raw materials for industry. Its large population also provided an important market for British goods.

Because India was important to Britain, the British did everything they could to protect India from other imperialistic countries. In the late 1800s, Russia threatened India on its northwest boundaries. To protect India, Britain took over neighboring Afghanistan.

This picture shows the Prince of Wales being welcomed to India.

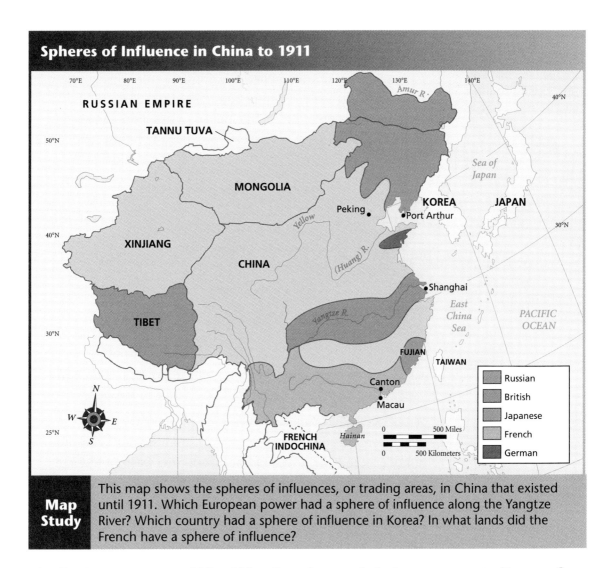

Spheres of Influence in China to 1911

Map Study

This map shows the spheres of influences, or trading areas, in China that existed until 1911. Which European power had a sphere of influence along the Yangtze River? Which country had a sphere of influence in Korea? In what lands did the French have a sphere of influence?

Reading Strategy:
Predicting

Based on what you have just read, predict what will happen to Southeast Asia as imperialism spreads.

Why Was Southeast Asia Important to Europe?

France also threatened British interests in India. France took over much of Southeast Asia, an area that became known as French Indochina. (Today, this area includes the countries of Vietnam, Laos, and Cambodia.) The British took over Burma to keep the French from expanding westward. (India lies to the west of Burma, now called Myanmar.) Soon Ceylon, Malaya, and Singapore also fell under British control.

When Did Europe Insist on More Trade with China?

China lies east of India. For years Chinese rulers had allowed only limited trade with other countries. By the late 1800s, however, this limited trade no longer satisfied the Europeans. They forced China to give them special trade rights. After 1842, Great Britain, France, Germany, and Russia took over Chinese land and important sea ports. These nations divided China up into four different trading areas. Each European power controlled the trade in one of these areas. Historians call this a **sphere of influence.** The Europeans said that China was still an independent country. However, its rulers had no say in the European-controlled trade.

What Happened in Japan in 1867?

For a while, people thought that Japan, too, might fall to Europe's imperialism. However, a revolution in 1867 ended the rule of the shogun and returned political power to Emperor Meiji. This revolution brought great change to Japan.

After 1867, new leaders governed Japan in the emperor's name. They introduced many reforms, and Japan set out to become a modern, industrialized nation. It adopted western ideas in transportation and education. It abolished feudalism. Then the Japanese leaders wrote a constitution based on the German system Bismarck had developed.

How Did Japan Become Imperialistic?

Next, Japan began to develop a western-style army. In 1876, its leaders passed a law that ordered all young men to serve in the army. Soon Japan had a modern army and navy. Japan used its new military power to become imperialistic. From 1894 to 1895, it went to war with China. China lost and had to give Japan some of its territory.

In 1904, Japan went to war with Russia and won again. It took over Korea and gained important trading rights in Russian-controlled lands in China. Like many European countries, Japan was now an imperialistic world power.

Word Bank
Afghanistan
France
Great Britain
Japan
Russia

Lesson 2 Review On a sheet of paper, use the words from the Word Bank to complete each sentence correctly.

1. In 1858, _____ took over direct rule of India.

2. In the late 1800s, Great Britain took over _____.

3. In the late 1800s, _____ took over much of Southeast Asia.

4. _____ became a military power after its revolution in 1867.

5. Japan became a world power after it defeated China in 1895 and _____ in 1904.

What do you think ?

China was once the most powerful and richest country in the world. But in the 1800s, Europeans began to control its trade. Why did that happen?

Objectives

◆ To identify colonies that Britain controlled in Africa

◆ To Identify other countries that controlled colonies in Africa

◆ To describe how Europeans treated native people

Reading Strategy: Predicting

Based on the first two lessons in this chapter, how do you think the Africans will be treated by other countries?

Protectorate

An independent country whose foreign policy is controlled by a major power

As you know, Europeans wanted colonies in Asia. They wanted them in Africa, too. In the 1870s, Europeans raced one another for colonies there.

What Colonies Did Britain Control in Africa?

By the end of the 1800s, Great Britain controlled what are now the nations of Sudan, Nigeria, Ghana, Kenya, and Uganda. In 1900, it took over Nigeria. South Africa became a British colony in 1909.

In 1859, workers began to build the Suez Canal. When it was finished over 10 years later, it connected the Mediterranean and Red Seas. The canal made the trip from Europe to India and the Far East much shorter. In 1875, Britain took control of the canal.

The Suez Canal was finished in 1869. It links the Mediterranean Sea and the Red Sea. This image shows the opening ceremony of this important waterway.

A few years later, Egypt became a British **protectorate.** As a protectorate, Egypt stayed independent, but Britain controlled its foreign policy. In return, Britain protected Egypt from attacks by other countries.

How Big Was the French Empire in Africa?

By 1847, France had gained control of Algeria. Soon, France established the largest European empire in Africa. This empire stretched 2,500 miles from the Atlantic Ocean eastward to Sudan. France's holdings in Africa were large, but not rich. Still, other countries respected France for having such a large empire.

Writing About History

Imagine you are attending the meeting in Berlin in 1900 as a representative from Africa. Write a short speech telling the European countries how you feel about having them decide boundaries in your country.

How Big Was the German Empire in Africa?

Germany united as a nation in 1871. It entered the race for African colonies late. Even so, by 1900, only France and Britain had larger empires in Africa. Germany's colonies were far apart and not rich. However, its military strength worried other European countries. When Germany asked these countries to come to a meeting in Berlin, they came. There they talked about African boundaries. However, no one asked any Africans to come to the meeting.

What Other European Countries Controlled Africa?

Many other nations had colonies in Africa. Spain and Portugal had the oldest colonies. Belgium had a large empire in central Africa. Italy, which came late to Africa, had little success there. It tried to take over Ethiopia, but was defeated. In 1912, Italy did take control of Tripoli in what is now the nation of Libya. Tripoli was large, but poor.

Many European nations scrambled for empires, but some nations got little or nothing of value. They felt angry at those who got wealth from their colonies. This led to fighting.

Reading Strategy:
Predicting

Think about your prediction. Was it accurate? Why or why not?

Was Imperialism Good or Bad?

Europeans said that imperialism was good. It brought great improvements in health, transportation, and education to Africa and Asia. It introduced the ideas of constitutional government. It also brought jobs and industry to the colonies.

However, many of the colonial people thought that imperialism was bad. They felt that Europeans got more out of imperialism than they did. Factories in Africa and Asia supplied cheap goods to Europe. But these factories—owned by Europeans—destroyed native industry and many people lost their jobs.

Also, the colonial people had no control over their government or their country's natural resources. Europeans took the best land and the richest sources of gold, iron, silver, copper, or other valuable natural resources found in the ground.

How Did Europeans Treat Native People?

Europeans thought they were better than the native people of Africa and Asia. They tried to change the religion, the language, and the way of life of these colonized people. This showed that they had little respect for native culture and customs. In time, this led to a wave of nationalism among the people of Africa and Asia.

Lesson 3 Review On a sheet of paper, write the letter of the answer that correctly completes each sentence.

1. The Suez Canal connected the Mediterranean Sea and the _____ Sea.

   A Algerian   **B** Asian   **C** Black   **D** Red

2. By 1847, France had gained control of _____.

   A Algeria   **B** Sudan   **C** Germany   **D** Britain

3. In 1875, _____ took control of the Suez Canal.

   A Britain   **B** Germany   **C** Italy   **D** Nigeria

4. Italy tried to take over _____, but was defeated.

   A Belgium   **B** Britain   **C** Ethiopia   **D** Spain

5. By 1900, only France and Britain had African empires larger than _____.

   A Belgium   **B** Germany   **C** Spain   **D** Egypt

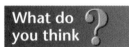

What do you think

Why would Europeans want Africans to give up their language, religion, and customs?

Biography

Leopold II of Belgium: 1835–1909

Leopold II was born in the Belgian capital of Brussels. At age 20, he entered the Belgian senate. As a senator, he urged the Belgian government to acquire colonies in Africa. When the government did not cooperate, Leopold used his own money to pay for an expedition to central Africa. In 1865, Leopold became king of Belgium, and in 1885, he founded the Congo Free State. Leopold used a private army to force Africans in the area to work. They helped Leopold gather a huge personal fortune. About a year before his death, Leopold turned over the Congo Free State to the Belgian government. It was renamed the Belgian Congo.

"That Was No Brother"

The first meeting between white explorers and Africans must have been terrifying to both groups. The Africans had never seen white-skinned people before. The whites were far from home and few in number compared to the Africans. Misunderstandings were likely to occur. This excerpt describes such a meeting from an African's viewpoint.

When we heard that the man with the white flesh was journeying down the [river] we were open-mouthed with astonishment. We stood still. All night long the drums announced the strange news— a man with white flesh! That man, we said to ourselves, has a white skin. He will be one of our brothers who were drowned in the river. All life comes from the water, and in the water he has found life. Now he is coming . . . home. . . .

We will prepare a feast, I ordered. We will go to meet our brother and escort him into the village with rejoicing! We donned our ceremonial garb. We assembled the great canoes. We listened for the gong which would announce our brother's presence . . . Presently the cry was heard: He is approaching. . . . Now he enters the river! Halloh! We swept forward, my canoe leading, . . . to meet the first white man our eyes had beheld, and to do him honor.

But as we drew near his canoes there were loud reports, bang! bang! and fire staves spat bits of iron at us. We were paralyzed with fright; our mouths hung wide open and we could not shut them. Things such as we had never seen, never heard of, never dreamed of— they were the work of evil spirits! Several of my men plunged into the water. . . . Some screamed dreadfully, others . . . were dead, and blood flowed from little holes in their bodies. "War! That is war!" I yelled. "Go back!" The canoes sped back to our village with all the strength our spirits could impart to our arms.

That was no brother! That was the worst enemy our country had ever seen. . . .

Now tell me: has the white man dealt fairly by us? Oh, do not speak to me of him! You call us wicked men, but you white men are much more wicked! You think because you have guns you can take away our land and our possessions. You have sickness in your heads, for that is not justice.

Document-Based Questions

1. Who did the Africans think the white man was?

2. How did the Africans prepare to greet the white man?

3. How did the white man greet the Africans?

4. Why does the writer call white men wicked?

5. After reading the excerpt, what is your opinion of what the white man did?

Source: From The Quest for Africa. *© 1957 by Dr. Heinrich Schiffers, G. P. Putnam's Sons, New York.*

"Dr. Livingstone, I Presume?"

For many years, Africa was called the unexplored continent. The African desert made it hard to travel there by land. Africa's rivers had many waterfalls and rapids that made travel difficult.

In the 19th century, religious explorers set out for Africa. They wanted to bring Christianity and education to the Africans. One of the most famous was David Livingstone. Livingstone went to Africa to spread Christianity. He also hated slavery and wanted to end the slave trade. In time, he became well known and was loved by many Africans.

Between 1841 and 1873, Livingstone made three long trips to Africa. In 1849, he crossed the vast Kalahari Desert. On this trip he explored the Zambezi River. Six years later, he followed that river eastward to the coast. On that trip, he explored a giant waterfall. He named it Victoria Falls after the English queen, Queen Victoria.

In 1865, he set out to find the source of the Nile River. He began at Cape Town on the southern tip of Africa and went north. For many years nothing was heard from him. Many people thought he had died or become lost.

An American newspaper, the *New York Herald,* sent a reporter to find Livingstone. The reporter, Henry Stanley, traveled for 126 days in search of Livingstone. He sent back daily accounts of what he was seeing and learning in Africa. Some African guides took him to Ujiji on Lake Tanganyika. In his newspaper account, Stanley described what happened next. "The expedition at last comes to a halt. . . . I alone have a few more steps to make. . . . As I come nearer I see the white face of an old man. . . .

Henry Stanley met up with David Livingstone near Lake Tanganyika in Africa.

We raise our hats and I say, "Dr. Livingstone, I presume?"

The two men became friends and explored together. By the end of the trip, Africa fascinated Stanley. In 1873, Dr. Livingstone died. Stanley continued to explore.

Explorers like Livingstone and Stanley were very important in the scramble for African territory. Their writings and speeches made people more interested in Africa. They also convinced some people that slavery was evil and should be stopped.

Wrap-Up

1. Why did African geography discourage its exploration?

2. Why did the missionary explorers go to Africa?

3. What river and waterfall did Livingstone explore on his expeditions?

4. On his first trip to Africa, for whom did Henry Stanley work? What did he do?

5. How did Livingstone and Stanley contribute to the scramble for Africa?

- In imperialism or colonialism, a stronger nation controls weaker ones for its own benefit. The Industrial Revolution contributed to this policy. Factory owners needed raw materials from colonies and used them as markets for their goods.

- Countries believed that having colonies made them important world powers. Since sea power was especially important, colonies were used as naval bases.

- In Asia, Britain took control of India, Burma, Ceylon, Malaya, and Singapore. France took Indochina.

- The Industrial Revolution made colonies into sources of raw materials and markets. Imperialism made large parts of Asia and Africa into European colonies.

- After 1842, Britain, France, Germany, and Russia divided China into trading areas. They were called spheres of influence.

- After 1867, Japan modernized and went to war against China and then Russia. It took over Korea and won trading rights in China.

- European powers divided Africa into colonies. Britain controlled Egypt and the Suez Canal, South Africa, and several other colonies. French colonies were mainly in West Africa. Germany, Portugal, Spain, and Belgium also had colonies.

Chapter 24   REVIEW

Word Bank

Algeria

Bismarck

British East India
  Company

China

Great Britain

India

Japan

Meiji

Mogul Empire

Suez Canal

On a sheet of paper, use the words from the Word Bank to complete each sentence correctly.

1. _____ won its independence in 1947.

2. After 1842, Great Britain, France, Germany, and Russia divided _____ up into four different trading areas.

3. Emperor _____ began to make Japan a modern and powerful nation.

4. _____ ruled most of India in the 1500s and 1600s.

5. _____ defeated Russia in 1904 and won control of Korea.

6. The _____ connected the Mediterranean and Red Seas.

7. After 1867, new leaders in Japan wrote a constitution based on the German system _____ had developed.

8. The British ruled India through their _____.

9. By the end of the 1800s, _____ controlled what are now the nations of Sudan, Nigeria, Ghana, Kenya, and Uganda.

10. By 1847, France had gained control of _____.

On a sheet of paper, write the letter of the answer that correctly completes each sentence.

11. A nation's warlike policy or practice is called _____.

    A imperialism   **C** nationalism
    B colonialism   **D** militarism

12. The control by a powerful nation of a weaker one is _____.

    A militarism   **C** nationalism
    B imperialism   **D** Kaiser

13. Europeans said that imperialism brought _____ to Africa and Asia.

    A improvements in health   **C** better education
    B jobs and industry   **D** all of the above

14. By the 1600s, _____ was the greatest sea power in the world.

    A Korea   **B** India   **C** Britain   **D** China

15. In 1904, Japan went to war with _____ and won.

    A Russia   **B** China   **C** Germany   **D** France

16. By 1900, only Great Britain had a larger empire in Africa than _____.

    A France   **B** Germany   **C** China   **D** Russia

On a sheet of paper, write the answer to each question. Use complete sentences.

17. What is imperialism?

18. Which countries became imperial powers during the 19th century?

Critical Thinking On a sheet of paper, write your response to each question. Use complete sentences.

19. Do you believe imperialism was more a force for good or a force for evil? Explain your answer.

20. Why do you think Europeans gained control over Africa so easily?

Test-Taking Tip

Restate the test directions in your own words. Tell yourself what you are expected to do.

Unit 5

Compare and Contrast

Comparing and contrasting reveals how things are alike and how they are different. People, ideas, and events are sometimes compared and contrasted in writing. Look for words that signal comparing and contrasting when you read.

> To compare, ask: "How are these things alike?"
>
> To contrast, ask: "How are these things different?"

- To decide if things are being compared, look for words, such as:

> also   both   like   similar
>
> Cavour, like Garibaldi, was a leader in the unification of Italy.

- To decide if things are being contrasted, look for words, such as:

> but   however   instead
> not   only   while
>
> Cavour was called the "brain" of the revolution while Garibaldi was called the "sword."

Decide whether each of these sentences compares or contrasts.

1. Mazzini's revolt was unsuccessful; however, Cavour's gained Sardinia's freedom.

2. Cavour worked to unite the northern Italian states while Garibaldi fought in the south.

3. Both Cavour and Garibaldi were Italian heroes.

4. Germany, like Italy, had many independent states.

5. Ironically, it was not a German, but Napoleon, who began German unification.

Compare and contrast the effects of imperialism. Focus on what happened between imperialistic European nations and the named areas. In your notebook, write one sentence about each item. Be sure to use words that compare and contrast.

6. India

7. Southeast Asia

8. China

9. Japan

10. Egypt

- Nationalism means that a group of people have one language, one culture, one government, and a common history.

- Giuseppe Mazzini was called the soul of Italian independence because he stood for its spirit of freedom.

- Count Camillo di Cavour was known as the brain of Italian unity. He got French support for Sardinia's war against Austria.

- Giuseppe Garibaldi was called the sword of Italian independence because of his military accomplishments. He and his Red Shirts freed Sicily.

- The German Revolution of 1848 failed. The Prussian ruler refused to become king of all the German states. German nationalists believed only Prussia could unite Germany.

- Prussia was the largest German state. In 1862, Otto von Bismarck became Prussia's prime minister. Bismarck did not believe in democratic rule.

- Bismarck used militarism to conquer the German states. He defeated Austria in seven weeks. A new empire, Austria-Hungary, was formed.

- In the Franco-Prussian War of 1870, Prussia defeated France and won French territory. The remaining independent German states joined Prussia to become Germany.

- In imperialism, a stronger nation controls weaker ones. The Industrial Revolution contributed to this because Europeans needed the raw materials and markets in Asia and Africa.

- Countries believed that having colonies made them important world powers. Since sea power was important, colonies were used as naval bases.

- In Asia, Britain took control of India, Burma, Ceylon, Malaya, and Singapore. France took Indochina.

- Many Europeans thought that imperialism was good because it improved health, transportation, and education. Also, it brought jobs and industry to the colonies.

- Many of the colonial people thought imperialism was bad. European factories in Africa and Asia destroyed native industry. The colonial people had no control over their government or natural resources.

- After 1842, Britain, France, Germany, and Russia divided China into trading areas, or spheres of influence.

- After 1867, Japan modernized and went to war against China and then Russia. It won Korea and trading rights in China.

"Human beings come in all sizes and shapes and in a variety of colors. This rich diversity is match by an equal diversity in regard to religion beliefs and political ideologies. We are thrown together on this planet. . . . That is why the Charter imposes the imperative on all human beings to . . . live together in peace with one another as good neighbors."

~U Thant, Secretary-General of the United Nations (1962–1971), speaking in 1964

Unit 6

World Wars and Revolutions

Wars unlike history had ever seen before filled the first half of the 20th century. World War I and World War II were large and devastating. Millions of people were killed or injured.

You will learn how World War I began in 1914 and lasted four long years. During this time, a revolution started in Russia. You will see how and why it started. After World War I, you will see how World War II started in 1939. After World War II, you will see how the United Nations formed. You will also learn how this organization got involved in a war in Korea in 1950 to try to prevent the spread of Communism.

25

World War I and the Russian Revolution

Y ou learned about imperialism, nationalism, and militarism in earlier chapters. Now you will see how these caused World War I. This war was unlike any before it. It featured modern weapons, terrible fighting conditions, and great loss of life. In this chapter, you will learn how it started, how it was fought, how it ended, and what it meant for those involved. You will also learn how powerful groups started a revolution in Russia.

Goals for Learning

◆ To explain how imperialism, nationalism, and militarism caused war

◆ To identify the countries that fought in the war

◆ To describe the different goals the Big Four powers had at the peace conference

◆ To describe the social, economic, and political effects of World War I

◆ To describe life in czarist Russia

◆ To list the causes and effects of the Revolution of 1905

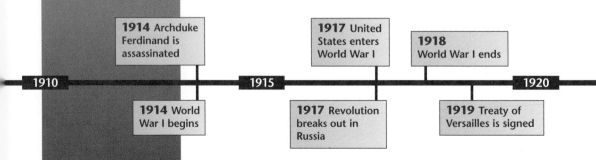

1914 Archduke Ferdinand is assassinated

1917 United States enters World War I

1918 World War I ends

1910

1915

1920

1914 World War I begins

1917 Revolution breaks out in Russia

1919 Treaty of Versailles is signed

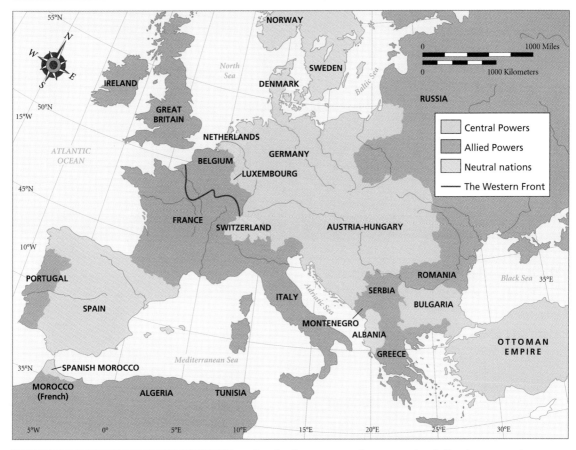

Map Skills

During World War I, Europe was divided into two alliances. Germany and Austria-Hungary were the major Central Powers. France, Russia, and Great Britain were the main Allied Powers. Some countries were neutral. That is, they took neither side. This map shows the central, allied, and neutral powers in Europe during World War I. It also shows the western front.

Study the map and answer the following questions:

1. To what alliance did Italy belong?

2. To what alliance did Bulgaria belong?

3. Where was the western front?

4. What are the names of three neutral countries shown on this map?

5. German U-boats were an important weapon against British naval power. In what sea would they have been most effective?

Reading Strategy:
Text Structure

Readers can look at the organization of the text to help them identify the most important information.

◆ Before you begin reading this chapter, look at the chapter title, the names of the lessons and the sections, the boldfaced words, and photographs.

◆ You will notice that the section titles are in the form of questions. The answer to each question is provided in the paragraph(s) in that section. In this way, the text is structured in a question and answer format.

Key Vocabulary Words

Lesson 1
Rival One who tries to outdo another country or person

Lesson 2
Central Powers The allied nations of Germany, Austria-Hungary, Turkey, and Bulgaria

Allied Powers The allied nations of Great Britain, France, Russia, Italy, and eventually, the United States and Japan

Trench A long narrow ditch

Barbed wire Wire that has sharp metal spikes on it

Unrestricted warfare War that is not limited to a certain area or boundary

Armistice An agreement to stop fighting

Lesson 3
Reparation Payment for war damage

Treaty of Versailles The treaty that ended World War I

League of Nations A group of leaders from many nations who met to solve problems between countries

Lesson 5
Autocracy A government in which one person rules with unlimited power

Standard of living A way to judge how well a person or a family is living

Democratic Having to do with a government in which all people have equal rights

Duma The Russian parliament

Lesson 6
Abdicate To give up power as a ruler

Socialism An economic and political theory in which the government owns and controls the major means of production

Objectives

◆ To explain how mistrust of one another led powerful nations to build bigger militaries

◆ To identify the event that directly started the war

Reading Strategy:
Text Structure

Preview this lesson. Notice the headings, features, and boldfaced words.

Rival

One who tries to outdo another country or person

In Chapter 24, you read about the powerful imperialistic nations of France, Great Britain, Germany, Austria-Hungary, Italy, and Russia. These imperialistic powers did not have equal shares of land and riches, so they became rivals. That is, they tried to outdo one another. At first, this led to jealousy. Then it led to mistrust. Finally, it led to war.

Why Did Imperial Nations Become Militarized?

As they became more mistrustful of one another, these imperial nations built bigger armies and navies. For example, Wilhelm II, Germany's kaiser, wanted his navy to be equal to Britain's. Britain then had to build an even larger navy. All these industrialized nations also built bigger, more deadly weapons. Countries were becoming more militarized.

What Was the Alliance System?

At first, the countries of Europe tried to prevent war. They formed alliances and agreed to aid one another if attacked. After all, one country would surely not attack another if that meant fighting with several countries instead of one. By 1914, two **rival** alliances were in place. Germany, Austria-Hungary, and Italy made up the Triple Alliance. Great Britain, France, and Russia made up the Triple Entente.

The assassination of Archduke Franz Ferdinand and his wife, Sophie, was the spark that caused World War I. This photo shows Ferdinand and Sophie just before they were killed.

What Event Started World War I?

Nationalism had helped nations like Italy and Germany to unite. But by the 1900s, the spirit of nationalism had become a problem for some nations.

Serbs living in Austria-Hungary wanted to be part of Serbia, a neighboring country. Many Serbs lived in Sarajevo, which was a city in Austria-Hungary. To try to improve relations with the Serbs, the Austrian emperor sent his nephew Franz Ferdinand to Sarajevo. On Sunday, June 28, 1914, Ferdinand and Sophie, his wife, were killed as they rode through the streets of Sarajevo.

Austria-Hungary blamed the Serbians. On July 28, 1914, Austria declared war on Serbia. Next, Russia said it would protect Serbia. A few days later, Germany declared war on Russia. France then came into the war in support of Serbia. Next, Great Britain honored its alliance with France. What started out as a small revolt exploded into a big war.

Lesson 1 Review On a sheet of paper, write the answer to each question. Use complete sentences.

1. How did imperialism cause World War I?
2. How did militarism cause World War I?
3. How did the alliance system cause World War I?
4. How did nationalism cause World War I?
5. What event in Sarajevo led to World War I?

What do you think

What could have kept World War I from happening?

Reading Strategy:
Text Structure

As you read the next paragraphs, use a graphic organizer to record the countries of the Central Powers and the Allied Powers.

Objectives

◆ To identify the Central Powers and the Allied Powers

◆ To describe trench warfare and new weapons used in World War I

◆ To explain why the United States entered the war

◆ To describe how the war ended

Central Powers

The allied nations of Germany, Austria-Hungary, Ottoman Empire, and Bulgaria

Allied Powers

The allied nations of Great Britain, France, Russia, Italy, and eventually, the U.S. and Japan

When fighting started in August 1914, millions of soldiers marched eagerly to battle. They thought they would be home by Christmas. But Christmas came and went and still they fought. In fact, they fought for four long years.

On one side of the war were Austria-Hungary, Germany, Bulgaria, and the Ottoman Empire. Historians call them the **Central Powers** because they were countries in central Europe.

Historians call the other side the **Allied Powers,** or the Allies. The Allies included France, Russia, Great Britain, Italy, and several smaller countries. Italy, originally allied with Germany, had now switched sides. Later, Japan and the United States joined the Allies.

Where Was the Western Front of the War?

The Central Powers and the Allies fought World War I all over the world. During the earliest months of the war, most fighting took place in Belgium and northern France. This was known as the western front. Germany wanted a quick victory over France. It could then turn east and defeat Russia on the eastern front. When the Allies stopped the Germans at the Marne River, Germany's hope for a quick victory over France ended.

Soldiers spent much of World War I fighting in trenches. Many new weapons made World War I the first modern war.

Many submarines, or "U-boats," were used to sink enemy ships in World War I.

What Was Trench Warfare?

For the next two years, both sides fought a bitter war on the western front. Soldiers dug **trenches,** or long, narrow ditches, where they ate, slept, and watched the enemy. **Barbed wire** protected these trenches. This type of wire has sharp metal spikes on it. Between the two series of trenches was an area the soldiers called "no man's land."

Many soldiers died fighting in the trenches, but neither side won much territory. For example, in the Battle of Verdun in 1916, each side lost more than 300,000 men. However, the German army advanced only four miles.

What Weapons Were Used in World War I?

During World War I, nations fought in the air for the first time. However, the use of airplanes in World War I was limited. But both sides used submarines on a large scale. Germany called its submarines U-boats. They sank many Allied and neutral ships carrying food and supplies.

Writing About History

In World War I, most American soldiers had never traveled far from home before. Imagine that you are an 18-year-old soldier in France. Write a letter home. What is happening? How does it feel?

Both sides also developed new weapons. The machine gun changed war forever. This type of gun fires bullets rapidly without reloading. It fired so fast that the only way an army could protect itself was to take cover in trenches.

Early in 1915, the Germans introduced poison gas. The Allies quickly followed the German example.

This cartoon shows the Allies fighting the Central Powers, represented here as a dragon.

This deadly gas settled in the trenches and blinded and choked the soldiers there. But gas was risky. If the wind suddenly shifted, the gas could drift back to the troops using the gas.

The tank was another new weapon. The British introduced it in 1916 to smash through the barbed wire that protected the trenches. By the end of the war, both sides were using tanks.

Who Fought on the Eastern Front?

Russians and Serbs fought Austrians, Germans, and Ottoman Turks along the eastern front. Allied soldiers were poorly prepared and sometimes went to battle without weapons. The Central Powers forced the Russians to retreat. But the Russian army kept thousands of German troops fighting for over three years.

In 1916, a million Russian soldiers died in an attack on Austria. Short on food, guns, and supplies, the Russians grew tired of war. They blamed their problems on the czar.

In 1918, after a revolution in Russia, Russia and Germany signed the Treaty of Brest Litovsk. It ended the war for Russia. Because of the treaty, Russia had to give Finland, Estonia, Latvia, Lithuania, the Ukraine, and part of Poland to Germany.

Where Else Did Fighting Take Place?

As the war expanded, fighting broke out in many places besides the western and eastern fronts. There was fighting in Italy and Asia. Japan moved to take over areas of China that were under German influence. Australia and New Zealand forces took over some islands Germany held in the Pacific. Some of the heaviest battles were fought in Turkey, part of the Ottoman Empire. The war even extended into Africa, where British and French troops took over former German colonies.

When Did the United States Enter the War?

In 1917, Germany announced that it would begin **unrestricted warfare** in waters around Britain. That is, German U-boats would sink any ship—even ones from neutral countries—that sailed into the waters surrounding the British Isles.

Technology Connection

German U-boats

Germans launched their first U-boat (for the German word *Unterseeboot,* meaning "undersea boat") in 1906. During World War I, Germany used U-boats in many successful attacks on British ships. Germany built more than 400 new, larger, and more powerful U-boats that sank more than 4,000 ships.

The Germans put hundreds of U-boats into use in World War II. During three days in October 1940, eight of these vessels destroyed 38 British ships. Not one of those U-boats was damaged. However, Germany was eventually overcome by the Allied forces. By the end of World War II, Germany had lost 821 U-boats. Its largest remaining boat, the U-234, was forced to surrender by an American destroyer in the North Atlantic as the war ended.

Germany knew that this plan would lead to war with the United States, which had been a neutral country. Its leaders thought that they could force Britain to surrender before American troops and supplies arrived in Europe. On April 6, 1917, the U.S. Congress declared war on Germany. Soon more than a million American soldiers landed in Europe.

When Did World War I End?

By 1918, after four long years of war, both the Central Powers and the Allies were tired. Germany no longer had trained troops to replace those killed in battle. The fresh American troops tipped the balance in favor of the Allies. On November 11, 1918, Germany agreed to an **armistice,** or an end to fighting. On the 11th day at the 11th hour of the 11th month, the great war ended.

Then and Now

The World War I "Doughboy"

In the early 1900s, most men became soldiers just for the length of a war. Then they returned to civilian life. World War I soldiers were called "doughboys." This may be because the buttons on soldiers' uniforms looked like doughboys—what we now call doughnuts. When America entered the war, the army was very small. A draft law was passed in 1917, calling up all men between 21 and 30. The ages later became 18 to 45. Draftees received combat training. They learned how to be part of a bayonet charge, use a gas mask, and fire a rifle.

Today, the United States has a professional volunteer army. Volunteers sign up for a set number of years. They can then choose whether or not to re-enlist. Besides combat training, the army trains people in medicine, languages, computers, and other fields. It has changed in other ways, too. The military was segregated in World War I. African Americans served in separate army units. In 1918, there were no black marines and few women in the military. Today, these groups make up almost 25 percent of the army.

Lesson 2 Review On a sheet of paper, write the letter of the answer that correctly completes each sentence.

1. _____ fought on the Allied side in World War I.

   A Turkey   **C** Austria
   B Bulgaria   **D** Great Britain

2. On the western front, soldiers lived in _____ and faced one another across a "no man's land."

   A tanks   **C** trenches
   B airplanes   **D** U-boats

3. World War I lasted for _____ years.

   A two   **C** six
   B four   **D** seven

4. The United States entered the war in _____.

   A 1914   **C** 1916
   B 1915   **D** 1917

5. World War I ended in _____.

   A 1917   **C** 1919
   B 1918   **D** 1920

What do you think ?

Germany decided to attack any ship in the waters around Britain. Why did this lead to war with the United States?

Objectives

◆ To identify Woodrow Wilson's Fourteen Points

◆ To describe what other countries wanted after the war

◆ To describe the League of Nations

Reparation

Payment for war damage

Reading Strategy:
Text Structure

As you read, look for words like *first, then, next,* and *finally.* These words will help you understand the order of the text

World War I ended in November 1918, and the Allies won. The next year, the Allied leaders met at Versailles in France to create a peace treaty. The "Big Four"—Britain, France, Italy, and the United States—made most of the big decisions. Each of them wanted something different from the peace meeting.

What Did the United States Want?

President Woodrow Wilson represented the United States at the peace meeting. He had written a peace plan called the Fourteen Points. Part of his plan was to end secret treaties between nations. He also wanted to reduce the size of armies and navies in each nation. Most of all, Wilson wanted to organize a league of nations to keep the peace.

What Did Other Countries Want?

The leaders from France, Great Britain, and Italy had plans that were different from Wilson's Fourteen Points. France had suffered greatly during the war. Premier Clemenceau, who represented France, wanted Germany to make **reparations** for the war. That is, he wanted Germany to pay for the cost of the war. He also wanted Germany to return land to France.

Prime Minister Lloyd George of Great Britain also wanted Germany to pay for the war. In addition, Britain wanted Germany's African colonies. However, they did not want the French to become too powerful. Prime Minister Vittorio Orlando represented Italy at the meeting. He wanted the Allies to honor a treaty that had been signed in 1915. The Allies had promised to give Italy more land if it entered the war on the Allied side.

The four Allied leaders at the peace conference were (from left): Vittorio Orlando (Italy), Lloyd George (Great Britain), George Clemenceau (France), and Woodrow Wilson (United States).

What Happened to Germany?

The leaders at Versailles finally agreed to a treaty. The **Treaty of Versailles** forced Germany to accept responsibility for causing the war. Germany also had to pay for the cost of the war. In addition, Germany gave the land of Alsace and Lorraine to France. It divided its African colonies between France and Great Britain. It also gave its colonies in the Pacific to Japan. Even though the German leaders thought the Allies had treated them unfairly, they signed the treaty in 1919.

What Happened to the Austro-Hungarian Empire?

The Treaty of Versailles broke up the Austro-Hungarian Empire. Austria and Hungary became two countries. The treaty also created two new countries—Yugoslavia and Czechoslovakia. Some Austro-Hungarian land went to Poland, Latvia, and Romania. The treaty carved Finland, Estonia, Latvia, and Lithuania out of the western part of the old Russian Empire.

What Was the League of Nations?

The Treaty of Versailles created the **League of Nations** to try to keep peace. This was a group of leaders from many nations who met to solve problems between countries. These leaders met in Geneva, Switzerland, to talk over their problems. However, the League was weak because some countries did not join. Also, the League could not force countries to obey its rulings.

Treaty of Versailles

The treaty that ended World War I

League of Nations

A group of leaders from many nations who met to solve problems between countries

Lesson 3 Review On a sheet of paper, write the answer to each question. Use complete sentences.

1. What countries were represented at the peace meeting in France?

2. What were the Fourteen Points?

3. Why did Germany think the Treaty of Versailles treated it unfairly?

4. What two new countries were created by the Treaty of Versailles?

5. Why was the League of Nations weak?

What do you think ?

The Treaty of Versailles treated Germany and the other Central Powers poorly. What were the problems this caused for those countries?

Map Study

The top map shows what Europe looked like just before World War I. The bottom map shows Europe after the war. Were there more countries in Europe before or after the war? What happened to Austria-Hungary after the war?

Europe Before World War I

Europe After World War I

Objectives

◆ To explain the loss of life and financial cost of the war

◆ To identify the problems caused by the Treaty of Versailles

Reading Strategy:
Text Structure
─────────────
As you read this lesson, use a graphic organizer to list the social, economic, and political effects of World War I

What Were the Social and Economic Effects of the War?

World War I was the first total war. Cities, farms, factories, and people living at home all become part of a total war. Because of this, there were many social effects of the war. The years between the wars were difficult for people everywhere. Russia, Germany, Austria-Hungary, and France lost a whole generation. A generation is all the people born around the same time. In fact, France lost one out of every five men between the ages of 20 and 44.

World War I also had economic effects. Historians do not know what the war cost. One guess is about $350 billion. Many governments raised taxes and borrowed large sums of money to pay for the war. However, by the end of the war, every major European country was bankrupt. They could not pay off their debts because they had no money. Cities and farms lay in ruins. Many people had no jobs. Because of the war, Europe lost much of its power and wealth. Countries like the United States and Japan took over the European markets.

What Were the Political Effects of the War?

Democracy spread because of the war. In Germany, Austria-Hungary, and Russia, governments elected by the people replaced monarchies. However, in Russia, a dictatorship soon replaced the new democratic government.

Many soldiers were wounded in the war.

The Treaty of Versailles created new countries. But some of these had large numbers of foreign people. For example, Poland and Czechoslovakia had large groups of German-speaking people. This caused problems in the future.

As a result of World War I, the United States emerged as a world power. Its economy was healthier than that of other countries. However, many Americans wanted the United States to stay out of world affairs. This would also create problems in the future.

Lesson 4 Review On a sheet of paper, write the answer to each question. Use complete sentences.

1. What is a "total war"?

2. How did World War I affect the economy of Europe?

3. What happened to the new democratic government of Russia?

4. What was one problem that the Treaty of Versailles caused?

5. What were three effects of World War I?

What do you think ?

How do you think the deaths of so many people in World War I made soldiers feel about the war?

Objectives

◆ To explain what an autocracy is

◆ To identify changes that Alexander II and III made

◆ To describe what happened under the rule of Czar Nicholas II

◆ To explain what happened on Bloody Sunday

Autocracy

A government in which one person rules with unlimited power

Standard of living

A way to judge how well a person or a family is living

Reading Strategy:
Text Structure

Choose an event in this section. Use a graphic organizer to illustrate cause and effect for that event.

One important result of World War I was the Russian Revolution of 1917. In less than a week, rebels overthrew the czar. But people before them had planted the seeds of the revolution.

What Was the Autocracy of Russia?

In the 1800s, Russia was an **autocracy**—a government in which one person rules with unlimited power. In Russia, that person was the czar. He controlled the lives of his people and expected them to obey without question.

In 1855, Alexander II became czar. He ended serfdom and introduced the jury system. He gave Russians more rights, and allowed more people to attend school. Around the same time, the Industrial Revolution reached Russia. When this happened, many farmers left their land to go to the cities to work. Russian cities of St. Petersburg, Moscow, and Baku became centers of industry. The Russian **standard of living**—a way to judge how well a person or family is living—also improved.

People in Russia were experiencing their first taste of freedom. But they wanted more. When the czar refused to give them more rights, the Russian people revolted. During one of these revolts, a young revolutionary killed Czar Alexander.

Czar Alexander II freed the serfs and their families in 1861, ending serfdom in Russia.

Democratic

Having to do with a government in which all people have equal rights

Duma

The Russian parliament

In 1894, Nicholas II became czar. He faced many problems. Educated Russians wanted a more **democratic** government in which all people had equal rights. Instead of listening to his people, Czar Nicholas II tried to get them to think about something else. Nicholas II declared war on Japan in 1904. This was called the Russo-Japanese War. When Russia lost the war, people demanded more change.

One cause of the Russian Revolution was the widespread suffering of peasants. The czar used soldiers called "cossacks" to control the peasants by force.

In 1905, another revolt took place. Russians call this day Bloody Sunday. Workers had marched in peace to the czar's palace in St. Petersburg. They wanted better working conditions, more freedom, and an elected national assembly. The czar's soldiers fired on the crowd and killed hundreds of workers.

After Bloody Sunday, Russian workers refused to work. Riots broke out. Peasants attacked the nobles and burned their estates. The czar promised to give the people more freedom if they would stop the violence. He even agreed to the election of a Russian parliament, or **Duma.** However, Czar Nicholas dismissed the Duma after three months. He believed that he alone had the right to govern.

Word Bank
serfs
Alexander II
Baku
Japan
Sunday

Lesson 5 Review On a sheet of paper, use the words from the Word Bank to complete each sentence correctly.

1. In the late 1800s, the nobles completely controlled the _____.

2. In 1855, _____ ended serfdom.

3. During the Industrial Revolution, the Russian cities of St. Petersburg, Moscow, and _____ became centers of industry.

4. In 1904 Czar Nicholas II declared war on _____.

5. Russian soldiers killed hundreds of workers on January 22, 1905; Russians call this day Bloody _____.

What do you think ?

Why would both Russian serfs and Russian nobles want reform?

Biography

Grigori Rasputin: c. 1872–1916

Rasputin was a Siberian peasant who became a monk and healer. Later, he moved to St. Petersburg. Although Rasputin lived an immoral life, he had an interesting personality.

The royal heir, Alexei, had hemophilia. With this disease, even minor bumps can cause severe bleeding. At that time, the bleeding could not be controlled. Rasputin was somehow able to help Alexei. Czar Nicholas II and Czarina Alexandra then began taking Rasputin's advice about officials and policies. However, Rasputin's advice was not very good, and it caused many problems. To end Rasputin's influence, some nobles assassinated him. First, they poisoned him, but he survived. Then they shot him several times and drowned him.

- To describe socialism
- To explain why Nicholas II gave up his power

Reading Strategy:
Text Structure

The section headings are written as questions. After you read each section, try to answer the question asked in the heading

After the Revolution of 1905, the spirit of rebellion continued to grow in Russia. But the revolutionaries could not agree on how change should happen. Some wanted to limit the czar's power and create a constitutional monarchy like Great Britain's. Others thought a completely new form of government was needed.

How Did World War I Affect Russia?

World War I was probably the single most important cause of the Russian Revolution of 1917. Millions of Russians were killed, wounded, or taken prisoner. The people had to live with little food, fuel, and other needed supplies. They became very angry at Czar Nicholas.

Women marched on St. Petersburg in 1917 demanding bread. This forced Czar Nicholas II to step down as ruler of Russia.

The Russian Orthodox Church

Byzantine missionaries took Christianity to Russia in the 900s. By the 1400s, the Russian Orthodox Church was self-governing. The patriarch, the head of the church, lived in Moscow. For centuries, Orthodox priests and monks had great influence. The church was central in the lives of many ordinary Russians. They kept icons in their homes. Some czars used the church to support their absolute rule.

The Russian Revolution was a disaster for the church. It lost power and property. Still, millions of people remained faithful. After the Soviet Union collapsed in 1991, Russia had a great religious revival. Some Russians have joined other churches. The Russian Orthodox Church, however, remains the most important.

Abdicate

To give up power as a ruler

Socialism

An economic and political theory in which the government owns and controls the major means of production

Why Did Czar Nicholas II Abdicate?

On the morning of February 24, 1917, news came that stores in St. Petersburg had no bread. Women became angry. "We want bread! We want bread!" they shouted. Soon a crowd formed. They carried banners, shouted, and sang. Some of their signs said "End the War" and "Down with the Czar."

His troops even refused to obey him. He had to **abdicate** as ruler. That is, he gave up his power. After the czar abdicated, no one was sure who would govern Russia. Many Russians thought **socialism** would solve the country's problems. Socialism is an economic and political theory in which the government owns and controls the major means of production

What Do Socialists Want?

Under socialism, the government controls the economy of a nation. Representing the people, the government owns all the land, industries, and transportation. The most influential of all the early socialists was a German named Karl Marx.

Lesson 6 Review On a sheet of paper, write the letter of the answer that correctly completes each sentence.

1. Under _____, a government owns all the land, the industries, and the means of transportation.

   A democracy   **C** socialism

   B monarchy   **D** constitutional monarchy

2. _____ was a German who influenced the Russian Revolution.

   A Czar Nicholas II   **C** Alexander II

   B Karl Marx   **D** Rasputin

3. Probably the single most important cause of the Russian Revolution was _____.

   A World War I   **C** a provisional government

   B Bloody Sunday   **D** the Duma

4. During World War I, conditions in Russia got worse because _____.

   A factories could not produce bullets and guns

   B food was scarce

   C millions of soldiers died or were wounded

   D all of the above

5. In 1917, the Russians forced _____ to abdicate.

   A Czar Nicholas II   **C** Alexander II

   B Karl Marx   **D** Rasputin

What do you think ?

Why do you think the czar's soldiers joined the workers who were rebelling on February 25, 1917?

The Next War

This picture, titled "Shadows," shows the bleakness of World War I.

In August 1914, European nations plunged into the Great War. World War I ended four years later. It had destroyed millions of lives. Many soldiers had gone to war with grand ideas of honor and glory. The reality was different. War was wet trenches, poison gas, and artillery fire. Soldiers saw lives being wasted. Their views quickly changed. This change is clear in the poetry written during the war. Early poems are often about heroism. Later poems show shock and anger.

Britain had many fine soldier-poets. One was Siegfried Sassoon. He wrote bitterly, "when it was all said and done, the war was mainly a matter of holes and ditches." The poem that follows is by Wilfred Owen, a young British officer. He was killed a week before the war ended.

War's a joke for me and you,

While we know such dreams are true. Out there, we've walked quite friendly up to Death;

Sat down and eaten with him, cool and bland,
Pardoned his spilling mess-tins in our hand.
We've sniffed the green thick odour of his breath,
Our eyes wept, but our courage didn't writhe.
He's spat at us with bullets and he's coughed
Shrapnel. We chorused when he sang aloft;
We whistled while he shaved us with his scythe.
Oh, Death was never enemy of ours!
We laughed at him, we leagued with him, old chum.
No soldier's paid to kick against his powers.
We laughed, knowing that better men would come,
And greater wars; when each proud fighter brags
He wars on Death for lives; not men for flags.

Document-Based Reading Questions

1. How have the soldiers in this poem become friendly with Death?

2. What weapons has Death used against the soldiers?

3. Death is often pictured with a scythe, a long blade used for cutting grass. How does Owen use that image?

4. Many soldiers could not talk about the war. Would civilians think of death like Owen did in this poem?

5. Owen says that a proud fighter, "Wars on Death for lives; not men for flags." What does he mean?

Death at Sarajevo

June 28, 1914, was a hot Sunday in Sarajevo. Despite the heat, crowds of people filled the streets. They were waiting for Archduke Franz Ferdinand and his wife, Sophie. People were curious to see the archduke. He would be the next emperor of Austria-Hungary. His visit was supposed to improve Austria's image.

Sarajevo was the capital of Bosnia, a small Balkan state. Bosnia's people were Slavs. They had become independent of the Ottoman Empire less than 40 years earlier. Then the Austro-Hungarian Empire had taken control of the area. Many Bosnians hated Austrian rule. They wanted to be part of nearby Serbia, a Slav state. Some joined a secret society known as the Black Hand. Its slogan was "Union or Death."

That June morning, the archduke and duchess rode to the town hall in an open car. With them was the military governor of Bosnia. No one realized that several Black Hand members were waiting along the route. Suddenly a man stepped forward and threw a bomb. It exploded in the street and wounded officers in the next car. The official party went on with the scheduled program. At its end, the archduke decided to visit a wounded officer in the hospital. The duke had his driver stop while he gave him new directions.

Standing only a few feet away was 19-year-old Gavrilo Princip. He was one of the Black Hand members in the plot. Princip pulled out a small gun and fired twice. The first shot struck the Duchess Sophie. She died instantly. The second bullet struck Franz Ferdinand near the heart. He uttered a few last words, then his head fell back. He died a few minutes later.

Police seized Princip, kicking and beating him. They took him to jail. Next, the Austrians arrested every known revolutionary in Sarajevo. Because he was young, Princip was sentenced to only 20 years in jail. That was the maximum sentence.

The sudden, brutal murders shocked the world. Austrian officials blamed Serbia. They were determined to punish Serbia. Austria called on its ally, Germany, for help. Then Austria declared war on Serbia. Serbia asked its ally, Russia, to come to its aid. Within a few days, Russia and Germany had declared war. Soon most of Europe was involved. Members of both European alliances immediately got ready for war. The shots in Sarajevo triggered World War I.

Wrap-Up

1. Who was Franz Ferdinand?

2. Why did many people in Sarajevo dislike Austrian rule?

3. What was the Black Hand?

4. Who killed the archduke and duchess? How was he punished?

5. What were the effects of the shootings at Sarajevo?

- In the late 1800s, powerful European nations competed for both land and military power. They formed alliances to aid each other in case of war. Germany, Austria-Hungary, and Italy made up the Triple Alliance. Great Britain, France, and Russia were the Triple Entente.

- A Serbian nationalist killed Austrian Archduke Franz Ferdinand and his wife in June 1914. This act triggered World War I. The alliance system brought the major European nations into the war.

- The nations in World War I divided into the Central Powers (Austria-Hungary, Germany, Bulgaria, and Turkey) and the Allied Powers (France, Russia, Britain, Italy, and smaller nations). Japan and the United States later joined the Allies.

- World War I relied on trench warfare. New weapons were also used: airplanes, submarines, machine guns, poison gas, and tanks.

- The United States was neutral until April 1917, when Germany declared unrestricted war on shipping. The United States joined the Allies. In November 1918, Germany agreed to an armistice.

- The "Big Four"—Britain, France, Italy, and the United States—shaped the peace treaty. Each nation had different goals.

- The Treaty of Versailles gave Germany's colonies to France, Britain, and Japan. Germany had to give land back to France and pay the costs of war. The treaty broke up the Austro-Hungarian Empire.

- In the 1800s, Russia was an autocracy. The czar was an absolute ruler. More than 80 percent of Russians were serfs.

- In the mid-1800s, Czar Alexander II freed the serfs, reformed education, and gave people more rights. Revolutionaries killed him. His son Nicholas II ignored calls for reform.

- The Industrial Revolution reached Russia in the late 1800s. The standard of living for factory workers improved, but most people remained poor.

- In 1894, Nicholas II became czar. He declared war on Japan in 1904. Russia lost.

- In 1905, workers held a peaceful march in St. Petersburg. Soldiers killed hundreds on that "Bloody Sunday."

- Many Russians wanted socialism, a system in which the government runs a nation's economy.

- World War I made things worse for the Russians. In 1917, a revolution forced Nicholas II to resign. Leaders of the Duma formed a government.

Chapter 25 REVIEW

Word Bank

Alexander II
alliance
armistice
bankrupt
Italy
neutral
Nicholas II
reparations
Russia
U-boat

On a sheet of paper, use the words from the Word Bank to complete each sentence correctly.

1. Before the war, many countries made a(n) _____ with one another and agreed to help one another.

2. Belgium was a(n) _____ country during the war because it chose neither side.

3. The Treaty of Brest Litovsk ended the war for _____.

4. The Germans used the _____, a type of submarine, to destroy Allied ships.

5. On November 11, 1918, Germany agreed to a(n) _____, or an end to the fighting.

6. After World War I ended, the "Big Four" nations—Britain, France, _____, and the United States—met to create a peace treaty.

7. As a result of the war, all the major European countries were _____ and had no money to pay their debts.

8. At Versailles, France demanded that Germany make ____, or payments for war debts.

9. Czar _____ introduced change into Russia and gave his people some freedom.

10. "Bloody Sunday" took place during the rule of Czar _____.

On a sheet of paper, write the letter of the answer that correctly completes each sentence.

11. _____ fought as part of the Central Powers in World War I.

    A Japan   **C** the United States
    B France   **D** Germany

12. During World War I, the industrial nations developed _____.

    A tanks   **C** machine guns
    B poison gas   **D** all of the above

13. _____ represented France at the Versailles peace meeting.

A Clemenceau   **C** George
B Wilson   **D** Ferdinand

14. _____ represented Britain at the peace meeting.

A Orlando   **C** Wilson
B George   **D** Clemenceau

15. Under the czars, Russia was a(n) _____.

A democracy   **C** autocracy
B constitutional monarchy   **D** duma

On a sheet of paper, write the answer to each question.
Use complete sentences.

16. What were the causes of World War I?

17. What were three terms of the Treaty of Versailles?

18. Why did the Russians revolt against Czar Nicholas II?

Critical Thinking On a sheet of paper, write your response to each question. Use complete sentences.

19. If you had been a German in 1919, how would you have felt about the Treaty of Versailles?

20. Do you think having a large and powerful military causes or prevents war? Explain your answer.

Test-Taking Tip

For multiple-choice or word bank questions, cross off answers you know are wrong. Then choose the correct answer from the remaining choices.

26

Nationalism, Revolution, and Totalitarianism Around the World

In this chapter, you will learn about the results of the Russian Revolution. You will witness the creation of Communism and the Soviet Union. You will also learn how nationalism and hard economic times led to the rise of dictators, including the Nazis in Germany. You will see how these changes affected Europe and Asia and set the stage for World War II.

Goals for Learning

◆ To explain how Russia became the Soviet Union

◆ To describe life in the Soviet Union under Stalin

◆ To explain why dictators came to power in Italy

◆ To explain how the Nazis gained power in Germany

◆ To describe how the Chinese began to build a modern nation after the overthrow of the government in 1911

◆ To explain how military leaders took over the government of Japan

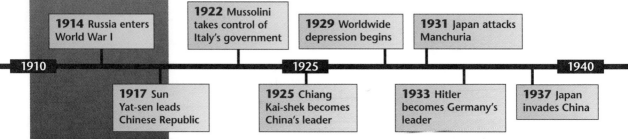

1914 Russia enters World War I

1922 Mussolini takes control of Italy's government

1929 Worldwide depression begins

1931 Japan attacks Manchuria

1910

1925

1940

1917 Sun Yat-sen leads Chinese Republic

1925 Chiang Kai-shek becomes China's leader

1933 Hitler becomes Germany's leader

1937 Japan invades China

The Development of the Soviet Union

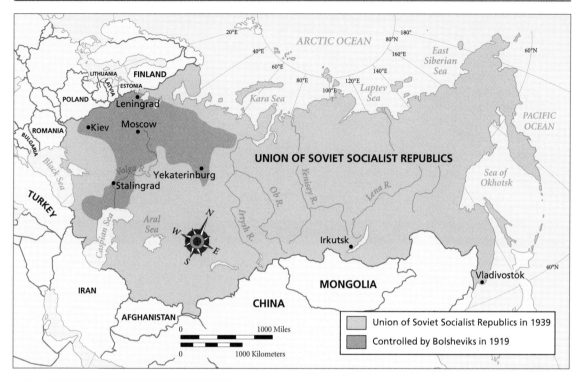

Map Skills

This chapter is about revolution and change in Russia. A group called the Bolsheviks led the revolution. This map shows the area that the Bolsheviks controlled in 1919. The map also shows the border of the Soviet Union in 1939. This was the new nation that formed as a result of this revolution.

Study the map, then answer the following questions:

1. What cities did the Bolsheviks control in 1919?

2. What seas are shown on this map?

3. What rivers are shown on this map?

4. What countries bordered the Soviet Union to the south?

5. What does this map tell you about the size of the Soviet Union in 1939?

Reading Strategy:
Visualizing

When readers create pictures in their head about what they are reading, they are using visualization. This is another strategy that helps readers understand what they are reading. Use the following ways to visualize a text:

◆ Notice the order in which things are happening and what you think might happen next.

◆ Look at the photographs, illustrations, and descriptive words.

◆ Think about experiences in your own life that may add to the images.

Key Vocabulary Words

Lesson 1
Bolshevik A revolutionary socialist group in Russia

Militia A group of people who can be called to military service when something dangerous happens suddenly

Communism An economic system in which there is little private property and the government produces goods

Minority A small group of like people within a larger group

Successor One who follows another in a position

Lesson 2
Heavy industry The manufacturing of products, such as machines and raw materials, for use in other industries

Consumer goods Products that people buy

Collective farm A large farm owned by the government and worked by many peasants

Totalitarian state A government in which a small group totally controls the lives of its country's citizens

Purge To remove from office; to clean by getting rid of unwanted things

Lesson 3
Veteran A person who has served in the military, especially during a war

Fascism A form of government in which a dictator and the dictator's party totally control a government

Lesson 4
Inflation A quick increase in prices

Swastika The Nazi symbol of a cross with its arms bent

Depression A time of economic collapse when businesses lose money and many people become poor

Reichstag The national assembly of the Weimar Republic

Fuehrer The name given to Adolf Hitler meaning "leader"

Gestapo Hitler's secret police force

Lesson 6
Great Depression The worldwide depression that began in the United States in 1929

Objectives

◆ To identify Lenin and the changes the Bolsheviks brought to Russia

◆ To describe the Russian Civil War

◆ To describe how Joseph Stalin came to power

Bolshevik

A revolutionary socialist group in Russia

Militia

A group of people who can be called to military service when something dangerous happens suddenly

Communism

An economic system in which there is little private property and the government produces goods

The **Bolsheviks** were a revolutionary socialist group. For many years, they plotted against the czar. Their party was small, but it was well organized.

A man who called himself Lenin led the Bolsheviks. He became a revolutionary when the czar's soldiers killed his brother. Many Russians liked his promise of "Peace, Land, and Bread." The Russian government arrested him and then exiled him. Lenin stayed away from Russia for 17 years.

What Was the Red Guard?

In the fall of 1917, the Bolsheviks took over the Russian government. They formed a **militia**—a group of people who can be called to military service very quickly when needed. This militia, called the Red Guard, seized the government by force on November 6 and 7. The Red Guard then arrested the leaders of the provisional government.

This change in government was almost bloodless. The Bolsheviks moved quickly to establish control. They gave their party a new name— the Communist Party. Lenin became its leader. This party believed in **Communism.** Communism is an economic system in which there is little private property and the government produces goods.

The Communist Party gave Russia a new name. It became the Union of Soviet Socialist Republics (U.S.S.R.), or the Soviet Union.

Lenin was the leader of the Communist Party, which took over the Russian government in 1917.

What Did the Communist Government Do?

Many Russians did not support the Communists. In the first free elections to choose an assembly, they received only one-third of the vote. The Communists simply closed the assembly after only one day. Lenin then kept his promise to the Russian people and pulled Russia out of World War I. The Communists signed a peace treaty with Germany in March 1918. Russia had to give up about a third of its European territory.

Some Russians opposed Lenin and the Communists. These non-Bolsheviks formed a "White" army. A number of national **minorities** in Russia supported the Whites. (A minority is a small group of like people within a larger group.) Countries like Great Britain, France, Japan, and the United States sent troops to fight the "Reds"—the Bolshevik army.

What Happened During the Russian Civil War?

The Whites and the Reds fought a civil war that lasted until 1920. Among those who died was Czar Nicholas II and his family. The Bolsheviks shot them because they did not want the White army to rescue the royal family.

The Reds finally defeated the Whites, but the civil war left Russia with many problems. Factories had closed and there was nothing to trade. Some of the millions who had died included the brightest and most skilled people in Russia.

What Did Lenin Do After His Victory?

After the Reds won the Russian Civil War, Lenin and the Communists changed Russia. The government took control of industry. They also divided land among the peasants. The government taxed extra grain. However, it allowed the peasants to sell their goods to make extra money. The Communists also removed Russia's class system and asked people to give up religion. They created a powerful dictatorship that controlled the government and the economy. Finally, they established a secret police that used terror to control the Russian people.

Writing About History

Choose one person from this chapter who was important in Russian history or culture. Research his or her life. Then write a short biography of that person in your notebook.

Many people starved during the Russian civil war. This picture shows barefoot and starving children during the war.

Successor

One who follows another in a position

What Happened After Lenin Died?

In 1922, Lenin became sick. Two Communist leaders began fighting to become his **successor**—the one who would take over the government.

Most people expected Leon Trotsky to become the new party leader. He had founded the Red Guard and had beaten the Whites in the civil war. He was a well-known, popular leader. He was also an excellent writer and speaker.

Trotsky's rival was Joseph Stalin. He was a quiet man and not well known, but he had a high-ranking position in the Communist Party. Stalin had used his power to appoint his followers to key positions in the government.

History in Your Life

The World's Largest Country

Russia is the largest country in the world. It sprawls across northern Europe and Asia. Russia has about 6,600,000 square miles of land. It is almost twice as large as China or the United States. The Volga is the longest river in Europe. It flows near Moscow into the Caspian Sea.

Steppes, or grasslands, cover much of western and central Russia. They run from Ukraine across Russia into Kazakhstan.

Summers are short and hot. Winters are long and snowy. A low mountain range, the Urals, separates the steppes from Siberia.

Siberia is the Asian part of Russia. It stretches east to the Pacific Ocean. Northern Siberia has a subarctic climate—the ground is partly frozen all year. Huge, thick forests cover other areas. Siberia has about three-quarters of Russia's mineral wealth.

Word Bank

Lenin

Reds

Stalin

Trotsky

Whites

Lesson 1 Review On a sheet of paper, use the words from the Word Bank to complete each sentence correctly.

1. The formerly exiled leader of the Bolsheviks was _____.

2. The Bolsheviks came to be called the _____.

3. The people who opposed the Bolsheviks became known as the _____.

4. The founder of the Red Guard was _____.

5. _____ became leader of the Soviet Union after Lenin's death.

What do you think ?

Why was Lenin smart to promise "Peace, Land, and Bread" to the Russian people?

Objectives

◆ To describe the ways Joseph Stalin changed Russia

◆ To describe a totalitarian state

Heavy industry

The manufacturing of products, such as machines and raw materials, for use in other industries

Consumer goods

Products that people buy

Collective farm

A large farm owned by the government and worked by many peasants

Reading Strategy:
Visualizing

What words in this paragraph help you visualize what you are reading?

When Lenin died in 1924, two leaders—Leon Trotsky and Joseph Stalin—fought to become Lenin's successor. They both wanted to be the one who would follow Lenin and take over the government.

How Did Stalin Change Russia?

Finally, in 1927, Joseph Stalin won the support of party members. Stalin wanted to industrialize Russia. He set up a series of Five-Year Plans. Stalin built **heavy industry**—factories that make basic products like steel or machines for use in other industries. The government gave a lot of money to heavy industry, but there was little money to produce **consumer goods.** These goods that people buy, like clothing and shoes, became scarce in Russia.

Stalin also set up **collective farms.** He believed that fewer workers could produce more food on these large farms. Each farm was owned by the government and worked by many peasants. The peasants had to sell their crops at fixed prices. The government paid the workers according to the amount of work they had done. Most peasants hated these collective farms. Some burned grain and killed farm animals. Stalin sent these people to Siberia. He ordered the death of thousands of farmers and their families. Historians believe that between 5 and 10 million peasants died.

Joseph Stalin ruled the Soviet Union harshly. He turned his country into an industrialized nation, but he used cruel methods to do it.

Stalin's "Great Purge" caused great suffering among the Russian people. Historians believe millions died from Stalin's plan to rid his enemies.

Stalin made the Soviet Union a **totalitarian state.** A totalitarian state is a government in which a small group controls the lives of its country's citizens. That is, people have no rights. Under Stalin, everyone in the Soviet Union lived in fear. People who spoke out against the government were sometimes never seen again. Stalin encouraged children to report their parents if they did or said anything disloyal. His secret police watched everyone. Stalin even **purged,** or removed from office, thousands of members of the Communist Party.

Stalin died in 1953. As a ruler, he had changed the Soviet Union—some for the good, but mostly for the bad. Millions of Russians suffered and died. Living conditions remained poor. The government completely controlled the lives of the people

But the Soviet Union became a powerful industrialized nation with improved health care and education.

Europe at the End of 1938

Countries Under Dictatorships

ATLANTIC OCEAN

NORWAY
FINLAND
60°N
SWEDEN
ESTONIA
North Sea
LATVIA
Baltic Sea
UNION OF SOVIET SOCIALIST REPUBLICS (U.S.S.R.) (Stalin)
IRELAND
DENMARK
LITHUANIA
50°N
GREAT BRITAIN
EAST PRUSSIA
50°N
NETH.
GERMANY (Hitler)
POLAND
BELG.
LUX.
CZECHOSLOVAKIA
FRANCE
SWITZ.
AUSTRIA
40°E
ALPS
HUNGARY
10°W
ROMANIA
PORTUGAL (Salazar)
PYRENEES
Corsica (France)
YUGOSLAVIA
Black Sea
SPAIN (Franco)
ITALY (Mussolini)
Adriatic Sea
BULGARIA
40°N
Sardinia (Italy)
ALBANIA
TURKEY
Sicily
GREECE
0°
Cyprus
500 Miles
Mediterranean Sea
Crete
0°
0°
500 Kilometers
10°E
20°E
30°E

Map Study

This map shows what Europe looked like at the end of 1938. It also shows the countries under the control of a dictator. What were the names of five European dictators? Which dictator controlled the most land? In case of war, why would Britain be more difficult to conquer than France?

Dictators

Throughout history, powerful leaders have taken power by force. They have absolute power and do not allow opposition. Their word is law. In the early 1800s, Napoleon Bonaparte conquered much of Europe. Napoleon began as an enemy of monarchy, but then he became a dictator. Also in the 1800s, most of Latin America won its independence from Spain. Since then, dictators called "caudillos" have often ruled these countries.

In the 1930s, Franco won the civil war in Spain and became its dictator. Two other dictators—Mussolini in Italy and Hitler in Germany—took the world to war.

In recent years, people have overthrown dictators in the Philippines and Indonesia. Yet dictators keep coming to power. Unfortunately, dictators still rule smaller nations around the world today.

Word Bank
collective farms
heavy industry
rights
Siberia
totalitarian

Lesson 2 Review On a sheet of paper, use the words from the Word Bank to complete each sentence correctly.

1. Stalin stressed _____, factories that make industrial products such as machines.

2. Stalin forced farmers to work on _____ owned by the government.

3. Under Stalin, the Soviet Union became a _____ state.

4. Under totalitarianism, people had no _____.

5. Peasants who disagreed with Stalin were sent to _____.

What do you think ?

How might the Russian people have felt when their factories produced only a few consumer goods?

Objectives

◆ To identify Benito Mussolini
◆ To describe fascism and its influence on others

During World War I, Italy fought on the side of the Allies. The Italians wanted to win territory from Germany and Austria-Hungary. After the war, the Treaty of Versailles disappointed them. They wanted more land than the treaty gave them.

World War I also brought economic and political problems to Italy. The war left the country in debt. Many people lost their jobs. Many political parties arose, and the government was weak.

Veteran

A person who has served in the military, especially during a war

Reading Strategy: **Visualizing**

Create a graphic organizer to help you remember some things about fascism.

Who Was Benito Mussolini?

Many Italians blamed the democratic government for all of their nation's problems. Some feared a Communist revolution in Italy like the one in Russia. Benito Mussolini used this deep fear of Communism and revolution to win power. Most of his followers were **veterans.** That is, they had fought for Italy in World War I. They became known as "Black Shirts." In 1919, Mussolini formed the Fascist Party. It opposed both Communism and democracy. Mussolini promised to make Italy as great as the ancient Roman Empire. In 1922, he became the dictator of Italy. His followers called him "Il Duce," or "the leader."

Mussolini became dictator of Italy in 1922. He was known as "Il Duce," which means "the leader."

What Is Fascism?

Fascism developed during the 20th century. This government system is a little different in each country, but they share the following:

1. They have only one party and one leader. All other political parties are banned.

2. All fascist governments demand obedience to the state and to its leader.

3. They take away individual rights and freedom. That is, the state takes away freedoms that belong to each person. The government censors all books and newspapers.

4. They preach extreme nationalism. They believe their country is the best and should be the strongest.

5. They build up military power. Fascists believe that military force wins land for their country and makes it great.

Whom Did Mussolini Influence?

Fascists from other countries admired Italy's fascist dictatorship and borrowed ideas from it. In Spain, a fascist named Francisco Franco set himself up as dictator. In Germany, Adolf Hitler carefully watched Mussolini. In a few years, Hitler would become the most feared fascist leader in the world.

The League of Nations Fails

When World War I ended, world leaders met to discuss peace. U.S. President Woodrow Wilson wanted to create an organization to which every nation belonged. He thought this organization could prevent war. That is, it could keep wars from happening.

The Treaty of Versailles formed this organization—the League of Nations. The nations of the league promised to defend the territory and independence of all its members.

A test of the league's strength came in October 1935 when Italy attacked Ethiopia. Ethiopian Emperor Haile Selassie asked the league for help. It voted to force Italy to withdraw through economic means. That is, member nations refused to buy goods from Italy or to sell it war materials.

However, Great Britain and France did not want to upset Italy. They wanted Italy's support against Germany. Great Britain continued to allow Italy to send troops and supplies through the Suez Canal. Italy was then able to defeat Ethiopia.

In 1935, the league failed to stop Italy. It tried to make everyone happy. Instead, it made everyone mad. Ethiopia lost its independence and the league lost its best chance of preventing war through nations working together.

Lesson 3 Review On a sheet of paper, write the answer to each question. Use complete sentences.

1. What problems led to the rise of Mussolini in Italy?

2. Who supported the Fascist Party in Italy?

3. Who were the "Black Shirts"?

4. What are five ways in which most fascist governments are alike?

5. What are the names of two fascist leaders influenced by Mussolini?

What do you think ?

Dictators often do terrible things. Why do you think people allow dictators to rule them?

Objectives

- To describe the conditions that allowed the Nazis to gain control
- To describe Hitler's rise to power

Inflation

A quick increase in prices

Swastika

The Nazi symbol of a cross with its arms bent

Depression

A time of economic collapse when businesses lose money and many people become poor

Reading Strategy:
Visualizing

Look for clues in this lesson that help you visualize how Hitler came to power.

When German soldiers returned home after World War I, they found little work. Because the war had destroyed many factories, people had few goods to sell at home or to foreign markets. Prices went up quickly. This is called **inflation.**

What Was the Weimar Republic?

At the end of the war, the Allies forced Kaiser William II of Germany to step down. Then the German people set up a democratic government and wrote a constitution. They called their new government the Weimar Republic. However, the new government had problems. Some Germans blamed it for accepting the terms of the Treaty of Versailles.

One party that opposed the new government was the Nationalist Socialist German Workers' Party. It was called *Nazi* for short. The Nazis adopted a red flag with a black **swastika** as its symbol. A swastika is a cross with its arms bent. Adolf Hitler became the Nazi leader.

In 1923, Hitler tried to take control of the German government by force, but he failed. Then the leaders of the Weimar Republic arrested and jailed him. During his jail term, he wrote *Mein Kampf,* which means "My Struggle."

In his book, Hitler said that the German people were better than other people. He also said that everyone else was less important than the German people. Hitler came up with a plan to make Germany a powerful nation once again.

How Did the Depression Help the Nazis?

In 1929, a long drop in business activity—a **depression**—took place all over the world. By 1932, nearly 40 percent of the factory workers in Germany had no jobs. Many turned to Communism. But the middle class and the wealthy were tired of inflation; they feared the Communists. Many of them turned to Hitler because he opposed Communism. Soon the Nazis became the largest political party in Germany.

What Did Hitler Do As Dictator?

In 1933, Hitler became head of the German government. Then he called for an election. (The Nazi Party still did not have a majority in the German assembly, or **Reichstag.** Hitler needed a majority to become really powerful.)

Just before the election, someone set the Reichstag building on fire. No one knows who started the fire, but Hitler blamed the Communists. In the election, many German people, fearing revolution, voted for the Nazis. The Nazis did not win the election, but Hitler later took control of the Reichstag.

Next, Hitler made himself dictator. He called himself the **Fuehrer,** which means "leader." As dictator, Hitler did the following:

1. Banned all other political parties and all labor unions.

2. Made all army officers promise to obey his orders.

3. Censored all books, magazines, newspapers, radio programs, and movies.

4. Burned all books that contained ideas opposed to Nazism.

5. Established a secret police force called the **Gestapo.** It made sure that no one said anything against Hitler or the Nazis.

6. Rebuilt the German army into a powerful war machine.

Lesson 4 Review On a sheet of paper, write the answer to each question. Use complete sentences.

1. Why did the government of the Weimar Republic have problems?

2. What is the symbol of the Nationalist Socialist German Worker's (Nazi) Party?

3. What economic conditions caused the people of Germany to turn to Hitler?

4. What did Hitler censor as soon as he became dictator?

5. What was the secret police force that Hitler established? What did it do?

Reichstag

The national assembly of the Weimar Republic

Fuehrer

The name given to Adolf Hitler meaning "leader"

Gestapo

Hitler's secret police force

What do you think ?

Hitler forced Jews to wear yellow stars. Why do you think he did so?

During the Age of Imperialism, Europe and Japan carved out spheres of influence in China. European powers controlled Chinese mines, railroads, and some factories. But Chinese nationalists hated imperialism. They wanted to free China from foreign influence.

What Did Sun Yat-sen Want for China?

Sun Yat-sen led the Chinese nationalists. He wrote a book called *Three Principles of the People,* which greatly influenced his country. In his book, he wrote that he wanted three things for China:

1. A strong national government free of foreign control.

2. A democratic government that the Chinese people controlled.

3. Better living conditions for all the Chinese people.

Sun Yat-sen was the leader of the Chinese nationalists. He wanted to free China from foreign influence.

Why Did the Soviet Union Help Sun Yat-sen?

In 1911, Sun Yat-sen and the Chinese revolutionaries overthrew the government and formed a republic. However, for the next five years, civil war tore China apart. In 1917, Sun Yat-sen became leader of the republic. But military leaders who wanted power for themselves still controlled much of China.

Sun Yat-sen asked the European nations for help. They would not help, because Sun Yat-sen had criticized them for being imperialists. Sun Yat-sen then turned to the Soviet Union. Lenin, the Russian leader at the time, agreed to send money and military supplies to China. He thought that his country and China faced the same enemies. Lenin also wanted to introduce Communism to China.

Reading Strategy:
Visualizing

How could this paragraph be written differently to create a stronger picture in your mind?

What Started a Civil War in China?

In 1925, Sun Yat-sen died. Then Chiang Kai-shek, an army general, became China's leader. Chiang did not trust the Soviet Union or the Communists. Soon after taking power, he ordered the Soviet advisers out of China and nearly wiped out the Chinese Communist Party. Only a few Communists managed to escape.

Mao Zedong was one of the Communists who fled to the Chinese countryside. With his supporters, he fought a long civil war against Chiang. Several times during this war, Chiang almost destroyed the Communists.

What United the Chinese People?

In this war, bankers and business people in the cities along China's coast supported Chiang. The peasants supported Mao Zedong because the Communists took land from the rich and divided it among the landless peasants.

China's civil war stopped for a while in 1937 when Japan invaded China. The Japanese killed many Chinese people and destroyed cities, farms, and factories. Then all the Chinese people united to fight their common enemy.

Lesson 5 Review On a sheet of paper, write the letter of the answer that correctly completes each sentence.

1. Chinese _____ hated foreign influence in China.

   A industrialists **C** imperialists
   B nationalists **D** Communists

2. Sun Yat-sen wanted _____ for the Chinese people.

   A a strong national government
   B a democratic government
   C better living conditions
   D all of the above

3. After Sun Yat-sen died, _____ led China.

   A Chiang Kai-shek **C** Hitler
   B Lenin **D** Mao Zedong

4. The leader of the Chinese Communists was _____.

   A Chiang Kai-shek **C** Mao Zedong
   B Sun Yat-sen **D** Lenin

5. In 1937, _____ invaded China and the Chinese people stopped their civil war.

   A Japan **C** Italy
   B Germany **D** Russia

What do you think ?

Why do you think some Chinese people hated imperialism?

Objectives

◆ To describe how the Great Depression in the United States affected Japan

◆ To explain how Japan's government was like the fascist governments of Germany and Italy

◆ To explain why Japan attacked Manchuria

Great Depression

The worldwide depression that began in the United States in 1929

Reading Strategy: Visualizing

What words in this paragraph help you visualize what you are reading?

The **Great Depression** started in the United States in 1929 and spread all over the world. It was hard on Japan, because people no longer had money to buy Japanese silk. Some Japanese companies that had exported goods to other countries went out of business. Many workers had no jobs. The Japanese people blamed its government for their problems.

Who Became the Real Leaders of Japan?

In the 1920s, the Japanese government had become more democratic. Before then, it had not allowed many people to vote. Now they had this right. When the depression hit in the 1930s, some people blamed democracy. Military officers did so because they wanted more power.

In the fascist countries of Italy and Germany, one military man ruled all the people. This was not true in Japan. In the 1930s, a small group of military men gained power in the government. They said that the emperor ruled. But in fact, the military ruled in his name. General Hideki Tojo—the minister of war—was the chief speaker for the military.

However, Japan's government had at least four things in common with the fascist governments of Germany and Italy.

1. It arrested anyone who spoke out against it.

2. It controlled the press and censored newspapers and radio.

3. It ordered schools to teach children that they must always obey.

4. Its secret police made people afraid to say or do anything against the government.

General Hideki Tojo led a group of military leaders in Japan. He would lead a government takeover in 1941.

Why Did Japan Attack Manchuria?

In September 1931, Japan attacked Manchuria. (This Chinese province bordered on Japanese-controlled Korea.) Japan quickly overran Manchuria. The Japanese said that they had freed the province from China. But Japan completely controlled this new state, which it renamed Manchukuo. Why had Japan attacked Manchuria? For two reasons. First, Japan's military leaders wanted Manchuria's coal and iron for industry. Second, Japan had too many people. But Manchuria had few people. The Japanese leaders wanted people from Japan to move to Manchuria and settle there.

What Alliance Developed?

During the 1930s, Germany and Italy had developed close ties. In 1936, Germany and Japan agreed to join together to fight the spread of Communism. In 1937, Italy agreed to this, too. The three nations would later agree to help each other if one of them went to war. That war—World War II—was coming closer and closer.

Word Bank

Germany
Great Depression
Italy
Manchuria
Tojo

Lesson 6 Review On a sheet of paper, use the words from the Word Bank to complete each sentence correctly.

1. Because of the _____, many Japanese companies went out of business after 1929.

2. In the 1930s, General _____ ruled Japan

3. Japan attacked _____ in 1931.

4. In 1936, _____ and Japan formed an alliance to fight the spread of Communism.

5. Japan, Germany, and _____ formed an alliance.

What do you think ?

In Chapter 13, you read about Japanese feudalism and the samurai. How might this tradition have prepared the Japanese people for military leadership?

The Importance of the Peasant Problem

Mao Zedong

Mao Zedong was leader of the People's Republic of China and first secretary of the Chinese Communist Party beginning in 1943. He died in 1976. Mao wrote this speech in 1927 after spending 32 days in Hunan Province investigating the concerns of peasants and their potential as revolutionaries. Mao went on to lead the Communists in the struggle to control China.

During my recent visit to Hunan I made a first-hand investigation of conditions in the five counties of Hsiantan, Hsianghsiang, Henshan, Liling and Changsha. In the thirty-two days from January 4 to February 5, I called together fact-finding conferences in villages and county towns, which were attended by experienced peasants and by comrades working in the peasant movement, and I listened attentively to their reports and collected a great deal of material. Many of the hows and whys of the peasant movement were the exact opposite of what the gentry [people of high social position] in Hankow and Changsha are saying. I saw and heard of many strange things of which I had hitherto been unaware. I believe the same is true of any other places, too. All talk directed against the peasant movement must be speedily set right. All the wrong measures taken by the revolutionary authorities concerning the peasant movement must be speedily changed.

Only thus can the future of the revolution be benefited. For the present upsurge of the peasant movement is a colossal event. In a very short time, in China's central, southern and northern provinces, several hundred million peasants will rise like a mighty storm, like a hurricane, a force so swift and violent that no power, however great, will be able to hold it back. They will smash all the trammels [things that limit movement] that bind them and rush forward along the road to liberation. They will sweep all the imperialists, warlords, corrupt officials, local tyrants and evil gentry into their graves. Every revolutionary party and every revolutionary comrade will be put to the test, to be accepted or rejected as they decide. There are three alternatives. To march at their head and lead them. To trail behind them, gesticulating [gesturing] and criticizing. Or to stand in their way and oppose them. Every Chinese is free to choose, but events will force you to make the choice quickly.

Document-Based Reading Questions

1. Why did Mao Zedong visit counties in the Hunan Province?

2. How did he respond to what he learned?

3. What was Mao Zedong's biggest concern?

4. What did he think might happen to the warlords?

5. What action did he decide to take?

Source: *"Report on the Investigation of the Peasant Movement in Hunan," Mao Zedong, March 1927.*

Hitler's Rise to Power

In 1919, Germany was defeated and in ruins. The Treaty of Versailles took away its military strength. The treaty also ordered Germany to pay $33 billion in war damages to the Allies. Germans were angry and bitter. Things got worse in the next few years. Inflation soared. By late 1923, German money was worth almost nothing. Many people were out of work and hungry. The Weimar government was too weak to do anything. The times were ripe for revolution.

Playing on these feelings, many nationalist groups formed. One was the Nazi Party. Adolf Hitler became its leader. In fiery speeches, Hitler blamed Germany's troubles on the Versailles Treaty. He attacked the Weimar government. He denounced capitalists and the Jews. Hitler organized a private army of 15,000 "brown shirts."

In 1923, the Nazis staged a *putsch*—an attempt to overthrow the state government of Bavaria. About 3,000 people, including government leaders, were holding a rally at a Munich beer hall. Hitler's "brown shirts" surrounded the hall. They set up a machine gun in the entrance. Hitler jumped up on a table and fired his gun into the air. He shouted, "The national revolution has begun!" He then led his men toward the center of the city, but police stopped them. They arrested Hitler and most of the top Nazi leaders.

Hitler and other top Nazi leaders were sent to prison for treason. It was there that he wrote *Mein Kampf* (My Struggle). The book stressed nationalism and racism. It also made Hitler famous in Germany.

From 1924 to 1929, the German economy began to recover. Many Nazis lost interest and drifted away. Then the worldwide depression hit Germany. Slowly, Hitler began to rebuild the Nazi Party.

By late 1932, the Nazi Party was the strongest in Germany. Hitler was getting valuable help from people who preferred Nazism to Communism. In 1933, another government crisis occurred. Hitler promised to support the government if he were made leader. On January 30, 1933, he took office as chancellor. Six months later, he was dictator of Germany.

The dictator in Germany was Adolf Hitler. He took control of the German government in 1933.

Wrap-Up

1. What conditions set the stage for the rise of nationalism in Germany?

2. Who did Hitler blame for Germany's hard times?

3. What happened at the Beer Hall rally?

4. What was *Mein Kampf*?

5. How did Hitler eventually become leader of Germany?

Chapter 26   S U M M A R Y

- The Bolsheviks were revolutionary socialists led by Lenin. They took over the Russian government in 1917 and became the Communist Party. They called Russia "the Soviet Union." It then dropped out of World War I.

- Non-Bolsheviks formed a "White" army to fight the Bolshevik "Red" army. Civil war continued until 1920.

- With the support of peasants and workers, the Red army won. Lenin took over industry, gave land to peasants, and set up a dictatorship.

- After Lenin died, Joseph Stalin defeated his rival, Leon Trotsky, and became the new leader of Russia.

- Russia became a totalitarian state. In the 1930s, Stalin held purges. Millions were arrested. Russia became a powerful industrialized nation, but its people had few freedoms.

- Italians felt that the Allies had cheated them in the Treaty of Versailles.

- In 1919, Mussolini formed the Fascist Party. It opposed both democracy and Communism. Italy's dictator, Mussolini, became known as "Il Duce."

- Fascism demands total obedience to one party and leader. The state censors books and newspapers and denies free speech. Fascists believe in nationalism and military power.

- In Germany, the Weimar Republic was the democratic government after World War I. Many small political groups opposed it.

- Adolf Hitler led a fascist party known as the Nazis. In 1923, Nazi leaders were jailed for trying to take over the government. While in jail, Hitler wrote *Mein Kampf.* It described Hitler's plan to make Germany strong again.

- An economic depression and fear of Communism helped Hitler gain power. By 1933, he was head of the government.

- In China, Sun Yat-sen led a nationalist movement. A revolution in 1911 overthrew the monarchy but led to civil war. Only the Soviet Union sent Sun Yat-sen help.

- After Sun Yat-sen died, Chiang Kai-shek led the Nationalists. He conducted a long civil war against Mao Zedong's Chinese Communists.

- Japan's government became more democratic after World War I. However, the depression hurt the economy. Military leaders used this as an excuse to gain power.

- In 1931, Japan invaded Manchuria, a Chinese province rich in iron and coal. Later Japan became allies with Germany and Italy against Communism.

Chapter 26   R E V I E W

Word Bank

Fuehrer

Hitler

Il Duce

Japan

Lenin

Mussolini

Totalitarian

Bolshevik

Stalin

Nazi

On a sheet of paper, use the words from the Word Bank to complete each sentence correctly.

1. When Russia lost its war with _____, people began to demand more change.

2. The leader of the Bolsheviks was _____.

3. In the Russian civil war, several foreign countries sent troops to fight the _____ army.

4. _____ had a plan to industrialize Russia.

5. _____ states are governments in which a small group totally controls the lives of all the citizens.

6. Benito _____ became Italy's dictator.

7. Italians called their dictator _____, which means "leader."

8. Adolf _____ led the Nationalist Socialist German Workers' Party.

9. _____ is another name for the Nationalist Socialist German Workers' Party.

10. Germans called their dictator _____, which also means "leader."

On a sheet of paper, write the letter of the answer that correctly completes each sentence.

11. After Lenin and his followers came to power, he _____.

   A took control of all industry

   B gave land to the peasants

   C swept away the class system

   D all of the above

12. Stalin conducted a _____ in which the government killed millions of workers that he thought were disloyal.

   A minority   **B** purge   **C** militia   **D** study

13. A person who has served in the military, especially during a war, is a _____.

    A veteran   **C** extremist

    B Gestapo   **D** swastika

14. The Nazi Party chose a cross with its arms bent, the _____ , as a symbol.

    A Reichstag   **C** swastika

    B Gestapo   **D** Nazi

15. The name of Germany's government after World War I was the _____.

    A Fascist Party   **C** Nationalist Party

    B Weimar Republic   **D** Communist Party

On a sheet of paper, write the answer to each question. Use complete sentences.

16. Why did Italy and Germany choose fascism and dictators after World War I?

17. What are six things Hitler did when he became dictator?

18. What are four things that Japan had in common with Nazi Germany and fascist Italy during the 1930s?

Critical Thinking On a sheet of paper, write your response to each question. Use complete sentences.

19. Stalin wanted to change Russia into a modern industrial power. What was it about the way he did it that prevented him from being successful?

20. Mussolini wrote that fascism "was born of the need for action." What do you think he meant?

Test-Taking Tip

Cross off items on matching tests as you use them. Be sure you use each item only once.

27

World War II and Its Aftermath

More than 50 countries fought in World War II. The war was fought in Europe, Asia, and North Africa. Millions of troops and civilians died. In this chapter, you will watch as Hitler ignores the Treaty of Versailles. You will read about the Battle of Britain, a German army facing a cold winter in the Soviet Union, and the destruction at Pearl Harbor. You will see what ended World War II and the result of that war. Then you will learn how Europe was rebuilt after the war.

Goals for Learning

◆ To explain the major causes of World War II

◆ To list the countries that fascist dictators and nations invaded and explain why appeasement failed

◆ To list the successes of the Axis Powers and the Allies

◆ To explain what brought an end to World War II

◆ To explain what the Holocaust was and why it happened

◆ To describe the social, economic, and political results of World War II

◆ To describe the makeup of the United Nations

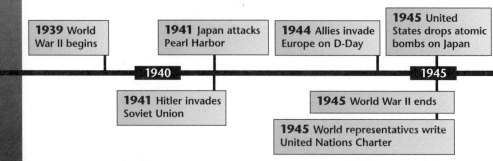

1939 World War II begins

1941 Japan attacks Pearl Harbor

1944 Allies invade Europe on D-Day

1945 United States drops atomic bombs on Japan

1935　　　　　　　　　1940　　　　　　　　　1945

1941 Hitler invades Soviet Union

1945 World War II ends

1945 World representatives write United Nations Charter

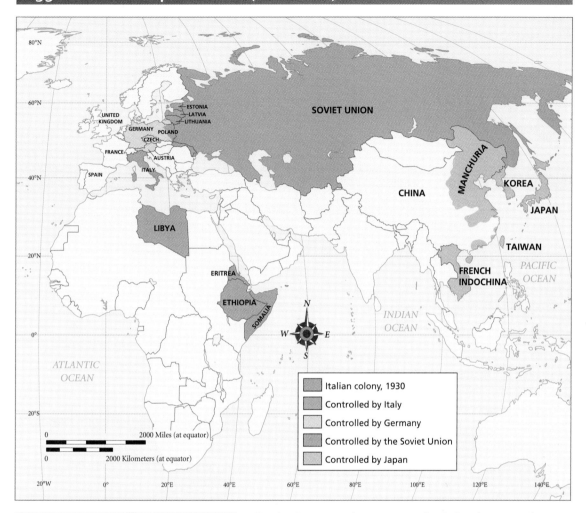

Map Skills

In the 1930s, Japan, Germany, Italy, and the Soviet Union took over the land and resources of neighboring countries. Because they were strong, they believed they had the right to rule other nations. This map shows aggression in Europe and Asia from 1930 to 1940.

Study the map, then answer the following questions:

1. What area of China did the Japanese conquer?

2. What French territory in Asia did the Japanese capture?

3. What countries did Germany conquer?

4. What African colonies did Italy control?

5. Which country—Germany, Italy, Japan, or the Soviet Union—controlled the most land?

Reading Strategy:
Inferencing

Sometimes the meaning of a text is not directly stated. You have to make an inference to figure out what the text means.

◆ What You Know + What You Read = Inference

◆ To make inferences, you have to think "beyond the text." Predicting what will happen next and explaining cause and effect are helpful strategies for making inferences.

Key Vocabulary Words

Lesson 1
Axis A make-believe line

Axis Powers The alliance of Germany, Italy, and Japan during World War II

Lesson 2
Appeasement Making others content

Front The place where armies fight

Lesson 3
Blitzkrieg The quick and forceful method of attack that Germany used in World War II

Arsenal A place where weapons are kept

Destroyer A small, fast warship that uses guns to protect ships from submarines

Lend-Lease program Franklin Roosevelt's program that allowed Britain to borrow war supplies from the U.S. during World War II

Lesson 4
Occupy To take over and stay in a place

Resistance Groups of people who used hit and-run tactics to fight the Nazis

Guerilla warfare A kind of fighting that involves small attacks against an enemy

D-Day The Allied invasion of France in 1944

Kamikaze A Japanese pilot who crashed his plane into an enemy ship

V-E Day The day the allies completed their victory in Europe: May 8, 1945

Atomic bomb A nuclear bomb

Nuclear Having to do with atoms

V-J Day The day the Allies completed their victory in Japan: September 2, 1945

Lesson 5
Holocaust Hitler's killing of many of the Jews in Europe

Ghetto The parts of cities where Jewish people had to live during World War II

Genocide The mass murder of a group of people

Concentration camp A prison death camp

Lesson 6
Refugee A person who is forced to flee from his or her country

Superpower A nation that has more power and money than other countries

Satellite A nation that is tightly controlled by another nation

Lesson 7
United Nations (UN) The international organization that works to settle disagreements

Charter A constitution; a set of statements that explains a group's purpose

Trust territory A territory that the Allies took from the countries that lost World War I and World War II

Objectives

- To describe how nationalism and imperialism led to war
- To explain how the formation of the Axis Powers led to war
- To identify four other causes of the war

Axis

A make-believe line that goes through the middle of an object that spins around it

Axis Powers

The alliance of Germany, Italy, and Japan during World War II

Reading Strategy:
Inferencing

What do you already know about the start of World War II?

The 1930s brought danger to the whole world. Once again, the countries of Europe stood ready to fight. In Chapter 25, you learned that nationalism, imperialism, and militarism caused World War I. They also led to World War II.

Why Did Nationalism Lead to War?

Italy's Mussolini and Germany's Hitler were nationalists. So were the military leaders of Japan. Mussolini promised to make Italy as great as the Roman Empire. Hitler called the German people the "master race." He preached that all other people were inferior. Italy, Germany, and Japan thought that they were superior. They believed that they had the right to rule all the other people in the world.

Why Did Imperialism Lead to War?

These three countries were also imperialistic. They wanted to take over the land and resources of other countries. Japan tried to create a new empire. Italy expanded into Africa and tried to make the Mediterranean Sea into an "Italian lake." Germany annexed Austria and Czechoslovakia.

Why Did Militarism Lead to War?

Italy, Germany, and Japan tried to form a military **axis** around which the world would turn. An axis is a make-believe line that goes through the middle of an object. The object spins on the axis. For this reason, historians called the three nations the **Axis Powers.**

The three Axis nations spent great sums of money on the military. They developed new weapons and built large armies. They welcomed war. They said that dying for their country was the highest honor a person could ever have.

What Are Four Other Causes of World War II?

Nationalism, imperialism, and militarism led to World War II. But four other things did, too.

First, the Treaty of Versailles, which ended World War I, punished Germany severely. Hitler and the German people wanted to make the Allies pay for what Germany had suffered.

Second, the breakdown of the world economy after 1929 helped nations turn to war. During the Great Depression, many businesses failed. World trade almost stopped. The money of some countries became almost worthless. The Treaty of Versailles made Germany and Austria pay for World War I damages. This destroyed the economies of these two countries. These hard times encouraged the rise of dictators. People were willing to follow leaders who promised a better way of life.

Third, the three Axis countries were totalitarian dictatorships. They did not believe in personal freedom or in free elections. They did not believe in freedom of speech or equality. They wanted to destroy democracy.

Fourth, the failure of the League of Nations was a cause of World War II. The league had little power to use against countries that broke its rules. The United States never joined the league. Germany and Japan dropped out in 1933; Italy left it in 1937. The league expelled Russia in 1939.

All of these set the stage for World War II. It would be even more destructive than World War I.

The Great Depression ruined the world economy. In the United States, people had to wait in line for food and jobs.

Writing About History

Pretend that you represent a world organization that tries to prevent wars around the world. In your notebook, write 10 things that your organization would do to try to prevent a world war.

Reading Strategy: Inferencing

How does what you already know about World War II add to what you have just read?

Lesson 1 Review On a sheet of paper, write the letter of the answer that correctly completes each sentence.

1. _____ was one cause of World War II.

   A Communism   **C** Revolution
   B Monarchy   **D** Nationalism

2. Germany, Japan, and Italy formed the _____ Powers.

   A Allied   **C** European
   B Axis   **D** democratic

3. All three countries felt _____ to other people.

   A superior   **C** weaker
   B inferior   **D** less powerful

4. The _____ was a cause of World War II.

   A failure of the League of Nations
   B Great Depression
   C Treaty of Versailles
   D all of the above

5. _____ never joined the League of Nations.

   A Russia   **C** The United States
   B Germany   **D** Italy

What do you think ?

What do you think was the most important cause of World War II?

Objectives

◆ To identify countries that Hitler invaded

◆ To explain the policy of appeasement and why it failed

◆ To identify the countries that fought in World War II

Conference

A meeting to discuss ideas and plans

Reading Strategy:
Inferencing

After reading this section, what inference can you make about Hitler's plans?

The Treaty of Versailles limited the size of Germany's army and the number of weapons it could have. Hitler ignored the treaty. He ordered all young German men to serve in the army. He ordered Germany's factories to produce guns, tanks, airplanes, and other weapons. Hitler said, "Today, Germany; tomorrow, the world!"

How Did Hitler Break the Treaty of Versailles?

The Treaty of Versailles barred German troops from the Rhineland, an area of Germany that bordered France. In March 1936, Hitler sent troops there. Great Britain and France protested, but did nothing because they feared war.

The Treaty of Versailles also said that Germany and Austria—who were allies in World War I—could not unite again. In 1938, Hitler said that all German-speaking people should be one. He ignored the treaty again by invading and annexing Austria. Once again, Britain and France took no military action.

Why Did Hitler Want the Sudetenland?

Hitler had invaded the Rhineland and Austria and no one did anything. He then demanded control over Czechoslovakia. (It was one of the new countries that the Treaty of Versailles created after World War I.) About three million Germans lived in the area of northwestern Czechoslovakia that bordered Germany. (People called this area the Sudetenland.)

What Did the Munich Pact Give Hitler?

The British and the French had promised to protect Czechoslovakia against its enemies. On September 29, 1938, British Prime Minister Neville Chamberlain met with Hitler in Munich, Germany. Chamberlain invited French and Italian leaders to participate in the **conference,** or meeting. However, he did not invite leaders from the Soviet Union or from Czechoslovakia.

At the conference, the leaders signed the **Munich Pact.** It gave Hitler control of the Sudetenland. In return, he promised not to attack the rest of Czechoslovakia. When Chamberlain returned to England, cheering crowds greeted him. He said that now they would have "peace in our time." However, six months later, Hitler took over the rest of Czechoslovakia.

Why Did Appeasement Fail?

Neither Great Britain nor France helped Austria or Czechoslovakia. They hoped to avoid war. They followed a policy of **appeasement.** That is, they gave in to the fascist dictators. Britain and France hoped that the dictators would be happy with what they had and would not attack other countries. This policy failed.

Why Did Germany and Russia Sign a Treaty?

Soon, Germany and Russia signed a treaty. They agreed not to make war against each other. No one could understand why Hitler and Stalin signed this treaty. After all, Hitler hated Communism, and Stalin hated Fascism.

Both countries gained something from their treaty. The Soviets got two things. First, the treaty allowed them to avoid war—for the time being. It gave them time to strengthen their military forces. Second, the treaty gave them control of Latvia, Estonia, and Lithuania.

Germany also gained two things from the treaty. First, it protected Germany against fighting a two-**front** war. (A front is the place where armies are fighting.) Second, the treaty left Germany free to invade Poland.

Hitler (right) met with European leaders in Munich, Germany, in 1938. There they signed the Munich Pact, which gave Hitler control of the Sudetenland. Pictured to the left is Britain's Prime Minister Neville Chamberlain.

Geography Note

During the 1800s, the Low Countries of Europe became the Netherlands, Luxembourg, and Belgium. The Netherlands remained neutral in World War II, while Germans occupied the other two countries.

What Sparked World War II?

In September 1939, Hitler, believing that Great Britain and France would do nothing, invaded Poland from the west. At the same time, the Soviet Union attacked from the east.

Now the British and French leaders gave up their policy of appeasement. They had proof that the policy did not work. On September 3, 1939, Britain and France declared war on Germany. World War II had begun.

Who Fought World War II?

Historians call the two sides in the war the Axis and the Allies. The three major Axis powers were Germany, Italy, and Japan. A few other nations supported them. When war broke out, the Allies included only France and Britain. Later, the Soviet Union, the United States, Canada, and 47 other nations joined the Allies.

Lesson 2 Review On a sheet of paper, write the answer to each question. Use complete sentences.

1. What countries did Italy and Germany invade during the 1930s?

2. How did Germany ignore the Treaty of Versailles?

3. Why did France and Great Britain do nothing to stop Hitler's annexation of Austria and Czechoslovakia?

4. What did the Soviet Union get from its treaty with Germany?

5. What happened in September 1939 that sparked the beginning of World War II?

What do you think ?

What does the saying from the Nazi Party, "Today, Germany; tomorrow, the world!" mean?

Objectives

◆ To identify the terms Maginot line and total war

◆ To describe the Battle of Britain

◆ To describe Hitler's invasion of the Soviet Union

Blitzkrieg

The quick and forceful method of attack that Germany used in World War II; "lightning war"

Maginot line

A line of concrete forts built by France along its border with Germany

Reading Strategy:
Inferencing

What can you infer about the damage and hardship resulting from a total war?

World War II began on September 3, 1939. But for seven months, no fighting took place. Then, in April 1940, German troops began to attack. Within days they conquered Denmark, Norway, the Netherlands, Luxembourg, and Belgium.

To do this, Germany invented a quick and forceful method of attack called the **blitzkrieg,** or "lightning war." Using the fastest new machines, the Germans rushed deep into enemy territory. They defeated an enemy country before it could defend itself.

What Was the Maginot Line?

After World War I, the French built a line of concrete forts along its border with Germany. France's defense was called the **Maginot line.** Hitler got around the Maginot line by conquering Belgium. On June 16, 1940, German troops marched into Paris. Six days later, the French surrendered to Germany. Hitler now controlled almost all of Western Europe.

How Was World War II a Total War?

Now Great Britain stood alone. It prepared for a German invasion. The new British Prime Minister Winston Churchill said, "We shall defend our island, whatever the cost may be. . . . We shall never surrender."

The Axis tried to force England's surrender by waging "total war." In a total war, both soldiers and civilians suffer from bombing, sickness, and lack of food. A country uses all its resources to destroy all the resources of another country.

Where Did the Battle of Britain Take Place?

The battle between Hitler's air force and the British air force began in August 1940 and lasted for over a year. Day and night, German planes bombed London, Britain's capital. To escape the bombs, thousands of Londoners slept in underground railroad stations.

In the Battle of Britain, as it was called, Germany lost 2,300 planes, while England lost only 900. In October 1941, Hitler stopped the air war. This was his first defeat. Now he decided to starve the English into surrendering. German submarines began sinking merchant ships headed for Britain. As British supplies got low, Churchill asked the United States for help.

How Did the United States Help Britain?

When war broke out in Europe, the United States declared itself neutral. However, President Roosevelt asked the United States to become an "**arsenal** of democracy." (An arsenal is a place where someone stores or makes weapons.)

Roosevelt sent 50 old **destroyers** to Britain. These small, fast warships used guns and other weapons to protect merchant ships from submarines. In return, the United States received the use of eight British naval bases along the Atlantic Coast. Roosevelt also developed the **Lend-Lease program.** Through this program, Britain borrowed supplies from the United States.

Why Did Hitler Invade the Soviet Union?

After the failure of the Battle of Britain, Hitler decided to attack his ally—the Soviet Union. He ignored their treaty because he wanted the Soviet oil fields, grain, and other resources.

Communication in History

Breaking the Enemy's Code

Even in peacetime, governments send messages in code. In wartime, breaking codes can help win the war. During World War II, the Allies broke several top-secret German and Japanese codes. Much of the information about these codes is still secret, however.

In 1939, Polish spies got a German coding machine. It was called "Enigma." British mathematicians and code-breakers worked for months to solve Enigma's system. When they did, it was called the "Ultra secret."

Ultra let the British decode messages between Hitler and his generals. Sometimes the British knew battle plans before the German generals did.

By August 1939, American code-breakers had cracked Japan's diplomatic code. The Japanese used it in messages between Tokyo and its embassies. The code-breakers named it "Magic." They then faced two problems until war broke out in 1941. First, they were a small team, but they received a huge volume of messages. Second, the decoded messages were in Japanese. Few Americans could read it.

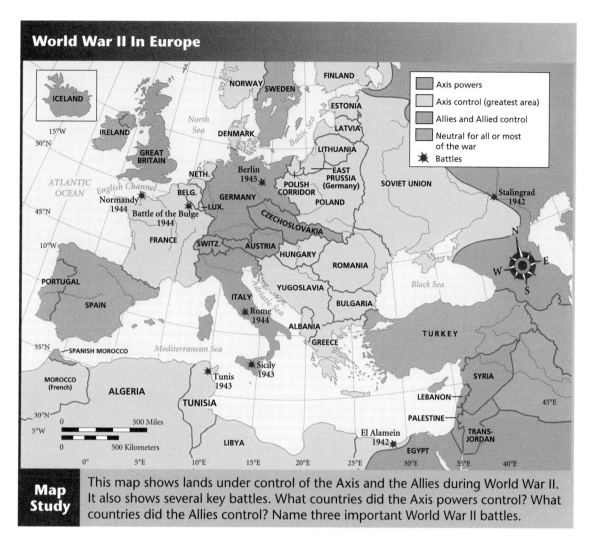

World War II In Europe

Legend:
- Axis powers
- Axis control (greatest area)
- Allies and Allied control
- Neutral for all or most of the war
- ★ Battles

Map Study — This map shows lands under control of the Axis and the Allies during World War II. It also shows several key battles. What countries did the Axis powers control? What countries did the Allies control? Name three important World War II battles.

At first, the Germans won one battle after another. But soon a terribly cold winter caught the Germans unprepared. Many soldiers in both armies died. Historians call the six-month Battle of Stalingrad a turning point in the war. Before Stalingrad, the Soviets retreated. After Stalingrad, the Germans did.

Hitler did not expect such a cold winter. The Russian army had destroyed anything that might help Hitler. They burned crops and blew up houses, dams, and bridges. By February 1943, they had defeated Hitler.

Tanks were very important weapons in World War II.

Reading Strategy:
Inferencing

What do you already know about this topic?

Where Else Did the Axis Fight?

In 1940 and 1941, the Axis invaded Greece and Yugoslavia. Then they attacked British possessions in North Africa. Next, they threatened the Suez Canal, which was the British lifeline to India. But in May 1943, the Axis forces in North Africa surrendered. Historians consider the Battle of El Alamein in Egypt another turning point in the war. As Churchill said: "Up to Alamein we survived; after Alamein we conquered."

Reading Strategy:
Inferencing

How does what you already know about Pearl Harbor add to what you have just read?

Why Did Japan Attack Pearl Harbor?

Between 1939 and 1941, Japan tried to gain more power. It depended on the United States for gasoline and old iron to help it wage war. Then the United States stopped selling the Japanese these materials. Japan prepared for war with the United States. Japanese leaders decided to cripple the U.S. Pacific Fleet, which was stationed in Pearl Harbor, Hawaii.

On Sunday, December 7, 1941, Japanese planes attacked Pearl Harbor. In this surprise raid, the Japanese killed over 2,500 Americans; sank or badly damaged 18 American ships; and destroyed 188 American planes. The next day, the United States declared war on Japan and its Axis partners.

Within months, Japan conquered northern and central China. It took over the Philippines, most of Southeast Asia, the Dutch East Indies, and French Indochina. Japan also helped to capture the island of New Guinea and then prepared to invade Australia.

Word Bank

Blitzkrieg

Britain

El Alamein

Pearl Harbor

Stalingrad

Lesson 3 Review On a sheet of paper, use the words from the Word Bank to complete each sentence correctly.

1. _____ war was different from fighting during World War I because it was a quick attack.

2. During the Battle of _____, Germany fought an air and bombing war and lost.

3. During the Battle of _____, Germany fought a bitter winter and lost.

4. The Allies won a major victory at _____ in Egypt.

5. On December 7, 1941, the Japanese attacked _____, killed many Americans, and destroyed many ships and planes.

What do you think ?

Americans were faced with a difficult problem when the Japanese bombed Pearl Harbor. What would have been your reaction to the problem?

Objectives

◆ To describe the Allies' victories in the Pacific and Europe

◆ To identify D-Day

◆ To describe the effects of the atomic bomb on Hiroshima

◆ To identify the resistance

From September 1939 to the summer of 1942, the Axis Powers had things pretty much their own way. Then the tide turned; the Allies began to win in the Pacific and in Europe.

In June 1942, the Allies won a great naval victory at Midway Island. Historians call this battle a turning point in the Pacific. The Allies forced Japan to go on the **defensive,** or to defend oneself rather than attack others. When the Allies captured Guadalcanal in 1943, Japan went into full retreat.

In 1943, the Soviets defeated Hitler at Stalingrad. At about the same time, Allied troops swept enemy troops out of North Africa.

What Was the Resistance?

During the war, Germany **occupied,** or took over, many European countries. In these occupied countries, even in Germany itself, civilians secretly fought against the Nazis. People with great courage secretly organized and fought for their freedom. They were members of "the **Resistance**." That is, they resisted, or opposed, the Germans occupying their country. They used **guerilla warfare** to get at the enemy. In this kind of fighting, Resistance fighters blew up bridges, railroads, and factories. Hitler sent thousands of troops into these occupied countries to guard important transportation and supply centers.

How Long Did the Allies Fight in Italy?

On July 10, 1943, the Allies invaded Italy and opened up a new front. They quickly overran the island of Sicily. This forced Mussolini to resign and a new government was formed.

This new government signed an armistice with the Allies. However, thousands of German troops remained in Italy. It was not until June 1944 that Allied troops freed Rome from German control. However, parts of Italy stayed under German control until the spring of 1945.

Defensive

Protecting oneself rather than attacking others

Occupy

To take over and stay in a place

Resistance

Those who opposed the Germans occupying their country

Guerilla warfare

A kind of fighting that involves small attacks against an enemy or the things it needs and uses

Based on the title
of the next section,
what can you infer
about the text in the
section?

D-Day

The Allied invasion of
France in 1944

Kamikaze

A Japanese pilot who
crashed his plane
into an enemy ship
and destroyed it and
himself

V-E Day

The day the allies
completed their
victory in Europe:
May 8, 1945; stands
for "Victory in Europe
Day"

What Was D-Day?

In the early morning hours of June 6, 1944, a large Allied army invaded France. Historians call this **D-Day.** By the end of August, Paris was free for the first time since 1940. The Allies had driven the Germans out of Paris. Now they prepared to attack Germany.

D-Day brought an Allied attack from the west. At the same time, Soviet forces attacked Germany from the east. During 1944, the Soviets successfully pushed the Germans back. By October 1944, almost all of eastern and central Europe was under Soviet control.

What Was the Allied Battle Plan in the Pacific?

In the Pacific, the Allies used a plan called "island hopping." They fought their way north to Japan by leapfrogging from one island to another. They attacked some Japanese-controlled islands but ignored, or leapfrogged, others. The Allies then cut off supplies to the islands they ignored.

Things were going badly for Japan. It called on its young pilots to die for their country with honor. These pilots were called **kamikazes.** They crashed their planes, loaded with bombs, into Allied ships.

What Ended World War II in Europe?

In March 1945, the Allies crossed the Rhine River on Germany's western border. Soviet forces marched toward Berlin from the east. In April, the Allied forces met at the Elbe River and Russian troops captured Berlin. On April 30, 1945, Hitler killed himself. On May 7, Germany surrendered. Historians call the next day, May 8, **V-E Day**—Victory in Europe Day.

What Ended World War II in the Pacific?

Now the Allies turned their full attention to Japan. Day and night, American planes bombed Japanese cities. President Harry Truman, who took office after President Roosevelt died in 1945, did not want to invade Japan. He knew that many American soldiers would be killed.

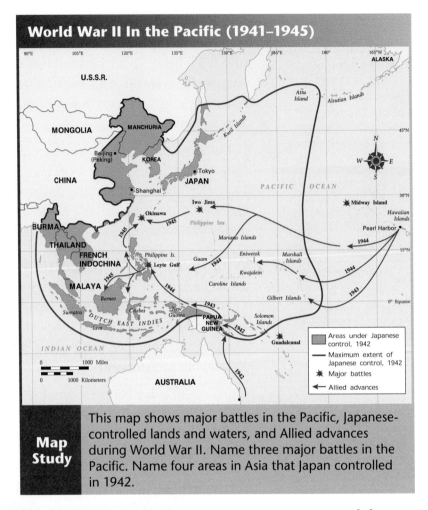

World War II In the Pacific (1941–1945)

Map Study

This map shows major battles in the Pacific, Japanese-controlled lands and waters, and Allied advances during World War II. Name three major battles in the Pacific. Name four areas in Asia that Japan controlled in 1942.

General Dwight D. Eisenhower was the Allied commander in Europe. He became president of the United States in 1953.

On August 6, 1945, Truman approved the use of the world's first **atomic bomb.** This type of bomb was **nuclear.** This meant it used energy from atoms, which gave it much destructive power. The United States dropped it on the Japanese city of Hiroshima. Japan did not surrender. Three days later, the United States dropped a second atomic bomb on the city of Nagasaki. On August 14, 1945, Japan agreed to end the war. On September 2, Japan officially surrendered. Historians call this **V-J Day**—Victory in Japan Day. World War II was over.

"A Blinding Flash Cut Sharply Across the Sky"

In May 1941, President Roosevelt set up a secret program—the Manhattan Project—to build a special bomb. On August 6, 1945, three American planes flew over Hiroshima, Japan. At exactly 8:15 a.m., a B-29 bomber called the *Enola Gay* dropped this ten-foot atomic bomb.

The bomb weighed about 8,000 pounds. It carried about two pounds of uranium, which gave it enormous energy. In fact, the bomb had the explosive power of 20,000 tons—or 40 million pounds—of TNT.

A Japanese man who was about three miles from the blast center described the scene. He said, "A blinding flash cut sharply across the sky. . . . At the same moment as the flash, the skin over my body felt a burning heat . . . and then a . . . huge 'boom.'" He saw a large mushroom-shaped cloud rise nearly 27,000 feet over Hiroshima.

The temperature at the center of the blast was at least about 10,800° Fahrenheit. Fires broke out everywhere. Then rain began to fall. It was made up of large, black drops. This black rain was radioactive. It caused blood cancer, loss of hair, high fever, and death.

No one knows how many people died in the attack on Hiroshima. Perhaps as many as 140,000 to 150,000 persons died immediately from burns. However, during the months that followed, more than 200,000 people died from the aftermath of the bomb.

In a park in downtown Hiroshima, the Japanese have built a monument to those who died. On it, they wrote "Let all the souls here rest in peace; For we shall not repeat the evil." Let us hope the world never does.

The atomic bomb that was dropped on Hiroshima destroyed almost everything it touched. Hundreds of thousands of Japanese people were killed.

The Nuclear Age

The Nuclear Age began in August 1945. Atomic fireballs burned Hiroshima and Nagasaki to the ground. Many people were grateful that the war had ended, but they were also horrified. They feared this immense new energy source. Soon several other countries developed this bomb. For years, nations competed in a nuclear arms race. Finally, many countries agreed to limit nuclear tests and weapons. Some have refused to follow these rules, however.

Nuclear energy has peaceful uses too. Some people believe it is a clean, safe source of energy. France, the Soviet Union, and other countries depend on nuclear power plants. But many people in the United States doubt its safety. Nuclear medicine is another peaceful use. Tiny amounts of radioactive materials find and treat disease.

Word Bank
Allies
D-Day
Midway
Resistance
Truman

Lesson 4 Review On a sheet of paper, use the words from the Word Bank to complete each sentence correctly.

1. Historians consider the Battle of _____ a turning point in the war in the Pacific.

2. Many European civilians fought the war as members of the _____.

3. The _____ invaded Italy in 1943.

4. _____ is the name for the Allied invasion of France on June 6, 1944.

5. President _____ gave the command to drop an atomic bomb on Japan to end the war.

What do you think ?

Do you think the United States did the right thing by dropping atomic bombs on Japan? Explain your answer.

- To explain why Germans thought the Jews were responsible for Germany's problems
- To describe how the Germans treated the Jews

Holocaust

Hitler's killing of many of the Jews in Europe

Ghetto

The special parts of cities where the Jewish people were forced to live during World War II

Reading Strategy:
Inferencing

What do you already know about the Holocaust?

At the end of the war, Allied forces discovered that the Nazis were guilty of horrible crimes against humanity. Hitler and the Nazis thought there were two groups of people. They thought the German people were a "master race." They said that everyone else was below them, or inferior. Nazi leaders told the German people that the Jews were responsible for Germany's problems. They discussed a plan to murder all the Jews of Europe. Nazi officials called this plan the "Final Solution." Historians call Hitler's carrying out his plan to kill Jews the **Holocaust.**

What Were the First Steps the Nazis Took?

The Nazis began to treat the Jews badly almost as soon as Hitler took power. All Jews working in the German government lost their jobs. Hitler also ordered all Jews to wear a yellow star on their clothes. Finally, Jews were forced to move to **ghettos,** which were special parts of the cities.

Biography

Anne Frank: 1929–1945
Anne Frank's diary has made her a symbol of Nazi cruelty. In July 1942, Nazi troops began rounding up Jews in Amsterdam. With her parents and sister, Anne went into hiding. She had just turned 13. The family and others lived in a secret attic above her father's former business. Anne also began a diary, writing about her hopes and dreams. For two years, non-Jewish friends brought them food. Then in August 1944, the Gestapo found and sent them to  concentration camps. Only her father survived. Anne died at Bergen-Belsen. After the war, her father found the diary and published it.

What Was Kristallnacht?

Soon Hitler took his hatred of Jews one step further. On November 9, 1938, non-Jewish Germans broke into and destroyed many Jewish owned businesses and many synagogues, where the Jews worshipped. Historians call this Kristallnacht, or "Night of Broken Glass."

What Happened in the Holocaust?

Starting in June 1941, the German government began an organized program of **genocide**. Genocide is the complete destruction of a culture or people. Hitler ordered millions of Jews arrested. The Nazis rounded up Jews from Germany and from all the countries the Nazis had conquered. Individuals and entire families were crowded into cattle cars and brought to large prison death camps called **concentration camps.**

A special Nazi army unit called the SS ran the concentration camps. Six of the camps, including Auschwitz and Dachau, were death camps. When the prisoners arrived, those who seemed strong and healthy were forced to work. Everyone else was put to death right away. This group included babies, young children, sick people, and elderly people.

Before the war, there were about 11 million Jews living in Europe. By the end of the war, the Nazis had murdered nearly six million Jews. Every Jewish community in Europe that the Nazis had taken over suffered losses. Experts guess that another five million non-Jews were killed.

Did the Jews Fight Back?

It was difficult and dangerous to resist the Nazis, but many Jews fought back. If a prisoner escaped or attacked a Nazi, the army would round up and kill a large number of Jews. The Jews were isolated and had no weapons. Nevertheless, during the war, some 20,000 to 30,000 Jews fought bravely against the Nazis. The fighters were completely outnumbered by the Nazis and had few weapons. Still, they led uprisings in many ghettos. Even though they knew they had little hope of success, fighters led uprisings in several camps.

Hitler and *Lebensraum*

Hitler wanted to rebuild Germany into a great power. To do this, Hitler said that Germany needed more living space, or *Lebensraum.* This idea was a basic part of his policy. In theory, Hitler meant empty lands where Germans could settle. But in reality, any land that Germany would take already belonged to other people. Germany was no more crowded than most of Europe.

Many historians think that *Lebensraum* was just an excuse. It justified Hitler's plans to conquer his neighbors. He found other reasons to claim their land, too. For example, many ethnic Germans lived in Czechoslovakia. Nearby Austria was another German-speaking country. Also, the Treaty of Versailles, which ended World War I, had deeply wounded German pride. France had gotten land from Germany. So had Poland. Beyond Poland were the rich farmlands of Ukraine in the Soviet Union. Taking more land would bring Hitler more power.

Hitler almost succeeded in destroying the Jewish culture and people. It is important to remember what happened during the Holocaust so that we can prevent it from ever happening again.

Lesson 5 Review On a sheet of paper, write the answer to each question. Use complete sentences.

1. Why did the German people think that Jews were inferior to them?

2. What was Kristallnacht?

3. About how many Jews were killed in concentration camps?

4. How did Jews fight back?

5. Why is it important to remember what happened in the Holocaust?

What do you think ?

What are some ways that reminders of the Holocaust have been kept alive through the years?

Objectives

◆ To identify ways that the war destroyed the economies of some countries

◆ To explain why refugees fled their countries

◆ To identify changes in Italy, Germany, Eastern Europe, and Japan

World War II ended in 1945. Millions of people had been killed or injured. The economies of many countries were destroyed, and the political power of the world shifted. We still live with the social, economic, and political results of the war.

Before the war, Europe had led the world's economy. Large empires had made Britain and France rich and powerful. Now they no longer controlled many of their colonies. Their economies had fallen apart.

Some historians have guessed that the war may have cost four trillion dollars. It wrecked the economy of most countries—except the United States. Most countries had borrowed money to pay for weapons. If they had goods to export after the war, they could pay back this money. But they had nothing to sell because the war had destroyed their factories.

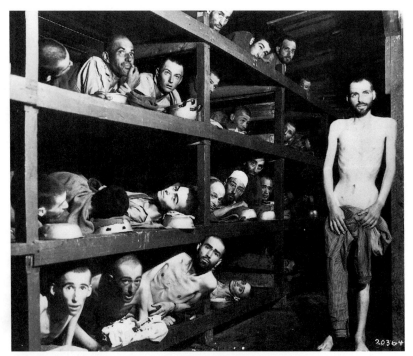

Those in concentration camps suffered through terrible treatment, including cramped living conditions. This photo shows prisoners at Dachau in Germany.

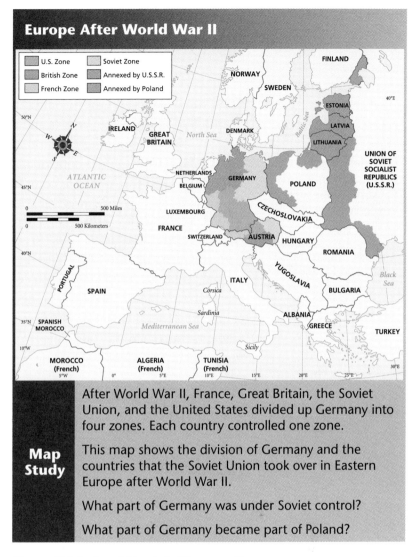

Europe After World War II

U.S. Zone
British Zone
French Zone
Soviet Zone
Annexed by U.S.S.R.
Annexed by Poland

Map Study

After World War II, France, Great Britain, the Soviet Union, and the United States divided up Germany into four zones. Each country controlled one zone.

This map shows the division of Germany and the countries that the Soviet Union took over in Eastern Europe after World War II.

What part of Germany was under Soviet control?

What part of Germany became part of Poland?

How Did the World Change?

The war also destroyed homes, farms, highways, bridges, and railroads. People had no food. Because of this, millions of **refugees** were forced to flee their countries. Their cities lay in ruins. The war damaged the capitals of Germany, Poland, Austria, the Netherlands, and Hungary. Many people went to other countries to find a new and better life.

Because of the war, the political power of the world shifted. The United States and the Soviet Union became much more powerful than any other country. For this reason, historians called them **superpowers.**

The United States and the Soviet Union had been allies in World War II. But after the war, they grew apart. Before long, an invisible boundary separated democratic Western Europe from Communist-controlled Eastern Europe. Winston Churchill called this invisible boundary the **Iron Curtain.**

What Changes Took Place in Italy and Germany?

After the war, the Italians voted to set up a republic. The Allies divided Germany into four zones. Britain, France, the Soviet Union, and the United States each controlled one zone. In 1949, the western zones united under a new democratic government called the Federal Republic of Germany, or West Germany. The Soviets set up a Communist government in their zone called the German Democratic Republic, or East Germany.

What Changes Took Place in Eastern Europe?

The Communists took control of Eastern Europe. Poland, Yugoslavia, Czechoslovakia, Romania, Bulgaria, Albania, and Hungary set up Communist governments. They became **satellites** of the Soviet Union. A satellite nation is tightly controlled by another nation.

What Changes Took Place in Japan?

After the war ended, the United States placed Japan under the control of General Douglas MacArthur. (He had been a leader in the war in the Pacific.) He introduced the Japanese to democracy. The Japanese wrote a new constitution that protected individual rights. The Allies told the Japanese they could have only a small military force for self-defense. The emperor remained as head of state, but the people no longer viewed him as a god.

Superpower

A nation that has more power and money than other countries

Iron Curtain

The invisible boundary between Western Europe and Eastern Europe after World War II

Satellite

A nation that is tightly controlled by another nation

Lesson 6 Review On a sheet of paper, write the letter of the answer that correctly completes each sentence.

1. Many countries in Eastern Europe became _____ of the Soviet Union.

   A refugees   **C** superpowers
   B satellites   **D** colonies

2. Bombs and troops destroyed _____ and left Europe in ruins.

   A factories   **C** homes
   B railroads   **D** all of the above

3. The Soviets set up a _____ government in East Germany after the war.

   A Communist   **C** Slavic
   B democratic   **D** military

4. After the war, the Allies divided Germany into _____ zones.

   A two   **C** four
   B three   **D** five

5. The invisible boundary separating democratic Western Europe from Communist-controlled Eastern Europe was known as the _____.

   A Iron Curtain   **C** superpowers
   B satellite   **D** Italian zone

What do you think ?

Why do you think refugees wanted to leave their countries and go to other European countries after the war?

Objectives

◆ To identify the six parts of the United Nations and the job of each

◆ To explain some successes and failures of the United Nations

Organization

A group of people joined together for a common purpose

United Nations (UN)

The international organization that works to settle disagreements, improve the way people live, and keep peace around the world

Charter

A constitution; a set of statements that explains a group's purpose

In August 1941, President Roosevelt and Prime Minister Churchill began to work together to establish safety in the world. In April 1945, representatives of many nations met in San Francisco, California. They met to establish an **organization,** or group, to replace the League of Nations. It was called the **United Nations** (UN). This is an international organization that works to settle disagreements, improve the way people live, and keep peace around the world. Its representatives wrote a **charter,** or constitution, for this new organization. It has six major parts. Each has a special job.

The first branch is the General Assembly. All member nations belong to it. Each nation—no matter how large or how small— has one vote. The assembly debates world problems. If it votes for UN action on an issue, the matter goes to the Security Council.

The Security Council tries to settle arguments between nations peacefully. It has 15 members. Britain, China, France, the United States, and the Soviet Union became the permanent members of the council. Ten other nations are elected to it. They serve two-year terms. The five permanent members of the council have veto power. Any one of them can stop the council from taking any action. The council members have used this power many times.

The Secretariat handles the day-to-day work of the UN. The Secretary-General of the UN heads the Secretariat. People from many countries help. They work in the UN building in New York.

The International Court of Justice handles questions of law that arise between member nations. It listens to arguments between countries and decides what can be done. However, it has no power to carry out the actions of its rulings.

What Does the Economic and Social Council Do?

The Economic and Social Council tries to stop wars by improving the way people live. It does this through five groups.

- The United Nations Educational, Scientific, and Cultural Organization (UNESCO) gives advice to needy countries in Africa, Asia, and Latin America.

- The United Nations International Children's Emergency Fund (UNICEF) cares for sick, starving, and homeless children in dozens of countries.

- The Food and Agricultural Organization (FAO) helps farmers grow more food.

- The World Health Organization (WHO) improves people's health.

- The International Labor Organization (ILO) improves working conditions and living standards around the world.

The Trusteeship Council takes care of all **trust territories.** These are territories that the Allies took from countries that lost World War I and World War II. The council prepares these territories to rule themselves. Most of them are now independent countries.

How Successful Has the UN Been?

The UN can be proud of what it has done since 1945. Over 150 nations are now members. It provides a place where nations can present their views to the world. It has helped colonial people gain independence. It has helped keep peace in many places in the world. It has protected millions of people from diseases.

However, the UN has failed to stop some wars. It has not been able to get nations to give up their weapons. It still does not have its own military force. Instead, it depends on its members to volunteer soldiers. Some nations refuse to obey UN orders or pay their share of the UN's costs.

Lesson 7 Review On a sheet of paper, write the answer to each question. Use complete sentences.

1. What are the six major branches of the United Nations?

2. Which five countries became the permanent members of the Security Council?

3. What are three agencies of the Economic and Social Council?

4. Why is the Trusteeship Council almost out of business?

5. What is one success and one failure of the UN?

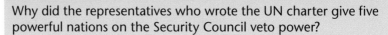

What do you think

Why did the representatives who wrote the UN charter give five powerful nations on the Security Council veto power?

The United Nations Charter

The United Nations Charter was signed in 1945.

One important result of World War II was the creation of the United Nations (UN). It replaced the League of Nations. The United States had refused to join the League, which weakened it. The League could not keep the peace.

During World War II, Allied leaders had met often to plan strategy and future cooperation. In January 1942, 26 Allied nations held a meeting. They first used the name "United Nations" to describe their group. In April 1945, before the war ended, representatives of about 50 nations drew up a charter, or constitution, for the new organization. The UN Charter begins:

We the people of the United Nations are determined to save future generations from the scourge of war, which twice in our lifetime has brought untold sorrow to mankind. We are determined to reaffirm our faith in fundamental human rights, in the dignity and worth of the human person, and in the equal rights of men and women and of nations large and small. We are determined to establish conditions under which justice and respect for the duties arising from treaties and other parts of international law can be maintained. We are determined to promote social progress and better standards of life in greater freedom. To achieve these goals, we will practice tolerance and will live together in peace with one another as good neighbors. We are also determined to unite our strength to maintain international peace and security, and to insure that armed force shall not be used except in the interests of all. And, finally, we are determined to use international means to promote the economic and social advancement of all peoples. To accomplish these aims we have resolved to combine our efforts. And so our Governments have agreed to present this Charter of the United Nations. And they do hereby establish an international organization to be known as the United Nations.

Document-Based Questions

1. What two wars is the Charter referring to in its opening sentence?

2. What rights does the Charter reaffirm?

3. What are two other goals of the United Nations according to the Charter?

4. How will member nations achieve those goals?

5. Does the Charter expect possible threats to international peace in the future? If yes, how will the United Nations deal with them?

Source: The United Nations Charter, 1945.

The Dachau Concentration Camp

Dachau was the first Nazi concentration camp in Germany. It became a model for camps built later. Dachau opened in March 1933. It was on the grounds of a former ammunition factory near Munich. Prisoners included political opponents, Jews, and people who were not considered normal. Some were religious leaders who spoke out against the Nazis.

It is hard to know how many people were held at Dachau. The camp originally held 5,000 persons. It was expanded in 1937. Between 1938 and 1945, the camp registered more than 200,000 people. Thousands more passed through on their way to other camps. Others died before their names were recorded.

The prisoners lived in 32 "blocks," or barracks. Each block was built for 180 persons. Later, more than 800 people lived in that same space. To prevent escapes, the camp was fenced with electric barbed wire and a wall. On one side was a water-filled ditch. Guards with machine guns kept watch. If one prisoner escaped, all the others were punished.

The camp crematorium and gas chamber stood outside the walls. A crematorium is where bodies of the dead are burned. New arrivals at Dachau were told to undress and shower. But the "showers" contained poison gas, not water. Thousands of people were gassed and then burned. The smell of burning bodies often filled the air. Perhaps 70,000 people died at Dachau.

Over the camp gate hung the sign reading *Arbeit Macht Frei.* That means, "Work makes you free." This was a lie. Prisoners worked in the gravel pits. They worked from sunrise to sunset. If workers stopped, Nazi guards kicked or hit them with rifles.

A prisoner of Dachau shows an American soldier the crematorium.

Prisoners never had enough food. On April 29, 1945, American troops freed Dachau. The camp had nearly 30,000 prisoners. Many looked like walking skeletons. Some were so ill and weak that they soon died. The soldiers were horrified by what they found. General Dwight D. Eisenhower wrote, ". . . I have never at any other time experienced an equal sense of shock."

Some years later, the acting mayor of Berlin said, "Every German . . . must feel responsible . . . for the sins committed . . . in the name of Germany." Today there are chapels and a museum at Dachau.

Wrap-Up

1. What and where was Dachau?

2. Who was sent to Dachau?

3. How did the Nazis try to prevent prisoners from escaping?

4. What happened in the "showers"?

5. What did American soldiers find when they freed Dachau?

- Italy, Germany, and Japan—the Axis Powers—were strongly nationalistic and imperialistic in the 1930s. They built strong military forces.

- German anger at the Treaty of Versailles and worldwide economic problems caused World War II. Other causes were the Axis dictatorships and the failure of the League of Nations.

- Hitler broke many provisions of the Treaty of Versailles. He invaded the Rhineland and Austria. In 1938, he demanded the Sudetenland section of Czechoslovakia.

- To avoid war, France and Britain followed a policy of appeasement. They did not act against Italy or Germany. The Munich Pact gave Hitler the Sudetenland.

- Germany and the Soviet Union signed a treaty not to attack one another. In September 1939, the two countries invaded Poland. Then Britain and France declared war on them.

- In 1940, Germany launched the "blitzkrieg" and quickly conquered most of Western Europe. The Maginot line of defense failed, and France surrendered.

- The Axis waged total war against Great Britain. German planes bombed England in the Battle of Britain. The United States aided Britain through the Lend-Lease program.

- Germany invaded the Soviet Union for its oil and grain. The Russian winter stopped the Germans, and after the battle of Stalingrad the Germans retreated.

- In December 1941, Japanese forces attacked the American fleet at Pearl Harbor, Hawaii. The United States declared war on the Axis Powers.

- To avoid invading Japan, President Harry Truman decided to drop atomic bombs on Hiroshima and Nagasaki in August 1945. Japan surrendered.

- World War II killed about 60 million soldiers and civilians. Millions of Jews and others were killed in Nazi concentration camps. This killing of innocent people is called the Holocaust.

- World War II hurt the economies of most nations except the United States. Major nations lost their colonial empires. Refugees moved to other countries.

- An invisible "Iron Curtain" separated Soviet-dominated Eastern Europe from democratic Western Europe. Germany was divided into democratic West Germany and Communist East Germany.

- The United Nations (UN) was formed in 1945 to prevent future wars. It has both succeeded and failed. Soldiers from member nations serve as peacekeepers.

Chapter 27 REVIEW

Word Bank

General Assembly

Hiroshima

Japan

League of Nations

Maginot Line

Munich Pact

Rhineland

Roosevelt

Secretariat

Security Council

On a sheet of paper, use the words from the Word Bank to complete each sentence correctly.

1. The _____ could not prevent World War II, because it was weak and its most powerful members would not cooperate.

2. When war broke out, President _____ asked the United States to become an "arsenal of democracy."

3. Hitler ignored the Treaty of Versailles when he sent German troops into the _____.

4. The _____ gave Hitler control of the Sudetenland.

5. France's line of concrete forts along its border with Germany was called the _____.

6. The United States dropped an atomic bomb on _____ on August 6, 1945.

7. World War II ended when _____ agreed to end the fighting on August 14, 1945.

8. Every member nation in the United Nations is represented in the _____.

9. Britain, China, France, the United States, and the Soviet Union became the five permanent members of the UN _____.

10. The _____ handles the day-to-day operations of the UN.

On a sheet of paper, write the letter of the answer that correctly completes each sentence.

11. Japan, Germany, and Italy were the three _____ Powers in World War II.

   A Allied   **B** Axis   **C** Pacific   **D** Western

12. Great Britain, France, the United States, the Soviet Union, Canada, and 47 other nations were the _____ in World War II.

   A Allies   **C** League of Nations
   B Axis   **D** Eastern Powers

13. The _____ was a turning point in World War II.

  A Battle of Stalingrad   **C** Battle of Midway
  B Battle of El Alamein   **D** all of the above

14. Japan tried to cripple the U.S. Navy with a surprise attack on _____.

  A Midway   **C** Pearl Harbor
  B Guadalcanal   **D** San Francisco

15. A special Nazi unit called the _____ ran the concentration camps.

  A Kamikaze   **C** Maginot line
  B Blitzkrieg   **D** SS

On a sheet of paper, write the answer to each question. Use complete sentences.

16. What caused the United States to stop being neutral and to enter World War II?

17. What is one social, one economic, and one political outcome of World War II?

18. After the Battle of Britain, Hitler attacked the Soviet Union. Why?

Critical Thinking On a sheet of paper, write your response to each question. Use complete sentences.

19. Why do you suppose appeasement was popular at first? What happened in World War I that might explain appeasement? Why did it fail?

20. Could Germany have won World War II if it had not attacked the Soviet Union? Explain your answer.

Test-Taking Tip

Spend most of your time on essay tests answering the question. Don't write long introductions or conclusions.

Political Cartoons

Political cartoons are drawings about political events. Some are intended to make people laugh. They may poke fun at a political figure. However, the main point of a political cartoon is to encourage people to think about current issues. Political cartoons express a viewpoint about a political issue or topic. Cartoonists reveal various opinions in a drawing. They can persuade others to support their opinion through the cartoon.

Cartoons often use symbols, or objects that stand for something else. In the cartoon on this page, the bomb-shaped object stands not just for the atomic bomb but also for the climate of fear around it. Notice that a house and family are perched on the bomb. What do you think they stand for?

Cartoonists use labels or captions to help readers interpret their drawing. This cartoon has three labels. One is "atomic bomb." The others are "world control" and "world destruction." The bomb is balanced on the cliff labeled "world control." It is teetering over a deep canyon called "world destruction." The cartoonist, Ruben Goldberg, has added a caption, too: "Peace Today." The cartoon was published in 1948, only three years after the first atomic bombs were dropped on Japan.

Peace Today

Study the cartoon. Then answer these questions.

1. What do the house and family stand for?

2. Why is the bomb balanced between "world control" and "world destruction"?

3. What does the cartoon show about people's feelings in 1948?

4. What does the caption "Peace Today" add to the cartoon?

5. Find a current political cartoon in your newspaper. Write what you think it means.

- Military alliances and nationalism led to World War I (1914–1918). The Allies were France, Russia, Britain, Italy, Japan, and the United States. They defeated the Central Powers (Austria-Hungary, Germany, Bulgaria, and the Ottoman Empire).

- World War I was a total war. Armies used trench warfare and many new weapons.

- The Treaty of Versailles blamed Germany for the war and broke up the Austro-Hungarian Empire. It created new democratic nations.

- Russia had begun to industrialize in the 1800s, but most people were poor. In 1905, workers rebelled and Nicholas II briefly gave in to some demands. A revolution in 1917 overthrew him.

- Lenin's Bolsheviks (later called Communists), took over the Russian government. Russia became the Soviet Union.

- Stalin made the Soviet Union a totalitarian state. The government developed heavy industry and collective farms. Stalin had opponents killed or sent to Siberia.

- Fascism opposed both democracy and communism. It demanded total obedience to the state. Mussolini gained power in Italy. Adolf Hitler led the Nazis in Germany.

- In China, Sun Yat-sen led a nationalist revolution in 1911. Later Chiang Kai-shek led a civil war against Mao Zedong's Chinese Communists. Military leaders took power in Japan in the 1930s.

- The Axis Powers (Italy, Germany, and Japan) were nationalistic. They seized territory in the 1930s, but France and Britain did not stop them. In 1939, Germany and the Soviet Union invaded Poland. France and Britain then declared war.

- Hitler conquered Western Europe. Japan conquered Southeast Asia and much of China. The United States entered the war in 1941.

- The battles of Stalingrad (Russia), El Alamein (North Africa), and Midway (Pacific) were turning points in the war. Allied forces invaded France in June 1944. Germany surrendered in May 1945. The United States used atomic bombs against Japan, which surrendered in August 1945.

"I have fought against white domination, and I have fought against black domination. I have cherished the idea of a democratic and free society in which all persons live together in harmony . . . It is an ideal which I hope to live for . . . but if needs be, it is an ideal for which I am prepared to die."

~Nelson Mandela, South African political leader and president; he said this at his trial in 1964 and repeated it on his release from prison in 1990

Unit 7

The World Since 1945

The contemporary world is the world in which you are living today. This world is an interdependent one. That is, you depend on people around the world. You eat food that farmers grew in Asia and Africa. You listen to Latin American music. Your family may drive a car made in Europe. These products, mass communication, and technology link you to people around the globe.

With this unit, you end your study of world history. What an adventure it has been! You have visited the past. Now you will look at the present. You will see new nations develop. You will also see how your global village changes. You will learn the lessons that prepare you to greet the future. Where will the 21st century take you? Changes lie ahead. Be ready to meet it and to grow into a good citizen of this global village we call the earth.

28

The Cold War

B oth the United States and the Soviet Union came out of World War II as superpowers. The United States lost 300,000 men and women in battle, but Germany and Japan had losses of several million people. More than 18 million Soviets lost their lives. The Soviet Union fought much of the war on its own soil.

Between the end of World War II and the collapse of the Soviet Union in 1991, the United States and the Soviet Union were engaged in a "cold" war. This was a war of ideas, not bombs.

Goals for Learning

◆ To explain how the cold war began

◆ To describe U.S. conflicts with the Soviets and explain the Korean War

◆ To explain why Communism failed in the Soviet Union and Eastern Europe

◆ To describe the changes in European countries

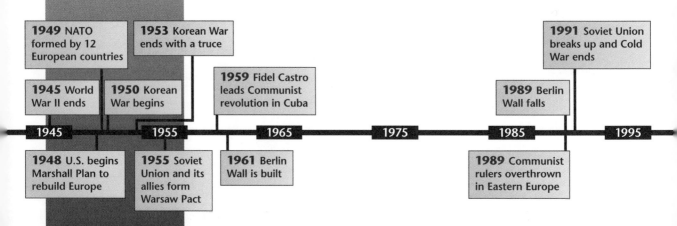

1949 NATO formed by 12 European countries

1953 Korean War ends with a truce

1991 Soviet Union breaks up and Cold War ends

1945 World War II ends

1950 Korean War begins

1959 Fidel Castro leads Communist revolution in Cuba

1989 Berlin Wall falls

| 1945 | 1955 | 1965 | 1975 | 1985 | 1995 |

1948 U.S. begins Marshall Plan to rebuild Europe

1955 Soviet Union and its allies form Warsaw Pact

1961 Berlin Wall is built

1989 Communist rulers overthrown in Eastern Europe

Europe Divided

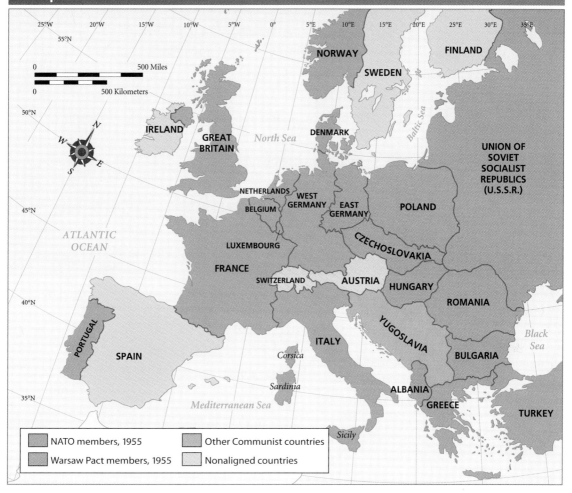

Legend:
- NATO members, 1955
- Warsaw Pact members, 1955
- Other Communist countries
- Nonaligned countries

Map Skills

This map shows how Europe was divided by two alliances—NATO and the Warsaw Pact. The map legend tells you what countries were NATO members in 1955, Warsaw Pact members in 1955, other Communist countries, and nonaligned countries, or countries that are not in any of these groups.

Study the map, then answer the following questions:

1. Which countries were NATO members in 1955?

2. Which countries were members of the Warsaw Pact?

3. Which alliance did most countries of Western Europe join?

4. Which country in the Warsaw Pact was probably the most powerful?

5. Which countries did not belong to either NATO or the Warsaw Pact?

Reading Strategy:
Metacognition

Metacognition means "thinking about your thinking." Use metacognition to become a better reader:

◆ Write the main idea, details, and any questions you have as you read the text.

◆ Make predictions and ask yourself what you already know about the topic.

◆ Summarize what you have read and make inferences about the meaning.

◆ Visualize what is happening in the text. If something doesn't make sense, go back and read it again.

Key Vocabulary Words

Lesson 1

Cold war The war of ideas between the United States and the Soviet Union after World War II

Propaganda One-sided information meant to change people's thinking

Truman Doctrine President Truman's plan to stop the spread of Communism

Marshall Plan The American plan to rebuild Europe after World War II

Lesson 2

Truce An agreement to stop a war for a time

Lesson 3

Glasnost A Russian word that means openness; under Gorbachev it meant openness in government

Perestroika An economic policy used by Gorbachev to encourage factories to produce the goods people wanted

Coup A takeover of the government

Lesson 4

Strike The act of refusing to work until certain demands are met

Solidarity The name of the Polish shipbuilder's union that went out on strike in 1980

Berlin Wall The wall that divided the people of East and West Berlin

Ethnic cleansing The act of getting rid of a group of people because their religion or race is different from the majority group

Tariff A tax that countries put on goods they import or export

Currency The form of money a country uses

Objectives

- ◆ To explain what the cold war was
- ◆ To identify the Truman Doctrine and the Marshall Plan
- ◆ To explain why NATO was formed

Reading Strategy:
Metacognition

Before you read this lesson, think about what you can do that will help you understand all the reasons for the cold war.

Cold war

The war of ideas between the United States and the Soviet Union after World War II

Propaganda

One-sided information meant to change people's thinking

Truman Doctrine

President Truman's plan to stop the spread of Communism

Soon after World War II, the United States and the Soviet Union began a **cold war.** That is, they became rivals who used words and ideas as weapons instead of bullets. They fought the cold war with **propaganda,** or one-sided information. They used this propaganda to change people's way of thinking.

Which Countries Did the Truman Doctrine Help?

At the end of the war, the Communists threatened to take control of Greece and Turkey. But American President Harry Truman wanted to prevent the spread of Communism.

In 1947, Truman announced the **Truman Doctrine.** This plan gave economic and military help to nations threatened by an outside power. The Truman Doctrine helped Greece and Turkey defeat the Communists. But it also showed the world that the United States would do everything short of war to stop the spread of Communism.

The Marshall Plan helped European nations rebuild after World War II.

Marshall Plan

The American plan to rebuild Europe after World War II

Reading Strategy:
Metacognition

Remember to ask yourself questions as you read. This will help you understand what you are reading.

Word Bank

Communism

Marshall Plan

NATO

propaganda

Truman Doctrine

What do you think ?

In Chapter 25, you learned that alliances led to World War I. Why do you think nations once again formed alliances?

Whom Did the Marshall Plan Help?

Both Communism and economic collapse threatened Europe. In 1948, the U.S. Congress approved the **Marshall Plan,** or European Recovery Program. It helped European nations get back on their feet after the war.

The Marshall Plan was a big success. By 1950, countries were producing more goods than they had before the war. Instead of being rivals, some European countries began to work together for economic growth.

What Two Military Alliances Brought Countries Together?

In 1948, the Communists took complete control of Czechoslovakia. They forced Finland to sign a treaty with them and tried to take over Berlin. The West was afraid that the cold war might suddenly become hot.

Several nations formed the North Atlantic Treaty Organization (NATO). They said that an attack on any one of them would be an attack on all of them. Today, NATO has 19 members. It has taken part in many missions to keep world peace.

In 1955, the Soviet Union established the Warsaw Pact. This treaty set up a military alliance between the Soviet Union and other Communist countries in Eastern Europe.

Lesson 1 Review On a sheet of paper, use the words from the Word Bank to complete each sentence correctly.

1. President Truman wanted to contain _____.

2. The cold war used _____ to try to change people's way of thinking.

3. The _____ helped rebuild Europe after World War II.

4. The _____ helped Greece and Turkey defeat the Communists.

5. _____ is an alliance among 19 countries of Western Europe.

Objectives

◆ To describe the blockade of Berlin and the Berlin Airlift

◆ To explain how the Korean War began and ended

In 1948, the cold war threatened to become a real war in Berlin. After World War II, Germany was divided into four sections. The United States, Britain, France, and the Soviet Union each controlled one zone. Its capital, Berlin, was located completely within the Soviet zone. The four countries agreed that each would control a part of Berlin.

Why Did the Soviets Set Up a Blockade?

In June 1948, the Soviets tried to take over all of Berlin by starving the people living there. To do this, they used a blockade. That is, they "blocked" all roads, waterways, and railroads into the city. The people of Berlin had no food, fuel, or other necessary supplies.

How Did the West Get Around the Blockade?

President Truman said, "The United States is going to stay. Period." Almost immediately the West began to use planes to fly in supplies. For more than a year, American and British planes brought tons of food and fuel to the people of Berlin. Planes took off and landed around the clock at the rate of one every three minutes. During the blockade, the pilots flew over 277,000 flights. They delivered more than two million tons of supplies.

Then and Now

The Mariinsky Theatre

The Mariinsky Theatre was named for Maria, wife of Tsar Alexander II. It was built in 1860 in St. Petersburg, Russia. It became a thriving center for the ballet. After the Russian Revolution, the Bolsheviks renamed it the Academic Theater. When government support ended, many performers had to leave. During the Cold War era, three famous dancers—Rudolf Nureyev, Natalia Makarova, and Mikhail Baryshnikov—defected to

Western nations from their ballet home at the Mariinsky (then called the Kirov). This caused strife between the theater management and Soviet authorities.

Today, the renamed Mariinsky Theater is a renowned performance center, featuring its own opera and ballet companies. Every year in June, it hosts the St. Petersburg White Nights Festival. Performers and tourists, once afraid of the Soviet Union, now visit St. Petersburg and the Mariinsky Theatre.

Why Did the Soviets Stop the Blockade?

Historians call this the Berlin Airlift because the West "lifted" supplies into the air and took them to Berlin. With this airlift, the Western powers showed one big thing—they would not let the Communists control any more European land. The West was not going to allow Communism to spread.

All this made the Soviets mad, but they did not shoot down any Western planes. They did not want to start a war. In May 1949, the Soviets stopped blockading Berlin.

What Started the Korean War?

Korea lies between China and Japan. In 1910, Japan made Korea part of its empire. When World War II ended, Soviet forces took over the northern half of Korea. American forces occupied the south. The 38th parallel of latitude became the border that divided the two republics. On June 25, 1950, Communist troops crossed this border into South Korea.

How Did the UN Help South Korea?

South Korea asked the United Nations to stop the North Koreans. The UN Security Council voted to send aid to South Korea. (The Soviet Union was not attending the UN meetings at that time. If it had been, the Soviets probably would have vetoed any UN action.) The United Nations sent soldiers to help South Korea. The Chinese and Soviet Union helped North Korea.

More than 54,260 American soldiers were killed in battle during the Korean War, which was fought 1950–1953.

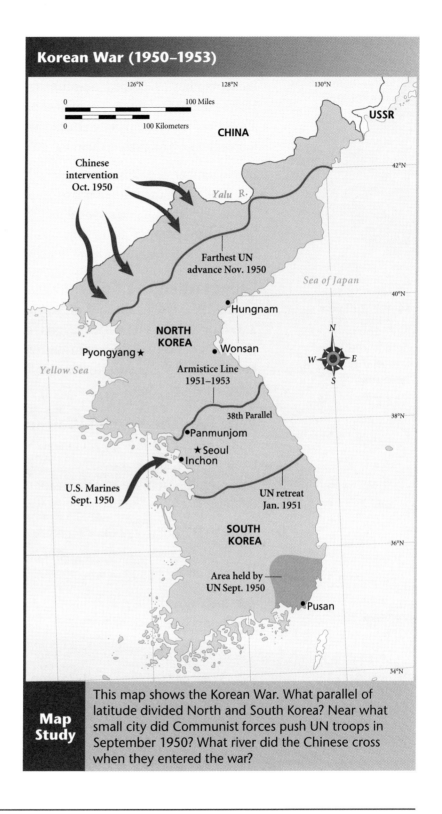

Korean War (1950–1953)

126°N   128°N   130°N

0   100 Miles

0   100 Kilometers

USSR

CHINA

42°N

Chinese
intervention
Oct. 1950

Yalu R.

Farthest UN
advance Nov. 1950

Sea of Japan

40°N

Hungnam

NORTH
KOREA

Wonsan

Pyongyang ★

Armistice Line
1951–1953

Yellow Sea

N

W   E

S

38th Parallel

38°N

Panmunjom

★ Seoul

Inchon

U.S. Marines
Sept. 1950

UN retreat
Jan. 1951

SOUTH
KOREA

36°N

Area held by
UN Sept. 1950

Pusan

34°N

Map Study

This map shows the Korean War. What parallel of latitude divided North and South Korea? Near what small city did Communist forces push UN troops in September 1950? What river did the Chinese cross when they entered the war?

Truce

An agreement to stop a war for a time

How Did the UN Troops Push Back the Communists?

By September 1950, the Communists controlled most of Korea. However, the UN forces got behind the North Korean lines. Then they made a surprise attack that cut the Communist forces in two and forced them to retreat.

By November, UN forces had pushed the Communists back to the Yalu River, the border between China and North Korea. It looked as if the war was over. The UN hoped that Korea would become one country again. But then China sent in thousands of troops to help the North Koreans. The fighting continued.

Reading Strategy:
Metacognition

Note the important details in this lesson. Summarize what you have read about the cold war.

What Ended the Korean War?

In July 1951, **truce** talks began. A truce is an agreement to stop a war for a time. The talks dragged on for two years. Finally, the two sides signed an armistice. It left Korea divided. The border between the two Koreas was almost what it had been before the war.

Why Was the Korean War Important?

The Korean War showed that the UN could stop an attack on a member nation. It showed that China could hold its own in a war that did not use atomic weapons. It also showed that the cold war between the two superpowers would continue.

Since 1953, the United States has continued to support South Korea. It has become an industrial powerhouse in Asia. North Korea remains Communist.

Lesson 2 Review On a sheet of paper, write the answer to each question. Use complete sentences.

What do you think

Since neither the Communists nor the UN troops won the Korean War, was it worth fighting?

1. Why did the Soviets blockade Berlin in June 1948?

2. What caused the Soviets to stop the blockade?

3. What event started the Korean War?

4. How did the United Nations help South Korea?

5. What were the effects of the war on Korea?

Objectives

◆ To describe the reform efforts of Khrushchev and Gorbachev

◆ To explain why the Soviet Union collapsed

◆ To describe Russia under Putin

Reading Strategy:
Metacognition

Note the main idea and important details of this paragraph. Summarize what you have read to make sure you understand this important event.

Throughout its history the Soviet Union has had serious economic problems. Soviet dictator Joseph Stalin tried to industrialize the Soviet Union. By the late 1930s, the Soviet Union had become a major industrial nation. Still, the standard of living in the Soviet Union remained very low.

Why Did Khrushchev's Reform Efforts Fail?

Stalin died in 1953. Nikita Khrushchev became the leader of the Soviet Union. He wanted to reform the weak Soviet economy and to end the government's cruel treatment of the Soviet people. To raise the people's standard of living, factories produced more consumer goods. Artists and writers were allowed some freedom to create what they wanted for the first time.

In 1964, all this changed. Leonid Brezhnev replaced Khrushchev. He opposed reform. Brezhnev punished anyone who spoke out against the government.

What Role Did Gorbachev Play in Reforming the Soviet Union?

In the 1980s and 1990s, Russian citizens had to wait in long lines to buy things they needed because goods were scarce. Prices were very high and wages were low.

In 1985, Mikhail Gorbachev became the new Soviet leader. Gorbachev was a younger man with new ideas. He faced big problems. The Soviet economy was falling apart. Almost one-third of the Soviet population lived in a state of poverty. People spent hours a day standing in lines to buy food and clothing. Prices were high and wages low. (A pair of winter boots cost the average citizen a month's wages!)

Soviet leader Mikhail Gorbachev (right) meets with U.S. President Ronald Reagan (left).

Gorbachev introduced a policy of **glasnost** or openness, in government. For the first time, people could speak out against the government. He allowed more freedom of the press. To help rebuild the economy, he introduced **perestroika**. That is, he let factories produce the goods people wanted. Gorbachev called for the beginning of a market economy with less government interference.

Then, Gorbachev moved his country toward a more democratic government by creating a new Soviet parliament. The Russian people elected representatives to this parliament. Other political parties besides the Communists were allowed to run candidates. In May 1989, the Soviet parliament met for the first time. The elected representatives were allowed to speak freely. The entire meeting was carried live on Soviet television. Glasnost was being put into practice.

Gorbachev struggled with the problems that resulted from his reforms. He began to back away from them. The army and the KGB, the secret police, were worried. They knew that a breakup of the Soviet Union would mean a loss of power and influence for them. They tried to arrest Gorbachev. The attempted **coup**, or overthrow of the government, failed. A new leader named Boris Yeltsin led thousands of Russians against the army and police. Yeltsin became a national hero.

What Caused the Collapse of the Soviet Union?

The Soviet Union continued to have economic and social problems. Part of the problem was that the Soviet Union was a country made up of more than 100 different ethnic groups. It had 92 nationalities and its people spoke 112 different languages. The new policy of glasnost encouraged some groups to demand an independent country of their own. Between 1988 and 1990, people in Soviet Georgia, Latvia, Estonia, Moldavia, Uzbekistan, Azerbaijan and Lithuania demanded independence.

Glasnost

A Russian word that means "openness"; under Gorbachev it meant openness in government

Perestroika

An economic policy used by Gorbachev to encourage factories to produce the goods people wanted

Coup

A takeover of the government

On December 1, 1991, the Ukraine voted for independence from the Soviet Union. Within days other Soviet republics declared their independence. Gorbachev tried to stop the breakup, but he could not. He resigned. On December 25, 1991, the Soviet flag was lowered from the Kremlin for the last time. The Soviet Union no longer existed.

Yeltsin was elected president of the new Russian republic. It had the most people and was the largest republic of the old USSR. He tried to maintain some unity among the newly independent republics by forming the Commonwealth of Independent States (CIS). Yeltsin had great difficulties governing. At the end of 1999, he resigned and was replaced by Vladimir Putin.

Boris Yeltsin (waving) became the president of Russia after the collapse of the Soviet Union. Though many Russians disagreed with how he ran the country, he was re-elected in 1996.

What Is Russia Like Under Putin?

One of the problems Yeltsin faced was an unpopular war in Chechnya. Chechnya is a largely Muslim area in southwestern Russia. Fighting continued for almost ten years. Putin took strong action to put down the rebellion. This helped him win election as president in 2000.

Since then, Putin has become more and more powerful. These moves are supported by most Russians. He has brought peace and stability back, but at a high price. The Russian people have lost some of their freedom. Newspapers that have criticized the president have been shut down. The government had taken over national television. The power of the country's governors has been greatly reduced. The Russian parliament has been turned into a rubber stamp. Many former members of the KGB, the secret police, hold positions of power.

The Russian people have been willing to support Putin because for many of them the quality of life has improved. His move to seize control over the nation's rich natural resources was popular. Russian oil, natural gas, and coal are in great demand and are its chief exports. The economy is booming. Russians, in particular those living in cities, are enjoying higher living standards. The Russian government is spending millions of dollars it earns on its vast natural resources to build roads, schools, shopping centers, and hotels.

Lesson 3 Review On a sheet of paper, write the word or name in parenthesis that best completes each sentence.

1. Under Communism, all major economic decisions are made by (government, consumers, investors).

2. The Soviet leader who introduced openness in government was (Khruschev, Gorbachev, Yeltsin).

3. The man who became a hero for putting down an attempt by the KGB and the army to overthrow the Soviet government was (Khruschev, Gorbachev, Yeltsin).

4. The Soviet Union broke up in (1981, 1991, 2001).

5. Under its President Vladimir Putin, Russia has become more of a (dictatorship, democracy, monarchy).

What do you think

Why do you think Russian President Putin is popular with many Russian people ?

Objectives

◆ To describe how Eastern Europe forced their Communist leaders out

◆ To describe the reunification of Germany and the fall of the Berlin Wall

◆ To explain the ethnic cleansing in Kosovo

Reading Strategy:
Metacognition

Remember to look at the photographs and maps as you read this lesson. Note the descriptive words. This will help you visualize what you are reading.

Eastern Europe revolted against Communist rule many times. The people of Hungary revolted in 1956. Their revolt was crushed by 2,500 tanks and 200,000 soldiers of the Soviet Union. Soviet tanks also put an end to a brief period of freedom in Czechoslovakia in the spring of 1968. Poland rebelled against the dictatorship of their Communist leaders in 1956, 1979, and in 1981. All these rebellions failed. Then, in 1989, the people of Eastern Europe finally were able to force their Communist leaders out.

How Did Hungary Cut a Hole in the Iron Curtain?

Since Gorbachev had encouraged a policy of glasnost, the Hungarian government began to allow its citizens more freedom of speech and assembly. Then, on May 2, 1989, Hungarian soldiers were ordered to begin cutting down the barbed-wire fence between Austria and Hungary.

The 150-mile fence and its minefield had been built in 1969. On one side of the fence was the Communist nation of Hungary. On the other was the democratic nation of Austria. The barbed-wire fence was part of the Iron Curtain. Cutting the fence that separated the two countries was historic. Hungary was the first country in Eastern Europe to allow people to freely travel to a Western nation. Word quickly spread that there was an opening in the Iron Curtain. Soon thousands of people from East Germany, Poland, and Czechoslovakia moved through Hungary to freedom in the West. For the first time in decades, people were being allowed to "vote with their feet" about whether they wished to live in a Communist country. In October of 1989, the Communist party in Hungary ceased to exist. Hungarian leaders set about trying to create a new democratic constitutional state.

How Did Communists in Poland Give Up Power?

In 1980, a group of workers in a shipyard in the city of Gdansk, Poland went on **strike**. That is, they refused to work until their working conditions improved. (Striking was not legal in Poland.) The workers wanted Poland's Communist government to recognize their union as legal. They called their union "**Solidarity**," or unity.

For eight years, Solidarity struggled to bring about reform. In the past, protests against the government would have led to a Soviet crackdown. But in 1989, things were different. The Soviet Union stayed out of the dispute. The Communist Polish government agreed to share power. In free elections held in June of 1989, the citizens of Poland elected representatives. Solidarity won a huge victory.

How Was Germany Able to Reunite?

In Chapter 27, you learned that after World War II, Germany was divided. Since 1949, there had been two Germanys. West Germany was a democracy; East Germany was Communist. In 1989, East Germans took to the streets demanding reform. In November 1989, the entire East German government gave up their positions. The new government now said its people were free to travel where they wanted, even to West Germany.

German citizens hammered down the Berlin Wall in 1989.

Thousands of Germans rushed to the **Berlin Wall.** (Since 1961 the wall had divided the people of East and West Berlin.) They climbed up on the wall and with hammers began to break down the wall. People danced and cried, and cheered. In February 1990, representatives of the East German and West German governments agreed to reunite.

What Caused the Breakup of Yugoslavia?

Like the Soviet Union, Yugoslavia was made up of many different ethnic groups. In 1990, the Yugoslav republics of Croatia, Bosnia-Herzegovina, Slovenia, and Macedonia began a push for independence. Slobodan Milosevic, who became the leader of the Serbian republic, rejected the idea. He made war against the other republics. His forces, helped by the Serbian minority in Croatia, captured one-third of Croatia's territory. In early 1992, Bosnia-Herzegovina declared its independence. Bosnia's large Muslim population favored independence, but the Christian Serbs living there did not. By mid-1993 over 70 percent of the republic was controlled by Serb forces. They began a policy of **"ethnic cleansing."** Bosnian Muslims were forced out of their homes and property. Over two million were left homeless and nearly 250,000 Bosnians were killed. Finally, a treaty was signed that divided Bosnia into two parts.

Secretary of State Madeleine Albright visits American troops in Kosovo in 1999.

Milosevic next began a war in Kosovo, a small province of Serbia. About 90 percent of its people are ethnic Albanians. They are related more to the people of Albania than they are to the Serbs. Just as he had in Bosnia, Milosevic tried to force the non-Serbs out. Thousands of refugees fled. Many of their villages were burned and many people were killed.

Writing About History

In recent decades, many nations have struggled to establish democratic governments. In your notebook, write an editorial for your local paper. Explain what you think democracy is. Tell how you feel about it

On March 24, 1999 NATO began air strikes against Serbia. NATO hoped that bombing would force Milosevic to stop his attacks in Kosovo. After two months of air strikes, Serbian leaders finally took their forces out of Kosovo.

The region still has many problems, but the fighting has stopped. Milosevic was put on trial for war crimes, but died during the trial. Yugoslavia no longer exists. All its former parts—Slovenia, Croatia, Bosnia and Herzegovina, Serbia, Montenegro, Kosovo, and Macedonia—are now all independent countries.

What Steps Has Europe Taken Toward Union?

After World War II a number of European countries sought closer ties. Many wanted to get rid of trade barriers and **tariffs**. A tariff is a tax that countries put on exports or imports. In 1952, six European nations agreed to create a tariff-free market for European coal and steel products. This was so successful that the same countries decided to reduce trade barriers even more. In 1970, they created the European Economic Community, also known as the Common Market.

During the 1980s and 1990s the European Community grew. In 1992, the name was changed to the European Union. In 2007, the EU had 27 members with nearly 500 million people.

Currency

The form of money a country uses

Just as people in all 50 states of the United States use the same **currency,** members of the European Union use the same euro. The EU has a parliament that makes rules and regulations about almost every aspect of economic and social life. It is working toward a common defense and foreign policy for all the members.

The European Union

Map Study This map shows the European Union, formed in 1993. The European Union works toward economic cooperation among its 27 members. Which country is the farthest south? What country lies between Estonia and Lithuania?

History in Your Life: Technology

The Jet Age

New technology often comes out of war. In 1939, Germany made the first successful flight of a plane powered by jet engines. By 1944, German Messerschmitt fighters were flying combat missions. They flew at nearly 550 miles an hour. The first American jet was built in 1942. After the war, the United States and the Soviet Union worked to build faster warplanes. By the Korean War in the 1950s, they had succeeded. The Americans had the F-86 Sabre jet. The Soviets had the MiG-15.

Jet planes soon changed passenger travel. Trips were faster, and there were fewer stops to refuel. Britain built the first large passenger jet in 1952. American companies soon followed. In 1958, a Boeing 707 carried passengers across the Atlantic. The first "jumbo jet" was the Boeing 747 in 1970. It could carry more than 400 people. Now, millions of people travel by jet every day.

Lesson 4 Review On a sheet of paper, write the answers to these questions. Use complete sentences.

1. Why was cutting the barbed-wire fence in Hungary important to the people behind the Iron Curtain?

2. What was Solidarity in Poland?

3. Why was the tearing down of the Berlin Wall important?

4. What caused the breakup of Yugoslavia?

5. What are some ways in which European countries are uniting?

What do you think ?

Would a United States of Europe be good or bad for the world? Why?

The Fall of the Berlin Wall

On November 11, 1989, the Berlin Wall, which had separated East Berlin from West Berlin since 1961, fell. This is an excerpt from a personal account of that event by Andreas Ramos. Ramos, an author and computer technology expert, was in Denmark when the wall fell.

From the East German side we could hear the sound of heavy machines. With a giant drill, they were punching holes in the wall. Every time a drill poked through, everyone cheered . . . People shot off fireworks and emergency flares and rescue rockets. Many were using hammers to chip away at the wall. There were countless holes. At one place, a crowd of East German soldiers looked through a narrow hole. We reached through and shook hands. . . .

Everything was out of control. Police on horses watched. There was nothing they could do. The crowd had swollen. People were blowing long alpine horns which made a huge noise. There were fireworks, kites, flags and flags and flags, dogs, children. The wall was finally breaking. The cranes lifted slabs aside. East and West German police had traded caps. . . . The final slab was moved away. A stream of East Germans began to pour through. People applauded and slapped their backs . . . Packed in with thousands, I stood at the break in the wall. Above me, a German

stood atop the wall, at the end, balanced, waving his arms and shouting reports to the crowd. With all of the East Germans coming into West Berlin, we thought it was only fair that we should go to East Berlin. A counterflow started. Looking around, I saw an indescribable joy in people's faces. It was the end of the government telling people what not to do, it was the end of the Wall, the war, the East, the West. If East Germans were going west, then we should go east, so we poured into East Berlin. Around me, people spoke German, French, Polish, Russian, every language. A woman handed her camera to someone who was standing atop rubble so that he could take her picture. . . . On top of every building were thousands of people. Berlin was out of control. There was no more government, neither in East nor in West. The police and the army were helpless. The soldiers themselves were overwhelmed by the event. They were part of the crowd. Their uniforms meant nothing. The Wall was down.

Document-Based Questions

1. How do you know this is an important event?

2. What did the Berlin Wall represent?

3. Why might someone want their picture taken atop the rubble of the wall?

4. Why do you think people were helping each other to climb on and through the wall?

5. People traveled from many surrounding countries to witness this event. Why do you think they did this?

Fall of an Empire

Some historians call the Soviet Union the world's last empire. In 1917, the Russian Revolution ended the empire of the czars. The Soviet Union, though, took over its territory. Officially, the country's name was the Union of Soviet Socialist Republics. It had 13 republics, based somewhat on ethnic groupings. The Russians made up the largest and most powerful group.

In 1985, Mikhail Gorbachev became the Soviet leader. Gorbachev's reforms changed Eastern Europe first. He gave the republics more independence. Events were quick and dramatic. In 1989, the Berlin Wall between East and West Berlin fell. Then Germany was reunited in late 1990. Later, other Iron Curtain countries formed democratic governments.

Inside the Soviet Union, events also moved quickly. In 1990, reform parties were formed in Russia. A reformer named Boris Yeltsin quit the Communist Party. In 1991, the Russian Republic held its first free election. The people elected Yeltsin president.

In August 1991, some hard-line Communists plotted to get rid of Gorbachev. He and his family were on vacation near the Black Sea. Armed men surrounded his country house. In Moscow, security troops tried to take control. Tanks blocked the streets. They surrounded the parliament building. But thousands of Russians who wanted democracy protested. Yeltsin climbed on a tank and encouraged them. The crisis soon ended, but the Soviet Union was crumbling. In late August, the Soviet legislature took away the Communist Party's power. Then even more republics broke away from the Soviet Union.

A Russian family shares a meal.

In December 1991, Russia, Ukraine, and Belarus formed a new alliance. It was called the Commonwealth of Independent States (CIS). Russia took over running most of the Soviet central government. Then on December 25, Gorbachev resigned. The huge red Soviet flag over the Kremlin came down. The Soviet Union, formed in 1922, was over.

Spotlight Story Wrap-Up

1. What was the structure of the former Soviet Union?

2. Who made up the largest and most powerful group in the USSR?

3. How did Gorbachev's reforms affect Eastern Europe?

4. Who plotted to get rid of Gorbachev in August 1991?

5. How did Boris Yeltsin become president of Russia?

- Rivalry between the United States and the Soviet Union became the Cold War. Under the Truman Doctrine, the United States helped Greece and Turkey resist Communist takeovers. The Marshall Plan helped Western Europe rebuild.

- In 1948, the United States and its European allies formed the North Atlantic Treaty Organization (NATO), a military alliance. In 1955, the Soviet Union set up the Warsaw Pact with its satellite countries.

- There were many conflicts between the superpowers, including the Berlin Airlift in Germany and the Korean War.

- Mikhail Gorbachev became the Soviet leader in 1985. He allowed more freedom (glasnost), reformed the economy (perestroika), and moved toward democracy.

- In 1991, the Soviet Union broke into independent republics. Boris Yeltsin was elected president of Russia. He tried to continue economic reforms, but crime and poverty hurt many Russians.

- Changes in the Soviet Union affected Eastern Europe. In 1989, people in Hungary, Poland, and East Germany overthrew Communist governments. The Berlin Wall came down, and Germany was reunited.

- The breakup of Yugoslavia brought conflicts. Serbian leader Slobodan Milosevic went to war against other ethnic groups in Bosnia and Kosovo.

- Western European nations worked toward economic unity. In 1992 they became the European Union. They adopted a new currency, the euro. In 2007, the European Union had 27 members, with nearly 500 million people.

Chapter 28   R E V I E W

Word Bank

Berlin

China

currency

glasnost

Marshall Plan

perestroika

South Korea

truce

Truman Doctrine

Warsaw Pact

On a sheet of paper, use the words from the Word Bank to complete each sentence correctly.

1. The _____ helped Europe recover from World War II.

2. In 1948, the Soviets tried to blockade _____.

3. In June 1950, the Communists tried to expand into _____.

4. A _____ is an agreement to stop a war for a time.

5. The _____ was an attempt to stop the spread of Communism.

6. Communist soldiers from _____ crossed into North Korea to join the fighting there.

7. Gorbachev introduced _____, or openness, to the Soviet Union.

8. Gorbachev also introduced _____, which was a looser economic policy.

9. The _____ set up a military alliance between the Soviet Union and its satellite nations.

10. Several European countries have also agreed to use one _____, or form of money.

On a sheet of paper, write the letter of the answer that correctly completes each sentence.

11. In 1985, _____ became the Soviet leader.

   A Joseph Stalin   **C** Nikita Khrushchev

   B Mikhail Gorbachev   **D** Boris Yeltsin

12. The Soviet Union came to an end in _____.

   A 1980   **B** 1986   **C** 1990   **D** 1991

13. When Boris Yeltsin resigned at the end of 1999, he was replaced by _____.

A Mikhail Gorbachev   **C** Vladimir Putin
B Nikita Khrushchev   **D** Slobodan Milosevic

14. Workers in Poland called their union _____.

A Gdansk   **C** Solidarity
B Iron Curtain   **D** Glasnost

15. All the countries of the European Union use the same _____.

A currency   **C** office building
B flag   **D** language

On a sheet of paper, write the answer to each question. Use complete sentences.

16. How did the Marshall Plan help Europe?

17. What was the purpose of NATO?

18. Why was the Korean War important?

Critical Thinking On a sheet of paper, write your response to each question. Use complete sentences.

19. The United States and Great Britain used an airlift to help the people in Berlin during the Soviet blockade. If they had not done this, what might have happened?

20. In Chapter 25, you read about the Russian Revolution of 1917. Which is more important—that revolution or the Russian Revolution of 1991? Explain your answer.

Test-Taking Tip

Be sure you understand what a test question is asking. Reread the questions if you have to.

29

New Nations Emerge

Before World War II, European nations controlled many colonies in Africa, Asia, and the Middle East. After the war, people in these colonies wanted to be free to make their own economic and political decisions.

In this chapter, you will watch colonies in Africa become independent and learn about apartheid. You will journey to the Middle East, where Israelis and Palestinians have been fighting for many years. You will read about Gandhi in India, and you will travel to China and Vietnam, where fierce wars were fought.

Goals for Learning

◆ To explain how the countries of Africa gained their independence, and to describe apartheid

◆ To explain the problems that exist between the Israelis and the Palestinians

◆ To explain the two problems that faced Gandhi in unifying India

◆ To describe the two groups that fought for control of China and to detail the outcome of this struggle

◆ To detail the events of the Vietnam War

1947 British India is divided into the free nations of India and Pakistan

1957 Vietnam War begins

1976 North and South Vietnam unite

1994 Nelson Mandela is elected president of South Africa

1945

1970

1995

1946 Nationalists and Communists begin to fight a civil war in China

1948 Israel becomes a nation; fighting begins with Arabs

1975 North Vietnamese take control of Saigon

1995 Israeli Prime Minister Yitzhak Rabin is assassinated

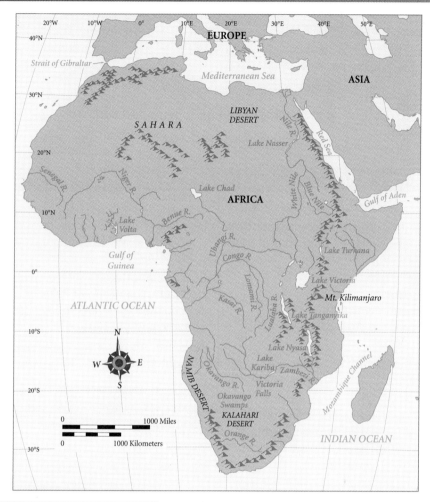

Map Skills

This is a topographic map of current-day Africa. That is, it shows Africa's mountains, deserts, lakes, swamps, and rivers.

Study the map, then answer the following questions:

1. Which African coast—the east or the west—has the most mountains?

2. What are the names of three deserts in Africa?

3. What are the names of three lakes in Africa?

4. What are the names of three rivers in Africa?

5. What ocean lies to the east of Africa?

Reading Strategy:
Summarizing

When readers summarize, they ask questions about what they are reading. As you read the text in this chapter, ask yourself the following questions:

◆ Who or what is this about?

◆ What is the main thing being said about this topic?

◆ What details are important to the main idea or event?

Key Vocabulary Words

Lesson 1

African Nationalism The struggle by native African people to gain their economic and political freedom from European colonial rulers

Pan-African Movement A group that planned ways in which Africans could achieve economic strength and political peace

British Commonwealth of Nations A group of nations that is loyal to the British monarch

Apartheid The official policy of the Union of South Africa that refused to give black and other nonwhite people any political, economic, or social rights

African National Congress (ANC) A black nationalist group in South Africa

Demonstrate To join together with other people to protest and march against something

Legalize To make lawful

Multiracial Having to do with all people and all races

Lesson 2

Displace To move people from their home or land; to force people to leave their home or land

Palestinian Liberation Organization (PLO) The group of Palestinians dedicated to regaining from Israel their homeland in Palestine

Terrorist A person who uses violence to frighten people and to get them to obey

Lesson 3

Passive resistance A nonviolent way of protesting for political and social change

Lesson 5

Election An act by which people choose someone or something by voting

Vietnamization The U.S. plan to turn the fighting of the Vietnam War over to the South Vietnamese army

Objectives

◆ To explain how African nations gained their independence

◆ To describe apartheid

African Nationalism

The struggle by native African people to gain their economic and political freedom from European colonial rulers

Pan-African Movement

A group that planned ways in which Africans could achieve economic strength and political peace

Between 1945 and 1990, more than 50 African countries became independent nations. The number is large because Africa is large. It has many different cultures.

Africa has three different geographic areas. The first is North Africa. It is the land between the Mediterranean Sea and the Sahara. Muslim Arabs and Muslim Berbers live there. But they have different cultural and religious roots.

The second geographic area in Africa is the sub-Sahara. It lies below the Sahara. People from many different cultures live on the land south of the Sahara. The third geographic area in Africa is its southern tip.

What Is African Nationalism?

For many years, native Africans struggled to gain economic and political freedom from their European colonial rulers. We call their struggle **African Nationalism.** Beginning in 1900, the Pan-African Movement met several times to plan for the political independence of Africa.

The **Pan-African Movement** wanted Africans to achieve economic strength and political peace. To do this, they had to work with what they had in common. The movement helped native Africans and their descendants in every part of the world. The group trained people who became political leaders of several new African nations.

What African Nations Were Independent After World War II?

When World War II ended, North Africa had only three independent nations—Egypt and Ethiopia, and Liberia. At the southern tip of the continent lay South Africa, which also had self-rule. Between North Africa and South Africa lay all the other land of this huge continent. Britain, France, Belgium, and Portugal controlled most of this in-between land.

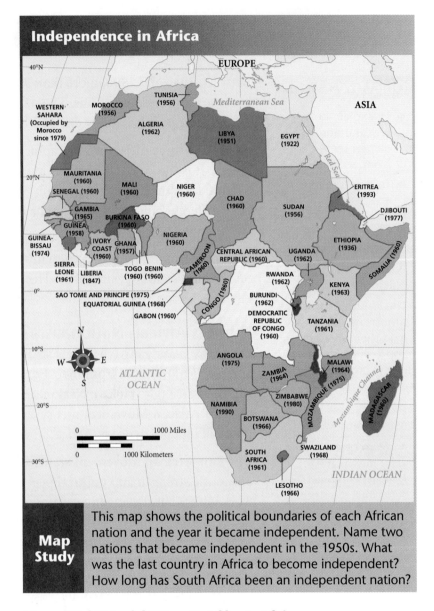

Independence in Africa

This map shows the political boundaries of each African nation and the year it became independent. Name two nations that became independent in the 1950s. What was the last country in Africa to become independent? How long has South Africa been an independent nation?

Map Study

How Did World War II Affect African Nationalism?

World War II weakened the political position of all the European colonial powers. During World War II, more than 200,000 Africans fought on the side of their British and French colonial rulers. After the war, these people felt they had earned the right to rule themselves.

Kwame Nkrumah (center) became the leader of Ghana after it gained its independence in 1957.

What French Colonies Became Independent?

The European colonial powers denied self-rule and independence. France in particular did not want to lose its colonies in North Africa. However, Morocco and Tunisia—both French colonies—gained their independence.

France wanted to hold on to the colony of Algeria. The French went to war with the Arab and Berber people living there. This war lasted from 1954 to 1961. But in 1962, Algeria, the last French colony in North Africa, finally won its independence.

What Was the First Independent Nation in Sub-Sahara Africa?

African Nationalism also spread to the European colonies in sub-Sahara Africa. The first new nation in this area was Ghana. Its people gained their independence in 1957.

Great Britain had ruled this area—called the Gold Coast—for 83 years. The people living there named their new nation after an ancient African empire. Kwame Nkrumah was the new African leader of Ghana. He said, "There is a new Africa in the world."

What Other Nations Became Independent?

Over the next 20 years, the "new Africa" continued to grow. In 1960 alone, 17 African nations gained their independence. Because of this, historians call 1960 "the year of Africa."

By the 1980s, more than 50 African countries had become independent nations. These new nations included Kenya, Mali, Nigeria, Senegal, Zaire, and Zimbabwe. Eritrea—the last area to gain its independence—became a nation in 1993.

What Is Apartheid?

Until the 1960s, the Union of South Africa was the only self-governing nation in the southern part of the continent. It belonged to the **British Commonwealth of Nations**—a group of nations that is loyal to the British monarch.

British Commonwealth of Nations

A group of nations that is loyal to the British monarch

Reading Strategy:
Summarizing

Stop often as you read. Try to sum up the events using your own words.

Apartheid

The official policy of the Union of South Africa that refused to give black and other nonwhite people any political, economic, or social rights

African National Congress (ANC)

A black nationalist group in South Africa

South Africa was different from the rest of Africa because whites living there controlled it. In 1948, the white-controlled government in South Africa made **apartheid** its official policy. This policy set blacks and other nonwhite South Africans apart from whites. White South Africans refused to give black and other nonwhite people any political, economic, or social rights. Whites also decided where nonwhites could live.

Great Britain and other nations protested this apartheid policy. South Africa then withdrew from the British Commonwealth. In 1961, South Africa became a republic.

How Did Black South Africans Fight Apartheid?

In 1976, a protest against apartheid turned into a riot. More than 500 people—mostly blacks—were killed. In 1983, a car bomb near a military base killed or injured more than 100 people. The **African National Congress (ANC),** a black nationalist group, said it had done the bombing.

As black South Africans struggled for equal rights, some used violence. Others did not. Bishop Desmond Tutu led nonviolent protests against apartheid. For his efforts to free South Africa from apartheid, Tutu was awarded the Nobel Peace Prize in 1984.

Biography

Jomo Kenyatta: c. 1890–1978

Jomo Kenyatta spent his life working for black rule in Kenya. As a boy, he attended a Scottish mission school. There he was called Johnstone Kamau.

As an adult, Kenyatta joined a political group. It was trying to change British colonial rule. Local government officials would not listen, however. In 1931, Kenyatta went to England to work there for the changes he desired. In England, he took the name *Jomo,* or "burning spear."

Kenyatta returned to Kenya in 1946 and worked for independence. Then he was jailed for his beliefs and actions. After Kenya gained independence in 1963, he became its first president.

Nelson Mandela (center) was sent to prison for 26 years for his actions against the white minority government in South Africa. However, when he was released from prison, he helped end apartheid and became the president of South Africa.

In 1986, the South African government said that blacks could no longer **demonstrate** against apartheid. That is, they could not join together with other blacks to protest and march against apartheid. But blacks continued to protest. The South African government put many black political leaders in jail.

Reading Strategy:
Summarizing

What important person is introduced in this section?

Demonstrate

To join together with other people to protest and march against something

Legalize

To make lawful

Why Was Nelson Mandela Jailed for 26 Years?

On the first day that young Rolihlahla Mandela went to school in South Africa, his teacher gave him an English name—Nelson. In his native language, *Rolihlahla* means "he who pulls the branch of a tree." The English translate this word as "trouble maker." As an adult, Nelson Mandela did make trouble for those who wanted apartheid. He changed the history of his country.

In June 1964, a South African court sentenced Mandela to life in prison. The court said that Mandela had tried to overthrow the white minority government. The government wanted to silence Mandela because he worked to gain political, economic, and social rights for black South Africans. For 26 years, he remained in prison.

Who Released Mandela from Prison?

The South African government locked Mandela behind prison walls. But he was still a hero for black South Africans. In 1989, F. W. de Klerk became president of the Republic of South Africa. By this time, the black protest to end apartheid was growing stronger. President de Klerk **legalized** the African National Congress. (That is, he said that people could join it without breaking the law.) In 1990, de Klerk released Mandela from prison.

How Did Mandela Help South Africans?

The ANC made Mandela its leader. Right away, Mandela called for an end to white privileges. For four years, Mandela and de Klerk negotiated over black political, economic, and social rights.

Finally, the two leaders agreed to a plan. It provided for South Africa's first **multiracial** election. *Multiracial* means all the people and all races. A multiracial election means people of all races can vote. Because of their work together, de Klerk and Mandela were awarded the 1993 Nobel Peace Prize.

In 1994, the people of South Africa elected Mandela to be their president. He served one term. Then, in 1999, at the age of 80, he retired from public office. People around the world honored him. He had broken down apartheid and united a divided nation.

Lesson 1 Review On a sheet of paper, write the answer to each question. Use complete sentences.

1. Into how many geographic areas is Africa divided?

2. What is African Nationalism?

3. What is the name of the first nation created south of the Sahara?

4. How was the nation of South Africa different from other African nations?

5. Why do many South Africans and other people think that Nelson Mandela is a hero?

What do you think ?

Why do you think the small white minority in South Africa adopted a policy of apartheid?

Objectives

◆ To explain the problems that exist between the Israelis and the Palestinians

◆ To describe the Arab-Israeli War and its outcome

More than 3,000 years ago, Palestine was the home of the Jewish people. But because of wars and troubles, many Jews moved to countries in Europe. However, in these places, some people persecuted them. That is, people were mean and unfair to the Jews because of their beliefs. For centuries, they dreamed of a Jewish homeland. There they would be safe; they could follow their own traditions.

What Homeland Did the Jewish People Choose?

In the 19th century, Jewish leaders began to discuss the idea of creating a Jewish nation in Palestine. By 1900, Jews were moving into the dry, desert land of Palestine. However, for many generations, Palestine had been the home of Palestinian Arabs.

How Did World War II Affect the Jewish People?

When World War I ended, Britain gained control of Palestine. In the 1930s, many Jews moved there to escape the Nazis in Germany. As you know, during World War II, the Nazis murdered over six million Jews. After the war, Jewish people wanted a homeland more than ever. They believed that only there would they be safe.

Reading Strategy:
Summarizing

What are some important details that help you understand why Israel was created?

How Did Israel Become a Nation?

After World War II, thousands of Jews left Europe to create their own nation in Palestine. The British could not stop them from settling there. Finally, Britain decided to leave Palestine. The United Nations was left to control it.

In 1947, the United Nations voted to divide Palestine into Jewish and Arab states. In May 1948, the new nation of Israel was declared by Jewish leader David Ben-Gurion. The neighboring Arab nations opposed the creation of a Jewish nation.

Dr. Chaim Weizmann took the oath as the first president of Israel in 1948.

Displace

To move people from their home or land; to force people to leave their home or land

What Was the Outcome of the 1948 Arab-Israeli War?

These Arab countries—Egypt, Iraq, Jordan, Lebanon, and Syria—attacked Israel. Nearly 400,000 Arabs in Palestine fled the area because of the fighting. These Palestinian refugees settled mostly in Lebanon, Jordan, and Syria.

The Israeli army quickly defeated the invading Arab armies. As a result, Israel gained most of the land in Palestine. Egypt and Jordan took the remaining land.

In the next 30 years, Israel fought four more wars against the Arab nations that surrounded it. Each time, Israel defeated their armies. However, the defeated Arab nations still refused to admit that Israel was a nation. Arab leaders even refused to meet with Israeli officials to discuss peace.

What Did the PLO Want?

These wars **displaced** many Palestinian Arabs. These people were forced to leave their homes. They ended up in refugee camps. They had no land of their own to live on. These displaced people demanded that they be given their own nation within Palestine.

Palestinian Liberation Organization (PLO)

The group of Palestinians dedicated to regaining from Israel their homeland in Palestine

Terrorist

A person who uses violence to frighten people and to get them to obey

Some Palestinian Arabs formed the **Palestinian Liberation Organization (PLO).** By the 1970s, many members of the PLO had become **terrorists**. They used violence to frighten Israeli citizens and to force them to leave Palestine. The PLO staged raids on Israel from neighboring Arab nations, such as Lebanon. In the early 1980s, Israel invaded Lebanon to rid it of the PLO.

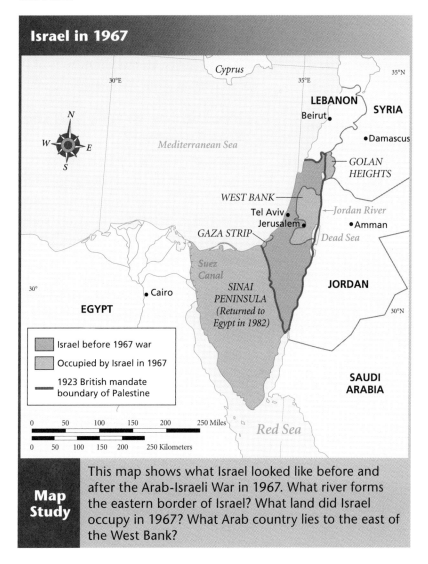

Israel in 1967

Map Study

This map shows what Israel looked like before and after the Arab-Israeli War in 1967. What river forms the eastern border of Israel? What land did Israel occupy in 1967? What Arab country lies to the east of the West Bank?

When Did Children Get Involved in the Fight?

In 1987, violence spread to areas that lay south of Lebanon called the West Bank and the Golan Heights. Young Palestinian children and women put up barriers in the streets. Then they threw rocks at Israeli soldiers. They killed a few soldiers and injured others. But the soldiers also killed and injured some Arab women and children.

After this, the Israeli soldiers arrested hundreds of Palestinians. Israel believed that controlling the West Bank was necessary for its security. In fact, hundreds of Israeli families had already built homes in the West Bank.

Reading Strategy:
Summarizing

What is the main idea of this paragraph?

How Did the Israelis and the Palestinians Work Together?

During the 1990s, the Palestinian Arabs began to work with the Israelis to obtain Palestinian self-rule. In 1994, the Israelis allowed the Palestinians to take control of much of the Gaza Strip and the West Bank. (A few hundred thousand Jewish settlers and more than two million Palestinians live in the West Bank and the Gaza Strip.)

Why Do the Israelis Not Want to Give Up Land?

In 1998, Israel celebrated because it had been a nation for 50 years. The Israelis had fought again and again to keep their homeland. However, the Palestinians did not celebrate.

Instead, the Palestinians called, once again, for the creation of their own nation. They began to argue and fight with the Israelis over land. The Palestinians wanted Israel to give up land in return for peace. The government of Israel thought that giving up land would weaken its security.

World leaders want the Israelis and Palestinians to negotiate again and to create peace in the Middle East. Both sides continue to search for the right solution.

Then and Now

Jerusalem

Jerusalem is one of the world's oldest cities. People have lived there for about 4,000 years. It was the center of ancient Jewish culture. Jewish kings ruled from there. King Solomon built the Temple on the Temple Mount. One of its walls still stands. It is called the Western Wall. Jews go there to pray.

Today the city is the capital of modern Israel. That country took control of East Jerusalem in the 1967 war. Palestinians also claim Jerusalem as their capital.

Jerusalem is holy to Christians and Muslims, too. Jesus taught in Jerusalem. The Last Supper and the Crucifixion both took place there. For Muslims, the Dome of the Rock is a holy shrine. They believe Muhammad rose to heaven from there.

Word Bank

Arabs

Ben-Gurion

Israel

Lebanon

PLO

Lesson 2 Review On a sheet of paper, use the words from the Word Bank to complete each sentence correctly.

1. _____ occupied Palestine when some Jewish people returned to it in 1900.

2. _____ became a nation in 1948.

3. Israel was declared a nation by Jewish leader David _____.

4. The _____ is an organization that wants the Arab Palestinians to have their own nation.

5. In the early 1980s, Israel invaded _____ to rid it of the PLO.

What do you think ?

Do you think the Arab Palestinians should have their own nation? Explain your answer.

Passive resistance

A nonviolent way of protesting for political and social change

Reading Strategy: **Summarizing**

As you read, notice the topic, the main thing being said about the topic, and important details.

India is located on the huge continent of Asia. For much of its history, many different people speaking many different languages have lived in India. This happened partly because many different groups of people have invaded India.

What European Countries Took Control of India?

Since the 1500s, Europeans have traded with India. By the 1700s, France controlled much of southern India. In addition, the British East Indian Trading Company sold Indian silks and other products throughout the world.

In 1763, Great Britain took control of large areas of India. As time passed, Britain drove the French from their trading posts in India. In 1858, Britain made all of India into a colony.

Why Did Indians Want Self-Rule?

Many Indians did not want their country to be a British colony. They wanted independence. They felt that the British treated them as second-class citizens in their own country. New industries and transportation served British needs, not the needs of the Indian people. The best jobs in India went to the British.

How Did Gandhi Bring Independence to India?

In 1885, a group of Indian leaders founded the Indian National Congress. Soon, it developed into the Congress Party. Its purpose was to gain political power for Indians.

In 1920, India's most important nationalist leader began to help India achieve independence. Mohandas Gandhi and his followers used **passive resistance** to fight British rule. This is a nonviolent way of protesting to get political and social change. For nearly 30 years, Gandhi led boycotts, protests, and work stoppages against the British. Finally, in 1947, Britain gave India its independence.

Gandhi wanted to make India a united nation. But he faced two major problems. The first problem was the caste system. The second problem was religious differences.

Why Was the Caste System a Problem for India?

There are four main castes, or classes, of people in India. These castes are divided according to work, money, skin color, and religious beliefs.

The members of each caste remained in the caste for life and followed its rules. For example, a person could marry only within the same caste. Another rule was that all the people in a caste did the same kind of work.

Gandhi knew that India could never be a true democracy as long as the caste system existed, so India's new constitution ended it. This constitution gave every Indian the right to vote. It opened schools that would educate all Indian children. It taught all these students Hindi, the national language. In time, India became the world's largest democracy.

Why Were Religious Differences a Problem for India?

The second problem that stood in the way of uniting India was religious differences. The majority of people in India were Hindus. They followed the Hindu religion. However, millions of Indians were Muslims. This Muslim minority wanted its own nation.

In August 1947, two new nations were created: India and Pakistan. Muslim Pakistan was further divided into East and West Pakistan. These two areas were more than 1,000 miles apart.

Reading Strategy:
Summarizing

What important details will help you remember how India and Pakistan were created?

Religious differences between Hindus and Muslims led to violence. More than 500,000 people died in this struggle. Gandhi wanted to stop the violence. As a protest, he did not eat food for many days. But on January 30, 1948, a Hindu assassinated him. This man believed that Gandhi no longer supported the Hindus.

Word Bank
Gandhi
Great Britain
Hindus
Muslims
Pakistan

Lesson 3 Review On a sheet of paper, use the words from the Word Bank to complete each sentence correctly.

1. In 1858, _____ took control of India and made it a colony.

2. In 1920, _____ began to lead the Indian people in passive resistance.

3. The majority of people in India were _____.

4. The minority of people in India were _____.

5. In 1947, part of India became the nation of _____.

What do you think ?

Why would the caste system have kept India from becoming a true democracy?

Objectives

◆ To describe the two groups that fought for control of China and the outcome of this struggle

◆ To explain the role the United States played in China's conflicts

European nations had colonies both in Africa and in Asia. China was not a colony. But Europe still had economic control over it. After World War II, China wanted to be independent from European nations.

What Two Groups Fought to Control China?

In Chapter 26, you read about the struggle between the Communists and the non-Communists for control of China. This struggle began in 1927. Mao Zedong led the Communist forces. Chiang Kai-shek led the Nationalists. For ten years their two armies fought each other. This civil war left China weak and divided.

What Happened When Japan Invaded China?

In 1937, Japan invaded China. Chiang Kai-shek and Mao Zedong stopped fighting each other; they united to fight the Japanese. But neither side trusted the other.

Each side fought the Japanese in a different way. The Communists used guerilla warfare against the Japanese. In this kind of warfare, bands of fighters made surprise attacks against the Japanese and their supplies. The Communists worked closely with the Chinese peasants. The Nationalists, however, did not use guerilla warfare. They stayed mostly in the cities of southwest China.

How Did the Two Groups Differ After World War II?

When World War II ended in 1945, the fighting between the Communists and the Nationalists started again. Their civil war lasted from 1946 to 1949.

Chiang Kai-shek's Nationalists had a large army. The United States sent them billions of dollars for weapons and training. But Chiang's government was both greedy and inefficient. His military officers argued with each other.

However, Mao Zedong's Communist forces were united in their cause. Many of the Chinese people supported them. The Soviet Union—the first Communist nation—sent them weapons and supplies.

Which Group Won Control of China?

Reading Strategy:
Summarizing

What is the main idea of this section?

By 1948, the Communists had the upper hand in China. One city after another fell to them. As this happened, thousands of soldiers deserted Chiang's army and joined Mao's forces. By the fall of 1949, Chiang Kai-shek and his government had lost control of China.

Chiang and his followers fled the mainland of China and crossed over to the small island of Taiwan. After 22 years of struggle, the Communists set up a new government in China. They called it the People's Republic of China.

Why Did Mao Zedong and the United States Not Trust One Another?

Mao Zedong did not trust the United States for two reasons. First, the United States had helped Chiang Kai-shek. Second, the United States had supported imperialism around the world.

The United States did not trust Mao either. The U.S. government thought that the Chinese Communists threatened

History in Your Life

"Made in Asia"

Where were your shoes made? Your CD player? Many products like these come from Japan, China, or Korea. Since 1945, Asian economies have grown quickly. Postwar Japan had the fastest-growing economy in the world. Other countries like South Korea, Taiwan, Singapore, and Hong Kong also grew. China, India, and Indonesia have developed more recently.

Asian nations differ greatly. Still, they share some attitudes. People will work hard for long hours. They want to learn new things.

For example, the Japanese studied other countries' methods. They became efficient at making quality products. In addition, most governments help industries develop.

At first, Asian countries depended on selling their goods to Europe and America. Things have changed in Asian societies, however. A middle class has grown up in these nations. People can buy cars, color TVs, and washing machines. They travel and use credit cards. Asian consumers have become the fastest-growing market for Asian goods.

freedom in Asia. The United States refused to recognize the Communist government as the legal government of China. Instead, the United States supported the Nationalist government on the island of Taiwan.

But in 1972, the United States changed its policy toward the People's Republic of China. For the first time, the United States recognized it as the legal government of the Chinese people.

Lesson 4 Review On a sheet of paper, write the letter of the answer that correctly completes each sentence.

1. The leader of the Chinese Nationalists was _____.

   A Mao Zedong   **C** Lenin
   B Chiang Kai-shek   **D** Gandhi

2. The leader of the Chinese Communists was _____.

   A Mao Zedong   **C** Tojo
   B Chiang Kai-shek   **D** Mandela

3. The Chinese Nationalists and Communists united to fight against the _____ in World War II.

   A Americans   **B** British   **C** Japanese   **D** French

4. After the war, the two groups fought one another again and the _____ won.

   A Nationalists   **C** Nazis
   B Republicans   **D** Communists

5. In 1972, the United States recognized that the legal government of China was the _____.

   A People's Republic of China **C** Nationalists
   B Nazis   **D** Chiang Kai-shek Party

What do you think ?

Why did Mao Zedong and his followers win the civil war in China?

Objectives

◆ To show the development of the Socialist Republic of Vietnam

◆ To explain the role of the United States in the Vietnam War

Election

An act by which people choose someone or something by voting

Writing About History

Choose a nation from this chapter that gained its independence. Research key events in its fight for independence. In your notebook, write the words for an imaginary national anthem.

After World War II, nationalist independence movements spread across Southeast Asia. In 1946, the United States gave the Philippine Islands their independence. South of the Philippines, the Netherlands gave freedom to Indonesia. However, France refused to free its colonial lands in Indochina.

What Did Ho Chi Minh Want for Vietnam?

Japan had conquered Indochina during World War II. The Vietnamese, under the leadership of Ho Chi Minh, fought against the Japanese. After the war, Ho Chi Minh wanted Vietnam to be an independent nation, not a French colony.

Between 1946 and 1954, Ho Chi Minh and his Communist followers fought a fierce guerrilla war against the French. The United States sent aid to the French. The United States did not want another Communist government in Asia. However, in 1954, the Vietnamese Communist forces captured a French fort. Because of this, the French government decided that it could not win the war.

What Happened After the Communists Defeated France?

Ho Chi Minh and the French agreed to divide Vietnam into two areas. The Communist area became known as North Vietnam. The non-Communist area became South Vietnam. Two other areas in Indochina became independent: Cambodia and Laos.

The division of Vietnam was not meant to be permanent. The government of South Vietnam was supposed to hold an **election**. In an election, people choose someone or something by voting. In this election, the Vietnamese people would choose how to unite their country.

Despite sending 500,000 American troops to fight in Vietnam, the United States could not win the war.

But this election never took place. North Vietnam began a guerrilla war to unite Vietnam into one Communist nation. Communists in South Vietnam, called the Vietcong, joined this struggle.

What Did the United States Do About the Guerrilla War?

In the early 1960s, the United States began to send military advisers to South Vietnam. Their job was simply to help the South Vietnamese government. But by 1968, nearly 500,000 American troops were fighting a war in South Vietnam. However, many Americans protested this war.

The Vietnam War lasted from 1960 to 1975. In 1969, the United States government started to gradually withdraw its forces from South Vietnam. The American plan was to turn the fighting of the war entirely over to the South Vietnamese army. The United States called this plan **Vietnamization.**

What United North and South Vietnam?

After the United States pulled all its soldiers out of Vietnam in 1975, the South Vietnamese government collapsed. The North Vietnamese took control of South Vietnam's capital city, Saigon.

The next year, North and South Vietnam united into one Communist country, the Socialist Republic of Vietnam. The government gave a new name to Saigon, the former capital of South Vietnam. It became Ho Chi Minh City.

After many years of struggle, the United States and the Socialist Republic of Vietnam found ways to work together. Trade between the countries increased, and the United States investment in Vietnam grew. There was more travel and tourism in the country. There was also a renewed effort to locate American soldiers that had been missing in Vietnam since the war.

Vietnamization

The U.S. plan to turn the fighting of the Vietnam War over to the South Vietnamese army

Reading Strategy:
Summarizing

What important details help you understand the events of the Vietnam War?

Southeast Asia

Map Study This is a current map of Southeast Asia. What large country lies on the northern border of Vietnam? Is Ho Chi Minh City (Saigon) in the northern or southern part of Vietnam? Which nation lies to the northeast of Thailand?

Lesson 5 Review On a sheet of paper, write the answer to each question. Use complete sentences.

1. Who controlled Vietnam until 1954?

2. Who led the Communists in their fight for an independent Vietnam?

3. What was the Communist area of Vietnam called? the non-Communist area?

4. Which army did the United States support in the Vietnam War?

5. What happened after the United States Army pulled out of Vietnam in 1975?

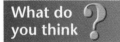

What do you think

Should the United States have fought in the Vietnam War? Explain your answer.

Statement of Nelson Mandela

This is an excerpt from the statement of the president of the African National Congress, Nelson Rolihlahla Mandela, at his inauguration as president of the Democratic Republic of South Africa. He spoke in Pretoria, South Africa, on May 10, 1994.

Today, all of us do, by our presence here, and by our celebrations in other parts of our country and the world, confer glory and hope to newborn liberty.

Out of the experience of an extraordinary human disaster that lasted too long, must be born a society of which all humanity will be proud.

Our daily deeds as ordinary South Africans must produce an actual South African reality that will reinforce humanity's belief in justice, strengthen its confidence in the nobility of the human soul and sustain all our hopes for a glorious life for all . . . each one of us is as intimately attached to the soil of this beautiful country as are the famous jacaranda trees of Pretoria and the mimosa trees of the bushveld.

Each time one of us touches the soil of this land, we feel a sense of personal renewal. The national mood changes as the seasons change.

That spiritual and physical oneness we all share with this common homeland explains the depth of the pain we all carried in our hearts as we saw our country tear itself apart in a terrible conflict . . .

We understand it still that there is no easy road to freedom

We know it well that none of us acting alone can achieve success.

We must therefore act together as a united people, for national reconciliation, for nation building, for the birth of a new world.

Let there be justice for all.

Let there be peace for all.

Let there be work, bread, water and salt for all.

Never, never and never again shall it be that this beautiful land will again experience the oppression of one by another and suffer the indignity of being the skunk of the world.

Let freedom reign.

The sun shall never set on so glorious a human achievement!

God bless Africa!

Document-Based Questions

1. What is the disaster Mandela refers to?

2. What does Mandela say happens when each South African touches the soil?

3. How does Mandela say is the way to achieve success?

4. To what animal does Mandela compare South Africa?

5. What does work, bread, water, and salt represent?

The Spinning Wheel and Salt—Weapons of the Indian Revolution

Mahatma Gandhi was the father of Indian independence. He was a man of ideas, trained as a lawyer. Gandhi believed in nonviolence. He thought that passive resistance was his people's best weapon. This is a form of nonviolent protest. It is used against laws seen as unfair. Gandhi believed that the force of truth could defeat British military force. Violence would not work.

In 1919, British colonial laws changed. Some Indian leaders organized strikes and riots against the laws. That led to a tragedy in the town of Amritsar, when British soldiers fired on a gathering of unarmed people. Hundreds were killed.

Gandhi decided to work for independence. In 1920, he became head of the Indian National Congress. The Congress Party became India's largest political party.

Indian leaders wanted both political and economic freedom. Great Britain sold India a lot of cotton cloth. That made the colony a valuable market for British industry. Gandhi urged Indians not to buy British cotton goods but to spin cotton thread and weave their own cloth. He hoped that this would make India less valuable to Britain. The simple spinning wheel became a powerful symbol. Gandhi himself wore only homespun cloth. He was often seen beside a spinning wheel.

Gandhi told his followers to disobey unfair British laws. One of those laws was the Salt Act. The law made it a crime to make salt from sea water. Indians had to buy expensive salt from the government. In 1930, Gandhi started a "salt march" to the sea in protest. He began the 200-mile march with 78 followers. Every day more and more people joined the march.

Gandhi (center) used passive resistance to gain India's independence.

The march lasted 24 days. When it reached the sea, there were hundreds of people. They began to make salt the traditional way. They boiled sea water to get the salt out of it. More Indians joined Gandhi and his followers. Thousands of people—including Gandhi— were arrested.

Under constant pressure, the British changed many laws. In 1935, India won some self-government. Full independence finally came in 1947. When the country was divided, violence did occur. Still, India had won independence with two simple weapons—salt and the spinning wheel.

Wrap-Up

1. What is passive resistance?

2. Describe what happened in Amritsar in 1919.

3. What political party did Gandhi lead?

4. Why did the spinning wheel become a symbol of Indian independence?

5. What was the salt march?

- In 1900, European nations controlled most of Africa. The Pan-African Movement led the struggle for African independence.

- African nationalism grew after World War II. Ghana, a British colony, became the first independent nation in sub-Saharan Africa in 1957.

- A minority of white settlers controlled South Africa. The policy of apartheid strictly separated nonwhite and white South Africans.

- The African National Congress was one nationalist group. Its leader Nelson Mandela spent 26 years in prison for protesting apartheid. In 1994, he was elected president in South Africa's first multiracial election.

- After World War II, many Jews moved to Palestine, but Arabs already lived there. In 1947, the United Nations divided Palestine into Jewish and Arab states. Jewish leaders declared the new nation of Israel.

- Israel won several wars against neighboring Arab countries. Because of these wars, many Palestinians became refugees. Some formed the Palestinian Liberation Organization (PLO), which led terrorist attacks on Israel. In the 1990s, some Arab and Israeli leaders worked toward peace and Palestinian self-rule.

- India was a British colony. Many Indians wanted independence. The Congress Party under Mohandas Gandhi fought the British, using passive resistance.

- India became an independent democracy in 1947. People in every caste had political rights. Religious differences led to the creation of Pakistan as a Muslim state.

- Beginning in 1927, Chinese Nationalists and Communists fought a civil war. They united to fight the Japanese in World War II.

- The Chinese civil war began again after World War II. The Communists won in 1949. Mao Zedong set up a Communist government—the People's Republic of China. In 1972, the United States accepted the People's Republic as a legal government.

- Southeast Asia was a French colony, Indochina. Ho Chi Minh, a Communist, led the Vietnamese fight for independence. After a French defeat, Indochina was divided into North and South Vietnam, Cambodia, and Laos.

- North Vietnam began a guerrilla war to unite Vietnam under Communist rule. The United States helped South Vietnam. After the United States left in 1975, all Vietnam became one Communist nation.

Chapter 29   R E V I E W

Word Bank

Ben-Gurion

Chiang

Ethiopia

France

Gandhi

Great Britain

Mao

Mandela

Tutu

Vietnam

On a sheet of paper, use the words from the Word Bank to complete each sentence correctly.

1. After World War II, _____ was one of the independent nations in Africa.

2. Bishop Desmond _____, who worked to get rid of apartheid, was awarded the Nobel Peace Prize in 1984.

3. The white minority in South Africa put Nelson _____ in jail for 26 years.

4. In 1948, David _____ announced a new nation: Israel.

5. _____ controlled India from 1858 to 1947.

6. Mohandas _____ used passive resistance to gain freedom for India.

7. The nationalist leader in China in 1927 was _____ Kai-shek.

8. The Communist leader in China in 1927 was _____ Zedong.

9. The Communist leader in _____ in 1946 was Ho Chi Minh.

10. _____ had colonies in Indochina after World War II.

On a sheet of paper, write the letter of the answer that correctly completes each sentence.

11. The South African policy of not letting blacks vote or choose where to live is _____.

   A Vietnamization   **C** apartheid
   B African Nationalism   **D** Pan-African Movement

12. In _____ soldiers hide, make surprise attacks, and set traps for the enemy.

   A guerilla warfare   **C** persecution
   B multiracial   **D** apartheid

13. _____ have fought the Israelis for land to set up a nation.

    A Arab Palestinians   **C** Chinese Communists

    B Vietnamese Communists   **D** Japanese

14. The United States used a plan called _____ to get out of a war in Southeast Asia.

    A African Nationalism   **C** Pan-African Movement

    B Vietnamization   **D** British Commonwealth

15. _____, the president of the Republic of South Africa, and ANC leader Nelson Mandela, were awarded the Nobel Peace Prize in 1993.

    A F. W. de Klerk   **C** Ho Chi Minh

    B Desmond Tutu   **D** Yitzhak Rabin

On a sheet of paper, write the answer to each question. Use complete sentences.

16. Why did India divide into two countries?

17. What two Chinese groups fought over control of China? Which side won? Why?

18. Why did the United States fight a war in Vietnam?

Critical Thinking On a sheet of paper, write your response to each question. Use complete sentences.

19. How would you solve the problems in the Middle East between the Palestinians and the Israelis?

20. Do you think Gandhi's passive resistance would have worked to end apartheid in South Africa? Explain your answer.

Test-Taking Tip

Learn from your mistakes. Review corrected homework and quizzes. Correct any errors you may have made.

30

The Developing World

In this chapter, you will learn about the many changes in world history that have taken place since the end of World War II. Japan and China became economic powers. Still, many challenges remain, especially in Africa and Latin America. The Middle East continues to be a troubled region. Many Africans face the problems of poverty, hunger and disease. Latin Americans are pushing for change.

Goals for Learning

◆ To explain the problems facing Africa today
◆ To describe why conflict still exists in the Middle East
◆ To explain the changes in Asian countries
◆ To list the problems Latin America faces

1959 Fidel Castro overthrows the pro-American leader of Cuba

1978 Israeli and Egyptian leaders sign Camp David Accords in United States

1989 Chinese students protest in Tiananmen Square

1991 Persian Gulf War begins and ends

2002 United States and allies begin Iraq War

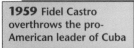

1960   1980   2000

1978 Deng Xiaoping begins economic reforms in China

1990 Iraq invades Kuwait

1997 Economic crisis in Asia

The Middle East

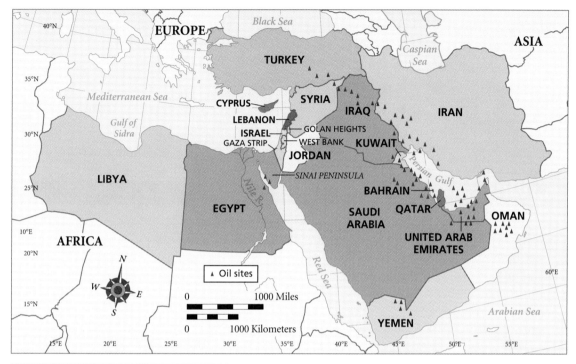

Map Skills

This map of the Middle East shows the oil sites in several countries. This area has oil resources that are important to many other countries. The countries with the largest oil reserves are Saudi Arabia, Iran, Iraq, Kuwait, and the United Arab Emirates. All of these nations belong to the Organization of Petroleum Exporting Countries (OPEC).

Study the map, then answer the following questions:

1. Which country is larger—Iraq or Iran?

2. In what direction does Kuwait lie from Iraq?

3. Where in the Middle East is the most oil?

4. What body of water lies between Iran and United Arab Emirates?

5. What body of water lies between Egypt and Saudi Arabia?

Reading Strategy:
Questioning

Questioning what you are reading helps you understand and remember more information. It also makes you a more active reader. When reading this chapter, ask yourself:

◆ Why am I reading this text?

◆ What key points can I draw from the facts and details in this text?

◆ How can I connect this text to experiences in my own life?

Key Vocabulary Words

Lesson 1

Investment Money given to a company to use to make more money

Drought A long period of time without much rain

Fertilizer A substance that helps the soil grow crops

Pesticide A substance that kills the bugs that eat the crops

Conflict Fighting; not being able to agree on something

Urbanization Becoming more like a city

Migrant A person who has left one place and moved to another

Slum An area of a city with too many people, poor housing, and low-income families

Lesson 2

Accords Agreements

Shah An Iranian ruler

Ayatollah A Muslim religious leader

Hostage Someone held against his or her will until certain demands are met

Lesson 3

Human rights Political and civil liberties, including the right to life, liberty and the pursuit of happiness

Lesson 4

Campesino A peasant who works the land but does not own it

Western Hemisphere The half of the earth that includes North and South America

Embargo An act that stops all trade

Objectives

◆ To explain the problems that African nations face today

◆ To list some reasons why African people suffer from a lack of food

Investment

Money given to a company to use to make more money

Reading Strategy:
Questioning

What do you think you will learn about by reading this lesson?

Africa is a continent in change. It has experienced many changes in a relatively short time. It has changed from being a colonial possession to a continent of independent nations.

Today, some African economies are growing at an average rate of over 5 percent. There has been real progress toward democratic rule. Trade and **investment** are growing, and Africa is reconnecting with the world economy.

What Are Africa's Biggest Problems?

Africa is also in crisis. Economic growth is uneven. The countries with natural resources, especially oil, have the fastest growing economies. Despite the progress, much of Africa still faces many problems.

Poverty is Africa's biggest problem. Between one quarter and one half of the population of Africa lives on less than two dollars a day. The average American makes more than 63 times what the average person in the Democratic Republic of Congo makes. One third of the people do not get enough food to eat. One out of every six children dies before the age of five.

Lack of food and water causes many problems in a number of African countries.

Why Do So Many People Go Hungry in Africa?

Famine is a big problem in Africa. Since the 1970s, many people have starved to death. There are five main causes of famine in Africa.

1. The population in Africa is growing at a rate of 3 percent per year, which is faster than any other region of the world. This means that the population will double in less than 24 years!

2. Since the 1970s, Africa has experienced several **droughts.** A drought is a long period without much rain.

3. Africa is growing less food, because its farmers have little **fertilizer, pesticides,** and fuel that are necessary for agriculture. Fertilizer helps the soil produce more crops; pesticides kill the bugs that eat the crops.

4. Many African countries pay more attention to industry than to agriculture.

5. In many parts of Africa, civil wars and armed **conflicts** have greatly damaged agriculture.

What Health Problems Does Africa Face?

Africa's people face many health problems. Many people become ill from malaria, a tropical disease spread by mosquitoes. About one million people in Africa die each year from malaria.

A big problem in Africa is AIDS. Africa accounts for 70 percent of the world's population infected with HIV/AIDS. The AIDS epidemic has a big effect on the economy. The death of so many farmers has cut food production. The number of orphans and old people that need care has grown. Some children cannot attend school because they have to take care of sick family members. Because most African countries are poor, they are unable to provide much medical care for people who are sick.

Drought

A long period of time without much rain

Fertilizer

A substance that helps the soil grow crops

Pesticide

A substance that kills the bugs that eat the crops

Conflict

Fighting; not being able to agree on something

Writing About History

This lesson describes things that are happening right now. Think of one way you could help stop the suffering of so many people.

In your notebook, state your goal, and then write the steps you would take to reach it.

Reading Strategy:
Questioning

Think beyond the
text. Consider your
own thoughts and
experiences as
you read about Africa.

Urbanization

Becoming more like
a city

Migrant

A person who has left
one place and moved
to another

Slum

An area of a city with
too many people,
poor housing, and
low-income families

How Has Rapid Urbanization Affected Africa?

One of the biggest problems in Africa is rapid **urbanization.** This means that African cities are growing at a very fast rate. Many people are leaving the countryside in hopes of escaping poverty and finding a better life in the cities. Often they are disappointed. Many of the newcomers have few skills and little education. There are few jobs available to them.

This large number of **migrants**—people who move from one area to another—puts a strain on city services. Housing is poor. Many people are forced to live in **slums** with no electricity, running water, or sewers. A slum is an area of a city with too many people, poor housing, and unhealthy living conditions.

Lesson 1 Review On a sheet of paper, write the word in parentheses that makes each statement true.

1. Malaria is a tropical disease spread by (fertilizer, mosquitoes, pesticides).

2. Because many African countries pay more attention to (democracy, malaria, industry) than to agriculture, there is not enough food in Africa.

3. Africa's greatest problem is probably (poverty, low birth rate, high prices).

4. (AIDS, Anorexia, Measles) is a big problem in many African countries.

5. Many rural people who migrate to Africa's cities live in (factories, slums, apartments).

What do you think ?

How would a civil war damage farming?

Accords

Agreements

The major countries in the Middle East continue not to trust in one another. The Middle East has been an area of conflict and violence for the last 100 years or so. One problem is that the Palestinians and the Israelis both claim Palestine as their own. You read about that in Chapter 29.

What Steps Have Been Taken to Bring Peace to the Region?

The United States has tried to encourage Israel and its neighbors to settle their differences. In 1978, U.S. President Jimmy Carter brought Egypt's President Sadat together with Israel's Prime Minister Begin at Camp David, Maryland. The Camp David **Accords,** or agreements, formed the basis for an Egyptian-Israeli peace treaty.

Israeli Prime Minister Yitzhak Rabin agreed to the idea of trading some of the land Israel had taken in the 1967 war for a guarantee of peace.

In November 1995 Rabin was killed by an Israeli who was against the peace process. The leaders who followed Rabin have made little progress in securing peace. Some Arabs opposed to the peace support terrorist groups like Hamas. Hamas uses violence like suicide bombings to try to prevent peace. On the other side, some Israelis fear that a self-ruling Palestine would be a threat to the security of their country.

Israel also reached out to its other Arab neighbors: Jordan and Syria. In 1994, Jordan signed a peace treaty with Israel. Talks were also held between Syria and Israel. The two sides distrust each other. Israel believes the Syrians must recognize the state of Israel as the homeland of the world's Jewish people. It also believes that Syria must control the Hezbollah. This is an organization close to Iran and Syria that Israel believes sponsors terrorism. Syria wants Israel to return the Golan Heights. This is an area overlooking the northeast corner of Israel that was taken over by Israel in the 1967 war. It also wants Israel to stop what it considers the racist attitude toward and treatment of Arabs.

In October 1998, leaders of the Middle East met with U.S. President Bill Clinton for nine days. Israel agreed to withdraw from more Palestinian land. The Palestinians agreed to get rid of terrorism. The United States agreed to guarantee security. Unfortunately, the agreement was broken and a lasting peace has not been achieved.

What Caused the Conflict in Lebanon?

In 2006, an Israeli soldier was kidnapped by Hezbollah. Even before the kidnapping, Hezbollah had fired many rockets at Israeli settlements. Israel invaded Lebanon to try to rescue their soldier. They also bombed Beirut, Lebanon's capital, killing many civilians and destroying many buildings. Thousands of people on both sides were forced to flee their homes. The UN arranged for the fighting to stop and Israel withdrew its soldiers.

Ayatollah Khomeini took control of Iran in 1979.

What Are the Roots of U.S. Problems with Iran?

Until 1979, Iran was ruled by a **Shah.** The Shah tried to make Iran into a modern nation. He began new industry. He built schools, highways, and factories. He gave women more freedom.

But many Iranians opposed the Shah. Many peasants were still without land of their own. Unemployment was high. The **ayatollahs,** the Muslim religious leaders of Iran, thought that the Shah was destroying traditional values. The Shah used his secret police to arrest and torture anyone who opposed him. He became a cruel dictator.

In the late 1970s, many people began to support Ayatollah Khomeini. Khomeini had long opposed the Shah. He wanted Iran to become an Islamic republic ruled by religious leaders. In January 1979 the Shah was forced to flee Iran. A new government under the Ayatollah took over Iran.

Much of the anger against the Shah was directed towards the United States. It was accused of being the "Great Satan," the protector of Israel, and the enemy of all Muslims. In November 1979, some Iranians took over the U.S. embassy. They captured 52 Americans and made them **hostages** for almost 15 months. Eventually, the hostages were released.

Since then, relations between the United States and Iran have been strained. The United States believes Iran is developing nuclear weapons. It accuses Iran of interfering in neighboring Iraq. It claims Iran is supplying Iraq with weapons used to kill American soldiers. Iran is accused of supporting terrorist groups like Hezbollah in Lebanon. Iran says it is not building nuclear weapons, but that it has the right to develop nuclear power. It also denies giving help to Iraqis fighting the United States.

Why Did Iraq and Iran Go to War?

Iran and Iraq are neighbors. Iranians are mainly Shiite Muslim; most Iraqis are Sunni Muslims. Iranians are Persians; most Iraqis are Arabs. Because of differences in language, culture, and religion, the two neighbors have a long history of conflict.

After its revolution in 1979, Iran tried to influence the large Shiite community in Iraq. This caused alarm among the Sunni Muslims who led the Iraqi government. In September 1980, Iraqi troops invaded Iran. The war between the two countries lasted eight years. More than one million people were killed. The oil industries in both countries were heavily damaged.

The Iraqis had better weapons, and they used poison gas. The Iranians, however, had the larger army and better airplanes. Both sides attacked international shipping. Because of this, the United States sent ships to the area. They protected the shipping lanes through which ships transported much of the world's oil. In 1988, the United States helped to end the war.

The Persian Gulf War in 1991 lasted only about 100 hours. UN forces defeated the Iraqis and freed Kuwait.

What Caused the Persian Gulf War?

The war with Iran left Iraq with a weakened economy and big debts. Iraq owed money to its neighbor, Kuwait. On August 2, 1990, Iraqi troops invaded Kuwait. They wanted to take over its rich oil fields. Saudi Arabia feared that Iraq might attack it too. If Iraq took over both Kuwait and Saudi Arabia, it would control nearly 40 percent of the world's oil. This would give it great power in the world.

The UN Security Council ordered Iraq to withdraw from Kuwait, but Iraq refused. In January 1991, an international force began an air war against Iraq. Iraq responded by firing missiles on Saudi Arabia and Israel. Iraqi soldiers did terrible things to the people of Kuwait. Gold and cash worth $1.6 billion was stolen from Kuwait's central bank and taken to Iraq.

Iraq would not leave Kuwait willingly. An international force of soldiers from 34 countries led by the United States invaded Iraq. After about 100 hours of fighting, the allies defeated Iraq. Kuwait was freed. Historians call this conflict the Persian Gulf War.

After the war, Iraq's leader, Saddam Hussein, remained in power. Two groups in Iraq—the Shiite Muslims and the Kurds—had not supported him in the war. Hussein made war against them. Hundreds of thousands were killed. Many people were forced out of their homes.

Why Did the United States Attack Iraq in 2002?

On September 11, 2001, the World Trade Center in New York was attacked. The United States suspected that Iraq was behind the attack. In December 2002, the United States and its allies attacked Iraq. There were several reasons given for the attack.

1. President George W. Bush believed that Hussein supported and cooperated with al Qaeda, a terrorist group led by Osama bin Laden. Bush called Iraq an evil country that supported terrorism.

2. The United States and others believed that Iraq's leader, Saddam Hussein, had weapons of mass destruction. These are weapons that can destroy large areas and kill many people.

3. The United States accused Hussein of taking away the basic rights of the Iraqi people.

4. President Bush believed the world was right to attack Iraq in self-defense; he believed that Iraq was a threat to the world.

At first, many other countries agreed with the United States. Hussein was quickly overthrown. At the beginning, most Iraqi people were happy to be free of their brutal dictator. Soon, however, some people began to view the foreign troops as invaders and occupiers, not as people bringing them freedom. Thousands of Iraqi people have been killed in what many people now call a civil war.

Lesson 2 Review Choose the letter of the answer that correctly completes each sentence. Write your answer on a sheet of paper.

1. The prime minister of Israel in the 1990s was _____.

    A Hamas   **B** Rabin   **C** Clinton   **D** Hussein

2. In 1979, Ayatollah _____ took over the Iranian government.

    A Shah   **B** Hussein   **C** Khomeini   **D** Hamas

3. In 1980, _____ invaded Iran.

    A Iraq   **C** Kuwait
    B Saudi Arabia   **D** the United States

4. In 1990, Iraq invaded _____.

    A Iran   **B** Libya   **C** Kuwait   **D** Israel

5. _____ fought Shiite Muslims and Kurds in his own country.

    A Rabin   **C** Hussein
    B Khomeini   **D** Shah

What do you think ?

Why is oil such an important resource for the Middle East?

Objectives

◆ To explain political changes in Asian countries

◆ To describe economic changes that have occurred in Asian countries

After Mao Zedong died in 1976, China began to change. China's new leader, Deng Xiaoping, proposed major economic reforms. His economic plan was called the Four Modernizations. The plan called for reform and change in agriculture, industry, science, and defense. There were many changes. One was that privately owned businesses and private property were again permitted. Another was that investment from foreign countries including the United States was welcomed. Although major industries were still controlled by the government, factory managers were given new powers to make them more efficient and profitable.

The new economic reforms resulted in a big increase in the standard of living for many people. Many Chinese families were able to buy such things as televisions, refrigerators, fans, and even cars. Until recently, these items were considered luxuries that most people could not afford. But the reforms had a bad side, too. A big gap developed between those people who had become successful and rich and those who had not. Crime and corruption increased. Food prices went up. Many people lost their jobs as some factories were closed.

China's economy is one of the fastest growing economies in the world today. Many foreign companies are investing in China. They are taking advantage of the low cost of labor in China compared to most developed countries. They also see China's huge population as a market for their products. One of China's biggest customers is the United States.

China's capital city is Beijing. Many people ride bicycles rather than motorized vehicles.

What Happened at Tiananmen Square?

In May 1989, more than 3,000 students went on a hunger strike in Tiananmen Square in Beijing, China's capital city. They wanted a democratic, not a communist, government. Soon, more than a million people went out on the streets and called for a change.

Through television, the whole world learned about the protest. But on June 4, 1989, soldiers marched into Tiananmen Square and killed hundreds of protestors. The government put many of the student leaders in jail and tortured or killed them.

Since the Tiananmen Square massacre, China's relations with the West have been strained. The West led by the United States has called for more **human rights** in China. Human rights refer to political and civil liberties, including the right to life, liberty, and the pursuit of happiness. They also include economic, social, and cultural rights.

Why Has Japan Become an Economic Power?

Japan is among the world's top producers of goods and services. It is the second largest economy in the world. (Only the economy of the United States is bigger.) People who study economics give three reasons for its success.

1. The government works with large companies to plan and promote industrial growth.

2. These companies get money from banks. Since Japanese people have one of the highest savings rates in the world, the banks have a lot of money to loan out. The Bank of Japan (owned by the Japanese government) guarantees the loans.

3. The Japanese people are group oriented. It is natural and easy for them to work with one another. They are generally hard workers who produce many products quickly and at low cost. Workers are well educated and highly skilled.

Biography

Aung San Suu Kyi: 1945–

Since 1988, Aung San Suu Kyi has led the fight for democracy in Myanmar (Burma). Leadership is a family trait. Her father, Aung San, is called the father of independent Burma.

In 1988, Myanmans protested against military rule. As a result, troops shot or arrested thousands. Aung San spoke out for human rights. She helped the National League for Democracy win 80 percent of the seats in parliament. The military rulers ignored this and kept her under house arrest for six years. In 1991, she won the Nobel Peace Prize. She was free for a short time; in 2003, she was returned to house arrest.

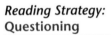

Reading Strategy:
Questioning

Ask yourself: "Did I understand what I just read?" If not, read the material again.

Who Are the "Little Tigers"?

Several other Asian nations have experienced economic growth in recent years. Known as the "little tigers," they are South Korea, Taiwan, Singapore, Hong Kong, and Thailand. South Korea builds ships and automobiles. Taiwan produces everything from toys to electronics. Singapore and Hong Kong are manufacturing and banking centers. Much of Thailand's economic growth is the result of huge foreign investment and loans. Investors were hoping to make money and take advantage of Thailand's lower cost of labor.

What Caused the Economic Crisis in Asia in 1997?

In June 1997, the money supply of Thailand collapsed. Soon, the crisis spread to Indonesia, Malaysia, the Philippines, and South Korea. Many Asian banks and businesses went bankrupt. This happened for two reasons.

First, many Asian businesses had borrowed too much money from banks in the 1980s. Then, factories began to produce more than they could sell and prices went down. The businesses could not pay back what they had borrowed. Soon, both the banks and the businesses had no money.

Second, foreign investors got worried. They pulled their money out of some Asian countries. Without this money, many Asian businesses could no longer stay in business.

Lesson 3 Review On a sheet of paper, write the answers to these questions. Use complete sentences.

1. How did Deng's Four Modernizations program change China?

2. Which group led the protest movement in China in 1989?

3. List at least two reasons why Japan became the most important economy of Asia.

4. Who are the "Little Tigers"?

5. What two problems led to the economic crisis in Asia?

What do you think ?

If you had to choose one human right that was most important to you, what would it be? Why?

Objectives

◆ To explain why campesinos demanded land reform

◆ To describe ways the United States has caused changes in Latin America

Campesino

A peasant who works the land but does not own it

One of the biggest problems facing Latin America is an extreme of wealth and poverty. Most Latin American countries have agricultural economies. The majority of people are poor people. They are peasants, landless farm workers, and factory workers. Poverty is widespread. It affects all groups but affects native peoples, minorities, women, and children the most. A small but rich elite controls much of the wealth. This group includes the landowners, factory owners, and military leaders.

Why Do Campesinos Want Land Reform?

A big problem is that a small group of people own so much of the land. For example, in Paraguay, a few big landowners control 80 percent of the land that can be farmed! This is true in most of the rest of Latin America. Many poor people, called **campesinos,** live and work on the land, but do not own it.

In many countries, campesinos are demanding land reform. They want the government to break up the large farms and divide the land among the poor. Land reform has been most successful in Mexico, Cuba, Peru, and Nicaragua.

Women buying and selling food in Guatemala, Central America.

Population growth is another big challenge. In 1940 Latin
America had about 126 million people. In 2007 there are nearly
600 million! Families are typically large. Improved health care
also means that fewer people die.

Economic development is another problem. The leaders of
Latin America believe that industrialization is the way to solve
many of the region's problems. In the 1980s and 90s, Latin
America made great progress. The region has large deposits
of oil, tin, copper, iron ore, and bauxite, the main ingredient
in aluminum. Export sale of these natural resources provides
much of the foreign income needed to finance development.
But relying on one product can be very bad. When the price
drops, governments are forced to borrow money to make up
the difference. Many Latin American countries got into trouble
when they began borrowing too much money.

How Do Latin America and the United States Get Along?

In Chapter 22, you read about the struggle for freedom in
Latin America. During this time, the United States encouraged
the wars of independence. In 1823, President James Monroe
warned European nations to stay out of the **Western
Hemisphere.** That is the half of the earth that includes North
and South America.

Conflict developed when Americans settled in territories of
northern Mexico in the 1830s and 1840s. In 1846, Mexico and
the United States went to war. At the end of the war, Mexico
had to give up California and all the land between Texas and
California.

In 1898, the United States went to war against Spain in the
Spanish-American War. Cuba, a Spanish colony, was given
its independence but U.S. forces stayed in Cuba for four more
years. The United States took control of Puerto Rico, another
Spanish colony. By now, the United States was becoming a
major world power.

Then and Now

The "Tourist Capital of Peru"

Cuzco is a city in southern Peru. It is believed to be one of the oldest cities in the world, dating back to 2000 B.C. Cuzco was the capital of the Incan civilization beginning in A.D. 1200. When Spain conquered the empire in 1533, they moved the capital to Lima.

Colorful reminders of Inca art and architecture are still found in Cuzco. Much of the Incan Temple of the Sun still stands, as do pieces of wall that once surrounded the city. The same is true of the Renaissance cathedral built by Spaniards, as well as explorer Francisco Pizzaro's palace. A major earthquake destroyed much of Cuzco in 1950. The historical buildings have been restored since that time. Cuzco, now a major center for archaeological research, is often called the "tourist capital of Peru."

The navy needed a fast way to move its warships from the Atlantic to the Pacific Ocean. It was decided to build a canal through Central America. The shortest route for a canal was through Panama, but Panama was a part of Colombia. The United States encouraged the people of Panama to revolt. U.S. President Theodore Roosevelt bragged, "I took Panama." The canal was built and opened to shipping in 1914.

The United States and Latin America have taken steps to reduce tariffs and trade barriers. They have joined together in regional trade agreements such as the North American Free Trade Agreement, or NAFTA. It took effect on January 1, 1994. It links together the economies of the United States, Mexico, and Canada. The United States has tried to promote free trade, that is, trade between countries that is free of taxes and other barriers.

Embargo

An act that stops all trade

What Major Problems Exist Between the United States and Latin America Today?

Several countries in Latin America have elected leaders who are critical of the United States government. In 1959, Fidel Castro overthrew the pro-American leader of Cuba. He became a dictator who would not allow free elections or a free press. He took over U.S.-owned businesses. The United States put an **embargo** on all trade with Cuba, which still exists. An embargo stops all trade. In 1961, a U.S.-trained group invaded Cuba and tried to overthrow Castro. The landing at the Bay of Pigs had little popular support. In July, 1962, the Soviet Union began to build missile sites in Cuba. The United States demanded their removal. It looked as if the United States and the USSR would go to war. Fortunately, the missile crisis ended peacefully. The Soviets agreed to remove the missiles, and the United States promised not to invade Cuba.

Venezuela's leader is Hugo Chavez. Like Castro, he is anti-American and wants to reduce America's influence in the region. His government has taken over several major oil businesses owned by foreign corporations. In Bolivia, Evo Morales, a critic of free market economics, is president.

Reading Strategy:
Questioning

Think about the purpose of this lesson. Ask yourself what you hope to learn by reading it.

History in Your Life

Baseball Around the World

Do you love béisbol? Do you play besoboru? These are the words for baseball in Spanish and Japanese. Baseball has been popular in countries around the world for more than a hundred years. Players from countries such as Cuba and Japan now play for American major league teams.

How did baseball spread outside the United States? American missionaries took it to Japan in the 1870s. During the Spanish-American War (1898), American soldiers brought the game to the Philippines.

The Japanese saw baseball as a new kind of martial art. By the early 1900s, it was the country's most popular sport. American major league players toured Japan in the 1920s and 1930s. Baseball then spread to Korea and Taiwan.

Baseball is played in Mexico, the Caribbean, and Central America, too. Tours and spring training also helped introduce it there. Each year, national teams from these areas play in the Caribbean Series.

Lesson 4 Review On a sheet of paper, write the answer to each question. Use complete sentences.

1. Why do you think that a few landowners, factory owners, and military leaders control most of Latin America's wealth?

2. Why did campesinos demand land reform?

3. How does poverty affect the people of Latin America?

4. What is the purpose of NAFTA?

5. Why did the United States try to overthrow Cuba's leader, Fidel Castro, in the Bay of Pigs invasion?

What do you think ?

What should the United States do to improve the life of poor people in Latin America?

Poverty Is a Threat to Peace

Muhammad Yunus received the Nobel Peace Prize in 2006 for starting Grameen Bank. This bank provides small loans—the average is $200—to poor people so they can invest in business and change their lives. Today the bank has 3.5 million borrowers. Most of them are women. Here is an excerpt from his acceptance speech.

Ladies and Gentlemen:
By giving us this prize, the Norwegian Nobel Committee has given important support to the proposition that peace is inextricably linked to poverty. Poverty is a threat to peace. . . .

Poverty is the denial of all human rights. Peace should be understood in a human way, in a broad social, political and economic way. Peace is threatened by unjust economic, social and political order, absence of democracy, environmental degradation and absence of human rights.

Poverty is the absence of all human rights. The frustrations, hostility and anger generated by abject poverty cannot sustain peace in any society. For building stable peace we must find ways to provide opportunities for people to live decent lives.

The creation of opportunities for the majority of people—the poor—is at the heart of the work that we have dedicated ourselves to during the past 30 years. . . .

We create what we want. We get what we want, or what we don't refuse. We accept the fact that we will always have poor people around us, and that poverty is part of human destiny. This is precisely why we continue to have poor people around us. If we firmly believe that poverty is unacceptable to us, and that it should not belong to a civilized society, we would have built appropriate institutions and policies to create a poverty-free world.

We wanted to go to the moon, so we went there. We achieve what we want to achieve. If we are not achieving something, it is because we have not put our minds to it. We create what we want.

I believe that this honor that you give us will inspire many more bold [projects] around the world to make a historical breakthrough in ending global poverty.

Document-Based Questions

1. How does Yunus define poverty?

2. How is poverty connected to peace?

3. What are the emotions that people experience from living in poverty?

4. According to Yunus, what do we achieve?

5. What does Yunus hope that his receiving the Nobel Peace Prize will inspire in others?

Source: Nobel lecture by Muhammad Yunus, December 20, 2006.

Themes in History

An old saying goes, "History repeats itself." Look back over the thousands of years you have studied. Probably you can see many continuing themes. Certain types of events seem to happen again and again.

One theme in history is the rise and fall of empires. In every time and place, leaders have wanted power. They have conquered and ruled other lands and people. The earliest empires began in Mesopotamia more than 4,000 years ago. Ancient history, in fact, sometimes looks like the history of empires. Babylon, Egypt, and Persia each ruled huge territories. Alexander the Great and Genghis Khan built the largest empires of all.

Empires fall for different reasons. Some, like Alexander's, depended on one strong leader. After the leader's death, the empire fell apart. Other empires grew weak before they were defeated. The Roman Empire declined for centuries. Finally, Germanic invaders brought it to an end. Sometimes empires were defeated by new technology. North Africans with guns defeated Songhai. Spaniards with guns and horses conquered the Incas.

The search for freedom is another major theme. Throughout history, individuals have rebelled against power. In the 1790s, the people of France began a bloody revolution. It ended the monarchy. In the 1800s, Latin American colonies won independence from Spain. After World War II, colonies around the world struggled to become independent. Some went to war. In India, Gandhi used a new way to win independence from Britain. He urged nonviolent methods like strikes.

Today there is a new emphasis on human rights. This issue combines justice with freedom. Human rights supporters want fair treatment for all people. They work particularly on behalf of people without power. Human rights is not a new issue. Gandhi wanted fair treatment for India's "untouchables." Today, activists work for the rights of children, the poor, and others.

Technology is another theme in human history. The earliest men and women made tools. Technology helped build civilizations. It has also changed history. Iron tools changed warfare and farming. The Chinese learned to make silk and porcelain. That encouraged trade ties between Asia and Europe. With better ships and navigation, explorers could make long sea voyages. Printing helped spread learning. Today, cell phones and the Internet link the whole world.

Wrap-Up

1. Name some empires from ancient times.

2. What are some causes for the fall of empires?

3. How have people shown their desire for freedom?

4. Name one advance in technology that changed history. What did it change?

5. Identify a theme in history that you have noticed. Include an example.

Chapter 30   S U M M A R Y

- Africa continues to face the challenges of poverty, famine, and disease.

- The United States has tried to bring peace to the Middle East. Israel made peace with Egypt (1978) and Jordan (1994). Conflicts continue in the Middle East.

- The Shah of Iran tried to modernize the country but used harsh methods. A religious leader, Ayatollah Khomeini, led a revolution against him in 1979.

- Iranians and Iraqis follow different branches of Islam and belong to different ethnic groups. Iraq invaded Iran in 1980, starting an eight-year war. The war threatened world oil supplies.

- In 1990, Iraqi leader Saddam Hussein invaded Kuwait to take control of its oil fields. In the Persian Gulf War, an international military force defeated Iraq.

- The United States and its allies invaded Iraq in 2002 because they suspected that Iraq was behind the attack on the World Trade Center on 9/11.

- After Mao Zedong's death, Chinese leader Deng Xiaoping made economic changes. He encouraged private business and foreign investment. Now, China has one of the fastest growing economies in the world.

- In 1989 in Tiananmen Square, soldiers attacked students. They were marching for democracy and human rights.

- Japan has the world's second largest economy. The economies of other Asian nations have also grown.

- An economic crisis hit Asian nations in 1997. Many banks and businesses failed.

- Land reform is an issue in many Latin American nations. Most people are poor.

- Mexico, Canada, and the United States signed the North American Free Trade Agreement (NAFTA) to encourage trade.

- Several countries in Latin America have elected leaders who do not like the United States government. Cuba's leader, Fidel Castro, came to power in 1959. The United States tried to overthrow him in 1961.

Chapter 30 REVIEW

Word Bank

Accords
ayatollah
campesinos
Japanese
Kuwait
malaria
Modernizations
Shah
Thailand
urbanization

On a sheet of paper, use the words from the Word Bank to complete each sentence correctly.

1. Because many people are flocking to the cities, Africa faces rapid _____.

2. The name for a religious leader in Iran is _____.

3. Millions of people in Africa suffer from AIDS or _____, which is spread by mosquitos.

4. The Camp David _____ formed the basis for an Arab-Israeli peace treaty.

5. Until 1979, Iran was ruled by a(n) _____.

6. In August 1990, Iraqi troops invaded _____.

7. Deng Xiaoping's economic plan was called the Four _____.

8. _____ people have one of the highest rates of saving money in the world.

9. In June 1997, the money supply of _____ collapsed.

10. The _____ in Latin America are demanding land reform.

On a separate sheet of paper, write the letter of the answer that correctly completes each sentence.

11. In 1979, _____ took 52 Americans hostage.

   A Iraq   **B** Iran   **C** Cuba   **D** Israel

12. The Persian Gulf War started after Iraq invaded _____.

   A Kuwait   **C** Iran
   B Saudi Arabia   **D** Israel

13. Pro-democracy protests in Tiananmen Square were led by _____.

   A peasants   **C** merchants
   B students   **D** government leaders

14. China's economy is the _____ largest economy in the world.

    A second   **B** third   **C** fourth   **D** fifth

15. In 1978, U.S. President _____ brought Egypt's Sadat and Israel's Begin together at Camp David, Maryland.

    A Nixon   **B** Reagan   **C** Carter   **D** Clinton

On a sheet of paper, write the answers to the following questions. Use complete sentences.

16. What is one problem that Africans face today?

17. What is one problem that people in the Middle East face today?

18. What is one problem that people in Latin America face today?

Critical Thinking On a sheet of paper, write your response to each question. Use complete sentences.

19. The conflict in the Middle East has gone on for many years. If you could talk to leaders in the Middle East, what advice would you give them about ending the conflict?

20. There are many countries in the world that suffer from extreme poverty. If you could choose one country to help, where would you go and what would you do?

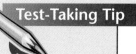

Test-Taking Tip

Make sure you have the same number of answers on your paper as there are items on the test.

31

The World Today

This is the last chapter of your world history book. In this text, you have traveled through time from ancient India, China, and Sumeria to modern nations. Now, in this final chapter, you will discover the global village that is Earth. You will see how the Internet and mass communication link the nations of our global village. Then you will learn how modern technology can be harmful. You will also learn about the joining together of the world economies. Finally, you will see what farming and industry have done to the environment. This chapter shows you what life is like today.

Goals for Learning

◆ To explain how technology and energy help build a global village

◆ To describe the economic interdependence of modern industrial nations and developing countries

◆ To identify some health concerns and environmental problems the world faces

◆ To describe how the threat of terrorism has changed the world

◆ To consider what the future may hold

1990s Internet expands the use of computers

1997 Recession begins in Thailand and spreads worldwide

2001 September 11 attacks; U.S. Department of Homeland Security created

1990   1995   2000

1992 International leaders meet to discuss environmental problems

1997 International leaders meet once again to discuss environmental problems

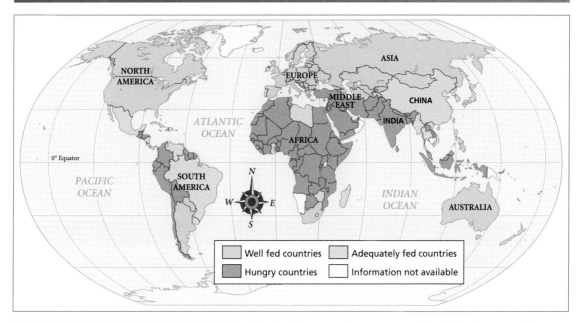

Map Skills

Many countries of the world have enough food to feed their people. But some countries do not. The climate is much hotter and drier near the equator than it is farther away, so that is where growing food is difficult. Many of these hungry nations have deserts in their land. This world map shows world hunger.

Study the map, then answer the following questions:

1. Which continent has the most serious problem with hunger?

2. What are three places where people are well fed?

3. On which coast of South America is there a hunger problem?

4. Do people in China have more or less food than people in Australia?

5. Do people in India have more or less food than people in North America?

Reading Strategy:
Predicting

In order to predict what will come next, it is helpful to first preview a text. Previewing helps readers think about what they already know about a subject. When making predictions, consider the following:

◆ Consider what you already know about the topic. Make your best guess as to what might happen next.

◆ Be sure to include details that support your prediction.

◆ As you read, you may learn new information that changes your prediction. Check your predictions as you read.

Key Vocabulary Words

Lesson 1

Technology The use of science to do practical things

Global village The term used to describe the sharing of ideas, cultures, and traditions throughout the world

Mass communication Messages directed at many people

Internet An international computer network

International Around the world; involving different nations

World Wide Web A network of information on the Internet open to businesses and individuals

Renewable Energy that will never run out

Photoelectric cell An invention that can produce electricity from light

Laser A tool that produces high-energy beams of light

Lesson 2

Interdependent Depending on one another

Free-market economy An economy in which manufacturers try to satisfy consumers' wants and needs

Northern Hemisphere The half of the earth north of the equator

Developing country A nation that is slowly developing its industry and economy

Southern Hemisphere The half of the earth south of the equator

Subsistence farming A type of farming in which people grow crops mostly for their own use, not to sell

Recession An economic slowdown

Lesson 3

Deforestation The destruction of forests

Fossil fuel Fuel made from coal, oil, or natural gas

Global warming The worldwide heating up of Earth, caused in part by human activity

Lesson 4

Regime The form of government

Tyranny Harsh, absolute power

Technology

The use of science to do practical things

Global village

The term used to describe the sharing of ideas, cultures, and traditions throughout the world

Reading Strategy:
Predicting

Preview the lesson title. Predict what you will learn in this lesson.

Today, the earth seems smaller than it used to be. Its physical size is the same as it was for the ancient Romans. The distance between Spain and Cuba is the same as it was for Christopher Columbus. The miles from France to Russia are still the same as they were for Napoleon. So what has changed?

What Has Made the World into a Global Village?

Today, people around the world share ideas, art, music, and different ways of living. This has happened because of advances in **technology.** Technology is the use of science to do practical things. Because of this technology, the world is changing into a **global village.**

What is a global village? The word *global* comes from the word *globe,* which means "the earth." As you know, a village is a place where a few hundred people live and work together. People who live in a village know most, if not all, their neighbors. Villagers share ideas and traditions. They share their lives. A global village, then, is a term used to describe the sharing of ideas, cultures, and traditions around the world.

Today, for the first time in history, modern technology— motion pictures, computers, video cameras, CD players, television—allows people from around the world to share their

lives. Technology also enables businesses to employ workers all over the world.

Technology links the whole world together. Technology makes the globe we live on into one village—a global village. We have begun to share our cultures around the globe.

We all live in Earth's global village. This picture shows Tokyo, Japan.

Reading Strategy:
Predicting

As you read, think about what might come next. Do you think that mass communication has played an important role in creating the global village?

Mass communication

Messages directed at many people

How Has Mass Communication Created Our Global Village?

Mass communication is one of the major reasons that the world is becoming a global village. Mass communication is messages directed at many people. Businesses and private or governmental groups prepare these messages.

Newspaper and magazine advertising provides mass communication in print. Advertising is the selling or the announcing of something. Motion pictures, television, radio, and musical recordings provide mass communication electronically.

Today, electronic communications connect people everywhere. Since the end of World War II, American television, movies, music, fast food, and clothing styles have helped to shape this new global culture. Around the world, many business people and government officials speak English.

But the global culture has also changed the United States. Music from Asia, Africa, and Latin America influences American popular music. Americans eat foods from around the world.

Communication in History

Your Phone Is Ringing

You hear them ringing everywhere. Cell phones ring in pockets and purses. People talk on the street and in their cars. Regular telephone messages move through wires and cables. Cell phones, however, send messages through the air. They travel much like radio waves. A World War II invention inspired the cell phone. It was the "walkie-talkie" used by soldiers in combat. After the war, inventors worked to adapt this technology. The first commercial cell phone clicked on in 1983.

Cellular phone technology spread quickly. Wireless networks put a low-power transmission tower in each area, or "cell." As the phone user travels, the call moves from cell to cell. Over longer distances, global networks use satellites to relay messages.

Cell phones are more than a convenience. People in a dangerous situation can call for help. In some places around the world, telephone wires did not reach distant towns. Cell phones have brought phone service there.

How Has the Internet Linked Our World?

The computer started a technological revolution as important as the Industrial Revolution. People use computers in businesses, schools, and homes. They are used to store information, figure math problems, and write things.

In the 1990s, the **Internet** expanded the use of computers. The Internet is an **international** computer network. (That is, the information on it goes around the world. It involves different nations.) This computer network connects millions of computer users all over the world. However, for some time, only universities and governmental agencies used the Internet.

All this changed with the development of the **World Wide Web.** It made the Internet easier to use and opened it to businesses and individuals. Because of the Internet, the whole world is linked electronically for the first time in history. E-mail lets us send messages to people anywhere in the world almost instantly.

How Does Space Exploration Create Our Global Village?

In October 1957, the Soviet Union placed *Sputnik,* the first space satellite, into orbit around the earth. Today, dozens of communication satellites send and receive radio, television, and telephone signals. Because of this, people around the globe can see television shows produced thousands of miles away. They can talk on the telephone to friends who live halfway around the globe.

On July 20, 1969, nearly a billion people watched on television as Neil Armstrong stepped from his spaceship. An American was the first person to land on the moon, but Americans do not own it. The nations of the world have agreed that the moon and all of outer space are international areas.

Internet

An international computer network

International

Around the world; involving different nations

World Wide Web

A network of information on the Internet open to businesses and individuals

"Space: the Final Frontier . . ."

In the 1500s, explorers needed courage and imagination. They sailed to new parts of the world. They had few maps to guide them. New technology helped, however. Better instruments measured speed and location. Shipbuilders designed sturdy ocean-going ships.

Nearly 500 years later, explorers traveled to new worlds in outer space. Courage and technology were still important. In April 1961, a Soviet cosmonaut became the first person in space. The first American space flight came a month later. From there, space exploration has reached greater and greater successes with many new types of spacecraft. Several unmanned ships have been sent deep into outer space. In 1996, *Pathfinder* landed on Mars and took many amazing photos of its surface. Some day, people may even live on the moon or on other planets.

Russia and the United States are now working together. U.S. space shuttles regularly delivered supplies and people to the Russian space station *Mir*. In 1998, work began on building the International Space Station. It is an orbiting science laboratory that goes around the earth more than 15 times a day. The station is serviced mostly by the United States and Russia. However, crew members have come from many countries. Fifteen governments are involved in the Space Station project. When the International Space Station is complete, it will have a mass of almost 1 million pounds and be larger than a five-bedroom house and measure 361 feet end-to-end. People have been living on it permanently since 2000.

What Have Coal and Oil Done to Our Global Village?

Coal was a source of energy in the 19th century. It produced energy for factories, homes, and steam locomotives. Oil has continued to be the major source of energy into the 21st century. It runs our factories, heats our homes, and powers our cars, trucks, trains, and planes.

But the burning of coal and oil has also created serious problems for our world. Air and water pollution creates health problems for humans. Pollution occurs when air, water, or land becomes unclean and unhealthy. Pollution threatens the life of many plants and animals. It threatens our environment—the land, sea, and air of our world.

What Is Wrong with Using Nuclear Energy?

Scientists have been looking for a clean source of energy that will not hurt our environment. They once thought that nuclear power was a clean source of energy. But it produces deadly waste products.

Also, people have died from accidents at nuclear power plants in the United States, Russia, and India. Even so, nuclear power plants produce about 20 percent of the electricity in the United States, Japan, and Great Britain. In France, 70 percent of the nation's electricity comes from nuclear power.

Some scientists look to wind, water in oceans and rivers, and the sun as clean sources of energy. These are **renewable** sources of energy. That means they'll never run out. Technology can use all of them to produce electricity. The **photoelectric cell** is an invention that can produce electricity from light. Today, many businesses and homes use photoelectric cells to create electricity. Engineers have designed cars that run on electricity produced by photoelectric cells.

Is nuclear energy the answer to the world's energy needs? Although it is used in many countries, it can be dangerous. This photo shows a destroyed nuclear power plant in Chernobyl, Ukraine. It exploded in 1986, killing 31 people.

How Has Technology Changed Medicine?

Doctors now remove a person's heart and fix it. They replace livers and hips. They sew fingers, arms, and legs onto a person who has lost them in an accident. Technology makes all this possible.

Engineers have invented new machines to help doctors figure out what diseases people have. One machine helps doctors see the inside of the body. Doctors use lasers to cut and seal wounds. A **laser** is a tool that produces high-energy beams of light.

What Is the Electronic Superhighway?

The electronic superhighway sends information from telephones, television, and computers. This information is now reaching many areas of the world. As this happens, cultures around the world influence one another. Today, some electronic programs translate one language into another. People can communicate even though they do not speak or write the same language. This "electronic culture" is going to change our global village.

The World's Major Consumers of Energy

Numbers indicate quadrillion British thermal units (Btu).

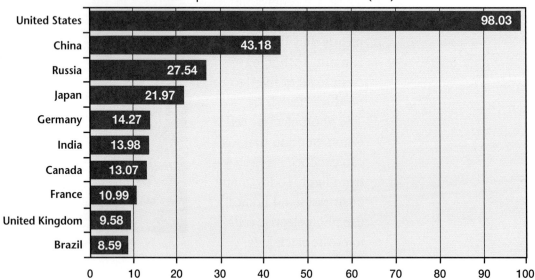

This graph shows the countries that use the most energy and how much they use (estimated). Which country uses the most energy? Why do you think this is true?

Can New Technology Harm Our Global Village?

In the early part of the 20th century, people predicted that technology would solve many of the world's problems. Electricity would provide the energy for many labor-saving machines. People would work only a few hours a week. Everyone would have an automobile. Airplanes would fill the sky.

At the time, people did not see how the military would use technology to fight World War I and II. They did not see what technology would do to our environment.

Today, some people think that we are losing our freedom. People can find out too much information about us. Every time we use a credit card, a computer files the information away. Computers also contain information about medicines we take. The government collects information about us and stores it on computers.

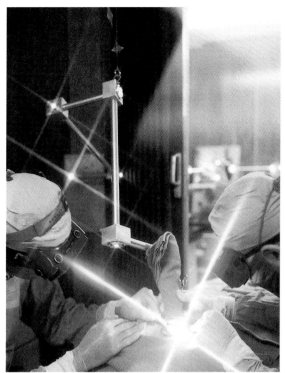

Doctors now use lasers and other technology to treat people. Medicine is one area that technology has influenced greatly.

But who will decide how to use all this information? How can we control what people know about us? Does having this information give some people control over us? If technology can cause harm, should we limit its development? Who will decide what that limit is? These important questions have no easy answers.

Biography

Stephen Hawking: 1942–

If you've ever heard of a black hole, you know something about Stephen Hawking. This physicist has made major discoveries about the universe. A black hole, for instance, is a region in space with intense gravity. The collapse of a huge star would have caused it. Not even light can escape a black hole. Hawking's main field is quantum physics, the study of units that make up the atom.

Hawking is a professor of mathematics at Cambridge University in England. Because of a disease of the nervous system, he uses a wheelchair. He speaks with the help of a computer.

Lesson 1 Review On a sheet of paper, write the answers to these questions. Use complete sentences.

1. How has mass communication changed our world?

2. What is one example of a clean source of energy?

3. What is one improvement that technology has brought to medicine?

4. What are one good thing and one bad thing about the Internet?

5. Why do some people consider nuclear energy very dangerous?

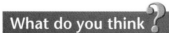

What do you think

What is your favorite form of mass communication and why?

Objectives

◆ To describe economies in developing nations

◆ To identify economic and other problems that developing countries have

Interdependent

Depending on one another

Free-market economy

An economy in which manufacturers try to satisfy consumers' wants and needs

Northern Hemisphere

The half of Earth north of the equator

Developing country

A nation that is slowly developing its industry and economy

Subsistence farming

A type of farming in which people grow crops mostly for their own use, not to sell

Southern Hemisphere

The half of Earth south of the equator

The global village is **interdependent.** What happens in one nation affects every other nation. For example, when the price of oil from the Middle East goes up, manufacturers in the United States have to spend more to produce goods. Consumers then pay more when they buy these goods.

What Is a Free-Market Economy?

Most rich countries have a **free-market economy.** In such an economy, manufacturers satisfy the wants and needs of consumers. The government lets factories produce what they like.

The **Northern Hemisphere**—the half of Earth north of the equator—contains most of the successful free-market countries. Among these are the United States, Canada, Germany, France, and Great Britain. Asia's strongest economy is in Japan. These countries have well-organized farming and industrial systems and make use of technology.

What Problems Do Developing Countries Have?

Developing countries are countries that are slowly developing their industries and economies. In these poor nations, most people do **subsistence farming.** This means that they grow crops mostly for their own use. They do not sell what they grow. Most of these nations are in the **Southern Hemisphere**— the half of Earth south of the equator.

These developing nations face many problems. First, they are overpopulated. More than half of the people in the world live in developing countries. This leads to hunger, pollution, and political unrest. It has also led to the destruction of the Amazon rain forest and the overuse of croplands in Asia. Second, in many developing countries, students attend school for only two or three years. Only about half the people in these countries can read and write. Third, industrialization requires money.

Most developing countries have only raw materials to sell. (The industrialized countries set the cost for these raw materials.) They have no consumer goods to trade to other countries. But poor countries want consumer goods, so they buy more than they sell. Money flows out of these countries.

What Is a Recession?

After the money supply of Thailand collapsed in 1997, the crisis spread to South Korea, Indonesia, Malaysia, and Russia. Soon, banks and businesses went bankrupt. People lost their jobs and had no money to buy things. Because no one was buying consumer goods, even more businesses closed down. Economists call this a **recession**, or an economic slowdown.

How Did the Recession Affect Japan and the United States?

Many people in Japan lost their jobs because of the recession. This is important because Japan is the economic engine for Asia. It keeps things moving there.

The recession also affected the United States. People in other countries had no money to buy goods from the United States. U.S. companies lost money, and some workers lost jobs. However, the bankrupted Asian companies no longer had a need for oil to supply energy to their factories. The Middle East lowered its oil price. This meant that the United States had to pay less for oil, so gasoline prices in the United States went down.

Who Is to Blame for the Recession?

Some people blame multinational corporations, which manufacture and sell goods in many countries. They compete with businesses in developing countries. These businesses cannot win when they are up against huge foreign corporations. For example, a small business might make the same product that a multinational makes. But the multinationals can sell their products cheaper. They can move their factories from one developing country to another to get the lowest cost for labor and materials.

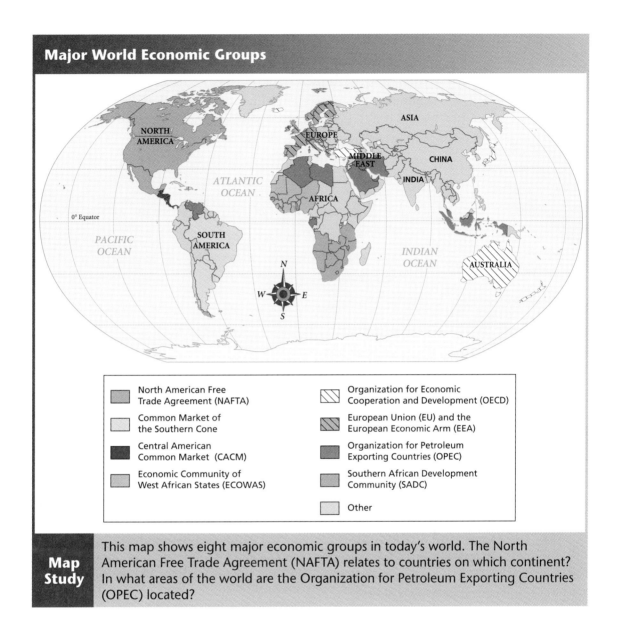

Major World Economic Groups

NORTH AMERICA

ATLANTIC OCEAN

0° Equator

PACIFIC OCEAN

SOUTH AMERICA

EUROPE

ASIA

MIDDLE EAST

CHINA

INDIA

AFRICA

INDIAN OCEAN

AUSTRALIA

N W E S

- North American Free Trade Agreement (NAFTA)
- Common Market of the Southern Cone
- Central American Common Market (CACM)
- Economic Community of West African States (ECOWAS)
- Organization for Economic Cooperation and Development (OECD)
- European Union (EU) and the European Economic Arm (EEA)
- Organization for Petroleum Exporting Countries (OPEC)
- Southern African Development Community (SADC)
- Other

Map Study

This map shows eight major economic groups in today's world. The North American Free Trade Agreement (NAFTA) relates to countries on which continent? In what areas of the world are the Organization for Petroleum Exporting Countries (OPEC) located?

Reading Strategy:
Predicting

Think about your prediction. What details can you now add to make your prediction more specific?

Who Helps Nations That Have Economic Problems?

For 50 years, industrialized nations have given money, food, medicine, tools, and machinery to developing nations. Each year, the 21 most industrialized nations provide billions of dollars to roughly 182 nations. In one third of these countries, people live on less than two dollars a day.

The industrialized nations send their money through two international organizations: the World Bank and the International Monetary Fund (IMF). The World Bank directs money from industrialized nations to developing ones. It helps build dams, mines, roads, and bridges. It also helps to improve education, health, and the environment. The IMF is an organization of 182 nations. It has a supply of money to help its members in times of economic crisis.

Word Bank

free-market

interdependent

overpopulation

recession

subsistence

Lesson 2 Review On a sheet of paper, write the word from the Word Bank that best completes each sentence.

1. The world's richest countries generally have a _____ economy.

2. People of less developed countries are often _____ farmers.

3. Economists call an economic slowdown a _____.

4. Nations of the world are _____, because what happens in one affects all the others.

5. Many developing countries face the problem of _____, which has led to hunger and pollution.

What do you think

Would the earth be in better shape if countries did not depend on one another? Explain your answer.

History in Your Life

What Will a Dollar Buy?

Do you have a dollar? If you were in Capri, Italy, you could buy a small pizza. In Sydney, Australia, you could buy a toy koala bear. First, though, you would have to exchange your dollar for the local money. In Italy, you would get about .75 euros for a dollar. In Sydney, you would get about $1.50 in Australian dollars.

In some countries, people like to be paid in U.S. dollars. This happens because the United States' economy is strong. That makes the U.S. dollar strong. The British pound is another strong currency.

In 1999, some members of the European Union agreed to gradually give up their national currencies. They now use a new currency called the "euro." A euro has the same value in every country that joins this agreement. This makes trade among these countries easier.

Objectives

◆ To identify important problems in our environment

Millions of people around the world die every day from illnesses related to unsanitary living conditions. Some do not have clean water to drink. Others simply do not have enough of the right foods to remain healthy. At the same time, air pollution and global warming are affecting every part of our world, from human beings to oceans, animals, and plants. These are serious concerns that need to be addressed.

What Diseases Are Threatening Our World?

AIDS continues to infect people all over the world. In 2006, nearly 40 million people worldwide were living with the HIV virus. New medications are helping more people with HIV live longer and avoid developing AIDS.

There is a growing crisis in developing countries, where many children have lost one or both parents to AIDS. One report says that by 2005, there were more than 15 million "AIDS orphans" worldwide. About 95 percent of the people who have HIV live in developing countries.

Several new diseases prompted concern in the 1990s and 2000s. A disease called SARS (Severe Acute Respiratory Syndrome) is believed to have been carried by Chinese horseshoe bats. More than 8,000 people in 26 countries have become infected with SARS. Lyme disease, spread by deer ticks, infected 25,000 people in the United States alone during 2002. The West Nile virus is most often spread to people and animals through mosquitoes. Scientists are working to learn more about how to control all of these diseases.

Deforestation

The destruction of forests

Fossil fuel

Fuel made from coal, oil, or natural gas

What Is the Growing Population Doing to Our Environment?

As the numbers of people increase all around the world, so do problems of damage to the environment. More people are driving cars. More factories are using more energy to make products. More space is needed to house and grow food.

Vehicles, factories, and energy-generating plants produce gases from burning fuels such as oil or coal. These gases pollute the air. They may contribute to breathing illnesses in people. They produce acid rain, which damages plants and harms animals that eat those plants. Dangerous global warming occurs when gases surrounding the earth trap the heat from sunlight. Factories, careless farming practices, and poor sewage disposal are affecting water quality in many countries of the world.

Lands that were once wilderness are becoming farms or towns. **Deforestation**, or the destruction of forests, is taking place all over the globe. When there are fewer trees and plants, the valuable oxygen they contribute to the earth's air also declines. Animals are losing the wild areas where they live. Many of those animals and the plants that once surrounded them are facing extinction. Some scientists estimate that around the world, up to 100 species become extinct every day!

What Pollutes Our Air and Water?

Air pollution affects our health, and it may change our climate. The burning of coal, oil, and natural gas causes most air pollution. These kinds of fuels are called **fossil fuels.** We also have water pollution. Farming and industry have poisoned lakes and rivers.

Farmers around the world now use fertilizers to help crops grow and pesticides to kill bugs. Rain makes these chemicals run off into rivers, lakes, and oceans. Then they end up in the bodies of fish and other animals. People who eat these animals or drink the water get sick. The problem is most serious in developing countries, where many people cannot get clean water.

Reading Strategy:
Predicting

What do you think the text will identify as the biggest sources of pollution?

What Is Global Warming?

Since the 1980s, scientists have warned us about **global warming.** Global warming is the worldwide heating up of Earth, caused in part by human activity. Scientists believe that gases from cars and factories are heating up the earth. Burning wood, coal, oil, or natural gas releases carbon dioxide. Trees remove this gas from the air and release oxygen into the air for us to breathe. But overpopulated countries are now cutting down forests and jungles to provide farmland and firewood.

Many people fear that this will increase the carbon dioxide in the air and raise the earth's temperature. This might change rainfall patterns around the world. Too much rain would cause floods; too little rain would cause droughts and famine. Scientists also believe that the polar ice caps are melting. This will raise the sea levels and flood cities like New York, which are on the coast. If this happens, two billion people around the world would have to move inland.

What Nations Have Environmental Problems?

Many American cities suffer from industrial air pollution. Russia and Eastern Europe suffer from it, too. When the Communists controlled them, they kept producing goods, no matter what happened to the environment.

Many developing African countries made the same mistake. They wanted to develop their economies quickly, but they ignored the environment. Now many Africans are starving to death. Farmers have killed their animals for food. Some ate the seeds they needed for next year's crop.

Asia depends on coal and oil for fuel. Its cars and factories are giving off high levels of carbon monoxide. The worst problems are in the cities. Most big cities have major problems with air and water pollution.

The developing countries of Latin America have problems, too. Just breathing the air in Mexico City is equal to smoking two packs of cigarettes a day. The city's pollution may cause 100,000 deaths a year.

How Are Nations Attacking Environmental Problems?

People all over the world care about the environment. In 1992, representatives from 178 countries met to talk about it. They agreed to reduce air pollution and to save forests.

In June 1997, world leaders met again. But many thought that the nations of the world had not made much progress since 1992. What is good for one nation may be bad for another. For example, many developing countries depend on the production and export of wood, coal, and oil. But what happens if the industrial countries cut back on the use of these fuels? The environment may improve, but the economies of the developing countries go downhill.

The truth is that the global environment is less healthy than it once was. Air pollution is growing. Also, people are using up resources like water, forests, topsoil, and fish faster than they can be replaced.

Reading Strategy:
Prediction

Think about your prediction. Were you right, or do you need to change your prediction?

Farming, industry, and carelessness cause water pollution.

How Can We Help Save the Environment?

We can do at least three things to help the environment. We can reduce the kinds of packages manufacturers sell things in. We can reuse things. We can recycle things that we no longer use. All of us depend on the same earth to supply us with our needs. Laws are being passed to preserve places where animals live and to protect endangered animals.

In fact, something happened as we entered the new century. The "greening" of countries around the world became more important as we learned about the costs of a polluted environment. *Greening* refers to the move toward cleaner power and technology. Although most people in developed nations were aware of the problem of global warming, industries were slow to change. Many companies are now using greener sources of energy. Green architecture is becoming more popular. New buildings are more energy-efficient and are built using recycled materials. People are making more environmentally sound choices in transportation, clothing, and food. However, there is still a long way to go.

The clear-cutting of trees, by loggers and others, damages the environment.

Lesson 3 Review On a sheet of paper, write your answers to the following questions. Use complete sentences.

1. What are the reasons that so many species are becoming extinct every day?

2. What are three things that cause damage to our environment?

3. Why is it important that forests are not destroyed?

4. What is global warming?

5. What are some environmental problems that developing nations have?

What do you think ?

What do you think is the single most important problem in the world today? Why?

Objectives

- ◆ To identify ways the world has changed since the attacks of 2001
- ◆ To describe the reasons for the war in Iraq that began in 2002
- ◆ To describe things that can be done to help prevent terrorist attacks

Regime

A form of government

Tyranny

Harsh, absolute power

After the September 11, 2001, terrorist attacks on the United States, all planes were grounded for two days. When they started flying again, airport security screening for all passengers was much more strict. Security was also increased near public places where large groups of people gather, such as sports arenas. Lawmakers in the United States began developing the new Department of Homeland Security. This department organizes all security and emergency agencies into one department.

How Has the Threat of Terrorism Changed the World?

The Taliban **regime,** or form of government, in Afghanistan was known to allow training camps for members of al Qaeda. The United States government had asked the Taliban to turn over Osama bin Laden, who had admitted leading the 9/11 terror attacks on America. The Taliban refused. The United States attacked Taliban sites in Afghanistan in October 2001. Taliban and al Qaeda members fled the country, as did bin Laden. American and NATO troops have remained in Afghanistan to help rebuild the country under a new government.

In 2002, a report by the American Central Intelligence Agency (CIA) warned that Iraq was hiding weapons of mass destruction. Iraq refused to cooperate with United Nations weapons inspectors. President George Bush insisted that Saddam Hussein's government was aiding terrorist groups. He said that the people of Iraq had to be freed of Hussein's **tyranny,** or harsh, absolute power. On March 19, 2003, troops from the United States, Britain, and many smaller nations invaded Baghdad, the capital of Iraq. Operation Iraqi Freedom had begun. Saddam Hussein went into hiding. Within 43 days the troops had taken over the country. In July 2003, Saddam Hussein's two sons were killed in a raid. Hussein was captured in December of the same year. An Iraqi court found him guilty of crimes against humanity, and he was executed in December 2006. The American and British troops found no weapons of mass destruction.

Americans wanted to help establish a democratic government in Iraq. Aided by other governments, the Iraqis began forming a representative government. They wrote a constitution and held their first free elections in 2005. Unfortunately, since that time, fighting between groups for control of the country has increased. As of early 2007, tens of thousands of Iraqi civilians had been killed. More than 3,000 American soldiers have been killed and about 20,000 injured.

Have There Been Other Terrorist Attacks?

According to the U. S. State Department, there were 9,474 terrorist attacks worldwide between 1982 and 2003. In the five-year period between 1998 and 2003, there were 1,865. Regular acts of terror continue in both Iraq and Afghanistan.

In many countries of the world, increased security has reduced the number of terrorist attacks. However, some have occurred. For instance, bombs planted on a subway and buses in London killed 52 people in 2005.

What Can Be Done to Prevent Further Attacks?

Further attacks can be prevented by increasing awareness of dangers. This is especially important with travel and in situations involving large groups of people.

Passengers on a flight from Paris to New York in December 2001 noticed another passenger acting suspiciously. They were able to subdue him before he could light explosives in his shoes.

In August 2006, British officials uncovered a plot to blow up 9 or 10 planes leaving London for the United States. The 24 men arrested were going to use liquid explosives in carry-on bags to destroy the planes mid-air. As a result, the airlines placed limits on the amount of liquid that travelers could carry on future flights.

The U.S. State Department has identified dozens of terrorist groups training members in different countries. One important task for the Department of Homeland Security is monitoring the activities of such groups. Agents and offices in foreign countries help them do this. A law called the Patriot Act allows the U.S. government more power to check the background of people in the country.

Lesson 4 Review On a sheet of paper, write the answers to the following questions. Use complete sentences.

1. How has security changed since the attacks of September 11?

2. What did Osama bin Laden admit to doing?

3. What information did the CIA report in 2002 contain?

4. Why have troops stayed in Afghanistan?

5. What is the purpose of the Patriot Act?

What do you think ?

Do you think it is OK for people to lose some of their freedoms in exchange for greater security?

Objectives

◆ To identify some good things and some bad things that could happen

◆ To suggest ways the world might change in the future

Spaceships to the moon, automobiles that speed people to their destinations, airplanes, television, telephone. At one time, all of these things existed only in the imaginations of inventors and dreamers.

Looking to the future, we can see promises and problems. Promises of new treatments for diseases; new technologies we cannot even guess at; new ways to feed the starving people of the world; promises of human rights and an improved standard of living for everyone, everywhere.

However, there are also problems--big problems that will require big solutions. Global problems such as extreme poverty and epidemics of diseases. Natural disasters that destroy the lives of people who have no way to rebuild and recover. Around the world, wars and the fear of terrorism continue. And problems that result from a growing world population, such as pollution and global warming.

What Is the Population Explosion?

At the time of the Roman Empire, the population of the world was 200 million. Since then, this is how it has grown:
- 1800: 1 billion
- 1920: 2 billion
- 1960: 3 billion
- 1975: 4 billion
- 1988: 5 billion
- 1999: 6 billion

Do you notice how the population is growing faster? The time between 1 billion and 2 billion was 120 years. The time between 5 billion and 6 billion was only 11 years. Scientists have calculated that by 2025, the population of the world will be 9 billion. By the year 2200, if we keep growing at the same rate, it will be 138 billion!

Writing About History

Imagine that you are making a time capsule. What would you like people to know about this time in history? In your notebook, list what you would include in the container.

In the past, increases in the food supply and control of disease allowed people to live longer. Today, however, the food supply is not growing as fast as the population is. The world's food supply is increasing at about 1 percent a year. The world's population, however, has been increasing at the rate of 1.5 percent a year.

In 1965, President Lyndon Johnson said that the most important thing we had to do was to work for peace on earth. But the next most important challenge to the human family was the "race between the food supply and the population increase." President Johnson said that the race was being lost. As time moves on, our growing population will continue to be a major problem for the governments of the world.

What Are Some Lessons of History?

Human history has been going on for thousands of years. What does it teach us? One thing we learn is that people from many different cultures faced hard problems in the past. We know the following about these people and their problems:

- Some met challenges with courage, good sense, and goodwill. They improved our world, and we owe them our thanks. We can learn from them.

- Others acted badly. They created terrible problems and caused many people to suffer. But even their terrible actions can teach us something—what not to do!

- Some ignored the past. We can do this, too, but then we will make the same mistakes others have made. The past shapes the present. It influences the future.

- No one has ever been able to predict for sure what the future will bring. But we can say one sure thing—the future belongs to all of us.

Lesson 5 Review On a sheet of paper, write the answers to the following questions. Use complete sentences.

1. What do you think is the most amazing invention of the last 50 years? Why?

2. Do you think that increased production of food will solve all the world's problems? Why or why not?

3. If you could fix one problem in the world today, what would you choose?

4. How can ignoring mistakes and problems of the past lead to problems in the future?

5. Name one person you admire and tell how he or she made a difference in the world.

What do you think ?

What do you think the biggest change in the world could be 50 years from now?

Al Gore on Global Warming

Former Vice President Al Gore has been very concerned about the environment for many years. In 1993, he wrote the book Earth in the Balance: Ecology and the Human Spirit. *In 2006, his book and documentary film* An Inconvenient Truth *brought attention to the urgent issues surrounding global warming. On September 9, 2005, Al spoke to the Sierra Club about the need to change the direction the world—the United States in particular—is heading. Here are some excerpts from that speech.*

Ladies and gentlemen, the warnings about global warming have been extremely clear for a long time. We are facing a global climate crisis. It is deepening. We are entering a period of consequences. . . .

Abraham Lincoln said, "The occasion is piled high with difficulty and we must rise with the occasion. As our case is new, we must think anew and act anew. We must disenthrall [free] ourselves and then we shall save our country."

My friends, the truth is that our circumstances are not only new; they are completely different than they have ever been in all of human history. The relationship between humankind and the earth had been utterly transformed in the last hundred years. We have quadrupled the population of our planet. The population in many ways is a success story . . . but the reality of our new relationship with the planet brings with it a moral responsibility to accept our new circumstances and to deal with the consequences of the relationship we have with this planet.

Document-Based Questions

1. What is Al Gore's greatest concern?

2. What is the purpose of the quote from Abraham Lincoln?

3. What does it mean to "rise with the occasion," as Lincoln said? What do people need to do to rise with (or to) the occasion?

4. Why has the relationship between humankind and the earth changed in the last hundred years?

5. What does Gore say we have to move beyond in order to change the situation?

Source: Excerpt from Al Gore's speech at the Sierra Summit, September 9, 2005.

The Search for New Sources of Energy

Today's high prices for energy have caused many countries to look for other ways to generate power. Cars and trucks are some of the biggest users of gasoline. Americans use about 382 million gallons of gasoline every day. Almost 65 percent of the oil used in the United States is imported from other countries.

Some countries have turned to ethanol as a substitute for gasoline. Ethanol is a fuel made from the sugar in plants. The United States and Brazil are the world's leaders in ethanol production. Brazil makes ethanol from the large amounts of sugar cane it grows. In the United States, most ethanol is made from corn.

Many countries have started using solar energy. Solar energy is energy from the sun that is converted into electrical energy. It is already used to heat homes and swimming pools. It is used to operate such things as lighthouses and road traffic warning signals. It could also be used to run cars and power plants.

Wind power is another energy source that does not harm the environment. Wind power uses wind turbines (similar to aircraft propeller blades) to generate electricity. They turn in the moving air and power an electric generator that supplies an electric current. Electricity from these turbines is fed into the local utility and then distributed to customers. However, the turbines are both noisy and dangerous to birds.

Other sources of energy are used in some countries. These sources include geothermal power, tidal energy, and hydroelectric power from falling water.

Wrap-Up

1. Why are many countries looking for new ways to generate energy?

2. What is ethanol and who are the world's biggest producers?

3. What are some of the uses of solar energy today?

4. How is wind used to generate electricity?

5. What are three other sources of energy besides solar energy and wind power?

Chapter 31   S U M M A R Y

- Modern technology has made the world a "global village." People around the world share ideas and cultures. Technology helps businesses become multinational corporations that have workers in many countries.

- Mass communication includes advertising and electronic communication. American culture influences other parts of the world.

- Computers have many uses. The Internet is an international computer network. The World Wide Web links people through electronics. These media are part of the "electronic superhighway."

- The United States and the Soviet Union competed in space for many years. Now, the two countries are among the 15 that are working on the International Space Station.

- Modern technology depends on energy from various sources. However, burning coal and oil pollutes the environment. Nuclear power plants produce deadly waste; accidents are a danger.

- Modern technology has also changed medicine with new equipment, such as lasers.

- Most rich countries have a free-market economy and well-developed industries and technology. Most of these nations are in the Northern Hemisphere.

- Developing nations are building their industries and economies. Many people in these nations live by subsistence farming. Overpopulation and education are problems. Developing nations also lack money. Most industrialized nations supply aid to poorer countries. Aid comes through the World Bank and International Monetary Fund.

- A recession in 1997 hurt the economies of Asian nations. This crisis affected the entire world economy. Some people blamed it on multinational corporations.

- Land, air, and water pollution is a global problem.

- Developing nations have pollution problems because of fast, uncontrolled growth.

- The threat of global terrorism has changed the world. There is more concern about security since the attacks of 9/11. There is a concern that this greater security results in the loss of privacy.

- More terrorist attacks are possible. It is important for everyone to be aware of their surroundings.

- In the future, a growing world population will strain the world's supplies of food and water.

Chapter 31   R E V I E W

On a sheet of paper, use the words from the Word Bank to complete each sentence.

1. The Internet is a(n) _____ computer network that goes around the world and among many nations.

2. Television, advertising, and movies are examples of _____, which is messages directed at many people.

3. The global village is partly the result of advances in _____, which is the use of science to do practical things.

4. Progress in technology depends on _____, which makes machines work and produces heat.

5. The _____ can produce electricity from light from the sun.

6. The burning of coal and oil threatens our _____, which is the land, sea, and air of Earth.

7. The Southern Hemisphere has many _____ countries, which are just beginning to grow their economies.

8. The nations of the world have become _____. They depend on one another.

9. Most industrial countries have a(n) _____ economy in which manufacturers meet the needs of consumers.

10. Many scientists are worried about _____, which could change the earth's temperature.

On a sheet of paper, write the letter of the answer that correctly completes each sentence.

11. A _____ is a tool that produces high-energy beams of light.

    A laser   **C** recession

    B technology   **D** subsistence

12. The _____ directs money from industrialized nations to developing countries.

    A IMF   **C** World Wide Web

    B Internet   **D** World Bank

13. The _____ has 182 members whom it helps in times of economic crisis.

   A World Bank

   B World Wide Web

   C International Monetary Fund

   D Internet

14. A _____ corporation does business around the world.

   A multinational   **C** advertising

   B electronic   **D** mass communication

On a sheet of paper, write the answers to the following questions. Use complete sentences.

15. What is one way that mass communication has helped create a global village?

16. What is one source of energy that may be safe and may not pollute our environment?

17. What is one problem that developing countries have?

18. What is the biggest problem facing the world today?

Read each question, then write your opinion on a sheet of paper. Use complete sentences.

19. Should the countries with the greatest wealth do more to help the less developed countries? Explain your answer.

20. What is one way you can reduce, reuse, or recycle to help the environment?

Test-Taking Tip

Read all test directions carefully. Do not assume that you know what you are supposed to do.

Unit 7

Voting

As American citizens, we vote to elect leaders and decide certain issues. As voters, we can do many things to find out about different candidates and issues. We can read newspapers. We can listen to political debates on radio and TV. Or we can attend political rallies and hear candidates speak in person. We can read articles about candidates in news magazines. We can get information from the political party of our choice. We can study the voting record of a candidate already in office.

Many people around the world vote for their political leaders. Each country has its own voting process. Here is how it works in the United States. To vote, qualified persons 18 and older must first register at a city or county clerk's office. In some places, they can register by mail or at the polls on election day. Polling places are usually open from 7 a.m. to 8 p.m. Each voter must vote at the assigned polling place in his or her district. Local newspapers usually list polling places and hours. Voters also can get this information from local government offices. Voters who will be out of town on election day may request an absentee ballot in person or by mail. They may then mark and send in the absentee ballot ahead of the election.

Voter Registration Application
For U.S. Citizens

At the polls, voters fill out a ballot. If necessary, election judges can show voters how to mark a ballot. Different districts use various machines and methods. Voters may have to pull a lever on a machine or punch holes. On paper, they may mark Xs with a pen. To ensure privacy, voters make their choices in a private booth.

After the polls close, election judges at each polling place count the votes. They deliver the count to the city or county clerk's office. When all the votes are counted, a winner is declared. Television, radio, and newspapers then give election results.

Find out the answers to these questions. Then you'll be ready to vote when the time comes.

1. How long must you live in your state and district before you can vote?

2. Where do you register to vote?

3. How do you register to vote?

4. Where do you vote?

5. How can you get an absentee ballot?

6. How do you fill out the ballot?

7. How are the votes counted?

8. In what day, month, and year can you vote in a national election for the first time?

As a future voter, explain how you would answer these questions.

9. How can you decide which candidates to vote for?

10. Why do you think it is important to vote in elections?

- The U.S. and the Soviet Union fought a "cold war" of words after WWII.

- In 1945, European nations controlled most of Africa. By the 1980s, there were 50 new African countries. African economies are growing quickly, but famine and overcrowded cities are problems.

- Apartheid hurt the black majority in South Africa. Nationalist leader Nelson Mandela helped end apartheid and became its president in 1994.

- The Jewish state of Israel fought several wars with Arab countries. Some displaced Palestinians became terrorists. By the 1990s, Arab and Israeli leaders were working toward peace. Palestinian self-rule is a major issue.

- Indian nationalists used passive resistance to gain independence from Britain in 1947. Pakistan was established as a separate Muslim state.

- In China, a Communist victory in the civil war established the People's Republic in 1949.

- The French colony of Indochina was divided into North and South Vietnam, Cambodia, and Laos. When Communist North Vietnam waged war against South Vietnam, the United States helped South Vietnam. Many Americans opposed the war. A Communist government united Vietnam in 1975.

- Oil and religion continued to cause conflict in the Persian Gulf region. A religious revolution in Iran overthrew the Shah. Iraq and Iran fought a long war. Iraqi leader Saddam Hussein invaded Kuwait but was stopped by an international force.

- The Chinese Communist government violently stopped pro-democracy demonstrators at Tiananmen Square in 1989.

- People in Eastern Europe overthrew Communist governments in 1989. Ethnic wars broke out in the former Yugoslavia. Western European nations moved toward economic union, with a common currency, the euro.

- Land reform is a major problem in Latin America.

- Modern technology made the world a "global village." Mass communication lets people share ideas and culture.

- Russia and the United States cooperate with other nations on space projects.

- Technology depends on energy. Many energy sources cause pollution or other hazards. World leaders try to balance the needs of rich and poor nations while protecting the environment.

- The threat of global terrorism has caused increased security since the attacks of 9/11. More terrorist attacks are possible.

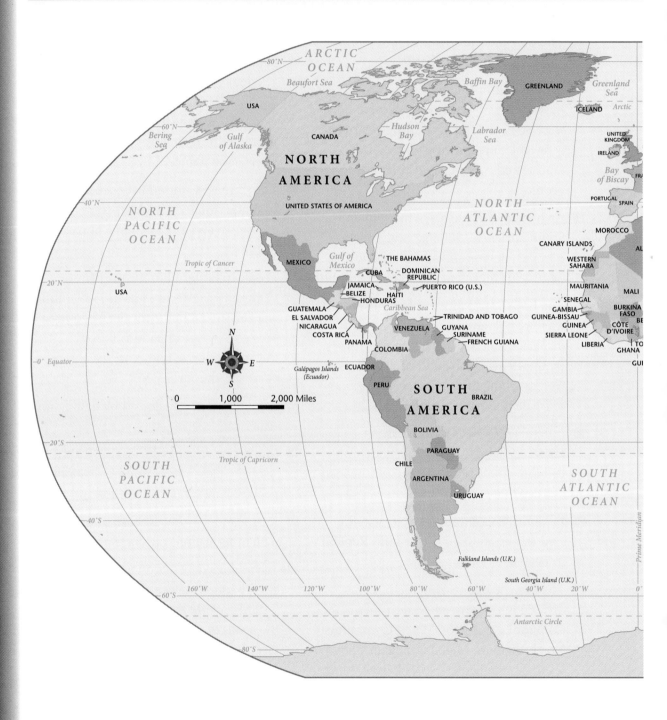

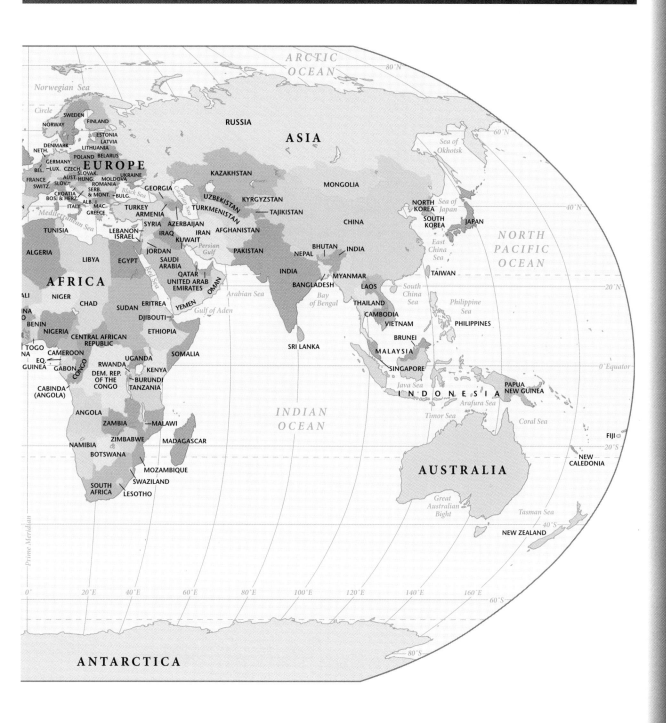

ARCTIC
OCEAN

80°N

Norwegian Sea

Circle

SWEDEN
NORWAY   FINLAND
                                    RUSSIA   ASIA   60°N
                    ESTONIA   Sea of
DENMARK   LATVIA   Okhotsk
NETH.   LITHUANIA
    GERMANY POLAND BELARUS
BEL. ─LUX. CZECH EUROPE   KAZAKHSTAN
FRANCE   AUST. HUNG. SLOVAK.   40°N
SWITZ. SLOV.┐   MOLDOVA UKRAINE   NORTH Sea of
        CROATIA   SERB. ROMANIA   GEORGIA   MONGOLIA   KOREA Japan
        BOS. & HERZ. & MONT.─BULG.   UZBEKISTAN KYRGYZSTAN   SOUTH   JAPAN
            ITALY ALB.┐ MAC.   TURKEY ─Black Sea─ TURKMENISTAN TAJIKISTAN   KOREA
                  GREECE   ARMENIA   CHINA
TUNISIA   LEBANON─┐ SYRIA AZERBAIJAN AFGHANISTAN   NORTH
        Mediterranean Sea   ISRAEL IRAQ   PACIFIC
                          JORDAN   Persian   PAKISTAN NEPAL BHUTAN INDIA   East   OCEAN
ALGERIA   Gulf   ─   China
        LIBYA   EGYPT SAUDI   INDIA BANGLADESH MYANMAR   Sea   20°N
                           ARABIA QATAR   TAIWAN
AFRICA   UNITED ARAB   LAOS South
MALI   NIGER   CHAD   ─Red Sea─ EMIRATES OMAN Arabian Sea Bay THAILAND China   Philippine
                    SUDAN ERITREA YEMEN   of Bengal   Sea   Sea
                          DJIBOUTI─ Gulf of Aden   CAMBODIA   PHILIPPINES
BENIN   VIETNAM
NIGERIA CENTRAL AFRICAN   ETHIOPIA   BRUNEI
TOGO   REPUBLIC   SRI LANKA   MALAYSIA
EQ.   CAMEROON   SINGAPORE   0° Equator
GUINEA GABON┐ RWANDA UGANDA SOMALIA   INDONESIA
        CONGO DEM. REP. KENYA   Java Sea PAPUA
              OF THE BURUNDI   NEW GUINEA
CABINDA   CONGO TANZANIA   INDIAN   Arafura Sea
(ANGOLA)   OCEAN   Timor Sea   Coral Sea   20°S
        ANGOLA   FIJI
            ZAMBIA ─MALAWI   NEW
NAMIBIA ZIMBABWE   MADAGASCAR   CALEDONIA
        BOTSWANA   AUSTRALIA
            MOZAMBIQUE
SOUTH   SWAZILAND   Great   40°S
AFRICA   LESOTHO   Australian
                                                     Bight   Tasman Sea
0° 20°E 40°E 60°E 80°E 100°E 120°E 140°E 160°E   60°S   NEW ZEALAND

80°S

ANTARCTICA

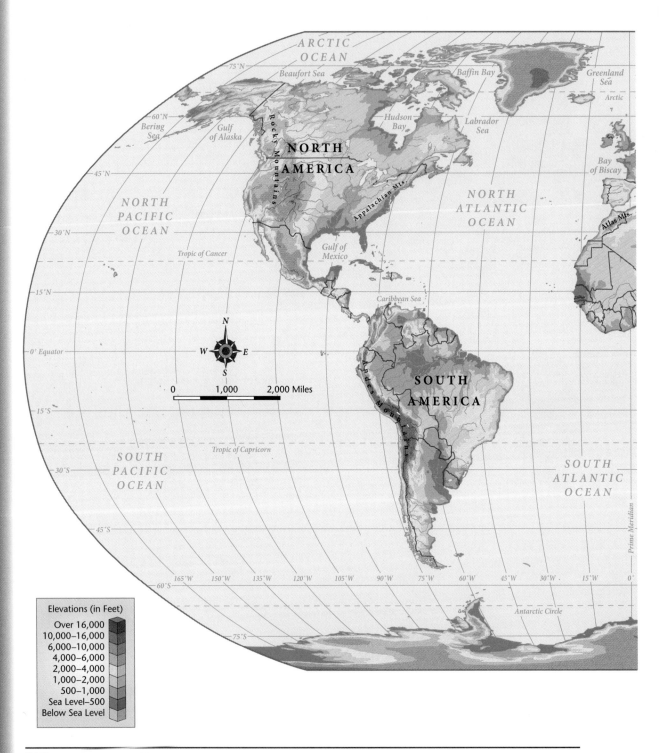

Elevations (in Feet)

Over 16,000
10,000–16,000
6,000–10,000
4,000–6,000
2,000–4,000
1,000–2,000
500–1,000
Sea Level–500
Below Sea Level

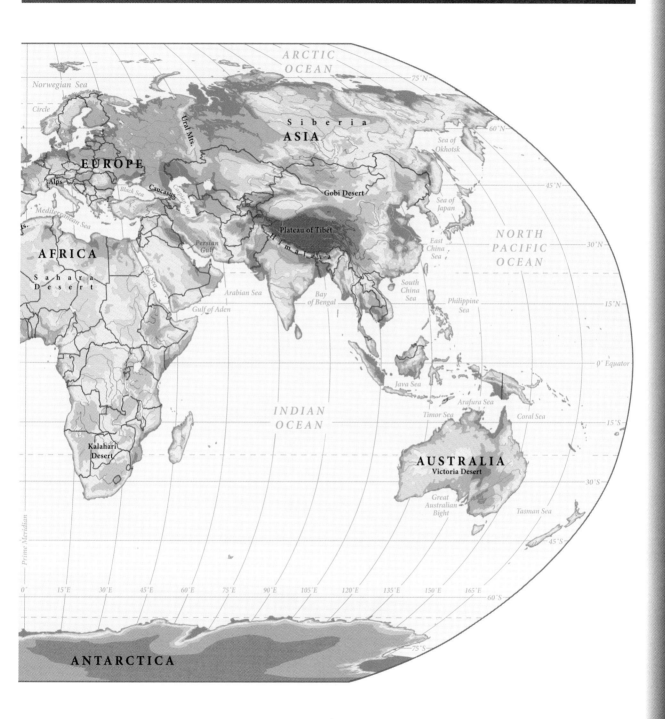

ARCTIC OCEAN

Norwegian Sea

Circle

75°N

EUROPE

Ural Mts.

Siberia

ASIA

60°N

Alps

Sea of Okhotsk

Black Sea

Caucasus

Caspian Sea

45°N

Gobi Desert

Mediterranean Sea

Sea of Japan

AFRICA

Persian Gulf

Plateau of Tibet

Sahara Desert

Red Sea

Himalaya

East China Sea

30°N

NORTH PACIFIC OCEAN

Arabian Sea

Bay of Bengal

South China Sea

Gulf of Aden

Philippine Sea

15°N

0° Equator

Java Sea

INDIAN OCEAN

Arafura Sea

Coral Sea

Timor Sea

15°S

Kalahari Desert

AUSTRALIA

Victoria Desert

30°S

Prime Meridian

Great Australian Bight

Tasman Sea

45°S

0°   15°E   30°E   45°E   60°E   75°E   90°E   105°E   120°E   135°E   150°E   165°E   60°S

75°S

ANTARCTICA

North America

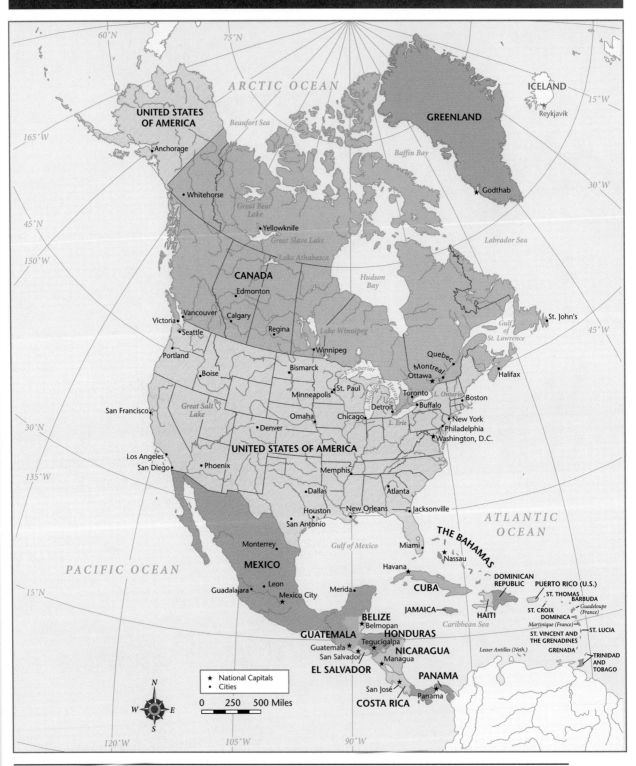

South America

Caribbean Sea

Managua ★

San José ★

Panama

Barranquilla ●

Caracas ★
TRINIDAD AND TOBAGO

Valencia ●

Cúcuta ●

Medellín ●

Bogotá ★

VENEZUELA

Georgetown ★
Paramaribo ★
Cayenne ★

GUYANA

SURINAME **FRENCH GUIANA**

COLOMBIA

Mitú ●

10°N

0° Equator

Quito ★

ECUADOR

Guayaquil ●

Manaus ●

Belém ●

Galápagos Islands (Ecuador)

Talara ●

PERU

Fortaleza ●

Trujillo ●

Pôrto Velho ●

Recife ●

Huánuco ●

10°S

Lima ★

BRAZIL

Ica ● Cuzco ●

Salvador ●

BOLIVIA

La Paz ★

★ Brásilia
Goiânia ●

Santa Cruz ●

Iquique ●

★ Sucre

20°S

PACIFIC OCEAN

Antofagasta ●

PARAGUAY

Rio de Janeiro ●

São Paulo ●

CHILE

★ Asunción

Córdoba ●

30°S

Santiago ★

Rosario ●

URUGUAY

Buenos Aires ★

Montevideo ●

ATLANTIC OCEAN

Concepción ●

ARGENTINA

N
W E
S

Valdivia ●

40°S

Puerto Montt ●

Comodoro Rivadavia ●

★ National Capitals
● Cities

Falkland Islands (U.K.)

50°S

0   250   500 Miles

South Georgia Island (U.K.)

90°W   80°W   70°W   60°W   50°W   40°W

Europe

Reykjavik ★ **ICELAND**

Norwegian Sea

Faroe Islands (Denmark)

NORTH ATLANTIC OCEAN

FINLAND

SWEDEN

NORWAY

Gulf of Bothnia

Helsinki ★

Oslo ★

Stockholm ★

Baltic Sea

Tallinn ★ **ESTONIA**

RUSSIA

LATVIA

Riga ★

Moscow ★

LITHUANIA

Vilnius ★

North Sea

Belfast ★

IRELAND

Dublin ★

UNITED KINGDOM

NETHERLANDS

Amsterdam ★

London ★

Minsk ★

RUSSIA

BELARUS

Copenhagen ★

DENMARK

Berlin ★

Warsaw ★

POLAND

Kiev ★

UKRAINE

English Channel

Brussels ★

BELGIUM

GERMANY

Prague ★

CZECH REP.

Paris ★

LUXEMBOURG

SLOVAKIA

45°N

LIECHTENSTEIN

Vienna ★ ★ Bratislava

MOLDOVA

Bern ★

Budapest ★

Chisinau ★

Bay of Biscay

FRANCE

AUSTRIA

HUNGARY

ROMANIA

SWITZERLAND

Ljubljana ★

SLOVENIA

Zagreb ★

Belgrade ★

Bucharest ★

Black Sea

ITALY

BOSNIA AND HERZEGOVINA

SERBIA AND MONTENEGRO

MONACO

CROATIA

Sarajevo ★

Adriatic Sea

BULGARIA

PORTUGAL

ANDORRA

Corsica

Tirana ★

Sofia ★

Skopje ★

Lisbon ★

Madrid ★

SPAIN

Sardinia

Rome ★

ALBANIA

MACEDONIA

Ankara ★

TURKEY

Balearic Islands

Tyrrhenian Sea

Aegean Sea

Gibraltar (U.K.) ★

GREECE

Athens ★

Algiers ★

Sicily

Ionian Sea

Rabat ★

Tunis ★

AFRICA

Crete

Valletta ★

MALTA

Mediterranean Sea

Alexandria ★

Tripoli ★

Red Sea

★ National Capitals

0   200   400 Miles

15°W   *0°*   *15°E*   *45°E*

60°N

N
W   E
S

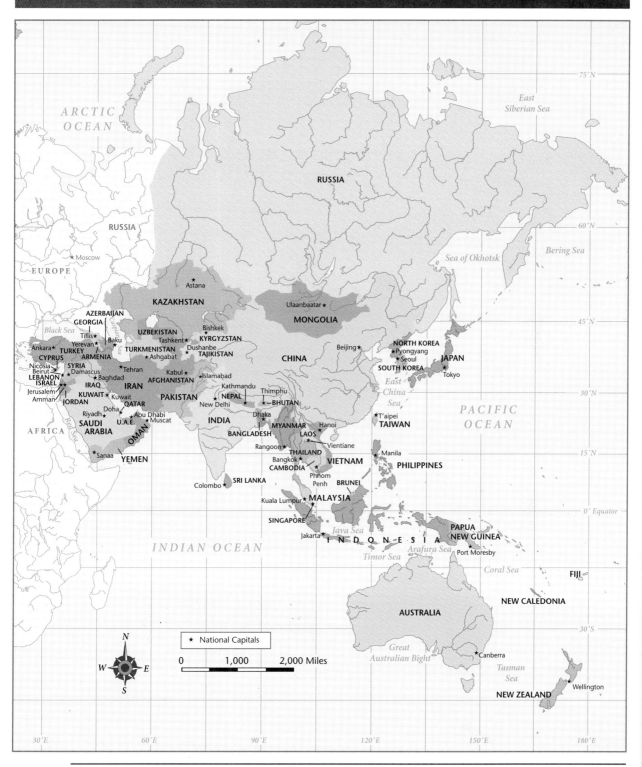

ARCTIC OCEAN

East Siberian Sea

RUSSIA

RUSSIA

★ Moscow

EUROPE

Bering Sea

Sea of Okhotsk

Astana ★

KAZAKHSTAN

Ulaanbaatar ★

MONGOLIA

AZERBAIJAN
GEORGIA
Tiflis ★
Ankara ★ Yerevan ★ Baku ★
TURKEY ARMENIA
CYPRUS
Nicosia SYRIA
Beirut ★ Damascus
LEBANON ★
ISRAEL
Jerusalem ★
Amman ★ JORDAN
AFRICA

Black Sea

UZBEKISTAN
Tashkent ★
TURKMENISTAN
Ashgabat ★
Bishkek ★
KYRGYZSTAN
Dushanbe ★
TAJIKISTAN

Beijing ★

CHINA

NORTH KOREA
Pyongyang ★
★ Seoul
SOUTH KOREA

JAPAN
Tokyo ★

Tehran ★

IRAN
Baghdad ★
IRAQ
KUWAIT
Kuwait ★
Riyadh ★
SAUDI ARABIA
OMAN

Kabul ★
AFGHANISTAN
Islamabad ★

PAKISTAN

Doha ★ QATAR
Abu Dhabi ★
U.A.E. ★ Muscat

Kathmandu ★
New Delhi ★ NEPAL
Thimphu ★
BHUTAN

INDIA

Dhaka ★
BANGLADESH

MYANMAR
Hanoi ★
LAOS

East China Sea

T'aipei ★
TAIWAN

PACIFIC OCEAN

Sanaa ★
YEMEN

Rangoon ★
Bangkok ★
THAILAND
CAMBODIA
Phnom Penh ★

Vientiane ★
VIETNAM

Manila ★

PHILIPPINES

Colombo ★
SRI LANKA

Kuala Lumpur ★
MALAYSIA
SINGAPORE ★
BRUNEI

INDIAN OCEAN

Jakarta ★ I N D O N E S I A

Java Sea

PAPUA NEW GUINEA
Port Moresby ★

Timor Sea

Arafura Sea

FIJI

Coral Sea

NEW CALEDONIA

★ National Capitals

N
W E
S

0   1,000   2,000 Miles

AUSTRALIA

Great Australian Bight

★ Canberra

Tasman Sea

NEW ZEALAND
Wellington ★

75°N

60°N

45°N

30°N

15°N

0° Equator

30°S

30°E   60°E   90°E   120°E   150°E   180°E

Africa

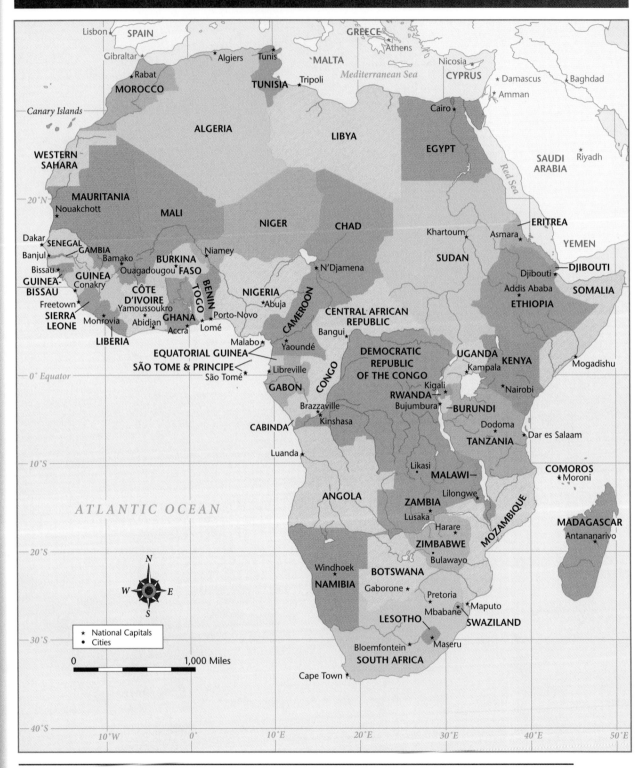

World Climate Zones

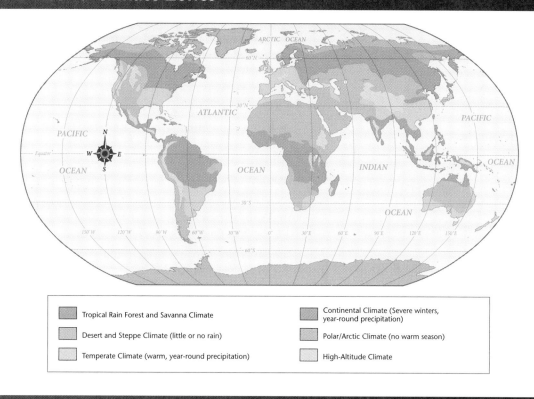

- Tropical Rain Forest and Savanna Climate
- Desert and Steppe Climate (little or no rain)
- Temperate Climate (warm, year-round precipitation)
- Continental Climate (Severe winters, year-round precipitation)
- Polar/Arctic Climate (no warm season)
- High-Altitude Climate

World Time Zones

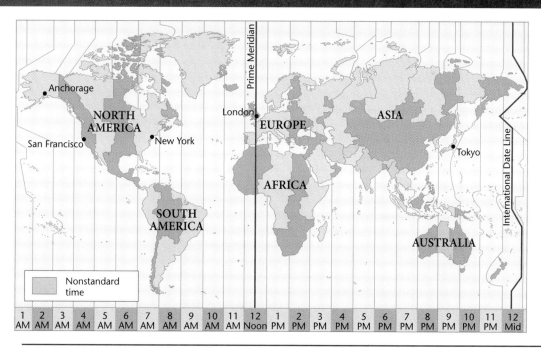

Nonstandard time

1 AM 2 AM 3 AM 4 AM 5 AM 6 AM 7 AM 8 AM 9 AM 10 AM 11 AM 12 Noon 1 PM 2 PM 3 PM 4 PM 5 PM 6 PM 7 PM 8 PM 9 PM 10 PM 11 PM 12 Mid

Glossary

A

Abacus (ab´ ə kəs) A tool that helps people add and do other things with numbers (p. 303)

Abdicate (ab´ də kāt) To give up power as a ruler (p. 633)

Abolish (ə bol´ ish) To get rid of something (p. 414)

Absolute monarch (ab´ sə lüt mon´ ərk) A king or queen who had complete and unlimited power over his or her people (p. 430)

Abundant (ə bun´ dənt) More than enough (p. 71)

Accords (ə kords´) Agreements (p. 762)

Acropolis (ə krop´ ə lis) A hill on which the people in a Greek city built their main temple (p. 122)

Advanced (ad vanst´) Beyond the beginning stage (p. 149)

Advisor (ad vī´ zər) A person who gives advice (p. 444)

African National Congress (ANC) (af´ rə kən nash´ ə nəl kong´ gris) A black nationalist group in South Africa (p. 734)

African Nationalism (af´ rə kən nash´ ə nə liz əm) The struggle by native African people to gain their economic and political freedom from European colonial rulers (p. 731)

Agency (ā´ jən sē) A group that provides a service (p. 693)

Alliance (ə lī´ əns) An agreement to help one another (p. 50)

Allied Powers (al´ īd pou´ ərs) The allied nations of Great Britain, France, Russia, Italy, and eventually, the United States and Japan (p. 617)

Ally (al´ ī) A friend; a country or person who helps another (p. 156)

Alms (ämz) The money or care that one gives to the poor and needy (p. 275)

Ambassador (am bas´ ə dər) A person sent to represent his or her government in another country (p. 582)

Amber (am´ bər) The hard, yellowish remains of a liquid that comes out of trees (p. 388)

American Revolution (ə mar´ ə kən rev ə lü´ shən) The American struggle against Great Britain for independence (p. 489)

Anatomy (ə nat´ ə mē) The structure of a human or animal body (p. 387)

Anglican Church (ang´ glə ken chėrch) The Church of England (p. 361)

Annex (ə neks´) To take over; to add a piece of land to one's country (p. 76)

Annul (ə nul´) To announce that a marriage never existed between two people (p. 360)

Anthropologist (an thrə pol´ ə jist) A scientist who studies the beginnings and the behavior of people (p. 9)

Apartheid (ə pärt´ hīt) The official policy of the Union of South Africa that refused to give black and other nonwhite people any political, economic, or social rights (p. 734)

Appeasement (ə pēz´ mənt) A policy of making others happy or content (p. 673)

Aqueduct (ak´ wə dukt) A structure that carries water from far away (p. 171)

Archaeologist (är kē ol´ ə jist) A scientist who finds and studies the things people left behind (p. 9)

Archbishop (ärch´ bish əp) The top religious leader in a church province (p. 361)

Archer (är´ chər) A soldier who fights with a bow and arrows (p. 47)

Architect (är´ kə tekt) A person who draws plans for buildings (p. 335)

Architecture (är´ kə tek chər) The art of building (p. 127)

Aristocrat (ə ris´ tə krat) A member of the powerful ruling class (p. 122)

Armada (är mä´ də) A large fleet of warships (p. 435)

Armistice (är´ mə stis) An agreement to stop fighting (p. 621)

Armor (är´ mər) A strong metal covering that protects the body in battle (p. 74)

Arsenal (är´ sə nəl) A place where someone stores or makes weapons (p. 676)

Artifact (är´ tə fakt) An object made by a person for a practical purpose (p. 9)

Artisan (är´ tə zən) A person who works with his or her hands to create something (p. 47)

Assassinate (ə sas´ n āt) To kill someone important (p. 160)

Assembly (ə sem´ blē) A meeting (p. 124)

Astronomer (ə stron´ ə mər) A person who keeps track of the sun, the planets, and the stars (p. 53)

Astronomy (ə stron´ ə mē) The study of the stars (p. 135)

Atomic bomb (ə tom´ ik bom) A bomb that uses nuclear energy and has much destructive power (p. 682)

Attract (ə trakt´) To pull something toward oneself (p. 385)

Authority (ə thôr´ ə tē) Power (p. 353)

Autocracy (ȯ tok´ rə sē) A government in which one person rules with unlimited power (p. 629)

Axis (ak´ is) A make-believe line that goes through the middle of an object that spins around it (p. 669)

Axis Powers (ak´ is pou´ ərs) The alliance of Germany, Italy, and Japan during World War II (p. 669)

Ayatollah (ä yä tō´ lə) A Muslim religious leader (p. 763)

B

Balance of power (bal´ əns ov pou´ ər) The condition that exists when all countries or all sections of government have equal strength (p. 544)

Ban (ban) To get rid of; to make something not legal (p. 471)

Baptism (bap´ tiz əm) A ritual by which a person becomes a Christian (p. 358)

Barbarian (bär bâr´ ē ən) An uncivilized person (p. 306)

Barbaric (bär bar´ ik) Not civilized (p. 252)

Barbed wire (bärbd wīr) Wire that has sharp metal spikes on it (p. 618)

Bastille (ba stēl´) A prison in Paris (p. 495)

Berlin Wall (bər lin´ wȯl) The wall that divided the people of East and West Berlin (p. 719)

Betray (bi trā´) To stop being loyal to someone (p. 178)

Bible (bī´ bəl) The Hebrew and Christian book that is thought to be holy (p. 36)

Biology (bī ol´ ə jē) The study of living things (p. 135)

Bishop (bish´ əp) A priest who is in charge of other priests and a number of churches (p. 239)

Blacksmith (blak´ smith) A person who works with iron and makes tools and weapons (p. 235)

Blitzkrieg (blits´ krēg) The quick and forceful method of attack that Germany used in World War II; "lightning war" (p. 675)

Bolshevik (bōl´ shə vik) A revolutionary socialist group in Russia (p. 643)

Boundary (boun´ dər ē) Dividing line (p. 429)

Boyar (bō yär´) A Russian noble who owned land (p. 257)

a	hat	e	let	ī	ice	ȯ	order	ủ	put	sh	she		a	in about
ā	age	ē	equal	o	hot	oi	oil	ü	rule	th	thin	ə	e	in taken
ä	far	ėr	term	ō	open	ou	out	ch	child	₮H	then		i	in pencil
â	care	i	it	ȯ	saw	u	cup	ng	long	zh	measure		o	in lemon
													u	in circus

Boycott (boi´ kot) To refuse to buy something; to refuse to deal with a person, business, or country (p. 488)

British Commonwealth of Nations (brit´ ish kom´ ən welth ov nā´ shəns) A group of nations that is loyal to the British monarch (p. 733)

Buddha (bü´ də) A name meaning the "Enlightened One"; the name given to Siddhartha Gautama, the founder of Buddhism (p. 100)

Bushido (bü´ shē dō) The Samurai code of honor in Japan (p. 311)

C

Calligraphy (kə lig´ rə fē) The art of beautiful handwriting (p. 311)

Calvinism (kal´ və niz əm) The religious movement founded by John Calvin (p. 363)

Campesino (käm pā sē´ nō) A peasant who works the land but does not own it (p. 772)

Canal (kə nal´) A waterway made by humans (p. 104)

Capital (kap´ ə təl) The city from which a ruler, or emperor, rules (p. 48); money used to start a business (p. 515)

Caravan (kar´ ə van) A group of traders traveling together, often through deserts (p. 69)

Cardinal (kärd´ n əl) A high official of the Roman Catholic Church (p. 444)

Caste (kast) A class of people in India (p. 98)

Catholic Reformation (kath´ ə lik ref ər mā´ shən) The Catholic Church's reforms that attempted to fight Protestant beliefs; also known as the Counter-Reformation (p. 366)

Cavalier (kav ə lir´) A person who fought for the king in the English Civil War (p. 440)

Cavalry (kav´ əl rē) Soldiers on horseback (p. 47)

Censor (sen´ sər) To prevent someone from reading or viewing something (p. 366)

Central Powers (sen´ trəl pou´ ərs) The allied nations of Germany, Austria-Hungary, Turkey, and Bulgaria (p. 617)

Chapel (chap´ əl) A small church (p. 343)

Chariot (char´ ē ət) A two-wheeled, horse-drawn carriage (p. 47)

Charter (chär´ tər) A constitution; a set of statements that explains a group's purpose (p. 692)

Christianity (kris chē an´ ə tē) The religion based on the teachings of Jesus Christ (p. 177)

City-state (sit´ ē - stāt) A city surrounded by smaller villages (p. 27)

Civilian (sə vil´ yən) A person who is not in the military (p. 300)

Civilization (siv ə lə zā´ shən) A large group of people who have cities and government, and a high level of development as a group (p. 17)

Civilized (siv´ ə līzd) Having good government and the things that make life easier (p. 172)

Civil service (siv´ əl sėr´ vis) A system of government run by civilians (p. 300)

Civil war (siv´ əl wôr) Fighting between people within their own country (p. 72)

Classical (klas´ ə kəl) A type of music from the 1700s and 1800s that is orderly and balanced; in the style of ancient Greece or Rome (p. 475)

Clergy (klėr´ jē) Leaders of religious groups (p. 329)

Co-emperor (kō - em´ pər ər) A person who rules part of an empire while another person rules the other part (p. 181)

Code of Napoleon (kōd ov nə pō´ lē ən) A code of law Napoleon passed that made all men equal in France (p. 506)

Cold war (kōld wôr) The war of ideas between the United States and the Soviet Union after World War II (p. 707)

Collective farm (kə lek´ tiv färm) A large farm owned by the government and worked by many peasants (p. 647)

Colonialism (kə lō′ nē ə liz əm) The controlling of colonies; another name for imperialism (p. 593)

Colonist (kol′ ə nist) A person who settles in a new place (p. 416)

Column (kol′ əm) A tall post used to support a building (p. 132)

Commandment (kə mand′ mənt) A rule, or a way to act (p. 37)

Communion (kə myü′ nyən) A ritual by which Christians grow in their faith (p. 358)

Communism (kom′ yə niz əm) An economic system in which there is no private property and the government produces goods (p. 643)

Community (kə myü′ nə tē) A group of people with something in common (p. 387)

Complaint (kəm plānt′) A statement about something that tells why a person is unhappy (p. 489)

Compromise (kom′ prə mīz) An agreement in which both sides give up something to stop an argument (p. 362)

Concentration camp (kon sən trā′ shən kamp) A large prison death camp (p. 686)

Conclude (kən klüd′) To decide by using facts (p. 380)

Conclusion (kən klü′ zhən) An answer; a decision reached through step-by-step thinking (p. 377)

Confederation (kən fed ə rā′ shən) A union, or group, of states or nations (p. 545)

Conference (kon′ fər əns) A meeting to discuss ideas and plans (p. 672)

Conflict (kon′ flikt) Fighting; not being able to agree on something (p. 760)

Congress of Vienna (kong′ gris ov vē en′ ə) An important meeting in 1814 and 1815 in which leaders restructured Europe (p. 543)

Conquistador (kon kē′ stə dôr) A Spanish conqueror (p. 406)

Conservative (kən sėr′ və tiv) A person who likes the old political order and is against revolution or change (p. 553)

Constitution (kon stə tü′ shən) A body of laws that states the rights of the people and the power of the government (p. 449)

Constitutional monarchy (kon stə tü′ shə nəl mon′ ər kē) A form of government in which a king and queen rule, but there are laws of a democracy to protect the people (p. 443)

Consul (kon′ səl) A Roman leader who served a one-year term in the government (p. 151)

Consumer goods (kən sü′ mər güds) Products that people buy (p. 647)

Contract (kon′ trakt) A legal agreement (p. 465)

Convention (kən ven′ shən) A group of people who meet to get something done (p. 497)

Core (kôr) The center of something (p. 388)

Coup (kü) A takeover of the government (p. 715)

Courtyard (kôrt′ yärd) A large open area inside the castle walls (p. 237)

Covenant (kuv′ ə nənt) An agreement (p. 38)

Creole (krē′ ōl) A wealthy landowner who had been born in a Spanish colony in the Americas but whose ancestors came from Spain (p. 549)

Cro-Magnon (krō - mag′ nən) The hominid *Homo sapiens*, a direct ancestor of modern humans (p. 14)

Crucify (krü′ sə fī) To hang someone on a cross to die (p. 178)

Crusade (krü sād′) Any of the military journeys taken by Christians to win the Holy Land from the Muslims (p. 229)

a	hat	e	let	ī	ice	ô	order	ů	put	sh	she	ə {	a	in about
ā	age	ē	equal	o	hot	oi	oil	ü	rule	th	thin		e	in taken
ä	far	ėr	term	ō	open	ou	out	ch	child	ᴛʜ	then		i	in pencil
â	care	i	it	ȯ	saw	u	cup	ng	long	zh	measure		o	in lemon
													u	in circus

Cubit (kyü´ bit) A measurement that is the length of an arm from the end of the middle finger to the elbow (p. 80)

Culture (kul´ chər) The values, attitudes, and customs of a group (p. 5)

Cuneiform (kyü nē´ ə fôrm) The writing invented by Sumerians (p. 29)

Currency (kėr´ ən sē) The form of money a country uses (p. 721)

Cycle (sī´ kəl) The events that keep happening, one after another (p. 97)

Cyrillic alphabet (si ril´ ik al´ fə bet) The alphabet invented by Cyril and Methodius and used to translate the Bible into Slavic languages (p. 255)

Czar (zär) The ruler of Russia; a Russian title that means "caesar" (p. 258)

D

Daimyos (dī´ myos) The highest nobles next to the shogun (p. 311)

D-Day (dē - dā) The Allied invasion of France in 1944 (p. 681)

Declaration of Independence (dek lə rā´ shən ov in di pen´ dəns) A document the American colonists signed in which they declared their freedom from Great Britain (p. 489)

Decline (di klīn´) To lose power (p. 175)

Defensive (di fen´ siv) Protecting oneself rather than attacking others (p. 680)

Deforestation (dē fôr´ ist ā shən) The destruction of forests (p. 798)

Delta (del´ tə) An area of fertile land at the mouth of a river (p. 67)

Democracy (di mok´ rə sē) Rule by the people (p. 123)

Democratic (dem ə krat´ ik) Having to do with a government in which all people have equal rights (p. 630)

Demonstrate (dem´ ən strāt) To join together with other people to protest and march against something (p. 735)

Depression (di presh´ ən) A time of economic collapse when businesses lose money and many people become poor (p. 654)

Desire (di zīr´) To wish for something (p. 101)

Destroyer (di stroi´ ər) A small, fast warship that uses guns and other weapons to protect ships from submarines (p. 676)

Developing country (di vel´ ə ping kun´ trē) A nation that is slowly developing its industry and economy (p. 793)

Dictator (dik´ tā tər) A leader who has full control of laws and rules with force (p. 151)

Direct democracy (də rekt´ di mok´ rə sē) A type of government in which each citizen votes on everything (p. 124)

Disciple (də sī´ pəl) A follower of someone (p. 178)

Displace (dis plas´) To move people from their home or land; to force people to leave their home or land (p. 738)

Divine right (də vīn´ rīt) The belief that God chooses the ruler of a nation (p. 437)

Dominate (dom´ ə nāt) To control (p. 47)

Drama (drä´ mə) A story that is acted out on stage (p. 338)

Drawbridge (dró´ brij) A bridge that can be raised or lowered over a moat (p. 236)

Drought (drout) A long period of time without much rain (p. 760)

Duma (dü´ mə) The Russian parliament (p. 630)

Dynasty (dī´ nə stē) A family that rules a country over a long period of time (p. 106)

E

Economist (i kon´ ə mist) A person who studies money (p. 518)

Economy (i kon´ ə mē) The system of making and trading things (p. 72)

Efficient (ə fish´ ənt) Working well with little loss of time or energy (p. 525)

Elder (el´ dər) An experienced, older person (p. 363)

Elect (i lekt′) A Calvinist term for those whom God has chosen to save (p. 363)

Election (i lek′ shən) An act by which people choose someone or something by voting (p. 748)

Ellipse (i lips′) The shape of an egg (p. 380)

Embargo (em bär′ gō) An act that stops all trade (p. 775)

Émigré (em′ ə grā) A French noble who fled France during the French Revolution (p. 497)

Emperor (em′ pər ər) A person who is ruler of an empire (p. 161)

Empire (em′ pīr) A large area of land ruled by one person (p. 47)

Encomienda (en kōmē′ endə) The Spanish system of forced physical labor (p. 410)

Enforce (en fôrs′) To make sure that people follow the laws and rules (p. 496)

Enlightened (en līt′ nd) The state of knowing the truth (p. 100); having a belief in reasoning; moving away from ignorance (p. 463)

Enlightenment (en līt′ n mənt) A time in European history when thinkers and writers tried to solve the problems of society by using reason (p. 469)

Enslave (en slāv′) To force people to become slaves (p. 126)

Equality (i kwol′ ə tē) The same rights for everyone (p. 496)

Estate (e stāt′) A large piece of land with a house on it (p. 311); a class of people in France (p. 493)

Estates-General (e stāts′ - jen′ ər el) The French governmental body made up of representatives from the three estates (p. 494)

Eternal (i tėr′ nl) Lasting forever (p. 171)

Ethics (eth′ iks) The study of what is right and wrong (p. 135)

Ethnic cleansing (eth′ nik klenz′ ing) The act of getting rid of a group of people because their religion or race is different from the majority group (p. 719)

Excommunicate (ek skə myü′ nə kāt) To say that someone can no longer be a member of a church (p. 358)

Executive (eg zek′ yə tiv) The branch of government that enforces laws (p. 499)

Exile (eg′ zīl) To send someone away from his or her own country and to order this person not to come back (p. 505)

Experimental science (ek sper ə men′ tl sī′ əns) The science that begins with and depends on careful experiments and measurements (p. 383)

Exploration (ek splə rā′ shən) The act of looking around some unknown place (p. 402)

Extinct (ek stingkt′) No longer existing; died out (p. 13)

F

Famine (fam′ ən) A time when crops do not grow and there is no food (p. 37)

Fascism (fash′ iz əm) A form of government in which a dictator and the dictator's party totally control a government (p. 652)

Fast (fast) To give up eating food for a while (p. 273)

Fertile Crescent (fėr′ tl kres′ nt) The area in the Middle East shaped like a quarter moon (crescent) where one of the earliest civilizations developed (p. 35)

Fertilizer (fėr′ tl ī zər) A substance that makes the soil grow crops (p. 760)

Feudalism (fyü′ dl iz əm) A political and military system based on the holding of land (p. 232)

Fief (fēf) The land and peasants who farmed it, which a lord gave to a vassal (p. 232)

a	hat	e	let	ī	ice	ô	order	ů	put	sh	she	ə	a in about
ā	age	ē	equal	o	hot	oi	oil	ü	rule	th	thin		e in taken
ä	far	ėr	term	ō	open	ou	out	ch	child	ŦH	then		i in pencil
â	care	i	it	ȯ	saw	u	cup	ng	long	zh	measure		o in lemon
													u in circus

Fleet (flēt) A group of ships (p. 128)

Foreign minister (fôr´ ən min´ ə stər) A person who handles one country's dealings with other nations (p. 543)

Formation (fôr mā´ shən) A shape or pattern (p. 436)

Fossil fuel (fos´ əl fyü´ əl) Fuel made from coal, oil, or natural gas (p. 798)

Founded (found´ əd) To have begun a country or city (p. 149)

Free-market economy (frē - mär´ kit i kon´ ə mē) An economy in which manufacturers try to satisfy consumers' wants and needs (p. 793)

French Revolution (french rev ə lü´ shən) The war that the common people of France fought against the king, nobles, and one another to achieve freedom (p. 495)

Fresco (fres´ kō) A painting done in wet plaster on a wall (p. 342)

Front (frunt) The place where armies fight (p. 673)

Fuehrer (fyür´ ər) The name given to Adolf Hitler meaning "leader" (p. 655)

G

Genocide (jen´ ə sīd) The mass murder of a group of people (p. 686)

Gentile (jen´ tīl) A non-Jew (p. 178)

Geometric (jē ə met´ rik) Simple designs made up of straight lines and circles (p. 199)

Geometry (jē om´ ə trē) The study of the measurement of flat and round things (p. 139)

Gestapo (gə stä´ pō) Hitler's secret police (p. 655)

Geography (jē og´ rə fē) The science that deals with land, weather, bodies of water, and plant and animal life (p. 91)

Ghetto (get´ ō) The special parts of cities where the Jewish people were forced to live during World War II (p. 685)

Glacier (glā´ shər) A thick sheet of ice (p. 195)

Glasnost (glas´ nost) A Russian word that means "openness"; under Gorbachev it meant openness in government (p. 714)

Global village (glō´ bəl vil´ ij) The term used to describe the sharing of ideas, cultures, and traditions throughout the world (p. 785)

Global warming (glō´ bəl wôrm ing) The worldwide heating up of Earth, caused in part by human activity (p. 799)

Glorious Revolution (glôr´ ē əs rev ə lü´ shən) The overthrow of James II and the crowning of William and Mary as monarchs of England (p. 442)

Goddess (god´ is) A female god (p. 132)

Gospel (gos´ pəl) One of four books of the New Testament part of the Bible; a word that means "good news" (p. 177)

Gothic (goth´ ik) A style of architecture with thin walls, pointed arches, many windows, and flying buttresses (p. 240)

Govern (guv´ ərn) To rule (p. 50)

Great Depression (grāt di presh´ ən) The worldwide depression that began in the United States in 1929 (p. 659)

Guerilla warfare (gə ril´ ə wôr´ fâr) A kind of fighting that involves small attacks against an enemy or the things it needs and uses (p. 680)

Guillotine (gil´ ə tēn) The machine used to execute people by chopping off their head (p. 499)

H

Habeas Corpus (hā´ bē as kôr´ pəs) A law that says that the government has to charge someone with a crime before putting the person in prison (p. 442)

Hajj (haj) The pilgrimage to Mecca that is a religious duty of all Muslims (p. 275)

Hari-kari (har´ ē - kar´ ē) To kill oneself with a knife (p. 311)

Heavy industry (hev´ ē in´ də strē) The manufacturing of products, such as machines and raw materials, for use in other industries (p. 647)

Hegira (hi jī´ rə) Muhammad's journey from Mecca to Medina; his flight from danger (p. 273)

Hellenism (hel´ ə niz əm) The blend of Western and Eastern cultures made possible by Alexander the Great (p. 138)

Hellenistic Age (hel ə nis´ tik āj) The time between 323 B.C. and 31 B.C., when Greek culture influenced the world (p. 139)

Helot (hel´ ət) A slave in Sparta (p. 126)

Heretic (her´ ə tik) A person who holds a belief that a religious authority thinks is false (p. 354)

Heritage (her´ ə tij) The traditions ancestors have passed down to their descendants (p. 576)

Heroic (hi rō´ ik) Being brave and bold (p. 119)

Hieroglyphics (hī ər ə glif´ iks) A kind of picture writing in Egypt (p. 77)

Hinduism (hin´ dü iz əm) The main religion of India that stresses the belief in the Vedas (p. 97)

Historian (hi stôr´ ē ən) One who is an expert in history (p. 5)

History (his´ tər ē) The record of past events (p. 5)

Holocaust (hol´ ə kȯst) Hitler's killing of many Jews in Europe (p. 685)

Holy Land (hō´ lē land) Palestine; the area where Jesus of Nazareth lived (p. 228)

Homeland (hōm´ land) The land that belongs to a people (p. 177)

Hominids (hom´ ə nids) A group that includes humans and their closest relatives (p. 13)

Hostage (hos´ tij) Someone held against his or her will until certain demands are met (p. 764)

Huguenot (hyü´ gə not) A French Calvinist (p. 364)

Humanism (hyü´ mə niz əm) A belief that human actions, ideas, and works are important (p. 331)

Human rights (hyü´ mən rīts) Political and civil liberties, including the right to life, liberty and pursuit of happiness (p. 769)

Hypothesis (hī poth´ ə sis) An educated guess based on what a scientist already knows (p. 377)

I

Ice Age (īs āj) A period of time when much of Earth and Earth's water was frozen (p. 13)

Icon (ī´ kon) A small picture of a saint or Jesus (p. 253)

Idol (ī´ dl) A statue of a god that people worship (p. 274)

Ikebana (i kā bä´ nə) One Japanese art of arranging flowers (p. 316)

Imperfection (im pər fek´ shən) Something that makes an object or person less than perfect (p. 184)

Imperialism (im pir´ ē ə liz əm) Control or influence a powerful nation has over a weaker nation (p. 593)

Independence (in di pen´ dəns) Being free; being able to govern one's self (p. 130)

Indulgence (in dul´ jəns) A church paper that says that a person will not be punished after death for their sins (p. 355)

Industrialization (in dus´ trē līz ā shən) The process of getting machines to do work (p. 517)

Industrial Revolution (in dus´ trē əl rev ə lü´ shən) An important change in the way people work (p. 515)

Infidel (in´ fə dəl) One who does not believe in the religion of another person (p. 283)

Inflation (in flā´ shən) A quick increase in prices (p. 654)

a	hat	e	let	ī	ice	ȯ	order	u̇	put	sh	she	ə	a	in about
ā	age	ē	equal	o	hot	oi	oil	ü	rule	th	thin		e	in taken
ä	far	ėr	term	ō	open	ou	out	ch	child	ᴛʜ	then		i	in pencil
â	care	i	it	ȯ	saw	u	cup	ng	long	zh	measure		o	in lemon
													u	in circus

Influential (in flü en´ shəl) Having the power to change things or to affect what happens (p. 543)

Inherit (in her´ it) To receive money, land, or a title from someone who has died (p. 433)

Inspector (in spek´ tər) A person who looks at how things are being done (p. 55)

Interdependent (in tər di pen´ dənt) Depending on one another (p. 793)

Internal combustion engine (in tėr´ nl kəm bus´ chən en´ jən) An engine that burns gasoline to produce power (p. 533)

International (in tər nash´ ə nəl) Around the world; involving different nations (p. 787)

Internet (in´ tər net) An international computer network (p. 787)

Invade (in vād´) To attack or march into another country (p. 104)

Investment (in vest´ mənt) Money given to a company to use to make more money (p. 759)

Iron Curtain (ī´ ərn kėrt´ n) The invisible boundary between Western Europe and Eastern Europe after World War II (p. 690)

Irrigate (ir´ ə gāt) To bring water to crops (p. 94)

Isolate (ī´ sə lāt) To keep apart or away from others (p. 103)

J

Jacobin (jak´ ə bən) A radical leader during the French Revolution (p. 498)

Jesuit (jesh´ ü it) A member of the Catholic religious order known as the Society of Jesus (p. 367)

Jihad (ji häd´) A holy war fought by Muslims to spread Muhammad's teachings (p. 278)

Joust (joust) A contest between two knights carrying lances and riding horses (p. 237)

Judaism (jü´ dē iz əm) The religion of the Hebrews that Jews practice today (p. 37)

Jury (jür´ ē) A group who listens to court cases and decides the outcome (p. 125)

K

Kabuki (kä bü´ kē) A Japanese play with exaggerated actions (p. 316)

Kaiser (kī´ zər) The emperor of Germany (p. 584)

Kami (ka´ mi) The spirits of the Shinto religion (p. 308)

Kamikaze (kä mi kä´ zē) A Japanese pilot who crashed his plane into an enemy ship and destroyed it and himself (p. 681)

Kiva (kē´ və) A small underground building used for ceremonies (p. 199)

Knighted (nīt´ əd) To be made a knight (p. 234)

Kremlin (krem´ lən) The center of the Russian church and the Russian government (p. 258)

L

Labor union (la´ bər yü´ nyən) An organized group of workers who try to improve their working conditions (p. 532)

Laborer (lā´ bər ər) A person who does hard work with his or her hands (p. 152)

Laser (lā´ zər) A tool that produces high-energy beams of light (p. 790)

League of Nations (lēg ov nā´ shəns) A group of leaders from many nations who met to solve problems between countries (p. 624)

Legalize (lē´ gə līz) To make lawful (p. 735)

Legislature (lej´ ə slā chər) The lawmaking body of government (p. 499)

Lend-Lease program (lend - lēs prō´ gram) A program developed by Franklin Roosevelt that allowed Britain to borrow war supplies from the United States during World War II (p. 676)

Liberal (lib´ ər əl) A person who wants change; a person who wants to limit the absolute power of kings and nobles and give power to the middle class (p. 553)

Literature (lit´ ər ə chür) The written works that have lasting influence (p. 260)

Locomotive (lō kə mō´ tiv) A self-propelled vehicle that runs on rails (p. 525)

Logic (loj´ ik) The science of thinking (p. 135)

Lord (lôrd) A king or a noble who gave land to someone (p. 232)

Lottery (lot′ ər ē) A system of picking names from a container so that each person has an equal chance of being chosen (p. 124)

Lutheran Church (lü′ thər ən chėrch) The church established by Martin Luther (p. 358)

M

Maginot line (mazh′ ə nō līn) A line of concrete forts built by France along its border with Germany (p. 675)

Majority (mə jôr′ ə tē) More than half of a group of people or group of things (p. 416)

Maneuver (mə nü′ vər) To move around easily (p. 130)

Manor (man′ ər) The part of a fief that peasants farm to support the lord's family (p. 235)

Manufacturer (man yə fak′ chər ər) A person who hires people to work with machines to make something to sell (p. 520)

Market (mär′ kit) A place to sell goods (p. 593)

Marshall Plan (mär′ shəl plan) The American plan to rebuild Europe after World War II (p. 708)

Massacre (mas′ ə kər) The act of killing many people who are often defenseless (p. 364)

Mass communication (mas kə myü nə kā′ shən) Messages directed at many people (p. 786)

Mass production (mas prə duk′ shən) A way of making large amounts of the same thing in a factory (p. 521)

Masterpiece (mas′ tər pēs) A piece of art that seems almost perfect (p. 303)

Mayflower Compact (mā′ flou ər kom′ pakt) The agreement made by the Pilgrims that set up a form of government for their new colony (p. 417)

Messiah (mə sī′ ə) A king sent by God to save people (p. 177)

Migrant (mī′ grənt) A person who has left one place and moved to another (p. 761)

Militarism (mil′ ə tə riz əm) A nation's warlike policy or practice (p. 581)

Military (mil′ ə ter ē) Having to do with the army (p. 27)

Military state (mil′ ə ter ē stāt) A place in which a leader rules through the military (p. 449)

Militia (mə lish′ ə) A group of people who can be called to military service when something dangerous happens suddenly (p. 643)

Minister (min′ ə stər) A person who can lead a religious ceremony in a Lutheran church (p. 358)

Minority (mə nôr′ ə tē) A small group of like people within a larger group (p. 644)

Minutemen (min′ it men) Colonial soldiers in the Revolutionary War who were ready to fight at any time (p. 488)

Moat (mōt) A dug-out area filled with water that circles a castle (p. 236)

Moderate (mod′ ər it) One who wants to change things little by little (p. 498)

Monarch (mon′ ərk) A king or a queen (p. 429)

Monk (mungk) A member of a religious order (p. 255)

Monsoon (mon sün′) A seasonal wind (p. 92)

Monument (mon′ yə mənt) An object or building honoring a person or event, usually made of stone (p. 16)

Mosque (mosk) A Muslim place of worship (p. 279)

Mother country (muᴛʜ′ ər kun′ trē) A nation that controls a colony (p. 593)

a	hat	e	let	ī	ice	ô	order	ů	put	sh	she		a	in about
ā	age	ē	equal	o	hot	oi	oil	ü	rule	th	thin	ə	e	in taken
ä	far	ėr	term	ō	open	ou	out	ch	child	ᴛʜ	then		i	in pencil
â	care	i	it	ȯ	saw	u	cup	ng	long	zh	measure		o	in lemon
													u	in circus

Multilingual (mul ti ling´ gwəl) A society in which a number of languages are spoken (p. 575)

Multiracial (mul ti rā´ shəl) Having to do with all people and all races (p. 736)

Mummify (mum´ ə fī) To wrap a dead body in strips of cloth to keep the body from decaying (p. 74)

Munich Pact (myü´ nik pakt) A 1938 agreement between Great Britain and Germany to appease Hitler (p. 673)

Muslim (muz´ ləm) A follower of the religion that Muhammad founded in Arabia in the 7th century (p. 228)

N

Nationalism (nash´ ə nə liz əm) Loyalty to one's country or nation (p. 429)

Nationality (nash ə nal´ ə tē) A group of people who share the same language, culture, and history (p. 546)

Natural resources (nach´ ər əl ri sôrs´ əs) Things—such as coal, ore, and water—that come from nature and help humans (p. 515)

Navigation (nav ə gā´ shən) The science of planning and directing a ship's journey (p. 399)

Negotiate (ni gō´ shē āt) To talk together, make bargains, and agree on something (p. 582)

Neolithic Age (nē ə lith´ ik āj) The age when people made polished stone tools; also called the New Stone Age (p. 15)

Neutral (nü´ trəl) Not choosing either side in a war or argument (p. 502)

Nirvana (nir vä´ nə) A condition of complete emptiness in which a person's soul finds perfect peace (p. 101)

Noble (nō´ bəl) A person of high birth (p. 106)

Noh drama (nō drä´ mə) A Japanese play with only two actors (p. 316)

Nomad (nō´ mad) A person who moves from place to place (p. 15)

Northern Hemisphere (nôr´ ᴛʜərn hem´ ə sfir) The half of the earth north of the equator (p. 793)

Nuclear (nü´ klē ər) Having to do with atoms or energy from atoms (p. 682)

O

Obelisk (ob´ ə lisk) A tall, pointed stone pillar (p. 77)

Occupy (ok´ yə pī) To take over and stay in a place (p. 680)

Ordinance (ôrd´ n əns) A law set forth by someone in government (p. 555)

Organization (ôr gə nə zā´ shən) A group of people joined together for a common purpose (p. 692)

P

Page (pāj) A young noble who learned to become a knight (p. 232)

Paleolithic Age (pā lē ə lith´ ik āj) The earliest period of human history; called the Old Stone Age (p. 14)

Palestinian Liberation Organization (PLO) (pal ə stin´ ē ən lib´ ə rā shən ôr gə nə zā´ shən) The group of Palestinians dedicated to regaining from Israel their homeland in Palestine (p. 739)

Palisade (pal´ ə sād) A wooden fence (p. 204)

Pan-African Movement (pan - af´ rə kən müv´ mənt) A group that planned ways in which Africans could achieve economic strength and political peace (p. 731)

Papyrus (pə pī´ rəs) A reed from the Nile River used to make paper (p. 80)

Parliament (pär´ lə mənt) The English council or lawmaking assembly (p. 241)

Passive resistance (pas´ iv ri zis´ təns) A nonviolent way of protesting for political and social change (p. 742)

Patriarch (pā´ trē ärk) A leader of the church (p. 253)

Patrician (pə trish´ ən) A Roman who owned land and helped a ruler govern (p. 149)

Patriotic (pā trē ot´ ik) Being loyal toward one's country (p. 127)

Patron (pā´ trən) A person who supports an artist with money (p. 342)

Pax Romana (paks rō mä´ nə) The Roman peace that began during the reign of Augustus Caesar (p. 172)

Peninsula (pə nin´ sə lə) A piece of land surrounded on three sides by water (p. 91)

Peninsular (pə nin´ sə lər) A person who came to South America from Spain and held an important office in the colonial government (p. 549)

Perestroika (per ə stoi´ kə) An economic policy used by Gorbachev to encourage factories to produce the goods people wanted (p. 714)

Pesticide (pes´ tə sīd) A substance that kills the bugs that eat the crops (p. 760)

Petition of Right (pə tish´ ən ov rīt) An English document that brought about more democracy (p. 437)

Pharaoh (fâr´ ō) An Egyptian ruler (p. 70)

Philosopher (fə los´ ə fər) A person who tries to understand the basic nature of knowledge and reality (p. 133)

Photoelectric cell (fō tō i lek´ trik sel) An invention that can produce electricity from light (p. 789)

Physics (fiz´ iks) The science of matter and energy (p. 135)

Pictogram (pik´ tə gram) A figure that tells a story (p. 95)

Pilgrim (pil´ grəm) A person who travels to visit a holy place (p. 228)

Plague (plāg) A disease that spreads from person to person and kills many people (p. 175)

Plantation (plan tā´ shən) A large area of farmland (p. 410)

Plateau (pla tō´) A flat area that rises above the land close by (p. 103)

Plebeian (pli bē´ ən) A common person in Rome who was not wealthy (p. 152)

Policy (pol´ ə sē) A plan that helps a person or a country make a decision (p. 581)

Polis (pō´ ləs) The Greek name for a city-state (p. 122)

Political (pə lit´ ə kəl) Having to do with governing (p. 153)

Politician (pol ə tish´ ən) A government leader (p. 159)

Politics (pol´ ə tiks) The work of government (p. 135)

Pope (pōp) The head of the Roman Catholic Church (p. 261)

Portrait (pôr´ trāt) A drawing of a person (p. 341)

Prehistory (prē his´ tər ē) The time before humans left written records (p. 13)

Prejudice (prej´ ə dis) An unfair and unreasonable opinion (p. 471)

Priest (prēst) A religious leader (p. 28)

Primary source (prī´ mer ē sôrs) A first-hand account of a historical event (p. 5)

Prime minister (prīm min´ ə stər) The leader in some democratic government systems (p. 577)

Prism (priz´ əm) A three-sided object that can be seen through (p. 385)

Proletariat (prō lə târ´ ē ət) The working class according to Marx (p. 560)

Propaganda (prop ə gan´ də) One-sided information meant to change people's thinking (p. 707)

Prophet (prof´ it) A person who speaks for God (p. 177)

Protectorate (prə tek´ tər it) An independent country whose foreign policy is controlled by a major power (p. 600)

a	hat	e	let	ī	ice	ô	order	u̇	put	sh	she	ə	a	in about
ā	age	ē	equal	o	hot	oi	oil	ü	rule	th	thin		e	in taken
ä	far	ėr	term	ō	open	ou	out	ch	child	ᴛʜ	then		i	in pencil
â	care	i	it	ȯ	saw	u	cup	ng	long	zh	measure		o	in lemon
													u	in circus

Protestant (prot´ ə stənt) A reformer who protested against the Catholic Church (p. 359)

Province (prov´ əns) An area, such as a state, that is part of a larger country (p. 50)

Purgatory (pėr´ gə tôr ē) A place of suffering after death (p. 356)

Purge (pėrj) To remove from office; to clean by getting rid of unwanted things (p. 648)

Purify (pyür´ ə fī) To make clean (p. 362)

Puritan (pyür´ ə tən) An English Protestant who wanted to purify the Anglican Church (p. 362)

Q

Quarter (kwör´ tər) To provide soldiers with a place to live (p. 485)

Qur'an (kô rän´) The holy book of the Muslims that contains the teachings of Islam; also spelled *Koran* (p. 274)

R

Radical (rad´ ə kəl) One who wants to change things all at once (p. 498)

Radiocarbon dating (rā dē ō kär´ bən dāt´ ing) A way of measuring the radioactivity of historic artifacts to determine how old they are (p. 10)

Raw materials (rȯ mə tir´ ē əls) The materials that are used to make things (p. 527)

Rebel (ri bel´) To disobey or fight against (p. 50)

Rebellion (ri bel´ yən) A fight by people against a government; a struggle for change (p. 330)

Recession (ri sesh´ ən) An economic slowdown (p. 794)

Reform (ri fôrm´) To make something better through change (p. 158)

Reformation (ref ər mā´ shən) A movement that challenged and changed the Catholic religion in Europe (p. 355)

Reformer (ri fôr´ mər) A person who tries to change something (p. 353)

Refugee (ref yə jē´) A person who is forced to flee from his or her country (p. 689)

Regime (ri zhēm´) A form of government (p. 803)

Reich (rīk) The German word for empire (p. 584)

Reichstag (rīk´ stag) The national assembly of the Weimar Republic (p. 655)

Reign (rān) To rule; the period of time a king or queen rules (p. 33)

Reign of Terror (rān ov ter´ ər) The one-year period in French history when radical leaders put many people to death (p. 499)

Reincarnation (rē in kär nā´ shən) The rebirth of the soul into a new body (p. 97)

Relic (rel´ ik) A holy object from the past (p. 251)

Renaissance (ren´ ə säns) Rebirth; a period in European history that focused on being an individual and expanding on creative thoughts and ideas (p. 330)

Renewable (ri nü´ ə bl) Will not run out; will last forever (p. 789)

Reparation (rep ə rā´ shən) Payment for war damage (p. 623)

Repeal (ri pēl´) To do away with a law (p. 486)

Representative (rep ri zen´ tə tiv) A person who speaks and governs for others (p. 151)

Republic (ri pub´ lik) A type of government with no king in which a few people represent, or speak for, everyone (p. 151)

Resistance (ri zis´ təns) Those who opposed the Germans occupying their country (p. 680)

Resolution (rez ə lü´ shən) A formal statement that a governmental body writes (p. 438)

Restoration (res tə rā´ shən) The period that saw monarchy return to England in 1660 (p. 441)

Retire (ri tīr´) To give up one's job (p. 161)

Revolve (ri volv´) To move around something (p. 379)

Ritual (rich´ ü əl) A ceremony (p. 358)

Rival (rī´ vəl) One who tries to outdo another country or person (p. 615)

Romanesque (rō mə nesk´) A style of building that was like what the Romans built with thick walls and arches (p. 240)

Roman Inquisition (rō´ mən in kwə zish´ ən) A Catholic court that inquired into people's religious beliefs (p. 366)

Roundhead (round´ hed) A Puritan who fought for Parliament in the English Civil War (p. 441)

S

Saint (sānt) A person who follows God's ways (p. 251)

Salon (sə lon´) A meeting of artists, writers, and thinkers in a Paris home during the Enlightenment (p. 469)

Salvation (sal vā´ shən) Eternal happiness for one's soul (p. 355)

Samurai (sam´ u̇ rī) A Japanese warrior who received land from a daimyo and fought for him (p. 311)

Sanitation (san ə tā´ shən) The act of keeping something clean and free from disease (p. 185)

Satellite (sat´ l īt) A nation that is tightly controlled by another nation (p. 690)

Schism (skiz´ əm) A permanent separation (p. 229)

Scientific law (sī ən tif´ ik lȯ) A pattern in nature that someone can predict (p. 386)

Scientific method (sī ən tif´ ik meth´ əd) A set of steps scientists follow for study (p. 377)

Scribe (skrīb) A person from ancient times who could read and write (p. 107)

Scroll (skrōl) A roll of papyrus (p. 80)

Sculptor (skulp´ tər) A person who carves statues (p. 335)

Secondary source (sek´ ən der ē sôrs) A second-hand account of a historical event; an account written by a person who was not there (p. 5)

Senate (sen´ it) A governing body (p. 149)

Senator (sen´ ə tər) A member of a senate, a governing body (p. 157)

Serf (sėrf) A peasant who was bound to the land and whose life was controlled by the lord of the manor (p. 235)

Shah (shä) An Iranian ruler (p. 763)

Shinto (shin´ tō) The Japanese religion that involves a love of nature and worship of spirits (p. 307)

Shogun (shō´ gun) A Japanese word that means "great general"; a military dictator (p. 310)

Siege (sēj) The act of surrounding a city or fort with an army and cutting off its supplies (p. 582)

Silt (silt) A rich layer of soil left behind after a flood (p. 67)

Slavery (slā´ vər ē) The owning of human beings as property (p. 413)

Slum (slum) An area of a city with too many people, poor housing, and low-income families (p. 761)

Socialism (sō´ shə liz əm) An economic and political theory in which the government owns and controls the major means of production (p. 633)

Socialist (sō´ shə list) A person who wants to end the private ownership of land and factories (p. 558)

Society (sə sī´ ə tē) A group of people whose members live together for the good of all (p. 107)

Solidarity (sol ə dar´ ə tē) The name of the Polish shipbuilder's union that went out on strike in 1980 (p. 718)

Sonnet (son´ it) A 14-line poem about one idea (p. 338)

Soul (sōl) A person's spirit (p. 101)

a	hat	e	let	ī	ice	ȯ	order	u̇	put	sh	she		a	in about
ā	age	ē	equal	o	hot	oi	oil	ü	rule	th	thin	ə	e	in taken
ä	far	ėr	term	ō	open	ou	out	ch	child	ᵀH	then		i	in pencil
â	care	i	it	ȯ	saw	u	cup	ng	long	zh	measure		o	in lemon
													u	in circus

Southern Hemisphere (suŦH´ ərn hem´ ə sfir) The half of the earth south of the equator (p. 793)

Sphere of influence (sfir ov in´ flü əns) An area in which only one foreign country can trade (p. 598)

Squire (skwīr) A 15-year-old page who learned how to ride a horse and use weapons to become a knight (p. 232)

Standard of living (stan´ dərd ov liv´ ing) A way to judge how well a person or a family is living (p. 629)

Static electricity (stat´ ik i lek tris´ ə tē) The electricity that builds up in something and is produced when one object rubs up against another (p. 388)

Strait (strāt) A narrow strip of water that connects two bigger bodies of water (p. 404)

Strike (strīk) The act of refusing to work until certain demands are met (p. 718)

Stupa (stü´ pə) A large building in which a monk is buried (p. 297)

Subcontinent (sub kon´ tə nənt) A large landmass that is somewhat smaller than a continent (p. 91)

Subsistence farming (səb sis´ təns fär´ ming) A type of farming in which people grow crops mostly for their own use, not to sell (p. 793)

Successor (sək ses´ ər) One who follows another in a position (p. 645)

Superpower (sü´ pər pou ər) A nation that has more power and money than other countries (p. 690)

Swastika (swäs´ tə kə) The Nazi symbol of a cross with its arms bent (p. 654)

Symbol (sim´ bəl) Something that stands for something else (p. 106)

Symphony (sim´ fə nē) A long musical work played by a group of musicians using many different instruments (p. 475)

T

Tactic (tak´ tik) A plan that helps someone win a game or a battle (p. 500)

Tariff (tar´ if) A tax that countries put on goods they import or export (p. 720)

Technology (tek nol´ ə jē) The use of science to do practical things (p. 785)

Temple (tem´ pəl) A place in which to honor gods (p. 28)

Terraced (ter´ ist) Going upward like steps (p. 52)

Terrorist (ter´ ər ist) A person who uses violence to frighten people and to get them to obey (p. 739)

Theory (thir´ ē) A statement that explains why or how something happens (p. 379)

Thesis (thē´ sis) A statement that people argue about or try to prove (p. 356)

Tory (tôr´ ē) A person who supported a strong monarchy in England (p. 442)

Totalitarian state (tō tal ə ter´ ē ən stāt) A government in which a small group totally controls the lives of its country's citizens (p. 648)

Tradition (trə dish´ ən) A custom, idea, or belief handed down from one person to the next (p. 429)

Translate (tran slāt´) To change the words of one language into those of another (p. 31)

Transportation (tran spər tā´ shən) The movement of people and things from one place to another (p. 524)

Treason (trē´ zn) The act of turning against the laws and people of your own country (p. 438)

Treaty of Versailles (trē´ tē ov ver sī´) The treaty that ended World War I (p. 624)

Trench (trench) A long narrow ditch (p. 618)

Tribune (trib´ yün) A representative who protected the rights of the plebeian class (p. 152)

Tribute (trib´ yüt) A payment given to a stronger ruler or nation (p. 48)

Triumvirate (trī um´ vər it) Rule by three people (p. 159)

Truce (trüs) An agreement to stop a war for a time (p. 712)

Truman Doctrine (trü´ mən dok´ trən) President Truman's plan to stop the spread of Communism (p. 707)

Trust territory (trust ter´ ə tôr ē) A territory that the Allies took from the countries that lost World War I and World War II (p. 693)

Tutor (tü´ tər) A teacher who teaches one person at a time (p. 332)

Tyranny (tir´ ə nē) Harsh, absolute power (p. 803)

Tyrant (tī´ rənt) A leader who rules by force and not by law (p. 122)

U

Unify (yü´ nə fī) To bring together as one (p. 55)

Unite (yü nīt´) To bring together as one (p. 69)

United Nations (UN) (yü nī´ tid nā´ shəns) The international organization that works to settle disagreements, improve the way people live, and keep peace around the world (p. 692)

Universe (yü´ nə vėrs) All the planets and stars that exist in space (p. 379)

Unrestricted warfare (un ri strik´ tid wôr´ fär) War that is not limited to a certain area or boundary (p. 620)

Urbanization (ėr bə nə zā´ shən) Becoming more like a city (p. 761)

Utopia (yü tō´ pē ə) A type of society in which everyone works peacefully together for the good of all (p. 559)

V

Vassal (vas´ əl) A person who received land from a king or noble (p. 232)

Vatican (vat´ ə kən) The home of the pope (p. 343)

Vaulted (vȯl´ təd) A ceiling that is high, arched, and covers a large space (p. 183)

V-E Day (vē´ - ē´ dā) The day the Allies completed their victory in Europe: May 8, 1945; stands for "Victory in Europe Day" (p. 681)

V-J Day (vē´ - jā´ dā) The day the Allies completed their victory in Japan: September 2, 1945; stands for "Victory in Japan Day" (p. 682)

Veche (ve´ chuh) The Russian assembly that represented all free, adult male citizens (p. 257)

Veteran (vet´ ər ən) A person who has served in the military, especially during a war (p. 651)

Veto (vē´ tō) To say no to a decision (p. 151)

Viceroy (vīs´ roi) An official who governs land for the king or queen (p. 410)

Vietnamization (vē et nə miz ā´ shən) The U.S. plan to turn the fighting of the Vietnam War over to the South Vietnamese army (p. 749)

Violate (vī´ ə lāt) To go against (p. 485)

Vision (vizh´ ən) A visit from God's angel (p. 273)

W

Western Hemisphere (wes´ tərn hem´ ə sfir) The half of the earth that includes North and South America (p. 773)

Whig (wig) A person who supported the English Parliament (p. 442)

World Wide Web (wėrld wīd web) A network of information on the Internet open to businesses and individuals (p. 787)

Worldly (wėrld´ lē) Having nothing to do with religion (p. 336)

Worship (wėr´ ship) To honor and praise a god (p. 28)

a	hat	e	let	ī	ice	ȯ	order	u̇	put	sh	she		ə	a	in about
ā	age	ē	equal	o	hot	oi	oil	ü	rule	th	thin			e	in taken
ä	far	ėr	term	ō	open	ou	out	ch	child	ᴛʜ	then			i	in pencil
â	care	i	it	ȯ	saw	u	cup	ng	long	zh	measure			o	in lemon
														u	in circus

Index

European, 232–34, 245, 312–13, 323

Japanese, 310–14, 319, 323

vs. nationalism, 429

Fief, defined, 232

Fire, discovery of, 15, 221

Florence, Italy, 334–37, 347

Folsom Point, 196, 217

Formation, defined, 436

Fossil fuels, 811
  defined, 798

Founded, defined, 149

Fourteen Points Plan, 623

France
  absolute monarchy in, 444–47, 453, 457
  African colonies, 733
  as American allies, 490, 509, 569
  Canada, colonization of, 417, 423, 457
  constitutional monarchy in, 496, 509, 569
  government, pre-Revolution, 493, 509, 569
  imperialism by, 598, 605, 609, 742
  maps, 483
  Napoleon, 500–506, 509, 545, 548–49, 569
  Protestantism in, 365
  revolution in, 493–99, 509, 554–59, 565, 569
  taxation, 493–94, 569
  timelines, 426, 482
  women's rights, 507
  in WWI, 623, 624, 627, 637
  in WWII, 672–74, 681, 697, 701

Franco-Prussian War, 581–82, 587, 609

Franklin, Benjamin, 388, 393, 564

Franks, 261, 267, 323, 432

Frederick II (the Great), 449, 453, 471–72, 479

Frederick Wilhelm IV, 580

Frederick William I, 449

Free-market economy, defined, 793

Fresco, defined, 342

Front, defined, 673

Fuehrer, defined, 655

Fugues, 474, 479

G

Galen, 185, 387

Galilei, Galileo, 382–84, 393, 457

Gandhi, Mohandas, 742–44, 752, 753

Ganges River, 91, 113

Garibaldi, Giuseppe, 578, 587, 609

Gasoline, 533, 534

Gautama, Siddhartha, 100, 113, 221

Genghis Khan, 305, 323

Genocide, defined, 686

Gentile, defined, 178

Geography, defined, 91

Geography Note
  Atacama Desert, 407
  Ellis Island, 576
  Fertile Crescent, 35
  Georgia, 716
  Wilderness Road, 485
  WWII, 674

Geometric, defined, 199

Geometry, defined, 139

George, Lloyd, 623, 624

George III, 488, 489

Germanic tribes, 263, 265, 267

Germany
  in Africa, 601
  Lutheran church in, 359, 363, 370, 371
  maps, 583
  Nazis, 654–55, 662, 663, 685–87, 697, 701
  reunification of, 718–19, 725
  the Second Reich, 582–83
  taxation, 370
  unification of, 580–84, 587, 609
  in WWI, 616, 617, 619–21, 623, 624, 627, 637
  in WWII, 669, 670, 672–79, 690, 697, 701

Gestapo, defined, 655

Ghana, 282–83, 291, 323, 733, 753

Ghetto, defined, 685

Gilbert, William, 388, 393

Glacier ,defined, 195

Glasnost, defined, 725
  defined, 714

Global village
  defined, 785
  disease issues, 797
  economic development in, 793–96, 811
  environmental issues, 798–802, 815
  factors affecting, 785–91, 815
  global warming, 799, 809
  history, lessons from, 807
  pollution issues, 798, 811
  population issues, 806–7, 811
  terrorism, 803–5, 811, 815
  timeline, 782

Global warming, 809
  defined, 799

Glorious Revolution, 453
  defined, 442

Goddess, defined, 132

Gorbachev, Mikhail, 713–15, 724, 725

Gore, Al, 809

Gospel, defined, 177

Gothic, defined, 240

Gothic architecture, 245, 323

Govern, defined, 50

Grand Canal of China, 104

Graph Study, 411, 530

Gravity, 385

Great Britain. *See* England

Great Depression, 670
  defined, 659

Great Plains Indians, 205–6, 217

Great Wall of China, 104, 113

Greece
  Alexander the Great, 137–39, 143
  architecture in, 132
  arithmetic in, 139
  Athens, 124–25, 134–35, 141, 143
  Europe, influence on, 330, 331
  government, 122–23, 143

Monument, 21
  defined, 16
Moors, 432, 453
Morales, Evo, 775
Morelos, José, 552, 565
Morocco, 733
Morse code, 532
Moscow, 258, 267
Moses, 37, 41
Mosque, 280
  defined, 279
Mother country, defined, 593
Moundville, 204
Mozart, Wolfgang Amadeus, 475,
  479, 569
Muhammad, 273–75, 277, 291,
  323
Multilingual, defined, 575
Multiracial, defined, 736
Mummify, defined, 74
Munich Pact, 672, 697
  defined, 673
Muslims, 228, 230, 245, 271, 291,
  323, 719
  defined, 228. *See also* Islam
Mussolini, Benito, 651–53, 663,
  669, 701
Mycenaeans, 119–21, 143
Mythos, 20

N

Napier, John, 389, 393
Nasca Lines, 216
Nationalism
  in Africa, 731, 732, 753
    defined, 429
  as disease, 545
  imperialism and, 593
  in Italy, 577–79
  overview, 453, 575–76, 587, 609
  rise of, 546–48, 553, 561, 569
  timelines, 426, 572
  war and, 616
  in WWII, 669, 697, 701
Nationality, defined, 546
Natural resources, defined, 515
Navigate, 35, 38, 41
Navigation Acts, 485
Navigation, 400, 423

defined, 399
Nazis, 654–55, 662, 685–87, 697,
  701
Neanderthals, 13, 21
Nebuchadnezzar, 51–53, 61
Negotiate, defined, 582
Neolithic Age, 15, 21
  defined, 14
Nero Caesar, 174–75, 189
Neutral, defined, 502
New Stone Age, 14, 15, 21
Newton, Isaac, 324, 385–86, 389,
  393, 457, 463–64, 479, 569
New Zealand, 620
Nicholas II, 630, 632, 633, 637,
  644, 701
Nigeria, 733
Nile River, 67–68, 75
Ninevah, 48–49, 61
Nirvana, defined, 101
Noble, defined, 106
Noh drama, defined, 316
Nomad, defined, 21, 195
  defined, 15
Normans, 263
North America
  Canada, colonization of, 417,
    423, 457
  colonization, results of, 416–
    20, 457
  slave trade in, 413–15
North American Free Trade
  Agreement (NAFTA), 774,
  779
North Atlantic Treaty
  Organization (NATO), 708,
  725
Northern Hemisphere, defined,
  793
North Star, 35, 41
Nuclear, defined, 682
Nuclear energy, 789, 811
Nuns, 227, 245

O

Obelisk, defined, 77
Occupy, defined, 680
Odoacer, 182, 189
Oil, 533, 788–89, 811

Old Stone Age, 14, 21
Olmecs, 193, 208, 217, 221
Opera, 305
Ordinance, defined, 555
Organization, defined, 692
Orlando, Vittorio, 623, 624
Ottoman Empire, 327

P

Pacific Coast Indians, 206, 217
Page defined, 232
Pakistan, 743, 753, 815
Paleolithic Age defined, 21
  defined, 14
Palestine, 38, 177, 228–30, 245,
  737–41, 753, 815
Palestinian Liberation
  Organization (PLO),
  738–39, 753
  defined, 739
Palisade defined, 204
Pan-African Movement, 753
  defined, 731
Panama Canal, 774
Pantheon, 184
Paper making, 80, 85, 109, 340
Papyrus, defined, 85
  defined, 80
Parliament, defined, 241
Parthenon, 132
Passive resistance, defined, 742
Patriarch, defined, 253
Patrician, defined, 149
Patriotic, defined, 127
Patron, defined, 342
Paul III, 366
Paul IV, 366
Pax Romana, 189
  defined, 172
Pearl Harbor, 678–79, 697
Peasants' War, 370
Peloponnesian War, 130, 143
Peninsula, defined, 91
Peninsular, defined, 549
Perestroika, defined, 714
Persian Gulf War, 756, 764, 765,
  779, 815
Persians, 54–59, 61, 79, 85,
  128–30, 143

Robespierre, Maximilien, 498, 509, 569
Roman Catholic Church
   authority, challenges to, 353–54, 371
   Edict of Worms, 358
   formation of, 254, 256, 267, 323
   indulgences, sale of, 355–56, 366
   land grants by, 402, 423
   the Middle Ages, 227–28, 245
   Reformation, 366–68, 371, 457
Roman Inquisition, 371, 457
   defined, 366
   science and, 382, 387, 393, 457
Roman Empire
   art/science, 184–85
   Augustus Caesar, 171–72, 189
   as builders, 183–84
   Christianity (See Christianity)
   decline of, 175
   fall of, 181–82, 221
   government, 172, 174–75, 183, 189
   map of, 169, 176
   timeline, 168
   vs. Byzantium, 251
   women's rights, 188
Romanesque, defined, 240
Romanesque architecture, 240, 245, 323
Roman Inquisition, 371, 457
   defined, 366
Romanov, Mikhail, 448
Roman republic
   Etruscans, 149–51, 165
   Europe, influence on, 330, 331
   First Triumvirate, 159, 165, 221
   government, 151–53, 165
   Latins, 149, 165
   Punic Wars, 154–56, 165
   reform in, 157–60, 165
   Second Triumvirate, 161, 165
   taxation, 157
   timeline, 146
   women's rights, 164, 188
Rome, map of, 150
Roosevelt, Franklin, 676, 681, 683, 692
Roots, 7

Roundhead, defined, 441
Rousseau, Jean Jacques, 467, 471, 479, 569
Russia. *See also* Commonwealth of Independent States (CIS); Soviet Union
   Christianity in, 266
   imperialism by, 598, 605
   Industrial Revolution in, 629, 637
   maps, 256
   monarchy in, 448–50
   Napoleon's invasion of, 502–5, 509, 569
   overview, 255–59, 267, 323
   pre-Revolution, 629–34, 637, 663, 701
   timelines, 248, 426, 612
   in WWI, 616, 617, 619–20, 627, 632, 701
Russo-Japanese War, 630, 637

S

Sadat, Anwar, 762
Saint, defined, 251
Salamis, battle of, 130
Salon, 479
   defined, 469
Salvation, defined, 355
Samurai, defined, 311
Sanitation, defined, 185
San Martín, José, 549, 550, 565, 569
Sanskrit, 99, 113
Sappho, 188
Sargon I, 31, 41
SARS, 797
Satellite, defined, 690
Saudi Arabia, 765
Savonarola, 336–37, 347
Schism, defined, 229
Scientific development
   arithmetic in, 389, 393, 457
   Bacon, Francis, 377, 391, 393, 457
   Copernicus, 379–81, 393, 457
   Franklin, Benjamin, 388, 393
   Galileo, 382–84, 393, 457
   Gilbert, William, 388, 393

Harvey, William, 387, 393
   maps, 375
   mathematics, 389, 393
   Newton, Isaac, 385–86, 389, 393, 457
   Roman Catholic Church, 382, 387, 393, 457
   scientific method, 377–78, 393, 457
   timeline, 374
   tools, 389, 457
   Vesalius, Andreas, 387, 393
Scientific law defined, 386
Scientific method, defined, 377
Scribe, defined, 107
Scroll defined, 80
Sculptor, defined, 335
Secondary source, 6, 21
   defined, 5
Senate, defined, 149
Senator, defined, 157
Seneca, 205
Senegal, 733
Serfs, 235, 329–30
Shah, defined, 763
Shah Jahan, 300, 318
Shakespeare, William, 338, 339, 347, 457
Shi Huangdi, 108
Shinto, defined, 307
Ship building, 35
Shogun, defined, 310, 323
Siege, defined, 582
Silk Road, 108
Silt, defined, 67
Singapore, 770
Sistine Chapel, 343–44
Skeleton finds, map, 3
Skill Builder
   cause and effect, 456
   compare and contrast, 608
   fact and opinion, 322
   political cartoons, 700
   reference materials, 568
   timelines, 220
   voting, 814
Slater, Samuel, 529, 537
Slavery, defined, 413
Slave trade, 413–15, 423
Slavs, 255–56, 266, 267

Slum, defined, 761
Smallpox, 408, 422
Socialism, defined, 633, 637
Socialist, defined, 558
Society, defined, 107
Socrates, 133–35, 221
Solidarity, defined, 718
Songhai, 286–87, 291, 323
Sonnet, defined, 338
Sonni Ali, 287, 291
Soul, defined, 101
South Africa, 734–36
South America. *See also* Latin
    America
    independence, wars for, 548–
      52, 565, 569
    maps, 541
    Spanish conquest of, 406–12,
      457, 549
    timeline, 540
Southern Hemisphere, defined,
    793
South Korea, 770, 794
Soviet Union. *See also*
    Commonwealth of
    Independent States (CIS);
    Russia
    Berlin, blockade of, 709–10
    in China, 656–57, 663
    in Cuba, 775
    development of, 643–46, 701
    environmental issues, 799
    maps, 641
    recession in, 794
    reformation/collapse, 713–16,
      724, 725
    Warsaw Pact, 704, 705, 708,
      725
    in WWII, 673, 676–77, 680,
      681, 690, 697
Space exploration, 787–88, 811,
    815
Spain
    Americas, conquest of, 406–12,
      457, 549
    English, defeat of, 435–36
    maps, 427, 434
    Moors in, 432, 453

rise/fall of, 432–36
slave trading, 413, 423
Sphere of influence, 605
    defined, 598
Spinning wheels, 519, 529, 537
Spotlight Story
    Babylonian Captivity, 60
    Beethoven, Ludwig van, 508
    Bismark's Kulturkampf, 586
    burying the dead, 84
    Chinese family ties, 112
    clocks, 392
    Dachau, 696
    David Livingstone, 604
    Diseases in Human History,
      422
    Dressing for Success, 564
    energy, search for, 809
    Farming in Africa and
      Oceania, 290
    Ferdinand, Franz, 636
    Germany, peasant's life in, 370
    Greek mythology, 142
    Hard Times (Dickens), 536
    Hitler, 662
    The Hundred Years' War, 346
    Indian independence, 752
    King John, 244
    Life In Rome, 164
    Maria Reiche, 216
    Playing the fool, 452
    Russian Christianity, 266
    Soviet Union collapse, 724
    Taj Mahal, 318
    technology, 40
    Themes in History, 778
    truth, 20
    Wollstonecraft, Mary, 478
    Women in Greece and Rome,
      188
Sputnik, 787
Squire, defined, 232
St. Bartholomew's Day Massacre,
    364
Stalin, Joseph, 645, 647–50, 663,
    673, 701
Stalingrad, Battle of, 677, 697, 701
Stamp Act, 485–86

Standard of living, defined, 629
Static electricity, defined, 388
Steam engine, 525–26, 537
Steel making industry, 522, 537
Stephenson, George, 526, 537
Stone Ages, 14–15, 21
Stonehenge, 16–17, 21
Strait, defined, 404
Strike, defined, 718
Stupa, defined, 297
Subcontinent, defined, 91
Submarines, 618
Subsistence farming, defined 793
Successor, defined, 645
Sumerians, 27–30, 41, 221
Sundiata Keita, 283, 291
Sung dynasty, 302–4, 319, 323
Sun Yat-sen, 656–57, 663, 701
Superpower, defined, 690
Swastika, defined, 654
Swift, Jonathan, 475, 479, 569
Symbol, defined, 106
Symphony, defined, 475
Synagogues, 60
Syria, 738, 762

T

Tactic, defined, 500
Taiwan, 770
Taj Mahal, 300, 318
Taliban, 803
Tamerlane, 298
T'ang dynasty, 301–2, 319, 323
Tanks, 619, 678
Tariff, defined, 720
Taxation
    of American colonies, 485–86,
      509, 569
    Assyrian Empire, 48
    Egypt, 77
    England, 438
    France, 493–94, 569
    Germany, 370
    Persian, 56
    Qin dynasty, 108
    Rome, 157, 172
    Sumer, 28
    WWI, 627

Photo Credits

Cover Image100/Punchstock; Cover © Robert Glusic/ Corbis; Cover © Reed Kaestner/Corbis; Cover © Steve Estvanik/Corbis; Cover Big Stock Photo; Cover © Blend Images/Superstock; page iii Digital Juice; page iv Digital Juice; page v Digital Juice; page vi Digital Juice; page vii Digital Juice; page viii Digital Juice; page ix Courtesy of Daren Hastings; page x Digital Juice; page xxiv Andres Rodriquez/Shutterstock; page xxvi © Steve Estvanik/ Corbis; page 7 Courtesy of Charmaine Whitman; page 9 Rechitansorin/Big Stock Photo; page 10 Kenneth V. Pilon/Shutterstock; page 11 © Bettmann/CORBIS; page 16 Photodisc/Getty Images; page 19 Photos.com/Jupiter Images; page 20 Vladislav Gurfinkel/Shutterstock; page 28 Dean Conger/National Geographic Image Collection; page 32 Marcel Lewinski; page 37 The Granger Collection, New York; page 39 © Bettmann/ CORBIS; page 40 The Granger Collection, New York; page 49 © Gianni Dagli Orti/CORBIS; page 52 Marcel Lewinski; page 57 The Granger Collection, New York; page 59 The Granger Collection, New York; page 60 Marcel Lewinski; page 70 Steve Vidler/ImageState/ Jupiter Images; page 72 Frederic Neema/Workbook Stock/Jupiter Images; page 73 Vladimir Korostyshevskiy /Shutterstock; page 76 Vova Pomortzeff/Shutterstock; page 77 Marcel Lewinski; page 81a CJ Photography/ Shutterstock; page 81b © SuperStock, Inc./SuperStock; page 83 © Kurt Scholz/SuperStock; page 84 The Granger Collection, New York; page 93 Tony Waltham/ Robert Harding/Jupiter Images; page 95 Kim Winship; page 97 Hitesh Brahmbhatt/Shutterstock; page 98 © SuperStock, Inc./SuperStock; page 100 The Granger Collection, New York; page 103 James Stanfield/ National Geographic Image Collection; page 106 Giraudon/Art Resource, NY; page 109 The Granger Collection, New York; page 111 Scala/Art Resource, NY; page 112 © Stephanie Maze/Woodfin Camp; page 120 © William Hubbell/Woodfin Camp; page 122 Albert Barr/Shutterstock; page 124 © Spiros Tselentis/ SuperStock; page 130 Vanni/Art Resource, NY; page 131 Scala/Art Resource, NY; page 132 Library of Congress; page 134 © SuperStock, Inc./SuperStock; page 135 The Granger Collection, New York; page 137 TAOLMOR/Shutterstock; page 141 Library of Congress; page 142 Scala/Art Resource, NY; page 151 © Bettman/ Corbis; page 154 © SuperStock, Inc./SuperStock; page 157 Library of Congress; page 160 Scala/Art Resource, NY; page 161 The Granger Collection, New York; page 164 Library of Congress; page 171a Pippa West/ Shutterstock; page 171b Richard Nowitz/National Geographic Image Collection; page 172 The Granger Collection, New York; page 175 Danilo Ascione/ Shutterstock; page 181 The Granger Collection, New York; page 184 Photos.com/Jupiter Images; page 187 wikipedia.org; page 188 The Granger Collection, New York; page 196 © Warren Morgan/CORBIS; page 200 IRC/Shutterstock; page 204 The Granger Collection, New York; page 209 Ales Liska/Shutterstock; page 211 Tomasz Otap/Shutterstock; page 212 © John Van Hasselt/CORBIS SYGMA; page 213 Photodisc/Getty Images; page 215 © Bettmann/CORBIS; page 216 SGM/ Stock Connection/Jupiter Images; page 222 © Atlantide Phototravel/Corbis; page 227 Marcel Lewinski; page 230 The Granger Collection, New York; page 231 © SuperStock, Inc./SuperStock; page 233 © Blue Lantern Studio/Corbis; page 235 © Musee Dobree, Nantes, France/Giraudon/The Bridgeman Art Library; page 237 © Castello del Buonconsiglio, Trent, Italy/ Alinari/The Bridgeman Art Library; page 239 © Bettman/Corbis; page 240 © Ray Manley/SuperStock; page 243 The Granger Collection, New York; page 244 The Granger Collection, New York; page 252 © SuperStock, Inc./SuperStock; page 255 © Bettman/ Corbis; page 257 Judy King; page 259 Andrey Armyagov/Shutterstock; page 261 © Bettman/Corbis; page 265 ©Musee Saint-Remi, Reims, France/Giraudon/ The Bridgeman Art Library; page 266 Scala/Art Resource, NY; page 274 © Murat Ayranci/SuperStock; page 280 The Granger Collection, New York; page 283 The Granger Collection, New York; page 285 The Granger Collection, New York; page 289 © Earl & Nazima Kowall/CORBIS; page 290 © SuperStock, Inc./ SuperStock; page 297 © Hubertus Kanus/SuperStock; page 302 The Granger Collection, New York; page 303 © Burstein Collection/CORBIS; page 305 The Granger Collection, New York; page 308 Victoria & Albert Museum, London/Art Resource, NY; page 311 The Granger Collection, New York; page 315 Manfred/ Shutterstock; page 317 © SuperStock, Inc./SuperStock; page 318 Photodisc/Getty Images; page 324 The Granger Collection, New York; page 329 The Granger Collection, New York; page 332 Erich Lessing/Art Resource, NY; page 333 The Granger Collection, New York; page 334 Scala/Art Resource, NY; page 335 The Granger Collection, New York; page 339 © Culver Pictures, Inc./SuperStock; page 340 Erich Lessing/Art Resource, NY; page 341 © SuperStock, Inc./SuperStock; page 342a © Bettman/Corbis; page 342b Scala/Art Resource, NY; page 343 The Granger Collection, New York; page 344 © Bettman/Corbis; page 345 The Granger Collection, New York; page 346 The Granger Collection, New York; page 353 The Granger Collection, New York; page 356 © Bettmann/CORBIS; page 360

The Granger Collection, New York; page 364 The Granger Collection, New York; page 367 The Granger Collection, New York; page 370 © SuperStock, Inc./SuperStock; page 379 © Bettman/Corbis; page 380 © Bettman/Corbis; page 383 © SuperStock, Inc./SuperStock; page 385 The Granger Collection, New York; page 389 The Granger Collection, New York; page 390 Judy King; page 391 © National Portrait Gallery/SuperStock; page 392 The Granger Collection, New York; page 399 © Bettmann/CORBIS; page 401 The Granger Collection, New York; page 408 The Granger Collection, New York; page 411 The Granger Collection, New York; page 414 The Granger Collection, New York; page 416 The Granger Collection, New York; page 417 © SuperStock, Inc./SuperStock; page 418 © SuperStock, Inc./SuperStock; page 421 Michel Zabe/Art Resource, NY; page 422 © Newberry Library/SuperStock; page 430 © Peter Willi/SuperStock; page 433 The Granger Collection, New York; page 435 The Granger Collection, New York; page 438 The Granger Collection, New York; page 439 The Granger Collection, New York; page 441 © National Portrait Gallery/SuperStock; page 444 The Granger Collection, New York; page 445 © Peter Willi/SuperStock; page 447 © National Gallery Collection; By kind permission of the Trustees of the National Gallery, London/CORBIS; page 449 The Granger Collection, New York; page 451 The Granger Collection, New York; page 452 © Christie's Images/SuperStock; page 458 © Christie's Images/CORBIS; page 465 The Granger Collection, New York; page 466 The Granger Collection, New York; page 469 The Granger Collection, New York; page 470 Bridgeman-Giraudon/Art Resource, NY; page 472 © Christie's Images/SuperStock; page 474 The Granger Collection, New York; page 475 The Granger Collection, New York; page 477 The Granger Collection, New York; page 478 Tate Gallery, London/Art Resource, NY; page 486 © Bettmann/CORBIS; page 487 The Granger Collection, New York; page 488 The Granger Collection, New York; page 489 The Granger Collection, New York; page 494 © SuperStock, Inc./SuperStock; page 497 The Granger Collection, New York; page 498 © SuperStock, Inc./SuperStock; page 500 © Bettmann/CORBIS; page 503 Photo Credit: Scala/Art Resource, NY; page 507 ©Musee de la Ville de Paris, Musee Carnavalet, Paris, France/Giraudon/The Bridgeman Art Library; page 508 Photo Credit: Erich Lessing/Art Resource, NY; page 517 The Granger Collection, New York; page 519 The Granger Collection, New York; page 520 © Bettman/Corbis; page 522 The Art Archive/JFB; page 526 The Granger Collection, New York; page 531 The Granger Collection, New York; page 533a © Culver Pictures, Inc./SuperStock; page 533b © SuperStock, Inc./SuperStock; page 534 © Culver Pictures, Inc./SuperStock; page 535 The Granger Collection, New York; page 536 © National Portrait Gallery/SuperStock;

page 548 The Granger Collection, New York; page 549 © Bettmann/CORBIS; page 550 The Granger Collection, New York; page 554 The Art Archive/Saint Sulpice Seminary Paris/Dagli Orti; page 555 Giraudon/Art Resource, NY; page 557 The Granger Collection, New York; page 558 The Art Archive/Musée National de la voiture et du tourisme Compiègne/Dagli Orti; page 560 Library of Congress; page 563 The Granger Collection, New York; page 564 The Granger Collection, New York; page 570 © Swim Ink 2, LLC/CORBIS; page 578 The Granger Collection, New York; page 584 The Granger Collection, New York; page 585 The Granger Collection, New York; page 586 Erich Lessing/Art Resource, NY; page 594 The Granger Collection, New York; page 596 The Granger Collection, New York; page 600 The Granger Collection, New York; page 602 © Stapleton Collection/Corbis; page 603 © SuperStock, Inc./SuperStock; page 604 The Granger Collection, New York; page 610 © Swim Ink 2, LLC/CORBIS; page 615 The Granger Collection, New York; page 617 © Bettmann/CORBIS; page 618 © Bettmann/CORBIS; page 619 The Granger Collection, New York; page 624 © Woodfin Camp; page 627 © Bettmann/CORBIS; page 629 The Granger Collection, New York; page 630 © Jaime Abecasis/SuperStock; page 631 © Culver Pictures, Inc./SuperStock; page 632 © Bettmann/CORBIS; page 635 © Hulton-Deutsch Collection/CORBIS; page 636 © SuperStock, Inc./SuperStock; page 643 Library of Congress; page 645 Library of Congress; page 647 The Granger Collection, New York; page 648 © Bettman/Corbis; page 651 Library of Congress; page 656 Library of Congress; page 659 The Granger Collection, New York; page 661 TAOMOR/Shutterstock; page 662 Library of Congress; page 670 © Bettmann/CORBIS; page 673 © Bettmann/CORBIS; page 678 The Granger Collection, New York; page 682 Library of Congress; page 683 © Woodfin Camp; page 685 © Reuters/Corbis; page 688 AP Images; page 695 © Bettman/Corbis; page 696 © Bettman/Corbis; page 700 The Granger Collection, New York; page 702 Volker Kreinacke/Shutterstock; page 707 © Bettmann/CORBIS; page 710 © Bettmann/CORBIS; page 713 © Dean Conger/CORBIS; page 714 © Larry Downing/Woodfin Camp; page 715 © Reuters/CORBIS; page 718 © Alexandra Avakian/Woodfin Camp; page 719 © Reuters/CORBIS; page 723 Carsten Medom Madsen/Shutterstock; page 724 © Gideon Mendel/CORBIS; page 733 © Bettmann/CORBIS; page 734 © Jason Laure/Woodfin Camp; page 735 © David Modell/Katz/Woodfin Camp; page 738 © SuperStock, Inc./SuperStock; page 749 © William Strode/Woodfin Camp; page 751 © Peter Turnley/CORBIS; page 752 Library of Congress; page 759 © Mike Goldwater/Alamy; page 763 © Bettmann/CORBIS; page 765 © John Ficora/Woodfin Camp; page 768 Kwan, Heungman/

Index Stock Imagery/Jupiter Images; page 770
© Reuters/CORBIS; page 772 © SuperStock, Inc./
SuperStock; page 777 Martial Trezzini/AP Images; page
778 http://visibleearth.nasa.gov/; page 785 © George
Hunter/SuperStock; page 789 © Chuck Nacke/Woodfin
Camp; page 791 © Tony Linck/SuperStock; page 792
© Mike Yamashita/Woodfin Camp; page 796 Nikolai
Okhitin/iStock Photo; page 800 © SuperStock, Inc./
SuperStock; page 801 David Hyde/Shutterstock; page
807 Juergen Sack/iStock Photo; page 809 © Jeff Morgan
Hay on Wye/Alamy; page 810 Jiri Castka/ Shutterstock

Staff Credits

Rosalyn Arcilla, Mel Benzinger, Karen Blonigen,
Carol Bowling, Laura Chadwick, Nancy Condon, Barb
Drewlo, Marti Erding, Daren Hastings, Brian Holl,
Patrick Keithahn, Mary Kaye Kuzma, Daniel Milowski,
Stephanie Morstad, Carol Nelson, Carrie O'Connor,
Julie Theisen, LeAnn Velde, Mike Vineski, Amber
Wegwerth, Susan Weinlick

Acknowledgments

Grateful acknowledgment is made to the following for
copyrighted material:

Andreas Ramos
"A Personal Account of the Fall of the Berlin Wall:
The 11th and 12th of November 1989" by Andreas
Ramos from www.andreas.com/berlin.html. Used by
permission of Andreas Ramos.

Estate of Moses Hadas
"How to Get Elected in Rome" by Moses Hadas from
A History of Rome. Courtesy of the Estate of Moses
Hadas.

Liveright Publishing Corporation
"The Travels of Marco Polo" by Manuel Komroff from
The Travels of Marco Polo. Copyright © 1926 by Boni
& Liveright, Inc., renewed 1953 by Manuel Komroff.
Copyright © 1930 by Horace Liveright, Inc., renewed
© 1958 by Manuel Komroff. Used by permission of
Liveright Publishing Corporation.

New Directions Publishing Corporation
"The Next War" by Wilfred Owen from *The Collected
Poems of Wilfred Owen,* copyright © 1963 by Chatto
& Windus, Ltd. Reprinted by permission of New
Directions Publishing Corp.

Norwegian Nobel Institute
"Nobel Lecture given by The Nobel Peace Prize
Laureate 2006, Muhammad Yunus (Oslo, December
10, 2006)" from Nobelpeaceprize.Org/Eng_Lect_
2006b. Copyright © Nobel Foundation. Reprinted with
permission from the Norwegian Nobel Institute.

Pearson Prentice Hall, Inc.
"A Manchester Housewife's Weekly Budget in 1833" by
Bernard from *Reading In European History.* Copyright
© 1958. Used by permission of Pearson Education
College Division.

Penguin Group U.K.
60 line (approximately 217 words) (pp. 62-63) from *The
Bhagavad Gita,* translated by Juan Mascaro (Penguin
Classics, 1962) Copyright © Juan Mascaro, 1962.
"Pericles' Funeral Oration" (approximately 3,355 words)
by Thucydides from *The History of The Peloponnesian
War,* translated by Rex Warner, with an introduction
and notes by M.I. Finley (Penguin Classics 1954,
Revised edition 1972.) Translation copyright © Rex
Warner, 1954. Introduction and Appendices copyright
© M.I. Finley, 1972. Used by permission of Penguin
Group U.K.

Random House, Inc.
"What is Enlightenment" by Immanuel Kant from
The Philosophy of Kant, translated by Carl Friedrich,
copyright © 1949 by Random House, Inc. Used by
permission of Random House, Inc.

**Roman Ghirshman, Vladimir Minorsky and
Ramesh Sanghvi**
"It's Hard to be Humble" by Roman Ghirshman,
Vladimir Minorsky and Ramesh Sanghvi from Persia,
The Immortal Kingdom.

University of Texas Press
"Royal Commentaries of the Incas and General
History of Peru" by Garcilaso de la Vega from *Royal
Commentaries of The Incas And General History of
Peru,* translated by Harold V. Livermore, Copyright
© 1966. Used by permission of The University of Texas
Press.

University of Utah Press
"The Capture and Death of Moctezuma" translated by
Arthur J.O. Anderson and Charles E. Dibble from *The
War of Conquest: How It Was Waged Here In Mexico.*

Westminster John Knox Press
"John Calvin's Strict Code of Conduct" translated by
Ford Lewis Battles, edited by John T. McNeill from
Institutes of The Christian Religion, Vol. Xx. Used by
permission of Westminster John Knox Press.

Note: Every effort has been made to locate the copyright
owner of material reproduced in this component.
Omissions brought to our attention will be corrected
in subsequent editions.